UNIVERSITY C

WITH

FROM THE

D1392654

EURO AIM
The Link

**Euro Aim is a promotion and information service
dedicated to assisting European independent
producers and distributors in the marketing and
distribution of their productions**

**Through our marketing initiatives and database
services, we provide the link between new
productions from Europe and buyers from around
the world**

MEDIA

**EURO AIM IS AN INITIATIVE
OF THE MEDIA PROGRAMME
OF THE EUROPEAN COMMISSION**

210, Avenue Winston Churchill B -1180 Bruxelles
Tél: 32-2/346 15 00   Fax: 32-2/ 346 38 42

EDITED BY PETER COWIE

VARIETY

INTERNATIONAL

FILM GUIDE

1992

LONDON
ANDRE DEUTSCH

HOLLYWOOD
SAMUEL FRENCH INC.

*The smallest
of the great
festivals.*

*The greatest
of the small
festivals.*

*Every evening
open-air
screenings.*

22 July - 1 August 1992

45th festival internazionale del film Locarno (Switzerland)

P.O. Box 1621 via della Posta 6 6600 Locarno   phone: (41-93) 310.232   fax:(41-93)317.465   telex:846.565fifl

IFG's Film of the Year: Irène Jacob in *The Double Life of Veronica*, directed by Krzysztof Kieślowski
photo: Sideral/M. Jeziorowska

The Editor's Choice of Films 1991

1. **La double vie de Véronique**, Kieślowski (France-Poland)
2. **The Suspended Step of the Stork**, Angelopoulos (Greece)
3. **Thelma and Louise**, Scott (U.S.A.)
4. **Van Gogh**, Pialat (France)
5. **Lune froide**, Bouchitey (France)
6. **The Birthday Trip**, Scherfig (Denmark)
7. **Edward Scissorhands**, Burton (U.S.A.)
8. **Raise the Red Lantern**, Zhang (China)
9. **Prospero's Books**, Greenaway (U.K.)
10. **Boyz N the Hood**, Singleton (U.S.A.)

CONTENTS

CREDITS

Editor: Peter Cowie
Consulting Editor: Derek Elley
Assistant Editor: Steve Pemberton
New York Liaison: Fred Lombardi
Cover Design: Stefan Dreja

Editorial and Business Offices:
Variety
34–35 Newman Street
London W1P 3PD
Tel: (071) 637.3663
Fax: (071) 580.5559

ISBN 0–233–98720–7
British Library Cataloguing in Publication Data
Variety International Film Guide 1992
I. Cowie, Peter
011.37
U.S. Library of Congress Catalog Card No: 64–1706.
Copyright © 1991 by Cahners Publishing Ltd.
Photoset, printed and bound in Great Britain by Cromwell Press Ltd.

INTERNATIONAL LIAISON

Africa: Roy Armes
Argentina: Alberto Tabbia
Australia: David Stratton
Austria: Jack Kindred
Belgium: Patrick Duynslaegher
Bolivia: Pedro Susz K
Brazil: Luis Arbex
Bulgaria: Ivan Stoyanovich
Canada: Gerald Pratley
Chile: Hans Ehrmann
Cuba: Carlos Mendoza
Czechoslovakia: Eva Zaoralová
Denmark: Ebbe Iversen
Egypt: Fawzi Soliman
Far East: Derek Elley, Fred Marshall
Finland: Matti Apunen

France: Michel Ciment
Germany: Jack Kindred
Greece: B. Samantha Stenzel
Hungary: Derek Elley
Iceland: Gísli Einarsson
India: Uma da Cunha
Ireland: Michael Dwyer
Israel: Dan Fainaru
Italy: Lorenzo Codelli
Japan: Frank Segers
Luxembourg: Jean-Pierre Thilges
Malaysia: Baharudin A. Latif
Mexico: Tomás Pérez Turrent
Netherlands: Pieter van Lierop
New Zealand: Mike Nicolaidi
Norway: Trond Olav Svendsen
Pakistan: Aijaz Gul

Philippines: Agustin Sotto
Poland: Wanda Wertenstein
Puerto Rico: José Artemio Torres
Romania: Manuela Cernat
South Africa: Martin Botha
Spain: Peter Besas
Sri Lanka: Amarnath Jayatilaka
Sweden: Peter Cowie
Switzerland: Christoph Egger
U.K.: Mark Le Fanu
U.S.A.: William Wolf
U.S.S.R.: Forrest J. Ciesol
Venezuela (and *Colombia*): Paul Lenti
Yugoslavia: Maja Vlahović

NEW AND FORTHCOMING FILMS

Jacques Dutronc in Maurice Pialat's *Van Gogh*
photo: Marie-Laure de Decker

Michel Piccoli, Jane Birkin and Emmanuelle Béart in
Jacques Rivette's *La belle noiseuse*
photo: M. Jamet/Sigma

Scene from Spike Lee's *Jungle Fever*
photo: David Lee/Universal

Still from Agnès Varda's tribute to the late Jacques
Demy, *Jacquot de Nantes*

Grey Wolf and Little Red Riding Hood, which won the
Grand Prix at Annecy and forms part of the 23rd
International Tournee of Animation

Still from Agnieszka Holland's *Europa Europa*, released
in the States by Orion Classics

NEW AND FORTHCOMING FILMS

John Goodman and John Turturro in *Barton Fink*, which captured the Palme d'Or at Cannes in 1991

Al Pacino and Donal Donelly in Francis Coppola's *The Godfather Part III*

photo: Paramount Pictures

Scene from *Truth or Dare (In Bed with Madonna)*, directed by Alek Keshishian

Scene from Xavier Koller's *Journey of Hope*, winner of the Academy Award for Best Foreign Film of 1990

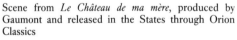

Scene from *Le Château de ma mère*, produced by Gaumont and released in the States through Orion Classics

U.S. ACADEMY AWARDS 1991 (for year 1990)

Kevin Costner's *Dances with Wolves* swept the Oscars
photo: Guild

Best Film: *Dances with Wolves*.
Best Direction: Kevin Costner for *Dances with Wolves*.
Best Actor: Jeremy Irons for *Reversal of Fortune*.
Best Actress: Kathy Bates for *Misery*.
Best Supporting Actor: Joe Pesci for *Goodfellas*.
Best Supporting Actress: Whoopi Goldberg for *Ghost*.
Best Original Screenplay: Bruce Joel Rubin for *Ghost*.
Best Adapted Screenplay: Michael Blake for *Dances with Wolves*.
Best Cinematography: Dean Semler for *Dances with Wolves*.
Best Art Direction: Richard Sylbert, Rick Simpson for *Dick Tracy*.
Best Costume Design: Franca Squarciapino for *Cyrano de Bergerac*.
Best Editing: Neil Travis for *Dances with Wolves*.
Best Original Score: John Barry for *Dances with Wolves*.
Best Original Song: "Sooner or Later (I Always Get My Man)" from *Dick Tracy*. Music and lyric by Stephen Sondheim.
Best Sound: Russell Williams II, Jeffrey Perkins, Bill W. Benton, Greg Watkins for *Dances with Wolves*.
Best Foreign-Language Film: *Journey of Hope* (Switzerland).
Best Documentary Feature: *American Dream*.
Best Documentary Short: *Days of Waiting*.
Best Live-Action Short: *The Lunch Date*.

Best Animated Short: *Creature Comforts*.
Best Special Effects: Eric Brevig, Rob Bottin, Tim McGovern, Alex Funke for *Total Recall*.
Best Make-Up: John Caglione Jr., Doug Drexler for *Dick Tracy*.
Best Sound-Effects Editing: Cecelia Hall, George Watters II for *The Hunt for Red October*.
Gordon E. Sawyer Award: Stefan Kudelski.
Irving G. Thalberg Award: Richard Zanuck and David Brown.
Honorary Awards: Sophia Loren and Myrna Loy.

FRENCH CÉSAR ACADEMY AWARDS 1991

Best Film: *Cyrano de Bergerac*.
Best Foreign Film: *Dead Poets Society*.
Best Director: Jean-Paul Rappeneau for *Cyrano de Bergerac*.
Best Actor: Gérard Depardieu for *Cyrano de Bergerac*.
Best Actress: Anne Parillaud for *Nikita*.
Best Supporting Actor: Jacques Weber for *Cyrano de Bergerac*.
Best Supporting Actress: Dominique Blanc for *Milou en Mai*.
Most Promising Young Actor: Gérard Thomassin for *Le petit criminel*.
Most Promising Young Actress: Judith Henry for *La Discrète*.
Best First Film: Christian Vincent for *La Discrète*.
Best Screenplay (original or adaptation): Christian Vincent and Jean-Pierre Roussin for *La Discrète*.
Best Cinematography: Pierre Lhomme for *Cyrano de Bergerac*.
Best Editing: Noëlle Boisson for *Cyrano de Bergerac*.
Best Art Direction: Ezio Frigerio for *Cyrano de Bergerac*.
Best Sound: P. Gamet, D. Hennequin for *Cyrano de Bergerac*.
Best Costumes: Franca Squarciapino for *Cyrano de Bergerac*.
Best Music: Jean-Claude Petit for *Cyrano de Bergerac*.
Best Documentary Short: François Amando for *La Valise*.
Best Fiction Short: Jean-Pierre Jeunet for *Foutaises*.

BRITISH ACADEMY OF FILM AND TELEVISION ARTS AWARDS: 1991

Best Film: *Goodfellas*.
Best Original Screenplay: Giuseppe Tornatore for *Cinema Paradiso*.
Best Adapted Screenplay: Martin Scorsese and Nicholas Pileggi for *Goodfellas*.
Best Director: Martin Scorsese for *Goodfellas*.
Best Actress: Jessica Tandy for *Driving Miss Daisy*.
Best Actor: Philippe Noiret for *Cinema Paradiso*.
Best Supporting Actress: Whoopi Goldberg for *Ghost*.
Best Supporting Actor: Salvatore Cascio for *Cinema Paradiso*.
Best Score for a Film: Ennio and Andrea Morricone for *Cinema Paradiso*.
Best Foreign-Language Film: *Cinema Paradiso* (Italy).
Best Short Film: *Say Goodbye*.
Best Short Animated Film: *Toxic*.
Fellowship Award: Louis Malle.
Michael Balcon Award: Jeremy Thomas.
Special Award: Deborah Kerr.
Flaherty Award: David Wallace for *The Last African Flying Boat*.

INDEPENDENT SPIRIT AWARDS OF INDEPENDENT FEATURE PROJECT/WEST

Best Film: *The Grifters*.
Best Foreign Film: *Sweetie* (Australia).
Best Director: Charles Burnett for *To Sleep with Anger*.
Best Actor: Danny Glover for *To Sleep with Anger*.
Best Actress: Anjelica Huston for *The Grifters*.
Best Supporting Actor: Bruce Davison for *Longtime Companion*.
Best Supporting Actress: Sheryl Lee Ralph for *To Sleep with Anger*.

Best Screenplay: Charles Burnett for *To Sleep with Anger*.
Best First Feature: Whit Stillman for *Metropolitan*.
Best Cinematography: Fred Elmes for *Wild at Heart*.
Special Distinction Award: Kevin Costner and Jim Wilson for *Dances with Wolves*.
Friends of Independents Awards: Sovereign Pictures and Eastman Kodak.
First Annual John Cassavetes Award for Bold, Creative Body of Work: Edward Pressman and Jon Jost (joint winners).
Reel Gold Award: Alpha Cine Laboratory.

EUROPEAN FILM AWARDS: 1990

Best Film: *Open Doors* (Italy).
Best Young Film: *Henry V* (U.K.).
Best Actor: Kenneth Branagh for *Henry V* (U.K.).
Best Actress: Carmen Maura for *¡Ay, Carmela!* (Spain).
Best Supporting Actor: Dimitri Pevsov for *Mother* (U.S.S.R.).
Best Supporting Actress: Malin Ek for *The Guardian Angel* (Sweden).
Best Screenplay: Vitaly Kanevsky for *Lie Still-Die-Revive* (U.S.S.R.).
Best Cinematography: Tonino Nardi for *Open Doors* (Italy).
Best Production Design: Ezio Frigerio and Franca Squarciapino for *Cyrano de Bergerac* (France).
Best Documentary: *Poperechnaya Street* (U.S.S.R.).
Special Jury Awards: *Open Doors* (Italy), *December Bride* (Ireland).
European Discovery of the Year: Ennio Fantastichini for *Open Doors* (Italy).
European Cinema Society Lifetime Achievement Award: Andrzej Wajda.
European Cinema Society Special Award: Association of the U.S.S.R. Film-makers.

PROFILES OF THE YEAR

Focus on an Actor:
DANIEL DAY-LEWIS

Midway through the 1980's, two British films were released within a few weeks of each other: *My Beautiful Laundrette*, directed by Stephen Frears, and the Merchant-Ivory production of *A Room with a View*. They had little in common – one a lean, raunchy satire of Thatcher-era South London, the other an elegantly-costumed rendition of E.M. Forster's Edwardian ironies. But what they did share was one actor: Daniel Day-Lewis.

Though top-billed in neither movie, it was Day-Lewis who attracted critical attention – not so much for either performance in itself as for the startling contrast between them. The streetwise gay punk of *Laundrette*, all blond-flashed hair and tough urban vowels, transmuted with total conviction into Forster's arch-prig Cecil Vyse, prissy-lipped and oozing conspicuous culture. Here, it was evident, was an actor in the risk-taking, chameleon tradition of Laughton and Olivier.

Day-Lewis's versatility, and the intensity of his presence, were confirmed when in 1986 he appeared at the National Theatre in *Futurists*, Dusty Hughes's powerful drama of the artistic revolution betrayed.

Daniel Day-Lewis in *My Left Foot*

Teamed with a superb cast (Jack Shepherd, Roger Lloyd Pack, Charlotte Cornwell), he played Mayakovsky with a searing fury of enthusiasm modulating into savage despair. The director was Richard Eyre who later directed him, again at the National, as Hamlet – a controversial performance, cut short towards the end of the run when Day-Lewis suffered a breakdown.

Daniel Day-Lewis was born in 1957. His pedigree is impressive, almost embarrassingly so: son of the Anglo-Irish Poet Laureate Cecil Day-Lewis and the actress Jill Balcon, grandson of the eminent film producer Michael Balcon. Having trained at the Bristol Old Vic Theatre School, he toured with the Old Vic company before landing his first major West End role in 1982 as Guy Bennett, British public-schoolboy turned Soviet spy, in Julian Mitchell's *Another Country*.

His screen career began with bit parts in *Sunday Bloody Sunday*, *Gandhi* and *The Bounty*. Though captivated by the theatre, which he once described as "an evil force drawing me on," Day-Lewis expresses a preference for movies. "Films tend to work – even bad films, in a strange way. Bad theatre doesn't work; and most theatre is bad." But he resisted the temptation to capitalise on his double triumph in *Laundrette* and *Room with a View*. Since then – barring a brief cameo as the heroine's bemused English boy-friend in Conny Templeman's *Nanou* – he has appeared in only four screen roles, each one seemingly chosen to stretch his eclectic range yet further.

As Tomas, the compulsively philandering Czech surgeon of *The Unbearable Lightness of Being*, his performance divided the critics – as did the film itself. Some found him miscast, implausibly middle-European, but there was no denying the edge of lithe,

Daniel Day-Lewis with Juliette Binoche in *The Unbearable Lightness of Being*

photo: The Saul Zaentz Company

dangerous sexuality he bought to his portrayal. With this film, Day-Lewis also gave notice of a professional dedication well beyond the norm: as part of his preparation for the role, he spent two weeks in a Prague operating theatre watching brain surgeons at work.

His next film flopped badly. Pat O'Connor's *Stars and Bars*, the comedy of an English innocent adrift amid deep-Southern dingbats, flailed wildly about in a vain quest for the right tone. Day-Lewis's performance, though, almost redeemed it: turning his lanky physique to a source of awkward embarrassment, he achieved (in Raymond Durgnat's phrase) "an adroit blend of the burningly romantic, the normally venal, and the comic schmuck." As an actor, he relishes the chance to make a fool of himself. "I want to be idiotic. It's a great relief from attempting in everyday life to retain some kind of dignity."

Day-Lewis defines what attracts him to a part as "the difficulties, the personal problems people have in giving of themselves." Pushing this principle to the outermost edge, he took on the role of the quadraplegic Irish writer Christy Brown in Jim Sheridan's low-budget *My Left Foot*, adapted from Brown's own autobiography. This time, his preparation included living for eight weeks in a Dublin clinic for the disabled and teaching himself, as Brown had done, to write and paint using only the eponymous foot. He also insisted, during the six weeks of filming, on remaining in his wheelchair throughout, being fed his meals and carried everywhere, experiencing for himself the resentment of the able-bodied towards the disabled.

The result was a performance of tangible ferocity flecked with a sardonic humour, resolutely uningratiating and making no concessions to audience sympathy. It earned him an Oscar, along with a stack of Best Actor awards from both sides of the Atlantic. Yet his next film, *Eversmile New Jersey*, an Anglo-Argentinian production directed by Carlos Sorin, with Day-Lewis as a travelling dentist in Patagonia, was released straight to video and vanished without trace.

Two more Day-Lewis performances are currently in the pipeline, both in adaptations of classic American fiction: *The Last of the Mohicans*, directed by Michael Mann, in which he plays the noble frontiersman Hawkeye; and as the New York socialite Newland Archer in Scorsese's version of Edith Wharton's *The Age of Innocence*. The versatility of Daniel Day-Lewis, it's fair to bet, is far from being exhausted.

Philip Kemp

Focus on a Producer:
EDWARD R. PRESSMAN

The recipient of this year's Indie Spirit's John Cassavetes Award for his contribution to independent film-making, Edward R. Pressman's career as a producer had already been commemorated by a 1988 retrospective at New York's Museum of Modern Art, an accord usually reserved for directors and stars. Other honours bestowed on him have included a retrospective at the French Cinémathèque and the Chevalier des Arts et des Lettres medal.

Pressman's main claim to fame has been his championing of new directors making offbeat, individualistic films. Appropriately, his career began in trying to launch a new director. Pressman, the son of a New York City toy manufacturer, while matriculating a degree in philosophy from the London School of Economics, met aspiring director Paul Williams when both were in their early twenties. Pressman produced Williams' short film *Girl* before they made their feature debut with *Out of It* (1969). This early Jon Voight effort plunged Pressman into the world of film financing even if it then only meant raising money from family and friends and borrowing the rest.

Pressman and Williams reteamed with Voight after he had attained stardom to film *The Revolutionary*. *Dealing* (1972) was the last of the three Pressman-Williams films. While Williams did not attain big time status Pressman was soon working with new directors who would be garnering acclaim. He produced Terrence Malick's first feature *Badlands*, and Brian DePalma's Hitchcockian breakthrough, *Sisters*. Pressman then produced the DePalma movie with the most dedicated cult following, *Phantom of the Paradise* (1974).

In the ensuing years Pressman has produced a wide range of films and even sauntered into the limited realm of political cinema. He helped launch Oliver Stone's career with an early feature, the 1981 horror movie, *The Hand*. He went on to produce some of Stone's more topical fare including *Wall Street* and *Talk Radio* while also producing Alex Cox's still more controversial *Walker* with its account of American adventurism in Nicaragua. Pressman has also worked with some of America's more righteous figures of the political right producing John Milius's *Conan the Barbarian* which helped boost Arnold Schwarzenegger to stardom and interestingly, contained a script credit for Oliver Stone.

Pressman's contribution to the international scene can be seen in his producing films for such foreign directors as Rainer Werner Fassbinder (*Despair*), Wolfgang Petersen (*Das Boot*) and the Taviani brothers (*Good Morning, Babylon*). Conversely, foreign capital has helped him produce films of unorthodox American directors such as Charles Burnett's *To Sleep*

Edward R. Pressman

with Anger, a winner of four Indie Spirit Awards including Best Director. Last April, Pressman made a deal with the Japanese computer and publishing company Asci Corp. which in its first phase pumped $15 million of capital into Pressman's production company.

Among Pressman's most recent films are *Reversal of Fortune* which won an Oscar for star Jeremy Irons, David Mamet's controversial police thriller *Homicide* starring Joe Mantegna, John Frankenheimer's *Year of the Gun*, and Hiro Yoshida's *Iron Maze*, a mystery involving a Japanese businessman in America. Pressman is still apparently trying to launch new directors as under his aegis, *Twin Peaks* co-creator Mark Frost has helmed the feature *Storyville*. A film bio, *Hoffa*, has also been announced to be directed by and co-star Danny DeVito.

Fred Lombardi

Focus on a Directing Team: THE COEN BROTHERS

Barton Fink won three awards at the Cannes Film Festival including best Film and Best Actor (John Turturro) but the award for Best Director created some confusion. The prize was designated to Ethan and Joel Coen yet the credits on all their films list only Joel as director, Ethan as producer and both as co-writers. Queried about the discrepancy Joel Coen replies, "At Cannes we listed ourselves both as director because that's closer to the case ... there's some slight, variate division of labour but it's very small." Adds brother Ethan, "Joel talks to the actors more than I do."

Such confusion may not be unusual from a pair that frequently confound critical expectations with their different kinds of films and playful variations on genre conventions. The brothers hail from Minnesota where as youngsters "just goofing around" they made Super 8 films. After attending film school at New York University older brother Joel found work as an assistant editor on low-budget horror films. Ethan, a Princeton graduate and philosophy major joined Joel to collaborate on scripts including Sam Raimi's *Crimewave*. Joel had worked as assistant editor on Raimi's cult horror favourite, *The Evil Dead*, but the most tangible way Raimi influenced the Coens was showing them how films can be financed. Raimi had bankrolled *Evil Dead* by going directly to various local investors and the Coens followed suit to produce their first feature, the 1985 release *Blood Simple*.

This modern day film noir was influenced, the Coens say, less by old movies than by pulp fiction and provided boosts to the careers of future Academy Award nominee Frances McDormand and character actor M. Emmett Walsh. In addition to establishing the Coens as film-makers, *Blood Simple* also provided a means for their

Joel Coen with John Turturro on the set of *Barton Fink*

future. The film was picked up by the Washington-based Circle Films for distribution and all their subsequent films have been produced by Circle which has given them "total freedom."

The Coens next made *Raising Arizona* (1987) which offered a live-action cartoon of American family life and marked John Goodman's first appearance in their films. The Coens used their protagonist's dreams to carry their extravagant visuals even farther and establish all kinds of primal connections. Their 1990 gangster epic, *Miller's Crossing*, was on more realistic ground. However, cartoon-like humour and dream imagery reappeared and an elusive hat became part of their visual poetry as it took on meanings of pride and integrity. John Turturro won acclaim for his portrayal of the small time hustler whose connivances provide the plot's dynamics.

Barry Sonnenfeld, the cameraman for their first three films, has left the Coens but his replacement on *Barton Fink*, Roger Deakins, has rendered yeoman service. Coen collaborators also include Carter Burwell who has scored all their films and Dennis Gassner who has been production designer for their last two. *Barton Fink* was also written with both Turturro and Goodman in mind.

Like their other films, *Barton Fink* is touched by the brothers' impishness as they added a non-existent genre, the Hollywood wrestling film, to their 1930's story. The Coens claim they had no idea that a Wallace Beery wrestling film, the cornerstone of their plot, actually did exist until one of their production staffers referred them to John Ford's 1932 *Flesh*.

Fred Lombardi

I.F.G. DOSSIER
ITALIAN CINEMA NOW

During the past decade, Italian cinema has lurched from crisis to crisis, and yet still contrives to capture world attention, winning awards at festivals, and attracting large audiences in the United States and elsewhere for certain titles. LORENZO CODELLI assesses the reasons for this roller-coaster experience, and traces the emergence of new themes and new maestros from an industry umbilically tied to Italian TV.

"Italy of the Miracle," it had been unanimously christened during the economic boom of the early 1960's. And that label was even more appropriate for the expansion of the Italian motion-picture industry, which during that radiant spell reached unparalleled peaks in quantity – almost 300 features annually (including a large number of co-productions) – quality and variety. The turbulent wave of the 1960's embracing Ermanno Olmi, Marco Ferreri, Marco Bellocchio, Pier Paolo Pasolini, Elio Petri, Bernardo Bertolucci, Valerio Zurlini, Mauro Bolognini, Dino Risi, Paolo and Vittorio Taviani, Ettore Scola and quite a few others, was competing with masters in full bloom like Federico Fellini, Luchino Visconti, Alberto Lattuada, Michelangelo Antonioni, and Pietro Germi, not forgetting several inventive popular craftsmen like Mario Bava, Riccardo Freda, Antonio Margheriti etc.

All were supported and encouraged by high-voltage tycoons, Carlo Ponti, Dino de Laurentiis, Franco Cristaldi, Angelo Rizzoli, Sr., Goffredo Lombardo. Their movies were frequently intended to subvert the national habits and ethics – e.g. the social impact of phenomena like *La dolce vita*, *Divorce Italian Style* or *Accattone* – which had usually been emasculated by the arch-conformist State television monopoly.

Thirty years and many thunderstorms later, it is clear that another "Italian miracle" has taken place: the actual endurance and reshaping of the motion-picture industry, thanks to a puzzling, seemingly irreversible symbiosis with the private and public networks.

Let the Sheep Sleep
The experiment in *laissez-faire* through which, for over fifteen years (1974–1990), the self-styled "free" networks were able to develop in total anarchy, broadcasting tons of movies interspersed with a flood of commercials, has permitted the rise and rise of Silvio Berlusconi's quasi-monopoly. This has greatly accelerated the decline in film attendances, but at the same time has given birth to a different breed of discriminating moviegoer – people who now prefer to leave home for their own special interests, for sophisticated pictures.

Unfortunately they turn their nose up at most national productions, assuming they

Silvio Berlusconi, President of the mighty Fininvest Group

chances to difficult or exotic pictures distributed by alert independents.

Rather than through bare statistics, the downfall of film experience could be illustrated by the disappearance of larger *cultural* debates about national pictures, those polemic struggles between opposing factions that were once the salt and daily bread of Italian cinema. Now the rare intellectual magazines have no followers outside academies, and their few readers are snoring in a unanimous trance. The show-business pages of most dailies are overrun with gossipy exchanges about TV-stars and TV-newscasts. The last furious battle engaging all film-makers, great and small, was fought in vain about the repellent 1990 law ratifying the commercial interruption of features by the private networks. But higher-minded discussions on provocative

Veteran director Alberto Lattuada

will be too similar to the daily TV-fodder they see on the small screen. They also more and more dread visiting those too many crumbling theatres in which the images and sounds sometimes appear worse than on any TV screen. From the 11,500 movie theatres in use in 1975, a mere 3,586 remained in 1989. Three-quarters of them anyway are obliged to close their doors during the long hot summers, practically from June to September, because during that time they can only get very sparse new releases of an inferior kind. Inflation has taken current movie tickets beyond 10,000 lire (over $8.50 dollars), and that's twice what a video rental costs.

Conversely, audiences for the admittedly more expensive stage and live music shows have increased during the last decade. But also the audience for the small but growing "cinéma d'essai" exhibitors has bucked the trend and has given unexpected box-office

topics advocated, for instance, by Francesco Rosi's **To Forget Palermo** (*Dimenticare Palermo*, 1990), or by Marco Risi's **Boys Out** (*Ragazzi fuori*, 1990), are deliberately stifled by the mass media in what looks like a not-so-casual conspiracy – in favour of television of course – which nobody cares to complain about any longer.

Bring on the Clowns!
Whereas the established genres have been streamlined to the core, their king is pumping fresh blood. The *commedia all'italiana*, once so beloved, prolific and incisive, has given way to the hyphenate-comedians trend. Rooted in their own towns' dialect and folk appeal, these performers coming frequently from cabaret or TV shows have supplanted unforgettable comic "monsters" like Alberto Sordi, Ugo Tognazzi, Nino Manfredi, and Vittorio Gassman.

The rustic **Roberto Benigni** (born in Arezzo, 1952) of Tuscan origins, has inherited Totò's formidable power of mesmerising audiences with torrid, nonsensical monologues verging on the blasphemous. Young people adore his non-conformist ardour. He has directed three and a half films, breaking all box-office records with **The Little Devil** (*Il piccolo diavolo*, 1987), and then starred in Fellini's **Voices of the Moon** (*La voce della luna*, 1990) as the poetic lunatic in love with the moon. **Johnny Stecchino**, his mafia spoof shot in Sicily, is expected to become this season's megahit.

Casting his mimicry in an updated version of Alberto Sordi's, the 101% Roman **Carlo Verdone** (b. 1950) has gone from early aggressive satires like **How Beautiful** (*Un sacco bello*, 1979), **White, Red and Verdone** (*Bianco, rosso e Verdone*, 1980), to tamer ones like **Compagni di scuola** (1988) and **This Evening at Alice's**

Roberto Benigni with Walter Matthau in *Il piccolo diavolo*

Carlo Verdone, star and director of *Bianco rosso e verdone*

(*Stasera a casa di Alice*, 1990). His rotund mask, good-boy shyness, droll linguistic distortions, and sexual hangups communicate well with upper class audiences.

Too lazy to be really impressed by his wide fame, the Neapolitan **Massimo Troisi** (San Giorgio a Cremano, 1953) has started with two Woody Allen-like intimate farces, **I Am Starting Again from Three** (*Ricomincio da tre*, 1981) and **Sorry I'm Late** (*Scusate il ritardo*, 1983), based on his brilliant stammering and his bashful relationships with girls. Then he directed an ambitious historic comedy set in the Fascist era, **The Lord's Ways Are Ended** (*Le vie del Signore sono finite*, 1987). Recently he has restricted himself to performing in three Ettore Scola movies. His chamber music kind of fragmented, philosophic tenderness sometimes

strikes one as not too far removed from the late Eduardo De Filippo's poetic disquisitions.

Another Tuscan original, **Francesco Nuti** (Prato, 1955) has established his Keatonesque character in a series of well-written pictures directed by Maurizio Ponzi, especially in the minor gem **Io, Chiara e lo Scuro** (1983). As a director, subsequently, of his own vehicles, he tried to assume more psychological nuances while nurturing his confirmed mass appeal. From **Casablanca, Casablanca** (1985), to **Bewitched** (*Stregati*, 1986) and **Willy Signori, I'm Coming from Afar** (*Willy Signori e vengo da lontano*, 1989), he created a fairytale universe tinged with crude undercurrents.

Even coming from an older generation and never having directed any films himself,

Paolo Villaggio (Genua, 1938) still has a very strong following among all ages and is rightly identified as the true author of his comedies. Refining his masochistic little clerk Fantozzi in a 15 year series of films – as well as in a parallel series of bestsellers – he has launched a violent attack against even the biggest institutions. He is capable of pure slapstick as in **The Comedies** (*Le comiche*, 1990), directed by his usual associate Neri Parenti, and of classic tragic acting as he demonstrated in Fellini's *La voce della luna* (1989).

The self-made equivalent to Jerry Lewis' "total film-maker", **Maurizio Nichetti** (Milan, 1948) provoked a torrent of laughter with his first *silent* comedy **Ratataplan** (1980), immediately imposing his bespectacled, moustacheoed, lovable marionette. His three subsequent pictures looked rather flat by comparison, but with **The Icicle Thief** (*Ladri di Saponette*, 1988) he created a memorable parody of De Sica's *Bicycle Thieves*, abruptly shifting that apologia for

poverty into the whirl of the contemporary advertising world. **To Wish To Fly** (*Volere Volare*, 1991) mixed cartoons and live gags to lampoon further excesses of consumerism, as well as unveiling Angela Finocchiaro's droll gifts.

Talents in the Ascendant

The era of wealth and glory, big budgets and boundless aspirations has unquestionably evaporated for Italian directors. New talents struggle hard to see the light and they can rarely build a professional career without prolonged, often fatal, interruptions, or without becoming anonymous TV hacks. The brightest and luckiest ones have emerged from a film family or have studied with top directors as mentors.

Marco Risi (Milan, 1951) had collaborated with his father Dino and his uncle Nelo, both directors, before making his debut in 1981 with **I'm Going to Live by Myself** (*Vado a vivere da solo*), a modest comedy for the limp jester Jerry Calà. Three

Maurizio Nichetti and Claudio G. Fava in *Ladri di saponette*

minor movies later he directed **Soldiers 365 Till Dawn** (*Soldati 365 all'alba*, 1987), a solid indictment of army life ending with an ominous warning. An unusual political commitment and a stylistic immediacy in his recent efforts have made him the leader of a hastily baptised "neo-Neorealism," the same trend pursued by a few film-makers not attached to any particular group, **Ricky Tognazzi** (*Ultrà*, 1991), **Michele Placido** (*Pummarò*, 1990), both connected to Claudio Bonivento, the intelligent producer of Marco Risi's works – not forgetting **Claudio Risi** (*Pugni di rabbia*, 1991), his elder brother. Marco Risi's pair of movies about Palermo's delinquent boys, **Meri For Ever** (*Meri per sempre*), and **Ragazzi fuori** (1990), vented the despair and fury of a wasted generation. His unashamed **Rubber Wall**

(*Muro di gomma*, 1991) exposed the ignominous military-political cover-up of the shooting down of a plane near Ustica.

Francesca Archibugi (Rome, 1960) opts for a rather more subdued realism. Fresh from studies at Centro Sperimentale under tutor Mario Monicelli and scriptwriter Furio Scarpelli, and a course at Ermanno Olmi's lab, she has written – with her team of friends Gloria Malatesta and Claudia Sbarigia – and directed **Mignon Has Left** (*Mignon è partita*, 1988), a very witty teenage romance inspired by personal experience. Thanks to this international success she was able to unite the superb duo of Marcello Mastroianni and Sandrine Bonnaire for her second opus, **Around Evening** (*Verso sera*, 1990); a father and daughter's tormented relationship that per-

Salvatore Termini and Santi Bellina in Marco Risi's *Ragazzi fuori*

Marcello Mastroianni and Sandrine Bonnaire in *Verso sera*

Celine Beauvallet and Leonardo Ruta in Francesca Archibugi's *Mignon è partita*

fectly recaptured the terrorist mood of the 1970's, and benefited from humorous dialogue and some whimiscal vignettes.

The Rise of Tornatore

Giuseppe Tornatore's 1990 Oscar for **Nuovo cinema Paradiso** (1988) has made him the most hyped and envied symbol of the Italian film renaissance. Born in Bagheria, Sicily, in 1956, he directed documentaries for Rai and won the support of shrewd producer Goffredo Lombardo for his first feature, **Il camorrista** (1986), starring Ben Gazzara as the infamous Neapolitan mob boss, Raffaele Cutolo. It was tepidly received. Giving free rein to his remembrances of cinema past, and enthusiastically supported by famed mogul Franco Cristaldi, he directed the $2\frac{1}{2}$ hour version of *Nuovo cinema Paradiso* originally rejected by most Italian exhibitors. Following its unexpected Cannes triumph in an abridged print, the film finally started a long run in Tornatore's own country, even if it was not as profitable as abroad. His third picture, **Everybody's Fine** (*Stanno tutti bene*, 1990), attempted a vast Felliniesque canvas about current social hypocrises. Tornatore is also a prolific maker of kitschy TV ads, which is a very remunerative business, employing many top directors (even Fellini, working incognito, of course).

Emerging unusually from a stage background as a much-admired director, **Gabriele Salvatores** (Naples, 1950) has brought to the movies an extraordinary flair for handling of ensemble performances, often using the same company. In 1972 he founded in Milan the celebrated Teatro dell'Elfo, which has fostered the brightest new players – among them Sergio Rubini, Margherita Buy, Sergio Castellitto, Ennio Fantastichini, Fabrizio Bentivoglio etc. His first film **A Summer Night's Dream**

Nanni Moretti appears in his own production of *Il portaborse*

(*Sogno di una notte d'estate*, 1982) was based on his rock Shakespearian shows. From **Kamikazen** (1987), to **Marrakech Express** (1988), **Turné** (1990) and **Mediterraneo** (1991), he has composed a polyphonic symphony mirroring his own generation's deceptions and impossible flights of optimism. His films constitute a series of biting allegories that his many real-life prototypes could enjoy and fully understand. Among Salvatores' most creative partners is Enzo Monteleone, a highly original screenwriter who has worked for Alessandro D'Alatri (*Red American*, 1991) and Cinzia TH. Torrini (*Hotel Colonial*), 1986), too.

Daniele Luchetti (Rome, 1960) studied and worked at Gaumont Italy (managed in the early 1980's by Renzo Rossellini, an illustrious name who left his own mark on the period), and then found Nanni Moretti as an enlightened producer for his first

feature, **It Will Happen Tomorrow** (*Domani accadrà*, 1987), conceived, like his subsequent pictures, together with the witty screenwriter Franco Bernini. *It Will Happen Tomorrow* is a metaphor for today's insurgent youth, narrated in the form of an Eighteenth-century picaresque novel. In the airy summer idyll **The Sphynx's Week** (*La settimana della sfinge*, 1990) he explored some bizarre provincial scenes. With **The Factotum** (*Il portaborse*, 1991) he delivered a brimstone tirade against everyday political corruption, erupting more from the bitter inspiration of his master-producer-star Nanni Moretti.

Veterans Take the Long View
The last decade has seen the death of Sergio Leone and the protracted illness of Michelangelo Antonioni. Seasoned directors from the 1950's and 1960's remain, however, the sharpest observers of Italy's

Bernardo Bertolucci

mutations. Federico Fellini above all, has predicted in sombre mood the horrific, absurd implosion of the private TV networks (**Ginger and Fred**, 1985), the sad abandonment of Cinecittà's glorious heritage (**Intervista**, 1987), and the savage coarsening of community life (**La voce della luna**, 1990). His powerful nightmares have become reality even against one's wishes.

Consciously declining to consider Italian themes anymore, and refusing to be confined by local producers, **Bernardo Bertolucci** has established an outstanding reputation worldwide, winning nine Oscars for **The Last Emperor** (1987) and a cult following for **The Sheltering Sky** (1990). On the other hand Francesco Rosi has come back home, after his international co-production, **Carmen** (1983) and **Chronicle of a Death Foretold** (1985), to

analyse the reigning Mafia-in-white-suits in **Dimenticare Palermo** (1990), a grim portrayal of our insoluble political crisis. **Paolo and Vittorio Taviani** have made a little jaunt to D.W. Griffith's Hollywood with **Good Morning Babylon** (1986), a co-production with the U.S.A., managed by their regular financial partner Giuliani G. De Negri; subsequently they have reverted to their favourite issue, the impasse of the idealist Left, in the ascetic parable **Night Sun** (*Il sole anche di notte*, 1990).

Ten years ago, on a Venetian mountain plateau near his house in Bassano del Grappa, Ermanno Olmi founded the unconventional school-laboratory "Ipotesi Cinema" with the aid of a meagre grant from Rai. He has supervised many remarkable shorts made there by young disciples like Maurizio Zaccaro, Francesca Archibugi, and Giacomo Campiotti. These

Placido Domingo and Julia Migenes in Francesco Rosi's *Carmen*

TWO PRODUCER-DIRECTORS

Pupi Avati

Together with his brother Antonio, Pupi Avati (Bologna, 1938) has fashioned a small but prolific factory, named DueA (from the two Avatis). With limited budgets partially supported by Rai, he has built a steadily growing audience for his annual pictures, working with the same technicians, often the same cast, basing fantastic or realistic legends in the familiar context of his Emilia Romagna. He has rediscovered underrated character actors like Carlo Delle Piane and Diego Abatantuono, and has made stars of several young actors, from Luca Barbareschi to Elena Sofia Ricci, Nik Novecento, Lino Capolicchio, Gianni Cavina and many others.

Under his banner ex-assistants and friends have found an opportunity to direct: Giuseppe Bertolucci (*Berlinguer ti voglio bene* 1977), in which Roberto Benigni made his first impact as a satirist, Luciano Manuzzi, and Cesare Bastelli. He has also used some of them in his musical show, *Hamburger Serenade* (1986), in his sitcom, *E' proibito ballare* (1988–89) and in a portmanteau experiment shot in one August week, *Sposi* (1988). To prepare for the complex shooting in Iowa of his jazz saga **Bix** (1991), he wrote and produced in the same city of Davenport a dark thriller directed by the newcomer Maurizio Zaccaro, **Where the Night Starts** (*Dove comincia la notte*, 1991). The uncompromising flow of his works looks amazing, but they were so subjective that for more than a decade they were rejected by most critics and had great difficulty in getting a release. Avati's two passions, jazz and the movies, brought him his earliest hits, the

autobiographical TV miniseries **Jazz Band** (1978) and **Cinema!!!** (1979).

Pupi Avati

Bryant Weeks in Avati's *Bix*

Nanni Moretti

Nanni Moretti

In the summer of 1976 some film society fans had enthusiastically applauded the very funny **I Am an Autarchic** (*Io sono un autarchico*), the first feature made in Super8 by an unknown named Nanni Moretti (Brunico, 1953); he had perfectly sent up the frustrations and political disillusionment of his not-so-revolutionary, rhetoric-ridden generation.

Moretti's psychoanalytical self-portrait was continued through extremely eccentric films, in which he has reviled the moviemaking world (**Golden Dreams** [*Sogni d'oro* 1981]), the decay of the Church (**The Mass Is Ended** [*La messa è finita*, 1985]), and the dismantling of the Communist Party (**Little Red Dove** [*Palombella rossa*, 1989]). Scorning the establishment, he decided with his friend Angelo Barbagallo to form his own company, Sacher Film (from his beloved Sacher chocolate tarts). He has since produced three ambitious pictures starring comedians Marco Messeri, Paolo Hendel, and Silvio Orlando: *Notte italiana* (1987) by Carlo Mazzacurati, an offbeat political diatribe, *Domani accadrà* (1988), and *Il portaborse* (1991), both by Daniele Luchetti; in the latter one he vengefully played a corrupt Socialist minister. Moretti's mounting indignation keeps pace with his visual imagination and especially his managerial calibre.

shorts are indeed the only worthy examples of the lost art of *cortometraggio*, because aspiring directors no longer have the patience to make them (when with the same microbudget they could do a feature instead!). The agreeable Bressonian feature, **Maicol** (1988), by Mario Brenta was generated inside his school. With their collective help Olmi directed **Long Live the Lady!** (*Lunga vita alla signora!*, 1987), an allegory about capitalism versus freedom. He gained the Golden Lion at the Venice Mostra for **The Legend of the Holy Drinker** (*La leggenda del santo bevitore*, 1988), starring Rutger Hauer, a limpid adaptation of Joseph Roth's novel shot in English and lusciously set in Paris. In the carefully planned travelogue **The River** (1991) he tracked the waters of the River Po.

The 1991 Berlin Festival awarded its Golden Bear to **House of Smiles** (*La casa del sorriso*), Marco Ferreri's return to his idiosyncratic obsession with seditious de-

Rutger Hauer in Olmi's *La leggenda del santo bevitore*

Niccolo' Paolucci in Luigi Comencini's *Marcellino pane e vino*

crepitude, investigated already in one of his early masterpieces, *El cochecito* (1960). **The Flesh** (*La carne*, 1991) managed to sublimate Ferreri's perennial sexual armageddon. **Captain Fracassa's Journey** (*Il viaggio di Capitan Fracassa*, 1990) displayed **Ettore Scola's** stylistic talents at their peak; it was an imaginative if studio-bound odyssey inspired by Théophile Gautier's classic, subtly rewritten as a gritty metaphor for current ills.

Comedy masters **Mario Monicelli, Dino Risi** and **Luigi Comencini** also spent the decade searching for new ideas. **Let's Hope It Will Be a Girl** (*Speriamo che sia femmina*, 1985), a misappreciated film about male identity, both illuminated Monicelli's utopian perspective. Working more frequently for TV, Risi teamed up once more with Vittorio Gassman for **I Won't Disturb You** (*Tolgo il disturbo*, 1991), a balanced parable about an incorrigible, elderly fool. A curious love story between two aging people

came under scrutiny in Comencini's **Merry Christmas, Happy New Year** (*Buon Natale, buon anno*, 1990). In the now neglected action genre, Antonio Margheriti, alias Anthony J. Dawson, excelled himself with **Indio** (1988) and **Indio 2, la rivolta** (1991), two save-the-Amazon-forest B-epics starring "Marvelous" Marvin Hagler.

Desperados in Limbo

Ever since the 1965 film law – the last comprehensive piece of legislation, forever waiting to be updated by successive governments – proclaimed in its much-criticised article 28 that a few million *lire* should be assigned annually by the State to pictures "inspired by artistic and cultural purposes," several new directors have seized their chance of a grant, with the result that hundreds of untrained film-makers shot their first and, yes, last picture simultaneously. Naturally, there were and are exceptions, because interesting directors like Peter Del Monte, Salvatore Piscicelli, Franco Piavoli, even the Tavianis, Avati and Moretti, did make use of that state-funding. Beyond the effects of this particular law, each season contains at least two dozen features made outside the system, which remain unreleased or appear sporadically at one of the various festivals. That means nearly one-fifth of the national output,

Marcello Mastroianni in Mario Monicelli's *Le due vite di Mattia Pascal*

Ermanno Olmi

SACIS

This associate member company of RAI Radiotelevisione Italiana is Italy's leading commercial audio-visual distributor. Apart from its direct sales work for RAI, SACIS has intensified its relations with the Italian film industry in recent years.

It handles the commercial exploitation, in Italy and abroad, of RAI's programmes or those in which RAI is the title-holder, in any capacity. SACIS also supervises the contents of radio and TV commericals broadcast by RAI and the related technical editing procedures.

Classic films distributed by SACIS include Olmi's *The Tree of Wooden Clogs*, Fellini's *Orchestra Rehearsal*, *Kaos* and *Good Morning Babylon*, by the Taviani brothers, Rosi's *Christ Stopped at Eboli*, and Angelopoulos's *Alexander the Great*. Recently SACIS has been distributing Pupi Avati's *Bix* (in competition in Cannes 1991), Gianni Amelio's award-winning *Open Doors*, and the sensational TV series, *The Octopus*.

At most film festivals, SACIS flies the Italian flag and remains for specialist distributors and TV buyers a key organisation where Italian film export is concerned.

Gian Maria Volontè in *Porte aperte*
photo: Umberto Montiroli

which appeared to be stable at around 110 and 120 units (excluding of course made-for-TV productions). But in 1990/91 that total was declining.

KEY PRODUCER-DISTRIBUTORS

Mario Cecchi Gori

The best comedies of the 1960's, as well as innumerable spaghetti westerns and dramas, were personally produced by Mario Cecchi Gori (Brescia, 1920). Together with his son Vittorio (Florence, 1942) he has built the largest film conglomerate in Italy. His Penta Film – allied with Berlusconi's holding and theatres – turns out almost 50 pictures a year, more than double the total of his bigger American-owned rivals.

His concern prospers thanks primarily to a repertoire of popular clowns like Paolo Villaggio, Carlo Verdone, and Francesco Nuti, opening on hundreds of screens during the lucrative Christmas period. He was bold enough to greenlight Fellini's *La voce della luna* (1990), Rosi's *Dimenticare Palermo* (1990), and Scola's *Il viaggio di Capitan Fracassa* (1990), expensive and not always financially rewarding gambles. The Italian video market too seems under his watchful control. And he obtained record sums for selling to Rai (his ex-partner) the rights to a whole slew of pictures.

Angelo Rizzoli, Jr.

The grandson of the late "commendatore" Angelo Rizzoli, Sr. – founder of a once powerful publishing dynasty and producer of *La dolce vita*, $8\frac{1}{2}$ and other milestones – was jailed and ousted from the ownership of his firm following the Banco Ambrosiano scandal. But Angelo Rizzoli, Jr. (Como, 1943), has risen from the ashes with some friendly help from Berlusconi and has formed Erre Produzioni, a company involved in prestigious European co-ventures such as Margarethe von Trotta's *Paura e amore* (1988), Jerzy Skolimowski's *Torrents of Spring* (1989), Paul Schrader's *The Comfort of Strangers* (1990), and Theo Angelopoulos' *The Stork's Suspended Step*, (1991). Erre has also produced some classy Italian movies such as Gianni Amelio's *Porte aperte* (1990), Giuseppe Tornatore's *Stanno tutti bene* (1990), Daniele Luchetti's *La settimana della sfinge* (1990), and Luigi Magni's *In nome del popolo sovrano* (1990).

Rizzoli's cultural leanings are confirmed by the names he has selected for his brand-new D.A.R.C. distributing arm: Bigas Luna, Hector Babenco, David Cronenberg, James Ivory. And he has announced his participation in the Eurotrustees consortium in order to finance joint-ventures with the U.S. Nowadays Gianni Amelio, Francesca Archibugi, Carlo Mazzacurati, and Giacomo Battiato are under contract to Rizzoli.

Mario (left) and Vittorio Cecchi Gori

TOP TEN GROSSING FILMS IN ITALY: 1990

	Admissions ($U.S.)
Dances with Wolves	18,285,477
Pretty Woman	17,752,361
The Little Mermaid	11,712,090
Ghost	10,190,848
Total Recall	9,258,317
Home Alone	8,826,891
Christmas Vacation '90 (Italian)	8,459,319
The Sheltering Sky	8,441,025
The Comics (Italian)	8,194,839
Rocky V	8,165,806

The long-awaited new law should encourage and provide decent outlets for those increasing numbers of debutant film-makers who are at work far beyond the grounds of Cinecittà. In Turin the Cinema Giovani Festival has stimulated various local film and video-makers; the best known are **Daniele Segre** (Alessandria, 1952), director of realistic documentaries and one fine feature, **Testadura** (1982), and **Corrado Franco** (Turin, 1957), who made **Running Downward** (*Corsa in discesa*, 1987). In Milan one could similarly find many neglected film-makers: **Silvio Soldini** (Milan, 1958), who directed the rarely seen **Landscape with Figures** (*Paesaggio con figure*, 1983), **Giulia in October** (*Giulia in ottobre*, 1984), and the minor hit **The Clear Air of the West** *L'aira serena dell'ovest* 1990); **Massimo Mazzucco** (Turin, 1954), who shot in New York his deeply-felt **Summertime** (1983), and then directed a second one, **Romance** (1986), his last to date; **Gianluca Fumagalli** (Milan, 1958), whose **A fior di pelle** (1987) was screened at several international festivals. In Sicily **Francesco Calogero** (Messina, 1957) produced and directed the extremely funny 16mm feature **The Kindness of Touch** (*La gentilezza del tocco*, 1987), applauded by all the reviewers.

The distribution system automatically banning these and innumerable other works coming from outside the mainstream is badly in need of some kind of modernisation. It appears paradoxical that all those thousands of festivals from the Alps to Sicily still contribute to the permanent throttling of releases, which barely reach an annual total of 350. The Italian films get an ever-decreasing slice of the gross, just 20%, whereas 68% goes to American productions, and a mere 6% to European ones. The chaotic video market has flourished much later than nearby countries, and it has partially improved the state of affairs, offering a huge bunch of unreleased pictures.

The Networks Battleground

The rating wars between Rai and Berlusconi for the control of audiences together with the enormously lucrative advertising revenue, have been fought for the most part by bombarding each other with home-made miniseries or down-market American imports.

Rai is long experienced in producing significant feature films, which have won several international awards since the 1970's. Its policies had to be divided among its three channels. **Rete 1**, the richest outlet with a guaranteed mass audience is run by the Christian Democratic Party and spon-

Fabrizio Bentivoglio in Soldini's *L'aria serena dell'ovest*

sors Fellini, Scola, Zeffirelli, the Tavianis, Olmi, Avati etc. – the established, and often costliest, film-makers. **Rete 2**, dominated by the Socialist Party, likes to support a younger group, including Marco Risi, Gianni Amelio – whose **Open Doors** (*Porte aperte*, 1990) was crowned by the top European Award – Andrea Barzini, and the controversial Marco Bellocchio. **Rete 3**, ruled by the Communist Party (now re-named "Democratic Party of the Left"), has co-sponsored no less than Giuseppe Tornatore's *Cinema Paradiso* and Francesca Archibugi's *Mignon è partita*, and it tries with a smaller budget to sustain promising directors.

Berlusconi's Fininvest and his three main channels – plus various subsidiaries – do not have to suffer any such political schizophrenia. Having built up his multi-media empire, Berlusconi acquired and then restored a major chain of theatres.

Nuovo Cinema Paradiso, co-sponsored by Rete 3

THE ONE AND ONLY

Among national shrines that everybody hopes will be around forever, **Marcello Mastroianni** (Fontana Liri, 1924) has experienced a really extraordinary renaissance in his fifth decade as a star. While the 1950's gave him an endless series of working-class roles, and the 1960's made him the suave cosmopolitan Casanova, the 1970's and early 1980's were the most stagnant period in his career. But ever since Nikita Mikhalkov's Chekhovian comedy *Dark Eyes* (1987), which won Mastroianni a best actor award and a standing ovation in Cannes, the ever-indolent Marcello has enjoyed a new lease on life. He mocked his *Dolce vita* role in Fellini's *Intervista* (1987), gloomily re-enacted the glorious past of Italian cinema in *Splendor* (Ettore Scola, 1988), played from within a mortified

Communist oldtimer in *Verso sera* (Francesca Archibugi, 1990), and lent considerable dignity to a self-exiled political leader in Angelopoulos's *The Stork's Suspended Step* (1991). By now, all the evils and pleasures of the world could be embodied in any one of his confident gestures or insolent glances.

Mastroianni with Jeanne Moreau in *The Suspended Step of the Stork*

Anita Ekberg and Marcello Mastroianni meet again in Fellini's *Intervista*

Giuseppe Tornatore

Settled in the country's business capital, Milan (incidentally a Socialist Party stronghold) he has willingly financed local filmmakers like Maurizio Nichetti, Gabriele Salvatores, and the great animator Bruno Bozzetto (for his live-action debut **Under the Chinese Restaurant** in 1986). But Berlusconi also helped Bertolucci's *The Sheltering Sky*, Ferreri's *The White Men How Good They Are* (1987), intriguing *auteurs* like Luciano Odorisio, Peter Del Monte, Luciano De Crescenzo, Franco Amurri, and most of all a series of lucrative farces starring the popular clowns of Italian cinema. American remakes of some of the latter are under way at his lively new Hollywood offshoot. His production output should valiantly expand now that the 1990 law is slowly going to regulate the airwaves without any radical change, so long as his international ventures made in English do not wholly vampirize it. Logically the same big "if" is hovering over Rai's future plans too.

In the Shadow of the Titans
Independent producers definitely require some degree of support from the TV-duopoly in order to undertake any kind of enterprise. The most effective among them are trying to specialise in particular genres or to expand their former teams.

Dario Argento, for instance, the renowned horror director of **Creeper** (*Phenomena*, 1984) and **Opera** (1987), has trained an informal group of adherents, Lamberto Bava – Mario's son – Michele Soavi, Luigi Cozzi, and special effects wizard Sergio Stivaletti. Mauro Berardi with his company Yarno has not only launched Roberto Benigni to superstardom, but has also given a first chance to fringe humorists such as Sergio Staino (*To Be Born a Horse*, 1988) and Francesco Salvi (*Let's Love Each Other Too Much*, 1989). Augusto Caminito and his Scena Film have produced Tinto Brass's successful whorehouse romp **Paprika** (1991), Abel Ferrara's **King of New York**

ITALIAN PRODUCTION 1980–1990

	1980	1981	1982	1983	1984	1985	1986	1987	1988	1989	1990
100% Italian Co-productions	130	79	99	101	87	81	94	106	103	102	98
Italo-Canadian	–	–	–	–	1	–	–	–	1	1	1
Italo-Brazilian	1	–	–	–	1	–	–	–	1	1	2
Italo-French	14	11	7	3	5	3	6	7	8	9	8
Italo-Spanish	9	6	4	1	2	–	3	1	1	1	–
Italo-German,	3	–	1	1	1	2	3	–	–	1	–
Italo-Russian	–	–	–	–	–	–	–	–	1	–	–
Italo-Hungarian	–	–	–	–	–	–	–	–	–	–	1
Italo-Swiss	–	–	–	–	–	–	–	–	–	–	1
Total Majoritarian Co-productions	26	17	12	5	9	5	12	8	11	12	12
German-Italian	1	–	–	–	–	1	–	–	1	–	–
Frano-Italian	1	2	3	1	5	1	1	–	5	2	5
Spanish-Italian	1	1	–	–	–	–	–	–	1	–	–
Anglo-Italian	–	–	–	–	–	–	–	–	1	–	–
Total Minority Co-productions	2	3	3	1	5	2	2	–	8	2	5
Tripartite Majoritarian	4	4	–	2	2	1	–	2	–	–	4
Tripartite Minoritarian	1	–	–	1	–	–	1	–	2	1	–
Total Multilateral Co-productions	5	4	–	3	2	1	1	2	2	1	4
Total Italian Films	163	103	114	110	103	89	109	116	124	117	119

FOUR ICONS

Fabrizio Bentivoglio

One of the most accomplished talents from the classic stage, Fabrizio Bentivoglio (Milan, 1957) studied at the Piccolo Teatro in his home city and then worked for ten years under the Italy's finest stage directors, Giorgio Strehler, Franco Enriquez, Giorgio De Lullo, and Giuseppe Patroni Griffi. In 1980 he began a parallel career on screen (*Masoch* directed by Franco Brogi Taviani, 1980; *Salomè* by Claude d'Anna, 1985; *Via Montenapoleone* by Carlo Vanzina, 1986). Thanks to another man of the theatre, director Gabriele Salvatores, he was given two remarkable roles: in *Marrakech Express* (1988) he played a forlorn Sahara traveller looking for his lost illusions, and in *Turné* (1989) he was a travelling actor jealous of his partner. His ironic verve and self-deprecating smile were also to the fore in *Italia-Germania 4 a 3* (1990) by Andrea Barzini, and above all in *Americano rosso* (1991) by Alessandro D'Alatri, a 1930's-type nostalgic comedy that made him a debonair seducer looking a dead ringer for Clark Gable.

Francesca Dellera and Sergio Castellitto in *La carne*

Margherita Buy

Sterotypes and sidekick roles are given to Italian young actresses nowadays rather than meaty parts that might breed another Claudia Cardinale or Stefania Sandrelli. However Margherita Buy (Rome, 1962) has distinguished herself in two totally different, three-dimensional roles in the same season. She was the dreamy, lighthearted blonde waitress falling madly in love with a fickle seducer in Daniele Luchetti's *La setti-*

mana della sfinge (1990). She deserved her award at the San Sebastian Festival. Guided by her husband Sergio Rubini, with whom she had played on the stage, in *La stazione* (1990) she became a coldhearted, indolent bourgeoise who deceives a petty stationmaster during a one-night stand just to repell a violent fiancé. A graduate of the Accademia of Rome, she first appeared in Nino Bizzarri's melodrama *La seconda notte* in 1985. Carlo Verdone has cast her in his upcoming comedy.

Sergio Castellitto

Sergio Castellitto's methodical progress towards stardom seems likely to make him a big name despite the difficulty of breaking into the Italian movie élite. This Roman actor (b. 1955) has worked on the stage and made his film debut in Luciano Tovoli's *L'armata ritorna* (1982). He has played honest-guy, minor roles and was noticed as one of the various members of Scola's *La famiglia* (1985). His thoughtful, nosey face can adapt either to comic parts as in *Sembra morto ... ma é solo svenuto* (1986) by Felice Farina, his first critical success, or to dramatic ones as in *Tre colonne in cronaca* (1990) by Carlo Vanzina, playing a sharp journalist detective. Carlo Verdone revealed his burlesque qualities in *Stasera a casa di Alice* (1990), a bedroom triangle in which they shared topbilling with superstar Ornella Muti. Through Marco Ferreri's *La carne* (1991) and Mario Monicelli's *Rossini Rossini* (1991) he has become a charismatic figure and an actor likely to dominate the decade ahead.

Francesca Dellera

Faithful to the grand lineage of *maggiorate*, the bosomy Gina, Sophia, Silvana, Anitona, cheerfully exploited by their respective Pygmalions, Francesca Dellera (Latina, 1965) first paraded her lavish curves in Tinto Brass's *Capriccio* (1987). This former model has unashamedly developed her outdated but so adorable public figure of the absent-minded, red-haired vamp, whose voluptuous lips and widescreen eyes devour every man like an octopus, and whose repartee owes a lot to Monroe. She was superbly sensual in the TV remake of *La romana* (1988) by Giuseppe Patroni Griffi, playing the part that had made a star of Lollobrigida in 1954, flanked by Gina herself as her mother; furious scuffles between them during the shooting were reported by the scandal sheets just like the old days. As an object of destructive desire she again burned up the screen in Marco Ferreri's *La carne* (1991).

Margherita Buy in *La stazione*

photo: Sandro Borni

Sophia Loren in Lina Wertmüller's *Sabato domenica e lunedì*

(1990), and has encouraged Klaus Kinski (**Paganini**, 1988) and Ben Gazzara (**Beyond the Ocean**, 1990) to take up directing. Luigi de Laurentiis, Dino's brother, has produced and released through his Filmauro the big-budget underwater adventure **Leviathan** (1988) by George Pan Cosmatos, as well as the mini-flop **Private Code** (1988) by Francesco Maselli.

Cinecittà itself, still one of the largest studios in Europe, has periodically become a production body, so that more features and TV-series can be drawn into its full-service facilities. The state body, Ente Gestione Cinema, has improved its equipment with the aid of Lucasfilm technicians. Recently the studios were invaded by the immense crews working on *The Adventures*

of Baron Munchausen (Columbia), *The Godfather Part III* (Paramount) and *Hudson Hawk* (Tri-Star) among others.

Right opposite Cinecittà, its cousin Centro Sperimentale di Cinematografia, also founded by the government in the mid-1930's which had once constituted a model international school-cum-library and archive, has been entrusted to the guidance of Lina Wertmüller with the aim of disentangling its potential energies from the clutches of Italian bureaucracy. It is to be hoped that the various regions of the peninsula will forge closer ties with such institutions as Centro Sperimentale, and with each other's film activity, in order to keep the best Italian talents here at home.

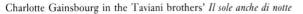

Charlotte Gainsbourg in the Taviani brothers' *Il sole anche di notte*

TECHNICAL WIZARDS

Vittorio Storaro

This brilliant director of photography (Rome, 1940) whose lighting genius has aided Bertolucci, Coppola, and Beatty, among others, and brought him a fistful of awards, is currently engaged on a lavish series of fifteen documentary features, **Roma Imago Urbis**. He is already preparing Bertolucci's next magnum opus about Buddha. As president of the Italian Association of Cinematographers (A.I.C.) he is battling to get the law to acknowledge the co-authorship status for his category; and he is supervising the publication of the Society's valuable Yearbook. Among the best cameramen of the new generation we should list **Italo Petriccione** (most of Salvatores' work), **Pasquale Rachini** (all Avati's films), **Alessandro Pesci** (*Traccie di vita amorosa*, 1990, *Il portaborse*, 1991), **Luca Bigazzi** (*L'aria serena dell'Ovest*, 1990), **Alessio Gelsini** (*La stazione*, 1990), and **Mauro Marchetti** (*Ragazzi fuori*, 1990).

Vittorio Storaro

photo: Giacomelli

Dante Ferretti

An inventive production designer (Macerata, 1943) who started working with Pier Paolo Pasolini, for whom he conceived the lavish and fantastic sets of *Medea* (1969), *Decameron* (1971), *The Arabian Nights* (1975), and *Salò* (1976). Then he created the extravagant sets for Fellini's *Orchestra Rehearsal* (1979) and for most of his subsequent movies. His gusto could be discerned in his designs for Terry Gilliam's *Munchausen* (1989) and Jean-Jacques Annaud's *The Name of the Rose* (1986). Other internationally-renowned production designers are **Francesco Bronzi** (*Kaos*, 1984; *Torrents of Spring*, 1989), **Andrea Crisanti** (all Rosi's films; *Nuovo cinema Paradiso*, 1988), **Luciano Ricceri** (Scola's partner), **Gianni Quaranta** (*The Legend of the Holy Drinker*, 1988; *The Comfort of Strangers*, 1990), and **Ferdinando Scarfiotti** (*Scarface*, 1983; *The Last Emperor*, 1987).

Enrico Sabbatini

Costume designer (Spoleto, 1932) who won an Oscar nomination for his creations in *The Mission* (1986), gave the unique, severe look to Francesco Rosi's characters in *Illustrious Corpses* (1976) and *Dimenticare Palermo* (1990), and has worked regularly on major TV miniseries (*Marco Polo*, 1982; *Anno Domini*, 1984; *Mamma Lucia*, 1987). His elegant western attire for *Old Gringo* (1989) was just one remarkable sample of Italian costume design for Hollywood productions. Think of Giorgio Armani's superb suits and dresses for Scorsese or De Palma, or Milena Canonero's imaginative tones and textures (*Tucker*, 1988;

Milena Canonero (right)

documentary on the shooting of the Bertolucci film. Among the most recent wave of editors one should mention **Mirco Garrone** (Nanni Moretti's films), **Cecilia Zanuso** (*Americano rosso*, 1991),, **Giancarla Simoncelli** (*Ultrà*, 1991), and **Roberto Missiroli** (*Verso sera*, 1990).

Dick Tracy, 1989; *Reversal of Fortune*, 1990; *The Godfather Part III*, 1990), and Elsa Zamparelli's ethnic costumes in *Dances with Wolves* (1990).

Gabriella Cristiani

This princess among film editors (b. Foggia, 1949) won an Oscar for *The Last Emperor* (1987). She had been the main pupil of Kim Arcalli, Bertolucci's greatest collaborator, and began working solo on *La luna* (1979) after Arcalli's premature death. For *The Sheltering Sky* she learned the secrets of editing with the new laser-disk technology, splicing together at the same time her own 16mm

Ennio Morricone

The maestro among Italian composers (b. Rome, 1928) has never abandoned his musical experiments, nor his off-screen activities. Among his most recent scores are Tornatore's *Nuovo cinema Paradiso* (1988) and *Stanno tutti bene* (1990); Folco Quilici's *Cacciatori di navi* (1991); and Carlo Vanzina's *Tre colonne in cronaca* (1989). His competitors include the prolific **Nicola Piovani**, who works for the Tavianis, Moretti, and Fellini; veterans **Riz Ortolani**, contributing his languid melodies to Pupi Avati's pictures, and **Armando Trovajoli**, composing melancholy rhythms for Scola's pictures; also pop songsmiths adored by young audiences like **Vasco Rossi, Franco Battiato**, and **Eugenio Bennato**.

Dante Ferretti's elegant sets enlivened Fellini's *Orchestra Rehearsal*

photo: Pierluigi Praturlon

Julian Sands in the Taviani brothers' *Il sole anche di notte*

Producers

AB Cinema
Largo Generale Gonzada del
Vodige, 4
00195 Roma
Tel: 3612534, 3200830
Fax: 3613251

Airione Cinematografica
Largo Olgiata 15, Isola 102
Tel: 3788200, 3789550
Fax: 3788200

Alia Film
Viale Gorizia, 52
00100 Roma
Tel: 858337

AMA Film
Via Pierluigi da Palestrina, 48
00193 Roma
Tel: 3611750, 3211143
Fax: 3220364

Cecchi Gori CG. Silver
Via Barnaba Oriani, 91
00197 Roma
Tel: 8084651, 8084654,
8088861
Fax: 874325, 8870378,
8088378

Clesi Cinematografica
Via Francesco Carrara, 24
00196 Roma
Tel: 3613771
Fax: 3610854

Cristaldi Film
Via Mangili, 5
00100 Roma
Tel: 3215010
Fax: 3221036

Dania Film – DMV Distrib.
Via Monti Parioli, 40
00197 Roma
Tel: 3610541, 3610542,
3610543
Fax: 3612107

Filmauro
Via Della Vasca Navale, 58
00146 Roma
Tel: 5560788, 5584875

Fulvia Film
Via Caroncini, 23
00197 Roma
Tel: 879659, 875232
Fax: 802117

**ICC Produzione
Distribuzione
Cinematografica**
Corso D'Italia, 92
00100 Roma
Tel: 8443421

Italian International Film
Via Delgi Scialoja, 18
00196 Roma
Tel: 3612109, 3610553,
3225965, 3721377
Fax: 3225965, 6799149

L.P Film
Via dei Banchi Vecchi, 58/61
00186 Roma
Tel: 6544932, 6875349,

Paolo Villaggio starring in *Ho vinto la lotteria di Capodanno*

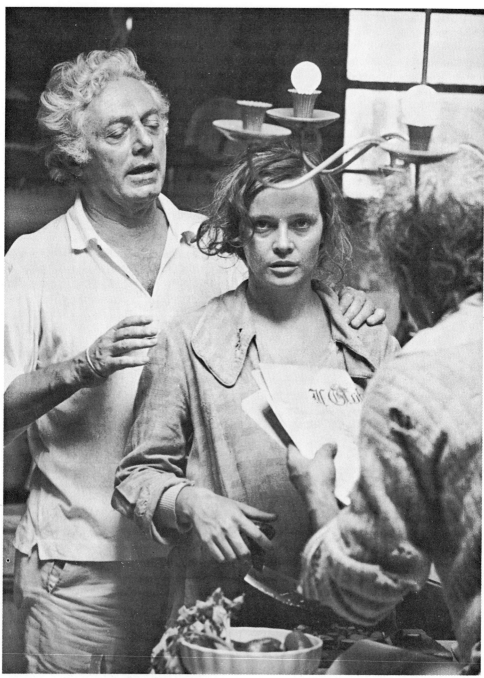

Dino Risi with Laura Antonelli on the set of *Sessomato* (1973)

6548747
Fax: 6548747

Massfilm
Via Bertoloni, 44
00197 Roma
Tel: 873757, 870679
Fax: 808397

Maura International Film
Via S. Godenzo, 154
00189 Roma
Tel: 3666203, 3650896
Fax: 3650556

Metro Film
Viale Carso, 22
00195 Roma
Tel: 3610547, 3610549

Numero Uno
Via Atanasio Kircher, 20
00197 Roma
Tel: 877686, 8082887, 472218
Fax: 8082755

Dean Film International
Via dei 3 Orologi, 10/E
00197 Roma
Tel: 8085500, 8083425
Fax: 8082823

Deantir
Via Eleonora Duse, 37
00196 Roma
Tel: 878483, 879275
Fax: 879331

Due A
Piazza Cola di Rienzo, 69
00192 Roma
Tel: 3214851, 3215108
Fax: 3215108

Eagle Pictures
Via Della Giuliana, 101
00195 Roma
Tel: 3748063, 386314
Fax: 3862314

Eidoscope
Piazza Adriana, 15
00193 Roma
Tel: 6548444, 6548445
Fax: 6875956

Erre Produzioni/Darc
Via Archimede, 164
00197 Roma
Tel: 873360, 873370, 872225
Fax: 878701

Excelsior Film
Via Caronicini, 58
00197 Roma
Tel: 873494, 8082760
Fax: 870465

Fandango
Via Salaria, 356
00199 Roma
Tel: 8441919, 8414687,
8842298
Fax: 8441633

Fanny Ardant and Vittorio Gassman in Ettore Scola's *La famiglia*

Filmapha
Via Asiago, 2
00195 Roma
Tel: 3612605, 3201975,
3612429, 3215211
Fax: 3220360

Pacific Pictures
Piazza Gentile da Fabriano, 15
00196 Roma
Tel: 3220200
Fax: 3220213

Penta Film
Via Aurelia Antica, 422
00165 Roma
Tel: 663901
Fax: 66390550

Racing Pictures
Via dei Tre Orologi, 10
00197 Roma
Tel: 8083692, 8083654
Fax: 8088691

RCS Produzioni
Via Ludovisi, 16
00197 Roma
Tel: 4820924
Fax: 4756583

Sacher Film
Viale Priamide Cestia, 1
00100 Roma
Tel: 5740483
Fax: 5740483

Scena Film
Via Archimede, 114
00197 Roma
Tel: 80887255
Fax: 8870258, 8088258

Schuhly Thomas
Via Tuscolana, 1055
00100 Roma
Tel: 72293489
Fax: 7222443

Titanus Produzione
Via Sommachampagna, 28
00100 Roma
Tel: 4957341

Vides Cinematografica
Via G. Magili, 5
00100 Roma
Tel: 32150110

Distributors

Academy Pictures
Via Fratelli Ruspoli, 8
00198 Rome
Tel: 08/884–0424 or 844–0860
Fax: 841–7043

Artisti Associati
Via Degli Scipioni, 281/283
00192 Rome
Tel: 08/321–0365 or 321–0367
Fax: 321–7245

Scene from *Kaos*, directed by Paolo and Vittorio Taviani

Marcello Mastroianni in Francesca Archibugi's *Verso sera*

Carlo delle Piane in Pupi Avati's *Festa di laurea*

Still from Marco Risi's *Ragazzi fuori*

Chance Film
Via Giuseppe Mercalli, 19
00197 Rome
Tel: 06/808–5041
Fax: 870–506

**Columbia Tri-Star Films
Italia**
Via Palestro, 24
00185 Rome
Tel: 06/494–1198
Fax: 446–9936

**Distribuzione Angelo Rizzoli
Cinematografica (D.A.R.C.)**
Via Archimede, 164
00197 Rome
Tel: 06/807–3360
Fax: 878–701

Filmauro
Via della Vasca Navale, 58
00146 Rome

Tel: 06/556–0788 or 558–
4875
Fax: 559–0670

**Italia International Film-
Pathe Group**
Via Degli Scialoia, 18
00196 Rome
Tel: 06/361–2109 or 361–2913
Fax: 322–5965

Istituto Luce/Italnoleggio
Via Tuscolana, 1055
00173 Rome
Tel: 06/722–0741 or 722–
2496
Fax: 722–2090

Life International
Via Cristoforo Colombo, 181
00147 Rome
Tel: 06/514–1297 or 513–
8483

Fax: 512–8846

Mikado Film
Lungotevere Flaminio, 26
00196 Rome
Tel: 06/322–5295 or 321–
8649
Fax: 321–9484

Penta Distribuzione
Via Aurelia Antica, 422/424
00165 Rome
Tel: 06/663901
Fax: 66390450

Titanus Distribuzione
Largo Chigi, 19
00187 Rome
Tel: 06/67031
Fax: 679–7507

**Twentieth Century Fox/
C.D.I**

Via Palestro, 24
00185 Rome
Tel: 06/444–0525 or 444–
0536
Fax: 444–0391

United International Pictures
Via Bissolati, 20
00187 Rome
Tel: 06/482–0626
Fax: 482–0628

Warner Bros Italia
Via Varese, 16B
00164 Rome
Tel: 08/446–3191
Fax: 444–0177

Useful Addresses

Agis
Via di Villa Patrizi, 10
0100 Roma
Tel: 884731259
Fax: 8848079

Anica
Viale Regina Margherita, 286
00198 Roma
Tel: 8841272
Fax: 47025179

Banca Nazionale del Lavor
Piazza San Bernardo, 101
00100 Roma
Tel: 47021
Fax: 47025179

Carlo Levy Associates
Via G. Carducci, 10
00100 Roma
Tel: 486961

Cinecittà
Via Tuscolana, 1055
00173 Roma
Tel: 74641, 722931
Fax: 7222155

Cinema 5
Via Aurelia Antica, 422
00100 Roma
Tel: 663901

Ente Gestione Cinema
Via Tuscolana, 1055
00173 Roma

Luciano Emmer enjoyed a comeback in 1990 with *Basta! Adessa tocca a noi*

Tel: 7222141
Fax: 7221883

Film Export Group
Via Polonia, 9
00198 Roma
Tel: 8554266, 8444187
Fax: 8550248

Finninvest
Largo del Nazareno, 3/8
00100 Roma
Tel: 67381
Fax: 67386044

International Recording
Via Urbana, 172
00184 Roma
Tel: 4821066, 4819006,
4827970
Fax: 4745246

Istituto Luce
Via Tuscolana, 1055
00173 Roma
Tel: 7222492, 72293370
Fax: 7222493, 7222090

Loeb and Loeb
Piazza Digione, 1
00197 Roma
Tel: 874557

MGM Pathe Studio
Via Pontina KM 23
00100 Roma
Tel: 5050242

**Ministero del Turismo e
dello Spettacolo**
Via Della Ferratella in
Laterano, 45
00184 Roma

Tel: 779309
Fax: 7574767

Pathe Communications
Via del Tritone, 46
00187 Roma
Tel: 6781151

**Rai – Radiotelevisione
Italiana**
Piazza Montegrappa, 4
00197 Roma
Tel: 3219995

Sacis
Via Tomacelli, 139
00166 Roma
Tel: 396841
Fax: 6878824

Shooting in Italy: Francis Coppola and Gordon Willis on *The Godfather Part III*

photo: John Seakwood

Maurizio Nichetti becomes a cartoon character, much to his inconvenience and his lover's frustration, in *Volere Volare*, co-directed by Guido Manuli (who made the animated segments)

Tribute to The International Tournee of Animation

The August 30, 1991 release of Expanded Entertainment's *The 23rd International Tournee of Animation* marked the 23rd anniversary of a venerable institution credited by many with playing a large role in turning independent animation around. Since 1965 The International Tournee of Animation has been feeding and sustaining an ever-growing American appetite for animation that is more than just "cartoons of kids," while at the same time returning 50% of profits to the animators.

The 23rd International Tournee of Animation highlights, as did each of its 22 predecessors, the very best of independent animation from around the world. The intent of The Tournee has always been to act as a showcase for new and notable films, techniques and animators, bringing to the fore the people and ideas that will shape the future of animation for years to come.

The 23rd International Tournee of Animation is notable for breathtaking debuts from new animators, such as Timothy Hittle, whose *The Potato Hunter* stands as a monument to both the classic western and the ingenuity that an animator and a shapely russet can show in front of a camera and Gregory Grant, whose *Ode to G.I. Joe®* was awarded the Student Academy Award, for the introduction of an exciting new technique in Chel White's visionary use of an ordinary office photocopy machine in *Photocopy Cha Cha*, for exceptional new films by animators familiar from past Tournees, including Bill Plympton's *Push Comes To Shove*, Vincent Cafarelli and Candy Kugel's *Fast Food Matador* and for the epic Annecy Festival Grand Prize-Winning *Grey Wolf and Little Red Riding Hood* by the Soviet Union's Garri Bardin.

Ultimately though, The 23rd International Tournee of Animation is most natable for the place it holds in a series that has grown steadily in the years since its introduction in 1965 to become the solid foundation from which have grown a biennial festival, a theatrical compilation of the best films from the festival, a magazine, a library of home video releases and, most recently, a television show.

Terry Thoren, president of Expanded Entertainment, comments, "When we began producing The Tournee we knew we'd be breaking new ground, but it amazes me to think of the different paths The Tournee has led us down. When we produced The Tournee it was clear that we could need to see more films if we were to programme the the best in the world, so we organised and hosted the First Los Angeles International Animation Celebration, a festival devoted solely to animation. From there things began to snowball." The event gave birth to a travelling feature that showcased the best festival films. This feature, *Animation Celebration*, is now in its fourth edition and will be released December 27, 1991. The Fourth Los Angeles International Animation Celebration took place October 31–November 7, 1991.

Newsletter Blossoms

In 1986 Thoren began publishing a newsletter devoted to animation industry news. The newsletter quickly blossomed, becoming *Animation Magazine*, today considered an animation industry necessity. In 1990 Thoren, while retaining the position of Editor in Chief, gave over publication of the magazine to VSD Publications where it has continued to prosper and grow and is now published bi-monthly. "We published *Animation Magazine* because the industry had

1985 Academy Award-winner: *Anna and Bella*

no way to communicate with itself, but publishing a magazine is a big job; coupled with the festival, The Tournee, the home video business and the television show it was too much for us. To ensure that *Animation Magazine* would continue at the level of quality we'd established we had to find a good home for it, and VSD is that home."

Expanded's entered the home video business in 1988 after countless requests to purchase The Tournees for repeat viewing. Today the company has some 24 videos for sale, encompassing the 19th, 20th and 21st Tournees as well as retrospectives and salutes to such famed animators as Bruno Bozzetto and Paul Driessen.

Expanded commitment is not only to the animation audience but to the artists who have made it all happen. The company has proudly maintained its co-op philosophy,

returning 50% of all profits from the Tournees of Animation to the film-makers, generating a cycle of incentive that keeps animators doing what they do best: animating more film for the next Tournee, or, with the explosion in animation creation, for prime-time TV shows, commercials and feature films. To date Expanded has returned more than $2,000,000.00 to animators and is able to guarantee a minimum of $1500.00 per minute for any film appearing in a Tournee.

The Tournee has grown considerably from its days of Museums and Colleges. Now appearing in more than 350 theatres around the country, The Tournee travels in much the same way that road-show musicals of the 1930's did, a limited number of prints playing in locked engagements. This arrangement allows The Tournee to reach its maximum audience quickly and with minimal marketing costs, leaving a greater share of profits for animators.

Throughout its 23 editions, The Tournee has contained hundreds of award-winning films, including the Academy Award-winners *Creature Comforts* (1990), *Balance* (1989), *Tin Toy* (1988), *The Man Who Planted Trees* (1987), *A Greek Tragedy* (1986), *Anna and Bella* (1985) and *Charade* (1984).

Today expanded is co-ordinating production of a TV show that will expose the breathtaking work of animators that has been stunning *Tournee* audiences for decades. The latest outlet is yet another example of the power of the independent animation that has made The International Tournee of Animation into a venerated institution.

Now well established, The Tournee betrays little evidence of its origin as an idea in the minds of a few prominent animators in 1965.

"The problem that existed in 1965 – and, to a certain extent still exists today – is that animated shorts weren't being shown in theatres in the United States," remembers animator Bill Littlejohn, one of The Tournee's founders. "Independent film-makers who didn't have a tie-in with network television, or anywhere else, needed a showcase. The world focus of animation had shifted to Europe, where major international animation festival were being held. The festivals were dominated by independent filmmakers with remarkable words. Animators were desperate for a place to show their films and we thought it was natural to put these short films into a package and show them where we could."

In fact, the genesis of The Tournee can be traced to 1964 when Pierre Barbin, the Director of the Festival d'Annecy in France, visited the United States as a guest of the State Department. Barbin brought with him amy of the films from the 1963 Festival which, through the efforts of producer Les

Prescott Wright (left) and Bill Littlejohn (right) guided the early development of the International Tournee of Animation

Goldman, were screened in Los Angeles. The success of these screenings and of a 1965 screening produced by animator John Wilson at the Huntington Hartford (now Doolittle) Theatre in Hollywood convinced Goldman, Littlejohn and colleagues in the local branch of the International Animated Film Association (ASIFA-Hollywood), that Los Angeles should have its own festival.

"The screenings were a great success," Littlejohn recalls. "They opened our eyes to the fact that short film packages were marketable, that an audience existed for this."

Encouraged, Goldman and Littlejohn approached Henry Hopkins, curator of the newly-opened L.A. County Museum of Art (LACMA), about organising a festival of animation at the Museum.

At this point Ward Kimball became involved. Kimball, a two-time Oscar-winning animator and one of the Disney's original "nine old men," had been a judge at Annecy and recognised that a local festival could be an important venue for the exciting diversity

1986 Aeademy Award-winner: *A Greek Tragedy*

he had seen at Annecy. With Hopkins's support, a selection committee was formed, and in 1965 the first International Animated Film Exhibition took place.

Littlejohn recalls, "The theatre was designed not for film but for stage presentations. They rented a portable screen and stuck it there. After the success of that show the Museum went into film in a big way, which is a major part of their function now."

A Second International Exhibition followed in 1967 and was even more successful. It marked the beginning of the short but influential tenure of Herb Kosower, an animation teacher at the University of Southern California (USC). Kosower organised and ran the 2nd, 3rd and 4th exhibitions and, more importantly, was the principal force behind the creation of the travelling Tournee. The programme also benefited from the participation of Phil Chamberlin, the Director of Education at LACMA and later the first curator of its new Film Department, and Clare Kitson, now with Channel Four in London.

While the exhibition had been conceived as a local event, the programme was shared from the start with at least one other institution. Dave Hilberman, one of the founders of UPA, then teaching at San Francisco State College, had arranged for the programme to be screened at the school. Other schools asked Hilberman for screenings at their institutions, It was a short step to the annual touring show, which, for a nominal rental fee, would bring the same selection of outstanding films to colleges and museums around the country.

Income for Animators

Since the purpose of the exhibitions was not only to make the films available to a wider audience, but also to provide some income to the animators, the founders decided that the majority of the rental money would be returned to the participating film-makers and distributors. This co-operative aspect directs 50% of net profits to the animators and remains one of the programme's most distinctive and commendable features. The original idea was that The Tournee would grow and exist only to the point where a major producer would see what a great idea it was and take it over.

With the many benefits of the proposed Tournee clear, it was necessary to gain the support of ASIFA-International. Littlejohn and Goldman presented a proposal to the organisation at that year's festival in Mamaia, Romania.

"There was some opposition to the concept. The purists in ASIFA-International didn't want the film-makers exploited," Littlejohn recalls. "We needed to assure them that the idea was not to exploit them, but to aid them by providing them with some income. They all saw Americans as exploiters, the businessman taking a buck from the animation and hell with the artists. . ." Goldman and Littlejohn received ASIFA's endorsement.

During its premier year of 1967 The Tournee travelled to about a dozen locations around the United States. Officially, the screenings in Los Angeles continued to be known as Exhibitions. (Thus, the 2nd Exhibition was the 1st Tournee, the 3rd Exhibition was the 2nd Tournee) In 1971, the Exhibition title was dropped and significant confusion was ended.

Expanded Entertainment President, Terry Thoren

One of the saddest periods for The Tournee was in 1969 when Herb Kosower, who had done such a masterful job of organising and establishing the programme, learned that he was dying from cancer. In a move that would presage the next stage in its development, Goldman brought in film educator and consultant Prescott Wright, who had just finished an assignment with the American Film Institute and begun his own distribution company, FilmWright, in San Francisco. Wright had previously headed the western branch of Brandon Films for six years and was experienced in programming and distribution. Wright took on responsibility for the Tournee's distribution in 1970, the year of the 5th Exhibition.

Prescott Wright's Influence

Wright's participation stabilised the distribution arm of The Tournee, and during the next several years the number of play-dates continued to grow. In 1973 the L.A. County Museum was no longer able to provide funding to produce The Tournee and FilmWright assumed responsibility for both the production and distribution of the programme.

By 1975, the 10th anniversary of both The Tournee and the Museum, the programme was screened at 50 locations around the country, including San Francisco Museum of Art, the Pacific Film Archive, the Cinémathèque Québécoise, the Walker Art Centre in Minneapolis and the High Museum of Art in Atlanta. The Tournee continued to be nurtured by loyal audiences who returned each year to see the latest animated treasures from around the world, and by the film-makers and exhibitors whose ongoing participation ensured The Tournee's survival.

In an essay written for the 1975 ASIFA Yearbook, Wright took note of the co-operative effort involved in the intensive and sometimes grueling selection process, "Through the co-operation of the major animation festivals in Zagreb and Annecy,

Poster Art from *The British Animation Invasion*

1989 Academy Award-winner: *Balance*

the Selection Committee members screen hundreds of films in Europe. The best of these are brought in for final screening in Los Angeles and San Francisco. . . and, by this process, some 300+ films are synthesised into a programme of between 15 and 20 and running about 100 minutes."

Ward Kimball, a veteran of many of those screening sessions, which also included such ASIFA stalwarts as June Foray, Bill Scott, Phil Chamberlain, Dale Chase, Jules Engel and many others, recalls that the Committee "would sit and watch – my God – two, three nights in a row of films. We tried all sorts of ways to pick out what we considered were the best films, we had arguments and so forth. . . lots of time we were looking for a variety of techniques – not just one slant, not necessarily Tom and Jerry-type animation all the time. Then we would get a hard time from the guys that

liked Bugs Bunny because we'd picked some 'art thing.' We wanted to show the variety of things that were being done."

"We only had 100 minutes of programme," Wright says, "so there had to be some synthesis and there had to be an understanding of who the audience was. One of our tasks was to build an audience, people sho had never seen this kind of thing before. So we had to make it an electric programme."

The Tournee premiered numerous films that went on to win Academy Awards or nominations, including Frank Mouris's *Frank Films*, Nedjelko Dragić's *Tup, Tup*, Emanuel Luzzatti and Giulio Giannini's *Pulcinella* and Steve Bosustow's *The Legend of John Henry*. Moreover, since 1973, The Tournee had began commissioing the programmes titles from students at different animation schools, offering them, in

1990 Academy Award-winner: *Creature Comforts*

Wright's words, "an opportunity to work on a professional level and exhibit their talents with the best in the world."

Economic realities, however, eventually forced Wright to institute a major change. Faced with diminishing support – both funding and available playdates – from the County Museum, Wright moved the Los Angeles premier, to Landmark's NuArt Theatre. It was, as he explains, a natural transition, "Landmark's Gary Meyer and I were friends and associates in San Francisco for many years; in fact, we studied at San Francisco State at the same time. Terry Thoren, president of Expanded Entertainment which is a subsidiary of Landmark, was the first to programme a Tournee at the Denver International Film Festival, which he founded. They had given us a lot of support and we had exhibited at the Landmark theatres more and more over the years. It just made sense to move the premiere to the NuArt."

In order to keep up with the changing times and expand the audience base, it was necessary for The Tournee to become more commercial. With Landmark's support, The Tournee market continued to grow until, by the time of the 16th Tournee, the number of playdates had reached 120.

Expanded Entertainment Era Begins

While The Tournee continued to grow and thrive under Wright's stewardship, the changing market indicated that The Tournee might best be served by expanding its base beyond the non-theatrical and limited theatrical venues with which it had always been associated. In 1985 Wright contracted with Expanded to take over production and distribution of the programme, beginning with The 19th Tournee in 1986. "It was clear that the success of The Tournee was dependent on more money being available to us. We needed to be able to pay the producers who wanted larger advances for their films. Expanded had not only the theatres, but the staffing and the financial resources to take The Tournee to the next level."

Along with the substantial increase in playdates came an improvement in quality. While past Tournees used 16mm, Expanded upgraded prints to 35mm and produced trailers and full-colour one-sheets to enhance the marketing of the programme. Yet, with all the changes, some things remained the same.

"The Tournee, now as then, is a true co-op," says Expanded Entertainment's Terry Thoren, "returning 50% of the profits back to the film-makers, with the goal of constantly replenishing the cycle so that we'll have great films for the 25th and 50th Tournees. All great animation, from the shortest short to the most epic feature, requires brash, unbridled creativity. The undiscovered talents of independent film-makers is the catalyst that drives the industry today and will continue to drive it when it's time to begin production on The 50th International Tournee of Animation!"

1987 Academy Award-winner: *The Man Who Planted Trees*

WORLD SURVEY

ARGENTINA

by Alberto Tabbia

Even if film production had not come to a halt in Argentina by May 1991, there was a feeling among the profession that the film industry as such had been stifled, most of its products the result of individual legerdemain, whether sure-fire commercial bets or the occasional creative venture. Most damaging is the certainty that at neither extreme the results are remarkable.

Aída Bortnik, the scriptwriter of, among others, the Oscar-winning *The Official History*, has recently published a "battle cry" calling to arms "against economic asphyxia and the mediocrity that denies any value to culture, even the need for it. (. . .) There is formal freedom in our cultural life, but films do not get made and theatres are closing down."

The reasons for this state of things are apparent. Between 1984 and 1989, coinciding with the years of return to democratic government. Manuel Antín, a distinguished director and a resourceful policy-maker in the cultural field, put Argentina back on the international film map. More than festival prizes or an Oscar, it was a question of image – something was happening in Argentine cinema. A closer inspection revealed some telling flaws in the picture. Box-office receipts showed a tendency to have one hit a year, at best two medium-range respectable attractions, and lots of titles nobody cared about. The audiences did not patronise Argentine films so much as events – Bemberg's *Camila*, Subiela's *Man Looking Southeast*, Solanas's *Gardel's Exile*. Coupled with the pretentious or near-miss products turned out by newcomers given financing by Antín at the head of the National Film Institute, this drift in film attendance prompted established producers to ask for fewer but more substantial credits, to be entrusted of course to their own capable hands. More unnerving, a certain conformism in subject matter had crept in – many films denounced the evils of yesterday's military régime, even placing any hint of corruption or violence in that recent past, but firmly closed their eyes to the new face of the same evils in the democratic context.

Scene from *La ultima siembra*, directed by Miguel Pereira

Recent projects, on the other hand, seem unaware of the need to seduce a new audience, such as has responded massively to, say, *Babette's Feast* or *Time of the Gypsies*, neither of them films from traditional sources, big names or boasting expensive special effects. Whether in "social comment" or in "broad farce," clichés that often seem to inhabit the mind of the film-makers themselves, not only of their local critics, there is little adventure to be seen.

Number of Screens Still Shrinking

There were a dwindling 2,300 cinemas in Argentina around 1980, less than a third of those operating in the 1930's and 1940's. Today there are only 510. With tickets costing around 4 dollars, and a good part of the population earning under $200 a month, it is not surprising that video clubs are still developing in Argentina. . . By early 1991, with the exception of Cuba, all of Latin America was safely in the hands of "democratic governments" of the kind the United States would approve of. Most of them were implementing liberal economic policies, trying not to have the social situation blow up in their faces after a strong dose of Reaganomics. Credits for government subsidised cultural activities were drastically cut, the effects of the measure in the shaky Argentine context being much stronger than in the U.S. or in Britain. Without the solid background that protects film production in France or Germany, the Argentine cinema is almost on the verge of extinction, second only to Brazil. Foundations prefer music and the plastic arts, money to be laundered seems less interested in films than expected.

After Manuel Antín, the Film Institute passed in quick succession through the hands of a traditional film-maker and of a former liberation ideologue before landing in those of a reliable, unadventurous official. He has attempted to revive the credit policy, although amounts returning for reinvestment are ludicrous in terms of actual production costs. Antín himself has devoted his efforts to the creation of a Foundation-based film university, adapting to the local scene features from UCLA and the Paris FEMIS. Gigantic and tantalising, the project is called by its creator "the dream of a sleeping Argentina." One may only wish that such a sleeping beauty may eventually awaken. With more than 800 applications and a capacity geared, optimistically, at 300, the University runs the risk of producing, like the rest of Argentine universities, frustrated title-holders or economic exiles. But then Antín is a visionary and of late realists have been offering mere mediocrity.

Hugo Soto in *Dios los cria*, directed by Fernando Ayala

Recent and Forthcoming Films

La Ultima Siembra (The Last Sowing). Script: Miguel Pereira based on *Los humildes (The Humble)*, a novel by Miguel Angel Pereira Sr. Dir: Miguel Pereira. Phot: Esteban Courtalon. Players: Patricio Contreras, Leonor Manso, Alberto Benegas, Mario Pasik, Gonzalo Morales. Prod: Jorge Estrada Mora Producciones and Yacoraite Films, with Channel Four (London).
The author of La deuda interna *returns to his native Jujuy, the northernmost province of Argentina, to enact a showdown of generations – old landowner, autocratic but close to elemental truths, against his U.S.-educated son, who destroys the land by trying to implant modern techniques in order to adapt it to an illusory foreign market; on the edges, pawns in a morality play, a coca-chewing Indian in touch with the old gods and a teenage native who has learned to read and write and, by the end, benefits from everybody's experience. Without the stylistic naiveté of his first film, Pereira strives for a momentous ideological statement. His film comes alive only occasionally.*
El Viaje (The Voyage). Script and Dir: Fernando Ezequiel Solanas. Phot: Félix Monti. Players: Walter Quiroz, Dominique Sanda, Franklin Caicedo. Prod: CineSur and Canal Plus (Paris).
From Tierra del Fuego, a teenage boy sets out North in search of his lost father. He explores not only his native Argentina but also the whole diversity of Latin American landscapes and cultures, meeting everywhere the same clash of spiritual richness and social exploitation. By the end, the enigmatic father is reached only to depart in a balloon – the child is left to make use of the fresh wisdom collected in his rites-of-passage journey. For a film-maker who has step by step liberated his work from father figures (whether historical like Perón, literary like Martín Fierro or pop myths like Gardel) this new film may turn out to be a welcome new stage in Solanas' gradual distancing from his authoritarian ideological tracts and his later, Fellini-inspired celebrations of Buenos Aires' urban lore.
Despues de la tormenta (After the Storm). Script: Tristan Bauer, Rubén Alvarez, Graciela Maglie. Dir: Tristan Bauer. Pho: Ricardo de Angelis. Players: Lorenzo Quinteros, Patricio Contreras, Ana María Picchio, Eva Fernández, Franklin Caicedo. Prod: Killarney S.A. and RTVE (Spanish Television).
Confronted with unemployment when a suburban factory closes down, a worker of 45 leaves his family and the big city to recapture his rural roots and his childhood landscape. He finds only a different kind of misery and hopelessness, and at the end returns to the city to face a new struggle.
Dios los cria (God's Children). Script: Fernando Ayala, Ricardo Talesnik. Dir: Fernando Ayala. Phot: Juan Carlos Lenardi. Players: Soledad Silveyra, Hugo Soto, China Zorrilla, Mau-

ricio Bruno, Hugo Grosso. Prod: ARIES Cinematográfica.

A woman attendant at a massage parlour and a transvestite decide to face life as a couple. A serious comedy by the dean of Argentine film directors.

Las tumbas (The Tombs). Script: Enrique Medina, Javier Torre, based on Medina's novel. Dir: Javier Torre. Phot: Javier Miquélez. Players: Norma Aleandro, Eduardo Saucedo, Federico Luppi, Lidia Catalano, Miguel Dedovich. Prod: Javier Torre.

Medina's novel, a best-selling exposé of gruesome daily life in and out of reform school, reaches the screen twenty years after its first publication. The director is himself a novelist, the son of film-maker Leopoldo Torre Nilsson whose first film, more than a decade ago, was his father's unrealised last project – La fiebre amarilla (Yellow Fever).

Vivir mata (Living Kills). Script: Gustavo Barrios, Ricardo Rodríguez, Bebe Kamin. Dir: Bebe Kamin. Phot: Juan Carlos Lenardi. Players: Mauricio Dayub, Jorge Petraglia, Cecilia Roth, Juan Leyrado. Prod: La Maga Films and RTVE (Spanish Television).

By the end of the Nineteenth century, Argentina opens up to European immigration. Among the shiploads of labour forces from Eastern Europe arrives the envoy of one Count Dracula . . .

Ya no hay hombres (There Aren't Any Men Left). Script: Elsa Ossorio, Alberto Fischerman. Dir: Alberto Fischerman. Phot: Rogelio Chomnalez. Players: Georgina Barbarossa, Giuliano Gemma, Katja Alemann, Tina Serrano, Gianni Lunadei. Prod: Víctor Bo for Argentina Sono Film.

An independent professional woman conjures up an ideal fantasy man, and sex object much more reliable than the real thing. Then one day, in real life, she meets a double of her imaginary lover.

Equinoccio, el jardin de las rosas (Equinox, Garden of Roses). Script and Dir: Pablo César. Phot: José Trela. Players: Mohamed Goulder, Saida Nasri, Ahmed Hmaied, Habib Mestiri, Walid Hafid. Prod: Equinoccio Produccions, in association with Tunisia.

Rompecorazones (Heartbreaker). Script and Dir: Jorge Stamadianos. Phot: Miguel Abal. Players: Teresa Costantini, Jorge Sasi, David Di Napoli, Jorge Díez, Grecia Levy. Prod: Cooperativa El Aniceto.

Que vivian los crotos (Long Live Hobos). Script: Ana Poliak, Willy Behnisch. Phot: Willy Behnisch. *Feature-length documentary.* Prod: Viada Producciones RTVE (Spanish Television) Channel Four (U.K.) National Film Board (Canada).

ALBERTO TABBIA is an Argentine film critic and cultural journalist. He co-edited the film series Flashback and is a regular contributor to the main Buenos Aires and Montevideo dailies, their literary supplements and other magazines as well.

TOP TEN GROSSING FILMS IN ARGENTINA: 1990

Dead Poets Society
Pretty Woman
The Bear
Cinema Paradiso
Look Who's Talking
Back to the Future, Part II
Driving Miss Daisy
When Harry Met Sally
Black Rain
Sea of Love

Producers

Gea Cinematográfica, S.A.
Pacheco de Melo 2141
(1126) Buenos Aires
Tel: 803–7779, 3421
Telex: 19051 GEACI AR

Jempsa
Jorge Estrada Mora
Producciones
Reconquista 609
(1003) Buenos Aires
Telex: 18783 TALA AR
Fax: (541) 311–4498

Argentina Sono Film
S.A.C.I.
Lavalle 1975
(1051) Buenos Aires
Tel: 49–0216/18

Cinesur
Córdoba 827–12° "24
(1054) Buenos Aires
Tel: 312 5174, 313 7692

Aries Cinematográfica
Lavalle 1860 (1051) Buenos
Aires
Tel: 45 6347, 40 3438
40 3430, 40 3439

MTC
Cabello 3791, 3rd M
(1425) Buenos Aires
Tel: 802–0329
Fax: 802–0611

Distributors

United International
Pictures S.R.L.
Ayacucho 520
(1026) Buenos Aires
Tel: 49–0261/64
Telex: 9051
Fax: 54–1111303

Theatrical S.A.
Tucumán 1938

Franklin Caicedo and Walter Quiroz in Fernando Solanas's *El viaje*

(1050) Buenos Aires
Tel: 45–6094/7, 953–7941
Telex: 27638 22–238
Fax: 953–7678

Transeuropa
Cinematográfica, S.A.
Ayacucho 586
(1026) Buenos Aires
Tel: 49–3417, 49–2653
Telex: 17387 TRAFI AR
Fax: 541–111191

Eurocine, S.A.
Tucumán 1978
(1050) Buenos Aires
Tel: 40–3731, 40–3631
Telex: 18320 EURO AR

Filmart
Ayacucho 595
(1026) Buenos Aires
Tel: 45–1739/9945, 47–4005
Telex: 17039 NORVI AR

Mundial Films
Ayacucho 595
(1026) Buenos Aires

Tel: 45–1739/9945, 47–4005
Telex: 17039 NORVI AR
Fax: 54–1–3256489

Distrifilms SA
Lavalle 2006
Buenos Aires 1051
Tel: 953–4182 6823
Fax: 54–1111632

Useful Addresses

Instituto Nacional de
Cinematografía
Lima 319 (1073)
Buenos Aires,
Argentina
Tel: 37–9091
Telex 21104 INCINE AR
Fax: 00 54 11–1–2559

Universidad del Cine
Pje. J.M. Giuffra
(1064) Buenos Aires
Tel: 362–0388, 362–0450
Fax: 541–782–0473

AUSTRALIA
by David Stratton

The progress and improved quality in feature film production noted in this section last year continued during the 1990–91 period, despite a few problems.

Most Australian feature films are basically now financed by the Film Finance Corporation; however, before a film can apply to the FFC, it now has to have 40% of its budget in hand, either by a pre-sale (which often means compromises, like foreign [mis]-casting) or by investment. Some of these "commercial" productions have been troubled, costly efforts like John Seale's $13 million *Till There Was You*, shot in 1989 and still (at the time of writing) unreleased, or Stephen Wallace's *Turtle Beach*. In addition, five films per year are so-called FFC "Trust Fund" pictures, lower-budget, supposedly less "commercial" pictures which are guaranteed by the FFC (recently, Trust Fund films included Gillian Armstrong's *The Last Days of Chez Nous*, Mark Joffe's *Spotswood* and Esben Storm's *Deadly*).

But an equally important area of film financing comes from the low-budget films backed by the Australian Film Commission, often in association with innovative Film Victoria – films like *Proof* and *Holidays on the River Yarra*, and the forthcoming *Romper Stomper* and *Greenkeeping*.

There is also a growing number of co-productions, mostly with France so far (*Green Card*, *Dingo*, *Isabelle Eberhardt*) but with other countries gradually joining in (Wim Wenders's *Until the End of the World* is an Australian–Franco–German co-production, while Bruce Beresford's *Black Robe* is a co-production with Canada, and *On My*

Own, starring Judy Davis, combines Australia, France, Italy and Canada).

Delayed Winner

The Australian Film of the Year really should have been the film of *last* year; John Duigan's **Flirting**, a sequel to his 1987 success *The Year My Voice Broke*, was completed in May, 1990, but, despite winning the AFI Award for Best Film in October, was kept under wraps and not released until March, 1991. Once again, Noah Taylor plays Danny Embling, a teenager from a New South Wales country town. It's the mid-1960's, and Danny is now a student at a smart private boarding school for boys, and proud of being a loner and a "dag." Duigan charmingly depicts Danny's romance with a girl boarding at a college for young ladies just across the lake from *his* school; but, in keeping with our hero's non-conformist attitudes, she's a black girl from Africa.

Despite its delayed release, *Flirting* (which at the moment looks like being the last feature film from the Kennedy Miller production company) was a box-office success, as was **Death in Brunswick**, another off-beat comedy. This feature debut for John Ruane (previously known for his medium-length film, *Feathers*) stars Sam Neill as a chronically lazy and disorganised character who's so broke he can't even pay the rent of his flat in the unfashionable Melbourne suburb of Brunswick. He gets a job as cook in a Greek restaurant, has an affair with a Greek girl (Zoe Carides) almost young enough to be his daughter, and accidentally kills his Turkish assistant. Neill

Andie MacDowell and Gérard Depardieu in Peter Weir's *Green Card*

gives a fine comic performance in a film which delights in switching moods, but John Clarke steals the picture as his sardonic, henpecked mate.

No Australian feature film competed at Cannes this year, but two were screened in official sections of the Festival. **Proof**, the first feature from writer–director Jocelyn Moorhouse, was selected to open the Directors' Fortnight, and scored quite a success. This is a black comedy about a blind photographer (Hugo Weaving) who hasn't trusted anyone since his mother died; he certainly doesn't trust the woman (Genevieve Picot) who cleans his house for him, though she longs to make love to him. So why does he trust a guileless young man (Russell Crowe) he meets in an Italian restaurant? The film doesn't answer all the questions it asks, but it's superbly acted and directed with fierce intensity.

The other Cannes entry, Leo Berkeley's

Holidays on the River Yarra, featured in the Un Certain Regard section of the festival. Despite the cheerful title (which, if you say it quickly, sounds like "Holidays on the Riviera"), *Holidays* is a rather grim depiction of teenage unemployment which leads to unthinking racism and violent crime. But Berkeley relieves the angst with some sharp humour and, again, there are fine performances in all the leading roles.

Cox in Melbourne

Death in Brunswick, *Proof* and *Holidays* were all made in Melbourne, and there's no doubt that, in recent years, the focus of quality production has shifted firmly from New South Wales to Victoria. Paul Cox makes his low-budget films, one a year, in Melbourne on what he calls "responsible" budgets (well under $1 million), and he is gradually building up an appreciative audience at home and abroad, though last year's film, the wonderfully quirky *Golden Braid*, didn't fare nearly as well as it should have. His latest is **A Woman's Tale**, a film written for Sheila Florance, the elderly actress who's been seen in small roles in nearly every Cox film to date. The actress herself was seriously ill with cancer but trying to stay independent and to live alone in her flat and not be placed in a hospital. Florance gives a brave, if at times a shade

Still from Jocelyn Moorhouse's *Proof*, released through Kim Lewis Marketing

Craig Adams and Luke Elliot in *Holidays on the River Yarra*

theatrical, performance, and is beautifully supported by Cox regulars like Gosia Dobrowolska, as the nurse who loves and cares for her, Chris Haywood as her troubled son, and Norman Kaye as an old man who lives next door. The film builds inexorably to a profoundly moving climax which takes a firm stand on the euthanasia question.

Roles for women certainly weren't in short supply in Australian films last year. Gillian Armstrong's **The Last Days of Chez Nous**, scripted by Helen Garner, is an emotional drama about a woman aged about forty (Lisa Harrow) happily married to her second husband (Bruno Ganz) and living with him and her teenage daughter (Miranda Otto) in a Sydney suburb. Their harmony is shattered with the return home from abroad of Harrow's younger sister, played by Kerry Fox (so memorable in Jane Campion's *An Angel at My Table*). Armstrong and Garner take their time establishing these characters, all of them human and flawed, and then hit the viewer with a dramatic final act.

In **Aya**, the first feature by Norwegian-born Solrun Hoass, a young Japanese war bride (Eri Ishida) tries to adjust to postwar Australia and isn't helped much by her boorish, unfeeling spouse (awkwardly played by Nicholas Eadie). More sympathe-

tic is her Japanese-speaking friend (Chris Haywood), and one wonders why she didn't marry him in the first place. More could have been made of this interesting, but ultimately uninvolving, theme.

Waiting is the second feature of Jackie McKimmie, and it's a pleasantly tart comedy about an unmarried woman (Noni Hazlehurst) awaiting the birth of her first baby in a remote house in a forest. She's surrounded by friends including the childless couple the baby is destined for, since this is a surrogate birth. McKimmie is good with her women characters but on less certain ground with her men; the film's an uneven one, but it has magical moments, like the opening scene in which a very pregnant Hazlehurst emerges nude, from a mountain stream.

Minimal Australian Content

The first official Australian co-production to reach cinemas really had only minimal Australian content: this was Peter Weir's **Green Card**, which was filmed entirely in New York, but with a number of Australians in key creative positions. On the French side there was Gérard Depardieu, and the film was a considerable local success (it grossed over $10 million in Australia), which should (one hopes) add to the coffers of the Film Finance Corporation, which

Eri Ishida and Nicholas Eadie in *Aya*

Sheila Florance and Gosia Dobrowolska in *A Woman's Tale*

backed it. A quality film, but not the best example of the co-production scheme.

More typical, but considerably less successful, were *Dingo* and *Isabelle Eberhardt*. **Dingo**, directed by Rolf De Heer and scripted by Marc Rosenberg, the talents behind *Incident at Raven's Gate*, has the great good fortune to feature Miles Davis, in his first dramatic screen role, as an American jazz trumpeter, who lives in Paris but who, in a whistle stop in a small Australian outback town in the 1960's, becomes an inspiration for a young boy who grows up to be Colin Friels. The film drags until Friels arrives in Paris to resume his friendship with Davis, and then it comes alive in some splendid jam sessions. **Isabelle Eberhardt**, a majority French picture directed by Ian Pringle, must rank as a lost opportunity; Eberhardt, a turn-of-the-century journalist and adventurer who seems to have been a

kind of French Lawrence of Arabia, must have been in real life more interesting than the character drably played by Mathilda May. It's left to Peter O'Toole to bring a touch of style to the flaccid proceedings.

Back to the mainstream, and away from co-productions, there's **Spotswood**, which looks like being one of the hits of the 1991–92 season (it achieved a profitable sale to the American independent distributor, Miramax). This Ealingesque comedy, beautifully directed by Mark Joffe, stars Anthony Hopkins as a time and motion study expert brought in to "save" an ailing shoe factory; it's the early 1960's, and old Mr. Ball (wonderfully played by veteran Alwyn Kurts) has decidedly not moved with the times. The film is witty and touching, and there are delightful supporting performances by Ben Mendelsohn and Russell Crowe, among many others.

From this and his previous film, *Grievous Bodily Harm*, you can tell Joffe knows his movies; so, too, does Ross Gibson whose clever first feature **Dead to the World**, looks like a mixture of *Johnny Guitar, Body and Soul* and *Force of Evil*. Gibson has taken a lot of risks with this ambitious picture (the soundtrack was entirely post-synched) but the result deserves, at the very least, to become a hit on the cult circuit.

Deadly is a more traditional thriller, but a good one. Esben Storm's first feature in nine years is set in a country town and deals with the controversial question of aboriginal deaths in custody. Jerome Ehlers is a city cop posted temporarily to the town to investigate such a death, and Storm generates plenty of tension – and social comment – as the mystery unfolds.

Backsliding, the first feature by British-born Simon Target, stars Tim Roth as a strange young man who gets work at an isolated weather station and disrupts the lives of a young married couple, both of them Born Again Christians. Target and cinematographer Tom Cowan use the vast expanses of the outback to add to the

Anthony Hopkins in *Spotswood*, released through Beyond International

tension in this suspenseful drama.

Sweet Talker, a vehicle for Bryan Brown, is more in the tradition of Frank Capra movies; it's a slightly whimsical yarn about a con-man who arrives in a small coastal town planning to swindle the locals, but winds up a local himself. Michael Jenkins, in his best film to date, deftly blends sentiment, romance (with Karen Allen) and humour.

The other feature films of the year rate only passing mention. **Beyond My Reach**, directed by Dan Burstall, is about Australian film-makers getting shafted in Hollywood; but the performances and direction are uncertain. **A Kink in the Picasso**, Marc Gracie's attempt at a *Mad World* style comedy, simply isn't funny; and **Dead Sleep** is a poverty row thriller starring Linda Blair which, with its plot about a shady doctor's experiments on his patients, should have been an awful lot better than it was.

Recent Films

Flirting. Script and Dir: John Duigan. Phot: Geoff Burton. Players: Noah Taylor, Thandie Newton, Nicole Kidman. Prod: Terry Hayes, Doug Mitchell, George Miller, for Kennedy–Miller Prods.

Death in Brunswick. Script: John Ruane, Boyd Oxlade, based on Oxlade's novel. Dir: John Ruane. Phot: Ellery Ryan. Players: Sam Neill, Zoe Carides, John Clarke. Prod: Timothy White, for Meridian Films.

Holidays on the River Yarra. Script and Dir: Leo Berkeley. Phot: Brendan Lavelle. Players: Craig Adams, Luke Elliot, Claudia Karvan. Prod: Fiona Cochrane, for Jungle Pictures Prods.

Proof. Script and Dir: Jocelyn Moorhouse. Phot: Martin McGrath. Players: Hugo Weaving, Genevieve Picot, Russell Crowe. Prod: Linda House, for House and Moorhouse Prods.

A Woman's Tale. Script: Paul Cox, Barry Dickins. Dir: Paul Cox. Phot: Nino Martinetti. Players: Sheila Florance, Gosia Dobrowolska, Norman Kaye. Prod: Cox, Santhana Naidu, for Illumination Films.

The Last Days of Chez Nous. Script: Helen Garner. Dir: Gillian Armstrong. Phot: Geoffrey Simpson. Players: Bruno Ganz, Lisa Harrow, Kerry Fox. Prod: Jan Chapman, for Chapman Prods.

Aya. Script and Dir: Solrun Hoass. Phot: Geoff Burton. Players: Eri Ishida, Nicholas Eadie, Chris Haywood. Prod: Denise Patience, Hoass, for Goshu Films.

Waiting. Script and Dir: Jackie McKimmie. Phot: Steve Mason. Players: Noni Hazlehurst, Deborra-Lee Furness, Helen Jones. Prod: Ross Matthews, for Filmside–ABC.

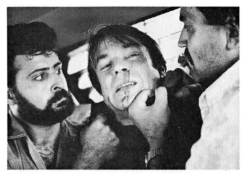
Sam Neill stars in *Death in Brunswick*

Isabelle Eberhardt. Script: Stephen Sewell. Dir: Ian Pringle. Phot: Manuel Teran. Players: Mathilda May, Tcheky Karyo, Peter O'Toole. Prod: Daniel Scharf, Jean Petit, Jacques Leclere, for Les Films Aramis–Seon Films.

Dingo. Script: Marc Rosenberg. Dir: Rolf De Heer. Phot: Denis Lenoir. Players: Colin Friels, Miles Davis, Helen Buday. Prod: Rosenberg, De Heer, for Gevest Australian–AO Prods.

Green Card. Script and Dir: Peter Weir. Phot: Geoffrey Simpson. Players: Gérard Depardieu, Andie MacDowell. Prod: Peter Weir, Jean Gontier, Duncan Henderson, for Lam Ping Ltd.

Spotswood. Script: Man Dann, Andrew Knight. Dir: Mark Joffe. Phot: Ellery Ryan.

TOP TEN GROSSING FILMS IN AUSTRALIA: 1990

	Rentals (AUS$)
Pretty Woman	26,010,000
Ghost	14,370,000
Look Who's Talking	13,800,000
Teenage Mutant Ninja Turtles	13,200,000
War of the Roses	9,770,000
Back to the Future, Part III	9,250,000
Dick Tracy	9,160,000
The Hunt for Red October	8,910,000
Bird on a Wire	8,870,000
Back to the Future, Part II	8,860,000

Players: Anthony Hopkins, Ben Mendelsohn, Alwyn Kurts. Prod: Richard Brennan, Timothy White, for Smiley Films–Meridien Films.

Dead to the World. Script and Dir: Ross Gibson. Phot: Jane Castle. Players: Richard Roxburgh, Agnieska Perepeczko, Tibor Gyapjas. Prod: John Cruthers, for Huzzah Prods.

Deadly. Script and Dir: Esben Storm. Phot: Geoffrey Simpson. Players: Jerome Ehlers, Frank Gallacher, Lydia Miller. Prod: Richard Moir, for Moirstorm Prods.

Backsliding. Script: Simon Target, Ross Wilson. Dir: Target. Phot: Tom Cowan. Players: Tim Roth, Jim Holt, Odile Le Clezio. Prod: Sue Wild, for Target Prods.

Sweet Talker. Script: Tony Morphett, from a story by Bryan Brown. Dir: Michael Jenkins. Phot: Russell Boyd. Players: Bryan Brown, Karen Allen, Chris Haywood. Prod: Ben Gannon, for New Town Prods.

Beyond My Reach. Script: Frank Howson, Philip Dalkin. Dir: Dan Burstall. Phot: Peter Bilcock. Players: David Roberts, Alan Fletcher, Terri Garber. Prod: Howson, for Boulevard Films.

A Kink in the Picasso. Script: Hugh Stuckey. Dir: Marc Gracie. Phot: James Grant. Players: Peter O'Brien, Jon Finlayson, Jane Clifton. Prod: Will Spencer, for Rosa Colosimo Prods.

Dead Sleep. Script: Michael Rymer. Dir: Alec Mills. Phot: John Stokes. Players: Linda Blair, Tony Bonner, Andrew Booth. Prod: Stanley O'Toole, for Village Roadshow Pictures.

Forthcoming Films

Black Robe. Script: Brian Moore, from his novel. Dir: Bruce Beresford. Phot: Peter James. Players: Lothaire Bluteau, Adam Young, August Schellenberg. Prod: Robert Lantos, Stephane Reichel, Sue Milliken, for Alliance Communications (Canada)–Samson Productions (Australia). *An Australian–Canadian co-production about a priest who, in Seventeenth-Century Québec, journeys north to convert the Indians.*

Breathing under Water. Script and Dir: Susan Dermody. Phot: Erika Addis. Players: Anne Louise Lambert, Kristoffer Greaves, Maeve Dermody. Prod: Megan McMurchy, for Periscope Prods. *An end-of-the-world drama set in an underground city.*

Eight Ball. Script: Ray Argall, Harry Kirchner. Dir: Argall. Phot: Mandy Walker. Prod: Timothy White, for Meridian Films. *The relationship between a young and successful architect and an ex-con.*

The Fatal Bond. Script: Phil Avalon. Dir: Vince Monton. Phot: Ray Henman. Players: Linda Blair, Jerome Ehlers, Donal Gibson. Prod: Phil Avalon, for Tovefelt Films. *A couple, about to start a new life in the country, become involved in murder.*

Flynn. Script: Frank Howson, Alister Webb. Dir: Frank Howson. Phot: John Wheeler. Players: Guy Pearce, Claudia Karvan. Prod: Howson, for Boulevard Films. *The adventures of the young Errol Flynn.*

Garbo. Script: Patrick Cook, Stephen Kearney, Neill Gladwin. Dir: Ron Cobb. Phot: Geoff Burton. Players: Stephen Kearney, Neill Gladwin, Max Cullen. *A comedy about a pair of philosophical garbagemen.*

The Girl Who Came Late. Script: Saturday Rosenberg. Dir: Kathy Mueller. Phot: Andrew Lesnie. Players: Miranda Otto, Martin Kemp, Gia Carides. Prod: Ben Gannon, for View Films. *A young woman is obsessed with horses – can she find a stable relationship?*

The Great Pretender. Script: John Cundill. Dir: David Elfick. Phot: Steve Windon. *A young man has an insatiable libido; a story set in the 1950's.*

Greenkeeping. Script and Dir: David Caesar. Prod: Glenys Rowe, for Central Park Films. *A low key, satirical view of urban life.*

Hammers over the Anvil. Script: Peter Hepworth, from a book by Alan Marshall. Dir: Ann Turner. Prod: Richard Mason, for the South Australian Film Corp.

Map of the Human Heart. Script: Vincent Ward, Louis Nowra. Dir: Vincent Ward. Phot: Eduardo Serra. Players: Jason Scott Lee, Patrick Bergin, Anne Parillaud. Prod: Tim Bevan, Vincent Ward, for Map Films Ltd–Working Title Prods–Les Films Ariane–V. Ward Prods.

The Nostradamus Kid. Script and Dir: Bob Ellis. Prod: Terry Jennings, for Simpson–Le Mesurier Films. *Set in the 1960's, it's a Coming of Age story of a Seventh Day Adventist who discovers drink, women and philosophy.*

On My Own. Script: Gill Dennis, Antono Tibaldi, John Frizzel. Dir: Tibaldi. Phot: Vic Sarin. Players: Judy Davis, Simon Henderson, David McIlwraith. Prod: Leo Pascarollo, Eilsa Resegotti, Rosa Colosimo, for Alliance Commu-

Mathilda May in Ian Pringle's *Isabelle Eberhardt*

nications–Ellepi Film. *A teenager's problems with his parents.*
Resistance. Script: The Macau Collective. Dirs: Paul Elliott, Hugh Keays-Byrne. Phot: Sally Bongers. Players: Donal Gibson, Helen Jones, Lorna Leslie. Prod: Christina Ferguson, Pauline Rosenberg, for The Macau Light Film Corp.
Romper Stomper. Script and Dir: Geoffrey Wright. Prod: Daniel Scharf, Ian Pringle, for Seon Films. *A savage study of the activities of a gang of inner-suburban racists.*
Round the Bend. Script: Robert Caswell. Dir: George [*Snowy River*, not *Mad Max*] Miller. Phot: David Connell. Players: Olympia Dukakis, Sigrid Thornton, Bill Kerr. Prod: Robert Caswell, Bernard Terry, for Glasshouse Prods. *A comedy about three generations of a family.*
Secrets. Script: Jan Sardi. Dir: Michael Pattinson. Phot: David Connell. Players: Dani Minogue, Beth Campion, Noah Taylor. Prod: Pattinson, for Victorian Intl. Pictures–Avalon NFU Studios.

Seeing Red. Script: Roger Pulvers. Dir: Virginia Rouse. Phot: Ian Jones. Players: Tony Llewellyn-Jones, Anne-Louise Lambert, Henri Szeps. Prod: Virginia Rouse, Tony Llewellyn-Jones, Carol Bennetto, for Goosey Films. *Various characters on the road from Sydney to Canberra are involved in the case of a missing boy.*
Stan and George's New Life. Script: Brian McKenzie, Deborah Cox. Dir: McKenzie. Phot: Ray Argall. Players: Paul Chubb, Julie Forsyth, John Bluthal. Prod: Margot McDonald, for Leo Films. *Forty-year-old Stan still lives with his parents; he meets George, a young woman from the country, and they plan a new life together.*
Strictly Ballroom. Script: Bax Luhrmann, Craig Pearce. Dir: Bax Luhrmann. Phot: Steve Mason. Players: Gia Carides, Paul Mercurio, Tara Morice. Prod: Tristram Miall, for M & A Films. *The adventures of a champion ballroom dancer.*
Turtle Beach. Script: Ann Turner, from the novel by Blanche D'Alpuget. Dir: Stephen Wallace. Phot: Russell Boyd. Players: Greta Scacchi, Joan Chen, Art Malik. Prod: Matt Carroll, for Roadshow, Coote & Carroll. *The personal and professional conflicts of an Australian woman journalist based in Malaysia.*
Until the Ends of the World. Script: Peter Carey. Dir: Wim Wenders. Phot: Robby Muller. *[See 1991 entry.]*

DAVID STRATTON was Director of the Sydney Film Festival (1966–1983) and divides his time between writing for Variety, and presenting movies on the S.B.S. TV network in Australia.

Noni Hazlehurst, Deborra-Lee Furness, Helen Jones and Fiona Press in *Waiting*

John Doyle and Tibor Gyapjas in *Dead to the World*

Australian Film Awards: 1990

Best Film: *Flirting* (dir: John Duigan)
Best Director: Ray Argall (*Return Home*)
Best Actor: Max von Sydow (*Father*)
Best Actress: Catherine McClements (*Weekend with Kate*)
Best Supporting Actor: Steve Bisley (*The Big Steal*)
Best Supporting Actress: Julia Blake (*Father*)
Best Photography: Jeff Darling (*The Crossing*)
Best Original Screenplay: David Parker (*The Big Steal*)

Best Editing: Robert Gibson (*Flirting*)
Best Music: Phil Judd (*The Big Steal*)
Best Production Design: Roger Ford (*Flirting*)
Best Sound: Anthony Gray, Ross Linton, Phil Judd (*Blood Oath*)
Best Documentary: *Handmaidens and Battleaxes* (Rosalind Gillespie)
Best Short Fiction: *Sparks* (Robert Klenner)
Best Animation: *Picture Start* (Jeremy Parker)
AFI Members' Prize: *Flirting*
Raymond Longford Award: Peter Weir
Byron Kennedy Award: Dennis O'Rourke

AUSTRIA

by Jack Kindred

It was "déjà vu" all over again in Austria's film industry in 1990. None of the made-in-Austria movies turned out to be outstanding, either in a critical or commercial way. The problems facing the landlocked Alpine nation's struggling directors, inadequate production subsidies, rising costs and a dearth of talented screenplay writers, refused to go away. The usual baker's dozen feature films made their debuts, but their low budgets precluded any lasting impact internationally. The production side of the industry focussed mainly on television product, TV commercials and to a limited extent industrial films. There was also some activity on the documentary and animation film scene. Neophyte directors and students dabbled in 16mm shorts and experimental films.

Even two award-winning pictures were not entirely Austrian. Werner Schroeter's **Malina**, best film at the German Film Awards, 1991, and the Bavarian Film Prizes, and Helmut Berger's **Never in Life**, (*Nie im Leben*) which grabbed the 12th annual Max-Ophüls 1991 award, were German-Austrian co-productions. Both directors were Austrian born, however. Another Austrian director, Wolfgang Murnberger, received the Saarland premier's award for his **Heaven or Hell** (*Himmel oder Hölle*) at the same Max-Ophüls minifestival. No shortage of talent there.

Comedy Strikes a Chord
Some Austrian directors apparently have a compulsion to make films with turgid existential, alienation or solipsistic themes designed to keep an entertainment-hungry public out of the theatres. On the contrary, however, Reinhard Schwabenitzky's bittersweet comedy **Ilona und Kurti**, whose plot involves an inheritance swindle with racist overtones, sparked enthusiasm for an Austrian film among moviegoers and critics alike after a long dry spell.

Not so merry was Götz Spielmann's **Erwin und Julia**, which had its premiere at the 1990 Austrian Film Days in Wels. Plot involves a life-hating failed writer, a would-be actor from the sticks, and a lovelorn waitress in a small café. All three are seeking a "new life" in "neurotic" Vienna. And on the solipsistic side was **Feldberg** from Michael Pilz, which, without much story or action, explores inner spaces, evidently hoping the auudience can do the same. This intellectual exercise also had its premiere in Wels before entering film limbo.

Pelter Patzak's fictional account of the symbiosis of power and corruption in politics, **Lex Minister**, was screened at Wels where it was said viewers would recognise this prototype of a politican. Evidently they did not for the film had a very modest run at the box-office and disappeared from the exhibition scene after three weeks.

Requiem for Dominic, Robert Dornhelm's true story of a hapless Romanian falsely accused of being the "Butcher of Timisoara," who died in hospital, did better despite its grim nature, perhaps because of the dramatic events of the Romanian revolution, which captured the world's attention. The movie was shown in New York and was the Golden Globe nominee for the best foreign film.

Milan Dor's **Pink Palace**, subtitled *Par-*

adise Beach, another film about seeking the blue bird of happiness, this time on a Mediterranean island, had a go at the competition in the Max Ophüls Preis but came away empty handed. However, **Meat Grinder** (*Fleischwolf*), Iranian-born Houchang Allahyari's harsh drama of an Austrian prison's subculture violence and sexual supression, received honourable mention at the Saarbrücken affair.

Wega's Many Projects
Most active on Austria's production scene was producer Veit Heiduschka's Wega Film, which perennially has four or five projects in the pipeline. He was executive producer on *Ilona und Kurti*, and has another project, Ernst Lauscher's petty criminal comedy *The Tatooed Heart*, in the can. *Death Flowers* from New York film school graduate Peter Illyl Huemer was set to roll later in 1991 and likewise the clapperboard was to sound on *The Piano Techer (Die Klavierspierin)* from Paulus Manker, as soon as budget requirements could be met, ditto Niki List's project, a *heimat* (homeland) film satire, *Land of Harmony*.

Like other Austrian producers, who film 10 to 12 features a year in total, Heiduschka faces a ceaseless struggle to finance his projects. The government's Federal Film Board FFA subsidises domestic directors to the tune of about 55 million *schillings* annually (some $1.5 million), a figure matched approximately by the public television broadcaster ORF in return for TV rights. Only a few companies like Michael von Wolkenstein's Satel Group, which has offices in Berlin, Budapest, Cologne, London and Munich, are involved occasionally in international co-productions to help meet the rising costs of production.

The Vienna Film Festival was due to reappear in 1991 after a two year hiatus following the resignation of the long-time director Helmut Dimko. The non-competitive Viennale shifted to an autumn date, October 17–27, under new management, with Wels Film Days director Reinhard Pyrker handling nitty-gritty chores and noted New German Cinema director Werner Herzog lending prestige to the event. Pyrker had selected the revamped Apollo cinema centre, five screens and 1,272 seats, for the Viennale's new flagship, provided renovation work could be completed in time.

Attendance at some 280 films released in Austria in 1990 totalled 10,149 million — down slightly from 10,256 million in the previous year. In other words, little change. The number of cinemas dropped from 290 at the end of 1989 to 278 on Jan. 1, 1991. Screens totalled 394, only five less than the total at the end of 1898. Average ticket prices in 1990 amounted to 65 *schillings* ($4.90) up from a top of 50 *schillings* ($3.85) the previous year.

Recent and Forthcoming Films

Himmel oder Hölle (Heaven or Hell). Script: Wolfgang Murnberger. Dir. Wolfgang Murnberger. Phot: Fabian Eder. Players: Adi Murnberger, Fabian Weidinger, Johannes Habeler, Lukas Habeler. Prod: Academy of Music and Dramatic Arts, Film and TV division Vienna.

Ilona and Kurti. Script: Reinhard Schwabenitzky. Dir: Reinhard Schwabenitzky. Phot: Frank Brühne. Players: Elfi Eschke, Hanno Pöschl, Louise Martini, Aviva Beresin, Milena Zupancic, Herbert Fux, Peter Pikl. Helma Gautier, Robert Hoffmann. Prod: SK Film with Wega-Film.

I Love Vienna. Script: Reinhard Jud with Houchang Allahyari. Dir: Houchang Allahyari. Phot: Helmut Pirnat. Players: Veredoon Varochsad, Dolores Schmidinger, Hanno Pöschl, Marisa Mell. Prod: EPO-Film Produktion GmbH.

Die Klavierspielerin (The Piano Teacher). Script: Michael Haneke. Dir: Paulus Manker. Prod: Wega-Film.

Lex Minister. Script: Peter Patzak, Hans Peter Heinzl. Dir. Peter Patzak. Phot: Martin Stingl.

Hans-Peter Hallwachs, Helmut Berger and Anica Dobra in Berger's *Nie im Leben*

Players: Hans Peter Heinzl, Iris Berben, Werner Stocker, Peter Patzak, William Berger, Immy Schell. Prod: K 6 K Theater.
Mindwalk. Script: Fritjof Capra and Floyd Byars. Dir: Bernt Capra. Phot: Karl Kases. Players: Liv Ullmann, Sam Waterston, John Heard, Lone Skye. Prod: Atlas Leasing Gesellschaft mbH.
Requiem für Dominic (Requiem for Dominic). Script: Michael Köhlmeier, Felix Mitterer. Dir: Robert Dornhelm. Phot: Hans Selikovsky. Players: Felix Mitterer, Viktoria Schubert, August Schmölzer, Angelica Schütz, Antonia Rados, Nick Vogel, Georg Hoffmann-Ostenhof. Prod: Terra Film Produktion.
Das tätowierte Herz (The Tatooed Heart). Script: Ernst Josef Lauscher, Peter Berecz. Dir: Ernst Josef Lauscher. Phot: Karl Walter Lindenlaub. Players: Françoise Montagut, Nino Prester, Beatrice Macola, Ernst J. Lauscher, Mahulena Bocanova, Hans-Michael Rebberg. Prod: Wega-Film.

JACK KINDRED, bon vivant and raconteur, is an ex-Variety staffer specialising in German media reporting, and based in Munich.

Producers

Satel Fernseh-und Filmproduktionsgesellschaft
Kirchengasse 19
A 1070 Vienna
Tel: (1) 523 7674
Fax: (1) 526 4328

Schönbrunn Film
Neubaugasse 1
A 1070 Vienna
Tel: (1) 937273
Fax: (1) 939658

TOP TEN GROSSING FILMS IN AUSTRIA: 1990

	Admissions
Pretty Woman	850,000
Look Who's Talking	600,000
The War of the Roses	360,000
The Little Mermaid	320,000
Dead Poets Society	300,000
Ghost	300,000
The Neverending Story 2	280,000
Oliver and Co.	257,000
Back to the Future	230,000
The Hunt for Red October	185,000

Wega Filmproduktionsgesellschaft
Hagelingasse 13
A 1140 Vienna
Tel: (1) 982 52424
Fax: (1) 982 5833

Distributors

Centfox Film
Neubaugasse 35
A 1071 Vienna
Tel: (1) 93 26 29
Fax: (1) 96 72 97

Columbia – Tri-Star Film Verlag
Waldgasse 21/1/1/9
A 1060 Vienna
Tel: (1) 597–15–15
Fax: (1) 597–15–16

Constantin Film
Siebensterngasse 37
A 1070 Vienna
Tel: (1) 93–13–53
Fax: (1) 93–14–02

Czerny Film
Neubaugasse 1

A 1070 Vienna
Tel: (1) 02–02–49
Fax: (1) 93–33–09

Fleur Film
Stadlgasse 1
A 4470 Enns
Tel: (7223) 2670
Fax: (1) 93–82–53 (Vienna Office)

Top Film
Lindengasse 56
A 1070 Vienna
Tel: (1) 96–19–19
Fax: (1) 96–19–18

UIP
Neubaugasse 1
A 1070 Vienna
Tel: (1) 93–46–31
Fax: (1) 96–75–48

Warner Brothers
Zieglergasse 10
A 1070 Vienna
Tel: (1) 93–86–26
Fax: (1) 93–94–62

Useful Addresses

Austrian Film Commission
Neubaugasse 36
A 1070 Vienna
Tel: (1) 526 33230
Fax: (1) 526 6801

Fachverband der Audivisions und Filmindustrie Österreichs
(*Association of Audiovisual and Film Industries*)
Federal Chamber of Commerce
Wiedner Hauptstr. 63
A 1045 Vienna
Tel: (1) 50105–3012
Fax: (1) 50206 253 (jointly with Exhibitors Association)

Österreichischer Filmförderungsfonds
(*Austrian Film Fund*)
Plunkergasse 3–5
A 1150 Vienna
Tel: (1) 92–56–01
Fax: (1) 92–01–63

BELGIUM
by Patrick Duynslaegher

Belgian film production has slowed down considerably in recent months. Only four films were released during the 1990–91 season, against more than a dozen during the period covered by the previous IFG report. Happily, two of the new films – **Toto Le Héros** and **Eline Vere**, both reviewed below – were of exceptional quality. After a triumphant reception at the Director's Fortnight of the Cannes film festival where director Jaco Van Dormael won the Caméra d'or for first feature, *Toto Le Héros* became the domestic sleeper of 1991. It attracted receipts of 20 million francs ($530,000) in its first 10 weeks in Belgium.

Harry Kümel's brilliant *Eline Vere* is another matter altogether, typifying the distribution problems local talent still encounters. As the IFG is going to press, this Dutch–Belgian–French co-production was only released in Holland. The film will be finally picked up by UIP, after local independent distributors, distrusting everything that's not easily marketable for the undemanding teenager audience, showed no interest at all.

L'Année de l'éveil, the eagerly awaited second feature by Gérard Corbiau, proved to be a lesser affair than his highly successful, Oscar-nominated *Le Maître de musique*. Based on the autobiographically-inspired novel by Charles Juliet, the film shows one decisive year in the life of fifteen-year-old François, an orphan boy sent to French military school in Aix-en-Provence in the late 1940's. Corbiau gets the psychological portrait right of the lonely, melancholy adolescent obsessed with the idea of dying in the Indo-China war. Less convincing is his amorous and sexual initiation, thanks to an affair with the Italian wife of the paternal commandant he betrays. The coming of age rituals and inner conflicts of the cadet are ponderously supported by a catalogue of classical music, as if the story is really taking place in a conservatory instead of inside a military barracks.

In **Janssen & Janssens draaien een film**, Robbe De Hert and Luc Pien show us twenty-five years of Movie Madness from Flanders. From a clever, ironic mixture of clips and interviews emerges a very diversified survey of the themes, pet subjects and characteristics of Flemish films. With mordant humour the difficulties are shown of making movies in a country without a film industry, a local audience and real interest from official bodies. The overall picture is rather bleak but De Hert and Pien pay homage to the many obsessed individuals who succeeded in realising their dreams against all odds.

The release of *Janssen & Janssens* coincided with the twenty-fifth anniversary of Fugitive Cinema, a socially committed film collective, created to stir things up in the arid Belgian film-scene of the mid-1960's. Robbe De Hert is still the most colourful member of this Antwerp-based group. Part of the madness he describes in his compilation film may be over now that the Flemish executive government issued a decree which regulates the granting of official funds. Until now film-makers have received their subsidies from the Ministry of Culture, a process that involves an abundance of red tape. Additional money was available from another ministry, that of Economic

Affairs. This so called "detaxation" system consisted of partially returning tax to the producers of indigenous films, based on the box-office grosses. With the new policy, drawn up by Cultural Affairs Minister Patrick Dewael and his colleague from Economic Affairs Norbert De Batselier, both sources of subsidy are united in the non-profit organisation "Stichting Vlaamse Filmproduktie" (SVF). The new industry organisation assists film-makers with script and production funds, eliminates direct ministerial involvement and aims to secure a continuous Flemish film production.

The new decree also met with some disapproval, mainly from the ranks of makers of animation shorts; they argue that with the repeal of the detaxation system there's no impetus left for distributors and exhibitors for showing these shorts.

While some people are still struggling to get our film industry off the ground, the success story in Benelux media circles is the smash victory of VTM (Vlaamse Televisie Maatschappij), the commercial station in Flanders that began broadcasting early 1989 and has since acquired a 40% share of the Flemish-speaking market. This promptly led to some childish friction with its main competitor, the state-supported BRT. The spectacular popularity of VTM is due to gameshows, the promotion of local musical talent and the sometimes crass appeal to a truly local Flemish identity. The success story has also a shadow side, called the "VTM-isation" of Flanders by its detractors, meaning everything is aimed at the lowest common denominator.

Kinepolis Now Taking 55%
Another Flemish success story is the dominance in the exhibition sector of Kinepolis, the 7,600 24-screen (all THX-sound) complex on the outskirts of Brussels. Kinepolis now represents 55% of the cinema market in the Belgian capital and the Bert and Claeys families who own the multiplex, also control the towns of Ghent, Hasselt and Kirtrijk and are soon starting up in Antwerp. The Kinepolis phenomenon is largely responsible for the 9% increase of cinema admission in 1990 (close to 5 million) but is also credited with the collapse of many downtown theatres.

Toto Le Héros

Script and Direction: Jaco Van Dormael. Photography: Walther van den Enden. Editing: Susana Rossberg. Music: Pierre Van Dormael. Art Direction: Hubert Pouille. Players: Michel Bouquet, Jo De Backer, Thomas Godet, Gisela Uhlen, Mireille Perrier. Produced by Pierre Drouot and Dany Geys for Iblis Films (Brussels)/Les Productions Phillippe Dussart (Paris)/Metropolis Filmproduktion (Berlin). 90 mins.

With the shorts and documentaries he made over the past ten years, Jaco Van Dormael already had a reputation among Belgian film professionals. Those who have seen his previous work won't be surprised how remarkably well-crafted his first feature is. For all the others, *Toto Le Héros* reveals Van Dormael as a surprising fresh talent.

French actor Michel Bouquet (veteran of a cycle of superb bourgeois thrillers by Claude Chabrol) plays an old man, Thomas, who is convinced since his early childhood that he was exchanged at birth with Alfred, the baby of his neighbours. In the twilight of his life he finally finds the energy to react against the cruel game that fate has played on him. He thinks back to his youth when he saw himself as the invincible Toto the Hero, and escapes from his old folks' home to seek revenge against his arch enemy Alfred, the man who has stolen his life, his love, his dreams.

Van Dormael instals the spectator inside the tortured mind of his protagonist, and develops this extremely subjective tale with an amazing narrative assurance. The three worlds of Thomas – as a bitter old man, a joyless adult and an imaginative child – are

Director Jaco van Dormael with Michel Bouquet on *Toto le Héros*

ingeniously intertwined. The overall structure is a puzzling murder mystery, but Van Dormael uses the conventions of the criminal film to his own benefit. *Toto Le Héros* is at once suspenseful, nostalgic (there's a wonderful use of the Charles Trenet song, "Boum"), mildly poetic and cheerful good fun.

Patrick Duynslaegher

PATRICK DUYNSLAEGHER is film critic for the leading Belgian weekly magazine, Knack. His articles have appeared in Variety, Sight and Sound, and other periodicals. Co-author of a book on André Delvaux.

Eline Vere

Script: Jan Blokker, Patrick Pesnot, based on the novel by Louis Couperus. Direction: Harry Kümel. Photography: Eduard Van Der Enden. Editing: Ludo Troch. Music: Laurens Van Rooyen. Art Direction: Ben Van Os, Jan Roelfs. Players: Marianne Basler, Monique Van De Ven, Thom Hoffman, Johan Leysen, Aurore Clément, Michael York. Produced by Matthijs Van Heijningen for Sigma Filmproductions (Amsterdam)/Paul Breuls for Silent Sunset Productions (Antwerp)/Yannick Bernard for Odessa Films (Paris). 140 mins.

Eline Vere marks a complete return to form for Harry Kümel (who didn't direct anything of real importance during the past decade). This lavish costume drama is

Marianne Basler in *Eline Vere*

based on the first and best novel (published in 1889) by Louis Couperus, hailed as the greatest Dutch novelist of the 1880 literary revival. *Eline Vere* describes the final years in the life of a young, over-sensitive and neurotic woman who feels herself doomed, tries to escape her suffocating upper middle-class environment in The Hague through romantic longing and who in the end unwittingly commits suicide. Fate plays an important part in her downfall as does repressed passion. Instrumental in her complete desintegration is her cousin Vincent who makes her doubt her own feelings every time she meets a man who attracts her.

Faithful to the spirit of Couperus, the film nevertheless reflects Kümel's own pre-occupation with people in decline and sex-ual ambiguity. It also shows his preference for a cruel humour, veering towards a camp sensibility (especially visible in the acting of Thom Hoffman as Vincent). As always Kümel makes it a principle to hide his real feelings towards his characters. His artistic detachment is always in evidence in what is above all an opulently designed exercise in pure style.

The director also finds the right visual equivalent for Couperus's ornate style. The stiffness, boredom and claustrophobia of petty-minded The Hague contrasts with the *fin-de-siècle* spirit of luxurious decadence in Brussels where Eline Vere finds temporary refuge, before her world finally collapses. Throughout the film, Kümel creates mean-ing and mood through lighting, movement, music and brilliant editing. The atmosphere of inescapable doom is intensified and made palatable through the imaginative symbo-lism in décor and costumes. The director of *Monsieur Hawarden* and *Malpertuis* revels in the sumptuous artifice of melodramatic convention and concludes the downward spiral of Eline's life with a virtuoso opera scene.

Patrick Duynslaegher

BOLIVIA

by Pedro Susz K.

This has again been a critical year for Bolivian cinema. Although *La Nacion clandestina* by Jorge Sanjines had a very enthusiastic reception at home and abroad, production difficulties again surfaced, preventing several current projects from being completed.

Throughout 1990, an intense campaign among film personalities here helped to raise the issue of a Film Law once again – this time with a majority of the public behind the drive too. But this had no impact on the members of Congress, who have been looking into this Law for the past six years. Congress, of course, has come under intense lobbying pressure from the video pirates to ignore the pleas for fresh legislation. The illegal buying, renting and selling of both films and videos is the worst crisis thus faced by the Bolivian cinema. But perhaps there is some hope that the Law will be approved eventually.

In Santa Cruz, in the east of Bolivia, filming was completed on the feature, **Los Igualitarios**. This is a film with an historical background, directed by Juan Miranda, a young film-maker with considerable experience in photography, for film, TV and video. *Los Igualitarios* recreates an authentic episode: the outbreak of federalism in the last years of the Nineteenth Century, headed by Andres Ibañez, a lawyer with progressive ideas. He was accused by the Bolivian authorities of seeking independence for the Santa Cruz province, in order to join up with Brazil. This argument gave the government a pretext to send in troops who snuffed out the uprising and shot its leader. Miranda tries to establish the true facts behind this incident, but the deficiencies of script and direction undermine his efforts.

BRAZIL

by Luis Arbex

The future of the Brazilian film industry looks appalling in 1991. The country's catastrophic economic situation continues to strike hard at the cinema, causing retrenchment in all sectors. The government withdrew all funds from the cinema branch, and Embrafilme, which sponsored most of the production in the past, has been closed. Even support for film periodicals has been halted.

At the Cannes Festival this year, Hector Babenco declared that the Brazilian cinema

TOP TEN GROSSING FILMS IN BRAZIL: 1990

Cinema Paradiso
Himmel über Berlin (Wings of Desire)
¡Atame!
Ladri di saponette
Dead Poets Society
Ghost
Pretty Woman
Driving Miss Daisy
Home Alone
My Left Foot

is dead, causing considerable turmoil among domestic directors. Two well-known film-makers are working abroad, some have changed profession or switched to TV, and the remainder have wisely kept silent.

The only quality features screened last season were Julio Bressane's **Sermons** and newcomer Nuno Cesar Abreu's **Proof of Evidence**. Besides, only nine films opened last season, although there are around 29 awaiting release. None of the joint ventures with foreign producers is ready for screening and some of the "Forthcoming Films" listed in last year's IFG have never surfaced. It is worth remembering that in 1979, Brazil ranked fourteenth among the world's largest film producers. But the days of the quota are gone: no cinema is obliged to devote 133 days' screening time to domestic product.

The only notable event of the year in São Paulo was Leon Cakoff's fifteenth International Film Festival. Cakoff continues to release original and uncut versions of films he brings in for the event, thus meeting the cultural enthusiasm and standards of a new generation. American films still dominate the market in São Paulo and in terms of art-house movies, a few new theatres have been equipped with the best in sound and screen comfort. Original versions can be seen at the Elétrico, Cinesesc, Mis and Bellas Artes (now under the management of former French director Jean-Gabriel Albicocco). These cinemas are in the Paulista area, with its selection of pleasant cafés, video stores, and film bookshops. The Goethe Institute, Alliance Française, and various embassies have all sponsored film weeks here recently.

Recent and Forthcoming Films

Boca de ouro (Mouth of Gold). Dir: Walter Avancini. Players: Tarcísio Meira, Cláudia Raia, Grande Otelo, Luma de Oliveira, Hugo Carvana. *Thriller.*
Corpo em delito (Proof of Evidence). Script and Dir: Nuno Cesar Abreu. Phot: Carlos Egberto. Mus: Raul do Valle. Players: Regina Dourado, Lima Duarte, Dedina Bernardelli, Wilson Grey.
O Grande mentecepto (The Great Madman). Dir: Oswaldo Caldeira. Players: Diogo Vilela, Imara Reis, Luis Fernando Guimarães, Déborah Bloch, Regina Casé, Osmar Prado.
Lua de cristal (Crystal Moon). Dir: Tizuka Yamasaki. Players: Xuxa Meneghel, Sérgio Mallandro, Cláudio Mamberti.
O mistéerio de Robin Hood (The Mystery of Robin Hood). Dir: José Alvarenga Jr. Players:

Renato Azragão, Mussum, Dedé Santana, Xuxa
Meneghel.
Nostalgia (Homesick). Dir: Túlio Becker, Sér-
gio Silva. Players: Romulo Viero, Sérgio Ku-
plich.
**Na rota do brilho (In the Course of
Brightness).** Dir: Deni Cavalcanti. Players:
Marcos Manzano, Alexandre Frota.
Os sermões (Sermons). Script and Dir: Júlio
Bressane. Phot: José Tadeu Ribeiro. Mus: Lívio
Tragtemberg. Players: Othon Bastos, José Lew-
goy, Ankito, Eduardo Tornaghi, Bia Nunes,
Caetano Veloso.
Sonho de verão (Summer's Dream). Dir:
Paulo Sérgio de Almeida. Players: Sérgio
Mallandro, Paquitas, Paquitos, Fafy Siqueira.
**Uma escola atrapalhada (A Plundered
School).** Dir: Antônio Rangel. Players: Renato
Aragão, Mussum, Dedé Santana, Angélica,
Supla.
A grande arte (The Great Art). Dir: Walter
Salles Jr. Mus: Jurgen Kniepper. Phot: José
Roberto Eliezer. Players: Peter Coyote, Tcheky
Karyo, Amanda Pays, Miguel Angel Fuentes,
Giulia Gam, Cássia Kiss, Raul Cortez. Prod:
Paulo Brito. *Filmed in English.*
**Brincando nos campos do Senhor (At Play in
the Fields of the Lord).** Dir: Hector Babenco.
Players: Tom Berenger, Daryl Hannah, Tom
Waits. *Filmed in English for the American market.*

José Mayer in *Gardenia's Perfume*

Perfume de gardênia (Gardenia's Perfume).
Dir: Guilherme de Almeida Prado. Prod:
Assunção Hernandes. Phot: Cláudio Portioli.
Players: Cristiane Torlonem, José Mayer, Walter
Queiroz. Prod: Star Filmes Lta.

*DR. LUIS ARBEX won a scholarship to the U.S. for
postgraduate medical training and remained there for
eight years. Now retired, he dedicates his time to
cinema research and travelling as a genuine movie
buff.*

Producers

**CDK-Produções
Cinematográficas Ltda**
c/o Carlos Diegues
Rua Miguel Pereira 62
22261 Rio de Janeiro.
Tel: (021) 266–7995

**L.C. Barreto Produções
Cinematográficas**
c/o Luiz Carlos Barreto
Rua Visconde de Caravelas 28
22271 Rio de Janeiro
Tel: (021) 266–5561

**Raiz Produções
Cinematográficas**
c/o João Batista de Andrade

Rua Epeira 59
05447 São Paulo
Tel: (011) 814–4491

Regina Films
c/o Nelson Pereira dos Santos
Rua Jornalista Orlando Dantas 1
Botafogo
Rio de Janeiro
Tel: (021) 552–3648

Distributors

Alvorada-Gaumont
Av. Ipiranga 318
São Paulo
Tel: 231–2361
Telex: 33221

Art Films
Av. Rio Branco 227/102
Rio de Janeiro
Tel: 210–1371
Telex: 30758

Bitelli International
Rua Traipu 210
São Paulo
Tel: 825–5599
Telex: 3255

CIC
Av. Rio Branco 245/28
Rio de Janeiro
Tel: 210–2400
Telex: 21202

Cinematográfica Sul

(F.J. Lucas)
Av. São João 1588
São Paulo
Tel: 220–5622

Haway
Rua Turiassu 716

São Paulo
Tel: 864–7199
Telex: 82255

Paris Films
Av. Pacaembu 1702
São Paulo

Tel: 864–9111
Telex: 83505

Severiano Ribeiro
Praça Mahatma Gandhi 2
Rio de Janeiro
Tel: 240–4242

BULGARIA

by Ivan Stoyanovich

Last year's dispatch for the IFG forecast bad times for Bulgarian cinema despite some small degree of hope for a miracle. Of course, there was no miracle. The film production studios, the bureaucrats, and centralised film distributors have or are about to cut their staff in half, if not disappear altogether. So far the survivors have only got a couple of millions and a host of dubious promises from the State just to finish those films already begun, and to fund two or three new ones without identifying them. A selected few cinemas in the major cities can still survive irrespective of the huge increase in ticket prices. The sense of insecurity conveyed in last year's article is doubled today, mainly due to the vague nature of the principled economic and political strategy of tomorrow's State.

New parliamentary and local elections lie ahead. If the opposition wins, and convincingly at that, we could expect a fuller privatisation programme including one in film production and distribution. The Grand National Assembly, however, has not passed, and the Government has not prepared, the respective documents for such legislation. If, on the other hand, elections are won by the present majority of Socialists (more or less followers of the Communists), we can expect even more complicated forms

of State-Co-operative-Private links in film production and distribution, for which there are no standards prepared either. In the meantime the bold and undoubtedly promising economic reform which puts to the test the domestic budget with regard to bread, meat, butter, sugar and energy, naturally distances viewers from the cinemas where tickets, like foodstuffs, rocketed up some four times while wages only doubled.

The International Monetary Fund as the protector, and, by the way, the entire Bulgarian democratic power which was welcomed so warmly, regard cultural funds as a mere footnote. At the current stage there is no hint of a lasting subsidy for film; not even of an initial credit to feed the turnover capital and which could possibly be refunded. No funds, that's the long and short of it.

The film branch, which up to now has reported directly to the Council of Ministers, is trapped in the bosom of the Ministry of Culture (boasting a modest budget anyway), but neither the film branch nor the Ministry have so far built any specific formula that accommodates both the artistic and industrial sides of this culture.

What has so far become clear is that the

Scene from *Love Is a Wilful Bird*

previous Cinematography Chief Lyudmil Staikov has quit his post, as did the Feature Film Studio Director Emil Angelov and other heads of studios and enterprises. As with an underaged monarch, the cinema here is ruled by triumvirates of regents with limited operative functions. The Union of Bulgarian Film-Makers leases its theatre, the restaurant, cafeteria and rest homes. The obvious aim of this bitter-sweet agony is to endure as long as possible while the major, priority issues are resolved and the State finds its feet.

Fair enough, the cinema is but a mirror of the trouble-stricken State which is now bearing the fruits, the rotten fruits of a malconceived political and economic social-ist system, where the natural historical course can only be the fastest possible eradication of this system. This, however, is the hardest part. Given today's young and fairly green democracy set against the skilled administrators, stock-exchange masters and political players of yesteryear, the heritage of a half million-strong communist party clinging to its privileges, it is hardly probable that the radical economic reforms, fully supported by the Euro-American world at that, and the radical legislation naturally channelled into private

property and entrepreneurship, will soon get the chance to put the derailed train back on its tracks.

In this wilderness, though, certain smart poachers have laid their traps in time and are now going to collect their prey. Rangel Vulchanov's **Love Is a Wilful Bird** – a picturesque absurdity illustrating our apocalyptic days – has already conquered the international, as well as the national circuit, not without the talents of Emil Hristov (cameraman), Georgi Todorov (art director), Stefan Dimitrov (music) and actors Emilia Tsaneva, Itsko Fintsi, Nikolai Binev, Todor Kolev and Ilka Zafirova.

I, the Countess, directed by Peter Popzlatev, and scripted by Raymond Wagenstein, with its serious socio-psychological analysis of drugs and young people attracted seven international awards. **Indian Games**, directed by Ivan Andonov and scripted by Victor Paskov, is a rich mixture of magic folkloric traditions and totalitarian paradoxes.

The first prize of our probably last national film festival went to **Silence** made by the young team of Dimiter Petkov (director and scriptwriter), Hristo Bakalov (camera), Vladimir Lekarski (art direction),

Scene from *Indian Games*

Still from *Silence*

with Hristo Gurbev, Peter Popyordanov and Zhoreta Nikolova in the main parts: a subtle, poetical study filmed with a strong visual texture but not sufficiently impressive for the viewer, as, for example, the philosophical parable of Ivan Pavlov, **Walks with the Angel**, a winner of a Strasbourg Silver Prize. **The Bronze Vixen**, a melodramatic story written by Ivan Golev and directed by Nikola Roudarov, made a bigger impact on audiences. And the comedy, **That Thing**, from a script by Hristo Boichev and directed by Georgi Stoyanov, was screened without much success.

Forthcoming Films

Protected Zone. Script: Edouard Zahariev, Plamen Maslarov. Dir: Edouard Zahariev. Phot: Emil Hristov. Players: Georgi Staikov, Evelina Borissova, Itsko Fintsi, Stoicho Mazgalov, Bogdan Glishev, Vassil Dimitrov. *An aesthetically accomplished tale told against the background of a political and moral clash – a son's striving to avenge the murder of his father in the Stalinist period.*
Silence. Script and Dir: Krassimir Kroumov. Phot: Wojciech Todorov. Music: Georgi Popov. Players: Yossif Surchadjiev, Vania Tsvetkova, Naoum Shopov. *Again, as in* Protected Zone, *the core of the film is a grave conflict arising out of a son's nemesis for a father killed during the communist repression.*

Oh God, Where Are You? Script and Dir: Krassimir Spassov. Phot: Plamen Somov. Players: Stefan Mavrodiev, Vassil Mihailov, Marin Yanev, Ivailo Hristov, Georgi Novakov. *Yet another generation gap drama. The countdown in this case is the murder of a father and the suicide of his son.*
I Want America. Script and Dir: Kiran Kolarov. Phot: Victor Chichov. Music: Kiril Donchev. Players: Nevena Kokanova, Stefan Danailov, Irina Yakovleva. *A family drama, the result of contradicting moral stands of children and parents of yesterday and today.*
Real Evidence. Script and Dir: Borislav Pounchev. Phot: Tsancho Tsanchev. Players: Ivailo Hristov, Kiril Gospodinov, Sasho Doinov. *Based on Yordan Radichkov's novelette* Goat's Beard, *this film is a tale of the sheep that has been unfairly taken away from the Socialist farm – an incident that provokes a bloody revenge.*
The Well. Script and Dir: Docho Bodjakov. Phot: Ivan Varimezov. Players: Lyuben Chatalov, Vania Tsvetkova, Peter Popyordanov. *A psychological analysis of changing morals – from anti-Fascist resistance to totalitarianism.*
Tony. Script: Rada Moskova. Dir: Dimiter Petrov. Phot: Kroum Kroumov. Music: Georgi Genkov. Players: Vania Bakalova, Lyubomir Chatalov, Iskra Radeva. *A film with children, for children and non-children, raising unpretentious children's issues.*
The Father of the Egg. Script: Boris Hristov. Dir: Henri Koulev. Phot: Svetlana Ganeva. Players: Ivailo Hristov, Lyuben Chatalov, Konstantin Kotsev. *We continue to wait for this complex mix of a film – an attempt at a screen version of the Apocalypse – as fantastic as it seems real.*
Plyontek. Script: Victor Paskov. Dir: Borislav Sharaliev. Phot: Emil Hristov. Players: Dimiter Popov, Kamen Tsonev, Radomir Balabanov, Elena Stoimenova.

IVAN STOYANOVICH has been a film critic and journalist for 35 years, author of several hundreds of articles and reviews, and has published books, brochures and reports on the cinema. Editor-in-Chief of Bulgarian Films Magazine for 30 years. Since 1991 he has been Editor-in-Chief of the "Intercine" Review, an independent film magazine on world and Bulgarian cinema.

Useful Adresses

National Film Centre
Ministry of Culture
17, Stamboliiski Blvd
Sofia
Tel: 87–21–54, 86–111

Boyana Feature Film Studio
Boyana 16 Film City
Sofia
Tel: 58–131
Telex: 22–376
Fax: 59–31–15

Vreme Popular Scientific and Documentary Film Studio
9 Biryuzov Blvd
Sofia
Tel: 44–28–23
Telex: 23–010

Sofia Animated Film Studio
Boyana 16 Film City
Tel: 58–131
Telex: 567

Bulgariafilm
Import–Export
96 Rakovski St
Tel: 87–66–11
Telegr: Bulgariafilm
Telex: 22–447
Fax: 88–24–31

Bulgarian Film Enterprises
(Bulgarian–British Joint Venture)
75 Biryuzov St
Sofia
Tel: 470–91–28
Fax: 470–91–48

Film Distribution
135A Rakovski St
Sofia

Tel: 88–12–91
Telegr: Bulgariafilm
Fax: 88–24–31

Bulgarian Video
60 Samokov Blvd
Sofia
Tel: 72–07–77
Telex: 22–812

Interfilm
(The Sofia Press Agency)
113 Lenin Blvd
Sofia
Tel: 70–20–48
Fax: 7–11–27

The "Intercine" Review
29 Slavianska St
Sofia
Tel: 88–58–31
Fax: 77–11–27

BURKINA FASO
by Roy Armes

For over twenty years Burkina Faso has been in the forefront of virtually every initiative to develop and promote cinema in black Africa. The Ouagadougou Pan-African Film Festival (FESPACO) was founded in a very modest way in 1969 and has since gone from strength to strength, becoming a regular biennial festival (alternating with the foremost Arab film festival – the Journées Cinématographiques de Carthage – in Tunisia). The festival in Ouagadougou has become the major show-case for new African cinema and the 1991 meeting was the twelfth and largest to date.

As early as 1970 the government of what was then Upper Volta took a leading role in moves to nationalise local film distribution and exhibition, setting up its own national film corporation. Though the battle to secure an adequate distribution of African-made films throughout Africa is still to be won, it was in Ouagadougou that the most serious efforts to control the power of the multinational film distributors were made in the 1980's. For a while at least it seemed as if the founding of a pan-African distribution consortium (CIDC), which took over previously French-owned commercial interests, offered real hopes, and there was a project for a parallel pan-African production organisation (CIPROFILM), to be funded from receipts from the distribution of foreign films. A further Burkina Faso initiative to offer professional training for African film-makers, by setting up a film school (INAFEC) in Ouagadougou in 1976, proved its immediate value and, though the organisation has now had to be wound up, there are moves to revitalise it in the 1990's. It was in Ouagadougou too that the first purpose-built privately owned film studio (CINAFRIC) was established, producing its first two features in 1983.

As far as production is concerned, the current Secretary General of the Pan-African Federation of Film-Makers (FEPACI) is the head of the Burkina Faso national film corporation, Gaston Kabore, and it is in Ouagadougou – alongside the Festival – that the organisation holds its meetings. Burkina Faso has been actively involved in recent steps to create inter-national co-production in Africa, giving support to such important films as Med Hondo's *Sarraounia* and Ousmane Sembene and Thierno Faty Sow's *Camp de Thiarrove*.

With respect to Burkina Faso's own national production, this remains at a fairly low level of about twenty features overall. As is the case in most parts of black Africa most of these have been first features by new young directors who have unfortunately not been able to create further features in which to develop their talent. The sequence begins in the 1970's with Mamadou Djim Kola's *Blood of the Outcasts*, Augustin Roch T. Taoko's *M'Ba-Raogo* and René Bernard Yonly's *On the Path to Reconciliation*. This trio was followed in the 1980's by Kollo Sanou with *Paweogo*, Paul Zoumbara with *Days of Torment*, Armand Balima with *The Dizziness of Passion*, and Emmanuel Sanou-Doba with *The Last Salary*.

At the 1991 FESPACO there were no fewer than four new debuts: Drissa Toure's **Laada**, Pierre S. Yameogo's **Laafi**, Boureima Nikiema's **My Daughter Will Not Be Circumcised**, and Abdoulaye D. Saw's co-production with Togo, **Yelbeedo**. Like Idrissa Ouedraogo's television film, co-funded by the German ZDF and French FR3 and also shown at FESPACO, **Karim and Sala**, none of these 1991 offerings by new directors proved to be of international status, but the force of Burkina Faso's support for black African cinema is indis-putable.

Burkina Faso's greatest contribution to cinema lies arguably in the work of its two world-class film-makers, Gaston Kabore and Idrissa Ouedraogo. Kabore's two features are deliberately contrasting explor-ations of film narrative. The first and more successful of the two, *Wend Kuuni*, draws on the resources of traditional oral story telling (a missing husband, a rebellious woman, a foundling) to build a complex pattern of variation and repetition. The second, *Zan Boko*, is perhaps less accessible, as it explores the implications for story telling of focussing not on an individual protagonist but taken the whole social group as hero. The tone is given in the opening childbirth sequence which is told not in terms of mother and baby, but as a social act involv-ing the whole village, and especially the men.

Ouedraogo's three cinema features show a steady growth in maturity and complexity. *Yam daabo*, a simple tale of a family taking its fate into its own hands, is a typically optimistic first feature from a young director working with state funding. *Yaaba*, the charming tale of a little boy who befriends an outcast old woman which made Oue-draogo's international reputation, shows a new sureness of touch. *Tilai*, perhaps his finest work, is a rigorous drama of irrecon-cilable family conflicts, told with all the stark authority of a Greek tragedy. Film-making is a difficult enterprise throughout black Africa, but the context for production seems most secure in Burkina Faso.

BURMA (MYANMAR)

by Fred Marshall

Although Burma (now known as Myanmar) has licensed private production films in the past two years, the government controls its own Motion Picture Corporation under the Ministry of Information. This has its own lab, and purchases raw stock (Fuji) for use by producers. Last year, 35 colour films were produced in Myanmar, all with Burmese soundtracks and aimed at the younger, working-class majority.

Myanmar is potentially one of the richest countries in Southeast Asia. It is endowed with a healthy and literate population of some 35 million people. All film-making activity is centred on the capital Yangon (formerly Rangoon), with its population of 2 million.

Among the most popular directors in Myanmar are War War Win Shwe, U Thu Kha, Maung Hla Myo, Maung Tin Oo, Aung Myint Myat, U Khi Myint, Than Htut Thein Htut, Thiha Kyaw Soe, Sein Than Mani, and Kyi Soe Tun. They are mostly in their fifties and regarded as key veteran figures in the Burmese film world. They can adapt themselves to make whatever type of film is required in order to suit the needs of story and stars alike.

U Thu Kha, a pioneer among pioneers, still commands respect as a film scholar and important literary personality. Although in his eighties, he remains a consultant for production companies. He is the only Burmese director ever to have had his work screened abroad (at the Manila International Festival of 1981). He recently completed a new film, **Lunch for a Monk** (*Yahan sa thaw sun tanta*), about a Buddhist monk.

All 400 cinemas in Myanmar are government-owned. All foreign films are screened in English versions only, and indeed foreign imports must have an English track attached before being unspooled in cinemas here (Hindi pictures being the sole exception). Strong censorship is applied where sex, violence, and politics are concerned. The emphasis is on family entertainment; audiences prefer stories from within the framework of their own society.

Many producers are now able to import films, thanks to new legislation. Most of the

U Thu Kha

buying and importing must be done with outside contacts through Asian cities like Hongkong, Bangkok, and Kuala Lumpur.

In domestic films, Burmese is spoken and sung, for local film dubbing does not exist. Most of these productions must be shot on locations up-country because of a lack of studio space and the high cost of filming abroad. Famous books and stories continue to be the prime source for film-makers, with character identification very important as well as a choice of superstars. Big-screen films are still preferred to TV and video.

The Burmese Academy Awards are forty years old. The Ministry of Information organises the event and is responsible for selecting the winners. Among previous winners are U Thu Kha (best director), Nyunt Khin (best actor), Wa Wa Win Shwe (best actress), Myint Myint Khin (best actress), and Moe Moe Myin Aung (best actress).

In 1990 the best film award went to **A Man Called Doe**. Kyi Soe Tun won best director, Kyaw Hein took best actor, and Moe Moe Myint Aung was best actress. These male and female superstars are judged by the public's acceptance of their character as well as their behaviour and morals. An actress must be able to swing and project sweetness for the family as well as sympathy for the older generation – and, like Mae Sweet, she must be able to preserve her youth for fifteen or twenty years.

CAMBODIA
by Fred Marshall

Kampuchea is once again known as Cambodia, but the country's media situation remains difficult to disentangle. Festivals are screening the Czech-Cambodian film, *The Ninth Circle*, about a Czech doctor who falls in love with a resistance worker-cum-nursing sister from Cambodia. Barrandov Studios shot it here on location some years back and it offers magnificent images of the country's lakes, waterfalls, mountains and temples including Angkor Wat. In addition, documentaries have been made by visiting film-makers about recent Cambodian history.

It is hard to say when the minuscule Cambodian film industry will revive and rival the heady days when Prince Sihanouk devoted so much time and talent to film-making. Pnom Penh, the capital, has some six operating cinemas, which have monthly performances. They depend on outside assistance from other major countries with whom Cambodia enjoys good relations. As in Laos, French is understood better than English. Films are often screened in Vietnamese, Chinese, or Thai depending on where they are available. Outside the capital, in areas like Battabang and Siam Reap, there are outdoor cinemas for workers and soldiers.

Pnom Penh has a public TV outlet which operates daily for three hours between 6 PM and 9 PM. Video is still the big attraction and pirate videos in Thai and English which come from Bangkok are readily available and are shown in many hotels, restaurants and public halls.

Prince Sihanouk was recently the subject of an Australian film, *The Prince and the Prophecy*, by a former cameraman and news editor, James Gerrand. Along with *This Is Cambodia*, this documentary has been seen worldwide at film festivals and at special screenings throughout Europe and the United States. Sihanouk was the first real head of his country's cinema, and an active film-maker in his day. He persuaded directors like Marcel Camus to shoot on location in Cambodia. A close friend of the Prince, Tee Lung Kang, directed the two most popular films ever made in Cambodia: *The Snake Woman* and *Return of the Snake Woman*. They were screened at the Asian Film Festival and were distributed outside the country in a Chinese-dubbed version. Both works were ghost stories stemming from Asian folklore.

CANADA

by Gerald Pratley

It has been a year much like all the others but with that degree of uncertainty always hovering over the business of film-making being sharply increased. The main factors here are the U.S.-Canada Free Trade Agreement and the decline of the CBC. These, combined with a severe economic recession, high unemployment, the introduction of the Goods and Services Tax (VAT), a weak and irresponsible national government, and a country torn apart by the intransigence of Québec and its threats to separate from Canada, have resulted in massive cuts in the funding of film and television production by the federal and provincial governments on which so much of our film-making depends.

Where Free Trade is concerned it is not a matter of our cinemas suddenly being flooded with American films to the exclusion of our own. As everyone abroad knows, 97% of our screentime is occupied by Hollywood – and Canadian feature films are hard to find. We are dominated, controlled and run from Los Angeles as part of Hollywood's domestic market (and always have been) and the millions of dollars of taxpayers' money poured into production over the past 25 years haven't changed this – and millions in profits each year continue to flow south. The policies advocated by supporters of a native cinema to change this situation have all been shelved over the years because governments were afraid of Washington. No, American companies which have their films printed in Canadian labs will not have to pay duty now on their negatives (a trifling amount anyway) and those few Canadian films and TV programmes going to the U.S. will not be charged duty either. These advantages are minor; the dangers lie in the conditions of the FTA calling for the elimination of all subsidies so that one country's "goods" do not compete unfairly with those of the other country. While the arts are supposed not to be affected by this, meaning that the Canada Council, and Ontario Arts Council and similar provincial and municipal funding bodies, are permitted to continue giving out grants, where does it leave Telefilm, the OFDC, SOGIC and five other provincial ministries funding film and TV production which the Americans do not consider as being Art in the same sense as composers composing and painters painting and so on; a situation not helped by the manner in which our governments will not use the term "Arts" (too elitist) and have lumped everything together as "Cultural Industries" including our hardpressed book and magazine publishers.

e Telefilm Canada

Action!

By providing support to the private sector, Telefilm Canada contributes to the development of the Canadian television, film and video industry.

As well, Telefilm is committed to promoting Canadian productions on the international scene. By maintaining offices abroad, the Corporation paves the way to co-production agreements that are key elements of a vigorous and dynamic industry.

Head Office
Montréal
Tour de la Banque Nationale
600, de la Gauchetière Ouest
14e étage
Montréal (Québec) H3B 4L9
Téléphone : (514) 283-6363
Télex : 055-60998
Télécopieur : (514) 283-8212

Offices in Canada
Toronto
2 Bloor Street West
22nd Floor
Toronto, Ontario
M4W 3E2
Telephone : (416) 973-6436
Fax : (416) 973-8606

Vancouver
350-375 Water Street
Vancouver, British Columbia
V6B 5C6
Telephone : (604) 666-1566
Fax : (604) 666-7754

Halifax
5525 Artillery Place
Suite 220
Halifax, Nova Scotia
B3J 1J2
Telephone : (902) 426-8425
Fax : (902) 426-4445

International Offices
Los Angeles
9350 Wilshire Boulevard
Suite 400
Beverly Hills, California
U.S.A. 90212
Telephone : (213) 859-0268
Fax : (213) 276-4741

Paris
15, rue de Berri
75008 Paris, France
Téléphone : (1) 45.63.70.45
Télécopieur : (1) 42.25.33.61

Londres
55/59 Oxford Street
Fourth Floor
London W1R 1RD
England
Telephone : (71) 437-8308
Telex : 923753
Fax : (71) 734-8586

Léo Munger and Marc Messier in André Forcier's *Une histoire inventée*

If the Americans take "industries" literally (and why shouldn't they as the Canadian government thinks this way) and refuse to accept the fact that the subsidising of films and books is an artistic rather than a commercial undertaking, and forces the government to drop this financial assistance, then what will happen to film-making – indeed to the National Film Board (itself a Government department)? Telefilm, the overgrown bureaucracy which provided $70M for TV production and $30M for films last year, has made matters worse by announcing that its funding from now on will be directed to "more commercial films." This seems to mean that the producers of *Porky's* and other horrors will once again be welcome. If anyone knew what films would be money-makers we could all get rich. Telefilm and its provincial cousins should be interested only in good films, but unfortunately there are few at Telefilm, including its script readers, who have the ability to recognise matrial of likely merit reflecting this country. While Telefilm and the others may claim to be banking institutions which expect their loans to be repaid (most are not) it is doubtful that the American FTA negotiators will accept this argument.

And so we await the FTA decision regarding subsidies for "cultural industries" and their effect on cinema if they are discontinued. Critics of the Mulroney government are unkind enough to say that with our national debt running into billions, and being greater per-population than that of the U.S. the PM would welcome the opportunity to cut out all funding to the arts to save money and put the blame on the Americans for forcing the issue under the FTA.

Commercials Travelin' South

Where Free Trade has made a serious impact on production is in the field of TV commercials. Now that customs duties have been abolished much of this work has shifted to Los Angeles. With so many of our advertising agencies being American-owned they are simply giving assignments to American commercial houses to be made by American directors, writers and actors and putting Canadians out of work. The agencies justify this on the grounds that most of the products advertised are American so why not use the same commercials. What works for the U.S. works for Canada. But what is to be said of the mentality of Canadian advertisers, such as Canadian Pacific, who use Americans and seem unconcerned over their lack of support for Canadian studios which produce commercials as effectively as the Americans? It is this "sell-out" attitude which has made Canada so dependent on much that is American – to our great cost in individuality.

As for factor two, the CBC, on which so much of our film-making depends, lost its head in more ways than one when, as a result of the government cutting 10% of its $1-billion budget, it dismissed 1,200 employees and closed down its TV stations in Calgary, Windsor and elsewhere, and eliminated much of its Canadian programming. For weeks after this it seemed that every columnist in every paper, every news broadcast, every editorial supported by letters to the editor, deplored the government's action and accused the Prime Minister of destroying the CBC and its

NATIONAL FILM BOARD OF CANADA
OFFICE NATIONAL DU FILM DU CANADA

INNOVATEUR
ESSENTIEL
ACCESSIBLE

INNOVATIVE
VITAL
ACCESSIBLE

ONF
Direction des communications
C.P. 6100
Succursale "A"
Montréal, Québec
H3C 3H5
Tél. : (514) 283-9247

NFB
Communications Divisions
P.O. Box 6100
Station A
Montreal, Quebec
H3C 3H5
Tel. : (514) 283-9247

Office
national du film
du Canada

National
Film Board
of Canada

Serge Thériault and Sophie Faucher in Alain Chartrand's *Ding & Dong: Le Film*

mandate to keep us all together while we are falling apart. But the truth of the matter is that the CBC deserves no sympathy at all. It has been in decline since the early 1970's. The rot began when it started to run commercials and chase ratings. The individuals who moved into power to run the CBC, a Crown company and a public broadcasting system, wanted the CBC to be American; it bid against private stations in buying American programmes most of which could be seen on U.S. stations; it wanted to be CBS and it wanted what little Canadian programming it did to look and sound American. It found itself being run by well-paid incompetents, and it is they who have destroyed a magnificent institution over the years. It has nothing to do with the lack of government funding which has always been generous; it has everything to do with lack of vision, imagination and a true concern to programme Canadian material. Skilled directors, writers and performers who could have accomplished so much, have been consistently neglected by the CBC. Its only future is to become our version of Channel 4, with one main headquarters, a small staff, with transmitters all over the country, with one knowledgeable individual in charge, and buying and initiating film and television programmes from outside producers and buying more from

Britain and Europe. In this way its funding would be more than adequate, commercials would be unnecessary, and the surge in Canadian film activity would be tremendous, resulting in work that would be seen by the public on a regular basis, reminding us of what makes us different from the Americans and strengthening our pride in the differences. It might then be perceived once again as a national public broadcaster. But few doubt that anyone has the courage to make a change of this magnitude. The CBC will become less and less a part of people's lives; its importance diminishes daily.

Québec

Four of the five highest-grossing Canadian films during the past year were produced in, and made their money in, Québec. The leading film was **Ding et Dong, Le Film**, starring the Québec comedy team called Ding and Dong. Shown only in the province it grossed $2,640,687 in just 13 weeks. Next came **Cruising Bar**, which took in $811,000; **In the Belly of the Dragon** and **Jesus of Montreal** continued their successful runs with the latter taking in another $609,0900 in addition to the $2.5 million it earned the previous year. (The fifth and non-Québec film on the list with $798,000 was the animated feature, **The Nutcracker Prince**, made in Ottawa).

In the other provinces **Beautiful Dreamers** grossed $350,000; **The Last Winter**, $320,000; **The Company of Strangers**, $350,000; **Bethune: The Making of a Hero** – reported to have cost $18 million ($305,000). Warner Bros. has agreed to dub French versions of all its releases in Québec. Under current regulations, films in English may only be shown for 60 days without a French version being available. Most Hollywood companies dub individual films for Québec; now, under pressure from the Québec government they are expected to follow the example of Warners. They must understand the "cultural

Graham Greene in *Clearcut*, from Alliance International

reality of Québec." Previously, Québec's new Cinema Bill 109 permits the major Hollywood studios to continue freely distributing their pictures to cinemas, TV and home video in the province, but specifically prevents Canadian-owned companies in Ontario or any other province from doing business in Québec unless they had offices and residences there prior to December 31 1982. To get their films into the province they must licence them through Québec-based distributors. Then why not Hollywood companies? The question is not answered by Québec.

Daniel Weinzweig, chairman of Ciné-phile Distributing Company says, "It's outrageous that the U.S. companies are allowed unfettered access to the Québec market and we are not . . ." Telefilm reports that 48 Canadian films (nearly all from

Québec) were shown in France during the eight years between 1982–89 attracting 13 million moviegoers with box-office receipts of $61 million. Denys Arcand's *The Decline of the American Empire* was the biggest draw, bringing in over a million viewers and about $6.2 million.

Other Happenings . . .
Two more reports for the shelving: *The Commission on Training Facilities for Artists* and *A Task Force on the Economic Status of Canadian Television*; after 50 years of waiting the NFB has at last been given its own headquarters in Toronto in a spiffy new building which includes three projection rooms and production facilities; Canada's Hollywood-style Genie Awards are postponed until after the *Festival of Festivals* and will revert to the Jury system which it discarded when taking over the Canadian Film Awards. Famous Players has shed its two-year old C/FP production and distribution company; a study commissioned by ACTRA (Alliance of Canadian Cinema, Television and Radio Artists) predicts that the total value of production will fall to just over $2 billion, a decline of $173–million from the levels of two years ago; a Brief from the CFTPA (Canadian Film and Television Production Association) representing 350 companies declares "the wholesale domination of Canadian film and TV screens by U.S. programming must end if the country is to endure culturally and even politically."

Irony: Filmline International, the company which did so badly with *Bethune*, is going to advise the Czechs on how to turn Barrandov into a successful commercial enterprise. Canada's cable companies are furious at being ordered by the Copyright Board to pay $50 million a year in royalties to programme producers, mostly American. Moviegoers will spend about $405 million visiting the cinemas this year (about $15 million less than last year) but will spend $1,278 billion to buy and rent movies on ideo to watch at home. Another shadow from free trade: the national government has eliminated its non-theatrical production fund which provided money for independent documentary film-makers to the tune of $1.8 million. The latest word from Washington: "Canadian actions to enforce the investment restrictions in the cultural sectors create irritants in bilateral relations." Irritants? It's hard to find in this country a film in cinemas, a programme on television, a song on the radio, a magazine on a news-stand, a book in a book store, which is not American!

Recent Films

The Adjuster (d. Atom Egoyan) More of the same from the director of *Speaking Parts*, this time with extra servings of kinky behaviour. A cold, hermetic film about voyeurism (perhaps), attractively photographed, communicating to very few. Script: Atom Egoyan. Players: Elias Koteas, Arsinee Khanjian, Maury Chaykin, Gabrielle Rose. Prod: Alliance Films. 102 mins.)

Ned Beatty in *Angel Square*

Angel Street (d. Anne Wheeler) Set in Winnipeg at Christmas 1945, this comedy-drama with animated sequences is a charming and sensitive tale of a young boy chasing down the attacker of his best friend's father. Somewhat in the tradition of *Hue and Cry* and *Emil and the Detectives*. (Script: James Defelice, Anne Wheeler. Players: Jeremy Radick, Ned Beatty, Prod: Festival Films 104 mins.)

Blood Clan (d. Charles Wilkinsen) Another entry in the horror class, this one concerning a Scottish immigrant family living in a remote Alberta prairie community haunted by killings from its ancestral past. (Script: Glynis Whiting. Players: Gordon Pinsent, Michelle Little, Robert Wisden. Prod: Festival Films. 87 mins.)

The Challengers (d. Eric Till) A pertinent, unaffected and likeable children's film, about love of family and friends, concerning an 11-year-old girl who joins a boys-only rock band in a small town in Manitoba. (Script: Clive Endersby. Players: Gwynyth Walsh, Eric Christmas, Steven Endrade. Prod: Lauron/CBC. 97 mins.)

City of Champions (d. Joseph Vismeg) A first film, quickly made on a low budget; a delightfully free and entertaining "going down the road" from Edmonton adventure, concerning three young people taking a funny and then dark look at the way money and love can drawn individuals together – and then push them apart. (Script: Joseph Vismeg. Players: Phil Zyp, Geraldine Carr, Kathryn Fraser, Marie Dame. Prod: Films Transit. 70 mins.)

Clearcut (d. Richard Bugajski) Based on a novel by M.T. Kelly, this important film deals with the land claims made by native peoples in Northern Ontario and their struggles to keep the logging companies from stripping the forests. On the personal level it brings a rebellious and militant Indian into deadly conflict with his lawyer and the mill owner – somewhat questionable given the circumstances. (Script: Rob Forsyth, Players: Ron Lee, Graham Greene, Michael Hogan, Rebecca Jenkins. Prod: C/FP Dist. 98 mins.

Cursed (d. Michael Arsenault) The obsessed chemist in back with dark-doings in the lab; this time a statue and its demonic inscriptions yield a formula for awful genetic experiments. (Script:

Jean-Marc Felion, Pierre Dalpe. Players: Ron Lea, Catherine Colvey, Tom Rack. Prod: Film Trust. 97 mins.)

Defy Gravity (d. Michael Gibson) A first feature trying hard to deal with a difficult style of high comedy-drama in telling of a manic inventor, alternating between good cheer and violent rage, and the effect this has on his family. It doesn't quite work. (Script: Gibson. Players: R.H. Thomson, Chapelle Jaffe, Simon Reynolds. Prod: Creative Exposure. 90 mins).

Ding et Dong, le Film (d. Alain Chartrand) The most successful film in Québec this year is a funny piece with the province's zaniest team, Claude Meunier and Serge Theriault, playing two poor actors who suddenly become millionaires and open their own theatre. (Script: Claude Meunier. Players: Meunier and Theriault, Raymond Bouchard, Sophie Faucher. Prod: Max Films. 96 mins.)

Divided Loyalties (d. Mario Azzopardi) Made for TV and with the hope of cinema showings (which it didn't get) this is a most unusual Canadian film: it actually deals with our British history, something our self-serving politicians at the mount of multi-culturalism would prefer to forget these days. It tells the true story of Joseph Brant, leader of the Mohawks and ally of the British during the American War of Independence. In spite of some lapses it is for the most part a colourful, moving, stirring and vivid chronicle, magnificently photographed by Vic Sarin and acted with power and passion. (Script: Peter Jobin. Players: Jack Langedijk, Chris Wiggins, Tantoo Cardinal. Prod: History Prods/CTV. 102 mins.)

Falling Over Backwards (d. Mort Ransen) A slight, over-long comedy-drama about a man in mid-life crisis who lives with his divorced, cantankerous father in Montréal, and who falls in love with their vivacious young landlady. Saul Rubinek sees it through. (Script: Ransen. Players: Paul Soles, Rubinek, Julie St. Pierre, Helen Hughes. Prod: Ranfilm/CBC. 103 mins.)

Getting Married in Buffalo Jump (d. Eric Till) Based on Susan Charlotte Haley's novel and set in the foothills of Alberta, this is a pleasing and often funny and sophisticated look at a cynical bar-lounge pianist from Toronto who goes out west to run her father's farm. To help her with the work she hires an old school friend of Ukrainian descent who proposes marriage. The complexities of love and the value of tradi-

tions are thoughtfully brought out. (Script: John Frizzell. Players: Wendy Crewson, Paul Gross, Victoria Snow. Prod: CBC Enterprises. 98 mins.)

Graveyard Story (d. B.D. Denedikt) A psychiatrist living in the Niagara region is haunted by a vision of a little girl buried in a nearby cemetery. A private detective finds out why. Conventional but in good taste. (Script: Denedikt. Players: John Ireland, Adrian Paul, Cayle Chemin. Prod: Golden Screen. 92 mins.)

H (d. Darrell Wasyk) A relentless drama showing the disintegration of two heroin addicts locked in a dreary basement room in a desperate struggle to break their habit. An enterprising low budget, more of a filmed play, production with only two characters who seem to live their roles it will leave most audiences uninvolved and out of sympathy with them. (Script: Darrell Wasyk. Players: Martin Neufeld, Pascale Montpetit. Prod: Cineplex. 90 mins.)

Highway 61 (d. Bruce McDonald) A follow-up to *Road Kill*, this is a blackly funny, knowingly played road comedy in which a streetwise girl takes a coffin with corpse and drugs from Northern Ontario to New Orleans accompanied by an innocent young man. It would have been a better film had its destination been Vancouver, but it's hard to break young film-makers of the American connection. (Script: Don McKellar. Players: Don McKellar, Valerie Buhagiar, Earl Pastko, Peter Breck. Prod: Cinephile. 110 mins.)

Looking for Miracles (d. Kevin Sullivan) Sentimental, depression-era, coming-of-age family tale taking place against an idyllic summer camp background in Northern Ontario. (Script: Kevin Sullivan, Stuart McLean. Players: Greg Spottiswood, Joe Flaherty, Patricia Gage, Zachary Bennet. Prod: Sullivan Films. 103 mins.)

Masala (d. Srinivas Krishna) A muddled racial multicultural carry-on set among an East Indian family in Toronto straining credibility as neither good comedy or melodrama. A case of a first film-maker doing too much and, in the bargain, wasting the talents of the international actor, Saeed Jaffrey. (Script: Srinivas Krishna. Players: Krishna, Zohra Segal, Sakina Jaffrey. Prod: Cinephile. 105 mins.)

Moody Beach (d. Richard Roy) A first feature in which a middle-aged man leaves his job in Montréal to live in his late mother's house in Florida. There he meets a French free-spirited girl who has taken up residence. Their subse-

Izabela Moldovan in *Reach for the Sky*, the twelfth in Rock Demers's celebrated *Tales for All* collection of family films

quent association is tedious, moody and monotonous. (Script: Richard Roy. Players: Michel Côte, Claire Nebout, Philip Spensley, Andrée Lachapelle. Prod: Cineplex. 90 mins.)

New Shoes (d. Ann Marie Fleming) A first feature in which Emily, a feminist film-maker, tries to discover why a man would buy new shoes before killing his lover and then himself. A bits-and-pieces film both slight and inconsequential. (Script: Ann Marie Fleming. Players: Ann Marie Fleming, Valerie Buhagiar. Prod: AMF Productions. 80 mins.)

No Apologies (d. Ken Pittman) An uncharacteristically pessimistic film from Newfoundland, set in a company town, concerning a film-maker back from the third-world who finds conditions at home just as depressing. An examination of nationalism and social justice through family relationships, the story manages to bring back the Newfie sense of humour for the final scenes. (Script: Ken Pittman. Players: Barrie Dunn, Bryan Hennessey, Maisie Rillie, Tony Quinn. Prod: Filmline Int. 90 mins.)

Le Party (The Party) (d. Pierre Falardeau) A well-made and convincingly played prison melodrama, but sordid and sensational in its depiction of a concert for the inmates given by a group of burlesque entertainers and of the brutal goings-on behind the scenes. Supposedly a film about hope and freedom, the characters are so sketchily drawn one feels nothing for them. (Script: Pierre Falardeau. Players: Lou Babin, Julien Poulin, Charlotte Laurier. Prod: C/FP Distribution. 100 mins.)

Perfectly Normal (d. Yves Simoneau) Much was expected from this Anglo-Canadian co-production, but the material, fanciful and quaint, is too slight to sustain the comedy antics of Robbie Coltrane, a shady entrepreneur with a love of food and opera, who makes friends with a shy, retiring young man working in a small town Ontario brewery. Like beer, it soon goes flat. (Script: Eugene Lipinski, Paul Quarrington. Players: Robbie Coltrane, Michael Riley, Kenneth Welsh. Prod: Alliance Releasing Co. 107 mins.)

Pictures at the Beach (d. Aron J. Shuster) A first feature about seven spoiled discontented Toronto "yuppies" spending a Sunday at the beach. They share common problems: not enough money, sex or time. This is a well-intentioned picture, but the conversations do not make these characters worth the time we spend with them. (Script: Shuster. Players: Paul Babiak, Bob Bidaman, Ann Curran. Prod: Fountainhead Pictures. 70 mins.)

The Pianist (d. Claude Gagnon). A lush, expensive, sentimental tear-jerker of immense banality moving between Toronto, Montréal and Vancouver in which two young girls fall in love with a Japanese pianist. (Script: Claude Gagnon. Players: Gail Travers, Macha Grenon, Eiji Okuda, Dorothée Berryman, Maury Chaykin. Prod: Aska Films. 113 mins.

Primo Baby (d. Eda Lever Lishman) A rebellious 15-year-old is placed in a foster home with a wealthy racehorse owner in Calgary and trains a half-blind racehorse to become a winner. The horse is not the only handicap in this unconvincing film. (Script: A.A. Lever. Players: Duncan Regehr, Janet-Laine Green, Esther Purves-Smith. Prod: Festival Films. 110 mins.)

Rafales (The Blizzard) (d. André Melançon) This is easily the best Québec film of the year. It is Christmas Eve and three men stage a hold-up in a shopping mall in Montréal. By accident, Santa Claus is shot. One man drives away in a raging blizzard, but he is followed by a radio announcer who has seen the robbery. What transpires is a thoughtful, suspenseful, percep-

Shirley Temple Black with Milos Forman, Henry Kissinger and the President of Czechoslovakia, Vaclav Havel, subject of Vojtech Jasný's documentary, *Why Havel?*

tive study in human relations; an entirely engrossing film of atmosphere and conviction. (Script: André Melançon, Marcel Leboeuf, Denis Bouchard. Players: Marcel Leboeuf, Denis Bouchard, Claude Blanchard, Guy Thauvette, Remy Girard, Monique Spaziani. Prod: Aska Film Distribution. 87 mins.)

Reach for the Sky (La Championne) (d. Elisabeta Bostan) The latest in Rock Demers' series *Tales for All* is different in that it has no Canadian characters this time, preferring to remain in Romania and take us into the world of youngsters training to become gymnasts. Their difficulties, disappointments, home lives and achievements are nicely dramatised. (Script: Vasilica Istrate, Elisabeth Bostan, Rock Demers. Players: Izabela Moldovan. Prod: Astral/Prima. 92 mins.)

Revenge of the Radio Active Reporter (d. Craig Pryce). A comic-strip sci-fi world of evil and corruption at the local nuclear power plant; the machinations of the dastardly president lead to an inquisitive reporter being dumped into a bubbling vat of radioactive waste. He emerges a nuclear mutant with unusual powers and goes after the villains in an orgy of revenge. Not quite funny enough. (Script: Craig Pryce. Players: David Scammell, Kathryn Boese, Derrick Strange. Prod: Astral Film. 85 mins.)

Sam and Me (d. Deepa Mehta) is another multi-racial family flare-up concerning the nephew of an overbearing East Indian doctor who comes to Toronto to take care of an elderly Jewish man considered to be awkward to manage. The entire film is awkwardly managed. (Script: Ranjit Chowdhry. Players: Chowdhry, Peter Boretski, Heath Lamberts, Kulbushan Kharbanda, Javed Jafri. Prod: Astral Films. 92 mins.)

Smoked Lizard Lips (d. M.B. Duggan) is another failed attempt at comedy, this time revolving around the misadventures of a South American dictator in exile in a small town outside Winnipeg. (Script: M.B. Duggan. Players:

Simon Magana, Andrée Pelletier, Victor Cowie. Prod: Cinephile. 95 mins.)
Terminal City Ricochet (d. Zale Dalen) This intended satire on what the world might well become – deadly space junk rains from the sky, the streets are glutted with obsolete consumer goods, environmental decay is everywhere – is neither good comic-strip, good fun or serious about its concerns. Much more could have been made of the party of Cultural Resistance Against Happy Face Fascism, but with five writers on the screenplay something was lost. Players: Peter Breck, Germain Houde, Jello Biafra. Prod: Festival Films. 107 mins.)
Une histoire inventée (An Imaginary Tale) (d. Marc-André Forcier) A strange collection of Fellini-like characters wend their way through this comedy-tragedy of theatrical and musical life, with jealousy, love and revenge occupying their time and attention under circumstances both real and imaginary. Beautiful Florence has always loved Gaston, the aging musician, but her young daughter eventually wins his heart. The complications involving the rest of the group take on a surreal note and, eventually, a somewhat tiresome whimsy. (Script: Jacques Marcotte, Marc-André Forcier. Players: Jean Lapointe, Louise Marleau, Charlotte Laurier. Prod: Astral Films. 90 mins.)
White Light (d. Al Waxman) A heavy-handed excursion into a detective's after-life experience in which he meets a beautiful woman. On returning to the living he searches for her. (Script: Ron Base. Players: Martha Henry, Martin Cove, Alison Hossack. Prod: Brightstar. 97 mins.)
White Room (d. Patricia Rozema) A would-be writer and sometime voyeur sees a popular singer murdered. At the funeral he meets her mysterious friend who invites him to her home. From here on the narrative turns into fantasy and confusion; but, according to the film-maker, it has much to do with feminism and the destructive effects of media attention on our private lives. The film has a nice finish to it, and what lies beneath is open to interpretation. (Script: Patricia Rozema. Players: Kate Nelligan, Maurice Godin, Margo Kidder, Sheila McCarthy. Prod: Alliance Releasing Co. 91 mins.)
... and some short dramas of note: **Altered Ego** (d. Maureen Judge) A Toronto author adopts a pen-name and has difficulty living two identities. (Script: M Judge, Martin Waxman.

Players: Peg Christopherson, Peter Spence. Prod: Makin Movies. 60 mins.); **Dory** (d. John Kozak) A beautifully realised story of two sisters living alone on the prairie, one of whom is mad. (Script: John Kozak. Players: Donna Lewis, Roscoe Handford. Prod: Winnipeg Film Group. 60 mins.); **The 24 Store** (d. Brian Stockton) A young Regina insurance salesman skips work and ends up in an all-night conveience store which sells everything. (Script: Brian Stockton. Players: George Dempster, Marsha Herle. Prod: Moving Images Ltd. 68 mins.)

National Film Board

Au Chic Resto Pop (d. Tahani Rached) Five ordinary folk get together with musician Steve Falkner to express their feelings about poverty in Montréal through rap, blues, rock and western songs. (85 mins.). **Burning Times** (d. Donna Read) Witch hunts and feminists during 300 years of persecution. (60 mins.). **Company of Strangers** (d. Cynthia Scott) A bus load of elderly ladies, stranded in the countryside, learn how to survive while getting to know each other; a spiritual experience, partly scripted, partly improvised, it takes place without identity suggesting that the participants are merely passengers on their way to Heaven. (100 mins.). **Creative Process: Norman McLaren** (d. Don Mcwilliams) A fascinating study, with rare and experimental footage, of the work of McLaren during his fifty years with the NFB. (116 mins.). **Five Feminist Minutes** (p. Mary Armstrong) An eclectic collection of sixteen five-minute films directed by women film-makers from the NFB's Studio D. A roundup of the usual subjects, the matters are serious, the treatment often humorous. (113 mins.). **Hotel Chronicles** (d. Léa Pool) A self-indulgent trip at the taxpayers' expense to permit the director to discover "the lives and dreams of Americans." (74 mins.). **Imperfect Union – Canadian Labour and the Left** (d, p, sc. Arthur Hammond) This is an ambitious, far-ranging, four-part study examining the relationship of organised labour and political parties of the left in Canada and the international background which influenced it. (Part I. 1890–1929 55 mins., Part 2. 1929–1938 50 mins., Part 3. 1939–1961 55 mins., Part 4. 1962–1989 60 mins.). **Princes in Exile** (d. Giles

Walker) Camp Hawkins is a summer retreat for children and young people with cancer – a camp which could be anywhere in an unidentified setting. A drama with a documentary look; the young players give a good account of themselves as their characters face up to their fatal disease with fortitude and even good humour. (104 mins.).

Simon and the Dream Hunters (d. Roger Cantin) A likeable children's film set in a small Québec town outside Montréal in which Simon and his friends dream of places far-away populated with unusual animals and characters. (82 mins.) **The Spirit Within** (d. Gil Cardinal/Will Campbell) Made by native film-makers, this is a sensitive and intimate study of the work of elders in attempting to bring meaning to the lives of the younger generation and to keep them from falling into idleness and crime. (56 mins.). **Uranium** (d. Magnus Isacsson) A thought-provoking and outspoken inquiry into the uranium mining industry and its legacy of deadly radioactive pollution expected to last a thousand years. (48 mins.)

Note: The NFB produced approx. 170 films last year, and has made 9,000 titles available on videocassettes for rent or purchase.

Independent Documentaries

Between Two Worlds (d. Barry Greenwald) An unusual and imaginative film about the Inuit people, and in particular, Joseph Idlout, a great hunter and trapper caught between the contradictions of traditional life and the ways of the white world. (Prod: Investigative Productions. 58 mins.). **Chile in Transition** (d. Gaston Ancelovici, Frank Diamond) Sixteen years of atrocities committed under military rule are revealed in a series of interviews and in the story of two cousins, one living in Chile, and other in Canada. (Canada-Netherlands-Chile. Prod: Films Transit. 125 mins.). **The Falls** (d., sc. Kevin McMahon) a powerful, outspoken study of the despoiling of Niagara Falls by pollution and commercial exploitation. (Prod: Alliance Films. 90 mins.) **The Famine Within** (d. Katherine Gilday) The contemporary obsession with body, shape and health among North American women is examined with candour and concern, and the media, fashion, food and diet

industries come in for some forthright criticism for the images they have created. (Prod: Films Transit. 120 mins.) **Island of Whales** (d., sc. Mike Poole) A research team sails around Vancouver Island to study the few remaining whales; an absorbing, concerned and critical survey, visually beautiful and sympathetically narrated by Gregory Peck. (Prod: Northern Lights. 55 mins.) **Leningradskaya: Southern Russia** (d. John Walker) Memories of a terrifying time in Soviet history when Stalin's industrialisation of farming in the 1930's took a terrible toll in human lives. The survivors remember. (Canada-UK. Prod: Atlantis. 58 mins.). **The Magic Season of Robertson Davies** (d. Harry Rasky) One of Canada's most accomplished and celebrated authors, Robertson Davies, talks about his life and work and tells us what he thinks of life today. Gracious, witty and thoughtful. (Prod: Rasky/CBC. 82 mins.). **Musicians in Exile** (d. Jacques Holender) Musicians forced by political situations to live in foreign capitals are the subject of this roving report, beginning with South African trumpeter, Hugh Masekela, and accompanied by a well-recorded musicial soundtrack. (Prod. Nemesis Productions. 75 mins.) **Why Havel** (d., sc. Vojtech Jasný) A timely documentary from Rock Demers in which Milóš Forman entertainingly introduces us to Vaclav Havel, his life and work. (Prod: Les Productions la Fête. 100 mins.) **Wisecracks** (d., sc. Gail Singer) An amusing compilation of excerpts from the club performances of "stand-up" comediennes and their comments on women's humour in this predominantly male activity. (Prod: Alliance. 90 mins.)

Experimental

A Bullet in the Head (d, sc. Attila Bertalan) A nightmarish fairytale about the absurdity and futility of war. (Prod: Creon Prods. 90 mins.). **Entry in a Diary** (d, sc. Bob Stampfl) A painter living in rural Ontario tries to renew his faith in life. (Prod: Entropy Pictures. 86 mins.). **I'm Happy, You're Happy, We're All Happy, Happy, Happy** (d, sc. Velcrow Ripper) In a city where everyone dresses in plaid suits and moves in surreal dream visions or silly nightmares, a mute fool emerges who works in a factory salting crackers. Video, animation, claymation and a mad soundtrack keep the images moving. (Prod: Transparent Films. 85 mins.). **La Liberté d'une statue (The Moving Statue)** A film within a film about a silent picture discovered in Egypt and a young girl's search for a heroic destiny. A puzzle picture of the deepest obscurity for theorists to delight in. (Prod: Amérique Films. 90 mins.)

Animation

Bicycle Ladies (Jill Haras) How to master the bicycle. (Prod: Siren Films. 14 mins.). **Dessine-moi une chanson (Draw Me a Song)** (Francine Desbiens) About love, solitude and music (Prod: NFB. 9 mins.). **Enfantillage (Kid Stuff)** (Pierre M. Trudeau) A child's drawings are influenced by the angry voices of his quarrelling parents. (Prod: NFB. 6 mins.). **L'Heure rêvée** (Pierre Veilleux) The expressiveness and universal symbolism of dreams. (Prod: NFB. 11 mins.). **Impact** (Jean-François DesBois) Everyone in pursuit of the mighty dollar. (5 mins.). **I Remember Sid** (Darren Brereton) The perils of life after death. (Prod: Techniflex. 8 mins.). **Jours de Plaine** (Réal Bérard/André Leduc) Music and images of Western Canada's francophones (6 mins.). **A Klondike Christmas** (Gordon Stanfield) Christmas almost doesn't arrive for the children of Big Fork. (Prod: GSA Films. 30 mins.). **The Nutcracker Prince** (Paul Schibli) Charmless and unfunny feature based on the fairytale ballet. (Prod: Hinton. 73 mins.), **Personality Software** (Sylvie Fefer) The type of person you've always wanted to be as a result of computer software. (Prod: BC Film/NFB. 8 mins.). **Premier Regard** (Pierre Sylvestre) A look at the world from a baby's point of view. (6 mins.). **To Be** (John Weldon) An eminent scientist's latest invention in reproduction. (Prod: NFB. 10 mins.). **25 Watts** (Pierre Sylvestre) A "couch potato" and his obnoxious cat. (4 mins.).

Forthcoming Films

John Gray's *Kootenai Brown*, a period Western filmed in BC; *Memory*, a France-Canada co-

Andrée Pelletier's *Petit drame dans la vie d'une femme*

production from Roger Frappier and Pierre Gendron; *Voyage de l'âge* from Jean Pierre Lefebrve; *La Demoiselle sauvage* by Léa Pool; *True Confections*, the recollections of Sandra Gotlieb, by Gail Singer; *Alexander Graham Bell: A Man out of Time* by John Kent Harrison; *Journey into Darkness*, the Bruce Curtis story written by Keith Ross Leckie; *Montréal vu par* as seen by Denys Arcand, Léa Pool, Michel Brault, Atom Egoyan, Patricia Rozema and Jacques Leduc, each directing a 15-minute episode.

Co-Productions

Jacques Dorfman's *Agaguk*; Bruce Beresford's *Black Robe*; *The French Revolution* (France-Canada, d. Robert Enrico/Richard Heffron); *Swan Lake – The Zone* (USSR-Canada, d. Yuri Illienko); *The Young Catherine* (U.K.-Canada, d. Michael Anderson).

Statistics Canada's Latest Report on Earnings and Attendance

Theatre attendance decreased 7% overall between the 1987–88 and the 1988–89 surveys of drive-in and regular movie theatres. Theatres continued to close, especially drive-ins. A total of 790 theatres – 658 regular and 132 drive-ins – operated in 1988–89, a drop of 4% from the year before. The number of drive-ins decreased 10% compared with a 3% decrease for regular theatres.

Meanwhile, box-office receipts in 1988–89 increased 4% over the previous year as the average ticket price rose to $4.76 from $4.24 the year before. The average price includes children's, students' and seniors' prices as well as adults; admission in large cities is $7. Movie theatres overall earned $375.3 million. Attendance dropped from 85 million to 78.8 admissions. The total number of multi-screen theatres has grown to an average of two screens per theatre in 1988–89 from 1.7 three years previously.

Average attendance in 1988–89 was three times per person – slightly lower than in recent years but a massive decline from 1952 when peak attendance was 18 times per person. Albertans continue to be the most avid moviegoers – attending an average of four times per person. Average attendance was lowest in New Brunswick, Prince Edward Island and Newfoundland where people went out to see a film less than two times per person. Theatre chains – primarily Cineplex Odeon and Famous Players – owned nearly two-thirds of all theatres and earned 90% of revenues.

GERALD PRATLEY, former CBC film critic and founder–director of the Ontario Film Institute, teaches film history at Ryerson Polytechnic Institute in Toronto.

Distributors

Alliance Releasing
920 Yonge Street
Suite 400
Toronto, Ontario
Tel: (416) 967–1174
Telex: 06–23776
Fax: (416) 960–0971

Alliance Vivafilm
355 Place Royale
3e étage
Montréal (Québec)
H2Y 2V3
Tel: (514) 844–3132
Telex: 05–25828
Fax: (514) 284–2340

Astral Films
175, boul. Montpellier
Bureau 600
Montréal (Québec)
H4N 2G5
Tel: (514) 748–6541
Telex: 05–826734
Fax: (514) 748–1348

720 King Street W.
Suite 600
Toronto, Ontario
M5V 2T3
Tel: (416) 364–3894
Telex: 06–22411
Fax: (416) 364–8565

Atlantis Releasing Inc.
Cinevillage
65 Heward Avenue
Toronto, Ontario
M4M 2T5
Tel: (416) 462–0016
Telex: 06–426129
Fax: (416) 462–0254

Brightstar Films Distribution Inc.
424 Adelaide Street E.
Toronto, Ontario
M5A 1N4
Tel: (416) 364–5144
Fax: (416) 364–5339

Canadian Filmmakers Distribution Centre
67A Portland Street
Toronto, Ontario
M5V 2M9
Tel: (416) 593–1808

Canadian Filmmakers Distribution West
1131 Howe Street
Suite 100
Vancouver, British Columbia
V6Z 2L7
Tel: (604) 684–3014

CBC Enterprises-TV Program Sales

415 Yonge Street
4th Floor
Toronto, Ontario M5B 2E7
Telex: 06–218269
Fax: (416) 975–3482

C/FP Distribution Inc.
8275, rue Mayrand
Montréal (Québec)
H4P 2C8
Tel: (514) 342–2340
Fax: (514) 342–1922

146 Bloor Street W.
3rd Floor
Toronto, Ontario
M5S 1P3
Tel: (416) 944–0104
Fax: (416) 964–3820

Cineplex Odeon Films Canada
1303 Yonge Street
Toronto, Ontario
M4T 2Y9
Tel: (416) 925–8246
Fax: (416) 324–5494

Cinéma Libre
3575, boul. Saint-Laurent
Bureau 704
Montréal (Québec)
H2X 2T7
Tel: (514) 849–7888
Fax: (514) 843–5681

Cinéma Plus Distribution Inc.
225, rue Roy E.
Bureau 204
Montréal (Québec)
H2W 1M5
Tel: (514) 848–0673
Telex: 05–267530
Fax: (514) 848–0714

131 Avenue Road
Suite 2
Toronto, Ontario
M5R 2H7
Tel: (416) 928–1044
Fax: (416) 924–6205

Ciné 360 Inc.
1590 avenue du Mont-Royal E.
Bureau 304
Montréal (Québec) H2J 1Z2
Tel: (514) 521–4114
Fax: (514) 521–3166

Cinephile Limited
388 King St. W.
Suite 211
Toronto, Ontario
M5V 1K2
Tel: (416) 581–1251
Fax: (416) 581–1382

Cinévidéo Inc.
360, Place Royale
3e étage
Montréal (Québec)
H2Y 2V1
Tel: (514) 284–9354
Fax: (514) 284–6715

Creative Exposure Ltd.
2236 Queen Street E.
Toronto, Ontario
M4E 1G2
Tel: (416) 690–0775
Telex: 062–17622
Fax: (416) 690–0775

Ellis Enterprises
1231 Yonge Street
Suite 201
Toronto, Ontario
M4T 2T8

Tel: (416) 924–2186
Telex: 06–22435
Fax: (416) 924–6115

Festival Films Inc.
203–2105 West 38th Avenue
Vancouver, British Columbia
V6M 1R8
Tel: (604) 264–0070
Fax: (604) 264–0071

Films du Crépuscule Inc. (Les)
55, avenue du Mont-Royal O.
Bureau 302
Montréal (Québec)
H2T 2S5
Tel: (514) 849–2477
Fax: (514) 849–5859

Films Transit Inc.
402, rue Notre-Dame E.
3e étage
Montréal (Québec)
H2Y 1C8
Tel: (514) 844–3358
Telex: 055–60074
Fax: (514) 844–7298

Imax Systems Corporation
38 Isabella Street
Toronto, Ontario
M4Y 1N1
Tel: (416) 960–8509
Telex: 065–24664
Fax: (416) 960–8596

Lapointe Films International Inc.
3575, boul. Saint-Laurent
Bureau 108
Montréal (Québec)
H2X 2T7
Tel: (514) 844–6613
Telex: 055–62322
Fax: (514) 844–5197

Libra Films
169 Liberty St
Ste 104
Toronto, Ontario
Tel: (416) 539–8432
Fax: (416) 534–0527

Malofilm Distribution Inc.
1207, rue Saint-André
Montréal (Québec)
H2L 3S8
Tel: (514) 844–4555
Telex: 055–61301
Fax: (514) 844–1471

8 Pailton Crescent
Toronto, Ontario
M4S 248
Tel: (416) 480–0453
Telex: 065–24090
Fax: (416) 480–0501

Nelvana Enterprises
32 Atlantic Avenue
Toronto, Ontario
MGK 1X8
Tel: (416) 588–5571
Telex: 06–22803
Fax: (416) 588–5588

Norstar Releasing Inc. 86
Bloor Street W.
5th Floor
Toronto, Ontario
M5S 1M5
Tel: (416) 961–6278
Telex: 06–219870
Fax: (416) 961–5608

Prima Films Inc.
1594 boul. Saint-Joseph E.
Montréal (Québec)
H2J 1M7
Tel: (514) 521–1189
Fax: (514) 521–2918

Productions La Fête Inc.
225. rue Roy E.
Bureau 203
Montréal (Québec)
H2W 1M5
Tel: (514) 848–0417
Telex: 055–62385
Fax: (514) 848–0064

Sullivan Films Distribution Inc.
16 Clarence Square
Toronto, Ontario
M5V 1H1

Tel: (416) 597–0029
Telex: 06–218692
Fax: (416) 597–320

**Thomas Howe Associates
Ltd.**
1100 Homer Street
Vancouver, British Columbia
V6B 2X6
Tel: (604) 687–4215
Telex: 04–508654
Fax: (604) 688–8349

**Vivafilm/Québec/Amérique
Distribution Inc.**
411, rue Saint-Jean-Baptiste
Montréal (Québec)
H2Y 2Z7
Tel: (514) 861–2400
Fax: (514) 398–0412

Winnipeg Film Group
304–100 Arthur Street
Winnipeg, Manitoba
R38 1H3
Tel: (204) 942–6795

Useful Addresses

Telefilm Canada
Tour de la Banque Nationale
600, rue de la Gauchetière
Ouest
14 étage
Montréal (Québec)
H3B 4L2
Tel: (514) 283–6363
Telex: 055–60998
Fax: (514) 283–8212

2 Bloor Street West
22nd Floor
Toronto, Ontario
M4W 3E2
Tel: (416) 973–6436
Telex: 06–218344
Fax: (416) 973–8606

5525 Artillery Place
Suite 220
Halifax, Nova Scotia
B3J 1J2
Tel: (902) 426–8425
Fax: (902) 426–4445

350–375 Water Street
Vancouver, British Columbia
V6B 5C6
Tel: (604) 666–1566
Fax: (604) 666–7754

9350 Wilshire Boulevard
Suite 400
Beverly Hills, California
U.S.A. 90212
Tel: (213) 859–0268
Fax: (213) 276–4741

15, rue de Berri
75008 Paris
France
Tel: (33–1) 45.63.70.45
Telex: 42–648082F
Fax: (33–1) 42.25.33.61

55/59 Oxford Street
Fourth Floor
London, England
W1R 1RD
Tel: (44–1) 437–8308
Telex: 923–753
Fax: (44–1) 734–8586

CHILE
by Hans Ehrmann

Production increased, theatre attendance dropped, the Viña del Mar Film Festival was revived after two decades and, although the law did not change, different criteria were applied and censorship eased in 1990, when an elected civilian government succeeded 17 years of military rule.

The release of seven Chilean films, after many years with two, one or none at all, was impressive although several had been shot earlier and delayed by censorship (Perelman's *Latent Image*) or postproduction problems (Caiozzi's *Moon in the Mirror*). One can hardly diagnose the birth of an

industry, a new wavelet, or a similar number of films next year but, whatever the shortcomings, there was once again hope of what the future might bring.

The prestige item was **The Moon in the Mirror** (*La luna en el espejo*), a competitive entry in Venice that earned Gloria Munchmeyer the best actress award. The screenplay by José Donoso, an internationally known novelist (with the director), was a key element, combined with Caiozzi's craftsmanship and the actors' artistry. This is a story of strong atmosphere, slow decay and frustrated relationships in which a retired and bedridden navy man, with a grown son perpetually at his back and and a spinsterish neighbour, live confined lives, although surrounded by Valparaiso's sun and sea. The one moment of hope is quickly crushed.

Gonzalo Justiniano's films sometimes begin realistically and evolve into a more symbolist mode. **Toffee or Mint** (*Caluga o menta*) commences with a group of tenement youngsters, whose grey environment breeds tedium and frustration. They have little in the way of family life and can expect even less in the way of work. Given this squalid existence, with practically no alternative, they slide naturally into petty crime, continually escalating until they finally engage in drugrunning. The film's tone changes during its last third with the appearance of Manuela, a mysterious and attractive middle class girl whose game of "toffee or mint" implies the illusion of choices (life and death, heaven and earth) that don't really exist for these people. The film was made with a partly non-professional cast.

Antonio Skarmeta's multimedia **With Burning Patience** (he also wrote a play and a novel) about poet Pablo Neruda and a postman during the Allende period and ending at the time of the coup, was shot in Portugal during 1983 with Chilean actors and German financing. It circulated in Chile for several years as a clandestine video and only recently made a 35m appearance in cinemas.

Something Is Out There (*Hay algo allá fvera*), is far removed from the realistic approach of most Chilean films. Although still lacking in craftsmanship, Pepe Maldonado is visually imaginative and creates a nightmarish atmosphere, but without really conveying what is going on.

The opposite is the case with two other first features; Alfredo Rates' **The Girl in the Dovecot** (*La niña en el palomera*), a melodrama that lacks the courage of its convictions, is based on a dated local play of

Gloria Munchmeyer in *La luna en el espejo*

the 1960's. Gerardo Cáceres' **Long Live the Bridegroom** (*Viva el novio*) is a piece of escapist entertainment with a case of popular soap opera stars as box-office insurance. The screenplay is repetitive but there are a few funny moments in this generally poor story of a swanky wedding, interrupted by the arrival of the groom's very much pregnant former girlfriend.

Although many of these films fail to transcend local interest, they do signal the birth and, in some cases, maturing of a new generation of directors.

The Importance of Viña del Mar

The importance of the 1990 Viña del Mar film festival was not simply the addition of one more to the already excessive number of similar events. Born in the late 1960's, it had been the home of the films and political debates, reprsentative of the period's Latin American cinema and was obviously suspended under military rule. Its profile, on returning to life, was still Latin American but non-competitive and quite different,

Mauricio Vega plays the lead in Gonzalo Justiniano's *Caluga o mento*

with more emphasis on the economics of film-making and little in the way of politics. The festival itself was organised on half a shoestring.

A whole generation of Chilean film-makers had been forced into exile and, in a perhaps unique phenomenon, they made over fifty features and a hundred documentaries in countries all the way from Australia, Brazil, Bulgaria, Canada, Cuba, France, Germany, Great Britain, Mexico, Nicaragua, the Soviet Union, Sweden, the U.S.A. and Venezuela, most of which have never been seen in Chile.

Viña del Mar, next to Valparaiso, now became the scene of their homecoming, with many returning for the first time in 17 years and their meetings with those who had remained behind, became an emotional event. Best known of the returnees are Raúl Ruiz, who is a major hero to young film-makers in this country, and Miguel Littin. Alejandro Jodorowsky, a sort of senior expatriate who had left Chile 38 years ago, sent his son Axel and a film (*Santa Sangre*).

The strangest case was probably that of Sebastián Alarcón, who had left on a scholarship in 1970, studied at the Moscow Film School and, since then, shot seven features in the Soviet Union, three of which

he brought to the festival where his Chekhovian sense of humour and atmosphere not only made them popular in Viña del Mar, but also led to their later arthouse exposure. Alarcón returned some time after the festival to prepare the first Soviet-Chilean co-production. *Even KGB Agents Fall in Love* was shot in early 1991.

It would be difficult to establish comparisons between Chilean films and those made abroad by local directors beyond the fact that the latter had larger budgets and were technically more polished. There are plans to establish Viña del Mar as an annual event, but it is not yet clear whether money will become available to run it on a more professional basis and what aims and general policy will eventually be established.

Attendances Decline

Although four of the seven Chilean films did quite well at the box-office, 1990 was by no means a good year for film business in general. For the first time the average weekly spectators in Santiago (over 3 million inhabitants) dropped below the 100,000 line and the decrease in audiences, as compared to 1989, came to 18.8%.

Only 19 films were seen by over 50,000 first run spectators. These were topped by Blake Edwards's *Skin Deep* with 288,000 followed by Peter Weir's *Dead Poets' Society* with 229,000. *Batman* came in a distant third with only 145,000. No others topped the 100,000 mark.

A little over 250 films opened in 1990 and the view from the bottom end is not encouraging: 50 films attracted between 5,000 and 10,000 first-run spectators; 73 came within the 2,000 to 5,000 range and 43 (mostly distributed by local independents) had less than 2,000.

Due to the inexperience of its manager, UIP broke up a long association with Chile Films, the largest circuit, and moved to the smaller Socine, a situation detrimental to both organisations that, after almost a year, seems to be heading towards a solution.

A commission has been studying changes in the censorship law and its findings may eventually go to Congress. But democracy has produced de facto changes, easily gleaned from the fact that *Henry and June*, Almodóvar's *Matador* and *Last Exit to Brooklyn* were approved and exhibited without hue and cry.

Another commission is studying financial support for local production and seems to be leaning towards some sort of soft loans, but this is not very likely to come about in the near future. Meanwhile, Spanish television (TVE) is co-producing Pablo Perelman's *Archipiélago* and Ricardo Larrain's *La Frontera*; this source presently appears to be unavailable for further financing.

The bleak production fund outlook does not apply to Raúl Ruiz. On a visit to Santiago he shot one of his four day wonders. Called **The Wandering Soap Opera** (*La telenovela errante*), it cost US$30,000. People worked on deferred salaries or just for the fun of it.

HANS EHRMANN has been a film critic since 1957 and Variety correspondent since 1961. He is a critic and editor on a Chilean newsmagazine.

Useful Addresses

Oficina de Difusión de la Cinematografía Chilena
Villavicencio 352
Santiago
Tel: 65 2 222 9874
Fax: 56 2 632 6389

Chile Films
(Studio, lab, distribution, exhibition)
La Capitanía 1200
Santiago
Tel: 56 2 220 3086
Fax: 56 2 211 9826

Producers' Association
Holanda 3660
Santiago
Tel: 56 2 223 7968
Fax: 56 2 499 069

Filmocentro
(production and distribution)
Jorge Washington 302
Santiago
Tel: 56 2 274 9269
Fax: 56 2 225 1228

Laboratorio Cinematográfico
Gamma
Bellavista 0112
Santiago
Tel: 56 2 371 085
Fax: 56 2 251 8360

Laboratorio Cinevisión
Av. República de Israel 1057
Santiago
Tel: 56 2 274 0038

As time goes by . . .

Average weekly spectators in Santiago

1974: 201,635	1983: 120,171
1975: 146,141	1984: 118,884
1976: 157,699	1985: 104,472
1977: 142,655	1986: 106,689
1978: 146,276	1987: 124,676
1979: 123,360	1988: 136,582
1980: 146,495	1989: 121,974
1981: 166,396	1990: 99,022
1982: 107,680	

CHINA

by Derek Elley

The dark days of mainland Chinese cinema seem to get ever darker. If 1989 was a dispiriting year, few could have expected the depressing litany of 1990 – seemingly harmless movies either banned internally or forbidden foreign screenings, miles of celluloid devoted to encomia of the Party and national heroes, and production falling through the floor. As of summer 1991 there was still no glimmer of light at the end of the long, gloomy tunnel.

Exact statistics are more and more shrouded in mystery, but those rough figures that do emerge tell a clear tale. From a previous average of 120–150 films a year, production was officially scaled back to some 100 for 1990, realistically taking account of the country's dire economy and shortage of state funds. But by the end of September 1990 only 58 movies had seen the light of day – and that figure included some productions from the previous year that had previously been blocked but were hastily passed after revisions in order to keep up a sufficient flow of product. At Shanghai Film Studio, only one of its 15 planned films had so far emerged.

The problem is not just a shortage of capital or lack of ideas; even when a script has been passed at studio level, the finished movie still has to get past the Peking censors. And with the post-Tiananmen atmosphere of caution affecting all areas of the country's bureaucracy, no civil servant is risking his career by passing a work that could later boomerang. So, if in doubt, ban it.

The fuss in spring 1991 over Zhang Yimou's **Judou** (*Ju dou*) summed up the present silliness. Though banned in China

itself, the Japanese-financed film (whose negative is luckily held in Tokyo) was entered in the foreign-film category of the Oscars by officials who later lived to regret their impetuousness. When word came down that it was to be withdrawn and Zhang forbidden to attend the Oscar ceremony, the U.S. Academy refused (as it has done in the past) and in March a large number of U.S. film-makers wrote an open letter to China's Radio, Film & Television Ministry deploring its decision. In the event, *Judou* did not win; the officials who entered it were forced to write self-criticisms; and it remains banned in China (more, it is thought, for its theme of repressive violence by the older generation than for its sexual content).

Officially, the film is still awaiting Zhang's re-editing; but he seems in no hurry to reach for his scissors. Meanwhile, in April 1990 Film Bureau chief Teng Jinxian announced that Zhang's latest movie, **Raise the Red Lantern** (*Da hong denglong gaogao gua*), was unacceptable, despite having been approved at script stage and shot in China itself (near Taiyuan, Shanxi province). As with *Judou*, this will have no effect on its international passage: the movie is funded by Taiwan's Era International (channelled through a Hongkong subsidiary for convenience) which also produced Hou Hsiao-hsien's *A City of Sadness*. Hou is also the movie's associate producer.

Based on a story by Mainland author Su Tong, *Raise the Red Lantern* deals with the sexual politics of a traditional 1920's household with several wives. (A red lantern is hung outside the room of the wife favoured by the husband on any particular night.)

Scene from Chen Kaige's *Life on a String*

Zhang's regular actress Gong Li plays the youngest wife. The movie was finally launched at the Venice festival where Era International head Ch'iu Fu-sheng had such a success in 1989 with *A City of Sadness.*

Muted Comeback
Zhang is currently the only international "name" director still based in the country. Of other so-called Fifth Generation directors, Chen Kaige, based in New York, made a muted comeback at Cannes in 1991 with **Life on a String** (*Bian zou bian chang*), a German-British-Chinese coproduction made for only $1 million about an elderly travelling musician and his young pupil, from a short story by Shi Tiesheng. The film was received with respect rather than excitement, but confirms Chen as an un-compromising poet of the medium. His next project is reported to be **The Despot's Lady** (*Bawang bieji*), from a script by Hongkong author Lei Pik-wa (*Rouge*), for Taiwan producer Hsü Feng.

Of other names, Wu Tianming, former head of the adventurous Xi'an Film Studio, was still in the U.S., planning a US-Taiwan co-production in English (from a short story by Nie Hualing) about a Chinese woman who comes searching for her father. Zhang Zeming (*Swan Song; Sun and Rain*), recently based in London, temporarily returned to Hongkong and Guangzhou in summer 1991 but expected to return to the UK later that year to shoot the script *Foreign Moon*, about a young Chinese girl's first experiences in London. Huang Jianxin (*The Black Cannon Incident*) is in the midst of a three-year teaching post in Australia.

Other members of the Fifth Generation have remained in China, even though not enjoying the high international profile of Zhang Yimou. Tian Zhuangzhuang's **Li Lianying, the Imperial Eunuch** (*Da taijian Li Lianying*), a co-production with Hongkong's Skai Film, emerged as a sturdy, talky costume drama little different from so many other Forbidden City movies, with Jiang Wen in commanding form as Li and local megastar Liu Xiaoqing repeating her Empress Dowager for the nth time. Both Jiang and Liu (who also co-starred together in *Hibiscus Town* and *A Woman for Two*) spent a large chunk of 1991 travelling outside China together and mulling over offers from Hongkong and Taiwan before returning home in mid-year.

Wu Ziniu (*Evening Bell*), based at the PLA-run August First Studio, has (like Tian) been content to bend with the wind back home by accepting routine assignments. But even his **The Big Mill** (*Damo fang*), about a Communist veteran's reminiscences of the 1930's, was forbidden to attend the 1991 Berlin festival, despite having been shown within China the previous year.

Huang Jianzhong (*A Good Woman*; *Two Virtuous Women*), after grinding out the crime thriller **Dragon Year Cops** (*Longnian jingguan*) with co-director Li Ziyu, has bounced back with **New Year's Day** (*Danian chuyi*), from a play by Jiang Yi. Shot in Jilin, northeast China, with a strong cast, the movie centres on an old man who returns home for a traditional family gathering that soon deteriorates into feuding and avarice. It features veteran Li Baotian in the lead and some pungent northeast-flavoured dialogue. Also of interest is the second film of Xia Gang, **Unexpected Passion** (*Zaoyu jiqing*), about a girl dying of leukemia who falls in love with a rough-and-ready stuntman. Despite its cliched plot, the movie has a light and mostly understated tone.

There is, too, little new about **The Girls to Be Married** (*Chujia nü*), another feudal/rural marriage drama picturesquely shot, this time by middle-generation Wang Jin, who made a mark three years earlier with China's first "X-rated" movie, *Village of Widows*. The protagonists here are five pubescent girls, and the movie settles down into series of vignettes before a surprise finale in which they try to hang themselves. Despite good direction, there is a terrible familiarity to the whole thing.

Banned Movies
Others have been less lucky in getting their wares shown. The current list of banned movies includes: Zhou Xiaowen's *Black Mountain Road*, about a group of hill traders during the Sino-Japanese War; Mi Jiashan's *Just Sixteen*; Li Shaohong's *The Bloody Morning*, modelled on Gabriel Garcia Marquez's *Chronicle of a Death Foretold*; and Zhang Yuan's *Mum*, about a librarian caring for her retarded young son. The hand of Radio, Film & TV Minister Ai Zhisheng even reached out to touch the Hongkong-Taiwan coproduction *My American Grandson* (*Shanghai jiaqi*), shot by Ann Hui in Shanghai: small cuts were demanded before the picture was premiered at the Hongkong festival in April 1991 – with the implied threat that, if the producer refused, he would not be allowed to use Mainland locations again.

The kind of films that do get shown at present are the endless streams of hagiographic war and political movies that recall production from the 1950's and 1960's. The titles themselves tell the story – *The Decisive Engagement*, made by five directors on an enormous 100 million yuan ($21 million) budget by August First Studio; *Warriors of China* (brave Chinese saving another country from terrorists); *The Meridian of War* (nasty Japanese in 1942); *Long Yun and Chiang Kai-shek* (nasty KMT); *Heroic Spirit* (more nasty Japanese, in 1931); and *Young Prisoners of War* (KMT ditto).

The classic of this school is already Wang Jixing's *Jiao Yulu*, about the eponymous selfless Party worker, premiered in February 1991 amid much publicity and released in some 420 prints. There is nothing new in such movies; what is new is the hoopla that now accompanies them, with people like Ai Zhisheng talking of "correct models" to follow and, when faced with foreign criticism, producing imperishable replies like "only the Chinese have the right to decide on the merits of Chinese movies."

Somewhere between the two extremes lie conventional, safe period pieces like another version of the classic **A Dream of Red Mansions** (*Hongluo meng*), in production for five years under veteran Xie Tieli, and **Old Restaurant** (*Lao dian*), a Peking-set character drama by young Gu Rong. Gu's next project is **The Red Dragonfly** (*Hong qingting*), set in a Cultural Revolution ballet company performing *Red Detachment of Women*.

Admissions for 1990 were officially 16 billion but the figure is largely meaningless in the face of mass ticket-buying by work units and compulsory attendance at "prestige" productions. The once-innovative Xi'an and Guangxi studios are effectively neutered under their new management. And even television has been forced to cut back its allotted airtime for foreign material to 15%.

As of summer 1991 there was still talk of an international film festival being held in Peking in the autumn. But given the prevailing climate, it is likely to be heavy on ceremony and light on any real achievements. As so often in Chinese history, change (when it happens) will come from the top and the film industry will follow. Meanwhile, everyone is marking time (or applying for exit permits) till the "old men" die or sort out their power struggles.

Recent and Forthcoming Films

Bian zou bian chang (Life on a String). Script and Dir: Chen Kaige, from a short story by Shi Tiesheng. Phot: Gu Changwei. Players: Liu Zhongyuan, Huang Lei, Xu Quing. Prod: Pandora (Germany)/Channel Four (U.K.) /Peking Film Studio, China Film (China). 120 mins.

Chujia nü (The Girls to Be Married). Script: He Mengfan, from a short story by Ye Weilin. Dir: Wang Jin. Phot: Zhao Xiaoshi. Players: Shen Rong, Tao Huimin, Je Xue, Ji Xueping, Chi Huaqiong. Prod: Pearl River (China)/Sil-Metropole (Hongkong). 96 mins.

Lao dian (Old Restaurant/Peking Duck Restaurant). Script and Dir: Gu Rong. Phot: Shen Xilin. Players: Chen Baoguo, Xu Songzi. Prod: Nanhai, Shanghai, Tianma, China Film.

Xuese qingchen (The Bloody Morning). Script: Xiao Mao, Li Shaohong. Dir: Li Shaohong. Phot: Zeng Nianping. Players: Kong Lin, Gong Zhaohui, Hu Yajie, Zhao Jun. Prod: Peking.

Qingliang si de zhongsheng (The Bell of Purity Temple). Script: Li Zhun, from his own novel. Dir: Xi Jin. Players: Ding Yi, Fang Chao. A China-Hongkong co-prod.

Guo nian (New Year's Day). Script: Jiang Yi. Dir: Huang Jianzhong. Players: Li Baotian, Zhao Lirong, Ma Xiaoqing, Ge You, Tan Xiaoyan, Ding Jiali. Prod: Peking.

Zaoyu jiqing (Unexpected Passion). Script: Zheng Xiaolong, Feng Xiaogang. Dir: Xia Gang. Phot: Zeng Nianping. Players: Yuan Fan, Lu Liping. Prod: Peking.

Mama (Mum). Script: Qin Yan. Dir: Zhang Yuan. Phot (b&w/colour): Zhang Jian. Players: Qin Yan, Huang Haipo. Prod: Xi'an.

Nüren, taxi, nüren (Woman, Taxi, Woman). Script: Qiao Xueju. Dir: Wang Junzheng. Phot: Li Yuebin. Players: Pan Hong, Ding Jiali, Liu Qiong. Prod: Peking.

The 10th Golden Rooster Awards

After the usual behind-the-scenes delays, the awards were finally announced in November 1990, along with those for the 13th Hundred Flowers Awards (voted in the spring by readers of the monthly magazine *Popular Cinema*). Both awards were for films released in 1989.

Best Film: *The Birth of New China.*

Best Director: Li Qiankuan, Xiao Guiyun (*The Birth of New China*);

Xie Tieli, Zhao Yuan (*A Dream of Red Mansions*).
Best Script: Zhang Tianmin, Zhang Xiaotian,
Liu Xing, Guo Chen (*The Birth of New China*).
Best Actor: Lu Qi (*The Baise Uprising*).
Best Actress: no award.
Best Supporting Actor: Sun Feihu (*The Birth of New China*).
Best Supporting Actress: Lin Moyu (*A Dream of Red Mansions*).
Best Photography: Li Chensheng (*Oh, Sweet Snow*); Zhao Junhong (*Spacious Courtyard*).
Best Art Direction: Chen Yiyun, Yang Zhanjia (*A Dream of Red Mansions*).
Best Music: Yang Yu (*Spacious Courtyard*).
Best Sound: Feng Deyao (*Spacious Courtyard*).
Best Editing: Wu Fanghai. (*The Birth of New China*).
Best Costumes: Xia Yayi, Zhao Ruhua, Zhang Xuan, Hong Jun, Liu Huiping, Jiang Jinming (*A Dream of Red Mansions*).
Best First Work: Huang Jun (*Childhood in Rijin*).
Best Documentary: *Love in the Bashan Mountains*.
Best Animated Film: no award.
Best Scientific/Educational Film: *Brain*.
Best Children's Film: *In Their Teens* and *The Private Teaching Company*.

The 13th Hundred Flowers Awards

Best Films: *The Birth of New China, Black Snow* and *The Kunlun Column*.
Best Actor: Gu Yue (*The Birth of New China*).
Best Actress: Song Jia (*Spacious Courtyard*).
Best Supporting Actor: Sun Feihu (*The Birth of New China*).
Best Supporting Actress: Lin Moyu (*A Dream of Red Mansions*).

DEREK ELLEY has been associated with IFG for more than 19 years. He is known as a specialist in Hungarian and East Asian cinema, and is author of The Epic Film: Myth and History (1984) and consultant editor of The Variety Movie Guide and Chronicle of the Movies (both 1991). A regular contributor to weekly Variety, he is currently completing A Handbook of Chinese Cinema.

COLOMBIA
by Paul Lenti

Colombia's official entry in the 1990 Cannes Film Festival, *Rodrigo D. – No Future*, which explored the hopeless world of Medellín's disenfranchised youth, can easily be seen as a broader metaphor for national reality with its bleak and violent vision of life.

While most Latin American film industries face crippling economic problems, these are nothing in comparison to the problems confronting Colombian cinema. Last year, the head of the state production company was kidnapped and held hostage by druglords for seven months while an upsurge in urban guerrilla violence and attacks on police for the first half of the year kept a terrorised citizenry at home. But, in June, the country's most notorious druglord Pablo Escobar, along with his most trusted henchmen, surrendered to officials, bringing an end what Colombia's president calls "narco-terrorism" and the wave of bombings and assassinations.

Maruja Pachón, latest head of the government film production company Focine, was kidnapped on November 7, 1990

– after a little over a month in office – and was held until May 20, when she was freed through the intercession of a priest. Pachón was taken because she is sister to Gloria Pachón Galán, widow of slain presidential candidate Luis Carlos Galán, who was killed by the drug cartels on August 18, 1989. It was this murder that sparked the government's two-year war on the drug barons, and the subsequent violence took its toll on the country. (National box-office attendance declined from 49 million in 1986 to an approximate 37.5 million in 1990, and all night-time entertainment venues have all reported sharp drops in clientele. The home video industry, plagued by rampant piracy and cheap contraband tapes smuggled from Venezuela or Panama, has replaced the cinema-going tradition for many, although the majority of video profits – an estimated 70% – end up in the pockets of pirates and bootleggers.)

Despite persistent violence, the new government of President César Gaviria has adopted a pragmatic approach in resolving the country's economic problems, among them, the long-standing stalemate with domestic exhibitors. Yet those in the film industry charge the government has sold them down the river by caving in to the exhibitors' interests.

President Gaviria's new administration took office in August, 1990, and immediately set about to resolve some of the country's major problems. Among new legal measures was a revised cinema law, which the state passed in December 1990. This law officially ended the government's near-six-year stalemate with domestic exhibitors by declaring a general amnesty on debt payments to the state production firm Focine, virtually cutting the debt in half.

Focine (Compañía de Fomento Cinematográfico) was founded by the Ministry of Communications in 1978 to produce and promote national films, funded by a 8.5% box-office tax. When the state upped this tax to 16% in 1985, exhibitors rebelled and

Director Sergio Cabrera (right) working on *Estrategia del Caracol*

withheld their entire quota and the matter remained in the courts for the past five and a half years. With bombs exploding in the streets, government efforts to crack down on exhibitors was given low priority. New directors at Focine were a common occurrence, staying only long enough to size up the problem before resigning in frustration.

Focine pursued legal recourses in a slow methodic fashion while the debt reached approximately 4,000-million *pesos* in 1990. After years of legal battles, several principal exhibitors finally admitted their debt officially in 1990 and began making monthly payments. (In 1990, Focine collected around 1,000-million *pesos*, which includes both debt payments and tariffs for the year.)

Thus, film-makers and producers feel the government's amnesty reverses their hard-won battle. Terms dictated an almost

50% cut in back taxes – from 16% to the original 8.5% – and awarded exhibitors favourable payment terms: exhibitors had between one and 11 months to make arrears. In addition, all interest accrued on this debt was likewise forgiven and the new law also reduced Focine's future box-office tax from 16 to 12%.

The amnesty was made official in January, when Focine's then temporary director Neftali Espinosa Rengifo signed a formal agreement with Munir Falh Issa, the new director at Cine Colombia, the nation's leading exhibition chain controlling almost 50% of national cinemas. Similar agreements with other exhibitors followed.

The new plan also relieves Focine of its role as tax collector. Instead, tariffs are now collected by the federal tax administration, which in turn passes this money on to Focine. One official calls this move "an entirely new ballgame. Since the federal government is collecting the money, they can always divert it to another project that they think has higher priority," he said.

Staff Trimmed at Focine

National film-makers also charge that rather than going to production, Focine's budget only finances the firm's oversized bureaucracy. Major restructuring efforts made by the organisation in 1990 reduced Focine's permanent staff from 66 to 64 employees, while production funds went to completing post-production on only one film, a movie that had been shot in 1989.

Since 1978, Focine had produced around 200 features, medium-lengths, shorts and documentaries. Yet owing to lack of funds over the past five years, production had slowly dried up. In 1990, Focine completed postproduction on only two films (**María Cano** and **Rodrigo D. – No Future**) and in 1991, it finished its final production venture, the ensemble comedy **Snail's Strategy** (*Estrategia del Caracol*), by Sergio Cabrera.

Colombian film-makers find it ironic that while Focine has finally won its legal battles, it has also decided to abandon the production business altogether. Current plan is for the state to act as middleman between film-makers and producers by stimulating domestic production through private-sector loans. This plan includes granting credits and low-interest loans, subsidising exhibition of Colombian films, promoting national cinema, marketing Colombian films abroad and granting cash prizes to films that have received awards at film festivals.

For a low-budget (U.S. $200,000) national film to recoup investment within the country, the picture needs approximately 1 million spectators at an average 500 *pesos* (U.S. $1) per ticket on initial release. (Last year's **Amar y Vivir** was considered a commercial hit, breaking all previous records set for a domestic film by selling 765,050 tickets through mid-May; *Batman*, a national blockbuster, sold only 800,900 tickets.)

As an incentive to make investment in film production a profitable venture, Focine has proposed to grant credits for production coupled with a three-year low-investment loan to producers. During the first year, nothing is owed on the principal. Interest rates are set at 16%, considerably lower than the 42–45% charged at private banks, due in part to the nation's approximate 25% annual devaluation of currency against the dollar, coupled with an even higher rate of inflation – around 3% a month. (Despite these figures, Colombia has one of the healthiest economies in Latin America.)

Film-makers charge that, despite production credits, the new plan does not stimulate investment in cinema. Most of Focine's new measures reward films after the fact, they say, based on box-office performance or festival recognition. They claim the success of *Amar y Vivir* was prompted by its being adapted from an already successful television soap opera and by the fact it received heavy promotion from the exhibition chain Cine Colombia, one of its producers. And, they claim that even though retrospectives of national cinema may draw awareness to Colombian films, paucity of product, due to Focine's legal battles, has made producers cautious.

New Activities in 1991

Meanwhile, Focine has been busy with a number of new activities to be funded by the 1,700–million *pesos* it expected to collect from back taxes in 1991. These include:

– A retrospective of Colombian cinema in Bogota and other cities.

– The acquisition and distribution of short films. Since federal law dictates mandatory screening of domestic shorts with all features, Colombia boasts a steady production of short films. In 1991, Focine planned to hold three national competitions where approximately 30 short films would be purchased. Winners receive 9-million *pesos* for one-year distribution rights at national cinemas.

– Control of Colombian box-office: National exhibitors are presently installing a new electronic ticket system to control the box-office. In the past, exhibitors have been accused of using what is referred to locally as "the carousel system," where sold ticket stubs are resold again and again, making accurate box-office assessments impossible. This new system will also streamline operations and reduce personnel.

– Promotion of National Film Festivals. Colombia touts two film festivals. The Cartagena International Film Festival, directed by Víctor Nieto, celebrated its 32nd edition in March, 1991, and – with the future of the Havana Film Festival uncertain – present plans are to promote it as a major showcase for new Latin American cinema. And, the Bogota International Film Festival, directed by Henry Laguado, celebrated its eighth edition in October at various locations in the capital.

Meanwhile, feature film-making in Colombia has fallen to a new low, with only four new productions for 1990–91:

1. Focine's final production, *Snail's Strategy*, was originally shot in 1989. Coproduced by director Sergio Cabrera's advertising firm Prods. Fotograma and Crear TV, post-production stalled until finishing funds could be secured from Spain and only completed in 1991.

2. The independent venture **Confession to Laura** (*Confesión a Laura*), filmed in 1990 in Havana, is a co-production between Colombia's Méliès Prods, Televisión Española and the Cuban film institute ICAIC.

3. The wholly commercial project, **To Love and Live** (*Amar y Vivir*), was coproduced in 1990 by the exhibition chain Cine Colombia, the TV production firm RTI Colombia and Colombiana de Televisión. By mid-May 1991, over 675,000 tickets had been sold.

4. Jorge Alí Triana began production on the short feature **The Hen with the Golden Eggs** (*La Gallina de los huevos de oro*) in Oct. 1991. This one-hour multinational production with an original script by Nobel Prize laureate Gabriel García Márquez and Eliseo Diego, was developed at García Márquez's writing workshop Taller de Guiones.

In documentaries, film-makers Patricia Castaño and Adelaida Trujillo have continued seeking European funds to produce their complex analytical works. In 1989, they made *Law of the Jungle* with British and German TV. Backed by funds from Britain's Channel 4 and BBC, last year the team produced two hour-long documentaries: *Behind the Cocaine War*, about how U.S. military aid to fight druglords is used to quash local civic and political organisations; and *Nothing Will Stop Us*, concerning the newspaper *El Espectador*, whose offices were bombed and editor assassinated.

Also finishing postproduction by year's end was the feature documentary *Silvia: Story of a Kidnapping*, co-produced, written and directed by Camila Motta. Shot in

Gustavo Londoño and Vicky Hernández in *Confession to Laura*

Colombia in 1990 with post-production in New York, this is the first documentary dealing with the problem of kidnapping in Colombia, which can be classified as a business venture. Every seven hours, someone in Colombia is kidnapped, 90% for money. The film centres on one case, that of Silvia, daughter of an influential banker, who was held from March-June 1985.

Among notable shorts are: Paola Panero's *And*, the story of two women, a public advocate assigned to defend a woman accused of a white-collar crime; the Colombian-French documentary *The Devil and the Rhumba*, directed by Gustavo Fernández and José María Tapías; and Patricia Cardoso's *The Air Globes*, which won best short fiction and best first work at the 1991 San Antonio Cine Festival.

Although many Latin American countries produce *novelas* (soap operas) featuring torrid love stories drawn out over many months, most Colombian TV companies have opted to produce miniseries, usually made up of 6–10 one-hour chapters adapted from Latin American literary classics. These companies have taken advantage of Colombia's lull in cinema production to hire some of the top film-makers.

Confesión a Laura
(Confession to Laura)

Script: Alexandra Cardona Restrepo. Direction: Jaime Osorio Gómez. Photography: Adriano Moreno. Editing: Nelson Rodríguez. Music: Gonzalo Rubalcabar. Players: Vicky Hernández, Gustavo Londoño, María Cristina Galvez. Produced by Méliès Producciones (Colombia), in co-production with Televisión Española (Spain) and ICAIC (Cuba). 90 mins.

A first feature by Jaime Osorio Gómez, *Confession to Laura* was produced under the auspices of Robert Redford's Sundance Institute and the New Latin American Cinema Foundation. Filmed entirely in Havana, the action takes place during the turbulence of the "Bogotazo," when widespreading rioting erupted in the streets of the capital following the assassination of presidential candidate Jorge Elíecer Gaitán on April 9, 1948.

In the midst of the chaos, this intimate story concerns a trio of characters, neighbours both united and separated by the violence outside and the unrest raging within. It is the catalyst for understanding that the larger canvas is only a metaphor for the individual.

The story concerns a cheerless middle-aged couple, Santiago and Josefina, who are virtual prisoners in their apartment because of the random violence taking place out in the street. While the husband is concerned, the wife tries desperately to block out reality by turning off the radio and baking a cake for Laura, a spinster living across the street, who is celebrating her birthday.

Urged on by his wife, Santiago manages to deliver the cake. But by now, snipers have taken position on the rooftops, shooting anyone in the streets below. It is impossible to return.

As the evening wears on and gunfire continues to resound outside, Santiago reveals the dissatisfied man inside. He confesses his frustrations to Laura. Rather than the small-time ineffective government bureaucrat, he fancies himself as an imposing figure, one who strikes a pose and smokes cigarettes with a certain sense of bearing, the potent man who sings and dances torrid tangos. Yet this intimacy does not go unobserved as Josefina watches from her window across the way.

At times, the film is reminiscent of Ettore Scola's *A Special Day* as historical events intrude upon individual intimacy, provoking catharsis and change. The reality of the masses becomes the reality of the individual developed through finely honed low-key acting and a polished script that should attract international attention.

Paul Lenti

Amar y Vivir (To Love and Live)

Script: Carlos Duplat Sanjuan, Luz Mariela Santofimio. Direction: Carlos Duplat Sanjuan. Photography: Julio Luzardo. Editing: Luis Alberto Restrepo. Music: Harold Orozco. Players: María Fernanda Martínez, Luis Eduardo Motoa, Waldo Urrego, Patricia Grisales, Horacio Tavera. Produced by RTI Colombia, Cine Colombia and Colombiana de Televisión.

A commercial melodrama, *To Love and Live* was adapted from the long-running popular television soap opera of the same name and stars María Fernanda Martínez and Luis Eduardo Motoa. Although the story meanders, the film is rife with national themes including violence, local crime bosses, the exodus of rural population to the cities, kidnapping, music and popular local characters.

The story begins in the small town of Bellavista, where young Joaquín (Motoa) is forced to leave by a local boss. Arriving in the capital, he finds a job at an auto shop and begins courting Irene (Martínez), a humble vender at the local market who enjoys singing in her spare time.

While Joaquín becomes involved in crime, Irene's persistence brings her to national fame as a singer, where she goes on to represent Colombia in the international OTI song festival. Although the soap opera ended with Joaquín's death, the film finishes with a reformed man exiting prison and reunited with his wife and now 15-year-old daughter.

Technically, the film is polished and well acted; there is also extensive location work. But *To Love and Live* suffers mostly from trying to be too faithful to the soap opera's extended storyline. It telescopes time and incidents to the point where the action jumps from one major scene to another. Also, various sideplots – such as Joaquín's search for his sister – could easily be cut since they distract from the overall story.

But no-one can deny the film's success at the national box office, due in part to its pre-existing loyal TV audience and the support of Cine Colombia's exhibition and promotion clout. Also, its treatment of national reality and frequent use of music helped propel the film to national blockbuster status.

Yet, all of these reasons that account for the film's domestic success may also work against its performance outside of Colombia, and it is doubtful the film would find such major acceptance in other territories.

Paul Lenti

Recent and Forthcoming Films

Estrategia del Caracol (Snail's Strategy). Script: Humberto Dorado, based on a screenplay by Sergio Cabrera and Ramón Jimeno. Dir: Sergio Cabrera. Phot: Carlos Congote. Editing: Manuel Navia. Music: Eduardo Carrisoza. Players: Frank Ramírez, Humberto Dorado, Florina Lemaitre, Gustavo Angarita. Prod: Focine, Crear T.V. and Producciones Fotograma. 100 mins.
Silvia: Historia de un Secuestro (Silvia: Story of a Kidnapping). Script and Dir: Camila Motto. Phot: Barry Ellsworth. Sound: Heriberto García. Editing: Esther Durán. Music: Nicolás Uribe. Prod: E.M. Films. 90 mins.

María Cano. Script: Camila Loboguerrero, Luis González, Felipe Aljure. Dir: Camila Loboguerrero. Phot: Carlos Sánchez. Editing: Luis Alberto Restrepo, Gabriel González. Music: Santiago Lanz K. Players: María Eugenia Dávila, Frank Ramírez, Jorge Herrera, Germán Escallón, Diego Vélez. Prod: Focine. 104 mins.

PAUL LENTI is a freelance journalist specialising in Latin American cinema. In addition to working eight years as a film critic for The Mexico City News and eight years with the trade publication Variety, he more recently co-ordinated the film section of the 1990 and 1991 New York Festival Latino.

Useful Addresses

Fundación Patrimonio
Colombiano
Carrera 13 No. 13–24, piso 9
Bogotá
Tel: 281–5241, 283–6495.

Focine
(Compañía de Fomento
Cinematográfico)
Calle 35 No. 4–89
Bogotá
Tel: 288–4661, 288–4575, 288–4712
Fax: 285–5749.

Festival de Cine de Bogotá
Calle 26 No. 4–92
Bogotá
Tel: 282–5196
Fax: 283–0141.

CUBA
by Carlos Mendoza

For the last few years there has been a sharp decline in both the quality and quantity of Cuban films. That trend has continued this past year as serious economic and political problems made themselves felt thus posing troubling questions about the future of an industry that had attracted wide praise at one time.

The five features released during the year included **Caravan** (*Caravana*) by Rogelio París, dealing with the participation of Cuban troops in the Angolan civil war; **Transparent Women** (*Mujer transparente*), a series of five short stories each by a different director on the problems of Cuban women. This was clearly the best release of the year and is a subject covered with some success in previous Cuban films of the 1960's and 1970's such as *Manuela, Lucia* and *Retrato de Teresa*. **Maria Antonia**, by Sergio Giral, Cuba's only major black director, which was virtually impossible to

understand for anyone not well versed in Afro-Cuban mythology and religion; **Hello Hemingway**, by Fernando Pérex, winner of top honours at the Latin American Film Festival in December, in a decision that proved very unpopular with both critics and spectators alike; and **The Useless Death of My Pal Manolo** (*La inútil muerte de mi socio Manolo*) by Julio Garciá Espinosa, about which the less said the better.

According to a report published in *Granma*, Cuba's leading national daily, for the last four years the industry has had earnings of just under U.S.$1.5 million while spending has been on the order of $2 million. Co-productions are one of the steps being taken to help overcome the shortfall. Noteworthy in this regard were **Explosion in a Cathedral** (*El siglio de las luces*), a film adaptation by director Humberto Solás, of the famous novel by Cuban writer Alejo Carpentier. This was being made with

Scene from *Maria Antonia*

French and Soviet help. The other joint venture was **For Rent to Dream** (*Me alquilo para soñar*) by Brazilian director Ruy Guerra, based on a short story by Gabriel García Márquez, with backing from Spanish TV. In the past Cuba had undertaken such projects with other Latin American and Third World nations such as Peru, Colombia and Angola, but economic problems in those countries where the film industry is in dire straits made any further progress in this area unlikely. If co-productions are to prove profitable in the long run, the source will have to be western Europe and chiefly Spain, but political tensions between the two countries make this seem doubtful.

Film School in Jeopardy
The International Film School in San Antonio de los Banos, on the outskirts of Havana, was in serious financial trouble and faced an uncertain future since no new donations had been received. Its director Fernando Birri had quit and gone to Germany. No public explanation of his departure had been given but it was widely reported in Havana that he was unhappy over financial and political problems and the failure of a recent film.

Controversy also developed as a result of a feud between Julio García Espinosa, head of the Cuban Film Institute (ICAIC), and Pastor Vega, No 2 at ICAIC and head of the organising committee for the Latin American Film Festival. The two traded charges and countercharges about personalities and politics that included alleged efforts to influence the jury at the December Latin American Film Festival and in the end Espinosa appeared to have won the power struggle.

The economic problems that we have talked about, which in the case of the film industry are very serious because it obtained much of its materials from the former socialist camp in Eastern Europe, and the growing political isolation, make it safe to say that not much of interest will come from Cuba in the near future in terms of film, for the days of revolutionary cinema are long gone.

CARLOS MENDOZA is a Cuban journalist and translator.

Forthcoming Films

Adorables Mentiras (Adorable Lies) Dir: Gerardo Chijona. Prod: ICAIC. Player: Isabel Santos.
Alicia en el pais de las maravillas (Alice in Wonderland). Dir: Daniel Díaz Torres. Prod: ICAIC.

Scene from *Hello Hemingway*

Useful Address

Instituto Cubano de Arte e Industria Cinematografica (ICAIC)
Calle 23 esq 12
Vedado
Habana

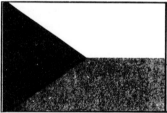

CZECHOSLOVAKIA

by Eva Zaoralová

At the end of 1990, the Central Management of Czechoslovak Film was definitively liquidated which (up to the fall of the totalitarian régime) controlled from Prague – together with the Department of Culture of the Central Committee of the Czechoslovak Communist Party – film production and distribution in Bohemia, Moravia and Slovakia. As far as competence is concerned, films now come under the Ministries of Culture of the Czech and Slovak Republics. The task of the appropriate ministerial department, however, is in the future to be not so much the ideological control of the cinema industry as the management of state funds for its support and, furthermore, the maintenance of non-commercial contact with foreign countries.

Film production is continuing its efforts at de-monopolisation, but this effort has been slowed by the fact that the Government has still not debated the new Film Law. So far, then, the state monopoly of the film industry has not yet been legally ended, but in spite of this, new private firms and companies are gradually being established. In the Czech region, for instance, there is Bonton, which in 1991 produced the first full-length feature film **Tank Regiment** (*Tankový prapor*), directed by Vít Olmar, from the novel with the same title by exiled author Josef Skvorecký. Then there are the firms Drufip and Bulšit, and in Slovakia were established the companies of Davay, Arttep or KIM–International which at the moment concentrate mainly on the production of publicity films and videoclips.

The leading producers, then, continue to be the Barrandov Film Studios, the Zlín (formerly Gottwaldov) Film Studio, concentrating mainly on documentaries and films for children, and the Film Studio Bratislava-Koliba. All these studios are undergoing considerable organisational changes. The Barrandov Film Studio, for instance, has reduced the number of its employees to half, dissolved creative groups even though they were staffed by completely new people, and released all the film directors (who until now were mostly in the position of employees, which means that they received a certain minimum wage even in periods when they were not making any films). The situation is similar in Slovakia, but there are still seven creative groups operating which are independent production units responsible for the realisation of films and also for the economic results of creativity.

On the one hand, all these changes may lead to the establishment of normal healthy competition, on the other hand, they understandably remove their former social security from the artists and apart from this the increased emphasis on economic effectiveness directs production towards commercialisation. Fearing such a consequence of the transition to market conditions in the film industry, the Union of Film and Television Artists (FITES) strove for the immediate creation of an independent film fund from which grants could be allocated for specific film projects. Both the Czech and the Slovak Governments *did* actually establish such funds in the national Ministries of Culture (in this direction also there was a shift of competency from the level of the Federation to the level of the Governments of the two Republics) and at present negotiations are under way concerning the manner of their allocation. The volume of these funds is not very large: in the Czech Republic there would be roughly enough for the production of six full-length

Still from Dušan Hanák's *Private Lives*
photo: Vlado Vavrek

films. It is expected, however, that not all expenses would be covered from this, but only a certain proportion. The provision of a grant should be decided by a commission which would be nominated always for just one year by the Minister of Culture.

Artists hitherto accustomed to the generosity of the state, provided at the cost of censorship pressures, must look elsewhere to acquire money for their films. Great hopes are placed in co-production partners, but already the first experiences are showing that accepting money from someone always means also accepting to a certain extent his orders. So far these are mainly the experiences of Slovak artists who also co-operated with foreign partners earlier, especially with German TV companies and in one case with a French partner.

Barrandov Still Prolific

The unfavourable financial situation of the Czechoslovak film studios, the largest of which – Barrandov Film Studios in Prague – is at present still the major producer because the authority of the abolished Central Offices of Czechoslovak Film has to some extent passed to them, is understandably reflected in the number of films produced. Nevertheless the situation is not as catastrophic as was forecast last year. Barrandov Film Studios alone have produced or are completing for 1991 a total of 16 full-length films (in comparison with the average of 25 films a year produced under

the Communist régime). It is true that the projects for these films came into being at a time when the studios still had an overall state subsidy. At present, when there are new "rules of the game," fewer and fewer new projects for future films are being made and this makes it all the more reasonable to assume that only projects with a certain guarantee of quality, or at least of commercial success, will get through the selection network to the stage of realisation.

The return on investment means, however, is less and less certain with every passing year: according to the latest statistics none of the Czech and Slovak films made in 1990 earned enough money to cover their expenses. The number of film-goers is declining constantly: in 1990 Czech and Moravian cinemas had attendances of 36,361 million (with a total of 10 million inhabitants) and the Slovak cinemas attracted 13,816 million (with 5 million inhabitants). This means a decline of roughly 30% in comparison with 1989. Only three

Czech films were among the twenty most successful: the formerly banned film **Larks on a String** by Jiří Menzel (in 8th place), the erotic comedy by Zdeněk Troška, **Sun, Hay and a Slap in the Face** (in 12th place) and the comedy by Milan Šteindler, **Ready for the Grave** (in 17th place). Not one of these films was seen by over a million cinema-goers – the only films seen by over a million were the French film *Emmanuelle* and the American imports *Dirty Dancing* and *Indiana Jones and the Temple of Doom*.

The decline in cinema-going in Czechoslovakia is due, apart from the usual factors (TV, video), to several definite causes. On the one hand there was a drop in the general interest in culture in connection with the considerably wider opportunities for other uses of free time in a free state and the increased interest in political activity. Also with the rise in the cost of living, the population is saving to a greater extent (the price of cinema and theatre tickets naturally rose also). And finally the cinemas in general are so poorly equipped technically, so out-dated and uncomfortable that visiting them is not in itself appealing. In connection with this it is also necessary to consider the transition of cinemas into private hands: so far they are still administered by district authorities. Multiplexes may solve some of the woes.

There have also been changes in the organisation of distribution: the former monopoly of the Central Hire of Films in the Czech Republic has become the joint-stock company Lucernafilm and this now has competitors in the shape of new firms, especially Interama. Czechoslovak Film-export, recently abandoned by its longtime director Jiří Janoušek, is no longer the only importer and exporter of films, but nevertheless in this sphere there have not yet been any basic changes in the existing situation.

In Czechoslovakia the number of VCR's has only recently expanded, but is still far from as great as in western countries. Nevertheless one of the most important problems is the black market in videocassettes and piracy which has not been withstood successfully in spite of all the efforts to establish a legitimate video rental system.

Film Production

The year 1990 showed the clear artistic and ideological prevalence of films which came into being at the close of the 1960's and languished for years in safe deposits. Sufficient to say that the Czechoslovak Film Critics' Prize went to the film by Jiří Menzel, *Larks on a String* (previously awarded a prize in Berlin) which was made in 1969. In 1991 the Critics' Prize went to the Slovak director, Juraj Jakubisko, for *Little Birds, Orphans and Fools*, also taken off the shelf. In 1990 around a dozen films were released which had been withheld for twenty years. Last year also some of these films were completed, such as **Decoy** by Hynek Bočan or **Ark of Fools** by Ivan Balada, which means that they are marked

1990, but differ considerably in style from contemporary films.

In the course of twenty years of constant ideological pressure the film-makers – even the relatively young ones – gradually learned not to think about man, the world and themselves and ceased to seek fresh ways of expressing themselves. The films emerging from Czechoslovak studios are mostly so alike that the directors could be interchanged. At least two of them, however, have maintained their originality: Jiří Menzel and Věra Chytilová. The former made the film version in 1991 of the play by Václav Havel, **The Beggars' Opera**, produced previously on the stage of the Drama Club (Cinoherní klub), and also became head of the Chair of Production at FAMU (Film and Television Faculty of the Academy of Fine Arts). In addition to this he is the only one who has kept his production team in Krátký film a.s. (Short Film Co. Ltd.). It looks probable that this company, originally a producer of documentary films, will become one of the producers of full-length feature films.

Věra Chytilová believed that with the fall of totalitarian power she would at last be able to realise her long-term project **The Face of Hope**, devoted to the life of the great Czech woman novelist Božena Němcová. During the Communist era this script came up against the resistance of the

Still from Karel Smyczek's *It's Alright for the Praguers*
photo: Komárek Jaromír

censors, because it seemed to them some-what disrespectful. However, in the new free-market situation the director is unable to find a producer with the courage to embark on such a demanding power with historical settings and so – in spite of the willingness of the French Centre National du Cinéma to provide a grant for the film – the efforts of Věra Chytilová have so far been in vain.

The Czech film industry expected an immense amount from the return of Jan Němec, the creator of *Diamonds of the Night* and *The Party and the Guests*, who spent many years in exile. His film, **In the Light of the King's Love**, inspired by the tale of the "cursed" writer and philosopher Ladislav Klíma (1878–1928) caused great controversy, especially due to the naturalism of the scenes of the "bloody novel" describing the considerably unusual course of marital hatred, because of Němec's obvious desire to shock, something also proper to the author's model. In any case this is the most interesting film of the Czechoslovak 1990–1991 season.

In some respects a further sensation is the film **Only Family Matters**, but this time not because of originality in form or content, but simply because the director, Jiří Svoboda, creator of this variation on *L'Aveu* (it is the tale of two Communist functionaries accused of treason in the 1950's and brought to court after months of psychological and physical pressure), became in the period between working on the script and realising it the Chairman of the Communist Party of Bohemia and Moravia!

Other directors also concentrated on the evocation of the atmosphere of the recent past and a critical view of the political development of Czechoslovaks: the Slovak director of the older generation, Martin Holly, made a film from a script by one of the President's present advisors, Jiří Křižan, **Silent Pain**, the story of a man who has suffered from childhood to adulthood for his origins – his father was executed at the end of the 1940's as a "class enemy." Thirty-year-old Václav Křistek set his second film **Vyžilý Boudník** (the title uses the names of two people: K. Vyžilý and L. Boudník) in the period of so-called normalisation, in other words in the 1970's, which marked the lives of two people brought together by chance.

A similar tone of bitter comedy was selected for his sarcastic condemnation of Mafia practices and bribery in the world of pop music and the moral stagnancy of this sphere in the time of the Jakeš régime by Vít Olmer, who called his film **Our Czech Songs II**. Unlike Křistek he had no hesitancy about taking advantage of the spectacular moments with which this material provided him.

Also on the subject of moral devastation is the second film **Smoke** by the talented Tomáš Vorel, one of the greatest hopes of the Czech film industry. The story of a young engineer who in his first post, thanks to his normal attitude, sets "local" history in motion is elaborated in a mélange of styles and genre elements, reality and absurdity.

The postwar history of a Slovak village is evoked by the tale of a man whose life is a series of compromises in **When the Stars Were Red** by director Dušan Trančik, which represented Czechoslovakia at the Berlinale. In the first film made in Czechoslovakia outside the state structure, Vít Olmer takes a comic look at the 1950's. His **Tank Regiment** shows conditions in the army during the period of the Cold War. Although the critics gave it a cool reception it looks as though this film will be one of the most popular this year. Also among the relative successes is the musical film by Karel Smyczek **It's Alright for the Praguers**, the script for which was also worked on by musician Michael Kocáb, who appears in the film and is now a Deputy to the Federal Assembly, formerly leader of the group "Prague Selection," (one of the pioneer groups of the "New Wave" not allowed to perform for most of the 1980's).

Zdeněk Troška is counting on success with audiences for his new film comedy, made at his own expense: **Sun, Hay and Eroticism**, which follows on from *Sun, Hay and Strawberries* and *Sun, Hay and a Slap in the Face*. Troška was one of the most talented and hopeful graduates from the Film Faculty of the Academy of Fine Arts, until he opted for easy success and commercialism with these films. Troška's slightly older colleague Miloš Zábranský is taking the opposite direction: after attracting the attention of the Czechoslovak and Slovak critics with the pyschological film *House for Two* (1988) in which he expressed his opinion courageously for the time on questions concerning materialistic lack of principles on the one hand and the moral code based on faith in God on the other, he attempted to intensify the religious motives in **Building** where he came to grief through lack of a more solid framework of action and ideas. The detective genre is represented this year only by the first film of Petr Šicha, **Stronger than Me**, based on the true case of a series of sexually motivated murders.

In Slovakia the young Martin Šulík made his début with **Tenderness**, following on in style from the avantgarde of the 1960's: very ambitious, but somewhat flat. Considerably more interesting is **Private Lives** by the well-known Slovak director Dušan Hanák, a stylistically elaborated probe into the alienated society of a totalitarian régime.

Interesting Debuts

There were more interesting débuts in Prague: the black-and-white film **Vojtěch the Orphan** (directed by Zdeněk Tyc) has already been screened in several festivals abroad as an interesting study of the conflict between individuality and a conformist environment. Oldřich Trojan's **Song Strip**, awaiting release, is an original confession of the emotional world of today's twenty-year-olds. The premieres are expected before the end of the year of two works arousing interest due to the personalities of the

Still from Tomáš Vorel's *Smoke*
photo: Knapp Vladislav

directors. Irena Pavlásková had an unexpectedly great success last year with her first work *The Time of Servants* which, after being included in the Critics' Week at Cannes, acquired considerable recognition in Montréal and Geneva. A further film by this director, **Corpus delicti**, also deals with the moral deformation of society in an atmosphere of totality and conformism. Jan Svěrák became famous both at home and abroad for his short mystification on an ecological theme *The Oilies* and so his first full-length feature film **Elementary School** is also awaited with considerable interest.

As can be seen, there are not as few new films from the 1990–1991 period as was feared when the old structure of the Czechoslovak film industry began to be broken down. But it is, of course, necessary to recall yet again that market mechanisms have not yet really made themselves felt and the great crisis in production and distribution is still to come. On the other hand, voices are beginning to be heard to an increasing extent criticising the quality of this production and pointing out that half of these films would have been better never made, that in the state of impotency which is clearly the result of the "shock of freedom" there would be no harm at all in producing less films. The main aim must be for those few actually made to find their public.

V žáru královské lásky (In the Light of the King's Love)

Script and Direction: Jan Němec, from the novel by Ladislav Klíma. Photography: Jiří Macháně. Editing: Alois Fišárek. Music: Jan Hammer. Players: Jiří Bartoška, Josef Abrhám, Pavel Landovský. Produced by Barrandov Film Studios. 87 mins.

This "bloody comedy" by Jan Němec is a transcription of the grotesque novelette by the "condemned" writer and philosopher Ladislav Klíma, *The Suffering of Count Sternenhoch* (first edition 1928). This book, crammed with unbridled imagery, sado-masochistic episodes and eccentric philosophy, has lost none of its impact and still shocks with its vocabulary and morbid fantasy. Jan Němec intended to make a film version in the 1960's but could not return to it until he came back from exile. He brought the action up to date by transferring it from an unspecified land at the beginning of the century to the "near" future and setting it is

contemporary Prague with its decaying houses, its magically beautiful panoramas and its monstrous television tower. In this macabre tale, reminiscent of a horror story, love comes dangerously close to hatred and vice-versa. The relationship of the decadent Count to the wife who scorns him culminates in the death of the antagonistic pair, which finally unites them.

The director makes no secret of the fact that many things attract him in the philosophy of the bizarre writer, a voluntary disinheritor of society, based on Nietzsche's extreme individualism exaggerated to idolisation of self, saturated with the desire for power and the cult of physical strength. His model gives him plenty of opportunity to shock, to attack the audience with rapid switches, tense eroticism, cruelty and an atmosphere of horror, providing him at the same time with key to the author's irony. The film is in harmony with the present post-modernist trend.

Eva Zaoralová

Still from Jan Němec's *In the Light of the King's Love*

photo: Karel Jesátko

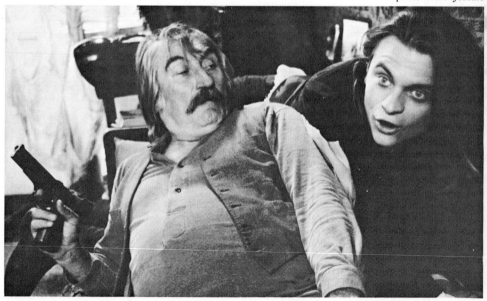

Sukromne životy (Private Lives)

Script: Dušan Hanák and Katka Benčičová. Direction: Dušan Hanák. Photography: Jozef Krivosik. Editing: Alfred Benčič. Music: Václav Hálek, Milan Svoboda. Players: Jana Šulcová, Magda Vašáryová, Václav Helšus. Produced by Bratislava Film Studios.

The central figures are two step-sisters: the elder, Nadia, is a psychologist, the younger, Elena, is an actress. They are different in nature and differently equipped for life and it is difficult for them to find common ground, especially as between them stands a man who first loved Nadia and then married Elena. All three characters are affected by the syndrome of totality: it is as if they lived in an aquarium, underwater, as if they had forgotten how to speak and communicate. And yet each yearns for a helping hand, each struggles with the burden of unfulfilled longings and ambitions. The masterful and apparently balanced Nadia is fighting the sense of futility after an operation which has left her sterile. Elena is torn between lover for her child and her husband and her desire for fame. Martin would like to live honestly and without compromises, but does not have the will-power.

This film by Dušan Hanák was shot before the revolution and is therefore full of hidden meanings and one eye on the ideological censors. In the context of the totalitarian régime the critics would admit the courage and undoubtedly critical tone of the film and its creator. Under the altered political conditions under which the film was completed many things have fallen somewhat flat. Nevertheless the film is admirably pure in style and it is clear that every component is well thought-out. The rigour of expression, sometimes bordering on aestheticism but translating very well the strange state of suppression which everyone who thought a little could observe in himself, places *Private Lives* among the best films of the recent period.

Eva Zaoralová

EVA ZAORALOVÁ (Hepnerová) is a Czech film critic and Editor of the magazine Film a Doba. She is author of many essays and two books and teaches film history at FAMU in Prague.

Useful Addresses

Film Department of the Ministry of Culture
Jindřišská 34
11000 Prague
Tel: (42.2) 22 66 67
Fax: (02) 22 37 51

Slovak Film Institute
National Centre of Film
ul. Červenej armády 32
811 09 Bratislava
Tel: (07) 529 29

Filmové Studio Barrandov
(*production*)
Kříženeckého nám. 322
150 00 Prague
Tel: (42.2) 54 16 22
Fax: (514) 288 8083

Slovenská filmová tvorba
(*production*)
Koliba
833 14 Bratislava
Tel: (42.7) 37 14 22
Fax: (42.7) 37 22 24

Lucernafilm
(*distribution*)
Národní tř. 28
110 00 Prague
Tel: (42.2) 22 70 41

Interama
(*distribution*)
Václavské nám. 28
110 00 Prague

Czechoslovak Filmexport
Václavské nám. 28
110 00 Prague
Tel: (42.2) 235.53 85
Fax: (42.2) 235 84 32

Czech Film Institute
Národní tř. 40
110 00 Prague
Tel: (42.2) 26 00 87

Association of Czech Film Artists (FITES)
Pod Nuselskými schody 3
12 0 00 Prague
Tel: (42.2) 691 13 10

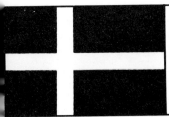

DENMARK

by Ebbe Iversen

Young director Lars von Trier kept Denmark visible on the international film map, when at the festival in Cannes this year his **Europa** was awarded both the Grand Prix Technique and the Prix de Jury, the latter shared with Maroun Bagdadi's *Hors la Vie*.

It is significant, however, that it would hardly have been possible to shoot *Europa* as a strictly Danish production. This ambitious film is a Danish-French-German-Swedish co-production, its main actors (Jean-Marc Barr and Barbara Sukowa) are not Danish, and the dialogue is partly in German, partly in English.

Although this is due to an artistic decision made by Lars von Trier, it also reflects the lack of money for larger film productions in Denmark. In a country with only 5 million inhabitants – and a language incomprehensible outside Scandinavia – a film industry cannot exist without heavy financial support from the government, and it is the eternal and increasingly desperate complaint of the Danish film world that this support is far from sufficient.

In recent years Danish films have enjoyed more success abroad than since the great days of the Danish silent cinema – with American Academy Awards for Gabriel Axel's *Babette's Feast* and Bille August's *Pelle the Conqueror*, the Palme d'Or in Cannes for the latter, an Academy Award nomination for Kaspar Rostrup's *Waltzing Regitze*, and two awards in Cannes for *Europa*, plus a number of awards at smaller festivals around the world for other Danish films. It is therefore argued that it is more relevant than ever to secure a continuous production of quality films in Denmark.

The amount for 1991 (DKK 66.1 million, approx US$ 10 million) allocated to the Danish Film Institute (DFI), which channels government grants to film producers, is inadequate for this goal, especially as part of the funds is earmarked for specific purposes such as the European Co-production and Distribution Fund (EURIMAGES), and the Nordic Film and Television Fund.

Additionally DKK 18.5 million is set aside for the so-called Fifty-Fifty Fund, which allows for automatic allocation to producers of 50% of production budgets provided they guarantee to put up the other half themselves. A mere DKK 26.9 million remains for the two film consultants at the DFI, whose task it is to select and support quality film projects for adults, while DKK 9.7 million is left for the consultant who deals with films for children and youngsters. The result is that only three or four quality films for adults can be produced each year.

Higher Funding Refused

Since last year an unofficial lobby, consisting of notable people from the film world and other cultural areas, has been trying to persuade parliament to grant an extra annual DKK 25 million to film production, pointing both to the artistic acclaim harvested abroad and to the need for more Danish films if local cinemas are to survive.

The attempt has not been successful, and an alternative method of financing Danish films has therefore been put forward by Bo Christensen, who this year took over as director of the DFI after a long career as producer at Nordisk Film, and business man Asger Aamund, who is managing director of the institution called "The Inter-

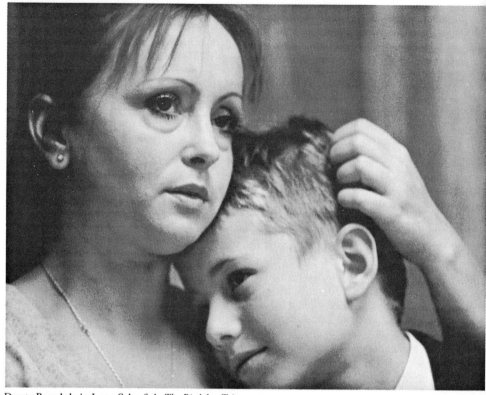

Dorota Pomykala in Lone Scherfig's *The Birthday Trip*

national Film Fund of Denmark", which is to secure sponsorship for new Danish films from the business world. The ambition is that the proposed fund will be able to invest an annual DKK 30 million in film production, DKK 10 million of the amount to be invested by larger Danish companies.

Minister of Culture Grethe Rostbøll (Conservative), supports the plan, but we have yet to see the film fund become a reality, whereas the establishment next year of a European Film High School situated in Ebeltoft in Jutland, catering for both "ordinary" people wanting to study film for shorter periods, and to professional film-makers from all Common Market countries wanting to meet, teach and discuss, is far more of a certainty.

Veteran film director Erik Balling is on record for having written that three or four films worth seeing are actually produced in Denmark every year, and to equal this on a pro rata basis, England or France would have to produce 30–40 such films annually and the U.S.A. 150–200, which is not the case. Danish films are therefore still worth fighting for.

Talents Emerge

During the past year the highly stylised and experimental **Europa** has been worth seeing, and so has new director Eddie Thomas Petersen's **Spring Tide** (*Springflod*), which is a modest, but gentle and romantic story of young love set against the barren landscapes of Southern Jutland. Another talented first time director is Lone Scherfig, whose melancholic comedy **The Birthday Trip** (*Kajs fødselsdag*) about a group of vulgar Danish men travelling to Poland in search of cheap booze and sex was no success with the Danish audience, partly because of a misleading promotion campaign. The film has, however, been well received at a number of festivals abroad, among them Berlin and Rouen.

The full-length animated film **War of the Birds** (*Fuglekrigen*) by the experienced Jannik Hastrup was awarded first prize at the Cannes Junior festival in May, while Ole Roos did not quite manage to capture the mood of danger and despair in Henrik Stangerup's novel **The Man Who Would Be Guilty** (*Manden der ville vaere skyldig*), on which he based his Danish-French co-production of the same title. The film was, at least, artistically ambitious, as can be said of Irene Werner Stage's first feature film **The Song About a Time of Cherries** (*Sangen om kirsebærtid*) delving into the mystical poetic symbols of the lonely life and strong memories of a woman who fell in love with a German soldier during the Occupation in 1940–1945.

Unintentional laughs were provoked by Preben Østerfelt's first feature **Dangerous Game** (*Farlig leg*), which tried in vain to be an erotic drama about strong and dark passions, while Kenneth Madsen's **A Day in October** (original title), shot in English with American actors in the leads, can only be praised for good intentions in its banal depiction of the Danish resistance movement and the situation of the Jews during the occupation.

Exciting Prospects

All in all it has not been an outstanding year for Danish films, partly because a number of the best directors have spent the year preparing films, which we have not yet seen. Bille August has been in Sweden directing **Best Intentions**, based on Ingmar Bergman's script, both as a television series and two feature-films for the cinema. Søren Kragh-Jacobsen has been working on the coming **The Boys of St. Petri** (*Drengene fra Sct. Petri*) about a group of young resistance fighters during the German occupation. This film, which is the Danish contribution to the Nordic Co-production Year, will be presented at the festival in Cannes in 1992. Nils Malmros has been shooting the psychological drama **Sorrow and Joy** (*Sorg og glaede*), and like Søren Kragh-Jacobsen's

Trine Dyrholm and Jesper G. Jensen in *Spring Tide*

Tommy Kenter in *Let the Polar Bears Dance*

film it is due to open domestically during the autumn.

In production are Morten Henriksen's **The Naked Trees** (*De nøgne traeer*), which is yet another story of the German occupation, controversial painter and film-maker Jens Jorgen Thorsen's **Return of Jesus**, (*Jesus vender tilbage*), Jørgen Leth's **Traberg**, about a journalist travelling in Spain and Latin America, Jytte Rex' experimental **The Mirrors of the Planet** (*Planetens spejle*), shot partly in Italy, and veteran director Edward Fleming's comedy **Hay Fever** (*Høfeber*).

Swedish director Stellan Olsson has come to Denmark to direct **The Great Day of Bathing** (*Den store badedag*), while Danish director Birger Larsen has gone to Sweden to direct **The Great Bear** (*Karlsvognen*). Norwegian actress and Bergman-veteran Liv Ullmann is going to direct her first film, **Sofie**, about the life of a Jewish family at the turn of the century, in Copenhagen this autumn. *Sofie* will be produced by Nordisk Film, which also financed Swedish actor Max von Sydow's first film as a director, the equally Danish *Katinka*.

EBBE IVERSEN has been a professional journalist since 1966. He has been film critic of "Berlingske Tidende" since 1973, and is a former co-editor of the magazine, "Kosmorama."

Finally a number of short feature films by promising young directors such as Jesper W. Nielsen and Niels Gråbøl are in production. These films, which are inexpensive to produce, are seen as a way of cultivating new talent and thus securing the future of the Danish cinema.

Europa

Script: Lars von Trier, Niels Vørsel. Direction: Lars von Trier. Photography: Henning Bendtsen, Edward Klosinsky, Jean-Paul Meurisse. Music: Joakim Holbek. Art director: Henning Bahs. Players: Jean-Marc Barr, Barbara Sukowa, Ernst-Hugo Järegård, Erik Mørk. Produced by Nordisk Film & TV, Gunnar Obel, Gerard Mital Production & PPC WMG, The Danish Film Institute, The Swedish Film Institute, Telefilm GMBH, Germany, EUR-IMAGES. 107 mins.

As in his earlier film *The Element of Crime*, Lars von Trier is fascinated by decay, destruction and despair. In *Europa*, which takes place in Germany just after the end of the Second World War, the main character is an idealistic young American, who arrives in Europe believing that somebody should be nice to the defeated Germans. He tries to live out his ideals by working as a sleeping car attendant for the train company Zentropa and marrying a beautiful German woman, but he ends up being used by the Nazi terror group Werewolf and even finds out that his wife is a member of Werewolf.

It is a disillusioned and rather cynical story, but it contains more humour than Lars von Trier's previous films, and it is told in a style inspired by the big Hollywood melodramas as directed by Douglas Sirk. Everything is larger than life in *Europa*, which can be seen as a dream or nightmare – at the beginning of the film the voice of Max von Sydow seeks to hypnotise the audience! The film is extremely stylised

Jean-Marc Barr in Lars von Trier's *Europa*

with a bold use of otherwise outdated background projections, mixing colour and black-and-white within the same image.

It may be regarded as an artistic weakness that Lars von Trier is much more preoccupied with style than with content – his film contains less than meets the eye – but as a daring combination of melodrama, thriller and dark comedy, *Europa* is very entertaining in a quite disturbing way. The acting by the international cast (in German and English) is uneven, but Jean-Marc Barr and Barbara Sukowa are fine in the main parts, and Joakim Holbek's impressive score is almost overwhelming, thus fitting the shamelessly grandiose images.

Lars von Trier is a master at captivating our senses. One would like him in the future to make films which also captivate our hearts.

Ebbe Iversen

National Film Board

1990 and 1991 were good years for Statens Filmcentral (which, by the way, changed its international name to National Film Board of Denmark) on the distribution side. A new audience was included when SFC launched a collaboration with the public libraries, distributing cassettes of film and video productions for free use in private homes. Statistically this meant about 50,000 loans of the shorts and documentaries in the SFC catalogue.

For film buffs, however, SFC still distributes on 16mm and has a yearly borrowing rate on this format covering around 150,000!

The international smash hit from SFC was the documentary **1700 Metres from the Future**, made by female director Ulla Boje Rasmussen. This warm and poetic portrait of a small Faroese society (16

inhabitants) is a feature-length film, which has participated in the most significant festivals all over the world.

Also a prize-winner was the one-hour documentary by the "green" film-maker Lars Brydesen, **Once There Was a Forest**, shot in Tanzania and telling the story of the disastrous ecological situation that the mountain people of Usambara must cope with.

Auteur-director Jon Bang Carlsen contributed this year with **Ich bin auch ein Berliner**, a bizarre view of a new Europe, where his two principal characters are not happy at all with no wall, having lived in peace right in the middle of East and West, cultivating their tomatoes and other vegetables.

Talented – and invited to several short film festivals – was **Speechless** by Poul Thomsen, a beautiful, poetic description of the fantasy world of autistic children. The film marks Poul Thomsen's début as a

Still from *1700 Metres from the Future*

photo: Andreas Fischer-Hansen

director. **The Wonderful Tale of Music** was widely acclaimed by the Danish audience at its premiere, and this animated film by Per Tønnes Nielsen, Anders Sørensen and Anders Koppel (composer) will certainly tour the world, as did their previous productions, also financed by Swedish, Norwegian and Canadian distributors.

The Danish documentary and short film and the existence of SFC helped very much in establishing two offices in Copenhagen, one being Nordisk Filmkontakt, an information tool for Nordic producers and distributors, the other being IVENS, a Media 95 Project, supporting the development and promotion of the European creative documentary. Both offices will be in operation from the autumn of 1991.

Tue Steen Müller

Danish Producers

ASA Film Production
Mosedalvej 14
DK-2500 Valby
Tel: 36 30 10 33

Crone Film Production A/S
c/o The Danish Film Studio
Tel: 45 87 27 00

Dagmar Filmproduktion A/S
Puggårdsgade 15
DK-1573 Copenhagen V
Tel: 33 93 92 91

The Danish Film Studio
52 Blomstervaenget
DK-2800 Lyngby
Tel: 42 87 27 00
Fax: 42 87 27 05
Telex: 37798 (studio dk)

Film-Cooperativet Danmark 1983 ApS
3 Bymandsgade
DK-2791 Dragør
Tel: 32 53 56 31

Fortuna Film
Ryesgade 106
DK-2100 Copenhagen Ø
Tel: 31 42 42 33

Per Holst Filmproduktion ApS
17 Livljaegergade
DK-2100 Copenhagen Ø
Tel: 31 26 42 00
Fax: 31 26 04 01

Hanne Høyberg Filmproduktion

Strandgade 4B
DK 1401 Copenhagen
Tel: 32 96 79 11

Kollektiv Film
Valkendorfsgade
DK-1151 Copenhagen 20
Tel: 33 12 69 96

M & M Productions
MS Valhal
Wilders Plads
DK-1403 Copenhagen K
Tel: 31 57 26 23

Metronome Productions A/S
Blomstervaenget 52
DK-2800 Lyngby
Tel: 45 93 00 97
Fax: 45 93 27 10

TOP TEN GROSSING FILMS IN DENMARK: 1990

Pretty Woman
Look Who's Talking
Waltzing Regitze (Danish)
Another 48 Hours
Back to the Future, Part II
Die Hard 2
The Jut Nuts 3 (Danish)
Dead Poets Society
Black Rain
Born on the Fourth of July

Nordisk Film Production AS
Mosedalvej
DK-2500 Valby
Tel: 31 30 10 33
Fax: 31 16 85 02

Gunnar Obel Film
Norgesvej 25
DK-9480 Lokken
Tel: 98 99 13 53

Victoria Film
c/o The Danish Film Studio
Tel: 45 87 27 00

Regner Grasten Film
Lykkevej 6
DK-2920 Charlottenlund
Tel: 31 63 44 24

Danish Distributors

AB Collection ApS
Hirsemarken 3
DK-3520 Farum
Tel: 44 99 62 00
Fax: 42 95 17 88

Bellevue Film
Strandvejen 451
DK-2930 Klampenborg
Tel: 31 63 49 00
Fax: 31 63 05 12

Camera Film
8 Mikkel Bryggersgade
DK-1460 Copenhagen K
Tel: 33 13 61 12
Fax: 33 15 08 82

Carina Film
231 Alekistevej
DK-2720 Vanløse
Tel: 31 71 58 00
Fax: 31 71 58 76

Cinnamon Film ApS
20 Slotsgade
DK-5000 Odense C
Tel: 66 12 17 16
Fax: 66 12 80 82

Constantin Film ApS
Skelbaekgade 1
DK-1717 Copenhagen K
Tel: 33 25 24 24

Dan-Ina Film
147B Trekronergade
DK-2500 Valby
Tel: 31 16 61 66
Fax: 31 16 61 92

Egmont Film
Rentermestervej 69A
DK-2400 Copenhagen NV
Tel: 31 19 80 00
Fax: 38 88 22 30

Kaerne Film ApS
17 Livjaegergade
DK-2100 Copenhagen Ø
Tel: 31 26 42 00
Fax: 31 26 04 01

Nordisk Film Distribution A/S
7 Axeltorv
DK-1609 Copenhagen V
Tel: 33 14 76 06

Saga Film International
3A Søndervang
DK-9800 Hjørring
Tel: 98 92 21 99

Scala Film
1 Gyldenbjergsvej
DK-5700 Svendborg
Tel: 62 21 88 66
Fax: 62 21 08 21

United International Pictures
13 Hauchsvej
DK-1825 Fr'berg C
Tel: 31 31 23 30
Fax: 31 23 34 20

Warner & Metronome ApS
16 Søndermarksvej
DK-2500 Valby
Tel: 31 46 88 22
Fax: 36 44 06 04

Useful Addresses

Danish Film Institute
Store Søndervoldstraede 4
PO Box 2158
DK-1419 Copenhagen K
Tel: 31 57 65 00
Fax: 31 57 67 00
Telex: 31465

Ministry of Cultural Affairs
2 Nybrogade
DK-1203 Copenhagen K
Tel: 33 92 33 70

The Danish Film Workshop
24 Vesterbrogade
DK-1620 Copenhagen V
Tel: 21 24 16 24

The Danish Video Workshop
4 Lermbekesvej
DK-6100 Haderslev
Tel: 74 52 86 95
Fax: 74 53 24 61

The Association of Danish Cinemas
c/o The Danish Film Institute

National Film Board of Denmark (Statens Filmcentral)
27 Vestergade
DK-1456 Copenhagen K
Tel: 45 33 13 26 86
Fax: 33 13 12 03

The Association of Danish Film Distributors
and
The Association of Danish Video Distributors
14 Oslo Plads
DK-2100 Copenhagen Ø
Tel: 31 42 21 66

The Association of Danish Film Clubs
20 Niels Hemmingsensgade
DK-1153 Copenhagen K
Tel: 33 15 67 60

The Association of Danish
Film Directors
22 Sankt Annae Gade
1416 Copenhagen K
Tel: 32 96 25 00
Fax: 32 96 75 55

The Danish Film Studio
52 Blomstervaenget
DK-2800 Lyngby
Tel: 45 87 27 00
Fax: 45 87 27 05

The Danish Film Academy
73 Bredgade
DK-1260 Copenhagen
Tel: 33 13 22 99
Fax: 33 32 10 26

The Film Workers' Union
21 Kongens Nytorv
DK-1050 Copenhagen K
Tel: 33 14 33 55

Nordisk Film Production AS
Mosedalvej
DK-2500 Valby
Tel: 31 30 10 33
Fax: 31 16 85 02

Risby Studios
DK-2620 Albertslund
Tel: 42 64 96 46

EGYPT

by Fawzi Soliman

The Gulf crisis was reflected in Egyptian cinema which was already in a crisis too. It lost its main market in Iraq and the Arab Gulf countries. In such an atmosphere of depression, which was felt more in Egypt, because of the return of more than 200,000 Egyptians from the Gulf Countries, people were not looking for entertainment in cinemas. They stayed at home to watch TV and CNN news. Moreover some new films were exposed to piracy before their video distribution. This was the reason for the Chamber of Cinema Industry to ask the producers to stop shooting new films for three months.

Nevertheless the Egyptian cinema did survive, and some good new productions were the proof. Out of 64 films – the production of 1990 – fourteen were appreciated by the critic and the public. After the war studio activity revived. Some of the cinemas belonging to the public sector were renewed, and new ones were established in the provinces. But there remains a shortage of well-equipped small-scale halls.

As far as production is concerned a different phase has started. Some film-makers were looking for a new system independent of foreign (Arab) distributors. They established production units together with scriptwriters and actors. In the framework of this new production system a very famous actor, Nour El Sherif, co-produced (with an art magazine) a film about the life of a Palestinian political caricaturist named Nagui El Aly. Other film-makers like Mohamed Khan took the

Still from *Prisoner 67*

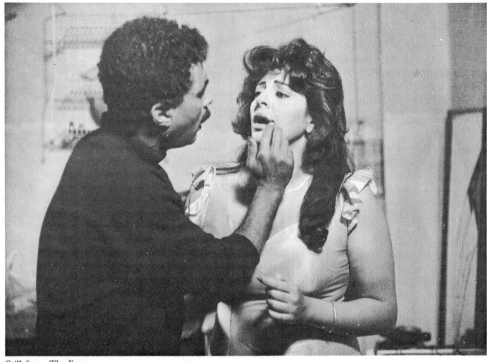
Still from *The Escape*

risk of producing their films with bank loans. The non-commercial directors try to deal with the real problems of society: the social and economic changes, the suffering of youth, and the growing problems of drug abuse.

Festivals in the Shadow of War

During the crisis, but before the war, two international manifestations took place: the First International Festival of Children's Films which included a symposium on "Cinema for Children" and the 14th Cairo International Film Festival with the participation of sixty countries. A third international event took place in Ismailia from April 25 to 29, 1991: the First International Festival for Documentary and Short films, in which 21 countries participated. The Ministry of Culture, i.e. the Cultural Development Fund, organised for the first time a competition to encourage and to promote films of quality by offering financial assistance to producers, directors, scriptwriters and actors.

1991 witnessed four newcomers, two of them graduates from the Cairo Film Institute, one from the Los Angeles Film Institute, the fourth coming from the documentary field. One of the most important film productions of 1991 is a 140-minute documentary on the life and work of Mohamed Bayoumi, the real pioneer of Egyptian cinema and author of the first Egyptian short feature films in 1923. The film, directed by Mohamed El Qalioubi and produced by the National Film Centre, marks the rediscovery of Bayoumi as cinematographer, graphic artist, writer and inventor.

One of the interesting cultural events was a symposium on "Film criticism – film culture – film journalism," arranged by the Egyptian Film Critics' Association in co-operation with the Goethe-Institute and FIPRESCI, represented by its Secretary-General Klaus Eder.

Recent Films

El Horoub (The Escape). Script: Mostafa Moharam. Dir: Atef El Tayeb. Phot: Mohsen Nasr. Players: Ahmed Zaky, Hala Sedky, Abdul Aziz Makhyoon, Mohamed Wafik. Prod: Medhat El Sherif. *A young man from Upper Egypt escapes from prison to take his revenge for an injustice. The authorities facilitate his escape as long as it keeps the people away from their real problems – until the fugitive becomes a national hero! Atef El Tayeb succeeds in combining two genres, the bloodthirsty action movie and the social document, in a tender, thoughtful manner.*

El Mowaten Masri (War on the Land of Egypt). Script: Mohsen Zaid. Dir: Salah Abou Seif. Phot: Tarek El Telmissany. Players: Omar Sharif, Ezzat El Alaily, Safeya El Emary, Abdullah Mahmoud. Prod: El Alameia for TV and Cinema (Hussein Kalla). *In June 1973 some parts of the land given to the peasants at the time of the 1952 revolution were turned to the landowners. In order to keep his three feddans, a peasant agrees to send his only son to the army instead of the landlord's son. But the peasant's son is killed . . .*

Fares El Medina (Knight of the City). Script: Fayez Ghaly. Dir: Mohamed Khan. Players: Mahmoud Hemeda, Lucy, Soad Nasr, Aida Riad. Prod: Khan Film. *A film about chivalry in hard times. A contemporary tale concerning a self-made businessman on a streak of misfortune. He tries to keep his ethics intact, selling all he owns in order to pay off his debts.*

Raghba Mutawahesha (Desert and Desire). Script: Wahid Hamed. Dir: Khairy Beshara. Phot: Samir Farag. Players: Nadia El Guindi, Soheir El Morshedy, Mahmoud Hemeda. Hanan El Turky. Prod: El Alameia for TV and Cinema (Hussein Kalla). *This film, inspired by an Italian play by Ugo Betti, deals with three women, a widow, her sister-in-law and her daughter, in hiding because of a crime committed by the late husband. Trouble brews when a man who was in prison with the husband arrives searching for hidden loot . . .*

Tasrih Bilkatl (Licence to Kill). Script and Dir: Taymour Serry. Phot: Samir Farag. Players:

Omar Sharif in *War on the Land of Egypt*

Mahmoud Yassin, Boussy, Salah Kabil. Prod: Hani Guirguis Fawzi. *In his first feature film, this young director continues his focus on the problem of pollution. It is essentially a drama about nuclear fallout and polluted film coming from Europe towards the Third World.*

Supermarket. Script: Assem Tawfik. Dir: Mohamed Khan. Phot: Kamal Abdel Aziz. Players: Nagla Fathi, Adel Adham, Mamdouh Abdelalim, Aida Riad. Prod: Nagla Fathi Films. *A study of relationships, between a pianist in a luxury hotel and a rich surgeon and tycoon who also happens to be a widower. This film won the Egyptian critics' prize last year.*

Useful Addresses

National Film Centre
City of Arts Giza
Al Ahram Avenue
Cairo
Tel: 854 801
Fax: 854 701

Chamber of Cinema Industry
23 Oraby Street
Cairo
Tel: 741 677, 741 638
Fax: 751 583
Telex: 92624 PERTX UN

SAUNA, SISU AND SÄÄTIÖ*)

WHICH ONE IS UNFAMILIAR?

FINNISH FILM FOUNDATION (FFF) IS THE ANSWER

FFF FOR FINANCING FILMS

FRIENDS, COMRADES / RAUNI MOLLBERG
ZOMBIE AND THE GHOST TRAIN / MIKA KAURISMÄKI
LA VIE BOHEME / AKI KAURISMÄKI

FFF FOR FINDING FILM FACTS FROM FINLAND

CINEMAS IN 1990: 340
ATTENDANCE: 6,2 MILLION
PREMIERES: 172
ASK FOR OUR ANNUAL CATALOGUE

FFF FOR FILMING FACILITIES

FILM HOUSE K 13
SOUND TRANSFER UNIT,
AUDIO POST PRODUCTION UNIT, MIXING UNIT,
ANIMATION STUDIO, EDITING UNITS

FIND US, WE'LL FIND THE ANSWER

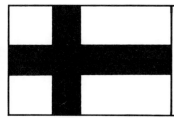

FINLAND

by Matti Apunen

The year 1990 at the Finnish box-office was a major disappointment for production and distribution companies. The total audience reached only 6.1 million, which is about 1.1 million (or 15.3%) less than in 1989. This figure is relatively the lowest ever, and means a serious reverse for Finnish film business and the promising development of the late 1980's.

Production companies were active in 1990: 13 feature films were completed, i.e. three more than the year before. All major productions, though, were box-office failures. **Paradise America** by Lauri Törhönen, **Friends, Comrades** by Rauni Mollberg, and **Amazon** by Mika Kaurismäki failed to live up to expectations. Also several of the heavily marketed Hollywood movies were disappointments, except *Pretty Woman* and *Die Hard 2* in 1990 and *Dances with Wolves* and *The Silence of the Lambs* in early 1991.

The Finnish production share of all films

Margi Clarke and Jean-Pierre Léaud in Aki Kaurismäki's *I Hired a Contract Killer*

was up to about 11% (7% in 1989), mostly due to the success of *Winter War* by Pekka Parikka. The film had its premiere in November 1989 but still in early 1990 it attracted an audience of over 300,000. The film was a smash hit (over 600,000 tickets sold in a country of 5 million inhabitants) but its production costs were far higher than expected, and led to the closure of its production company National-Filmi in July 1990. At the time of closing National-Filmi was the largest of the Finnish production companies. For the time being, there are practically no production companies capable of assuming large-scale financial risks, such as *Winter War*.

Foundation Increases Its Stake

The state-backed, film-financing organisation Finnish Film Foundation remarkably increased its contribution to domestic production. Until now the the FFF has supported a new production with approximately 60% of the budget; from now on it will advance a share of up to 80%. The new funding policy is the latest attempt to help the Finnish production business whose condition can be diagnosed as unstable and critical. Small production companies live in an atmosphere of uncertainty and under constant threat of bankruptcy. During the late 1980's the average negative costs escalated rapidly. In 1989 and 1990 the funding policy of the Foundation favoured some rather big-budget epics with broad subjects like *Winter War*, *Friends, Comrades* and *Amazon*.

Under these circumstances the negative cost of future films will most likely be limited. The outgoing managing director of

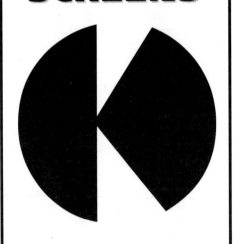
the Finnish Film Foundation, Jukka Vilhunen, feels that in the near future Finnish production policy must be concentrated on "reasonable, normal-size" productions, i.e. films with average budgets running about FIM 4–6 Million (about U.S. $1–1.5 million).

Vilhunen believes that the financial structure of Finnish films will undergo some basic changes. Scandinavian and all-European financing channels like Eurimages will play a bigger role alongside multilateral co-productions. In the last four years Finnish film production has settled at about 10 to 13 long feature films a year.

"I believe the volume of domestic production can be maintained. The situation is unstable but I don't see the domestic production as collapsing." says Vilhunen.

Turmoil in the Film Foundation
Vilhunen himself resigned suddenly in April 1991. Vilhunen says he is quitting because of the recent public debate over misappropriations in the Film Foundation. The damaging public campaign was launched by Antti Tuuri, the writer of two box-office hits, *Winter War* and *Plainlands*. Tuuri and a number of film-makers claimed that in the Film Foundation an "inner mafia" illegally manipulates the public support meant for film production. The FFF channels the public support for film production, about FIM 31.5 million annually.

The auditors were unable to find any serious mistakes, but Vilhunen says he cannot continue "in this atmosphere poisoned by malicious accusations." Vilhunen's successor will be named later.

The Chairman of the Film Foundation, Jukka Mäkelä of Finnkino, also left his chair but stayed as a member of the board. He was replaced by Mr. Hannu Tarmio, former general director of WSOY, the biggest publishing house in Finland.

White 'n' Blue Sales, the foreign sales arm of FFF, closed its doors in September 1990, after operating for less than a year.

TOP TEN GROSSING FILMS IN FINLAND: 1990

	Admissions
Pretty Woman	379,306
Die Hard 2	308,186
The Winter War (Finnish)	288,995
Numbskull Emptybrook's Wild Bachelor Years (Finnish)	232,397
Dead Poets Society	161,383
Back to the Future, Part III	155,532
Black Rain	147,707
Born on the Fourth of July	147,451
Bird on a Wire	144,085
The Hunt for Red October	139,681

A Push for Young Talents

The Finnish Film Foundation and Finnish television companies will pump up 10.4 million extra marks (about U.S. $3.8 million) for the declining film production. The state-financed Film Foundation, copyright organisation Kopiosto/AVEK, Finnish Broadcasting company Yleisradio and the independent TV company Mainos-Televisio have agreed on supporting young, talented film-makers through a new project they call "The Sparring Ring."

"The Sparring Ring" is a three-year plan during which the total sum of FIM 10.4 million will be distributed to eight young directors. The first three projects were announced in January 1991, the next three will be chosen in 1992, and the remaining two in 1993. The project is aimed at developing young film-makers' skills by giving them a chance to direct a financially assured project. Each director will be supported by FIM 1.3 million in order to make a "medium-length" feature film, i.e. a fiction effort of about 45–50 minutes. The films will have a screening forum on television, the two television companies with their three channels giving air time for those titles completed.

A similar type of incentive for young talents, a 100,000 mark ($36,000) competition for original scripts was launched in 1990 by the Finnish Film Foundation. The results, announced in December, were extremely encouraging: almost 400 scripts were entered, most of them by new writers. Many of them were described as "very promising," including the winning script by Juha Lehtovuori. The competition will be repeated in 1991.

A Helping Hand to Baltic Countries

Scandinavian countries are extending a friendly hand to the film-makers in Baltic countries striving for independence. Scandinavian Films, the joint organisation of the Scandinavian countries, and the Soviet Baltic states of Estonia, Latvia and Lithuania have agreed on founding a co-operative organisation known as "Baltic Camera".

Baltic Camera aims at creating a film system independent of the Soviet Union, and on the other hand at making use of the Baltics' experience and knowledge. Baltic Camera provides a non-commercial basis for renting out shooting equipment. The organisation will be located in Tallinn, Estonia.

Scandinavian Films plans to gather film equipment to be sent to Baltic countries. Most of the Soviet-made equipment used by the Baltic film-makers is out-of-date and in poor repair. Scandinavian Films will arrange Baltic film weeks in Nordic countries. It is also trying to find ways of introducing the Estonian, Latvian and

Lithuanian films to the European market through the existing marketing organisations of the Scandinavian countries.

Baltic Camera also plans to distribute Scandinavian films in Baltic countries and in the Soviet Union. The Baltic organisers believe that the distribution can be effected horizontally, through the network of small independent distributors in different parts of the U.S.S.R.

As long as the Soviet rouble is not a convertible currency, Baltic Camera cannot transfer its box-office income to Scandinavian producers. Instead, compensation will be paid in various forms of general know-how and production services (for example, the studio facilities in Tallinn, Riga and Vilnius). Estonian animation is of particularly high quality and this craftsmanship could be valuable to Scandinavian filmmakers.

Still from *Prince of the Hit Parade*

Iskelmäprinssi (Prince of the Hit Parade)

Script: Juha Tapaninen, Harri Rinne, Jukka Alihanka. Direction: Juha Tapaninen. Photography: Ulf Sundwall. Editing: Arturas Pozdniakovas. Players: Tina Isohanni, Saija Hakola, Mart Sander, Tarmo Ruubel. Produced by Tulta Tuotanto.

Prince of the Hit Parade marks the feature film debut of director Juha Tapaninen. It is a bright, funny and a little silly everyday comedy about an innocent era and people with big dreams. There is no message and no troubles: all that counts is the feathery visual style that carries the light plot easily along.

Juha Tapaninen is an experienced maker of TV commercials, which is quickly evident. His film has the same happy-go-lucky tone as the old commercials, Tapaninen's film also includes some enjoyable make-believe commercials or parodies of 1960's TV spots.

Prince of the Hit Parade refers to a certain type of Finnish musical comedy from the 1950's and 1960's – most memorable of which was *The Great Hit Parade* (1959) – mixtures of chart hits of those times, loose plots and terrible characterisation. The story itself is about small-town kids amid big dreams, all planning to make the headlines one way or another: modelling, singing or racing. The main roles are played by young actors, rather unknown but very easy-going and natural. They have been placed among some true pop stars (including Paul Anka) and princes of the Finnish 1960's hit parades.

The rhythm of the film is constituted by repeating black and white flashes, which blur the borderline between reality and fantasy by imitating the look of 1960's b & w documentaries. Tapaninen and his crew have scrupulously recreated the epoch of early 1960's, or actually made a postmodernist adaptation of it. The film is faithful to small details without being just a decorative display of old things.

Prince of the Hit Parade represents a fresh approach in Finnish film-making. For years the only practical alternatives have been the heavy epic realism à la Mollberg or the inimitable Kaurismäki touch. To the nostalgic tone Tapaninen has blended a spoonful of irony, but only seldom is he caught being too smart or pretentious. *Prince of the Hit Parade* may well be the most promising

Finnish feature debut since *Crime and Punishment* (1983) by Aki Kaurismäki.

Matti Apunen

Ystävät, toverit (Friends, Comrades)

Script: Joni Skiftesvik, Rauni Mollberg. Direction: Rauni Mollberg. Photography: Kjell Lagerroos. Editing: Kai-Ene Rääk, Olli Soinio. Music: Kari Rydman. Players: Mikk Mikiver, Stina Ekblad, Hannu Lauri, Paavo Liski, Tuire Salenius. Produced by Filmi-Molle Oy/Swedish Film Institute. 118 mins.

Mollberg's pungent new satire strikes a chord in a world so recently threatened by Saddam Hussein, but its ostensible theme of an arms magnate enjoying the tribute of East and West, Fascist and liberal, friend and foe, is in the end less significant than the craving for natural fulfilment that courses through the film like a powerful current.

Arno Jurmala, lord of his Lapland domain, extracts millions of tonnes of ore from the fells, creating ammunition for the guns of Hitler, Franco, Churchill, and the oh-so-neutral Swedes. Like Coppola's Godfather, Jurmala regards the world in terms of Family, and everyone has his price. Behind the exotic celebrations that mark his birthday at the start of the film lies a dark cloud of intrigue and coercion. Like the Godfather too, Jurmala never kills with his own hands; his gory deeds are performed by others at his discreet command.

At the heart of *Friends, Comrades*, however, stands a more fascinating personality even than Jurmala. Stina Ekblad's Lisa, the magnate's wife, dreams of giving birth to a son, of complying with the eternal rhythm of the Nature she sees and appreciates all about her.

Mollberg's taste for the ironic aside, as well as the earthy humour familiar from his previous films, embellishes *Friends, Comrades*, even when the annihilation and slaughter of war have left their mark on this Nordic landscape. For Mollberg, of course, Nature has her own means of purging such desecration, and the images one bears away from this film remain those of open skies and undulating fells.

Peter Cowie

Stina Ekblad in Rauni Mollberg's *Friends, Comrades*

Kari Väänänen (right) in Mika Kaurismäki's *Amazon*

by the imagery; Kaurismäki's film includes some unforgettable scenes from real-life Brazilian gold mines, immense hellish pits with thousands of ant-like workers climbing the muddy slopes. The film is immaculately shot by Timo Salminen who shows his craftsmanship in some beautiful jungle scenes.

The original film of three-and-a-half hours was cut by an hour for Finnish distribution and then to less than two hours for international release. At the same time, the American star Robert Davi was given top billing above the Finn, Kari Väänänen.

Matti Apunen

Amazon

Script: Mika Kaurismäki, Richard Reitinger. Direction: Mika Kaurismäki. Photography: Timo Salminen. Editing: Michael Chandler. Players: Kari Väänänen, Robert Davi, Rae Dawn Chong. Produced by Villealfa Filmproductions/ Noema Pictures. Sales: Scorer Films Ltd. (London).

Amazon is a half-bred adventure story with ecological undertones. It is set in the darkest jungles of the Amazon: a bank manager from Helsinki loses his wife in a car accident and tries to escape her memory by flying to Brazil with his two small daughters.

From the beginning it is very obvious that the longer they go on, the bigger their troubles will grow. They join an American adventurer who inveigles them into a gold-digging business with an abandoned caterpillar. There is only one problem: the caterpillar is a few thousand miles away, in the wrong place, deep in the jungle.

Amazon starts as a sort of "Heart of Darkness"-type adventure film, but changes its tone and wakes up to ecological consciousness. Nature, and finally the bank manager, too, finds peace of mind in a remote Brazilian village.

The slips in characterisation are balanced

Recent and Forthcoming Films

Boheemielämää (Bohemian Life). Script and Dir: Aki Kaurismäki. Phot: Timo Salminen. Players: André Wilms, Evelyne Didi, Kari Väänänen. Prod: Sputnik Films. *An adaptation of Henri Murger's classic novel from 1851; shot in Paris with an international cast.*

I Hired a Contract Killer. Script and Dir: Aki Kaurismäki. Phot: Timo Salminen. Players: Jean-Pierre Léaud, Margi Clarke, Kenneth Colley, Serge Reggiani. Prod: Villealfa/Aki Kaurismäki/The Swedish Film Institute. *A man tries to commit suicide but lacks the courage. He contacts a professional killer and hires him to do the job. Almost immediately he regrets his decision but he cannot reach the killer who is set on performing his part of the deal. . .*

Kadunlakaisíjat (The Street-Sweepers). Script and Dir: Olli Soinio. Players: Kari Sorvali, Mikko Kivinen, Soli Labbart. Prod: Filminor/ Heikki Takkinen. *A black, grotesque horror comedy: based on the characters created for The Moonlight Sonata (1988) by the same director.*

Kaivo (The Well). Dir: Pekka Lehto, Script: Outi Nyytäjä. Phot: Esa Vuorinen. Players: Auvo Vihro, Merja Larivaara. Prod: Kinofinlandia. *A sinister true story of a desperate mother who drowns her two little children in a remote village.*

Muutolinnun aika (Katya's Autumn). Script and Dir: Anssi Mänttäri. Phot: Heikki Katajisto. Players: Antti Litja, Hanna Manu, Tarja Markus. Prod: Reppufilmi/Petra Tarjanne. *A*

warm, human comedy about a divorced family and the reunion of the father and daughter.
Nikita: Elements of War. Dir: Sergei Skvortsov, co-dir: Marjaana Mykkänen. Script: Aleksei Adzhubei, Boris Karadchev. Phot: Boris Titov. Produced by Finnkino/Jukka Makelä. *Portrait of the controversial Soviet leader Nikita Khruschev, partly based on archive footage that was shelved for 30 years. Focus on Cuban missile crisis in 1962; interviews with close relatives and political opponents.*

Zombie ja kummitusjuna (Zombie and the Ghost Train). Dir: Mika Kaurismäki. Phot: Timo Salminen. Players: Silu Seppälä. Prod: Maríanna Films. *A rock'n'roll road movie; Mika Kaurismäki's return from expensive multinational productions to a domestic shoestring comedy.*

MATTI APUNEN is film critic for the Tampere-based morning newspaper, Aamulehti.

Producers

Filmi-Molle Oy
Siltakatu 12 A 5
SF–33100 Tampere 10
Tel: (31) 12 64 65

Filminor
Laivastokatu 8–10 D
SF–00160 Helsinki
Tel: (0) 65 14 22
Telex 125032 sesti sf.
Fax: 17 68 60

Filmiryhma Oy
Vyökatu 8
SF–00160 Helsinki
Tel: (0) 17 10 55
Fax: 66 26 02

Finnkino Oy
Kaisaniemenkatu 2 B
SF–00100 Helsinki
Tel: (0) 13 11 91
Telex: 100 1658
Fax: 13 11 93 00

Franck Films/Michael Franck Productions Oy
Iso Roobertinkatu 42 B
SF–00120 Helsinki
Tel: (0) 62 45 11
Telex: 100 0566 forumsf
Fax: 62 40 04

Jörn Donner Productions
Pohjoisranta 12
SF–00170 Helsinki
Tel: (0) 135 60 60
Fax: (0) 135 75 68

Giron Filmi Oy
c/o Jörn Donner Productions Oy
Pohjoisranta 12
SF–00170 Helsinki
Tel: (0) 135 60 60

Kinotuotanto Oy
Katajanokankatu 6
SF–00160 Helsinki
Tel: (0) 66 32 17
Fax: (0) 66 20 48

Matti Kassila Ky
Piikkikuja 6 A
SF–01650 Vantaa
Tel: (0) 843755

Nelimarkka Riitta – Seeck Jaakko
Marjaniemenranta 4
SF–00930 Helsinki
Tel: (0) 33 12 29

Reppufilmi Oy
Nervanderinkatu 12 B 22
SF–00100 Helsinki
Tel: (0) 49 83 78
Fax: (0) 49 84 59

Spede-yhtiöt
Ilmalankatu 2
SF–00240 Helsinki
Tel: (0) 14 16 33
Fax: (0) 14 08 15

Villealfa Filmproductions Oy/Sputnik Oy/Marianna Films Oy
Väinämöisenkatu 19 A

SF–00100 Helsinki
Tel: (0) 49 83 66
Fax: 49 86 61

Distributors

Finnkino Oy
Kaisaniemenkatu 2 B
SF–00100 Helsinki
Tel: (0) 13 11 91
Telex: 1001658
Fax: 13 11 93 00

Cinema Mondo
Museokatu 44
00100 Helsinki
Tel: (0) 44 62 08
Fax: (0) 44 64 28

Gaudeamus Elokuva
Vuorikatu 4 A 7
SF–00100 Helsinki
Tel: (0) 13 11 4 285
Telex: 121395 libacsf
Fax: (0) 13114346

Miofilm Oy
Torpantie 36
SF–90230 Oulu
Tel: (81) 22 86 60
Telex: 32300 urfil sf.

Senso Films Oy
Väinämöisenkatu 19 A
SF–00100 Helsinki
Tel: (0) 49 83 66
Fax: 49 86 61

United Pictures Finland
Lastenkodinkuja 1
SF–00180 Helsinki
Tel: (0) 694 08 11
Telex: 121808 uip sf.

Urania Film Oy/Ltd
Torpantie 36
90230 Oulu
Tel: (81) 22 86 60

Warner Bros Finland Oy
Lastenkodinkuja 1
SF–00180 Helsinki
Tel: (0) 69 40 522
Telex: 122530

Useful Addresses

**Central Organisation of
Finnish Film Producers**
Kaisaniemenkatu 3 B
SF–00100 Helsinki.
Tel: (0) 63 63 05

Finnish Film Foundation
Kanavakatu 12
SF–00160 Helsinki
Tel: (0) 17 77 27
Telex: 125032
Fax: 17 71 13

**Federation of Finnish Film
Societies**
Annankatu 13 C 18
SF–00120 Helsinki
Tel: (0) 64 83 72

**Finnish Cinema Association
Finnish Film Chamber**
Kaisaniemenkatu 3 B 29
SF–00100 Helsinki
Tel: (0) 63 63 05
Fax: (0) 17 66 89

**Finnish Broadcasting
Company (YLE)**
TV Centre
SF–00240 Helsinki
Tel: (0) 14801
Telex: 121055

FRANCE

by Michel Ciment

Although the French cinema has won the Academy Award for Best Foreign Film six times in the past twenty years, the reaction after the victory of Xavier Koller's *Journey of Hope* over *Cyrano de Bergerac* was unanimously hostile. Almost nobody had seen the Swiss film, but everyone still complained that Rappeneau's adaptation of Rostand's play had lost for political reasons: either because Depardieu had given *Time* magazine a controversial interview, or because the voting system was subject to manipulation.

The same oversensitive reaction was felt a few weeks later when three prizes went to the Coen brothers' *Barton Fink* at Cannes. Cries of "American imperialism!" were heard, although the film is a typical auteurist work and far removed from the mainstream of Hollywood cinema. People forgot that the French cinema was greatly honoured with the Grand Prix du Jury awarded to Jacques Rivette's *La belle noiseuse*, the Jury Prize (shared) to Maroun Bagdadi's *Hors la vie*, and the Best Actress award to Irène Jacob.

These signs of nervousness and chauvinism were all the more surprising since the French cinema continues to fare

Jacques Dutronc (centre) in Pialat's *Van Gogh*

photo: Luc Roux Studio

relatively well by comparison with its neighbours. With 4,518 screens, it still has the largest number of seats in Europe (apart from the U.S.S.R.), and those seats were filled in 1990 by 121.8 million spectators, an increase of 0.7% over the previous year, also a European record. It should be added, however, that the American cinema has increased its popularity by 20% over the last decade, while the French cinema has lost half its audience.

Nevertheless in 1990 French films progressed from 33.8% to 37.1% but this improvement was matched by the American imports. The conclusion of course is that these two industries occupy a dominant position in the French market to the detriment of all other national cinemas. The rest of the world represents just 5.6% of cinema attendances by comparison with 10.7% in 1989. Thus, France, a reputedly "film buff" society, is witnessing a narrowing of its cultural choices, all the more so since TV programmes are almost entirely devoted to Hollywood or French films. Out of the 370 features released in 1990, 129 were French and 138 American.

The average moviegoer is male, young, urban, and comes from a well-off family. As in most countries the 15–24 age group is the most eager to go to the cinema although there are less regular moviegoers than before.

In order to capture an audience both government (the French cinema is of course well subsidised) and industry have encouraged the production of big-budget films. Twelve features in 1990 cost more than 50 million francs as against seven the year before. 3,289 million francs were invested in the 146 films produced (10 more than the preceding year) with an average cost of 20.25 million francs, an increase of 15.5%. The need for more financing explains the development of co-productions (65 as against 81 with purely French backing).

Another interesting factor is the progress of co-production with more than one foreign partner: 3 films in 1988, 13 in 1989, 20 in 1990. No doubt the European aid fund, Eurimages, has played a role in this widening of the spectrum. Italy remains the favourite partner (16 films) followed by Germany (10) and French-speaking countries Canada (8), Belgium (7), and Switzerland (7). Conversely the best export markets are primarily Europe (50%), followed by North America (14%), and Asia.

It is television, however, which more and more dictates affairs here. The share of TV money invested in feature films is increasing each year, reaching 19.8% in 1990. The TV investors who want films for their primetime programmes tend to favour non-controversial, family entertainment, thus reducing the possibility of really innovative films.

The trend towards bigger-budget films that might appeal to the international market does not encourage the production of bold and provocative work either. Everybody runs for cover when faced with the costs and relies heavily on a classical French tradition which Truffaut strongly attacked as a critic in the 1950's: the quality film based on literary adaptations. *La Gloire de mon père* and *Le Château de ma mère* are based on Marcel Pagnol, *Uranus* is taken from Marcel Aymé, *Cyrano de Bergerac* from Rostand, and *Madame Bovary* from Flaubert.

With the exception of the last title these cultural enterprises at least paid off and French audiences greeted them enthusiastically as if the ultimate goal of the cinema was to flatter their literary tastes. Some costly films, though, proved to be disastrous, such as *Jean Galmol aventurier*, *Lacenaire*, and especially Eric Barbier's first feature **Le Brasier**, a Zolaesque social epic about a mining town in the 1930's, which plummeted at the box-office. Its 100,000 spectators in Paris against a 20 million franc budget compared unfavourably with the 500,000 people who queued to see Christian Vincent's **La Discrète**, made on a shoestring budget of 5 million francs, a ratio of 100 to 1!

Ambitious First-Timers

But Barbier and Vincent were equally ambitious beginners even if the first one failed where the latter succeeded. They both confirmed the constant and surprising renewal in French cinema. 29 new directors appeared in 1990 and a few of them came up with some of the best films of the year. *La Discrète* of course achieved the most spectacular breakthrough the same producer as Eric Rochant's first feature, *Un Monde sans pitié*, which also made headlines in 1989. Christian Vincent has woven a moral tale in the manner of Guitry, about a man who decides to seduce cold-heartedly a shy young girl, and ends up by being trapped in his own snare. Brilliantly written and superbly acted by Fabrice Luchini (one of Rohmer's favourite actors), this film reveals an assured director.

Brigitte Rouan's **Outremer** marks a no less striking debut. Drawing on memories of her childhood in North Africa she tells in a highly original way the story of three sisters at the time of the Algerian War, each episode in their family and private life being successively viewed through the eyes of one of the characters. Brigitte Rouan, an actress herself, plays one of the leading roles and gives a subtle portrayal of the colonial period.

Another actor turned director, Patrick Bouchitey adapted a story by Charles Bukowski and in **Lune froide** manages to express the necrophilia of the original tale without any trace of vulgarity. Bouchitey plays the lead together with Jean François Stevenin in this French road movie with its two idle bums who spend their time drifting from bar to bar and wind up making love to

Jean-François Stevenin and Patrick Bouchitey in *Lune froide*

a corpse. Olivier Schatzky's **Fortune Express** is likewise a very original first effort, combining the sense of action of a Huston (the central plot concerns a heist executed by paraplegics) and the surreal fantasy world of a Franju. Schatzky, a former scriptwriter, creates a weird atmosphere in an institution in a seaside town where power games are played out among invalids.

The fifth discovery of the year, last but not least, is **Delicatessen**, directed by an animator, Jean-Pierre Jeunet, and a comic strip cartoonist, Marc Caro. Far from the realistic style of most French movies, they have imagined a house peopled with extravagant characters – among them a butcher with cannibalistic tendencies – drawn with a sure sense of caricature and

Still from *L'Equilibriste*

close to the stylised universe of Carné and Prévert, and their poverty of the suburbs. *Delicatessen* did not attract any financial support (although it fared well at the box-office), either from the various government aid bodies or from TV, an interesting commentary on the conventional choices that are prevalent among many committees. These five first works, to which should be added a flawless 50-minute film by Arnaud Desplechain, **La Vie des morts**, about a gathering of friends during the death throes of one of them, all brought a whiff of fresh air to the current scene and proved more daring than most films by older directors.

Auteur Cinema Still Flourishing
Yet among so many mediocre films in their annual harvest there have been enough original works to confim that France is probably the country where auteur cinema is still the most alive, where people still try to express a personal vision of life as a painter or writer would do. A rather comforting thought when one considers the state of world production. Nico Papatakis's **Les Equilibristes**, for example, is a film of extraordinary power, coming from a 70-year-old artist who produced Cassavetes' *Shadows* and Genet's *Un Chant d'amour*. It is Genet who inspired him to tell the story of a famous old homosexual writer (Michel Piccoli) who, Pygmalion-like, dominates and transforms a young Arab into a daring circus tightrope dancer. Like all Papatakis's films (five in 25 years), *Les Equilibristes* is a tale of possession and manipulation which has the strength and inexorable development of a Greek tragedy.

Catherine Breillat, after *Virgin*, confirms herself as a painter of desire in **Sale comme un ange**. Few directors are able to express as well the power of sexuality, to come close to the intimacy of bodies in love, to depict the ambiguities of male–female relationships. Set against a crime film background (police precincts, drug dealers, seedy bars), *Sale comme un ange* is a tight

Jean Rochefort and Anna Galiena in *Le mari de coiffeuse*

Gérald Thomassin in *Le petit criminel*

study of an affair between an older cop (Claude Brasseur) and the wife (Lio) of his younger colleague (Niels Tavernier). Its Dostoievskian title perfectly reflects the tone of a film which leaves no room for the viewer to adopt a comfortable moral stance.

Le Mari de la coiffeuse is perhaps the most daring of the three recent remarkable films directed by Patrice Leconte. Jean Rochefort has fallen in love with a hairdresser and watches her using her scissors with extraordinary dexterity while he abandons himself to the sensuousness of belly-dancing. With a real freedom of inspiration and a sense of humour that does not preclude more tragic overtones from creeping in, Leconte can be counted as one of the more original French directors.

Originality is also the label that can readily (perhaps too readily) applied to Bertrand Blier. In **Merci la vie** this remarkable director has tried to create a surreal slice of life that mixes past and present, reality and fantasy in recounting the story of two girls on the run. But he has perhaps overreached himself (even if the film met with almost unanimous praise from the French press) in seeking to combine Fellini, Godard, Buñuel, Ferreri, and why not Lelouch?

On the other hand, Christian de Challonge's **Docteur Petiol** deserves a better reception than the one it received. With an extraordinary performance by Michel Serreau, who embodies a famous French doctor who, during the German occupation, burned in his private furnace Jews who he pretended to help escape from the Nazis, the film is a stunning metaphor for the Holocaust as well as a major expressionist work. Once more in this decidedly fruitful year, a film expands beyond the psychological and realistic boundaries of so much French cinema.

In this psychological tradition, however, three films are outstanding. Philippe Garrel's **J'entends plus la guitare** (which together with *Les Equilibristes* represented France at the Venice Festival) is one of the best efforts by this particularly offbeat director, who began his career in 1968. Its couples in disarray, its muted conversations, its subtle atmosphere create a little night music with a real resonance. **Un Cœur qui bat**, the second feature by François Dupeyron, plays with the banality of its subject-matter (an adulterous love story between two average personalities) and redeems it by means of a stylised, literary style.

Le petit criminel by Jacques Doillon shows the director on top form: tense, highly sensitive, with a remarkable control of his young performer (Gérald Thomassin). Doillon once again deals with a marginal character, a young boy who stages a holdup to reassure himself but who in fact only reveals his solitude and his anguish. The same theme is dealt with less successfully by Eric Rochant in **Aux yeux du monde**, his second feature after *Un Monde sans pitié*. Closer to an American genre movie (*Dog Day Afternoon*, for instance) it betrays a certain lack of rhythm and invention. All the aforementioned films, however, represent – with a few exceptions – the best of the crop and they are for the most part directed by young film-makers.

The remainder of the French production proved disappointing. There was the usual slew of French comedies, from which emerged only **Une époque formidable**, directed by the actor Gérard Jugnot; the social films à la Yves Boisset (including Boisset's own **La Tribu**, about the world of medicine) which on the whole seem to be running out of breath and lacking in conviction; the stale and academic historical reconstructions (**Les Dames galantes** by Jean Charles Tacchella, **Jean Galmot aventurier** by Alain Maline); the political thriller (Jacques Deray's **Netchairu est de retour**, from a story by Semprun) in total limbo; and finally the great classics ranging from the academic reading of **Madame Bovary** by Chabrol (the book is even read quite frequently on the soundtrack) to the rather pungent **Uranus** by Claude Berri, a bleak view of France after the Liberation adapted from Marcel Aymé's controversial book, not to mention the tepid variations on Pagnol (**La Gloire de mon père** and **Le Château de ma mère**) by Yves Robert.

Varda's Touching Hommage

The elder statesmen of the French cinema were not in particularly good shape this year with a few notable exceptions, among which one should mention Agnès Varda's **Jacquot de Nantes**, an hommage to her late husband Jacques Demy, in which she blends, in her usual collage style, reconstructed childhood scenes of a young boy who wants to become a film director,

Still from Agnès Varda's tribute to Jacques Demy, *Jacquot de Nantes*

excerpts from Demy's films, and documentary footage on the health of the dying artist. As often with Varda (and Demy) there is horror lurking behind the sweetness and light.

But two towering achievements must be singled out. **Van Gogh** and **La belle noiseuse**, both screened at Cannes and both marking a peak in their directors' careers. Curiously, both films deal with painters, although they could not be further apart from each other. Maurice Pialat, a former painter, decides *not* to show Van Gogh at work (with the exception of a few brief shots), an option close to that chosen by Tarkovski for *Andrei Rublev*. Pialat chronicles for three hours the last months of Van Gogh at Auvers sur Oise and does so in a style worthy of Jean Renoir, where the past seems to be shot *live* without any sense of stilted reconstruction. The light and the sound are superb, the sensuousness overwhelmingly present. The director avoids all the pitfalls associated with the romantic vision of the artist. With the aid of an extraordinary Jacques Dutronc he shows a man full of contradictions, in love with life (food and women), obsessed by his art, consumed with self-doubt, and torn by conflicting feelings towards his brother. It is undoubtedly one of Pialat's greatest films.

The same holds true of *La belle noiseuse*, freely adapted by Jacques Rivette from Balzac's *Le Chef d'oeuvre inconnu*. Perhaps because he deals with an imaginary artist called Frenhofer (brilliantly played by Michel Piccoli), Rivette takes the risk of showing the painter at work (the hand is that of Bernard Dufour) and his troubled and possessive relationship with the model. It is also a long film (four hours) but a unique experience, one of the few works in the history of the cinema that really makes us *feel* the creative process. In his prelude, set in a country house in the south of France, Rivette steps into Rohmer territory: it is all conversation pieces, charm and sunshine, with digs and double entendres flying between Piccoli, his wife Jane Birkin and the superb guest and future model Emmanuelle Béart who has come to visit with her lover. Progressively the film takes on more sombre tones and becomes more conceptual – as usual with Rivette – even systematic (with its overemphasis on the contact of the brush with the canvas) although its provocative length is justified by the genuine physical presence of the actors and the paint.

As befits the French cinema – so auteur-conscious – these two major films demonstrate at their best two tendencies dear to all artistic ambition: the realistic grain (Pialat) and the intellectual gropings (Rivette).

MICHEL CIMENT is one of the key figures behind the well-known French magazine Positif, and the author of numerous books on film, including the award-winning studies of Kubrick, Losey, Rosi Kazan, and Boorman.

Recent and Forthcoming Films

Adieu princesse. Script: Joaquim Leitao, Jorge Paixao Da Costa, Jean Léon. Dir: Jorge Paixao Da Costa. Phot: Dominique Brenguier. Players: Judith Henry, Antonio Capelo, Herman José, Lydia Bosch, Miguel Molina. Prod: Cinequanon/3B Productions.

L'Amant. Script: Gérard Brach and Jean-Jacques Annaud, based on Marguerite Duras' novel. Dir: Jean-Jacques Annaud. Phot: Robert Fraisse. Players: March Jane, Tony Leug. Prod: Renn Productions.

Les Amants du Pont Neuf. Script and Dir: Léos Carax. Phot: Jean-Yves Escoffier. Players: Juliette Binoche, Denis Lavant, Klaus Gruber. Prod: Christian Fechner.

L'Amoureuse. Script and Dir: Jacques Doillon. Phot: Christophe Pollock. Players: Charlotte Gainsbourg, Yvan Attal, Thomas Langman. Prod: Sara Films.

Les Années campagne. Script and Dir: Philippe Loriche. Phot: Etienne Faudue. Players: Charles Aznavour, Benoît Magimel, Françoise Arnoul, Clémentine Célarié. Prod: Baccara Productions.

L'Année de l'éveil. Script: Zoé Zurstrassen. Dir: Gérard Corbiau. Phot: François Catonné. Players: Laurent Grevill, Martin Lamotte, Chiara Caselli, Grégoire Colin, Johan Rougeul, Roger Planchon. Prod: Capricorne Production/FR3 Films Production/K2TWO/RTBF.

Août. Script and Dir: H. Herré. Phot: Luc Pagès. Players: Anouk Grinberg, Patrick Pineau, Dominique Pinon, Jean-Claude Brialy, Hélène Lapiower. Prod: Lazennec Production.

Les Arcandiers. Script and Dir: Manuel Sanchez. Phot: Miguel Sanchez. Players: Charles Schneider, Dominique Pinon, Simon de la Brosse, Géraldine Pailhas. Prod: Lazennec Production.

L'Atlantide. Script: Nicola Badalucco, Franco Bernini, Jonathan Meades, Angelo Pasquini, Bob Swaim, based on Pierre Benoit's novel. Phot: Ennio Guarnieri. Players: Tchéky Karyo, Jean Rochefort, Anna Galiena, Fernando Rey, Victoria, Christopher Thompson. Prod: RCS Produzione TV/Aura Film/Rai Uno/CFC.

Atlantis. Script and Dir: Luc Besson. Phot: Christian Pétron. Prod: Gaumont Productions.

Aujourd'hui peut-être. Script: Isabelle Mergault, Jean-Louis Bertucelli. Dir: Jean-Louis Bertucelli. Phot: Bernard Lutic. Players:

Julien Ciamaca and Joris Molinas in Gaumont's worldwide hit, *La Gloire de mon père*

Giulietta Masina, Véronique Silver, Eva Darlan, Jean Benguigui, Jean-Paul Muel, Muni, Jean Mercure. Prod: Agepro Cinéma/MF Productions/S.E.D.P.A./S.G.G.C./Cité Films.

Aux Yeux du monde. Script and Dir: Eric Rochant. Phot: Pierre Novion. Players: Yvan Attal, Kristin Scott-Thomas, Marc Berman, Charlotte Gainsbourg. Prod: Lazannec Production/FR3 Films Production/SGGG/La Générale d'Images.

La Belle histoire. Script and Dir: Claude Lelouch. Phot: Jean-Yves Le Mener. Players: Béatrice Dalle, Gérard Lanvin, Marie-Sophie, Patrick Chesnais, Vincent Lindon. Prod: Les Films 13.

La Belle noiseuse. Script: Pascal Bonitzer, Christine Laurent, Jacques Rivette. Dir: Jacques Rivette. Phot: William Lubtchansky. Players: Michel Piccoli, Jane Birkin, Emmanuelle Béart. Prod: Pierre Grise Productions/FR3 Films Productions/George Reinhart Productions.

Les Carnassiers. Script: Yves Boisset and Alain Scoff. Dir: Yves Boisset. Phot: Jacques Loiseleux. Players: Catherine Wikening, Wadeck Stanzak, Jean Carmet, Jean-Pierre Bisson, Yves Afonso, Maxime Leroux, François Dyrek. Prod: Les Films Oramax/Canal Plus/Films A2.

Céline. Script and Dir: Jean-Claude Brisseau. Phot: Romain Winding. Players: Isabelle Pasco, Lisa Heredia, Danièle Lebrun, Yves Jeannin. Prod: Jean-Claude Brisseau/LSR/Gaumont.

Cheb. Script: Abdelkrim Bahloul, Rachid Bouchareb, Christian Zerbib. Dir: Rachid Bouchareb. Phot: Youcef Sahraoui. Players: Mourad Bounaas, Nozha Khouadra, Pierre-Lou Rajot, Boualem Benani, Faouzi Saichi. Prod: 3.B Productions/E.N.P.A./Artédis/C.R.R.A.V.

Cherokee. Script and Dir: Pascal Otega. Phot: Gérard Stérin. Players: Alain Fromager, Roland Blanche, Jean-Paul Roussillon, Bernadette Lafont, Gérard Desarthe, Daniel Railet. Prod: Quartet Productions/Ciné Cinq/Téléma.

Le Ciel de Paris. Script: Michel Béna, Isabelle Coudier-Kleit and Cécile Varguaftig. Dir: Michel Béna. Phot: Jean-Marc Fabre. Players:

Charlotte Gainsbourg in *Aux yeux du monde*

Sandrine Bonnaire, Evelyne Bouix, Paul Blain, Marc Fourastier, Tanya Lopert. Prod: Sara Films.

La Cinquième génération. Script: Michel Wollensack and Gilbert Roussel. Dir: Gilbert Roussel. Phot: Marcel Combes. Prod: Nakipa Productions.

Les Clés du paradis. Script: Alexandre Jardin. Dir: Philippe de Broca. Phot: Jean-Yves Le Mener. Players: Gérard Jugnot, Pierre Arditi. Prod: Messine Productions.

Un Coeur en hiver. Script: Claude Sautet, Jérôme Tonnerre, Jacques Fieschi. Dir: Claude Sautet. Players: Emmanuelle Béart, Daniel Auteuil. Prod: Cinéa/Film par Film.

Un Coeur qui bat. Script and Dir: François Dupeyron. Phot: Yves Angelo. Players: Dominique Faysse, Thierry Fortineau, Jean-Marie Wiling. Prod: René Cleitman.

Comme des Chiens. Script and Dir: Jeanne Labrune. Phot: André Néau. Players: Lio, Rémi Martin, Nicolas Privé, Vittoria Scognamiglio, Marie Cella-Stella, Jean-Jacques Benhamou, Jean-Louis Cordina. Prod: French Productions/Art-Light Productions.

La Contre-Allée. Script and Dir: Isabel Sebastian. Phot: Willy Kurant. Players: Caroline Cellier, Jennifer Covillault, Jacqueline Maillan, Jacques Perrin. Prod: Baccara Productions/Films Ariane/TF1 Films Productions.

Delicatessen. Script: Gilles Adrien. Dir: Jean-Pierre Jeunet and Marc Caro. Phot: Darius Khondji. Players: Jean-Claude Dreyfuss, Dominique Pinon, Marie-Laure Dougnac, Karin Viard, Jean-François Périer. Prod: Claudie Ossard/UGC.

Dien Bien Phu. Script and Dir: Pierre Schoëndorffer. Phot: Raoul Coutard. Players: Jean Rochefort, Donald Pleasence, Patrick Catalifo, Richard Bohringer. Prod: Mod Films.

Dieu vomit les tièdes. Script: Sophie Kepes and Robert Guediguian. Dir: Robert Guediguian. Phot: Bernard Cavalie. Players: Arianne Ascaride, Pierre Banderet, Jean-Pierre Darroussin. Gérard Meylan. Prod: Alain Guesnier and Gilles Sandoz.

Les Enfants volants. Script and Dir: Guillaume Nicloux. Phot: Jean Badal and Raoul Coutard. Players: Anémone, Didier Abot, Michel Debrane, Dominique Frot, Nicolas Jouhet. Prod: Jean-Paul Alram.

L'Entraînement du champion avant la course. Script and Dir: Bernard Favre. Phot: Michel Amathieu. Players: Richard Berry, Valérie Mairesse, Mireille Perrier. Prod: Productions de Flandre/Les Productions Belle Rives/SGGC/Parma Films.

L'Evanouie. Script: Jacqueline Veuve and Sandra Joxe. Dir: Jacqueline Veuve. Phot: Renato Berta. Players: Jean-Pierre Léaud, Daniel Gélin, Stéphane Audran. Prod: EIA Films/Aquarius Film/RTSR Cinergie Films/Productions Crittin Thiebault.

La Femme du déserteur. Script and Dir: Michal Bat-Adam. Phot: Fabio Conversi. Players: Fanny Ardant, Alexander Charon. Prod: Mod Films/Cléa Productions France/Mimar Production.

La Fille du magicien. Script: Claudine Bories and Paul Vecchiali. Dir: Claudine Bories. Phot: Jean Monsigny. Players: Anouk Grinberg, Patrick Raynal, Jean-Paul Roussillon, Hélène Surêne, Jean-Pierre Sentier. Prod: Diagonale/Périphérie Production/SGGC.

Le Fils du Mékong. Script: Tchee, Lin Dao, François Leterrier. Dir: François Leterrier. Phot: Martial Thuri. Players: Tchee, Jacques Villeret. Prod: Paradise Production.

Fortune Express. Script: Olivier Schatzky and Pierre Jolivet. Dir: Olivier Schatzky. Phot: Carlo Varini. Players: Thierry Frémont, Cris Campion, Hervé Laudière, Luc Bernard. Prod: Altair Production/Andromède/Blue Films/Films A2.

La Fracture du myocarde. Script and Dir: Jacques Fansten. Phot: Jean-Claude Saillier. Players: Sylvain Copans, Nicolas Parodi, Cécilia Rouand, Dominique Lavanant, Jacques Bonnaffe. Prod: Belbo Films.

Gaspard et Robinson. Script and Dir: Tony Gatlif. Phot: Dominique Chapuis. Players:

Gérard Darmon, Vincent Lindon, Suzanne Flon, Bénédicte Loyen. Prod: Les Films de la Colline/SGGC/SOFIARP.

Gawin. Script: Alexandre Jardin and Arnaud Sélignac. Dir: Arnaud Sélignac. Phot: Jean-Claude Larrieu. Players: Jean-Hughes Anglade, Bruno, Wojtek Pszoniak, Catherine Samie. Prod: Loco Films/Corto Films/International Productions/TF1 Films Production.

Génération oxygène. Script and Dir: Georges Trillat. Phot: Gérald Thiaville. Players: Denis Lautriat, Corinne Touzet, Edward Meeks, Marc de Jonge, Christine Paillard. Prod: Magic Company.

Génial, mes parents divorcent. Script and Dir: Patrick Braoudé. Phot: Thierry Arbogast. Players: Adrien Dirand, Volodia Serre, Gianni Giardinelli, Jennifer Lauret, Joachim Mazeau. Prod: AFCL Productions/CFC/Ciné Cinq.

L'Homme au Masque d'or. Script: Alain Gillot and Eric Duret. Dir: Eric Duret. Phot: Ennio Guarnieri. Players: Jean Réno, Marlee Matlin, Marc Duret, Patrick Fontana, Xavier Masse. Prod: Jean-Marie Duprey and Marc Chayette.

L'Homme de ma vie. Script and Dir: Jean Charles Tacchella. Players: Christophe Malavoy, Maria de Medeiros, Anne Letourneau, Alain Doutey, Ginette Garcin. Prod: Gabriel Boustani.

L'Homme imaginé. Script and Dir: Patricia Bardon. Phot: Pascal Caubère. Players: Marie Carré, Jacques Spiesser, Hélène Bascoul, Paul Blain. Prod: CDN Production/Oculis Production.

Hors la Vie. Script and Dir: Maroun Bagdadi. Phot: Patrick Blossier. Players: Hippolyte Girardot, Rafic Ali Ahmad, Hussein Sbeity, Habib Hammond. Prod: Galatéé Films/Films A2/Filmalpha Roma/Lamy Films Bruxelles.

Indochine. Script: Régis Wargnier, Louis Gardel, Erik Orsenna, Catherine Cohen. Dir: Régis Wargnier. Phot: François Catonné. Players: Catherine Deneuve, Vincent Perez, Jean Yanne, Dominique Blanc, Pham Linh Danh. Prod: Paradis Films/Générale d'Images.

Isabelle Eberhardt. Script: Stephen Sewell. Dir: Jan Pringle. Phot: Manuel Teran. Players: Mathilda May, Tcheky Karyo, Peter O'Toole, Richard Moir, Arthur Dignam. Prod: Les Films Aramis/Flach Films/Scon Films.

Jacquot de Nantes. Script: Agnès Varda and Jacques Demy. Dir: Agnès Varda. Phot: Patrick Blossier. Players: Phillipe Maron, Edouard

Philippe Noiret and Jean-Pierre Marielle in Claude Berri's *Uranus*

Joubeaud, Laurent Monnier, Brigitte de Villepoix, Daniel Dublet. Prod: Ciné Tamaris.

Jalousie. Script and Dir: Kathleen Fonmarty. Phot: Richard Andry. Players: Lio, Christian Vadim, Odette Laure, Véronique Delbourg. Prod: Paradis Films/La Générale d'Images/Ciné Cinq/Ellepi Films.

J'embrasse pas. Script: Jacques Nolot, André Téchiné, Michel Grisolia. Dir: André Téchiné. Players: Philippe Noiret, Emmanuelle Béart, Manuel Blanc. Prod: Paradis Films/Président Film/ACF.

Le Joueur de violon ... Script: François Dupeyron, Jean-François Goyet, Charlie van Damme. Dir: Charlie van Damme. Phot: Etienne Becker. Players: Sami Frey, Barbara Sukowa. Prod: Hachette Première.

Juste avant l'orage. Script and Dir: Bruno Herbulot. Phot: Guillaume Schiffman. Players: Zabou, Christophe Malavoy, Hanns Zistchler, Laura Morante, Dominique Valadié. Prod: Les Films du Phare.

Lacenaire. Script: Georges Conchon and Francis Girod. Dir: Francis Girod. Phot: Bruno de Keyzer. Players:. Daniel Auteuil, Jean Poiret, Marie-Armelle Deguy, Jacques Weber, François Périer. Prod: Partner's Production/UGC/Ciné Cinq/Hachette Première.

Lola Zipper. Script and Dir: Ilan Duran Cohen. Phot: Philippe Lavalette. Players: Judith Reval, Jean-Paul Comart, Arielle Dombasle, François Perrot, Thibault de Montalembert. Prod: Thierry Forte.

Lune de fiel (Bitter Moon). Script: Gérard Brach, Roman Polanski and John Brown John. Dir: Roman Polanski. Phot: Tonino Delli Colli.

Hippolyte Girardot in Maroun Bagdadi's *Hors la vie*

Players: Emmanuelle Seigner. Prod: R.P. Productions.

Lune froide. Script: Jacky Berroyer. Dir: Patrick Bouchitey. Phot: Jean-Jacques Bouhou. Players: Jean-François Stévenin, Patrick Bouchitey, Jean-Pierre Bisson, Laura Favali, Marie Mergey. Prod: Les Films du Dauphin.

Madame Bovary. Script and Dir: Claude Chabrol. Phot: Jean Rabier. Players: Isabelle Huppert, Jean-François Balmer, Christophe Malavoy. Jean Yanne. Prod: MK2 Productions/CED Productions/FR3 Films.

Le Mari de Léon. Script: Fréderic Dard and Jean-Pierre Mocky. Dir: Jean-Pierre Mocky. Players: François Cluzet, Alain Bashung. Prod: Norbert Saada.

Mauvaise fille. Script: Régis Franc and André Téchiné. Dir: Régis Franc. Phot: Jean-Claude Larrieu and Christophe Artus. Players: Daniel Gélin, Florence Pernel, Yvan Attal, Christian Vadim. Prod: Les Films du Phare/Strada Films/TSR.

Ma vie est un enfer. Script: Josiane Balasko and Joël Houssin. Dir: Josiane Balasko. Phot: Dominique Chapuis. Players: Josiane Balasko, Daniel Auteuil. Prod: Ciby 2000.

Mayrig et 588 rue Paradis. Script and Dir: Henri Verneuil. Phot: Edmond Richard. Players: Nathalie Roussel, Claudia Cardinale, Richard Berry, Omar Sharif. Prod: Carthago Films/V Films/TF1 Films Production.

Méchant garçon. Script: Charles Gassot and Catherine Foussadier. Dir: Charles Gassot. Phot: Jean-Jacques Bouhon. Players: Catherine Hiegel, Joachim Lombard, Patrick Bouchitey. Prod: Charles Gassot.

Merci la vie. Script and Dir: Bertrand Blier. Phot: Philippe Rousselot. Players: Charlotte Gainsbourg, Anouk Grinberg, Gérard Depardieu, Michel Blanc, Jean Carmet, Catherine Jacob, Thierry Frémont. Prod: Ciné Valse/Film par Film/Orly Film/D.D. Production/SEDIF/Films A2.

Milena. Script and Dir: Véra Belmont. Phot: Dietrich Lohmann. Players: Valérie Kaprisky, Stacy Keach, Gudrun Landgrebe, Nick Mancuso. Prod: Stephan Films/FR3 Films Production/Farena Films/Sofinergie/Les Films l'Amante Inc/Bavaria Films/GmbH.

Mima. Script and Dir: Philomène Esposito. Phot: Carlo Varini. Players: Virginie Ledoyen, Nino Manfredi, Margarita Lozano, Vittoria Scognamiglio. Prod: Paris–New York Production.

Molosse. Script and Dir: Jeanne Labrune. Phot: André Neau. Players: Lio, Rémi Martin. Prod: French Production/Art-Light Productions.

Mon père, ce héros. Script and Dir: Gérard Lauzier. Phot: Patrick Blossier. Players: Gérard Depardieu, Marie Gillain, Patrick Mille, Catherine Jacob, Charlotte de Turckeim. Prod: Film par Film.

Netchaiev est de retour. Script: Dan Franck and Jacques Deray. Dir: Jacques Deray. Phot: Yves Angelo. Players: Yves Montand, Vincent Lindon, Miou-Miou, Carolina Rosi, Patrick Chesnais, Maxime Leroux. Prod: Les Films de l'Ecluse.

Nord. Script: Arlette Langmann and Xavier Beauvois. Phot: Fabio Conversi. Players: Bulle Ogier, Xavier Beauvois, Jean-René Gossart, Fernand Kindt. Prod: BVF/Gueroilms/LTC.

La Note Bleue. Script and Dir: Andrzej Zulawski. Phot: Andrzej Jaroszewicz. Players: Janusz Olejniczak, Marie-France Pisier, Sophie Marceau, Noémie Nadelmann. Prod: Oliane Productions/Erato Films/G Films/Genimini Filmproduktion GmbH.

On peut toujours rêver. Script: Olivier Dazat and Pierre Richard. Dir: Pierre Richard. Phot: François Lartigue. Players: Pierre Richard, Smaïn. Prod: Fideline Films/Film par Film/Renn Productions/Orly Films/Films A2.

Opération Corned-beef. Script: Christian Clavier and Jean-Marie Poiré. Dir: Jean-Marie Poiré. Phot: Jean-Yves Lemener. Players: Christian Clavier, Jean Reno, Isabelle Reno, Valérie Lemercier, Jacques François. Prod: Alter Films/Gaumont Production/TF1 Films Production/Alpilles Productions/Amigo Productions.

La Pagaille. Script: Pascal Thomas and Agenore Incrocci. Dir: Pascal Thomas. Phot: Renan Polles. Players: Rémy Girard, Coralie Seyrig, François Périer, Clement Thomas, Emilie Thomas, Sabine Haudepin, Patrick Chesnais. Prod: R. Films/Les Films Français/Films A2.

Parfois trop d'amour. Script and Dir: Lucas Belvaux. Players: Joséphine Fresson, David Martin, Bernard Mazzinghi. Prod: Oan Films/Les Films de la Drève.

Père et fille. Script: Robert Boner and Christine Pascal. Dir: Christine Pascal. Phot: Pascal Marti. Players: Richard Berry, Anémone, Lucie Phan, Amandine Bousson. Prod: French Production/Cinémanufacture.

La Poste. Script and Dir: Luis Puenzo. Phot: Felix Monti. Players: William Hurt, Sandrine Bonnaire, Jean-Marc Barr, Raul Julia, Robert Duvall. Prod: CFC/Pepper/Prince/Oscar Kramer.

Le Petit criminel. Script and Dir: Jacques Doillon. Phot: William Lubtchansky. Players: Richard Anconina, Gérald Thomassin, Clothilde Courau, Jocelyne Perhirin. Cécile Reigher. Prod: Sara Films.

Plaisir d'amour. Script: Nelly Kaplan and Jean Chapot. Dir: Nelly Kaplan. Phot: Jean-François Robin. Players: Pierre Arditi, Françoise Fabian, Dominique Blanc, Cécile Sanz de Alba, Heinz Benent, Pierre Dux. Prod: Cythère Films/Les Studios de Boulogne/Pathé Cinéma.

Pour Sacha. Script: Alexandre Arcady and Daniel Saint-Hamont. Dir: Alexandre Arcady. Phot: Robert Alazraki. Players: Sophie Marceau, Richard Berry, Fabien Orcier, Niels Dubost. Prod: Alexandre Films/S.G.G.G./TF1 Production/SOFIARP.

Prague. Script and Dir: Ian Sellar. Phot: Darius Khondji. Players: Sandrine Bonnaire, Bruno Ganz, Alan Cumming. Prod: Christopher Young Films/Constellation/LTD Production/Barandov.

Premier amour. Script: Christian Caillo, René Feret. Dir: René Feret. Phot: Pierre L'homme. Players: Valérie Stroch, Jean-Yves Bertheloot. Prod: Film Alyne/Film du Roseau.

La Provocation. Script: Zivko Nikolić and Dragan Nikolić. Dir: Zivko Nikolić. Phot: Savo Jovanovic. Players: Alain Noury, Dragana Mrkić, Boro Bergović. Prod: Zeta Film/Beograd Films/Aria Films.

Quand les étoiles étaient rouges. Script: Eugen Gindl. Dir: Susan Trancik. Phot:

Vladimir Smutny. Players: Dezsö Garas, Vasclav Koubek, Eva Salzmannova, Alena Ambrova. Prod: Constellation/UGC/Hachette Première/Slovesca Filmova Tvorba.

Quelque part vers Conakry. Script and Dir: Françoise Ebrard. Phot: D. Gentil. Players: children and Philippe Jutteau, Pascal N'Zonzi, Delphine Rich, Ionna Craciunescu. Prod: Les Films de l'Ecluse.

Le Raccourci. Script: Furio Scarpelli. Dir: Giuliano Montaldo. Phot: Blasco Giurato. Players: Nicolas Cage, Ricky Tognazzi, Patrice Flora Praxo, Giancarlo Giannini. Prod: Ellepi Film/Ital France.

Ragazzi. Script: Ivan Taieb and Stéphane Kelin. Dir: Mama Keita. Phot: Thomas Cichawa. Players: Ivan Taieb, Ken Amrani, Sabrina Colle, Marie-France Gantzer, Romane Bohringer. Prod: Performance Production.

Rei Dom ou la légende des kreuls. Script and Dir: Jean-Claude Gallota. Phot: Bernard Cavalie. Players: Pascal Gravot, Christophe Delachaux, Eric Alfieri, Muriel Boulay, Mathilde Altharaz. Prod: Marin Karmitz/La Sept/CDN Productions.

La Reine Blanche. Script and Dir: Jean-Loup Hubert. Phot: Claude Lecomte. Players: Catherine Deneuve, Richard Bohringer, Bernard Giraudeau, Jean Carmet, Laure Moutoussamy, Isabelle Carré. Prod: Caméra One/TF1 Films Production/Ciby 2000.

Rien que des mensonges. Script: Paule Muret, Jean-François Goyet. Dir: Paule Muret. Phot: Rénato Berta. Players: Fanny Ardant, Alain Bashung, Jacques Perrin. Prod: Aréna Films/Véga Films.

Le Rouge du couchant. Script and Dir: Jean-Claude Guiguet. Phot: Alain Levant. Players: Fabienne Baba, Véronique Silver, Marco Hofschneider, Louise Marleau. Prod: Molécule/Artémis/CCC/Les Films Stock.

Rue du Bac. Script: Yves Dangerfield and Gabriel Aghion. Dir: Gabriel Aghion. Phot: Fabio Conversi. Players: Geneviève Bujold, Frédéric Constant, Vincent Vallier, Françoise Brion, Edith Scob. Prod: Sara Films.

Sale comme un ange. Script and Dir: Catherine Breillat. Phot: Laurent Dailland. Players: Claude Brasseur, Lio, Niels Tavernier. Prod: French Production.

Sam Suffit. Script: Michka Assayas and Virginie Thévenet. Dir: Virginie Thévenet. Phot: José Luis Alcaïne. Players: Aure Atika, Bernadette

Laffont, Claude Chabrol, Philippe Bartlet, Jean-François Balmer. Prod: Les Productions du Troisème Etage/Paravision International/Paris-Eiga/AFDM.

Le Secret de Sarah Tombelaine. Script: Claude Gilbert and Daniel Lacambre. Dir: Daniel Lacambre. Phot: Philippe Théaudière. Players: Irène Jacob, Marc de Jonge, Harry Cleven, François Caron. Prod: S.M.P.

Les Secrets professionnels du docteur Apfelglück. Script: Philippe Bruneau and Thierry Lhermitte. Dir: Hervé Palud, Alessandro Capone, Mathias Ledoux, Stéphane Clavier and Thierry Lhermitte. Phot: Jean-Jacques Tarbes, Roberto Girometti, Claude Agostini, Gérard Sterin. Players: Thierry Lhermitte, Jacques Villeret, Micha Bayard, Claire Nadeau, Ticky Holgado, Roland Girard. Prod: Son et Lumière/Ice Films/Belt Productions/Films A2.

La Sentinelle. Script and Dir: Arnaud Desplechin. Phot: Caroline Champetier. Players: Emmanuel Salinger, Bruno Todeschini, Marianne Denicourt, Thibault de Montalembert, Valérie Dréville. Prod: Why Not/La Sept/2001 Audiovisuel/Films A2.

She. Script: Sergio Gobbi and Daniel Ubaud. Dir: Sergio Gobbi. Players: Joanna Pacul. Prod: GICA/Candice Productions/Aquila Cinematografica 85/Slovenska Filmova Tvorba.

Soleil Levant. Script and Dir: Roger Planchon. Phot: Gérard Simon. Players: Carmen Maura, Paolo Graziosi, Maxime Mansion, Jocelyn Quivrin. Prod: Les Films du Losange/Films A2.

Soupe de poisson. Script and Dir: Fiorella Infascelli. Phot: Acacio de Almeida. Players: Philippe Noiret, Chiara Caselli, Andrea Prodan. Macha Méril. Prod: French Productions.

Sup de fric. Script: Jean-Noël Fenwick. Dir: Christian Gion. Phot: Bernard Joliot. Players: Jean Poiret, Anthony Delon, Cris Campion, Valérie Mairesse, Laurence Ashley. Prod: Lapaca Productions.

Sushi, Sushi. Script: Laurent Perrin and Michka Assayas. Dir: Laurent Perrin. Phot: Dominique Le Rigoleur. Players: André Dussolier, Jean-François Stévenin, Sandrine Dumas, Eva Darlan, Michel Aumont. Prod: Titane/Christian Bourgeois Productions/Films A2.

La Totale. Script: Simon Michael and Claude Zidi. Dir: Claude Zidi. Phot: Jean-Jacques Tarbès. Players: Thierry Lhermitte, Miou-Miou, Eddy Mitchell. Prod: Film par Film/Films 7.

Toubab Bi. Script and Dir: Moussa Toubé. Phot: Alain Choquart. Players: Makena, Moussa Diouf, Hélène Lapiower, Monique Mélinand. Prod: Valprod.

Tous les matins du monde. Script: Pascal Quignard and Alain Corneau. Phot: Yves Angelo. Players: Gérard Depardieu, Jean-Pierre Marielle, Anne Brochet, Guillaume Depardieu, Michel Bouquet. Prod: Film par Film.

Toto le Héros. Script and Dir: Jaco van Dormael. Phot: Walther van den Ende. Players: Michel Bouquet, Jo de Backer, Thomas Godet, Mireille Perrier. Prod: Iblis Films/Les Productions Philippe Dussart/Metropolis Filmproduktion/RTBF/Jacqueline Pierreux/FR3 Films Production.

Toujours seuls. Script and Dir: Gérard Mordillat. Phot: François Catonné. Players: Annie Girardot, Marius Colucci, Yan Epstein, Claude Evrard. Prod: Partner's Production/Films A2.

Le Trésor des Iles Chiennes. Script and Dir: F-J Osang. Phot: Darius Khondji. Players: Stéphane Ferrara, Michel Albertini, Mapi Galan, Diogo Doria. Prod: Paula Branco and Oskar Leventon.

La Tribu. Script: Alain Scoff and Yves Boisset. Dir: Yves Boisset. Phot: Fabio Conversi. Players: Stéphane Freiss, Catherine Wilkening, Maxime Leroux, Jean-Pierre Bacri. Prod: Sara Films/Ciné Cinq.

Triplex. Script: Didier van Cauwelaert. Dir: Georges Lautner. Phot: Yves Rodallec. Players: Patrick Chesnais, Cécile Pallas, François-Eric Gendron, Jacques François. Prod: Gaumont Production/TF1 Films Production.

Twin Sisters. Script: André Koob and J-M Paland. Dir: Tom Berry. Phot: Rodney Gibbons. Players: Stéphanie Kramer, Frederic Forrest. Prod: Eurogroup/Allégro Films.

Un été après l'autre. Script and Dir: Anne-Marie Etienne. Phot: Jean-Claude Neckelbrouck. Players: Annie Cordy, Paul Crauchet, Olivia Capeta, Françoise Bette. Prod: Legend/Ciné-Contact/Alain Keytsman Production/R.T.B.F.

Un type bien. Script and Dir: Laurent Bénégui. Phot: Luc Pages. Players: Alain Beigel, Raoul Billerey, Agnès Obadia, Daniel Gélin. Prod: Cinq et Cinq Films/Alain Keytsman Productions/Gemka Productions/Films A2.

TOP TEN GROSSING FILMS IN PARIS: June 1990–June 1991

	Admissions
Dances with Wolves	1,266,891
Pretty Woman	1,046,602
La gloire de mon père (French)	865,009
The Little Mermaid	697,886
Uranus (French)	687,628
Ghost	657,861
Le Château de ma mère (French)	602,262
Total Recall	560,283
The Silence of the Lambs	559,813
Alice	549,124

Une époque formidable. Script and Dir: Gérard Jugnot. Phot: Jean-Pierre Fizet. Players: Gérard Jugnot, Richard Bohringer, Victoria Abril, Roland Blanche. Prod: Ciby 2000.

Uranus. Script: Claude Berri and Arlette Langmann. Dir: Claude Berri. Phot: Renato Berta. Players: Philippe Noiret, Gérard Depardieu, Jean-Pierre Marielle, Michel Blanc, Michel Galabru. Prod: Renn Productions.

Le Vent de la Toussaint. Script: Louis Gardel and Gilles Béhat. Dir: Gilles Béhat. Phot: Roland Bernard. Players: Etienne Chicot, Michel Albertini, Lydia Andrei, Patrick Bouchitey, Eva Darlan. Prod: Simone Halberstadt-Harari.

Vézaz. Script: Noël Sisini. Dir: Xavier Castano. Phot: Dominique Chapuis. Players: Kirk Douglas, Richard Bohringer, Jean-Michel Portal, Marie Fugain. Prod: Ariès Productions et Investissements/Pyramide Production/Ciné Cinq/Darblay S.A./Les Auditoriums de Joinville/Cartel S.A./Sogetel S.A. Ellepi Films.

La Vie des morts. Script and Dir: Arnaud Desplechin. Players: Thibault de Montalembert, Roch Leibovici. Marianne Denicourt, Suzej Goffre. Prod: Odessa Films/RGP Production/ La Sept.

La Vieille qui marchait dans la mer. Script: Dominique Roullet. Dir: Laurent Heyneman. Phot: Robert Alazraki. Players: Jeanne Moreau, Michel Serrault. Prod: Blue Dalhia Production.

Villa à vendre. Script: André Ruellan and Jean-Pierre Mocky. Dir: Jean-Pierre Mocky. Phot: Jacques Loiscleux. Players: Michel Serrault, Jean Poiret, Jacqueline Maillan, Lambert Wilson, Philippe Léotard, Jeanne Moreau, Claude Brasseur, Dominique Lavanant, Andréa Ferréol, Jean-Pierre Bacri, Clémentine Célarić. Prod: Sara Films/Studio Canal Plus.

Villa beau soleil. Script: Philippe Alard and Frédéric Duedal. Dir: Philippe Alard. Phot: Fabrice Richard and Philippe Alard. Players: Gwennola Bothorel, Thérèse Nivet, Frédéric Gelard. Prod: Collections Feux et Anges S.A.

Vincent et moi. Script and Dir: Michaël Rubbo. Phot: Andréas Poulsson. Players: Nina Petronzio, Christopher Forrest, Paul Klerk, Alexandre Vernon Dobtcheff. Prod: Rock Demers and Claude Nedjar.

La Voix. Script: Pierre Granier-Deferre and Christine Miller. Dir: Pierre Granier-Deferre. Phot: Pascal Lebògue. Players: Nathalie Baye, Sami Frey, Laura Moranic. Prod: Ciné Feel Productions/FR3.

Le Voleur d'enfants. Script: Dominique Garnier and Christian de Chalonge. Dir: Christian de Chalonge. Phot: Bernard Zizermann. Players: Marcello Mastroianni, Michel Piccoli, Angela Molina, Virginie Ledoyen, Loïc Even. Prod: GICA/International Deal Film/Starlet Film/Lotus Film.

GERMANY

by Jack Kindred

With Germany reunited at last, 1990 was a happy year for many Germans. Not so for the German film, which suffered its worst spell at the box-office in more than a decade. Made-in-Germany movies barely attained 10% of the market.

Until the fantasy film **The Neverending Story – the Next Chapter** and the semi-animated **Werner – Beinhart**, based on a popular comic strip, were released in the autumn, German films had slumped to a paltry 5.7% of the market. By year's end, however, *Werner* had drawn 3.2 million visitors and Part II of the *Neverending Story* some 2.9 million, rescuing the German film from almost total disaster. Even then, producer Dieter Geissler's fantasy film based on Michael Ende's best-selling novel, was hardly classifiable as a German film. Shot in English, it had an American cast, an Austrialian director, and an international team of special effects experts.

Out of the 79 feature films produced, only 48 were actually released in 1990 and most of these were flops. Ex-ski champ Willy Borgner's **Fire, Ice and Dynamite**, which caused wrath among certain exhibitors for its near-shameless product placement, had a fair box-office run of over 700,000 patrons, many of them doubtless skiing fans. Director Gabriel Barylli's **Bread and Butter** (*Butterbrot*), whose plot concerned three men holed up in a secluded house, who fret over problems with the opposite sex, scarcely paid for its negative with only 263,000 visitors. Hamburg's pride and joy, director Hark Bohm's **Crossing Borders** (*Herzlich Willkommen*), a stark portrayal of an East German escapee's trials

and tribulations in postwar West Germany, drew just under 200,000 viewers.

Even Michael Verhoeven's **The Nasty Girl** (*Das schreckliche Mädchen*), nominated in the best foreign film category at the 1991 Academy Awards, attracted only 115,613 visitors in a limited, art-house release. The well-crafted picture, at times viciously funny, evidently conjured up too many closet skeletons from the Nazi era to lure Germans away from lighter entertainment on television.

In the same vein, the 1966 East German film **Traces of the Stones** (*Spur der Steine*), on the East German censor's shelf for over 20 years, received critical acclaim, but was confined to the art-house and festival circuit. Frank Beyer's probing and witty exploration of the way the Communist system worked in East Germany was filmed in black-and-white at the DEFA studios in Babelsberg, just outside of Berlin.

Joseph Vilsmaier's eagerly awaited *Heimat* (homeland) film, **Rama Dama**, failed to live up to his previous opus, the surprise 1988 hit *Autumn Milk*. In Bavarian dialect, the title refers to rubble clearing after the Second World War, symbolic of the shattered nation's new beginning. The love story of a young woman, whose soldier husband is missing in Russia, revolves around the courage of ordinary people in the critical postwar period.

Unspooling at Berlin Festival
The cream of Germany's production mills unspooled in the New German Film section of the 41st International Film Festival in Berlin. Among the 24 movies selected were

Wolfgang Stumph in *Go, Trabi, Go*

photo: Neue Constantin Film

Franz X. Bogner's crime thriller **Cafe Europa**, Werner Herzog's **Echoes from a Sombre Empire** based on the central African Republic's deposed dictator Jean Bokassa, Reinhard Münster's sci-fi thriller **The Eighth Day** (*Der achte Tag*), and the horror movie, Michel Bergmann's **My Lovely Monster**.

Others included Jan Schütte's **Winckelmann's Travels** (*Winckelmanns Reisen*), a travelling salesman's adventures and loves, **The Serbian Girl** (*Das Serbische Mädchen*), Peter Sehr's first feature, a vacation love story between a German man and a high-spirited Yugoslav girl, and Peter Timm's spoof on the famed (or notorious) East German car, **Go, Trabi Go**. Apart from the above mentioned, some of the films in the series failed to find a distributor, a clear reflection on the unhappy state of the German film.

Financially speaking, 1990 saw the worst showing of German-produced movies since 1980 when their share in the domestic market amounted to an all-time low of 9.3%. However, a handful of German films did well in the first quarter of 1991, giving rise to cautious optimism. Two comedies, Loriot's (Vicco von Bülow) **Papa ante portas** (3.3 million visitors in 13 weeks) and Peter Timm's **Go, Trabi, Go** (1.3 million visitors in nine weeks), led the German releases while "New German Cinema" director Volker Schlöndorff, back from a stint of filming in the U.S., saw his latest opus **Voyager** (*Homo Faber*) attracting nearly 700,000 patrons in its first nine weeks. A number of interesting German films are also in the pipeline including Tevfik Baser's *Farewell Stranger*, an entry in the competition of Cannes, Doris Dörrie's *Happy Birthday, Türkel*, Percy Adlon's *Salmonberries*, Werner Herzog's *Scream of Stone* and Wim Wenders' long-awaited *Until the Ends of the World*.

Signs of an Upswing

Further room for optimism – the Federal Film Board (FFA), which keeps a tally on box-office returns, said there was an average 21% upswing in attendance in the first two months of 1991, largely due, however, to American blockbusters like *Home Alone, Dances with Wolves* and *Look Who's Talking Too*. The number of screens in the western part of reunited Germany in 1990 remained fairly constant at 3,112, down only slightly from 3,261 the previous year, according to the FFA. More than 102 million people went to the movies in the west, up 0.6% from 1989. Box-office returns in 1990 totalled 828 million *Deutschmarks* ($511 million) up 4.4% from the 792 million DM $460 million) in 1989.

Donald Sutherland and Mathilda May in Werner Herzog's *Scream of Stone*, released via Cine-International

Returns from exhibitors from the five states in the former DDR will not be tallied before the end of 1991 because of structural differences and communication difficulties. Trade sources estimate an overall 8% to 15% increase in revenues, and, in time, up to 20%.

The protracted malaise of the German film has generated much discussion as to what to do about the industry's flawed system of production subsidies, since the current film support law (Film Förderungs Gesetz), expires in 1993. Much criticism has been voiced about "Rucksack" producers (so called because of their transient business practices), some of whose skill in obtaining subsidy funds from the committees is legendary. They pocket the money up front, grind out a potboiler often based on a German literary classic (culture), and keep spectators out of the theatres in droves. However, one of the criteria for meting out film support is the "cultural" requirement, in line with Germany's commitment to the arts. Left in the lurch, however, are the distributors and exhibitors, who shoulder most of the risk in any highly subsidised film production project.

Most critics of the system have called for a drastic revision of the law, a clear separa-

tion of support for "cultural" and "commercial" film projects. The representatives of the FFA, the Bonn Economics Ministry, the exhibitors' and distributors' associations, and the producers, will have their work cut out for them when they meet next year. That the average German filmgoer prefers comedy to culture when it comes to film is clearly shown in box-office takings.

Fate of Babelsberg in the Balance

What to do about the DEFA studios, is another question facing Germany's film industry in the east, which is in the throes of restructuring state-run central planning and price controls into a capitalist free market, with private ownership, convertible currencies and access to foreign investors. DEFA's technical equipment, like much of industry in the former communist DDR, has become obsolete and in disrepair. The studio, sprawled over more than 500,000 square yards, has a higher production capacity potential than Bavaria Film and Studio Hamburg, Germany's major studios in the west, combined. DEFA is expected to operate as a holding company after receiving government funding for renovations. The government may grant tax advantages as well to lure private investors. But insiders say that at least 150 million marks ($88 million) will be needed for renovation. The studio is in the hands of the Truehand, a privatisation agency, but decisions on DEFA's future remained in limbo after the agency's chief, Detlav Rohweeder, was murdered by terrorists.

Director Werner Schroeter walked off a Berlin stage with a "Golden Film Band" in hand for his **Malina**, the winner of the Deutsche Filmpreis 1991. *Malina* also won the Bavaria Film Prize and was screened in competition at the 1991 Cannes film festival. Like **Success** (*Erfolg*) from Munich producer-director Franz Seitz, *Malina* was based on a famous novel. And again like *Erfolg*, the screenplay of which was adapted from Lion Feuchtwanger's renowned book, *Malina* fulfills the cultural conditions requisite for obtaining film production subsidies.

While the Seitz opus flopped completely with less than 10,000 vistors, *Malina* attracted some 170,000 box-office patrons, not bad for the art house circuit.

Despite its critical acclaim, however, *Malina* appears to be symptomatic of what has doggedly plagued the German film ever since the New German Cinema directors proclaimed the Oberhausen Manifesto back in 1962, in a reaction against the industry's low standards of escapist entertainment. The awards and kudos came but not the commercial success so necessary for all sectors of the industry – production, distribution and exhibition – to revive and flourish.

Erfolg
(Success)

Script and Director: Franz Seitz. Photography: Rudolf Blahacek. Editing: Gisela Haller. Music: Friedrich Meyer, Karl Amadeus Hartmann. Sound: Gunther Stadelmann. Production Design: Rolf Zehetbauer. Costumes: Monika Ludwig. Players: Bruno Ganz, Franziska Walser, Peter Simonischek, Matthieu Carrière, Gudrun Gabriel, Jutta Spiedel, Gerd Anthoff, Bernhard Wicki. Produced by Franz Seitz. 122 mins.

Franz Seitz tackles another famous German book, Lion Feuchtwanger's *Erfolg*, and comes up with *Success*, a handsome production that should do well in German territories, but is too literary and stolid to find audiences elsewhere. Seitz, who specialises in film versions of novels (*The Magic Mountain* in 1981 and *Doctor Faustus* in 1982, both based on Thomas Mann works), here focuses on Munich in the early 1920's as the Nazi Party was starting to emerge.

The theme is miscarriage of justice. Peter Simonischek plays the curator of an art gallery that exhibits controversial paintings. He champions the work of an eccentric woman artist, and one painting of a nude woman creates a scandal. The curator is unjustly accused of sleeping with the artist, who had committed suicide after he rejected her. He is found guilty and imprisoned.

His girlfriend, who marries him in prison, set about trying to have him released, but encounters cynicism and hypocrisy from the Bavarian authorities. A Swiss writer (sympathetically played by Bruno Ganz) helps her, and they fall in love even as they continue badgering the powers-that-be to reopen the case.

The finale depicts an armed encounter between Hitler and his followers and a German army unit, a seldom-remembered incident of great political importance at the time.

The depiction of Bavarian society during the period of hyper-inflation and the rise of fascism is a fascinating one for those interested in European history, but most non-German audiences will find *Success* too long and too wordy. However, the performances are solid down the line: Ganz, Franziska Walser, appealing as the woman fighting for justice, and Matthieu Carrière, hissable as a fanatical Nazi. Veteran director Bernhard Wicki has a scene as an exiled political part leader who, like most other influential people shown in the film is unwilling to help the unfortunate and ailing curator.

Go, Trabi, Go

Script: Reinhard Kloos and Peter Timm. Direction: Peter Timm. Photography: Axel Block. Editing; Christel Suckow. Music: Ekki Stein. Art Direction: Goetz Weidner. Costumes: Ute Schwippert. Players: Wolfgang Stumph, Claudia Schmutzler, Marie Gruber, Ottfried Fischer, Billie Zoeckler, Dieter Hildebrandt, Barbara Valentin, Konstantin Wecker, Diether Krebs, Monika Baumgartner. Produced by Reinhard Kloos. 96 mins.

Go, Trabi, Go, is the first German film to exploit the funny side of German unification. While the laughs may be few and far between, the movie could generate some revenue for exhibitors outside of Germany.

Audiences in eastern Germany are bound to go for it, but western film buffs will find it old fashioned. At times, the movie resembles a vintage Ma and Pa Kettle knee-slapper about pore ole country folks a-takin' their first vacation abroad (translated into East Germans motoring in Italy).

Real star of the show is a Trabant 601, familiar, homely, two-cylinder East German cars. This "Trabi" has the task of carrying Ma and Pa Struutz (Wolfgang Stumph and Claudia Schmutzler) and their daughter (Marie Gruber) from grimy Leipzig all the way over the Alps and down to sunny Naples. The Kettles never undertook a more treacherous journey. Stunt drivers went through a dozen Trabants!

Corny dialogue is helped along by the able comic talents of Stumph, a long-time regular on former East German TV. A strong supporting cast includes veteran West German funny man Dieter Hildebrandt as a garage mechanic who manages to get a laugh out of the hokey line, "After all, cars are only human."

Director Peter Timm, 41 was thrown out of his native East Germany in 1973, and only recently turned to film-making. This picture bodes well for his future ventures.

Malina

Script: Elfriede Jelinek. Direction: Werner Schroeter. Photography: Elfi Mikesch. Editing: Andrea Wenzhler. Music: Giacomo Manzoni. Art Direction and Costumes: Alberte Barsacq. Players: Isabelle Huppert, Matthieu Carrière, Can Togay, Fritz Schediwy, Isolde Barth, Peter Kern. Produced by Thomas Kuchenreuther. 123 mins.

Opera director Werner Schroeter, a protégé of the late Rainer Werner Fassbinder, has come out with yet another visually fascinating, but thoroughly inscrutable film which will appeal to a small circle of German intellectuals – and to almost no one else.

Colours are vibrant, the sets and lighting are superb. Beyond that, the film has precious little to offer, and certainly nothing to say.

French actress Isabelle Huppert runs wild-eyed through this story based on an autobiographical novel by an Austrian writer who ultimately immolated herself some years ago.

Huppert portrays a stifled writer torn between two lovers, although it is hard to understand her turmoil as supporting actors Matthieu Carrière and Can Togay turn in limp performances as her boring husband and uncaring lover. That is the main problem with this film. The dull screenplay and

Isabelle Huppert and Matthieu Carrière in *Malina*

stiff acting leave the audience totally indifferent to the human tragedy which literally ends in a roaring inferno.

In the throes of melodrama, Huppert repeatedly drops writhing and quaking to the floor, rips up curtains and clothes, scratches with her bare fingernails at the door, vomits in her handbag, bangs her head against a wall until it is bleeding and finally sets a myriad of small fires around her home. This goes on for two hours.

Schroeter's first love is the opera. So, at the movie's fiery climax, with flames crackling up the walls of a formerly pristine Vienna apartment, an opera singer appears singing arias from *Fidelio*, *Oberon* and *Antigone* as Huppert's character – and the audience – go on suffering.

Ernest Gill

Recent and Forthcoming Films

Babylon. Script: Andy T. Hoetzel, Ralf Huettner. Dir: Ralf Huettner. Phot: Diethard Prengel. Players: Natja Brunckhorst, Dominic Raacke, Ditte Schupp, Ina Siefert, Veronica Ferres, Michael Greling. Prod: Tyrannos Rex Filmproduktion GmbH.
Buster's Bedroom. Script and Dir: Rebecca Horn. Phot: Sven Nykvist. Players: Donald Sutherland, Geraldine Chaplin, Amanda Ooms. Prod: Metropolis/Limbo.
Happy Birthday, Türke!. Script: Doris Dörrie, Jakob Arjouni. Direction: Doris Dörrie. Phot: Helge Weindler. Players: Hansa Czypionka, Özay Fecht, Ulrich Wesselmann, Stefan Wigger, Lambert Hamel, Meret Becker, Doris Kunstmann, Sevgi Özdamar. Prod: Cobra Produktionsgesellschaft.
Herz in Der Hand (Heart in the Hand). Script: Johnny Ehp. Dir: Uwe Janson. Photo: Tom Fährmann. Players: Barbara Feltus, Michael Dick, Michael Heicks, Timo Paprotny. Prod: Volcano M.
Knight Moves. Script: Brad Mirman, Carl Schenkel. Dir: Carl Schenkel. Phot: Dietrich Lohmann. Players: Christopher Lambert, Diane Lane, Tom Skerritt. Prod: CineVox/Deal/Knight Moves Productions.
Lebewohl, Fremde (Farewell Stranger). Script and Dir: Tevfik Baser. Phot: Hans-Günther Bücking. Players: Grazyna Szapolowska, Müsfik Kenter, Ayub Khan Din, B. Uzzaman. Prod: Lichtblick/Tevfik Baser/Haro Senft.
Leise Schatten (Soft Shadows). Script and Dir: Sherry Hormann. Photo: Klaus Eichhammer. Players: Stefano Dionisi, Thomas Heinze, Ann Gisel Glass. Prod: Hager & Moss Film.
Liebe auf den ersten Blick (Love at first Glance). Script and Dir: Rudolf Thomé. Phot: Sophie Maintigneux. Players: Julien Benedict, Gero Lechner, Broich Margarita, Vera Tschechowa, Kyana Kretchmar, Hans Mich Reberg. Prod: Moana.
Moebius. Script and Dir: Matti Geschonneck. Phot: Frank Brühne. Players: Jörg Gudzuhn, Diether Krebs, Günter Lambrecht. Prod: Runze Filmproduktion.
My Lovely Monster. Script and Dir: Michel Bergmann. Phot: Fernando Arguelles. Players: Silvio Francesco, Nicole Fischer, Matthias Fuchs. Prod: Xenon.

TOP TEN GROSSING FILMS IN GERMANY: 1990

	Admissions
Pretty Woman	9,340,888
Look Who's Talking	5,198,644
The War of the Roses	4,086,078
Dead Poets Society	3,287,153
Ghost	3,283,209
Werner-Beinhart	3,221,322
The Neverending Story 2	2,960,167
Gremlins 2	2,566,041
Turner and Hooch	2,274,012
Ghostbusters 2	2,103,726

Nie im Leben (Never in Life). Script: Helmut Berger, Nina Grosse. Dir: Helmut Berger. Phot: Hans-Günther Bücking. Players: Anica Dobra, Helmut Berger, Hans-Peter Hallwachs. Prod: Marwo, Voissfilm.

Salmonberries. Script and Dir: Percy Adlon. Phot: Tom Sigel: Players: K.D. Lang, Rosel Zech, Chuck Connors. Prod: Pelemele.

Schrei aus Stein (Scream of Stone). Script: Hans Ulrich Krenner, Walter Saxer. Direction: Werner Herzog. Photography: Rainer Klausmann. Prod: Sera, Cinefilm.

Schtonk. Script and Dir: Helmut Dietl. Phot: Xaver Schwarzenberger. Players: Götz George, Uwe Ochsenknecht. Prod: Bavaria Film.

Der Tangospieler (The Tango Player). Script: Christoph Hein. Dir: Roland Gräf. Phot: Petr Ziesche. Players: Michael Gwisdeck, Corinna Harfouch, Herrmann Beyer. Prod: DEFA.

Die Trillertrine (Looking for Mozart). Script: Rolf Müller, Karl Heinz Lotz. Dir: Karl Heinz Lotz. Phot: Claus Neumann. Players: Maria Ferrens, Peter Raasch, Rolf Schill, Klaus Pönitz, Werner Godemann, Susanne Böwe, Peter Dommisch, Theo Adam. Prod: Regina Ziegler, DEFA.

Die Ungewisse Lange des Paradieses (The Uncertain Situation of Paradise). Script and Dir: Franziska Buch. Phot: Laszlo Kadar. Players: Cornelia Provis, Isolde Barth, Martin Schwab, Sabine Wegner. Prod: Vulcano M.

Der Verdacht (Suspicion). Script: Ulrich Plenzdorf. Dir: Frank Beyer. Phot: Peter Zie-sche. Players: Michael Gwisdek, Christine Schorn, Christiane Heinrich. Prod: DEFA.

Verfehlung (Transgression). Script: Wolfram Witt. Dir: Heiner Carow. Phot: Martin Schlesinger. Players: Angelica Dornröse, Gottfried John, Jörg Gudzuhn, Justus Carriere, Dirk Kummer, Dagmar Manzel. Prod: DEFA, Vietinghoff.

Die wahre Geschichte von Männern und Frauen (The True Story about Men and Women). Script: Robert Van Ackeren, Catharina Zwerenz. Dir: Robert Van Ackeren. Phot: Jürgen Jürges.

Wildfeuer (Wildfire). Script. Reinhold Klooss, Jo Baier. Dir: Jo Baier. Phot: Gernot Roll. Players: Anica Dobra, Karl Tessler, Josef Bierbichler, Johannes Thanheiser, Branko Samarovski, Eva Hörbiger. Prod: Bavaria Film.

Wunderjahre (Wonder Years). Script and Dir: Arend Athe. Phot: Michael Wiesweg. Players: Gudrun Landgrebe, Jens Weisser, Christian Müller-Stahl. Prod: Objectiv Film, DEFA.

JACK KINDRED, bon vivant and raconteur, is an ex-Variety staffer specialising in German media reporting, and based in Munich.

Producers

Allianz Filmproduktion GmbH
Leibnitzstr. 60
1000 Berlin 12
Tel: (30) 323 9011
Fax: (30) 323 1693

Anthea Film GmbH
Widenmayerstr. 4
8000 Munich 22
Tel: (89) 226 194
Fax: (89) 221 251

Alpha Entertainment
Haselburg str. 14
8000 Munich 90
Tel: (89) 642 1588
Fax: (89) 54 39 82

Bavaria Film GmbH
Bavariafilmplatz 7
8022 Geiselgasteig/Munich
Tel: (89) 6499 2389
Fax: (89) 649 2507

BioSkop-Film GmbH
Türkenstr. 91/111
8000 Munich 40
Tel: (89) 394 987
Fax: (89) 396 820

Capitol Film + TV International GmbH & Co. Vertriebs KG
Harvestehuder Weg 43
2000 Hamburg 13
Tel: (40) 411 79–0
Fax: (40) 411 79–199

Connexion-Film Vertriebs & Produktions GmbH & Co.
Harvestehuder Weg 45
2000 Hamburg 13
Tel: (40) 411 79 300
Fax: (40) 411 79 399

Franz Seitz Produktions GmbH
Beichstr. 8
8000 Munich 40

Tel: (89) 391 1123
Fax: (89) 340 1291

Willy Bogner Film GmbH
Sankt Veitstr. 4
8000 Munich 80
Tel: (89) 436 06–0
Fax: (89) 436 06 429

CCC Filmkunst GmbH
Verlängerte Dammstr. 16
1000 Berlin 20
Tel: (30) 334 200–1
Fax: (30) 334 0418

CineVox Film GmbH
Bavaria Filmplatz 7
8022 Geiselgasteig
Tel: (89) 649 541
Fax: (89) 791 2164

Delta Film GmbH
Otto Suhr-Allee 59
1000 Berlin 10
Tel: (30) 342 4075
Fax: (30) 342 5082

Manfred Durniok Produktion
Hausotterstr. 36
1000 Berlin 51
Tel: (30) 491 8045
Fax: (30) 491 4065

Impuls Film
Grazerstr. 20
3000 Hanover 81
Tel: (511) 835 001
Fax: (511) 838 6253

Hermes Film GmbH
Kaiserplatz 7
8000 Munich 40
Tel: (89) 394 368
Fax: (89) 344 363

Lisa Film GmbH
Wildenmayerstr. 48
8000 Munich 22
Tel: (89) 227 195
Fax: (89) 291 156

Mondada Film
Klausenerstr. 19
8000 Munich 90
Tel: (89) 692 5884
Fax: (89) 691 6709

Neu Constantin Film GmbH
Kaiserstr. 39
8000 Munich 40
Tel: (89) 3860 9221/2
Fax: (89) 3860 9242

Oko-Film GmbH
Mauerkircherstr. 3
8000 Munich 80
Tel: (89) 987 666

Olga Film GmbH
Tengstr. 16
8000 Munich 40
Tel: (89) 271 2635
Fax: (89) 272 5768

Primodessa Film GmbH
Cuvillierstr. 8
8000 Munich 40
Tel: (89) 982 568
Fax: (89) 982 8506

Studio Hamburg
Tonndorfer Hauptstr. 90
2000 Hamburg 70
Tel: (40) 6688–0
Fax: (40) 665 601
(40) 6688 4370

Rialto Film GmbH
Bismarckstr. 108
1000 Berlin 12
Tel: (30) 310–000–0
Fax: (30) 310 00 559

Roxy-Film GmbH
Schützenstr. 1
8000 Munich 2
Tel: (89) 555 341
Fax: (89) 594 510

Tele-München GmbH
Kaufingerstr. 25
8000 Munich 2
Tel: (89) 296 661
Fax: (89) 227 875

Vision Film GmbH
Kurfürstenplatz 4
8000 Munich 40
Tel: (89) 390 025
Fax: (89) 395 569

Von Vietinghoff
Filmproduktion
Potsdamerstr. 199
1000 Berlin 30
Tel: (30) 216 8931
Fax: (30) 215 8219

Regina Ziegler
Filmproduktion
Budapesterstr. 35
1000 Berlin 30
Tel: (30) 261 8071
Fax: (30) 262 8213

Distributors

Ascot Filmverleih GmbH
St. Annastr. 16
8000 Munich 22
Tel: (89) 29 69 95
Fax: (89) 33 18 39

Columbia Tri-Star
Filmgesellschaft mbH
Ickstattstr. 1
8000 Munich 5
Tel: (89) 23 69–0
Fax: (89) 26 43 80

Concorde Filmverleih
GmbH
Widenmayerstr. 5/6
8000 Munich 22
Tel: (89) 22 07 44
Fax: (89) 29 64 50

Delta Filmverleih GmbH &
Co KG
Rosenheimerstr. 2
8000 Munich 80
Tel: (89) 48 30 35–7
Fax: (89) 48 36 52

FIFIGE Hamburgische
Filmeikaufsgesellschaft
GmbH-AG Kino
Allendeplatz 3
2000 Hamburg 13
Tel: (40) 44 40 06
Fax: (89) 41 85 71

Futura/Filmverlag GmbH
Rambergstr. 5
8000 Munich 40
Tel: (89) 38 170–1
Fax: (89) 38 17 00 20

Highlight Film Verleih
GmbH
Herkomerplatz 2
8000 Munich 80
Tel: (89) 92 69 66 02
Fax: (89) 98 15 43

Impuls Film
Grazerstr. 10
3000 Hanover 81
Tel: (0511) 83 50 01
Fax: (0511) 838 6253

Jugend Film Verleih GmbH
Lietzenburgerstr. 44
D–1000 Berlin 30
Tel: (30) 219 9010
Fax: (30) 219 90111

Metropol Filmverleih GmbH
Viktoriastr. 34
8000 Munich 40
Tel: (89) 39 30 96
Fax: (89) 39 63 03

NEF 2 Filmverleih GmbH
Erhardstr. 8
8000 Munich 40
Tel: (89) 201 1747
Fax: (89) 201 1634

Neue Constantin Film
GmbH & Co. Verleih KG
Kaiserstr. 39
8000 Munich 40
Tel: (89) 38 60 90
Fax: (89) 38 60 92 42

Scotia International
Filmverleih GmbH
Deutschland
Possartstr. 14
8000 Munich 80
Tel: (89) 41 30 90–
Fax: (89) 470 6320

Senator Film Verleih GmbH
Kaiserstr. 35
8000 Munich 40
Tel: (89) 381 9030
Fax: (89) 3819 0325/0326

Tobis Film Verleih GmbH
Bismarckstr. 108
1000 Berlin 12
Tel: (30) 310 0050
Fax: (30) 3100 0559

Transit Film GmbH
Dachauer Str. 35
8000 Munich 2
Tel: (89) 55 52 61
Fax: (89) 59 61 22

20th Century Fox of
Germany GmbH
Hainer Weg 37–53
6000 Frankfurt
Tel: (69) 60 90 20
Fax: (69) 62 77 16

Warner Bros. Film GmbH
Rosenheimerstr. 143b
8000 Munich 80
Tel: (89) 418 0090
Fax: (89) 4180 0945

Useful Addresses

Verband der Filmverleiher
e.V (VDF)
(Assn. of Distributors)
Langenbeckstr. 9
6200 Wiesbaden
Tel: (6121) 1405–0
Fax: (6121) 140512

Dana Vavrova and Werner Stocker in Joseph Vilsmaier's *Rama Dama*

Still from Joachim Kreck's latest documentary, *The Linesman*

Hauptverband Deutscher Filmtheater e.V (HDF)
(Assn. of German Exhibitors)
Langenbeckstr. 9
Postfach 2927
6200 Wiesbaden
Tel: (6121) 30 66 60
Fax: (6121) 37 64 05

Filmförderungsanstalt (FFA)
(Federal Film Board)
Postfach 301808
1000 Berlin 301
Tel: (30) 261 6006
Fax: (30) 262 8976

Spitzenorganisation der Filmwirtschaft e.V (SP10)
(Film Industry Trade Organisation)
Langenbeckstr. 9
6200 Wiesbaden
Tel: (6121) 1727–0
Fax: (6121) 17 27 39

Export Union
Türkenstr. 9
8000 Munich 40
Tel: (89) 39 00 95
Fax: (89) 39 52 23

GREECE

by B. Samantha Stenzel

Greek films have developed a reputation internationally for being ponderous and slow-moving, very often focusing on political themes. Even though most are well-made, often with outstanding cinematography, almost all have failed at the box-office in the last few years.

A conservative government came to power in April 1990, ending over eight years of socialist rule. Manos Zacharias was re-placed as president of the board of directors of the Greek Film Centre (GFC) by Errikos Andreou. According to Andreou, an experienced feature and television director, "The way it was put to me, what the GFC needs is a professional from the film community itself, one who can confront the problems facing the industry and help curb the downward trend."

One of Andreou's primary goals is to lure

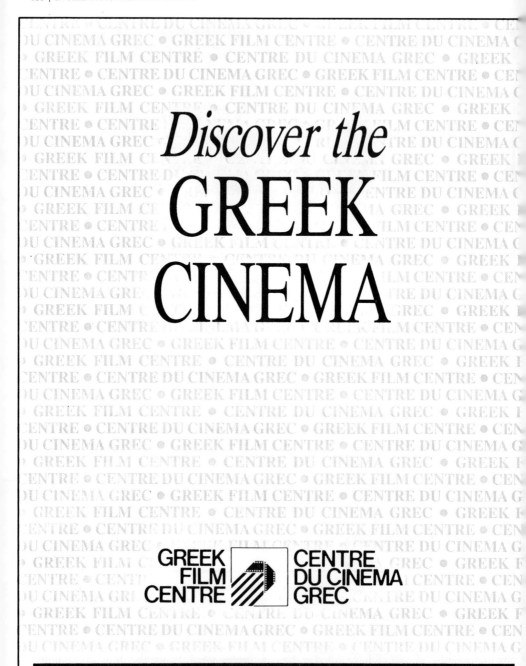

Marcello Mastroianni in *The Suspended Step of the Stork*

independent producers back into the fold through using tax shelters and other financial incentives. The GFC is now almost the only backer of domestic films and funding has been cut. For the past few years it has operated on a yearly budget of between 400–500 million drachmas ($20–30 million). This sum was cut to 275 million drachmas ($14¼ million), 100 million ($5.2 million) of which went for film production. Andreou recommended it be raised.

Box-office admissions dropped 20–30% in 1990–91 compared to the previous 1989–90 season. It is encouraging that renovated cinemas with Dolby sound or an equivalent system held their own. Partners George Michaeldides and Manos Krezias of Home Video Hellas, a branch of Elke distribution company, were the trailblazers four years ago when they completely refurbished the rundown central Opera and Radio City cinemas. They were once again trendsetters when they introduced fresh popcorn to Greeks, highlighting the booming business in snack bars, which serve liquor along with sandwiches and sweets.

George, Alexander and Spiros Spentzos, scions of their father's 50 year-old business Spentzos Films, saw their dreams of creating a luxury house from an old grade B cinema come true. The Ideal is one of Athens most magnificent theatres. It has Europe's second largest commercial cinema screen, state-of-the-art sound via Kodak's Cinema Digital Sound System, and plush armchairs. The centrally located Astor Cinema, converted from a stage theatre, had a highly successful first season.

Ticket prices were increased to 800 drachmas ($4.15) but this didn't even keep up with the almost 20% annual inflation.

The past season has been marked by great turbulence. Hardtops reopened when outdoor cinemas closed in September, as usual. However, last year, the beginning of the autumn season was marred by general strikes that lasted over three weeks. In the beginning of the year, violent demonstrations resulted in buildings being torched in central Athens, causing several casualties. The Persian Gulf war renewed terrorist incidents and bomb threats. No sooner was the war ended than public transport strikes began.

Couch Potatoes

All this chaos provided additional incentive for Greeks to become couch potatoes and amuse themselves with movies offered on pubcaster ERT or one of the newer private stations. The 50 or so outdoor cinemas still remaining in Athens are lobbying behind union president Theodore Rigas to reduce the VAT from 8 to 4%, the rate applied to theatre tickets, to remove the 6% tax levied by the Ministry of Culture for Greek film production and to place a ceiling on rents paid by exhibitors, now set quite high, with an average payment of between $2,500–$5,000 per four month season.

The 31st Greek Film Festival in Thessaloniki, this year held from October 1 to 7, has a reputation for offscreen shenanigans that in recent years have overshadowed the onscreen action. Last year was no exception.

Tassos Boulmetis's **The Dream Factory**, the festival opener, is unusually arresting, with sepia futuristic scenes in grim warehouses influenced by German expressionism alternating with brilliantly-coloured contemporary sequences and dream enactments. The approach is similar to *1984* with a peek into the future when clients pay a master dreamer to envision on a large screen the dreams they had before the "epidemic." The basic premise is interesting and contains traces of theories of both Freud and Jung, bound to appeal to viewers in analysis. Audience reaction was divided but nevertheless the film shared the Best First Feature Director award.

Panos Kokkinopoulos' **Scars of the Night**, which shared Best First Feature Award with *The Dream Factory*, is a routine thriller about a recently released convict's search for the money owed him by a friend who set him up for a five-year rap. His quest takes him to an island, in time to witness his friend's funeral. As he attempts to piece together the events surrounding his death, he is smitten with a lovely islander, witnesses bizarre rituals and is chased by an invisible demon. The stunning scenery and comely leads (Stratos Tzortzoglou and Katerina Lehou) cannot compensate for stilted acting and a cliched plot.

Takis Antonopoulos's **Impossible Encounter**, about a biker who gets involved with an older intellectual, is more suitable for video or television viewing than the wide screen. Dimitris Mavrikios's **Enigma Est**, a rich study of artist Giorgio de Chirico which captured the Best Documentary and Best Music prizes, is a natural for educational TV and documentary screenings. Excerpts of de Chirico's writings and views of his paintings are alternated with tasteful scenes from the many cities which influenced his work including Athens, Munich, Torino, Paris, and Florence.

Nikos Fatouros' documentary **Nikos Kessanlis** is notable for the intimate glimpse it gives of the character of the fascinating artist who is often before the camera. It is also worthy of educational TV and academic screenings.

Dimitris Spyrou's **The Flea**, a touching real-life tale of a twelve-year-old's struggle to write a village newspaper, was inexplicably omitted from the official competition. Filmed in the picturesque mountain villages around ancient Olympia, it is a subtle portrait exploring contemporary issues such as public education, mass emigration from the provinces to cities and childrens' rights. The performance by Pantelis Trivizas, a young drifter who plays the "Flea", is memorable. *The Flea* has been screened with great success at a number of international festivals.

Vasilis Alexakis' **The Athenians**, a technically adept comedy with razor-sharp photography by Andreas Bellis and a rousing score by popular composer Lukianos Kelaidonis, starts out with great promise but fizzles midway through, despite conveying some of the quirks and follies of modern-day Athens.

Far more successful is Stavros Tsiolis's **Love under the Date Tree**, which won awards for Best Film and Best Actor for Lazaros Andreou who plays the gentle Maestro, a perfect foil for Panayiotis (popular singer Argiris Bakirtzis), a self-centred obsessive who is irresistible to women.

Early scenes are brilliantly paced as this odd couple agrees to search through the Peleponnese for a significant date tree after Panayiotis' wife dies. Eventually the timing lags and the plot itself never sustains its early interest, although it is enjoyable, with breathtaking views of mountainous terrain and quaint traditional houses.

Women Directors Score Well

Several women debuted with feature films this past year. Vassiliki Iliopoulou won the Best Screenplay award for **The Crossing**, a psychological drama in which a hitchhiking soldier kills a gas station attendant and tries to flee the country aided by a sultry femme fatale. Illiopoulos is successful in fleshing out her characters and imparting feminine nuances to the lead and her daughter.

Gay Angeles's **Moira**, a black-and-white drama about a nameless heroine who lusts for books in a world dominated by TV and computers, is more preoccupied with visual effect than characterization. Lucia Rikaki's **Trip to Australia**, based on a true story about two youngsters who escape from their house to on the road, is a poorly rendered debut.

Still from the village drama, *The Flea*

The biggest flap in the cinema world last year was caused by Nikos Nikolaidis's **Singapore Sling**, a highly stylised exercise in kinky sex and explicit torture and violence among a trio in an isolated mansion. Nikolaidis extracts good production values from a low budget with veteran cameraman Aris Stayrou's highly atmospheric black-and-white lensing and Marie-Louis Bartholomew's costumes real standouts. Although Nikolaidis claims he intended movie to be a sendup of typical thrillers, the shock value far outweighs the humour.

Nikolaidis is one of Greece's most talented directors. One can only hope he has run the gamut of his obsession with the apotheosis of death, a dominant theme in all recent productions, and can now focus on other more humanistic concerns.

Dimos Avdeliodis's eargerly awaited second feature **Nike of Samothace** focuses on

Love in bloom in *Take Care*

the humorous rivalry between two families, the Peacocks and the Partridges, is a broad sweeping adventure with mythological overtones. It is sometimes very funny, often visually arresting, but overall lacks proper continuity.

Vorgos Tsemberopoulos's **Take Care**, a likeable portrait of an Athenian family, relies heavily on the excellent cast's sensitive performaces. The subtle charm of the tale of a cryptic loner who becomes involved with both the wife and daughter of his employer after his death, proved that a domestic film placed in a good house with a run long enough for word-of-mouth to buttress its effect, can still be a success. However it was one of the few Greek films to do solid business in the last few years; most have lasted only a week or two in local runs.

Voulgaris Again on Form
Another film completed after the Salonika Fest was veteran film-maker Pantelis Voulgaris's **Quiet Days in August,** a thoughtful film about lonely people spending the vacation period in deserted Athens. *Quiet Days* received an honour from the Berlin Film Festival's Protestant Film Jury and attracted favourable notices, especially for the performance of Aleka Paizi, the delightfully expressive lead of *Wedding on the Fringe*. She plays a reclusive elderly woman who spends her days reminiscing about a man she loved during the war and calling in

song requests at radio stations. Also outstanding are popular comic Thanassis Vengos's characterisation of retired seaman Nikos, Dinos Katsouridis's fine camerawork and Manos Hadjidakis's memorable score.

Voulgaris, whose last film was the action-packed drama *Striker with the No. 9* is more effective with this delicately rendered character study and *Quiet Days in August* joins *The Engagement of Anna* and *Stone Years* as one of his finer films.

Foremost Greek director Theo Angelopoulos's **The Suspended Step of The Stork** was completed just days before its Cannes premiere. It is his second film starring Marcello Mastroianni, reunited with Jeanne Moreau for the first time since Antonioni's *La notte*, made in 1960. In *The Suspended Step*, Gregory Karr is cast as a TV journalist who is in northern Greece covering the arrival by train of Iranian, Albanian and Kurdish refugees. He spies Mastroianni, whom he recognises as a Greek politician who disappeared some years ago. The journalist locates the man's ex-wife (Jeanne Moreau) who comes there to see if she can identify him. Although she claims it is not her ex-husband, there is reason to believe she is lying.

The plaintive accounts of the refugees emphasise Angelopoulos's underlying contention that borders are arbitrary divisions that often cause human suffering and confusion. This view was considered anti-national by a bishop in Florina, an area with a history of shifting borders and ethnic strife, and he and his fervid followers disrupted the shooting after he performed a ceremony to excommunicate Angelopoulos, although it was not in his power to do so.

The Suspended Step continues all of Angelopoulos's distinctive stylistic traits, finely honed throughout his highly regarded trilogy *Journey to Cythera*, *The Beekeeper* and *Landscape in the Mist*. In *The Suspended Step*, Angelopoulos's extraordinary longtime cameraman Giorgos Arvatnitis, assisted by

TOP TEN GROSSING FILMS IN ATHENS: 1990

	Admissions
Dead Poets Society	318,546
Pretty Woman	225,508
War of the Roses	120,037
Look Who's Talking	117,061
Born on the Fourth of July	111,871
The Sheltering Sky	100,000
Ghost	94,441
Back to the Future, Part II	84,758
Home Alone	78,812
Licence to Kill	78,589

Andreas Sinanos, perfectly captures poetic landscapes as well as utilising the trademark tracking shots, and talented composer Eleni Karaindrou has created an electric and highly atmospheric score. Angelopoulos refuses significantly to alter his style to suit popular tastes, winning him the admiration of cineastes. General audiences, however, sometimes do not have the patience for his slow pace and minimalist style.

Lefteris Xanthopoulos's **Master of the Shadows** premiered in the Directors' Fortnight at Cannes. In *Master of the Shadows*, Antonis Barkas (played by Kostas Kazakos), is a famous Karaghiozis (shadow theatre) player who sees his art dying out. This sensitive study of an artist's quandary when his creative outlet becomes obsolete, is sad but uplifting as well because it symbolises the passages necessary for a rebirth of creativity.

It was generally agreed that the quality of this year's crop of films was a great improvement over last year's. The thrust of the Greek Film Centre, under the guidance of President and General Manager Errikos Andreou, is to create quality films that blend artistic merits with commercial potential, a goal often desired but infrequently accomplished.

B. SAMANTHA STENZEL is a Chicagoan who has resided in Athens for the past eleven years. She is the Variety Athens correspondent, Cinema Editor for The Athenian Magazine and organises seminars and film programmes at cultural centres and schools.

Production Companies

Dimitri Dimitriadis
9 Hadjiyanni Mexi Street
Athens 115 28
Tel: 721–4976
Fax: 724–8131

Gemini Film Productions
2 Therianou Street
Athens 114 73
Tel: 643–3626, 642–3103
Fax: 364–7608

Yannis Petropoulakis
13/14–16 Sissini Street
Athens 115 28
Tel: 722–3053, 722–8884

Stefi
4 Agelikara Street
Athens 117 42
Tel: 902–5560

Distributors

ELKE
96 Acadimias Street
Athens 106 77
Tel: 362–3801
Fax: 360–3611

Nea Kinisi
Motion Pictures Enterprises
9–13 Gravias Street
Athens 106 78

Tel: 362–8454
Fax: 363–9008

Prooptiki
40–42 Koletti Street
Athens 106 82
Fax: 361–3762
Tel: 364–4541

Spentzos Film
9–13 Gravias Street
Athens 106 78
Tel: 362–956
Fax: 362–1438

UIP
4 Gambetta St.
Athens 106 78
Tel: 361–1472

Useful Addresses

Ministry of Culture
Aristidou 14
Athens 101 86
Tel: 322–4737

Greek Film Centre
Voula Georgakakou
Panepistimiou 10
Athens 106 71
Tel: 363–4586
Fax: 361–4336

Worldwide Sales
Exportfilm Bischoff & Co.
Isabellastr. 20
8000 München 40
Tel: 089/271–9940.
Telex 528290

**Cinema and TV
Technicians' Guild**
Veltetsiou 25
Athens 106 80
Tel: 360–2379

Greek Directors' Guild
Tossitsas 11
Athens 106 73
Tel: 822–3205, 822–8936

Greek Actors' Guild
Kaningos 33
Athens 106 82
Tel: 363–3742, 361–7369

**Assn. of Greek Motion
Picture Video and
TV Producers**
Skalidi 16–18
Athens 115 25
Tel: 671–7297
Fax: 647–5057

**Assn. of Open-Air Cinema
Owners**
Acadimies 95
Athens 106 77
Tel: 361–9239

**Panhellenic Theatre Owners
Assn.**
Acadimias 96
Athens 106 77
Tel: 801–1045

(*continued from page 210*)

Rahardjo Djarot, who is also one of the nation's leading directors.

Among other titles screened in New York were **Naga Bonar**, M.T. Risyaf's 1987 farce about the Indonesia fight for independence; Imam Tantowi's 1987 feature, **The Knight of Madangkara**, an epic blending martial arts and the supernatural; Ami Priyono's **Roro Mendut**, Indonesia's *Romeo and Juliet;* **Sangkuriang**, director Gautama Sisworo Putra's bizarre 1982 film combining Sudanese legend and the Oedipus myth. In addition, there were panel sessions on Indonesian cinema complete with American critics airing their views. In all, a remarkable event, co-sponsored by the government, private investment and Garuda Airlines.

Back home, comedian Didi Petet remains popular as **Si Kabayan Dan Gadis Kota,** a continuation of the "Si Kabayan" series, a reworking of the city-mouse, country-mouse story with Petet playing the bewildered rube from the provinces in the big city. Indonesia has a fair sampling of producers who prepare films for both the domestic and international markets. One such outfit, Rapi Films (which made Bellina's latest weeper) distributed earlier this year **Triple Cross**, with American-born action heroine, Cynthia Rothrock, in evidence. Rapi is back at it again in summer 1991, filming **Lady Dragon**, again with Rothrock aboard, directed by David Worth, the man responsible for the *Kickboxer*. Shooting in Los Angeles and Indonesia should push the production budget to $2.7-million, a fortune by domestic standards.

GUINEA-BISSAU

by Roy Armes

The late 1980's saw the entry of yet another small West African state into film history with a first feature-length film, when the National Film Institute in Guinea-Bissau produced *Mortu Nega*. The film's director, Flora Gomes, was born in Cadique in Guinea-Bissau in 1949 and had completed his training as a film cameraman at the Cuban Arts Institute by the early 1970's. But a decade or more passed before he could even begin work on his first feature film. During this period he worked as cameraman on a number of African and international projects and directed a number of small Ministry of Information documentaries.

Mortu Nega is a deeply committed look at Guinea-Bissau's war of independence against the Portuguese and a study of developments in the war's aftermath, following the humiliating defeat inflicted on the colonisers. It begins in 1973, the year in which Portuguese agents assassinated Amilcar Cabral, the leader of the independence movement and a man widely recognised as one of Africa's leading political theorists. Though the film is obviously designed as a national epic, it is couched in an almost documentary style, capturing the quality of practical idealism which was a feature of Cabral's philosophy. Indeed its depiction of the struggle bears out Cabral's dictum that "national liberation is necessarily an act of culture." The Portuguese themselves are hardly shown – except in their helicopters – and the film concentrates on the efforts of the revolutionaries as they bring not only liberation but also medicine and literacy to the people. The latter were vitally needed, as the illiteracy rate during Portuguese rule was around 99% and there were never more than 11 doctors for the entire rural population.

Much of the strength of *Mortu Nega* – rendered into English as "Those Whom Death Refused" – comes from the fact that, though politically committed, it does not attempt to hide the fact that some Party workers grow indifferent to the people. Moreover the film's climax comes when the people turn not to the Party but to their national past, as with songs and dances they consult the spirits of their ancestors in search of wisdom.

HONGKONG

by Derek Elley

The wild partying prior to China's mid-1997 takeover of the territory shows a few signs of running out of puff. Despite all its problems (which film-makers are never slow to mention), Hongkong is still the engine of East Asia's movie industry, dominating exhibition in areas like Taiwan, Singapore and Malaysia, having major followings for its stars in Japan, and exporting its product worldwide through Chinatown circuits. In terms of sheer quality, the 1990–91 season was not on a par with 1989–90; but there was little lack of energy on the production side.

The bald facts and figures (see below) show production for calendar 1990 about equal to 1989's; total box-office receipts were slightly down, and not helped by the absence of a new Jackie Chan movie (traditionally a big grosser). The most surprising fact was the sudden increase in foreign film's share of the market, up from a fifth to a third; but even the biggest of these (*Pretty Woman*) only ranked seventh in a combined Top Ten. Even in the year of Hollywood's biggest worldwide blockbusters, plus competition from home video and laser disc, Hongkong audiences during 1990 showed once again that they will still turn out for local product.

When Jackie Chan finally emerged in February 1991 with **The Armour of God 2: Operation Condor** (*Feiying gaiwak* – literally *Project Eagle*), it went on to take HK$40 million, hitting the current local benchmark for a mega-hit. That came as a major relief to Golden Harvest, which had seen the original budget treble to HK$115 million in the two years Chan had taken to shoot the movie in Hongkong, Spain, Morocco, Austria and the Philippines, including three months in the Sahara alone. The most expensive Hongkong film ever, it is hardly a real sequel to the 1987 original (co-star Alan Tam is dropped, for a start), more an action-adventure with an international cast revolving around the search for some hidden Nazi gold.

Other box-office hits of early 1991 included Poon Man-kit's local mafia comedy **To Be Number One** (*Bo hou*), which took HK$38 million, and yet another in the "gambling" cycle, Wong Tsing-wa's **All for the Gamble** (*Dou tsun*). And as of June, there was a major tussle shaping up between the summer releases of the top four male stars – Chow Yun-fat, Stephen Chow, Andy Lau and Jacky Cheung – who had some nine films ready between them.

Preparing to Parachute

Despite such activity, film-makers are still packing their parachutes. Recent emigrants to Canada include mega-star Leslie Cheung and director Clifford Choi. D&B Films has been shooting a string of low-budget action movies there, and Golden Harvest is investing US$25 million in British Columbia for the third *Teenage Mutant Ninja Turtles*. With HK$2 billion already invested in the Vancouver property market by Chinese emigrants, the Canadian city is becoming a de facto Hongkong Mark II and a natural film-making base. Under Canada's immigrant-investor programme, a minimum investment of C$250,000 (for B.C., Ontario, Alberta and Québec; the other six provinces require only C$15,000) guarantees residency for the investor and his family.

However, not many film-makers stay long once the paperwork is fixed: apart from bilingual action quickies, Hongkong itself is still the place to actually make movies. Singapore could suffer the same fate of being a convenient service centre that no one actually wants to live in: aggressive newcomer Impact Films became the first company officially to produce a feature on the island (Wong Ching's thriller *Gingtin supyi siusi*), and Golden Harvest is looking hard at the territory, but there are doubts whether Singapore's highly regulated environment will prove congenial to longterm investment, especially given the fact that more and more Hongkong film companies are simply laundering operations for triad money. Singapore's main benefit over Canada is its Asian location and majority-Chinese culture; Canada's is its window to the English-language market (still the dream of Hongkong film-makers, although even Jackie Chan has failed to penetrate it).

Meanwhile, despite some cutbacks in local production during the first half of 1991 (Golden Harvest was planning only some 16 pictures, compared with 24 in 1990), and the continuing conversion of large cinemas into multiplexes, there is still a frenzy of activity to reap the whirlwind before 1997, with actors like Andy Lau and Stephen Chow shooting back-to-back in an orgy of work (actress Joey Wang was the 1990 champ, with 16 movies).

The biggest craze of the past year has been "gambling" movies – launched by the 1989 success of Wong Ching's *Casino Raiders* (*Tsi tsun mou seung*), confirmed by the smash *God of Gamblers* (*Dou san*), and topped by 1990's all-time box-office champion **All for the Winner** (*Dou Sing*), which clocked up HK$41.3 million and broke every other financial record in the book as well. During 1990–91 the mass of movies with *dou* (gamble) in the title reached epic proportions, and the craze has already made a sudden star of young Stephen Chow, a likable young ex-TV actor who was the hottest thing of 1990.

Other newish trends include the resurgence of softcore historical dramas, providing veteran Run Run Shaw's dictum that "when business is poor, it's time to make erotic movies" (something he put into practice during the 1970's with director Li Han-hsiang). Golden Harvest led the way with **Erotic Ghost Story** (*Liu tsai yim tam*), since followed by others including **Liu Jai, Home for Intimate Ghosts** (*Liu tsai fa lung yut*), all fodder for Hongkong's "III" category (forbidden to under-18s). More productive has been the emergence of comedies directly satirising Mainland attitudes to Hongkong, a trend begun discreetly a few years ago but, post-Tiananmen, given the full treatment with

Front of house still for *Red Dust*

Alfred Cheung's **Her Fatal Ways** (*Biutse nei ho ye* – literally, *How's Things, Cousin?*), a witty *Ninotchka*-like comedy with the wonderful Dodo Cheng as a straitlaced Communist cadre meeting her come-uppance in free-wheeling Hongkong.

Other standouts from the 1990–91 season include Yim Ho's **Red Dust** (*Gungun hong chen*, in its Mandarin version), sumptuously mounted *Zhivago*-like melodrama set on the Mainland and scripted by the late Echo Chen; starring Taiwan's Lin Ch'ing-hsia and Ch'in Han and Hongkong's Maggie Cheung, it swept Taiwan's Golden Horse Awards in late 1990. (Finance was from the Hongkong Subsidiary of Taiwan's Tomson Films.) Eddie Fong's **Last Princess of Machuria** (*Chundou Fongtsi* – known as *Yoshiko Kawashima* in its international version) is a visually resplendent vehicle for Anita Mui as the famous bisexual wartime Mata Hari. And Tony Au's **Au revoir, mon amour** (*Hoyat gwan tsoi lei*) is a similarly well-mounted wartime love story with the same singer-actress opposite Leung Kar-fai.

Wong Kar-wai's **Days of Being Wild** (*A-fei tsingchun*), two years in production and costing a giant HK\$50 million, failed at the box-office (despite starring Leslie Cheung and Maggie Cheung) but looks like attracting festival attention overseas. A patchwork sexual society portrait of Hongkong from the 1960's to 1990 (with a sequel scheduled), it is seen by some as a masterpiece and by others as a self-indulgent piece of designer art, like Wong's 1988 cult hit *As Tears Go by*.

High Octane Follow-up

No such pretensions were attached to Ching Siu-tung's **A Chinese Ghost Story II** (*Sinnui yauwan II* – *yangan dou*), a high-octane follow-up to the successful original that showed the guiding hand of producer Tsui Hark. Nor John Woo's power-packed **Bullet in the Head** (*Diphut gaitau*), about three Hongkong buddies who meet death in the face in Vietnam during the late 1960's. Woo reined back on the bloodletting in his subsequent **Once a Thief** (*Tsungwang seihoi*), a cross between *Jules et Jim* and Hitchcock, set in Paris with attractive playing by Chow Yun-fat, Leslie Cheung and Cherie Chung. As of mid-1991 he was planning to produce (but not direct) a sequel to *The Killer*, which enjoyed a cult success abroad in 1990.

Further down the pole, the three Hui brothers returned together in **Front Page** (*San bungan batleung*), a predictable satire on Hongkong's exploitative press directed by Philip Chan that lacked the edge of Michael Hui's recent efforts with director Clifton Ko (*Chicken and Duck Talk; Mr Coconut*). Sammo Hung's **Pantyhose Hero** (*Tsifan seunghung*), starring Hung and Alan Tam, deserves a footnote as a boldly comic look at Hongkong's sizable gay scene, despite being modelled on the U.S. movies *Cruising* and *Partners*.

Finally, two quieter movies also deserve mention. Chan Ho-sun's clumsily-titled **Alan and Eric between Hello and Goodbye** (*Seungsing gusi* – literally *A Tale of Two Cities*) is a charming, *Jules et Jim*-like threesome set in Hongkong and San Francisco with genuinely likable playing by Eric Tsang, Maggie Cheung and Alan Tam. And Wu Ma's **Stage Door Johnny** (*Moutoi tsemui*), a nostalgic look at 1930's drama groups in Shanghai that between the formulary action bits is clearly made with much love and attention.

With Stanley Kwan finally starting shooting his long-planned biopic of actress Ruan Lingyu who committed suicide in March 1935 (with Maggie Cheung replacing Anita Mui in the lead); with Chen Kaige planning a movie in summer 1991 from a script by *Rouge* novelist Lei Pik-wa; with Tsui Hark, in between directing about four movies at the same time, looking as if he may finally start *Journey to the West* with Japanese finance; and with people like Clara Law, Sylvia Chang, Ann Hui and Lawrence Ah

Mon behind the camera, the 1991–92 season looks like having no shortage of name material.

DEREK ELLEY has been associated with IFG for more than 19 years. He is known as a specialist in Hungarian and East Asian cinema, and is author of The Epic Film: Myth and History (1984) and consultant editor of The Variety Movie Guide and Chronicle of the Movies (both 1991). A regular contributor to weekly Variety, he is currently completing A Handbook of Chinese Cinema.

Recent and Forthcoming Films

Yun Ling-yuk. Dir: Stanley Kwan. Players Maggie Cheung, Carina Liu, Leung Kar-fai, Cecilia Yip. Prod: Golden Way/Golden Harvest.
Sinnui yauwan III tsi dou dou dou (A Chinese Ghost Story III). Dir: Tsui Hark. Players: Tony Leung, Joey Wang. Prod: Film Workshop.
Seunghoi 1920 (Shanghai 1920). Dir: Po-chi Leong. Players: John Lone. Prod: Fu Ngai.
Tsoi Suk tsi wangsou tsin gwan (The Raid). Dir: Ching Siu-tung. Players: Dean Shek, Jacky Cheung, Leung Kar-fai, Fannie Yuan.
Gikdou tsuitsung (Zodiac Killers). Script: Wu Nien-chen. Dir: Ann Hui. Players: Andy Lau, Cherie Chung. Prod: Golden Harvest.
Bawang bie ji. Script: Lei Pik-wa. Dir: Chen Kaige. Players: Leslie Cheung, Xu Qing. Prod: Tomson (HK).
Gamyuk fungwan II tsi toufan (Prison on Fire II). Script: Nam Yin. Dir: Ringo Lam. Players: Chow Yun-fat, Ch'en Sung-yung. Prod: Cinema City.
Lung Man. Dir: Jacob C.L. Cheung. Players: Roy Chiao, Yim Ho, Lawrence Ah Mon.
Sa-sa yu Ga-ga. Dir: Sylvia Chang. Players: Sylvia Chang, Sally Yeh.
Yes yattsuk. Dir: Clara Law. Players: Lei Ming, Vivian Chow.
Wong Fei-hung. Dir: Tsui Hark. Players: Li Lianjie, Yuen Biao, Rosamund Kwan, Jacky Cheung, Kent Cheng. Prod: Film Workshop.
Lui Lok chun. Dir: Lawrence Ah Mon. Players: Andy Lau.
Hak sut (Will of Iron). Dir: John Chiang. Players: Jacky Cheung, Maggie Cheung.

Da hong denglong gaogao gua (Raise the Red Lantern). Dir: Zhang Imou. Players: Gong Li, Li Baotian, Ma Jingwu. Prod: Era International (HK).

Tenth Hongkong Film Awards

The awards for 1990, announced on April 21, 1991, were:
Best Film: *Days of Being Wild.*
Best Director: Wong Kar-wai (*Days of Being Wild*).
Best Script: Chan Man-keung (*Queen of Temple Street*).
Best Actor: Leslie Cheung (*Days of Being Wild*).
Best Actress: Dodo Cheng (*Her Fatal Ways*).
Best Supporting Actor: Ng Mang-dat (*A Moment of Romance*).
Best Supporting Actress/Best Newcomer: Rain Lau (*Queen of Temple Street*).
Best Photography: Christopher Doyle (*Days of Being Wild*).
Best Editing: John Woo (*Bullet in the Head*).
Best Art Direction: William Cheung (*Days of Being Wild*).
Best Martial Arts/Action Choreography: Ching Siu-tung (*Swordsman*).
Best Music: Joseph Koo, James Wong, Romeo Diaz (*A Terra-Cotta Warrior*).
Best Song: *Swordsman.*
Best Technical Award: *The Last Princess of Mancuria/Kawashima Yoshiko.*
Life Achievement Award: Pang Ngan-lun.

Facts and Figures

In 1990, 119 local productions were released in Hongkong, about the same as the previous year, with *All for the Winner, Front Page* and *When Fortune Smiles* brightening up the second half of the year. Total box-office receipts were HK$1,203 million, down by some 6% on 1989's HK$1,290 million. The absence in 1990 of a new Jackie Chan movie skewed the Top Ten slightly, but was partly compensated for by several successes of new star Stephen Chow (*All for the Winner, When Fortune Smiles, Curry and Pepper,* etc).

Some 110 foreign movies were released during the year, with their share of the total box-

TOP TEN GROSSING LOCAL FILMS IN HONGKONG: 1990

	Rentals ($HK)
All for the Winner	41,300,000
God of Gamblers*	37,000,000
Front Page	26,300,000
Heart into Hearts	23,300,000
A Terra-Cotta Warrior	20,900,000
A Chinese Ghost Story II	20,800,000
Her Fatal Ways	20,500,000
The Fun, the Luck and the Tycoon	20,300,000
No Risk, No Gain (Casino Raiders – The Sequel)	19,100,000
When Fortune Smiles	18,800,000

Total Gross, including end–1989

office being 32% (up from 1989's 22%). The highest grossing foreign film in 1990 was *Pretty Woman* (HK$20.5 million), followed by *Back to the Future Part II, Total Recall, Back to the Future Part III, Die Hard II, The Gods Must Be Crazy II, Robocop 2, Gremlins 2, Black Rain* (Ridley Scott) and *Batman* (HK$8.5 million).

Useful Addresses

Golden Harvest (HK)
8 Hammer Hill Rd
Ngau Chi Wan
Kowloon
Tel: 352–8222
Fax: 351–1683

Cinema City Co.
121 Waterloo Road
Kowloon Tong
Tel: 338–6281
Fax: 336–2767

Film Workshop Co.
121 Waterloo Road, G/F
Kowloon Tong
Tel: 338–9973
Fax: 338–9079

D&B Films
5 Kent Rd
Kowloon Tong
Kowloon
Tel: 338–7888

Sil-Metropole Organisation
15/F, Sunbeam Commercial
Bldg
469 Nathan Rd
Kowloon
Tel: 780–5355
Fax: 780–0719

Molesworth
Unit A, 4/F, Ka Cheong Bldg
2–4 Sunning Rd
Causeway Bay
Tel: 577–6255
Fax: 895–4104

Southern Film Corporation
19/F, Dominion Centre
37–59 Queen's Road East
Hongkong
Tel: 527–7284

Magnum Films
Unit 1–4, 17/F
Pacific Trade Centre
2 Kai Hing Road
Kowloon Bay
Kowloon
Tel: 796–6556
Fax: 799–2875

Impact Films-Movie Impact
Blk. 2, 6/F, Tien Chu Centre
1E, Mok Cheong Street
Tokwawan
Kowloon
Tel: 715–6545, 761–1703
Fax: 761–1020
Telex: 51533 enimp hx

Mobile Film Production
11 Wiltshire Road
Kowloon Tong
Kowloon
Tel: 794–0761
Fax: 338–8316

HUNGARY

by Derek Elley

In the summer of 1990 Hungarian cinema was at its lowest point in living memory: production had virtually ground to a halt in the first six months of the year; closed-door discussions on the future of the industry were attracting the wrath of young turk filmmakers; and there was a growing feeling that even the Hungarian Film Week, held annually every February and the industry's main international showcase, would not take place in 1991.

But rumours of the patient's death have proved premature. By summer 1991 some 15 or so features (excluding a mass of documentaries) had already been completed and/or shown, and a similar number either scheduled or in post-production. All the talking of the past year had finally yielded a Motion Picture Foundation of Hungary (Magyar Mozgókép Alapítvány) with a structure for dispersing state funds. And rumours were that the film week would be resurrected (without documentaries) in late 1991 or even in its regular early February, pre-Berlin slot.

So what has changed? On the surface, little, it would seem. Though Hungary's economy is well on the way to completing its transition to market capitalism, the film industry is still supported by state funds, Hungarians are still going to see western movies out of choice, and feature production is still around the 15–20 level of recent years. But look below the surface and it's a different story.

As of summer 1991 discussions were still going on about the exact system of disbursing state money, but the broad structure was already in place. Officially set up on April 24, 1991, and with Ferenc Köhalmi (in charge of film at the Culture & Education Ministry) as its secretary-general, the foundation functions as a conduit through which state monies pass, via a National Advisory Board, to half-a-dozen Special Advisory Boards, each representing a section of the industry – features, documentaries, animation, scientific/educational, etc.

The members of the special boards are nominated by individual guilds within their section (e.g. cameramen, directors, scriptwriters) to serve for three years, with the job of assessing the merits of projects submitted

for funding. This is the biggest change: no longer will the main studios be allocated a lump sum every year to be spent at the discretion of their heads with little or no accountability; projects will be judged and funded individually.

Here lies the final catch: of the feature film board's allocation, a maximum of 60% is to go to projects submitted by the major studios, with a giant 40% reserved for individuals and other companies. It is also understood that studios' past records will be taken into account when considering their applications. This could be bad news for some that conspicuously under-produced in recent years (when each studio got the same lump sum).

Magical Compromise

The structure may still look unnecessarily bureaucratic to foreign eyes, and may well end up simplified in the future; but its purpose is to ensure that fair play is seen to be done, and to build in sufficient checks to stave off accusations of favouritism. In a country and film industry as small as Hungary's, this is vital to maintain a broad consensus and escape factional in-fighting and score-settling during the break with the past. It also has a uniquely Hungarian flavour of magical compromise at the last moment – or, to put it another way, a tribute to that special Magyar adaptability that has managed to rescue its economy (and now its cinema) from the dire straits plaguing most of its East European neighbours.

That is not to say that everything is now roses. Many tensions still remain to be worked out; some of the established studios may disappear in coming years; the country still has major economic problems (inflation in mid–1991 was running at 35–40% in real terms); and state funds are not the only solution for the film industry. The 1991 allocation was almost unchanged from previous years at Ft 800 million (officially $10.5 million as of summer 1991); and half of that had already been given out under the old system at the start of the year, simply to get production under way.

With the average feature film budget now some Ft 25 million, companies need to get foreign funds as well if production is to remain at previous levels. Some, like the Hungarian-German venture Novofilm, do this by acting as service companies for western movies shooting in Hungary and ploughing the money back into their own productions; others go straight for co-productions. There is even talk of local television entering the arena in a more positive way, as with the U.K.'s Channel Four or French and German networks. In 1990 Péter Bacsó's Stalin's Fiancée became the first feature to receive subvention from Eurimages.

It will be a while before the new system settles down; meanwhile, in late May 1991 more theoretical discussions began on the future "form" of the Hungarian movie. No one wants to try to take on American movies at the box-office (not yet, anyway); and as long as the industry receives state funds it is also under some obligation to contribute to the country's cultural life. In practice that means Hungarian movies will still inhabit the art film/festival territory that they have done with such distinction over the years (even though foreign sales are proving tougher). And within Hungary itself, most movies will go out through a small "artkino" circuit separate from the U.S.-dominated mainstream theatres.

Focus on New Freedoms

To judge by production of the past year, little has changed in overall tone. No political barriers are left to topple, but production was still marked by the same delight in irony, love of obscure parables and tendency towards self-examination that has been a feature of Hungarian movies since 1949. As the East European country that first practised glasnost, and which has had the longest and most gradual transition, it is hardly surprising that many films have now openly focused on the new freedoms, following the official watershed of the democratic elections in spring 1990.

The best of the bunch – though not the obvious "artistic" champion – is Péter Timár's **Slap-Jack** (*Csapd le csacsi!* – the name of a crude card-game), a sharp, lively comedy produced by Novofilm, headed by director Pál Sándor. The loopy plot has a young couple feuding in their snazzy new dreamhouse while their nosy neighbour (Károly Eperjes) is training a group of (now-banned) Workers Militia in an underground shelter to reinstall a Stalinist government. The satirical blend of politics and materialism is never allowed to get in the way of the comedy as the couple's relationship takes on a *War of the Roses*-like nihilism. But its central theme – that Hungarians' real problems only started *after* the elections – reflects a deep chord in popular feeling; and the film's ending, with both neighbours rebuilding their separate dreams again, would be drepressing if it were not so wittily handled.

At the opposite end of the spectrum is Zsolt Kézdi-Kovács' **After All** (*És mégis*), an engrossing but typically dry meditation on the changes of the past 50 years, seen through the brain of a fifty-something journalist (András Kozák) who reckoned himself a liberal but is suddenly tarred as a Stalinist during the heady days of 1989. A complex collage of newsreels, contemporary fiction, and intellectual self-doubts, the film does not escape the pitfall of having the central figure retreat into silence for most of the running time. But it is a movie that had, as they say, to be made.

Somewhere between these two extremes is Miklós Jancsó's **God Walks Backwards** (*Isten hátrafelé megy*), which goes a long way to restoring the veteran director's tattered reputation of the past few years. Less obscure than his previous films, but still chockful of Jancsó trademarks (long takes, female nudity, mass groupings and songs, etc), it follows two media types as they

András Kozák in *After All*

observe rival groups in a deserted Police Academy after the Soviet withdrawal. The tongue-in-cheek ending sees the return of the Russians and the annihilation of the feuding Hungarians; and a surprise coda then turns the film into a moving tribute by Jancsó and regular scriptwriter Gyula Hernádi to friends past and lost. It has the feel of a final movie by two veterans who have come through the fires; hopefully it will mark a new beginning for the legendary Jancsó as well.

Two other veterans came up with disappointing (and, in local terms, expensive) films. Károly Makk's German co-production, **Hungarian Requiem** (*Magyar rekviem*), somehow managed to spend Ft 60 million on a lacklustre, and in its fantasy sequences very silly, drama about a cell-full of condemned political prisoners two years after the 1956 uprising. Despite a starry cast (György Cserhalmi, Károly Eperjes, Péter Andorai, Mathieu Carrière) the story lacks credibility, point and any real insight. Peter Bacsó's Hungarian-German-Swiss **Stalin's Fiancée** (*Sztálin menyasszonya*), a Ft 75 million black comedy set in a Ukrainian village during collectivisation, at least sported an astounding make-up job on Juli Básti, almost unrecognisable as the village idiot who is mistaken first as a spy, then as Stalin's fiancee, and finally turns the tables

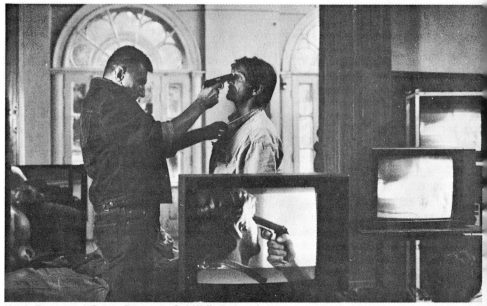

Károly Eperjes and György Dörner in *God Walks Backwards*

on her persecutors before a tragic finale. Pleasant, professionally mounted, but very thin, the movie has a curiously old-fashioned, dated feel.

The same could also be said for **Diary for My Father and Mother** (*Napló apámnak, anyámnak*), the final segment of Márta Mészáros' semi-autobiographical trilogy – though through no fault of the director. This takes the tale of "Juli" (the excellent Zsuzsa Czinkóczi) through the upheavals of 1956–58 and ends with the death of her father-figure, János (Jan Nowicki). A much more cinematic movie than the previous two instalments (helped along by Zsolt Döme's dynamic score), it forms a fitting climax to the whole opus, begun back in 1982. But with the recent changes in Hungary the last segment is robbed of its proper clout, a historical memoir ironically beached by the tide of history itself.

An old-fashioned feel of a different kind is also apparent in Pál Erdöss' **Homo Novus**, a Soviet co-production set in Russia and with an entirely Russian cast. Hard to judge properly in its Hungarian-dubbed version, despite good dubbing of Irina Kupchenko by Juli Básti, it tells of a schoolteacher in her thirties harassed almost to breaking-point by her spiteful, unruly students. Neatly shot in black-and-white, and with Kupchenko in top form, its moralistic ending carries a faint whiff of more overtly political tracts of the past.

Much more lively and contemporary, though somewhat of a mess structurally, is Péter Vajda's **Voila la liberté!** (*Itt a szabadság!*), with Péter Andorai heading a carload of bozos on a shopping spree to Vienna and being stranded on his return. Dated even in its own terms (such sprees were more a feature of 1989 than the present), it starts with much scatalogical brio but, like the hero, loses its way in the second half in a bad dose of maudlin introversion. Vajda's co-director was András Salamon.

Better organised, and showing a more experienced hand, is Péter Gothár's **Melodrama** (*Melodráma*), subtitled **Love and Freedom** (*Szabadság és szerelem*). Opening in 1968, with Hungarian troops crossing the border to "help" the Czech government and one of their number trying to hijack his tank to Vienna, it then flashes forward 20 years as our hero leaves prison and tries to track down the colleague who "stole" his Czech girl and their unborn son. Thankfully free of Gothár's more grotesque excesses, the film is chiefly remarkable for its fast-paced dialogue and ever-so-slightly ditzy atmosphere – no masterpiece but an entertaining, and pointed, near-hit.

Notable Debuts

Further down the allegorical trail are two notable first works that exist in abstract universes. **Shadow on the Snow** (*Árnyék a havon*, by Atilla Janisch (born 1958), is a fascinating man-on-the-run mystery, strikingly composed in black-and-white and scope, that shows a visionary talent at work (even if not yet fully organised). More of a piece is Zoltán Kamondi's **Paths of Death and Angels** (*Halálutak és angyalok*), a confident, highly cinematic drama about an old man (Czech actor Rudolf Hrušinský) with powers of life and death, his ambitious son (Russian actor Grigoriy Gladiy), and the woman between (Enikö Eszenyi). First written back in 1982, the script has a depth that manages to sustain interest even though its Sándor/Kafka-esque images are often obscure on first viewing. But its theme – of a fresh beginning, of an end to old practices – shines through.

Almost totally opaque (and obscure even to Hungarians) is Tamás Tolmár's **The Prince of Absence** (*A távollét hercege*), which opens with a quote from surrealist writer Frigyes Karinthy and is something to do with an obscure clerk who fantasises about a beautiful woman (Juli Básti) and some gangsters, and ends with him "opening the door" (à la *Magic Flute*) and walking into a vast desert. Those in search of more alternative viewing are directed instead to **Where**, an independent first production by Gábor Szabó, shot in

Peter Andorai (centre) in *Voila la liberté!*

Budapest and Los Angeles on $500,000 raised by the director himself. Starring the original angry young 8mm man of Hungarian cinema, Miklós Ács (see recent IFG's), in parallel stories of lovelessness and lack of communication, *Where* is a highly finished first work (excellent 35mm monochrome photography by Nyika Jancsó) that is only flawed by an unyielding, over-schematic approach and the shallowness of its central character.

Strangely enough, amongst all the array of works dealing with the recent changes, the long-term future of Hungarian cinema may lie instead in works like **Cruel Estate** (*Szoba kiáltással*), a fine fourth feature by young János Xantus. Far tighter than previous works like *Eskimo Woman Feels Cold* (1984), this grand guignol mystery-thriller, about a couple who move in with an old woman and later plan her murder, is completely free of political baggage but still thoroughly Hungarian in flavour. Confidently put together and with a fine trio of performances, it is the kind of movie that may well start turning up more often when the country settles down to a less haunted life in the 1990's.

Recent and Forthcoming Films

King Tit. Dir: Zoltán Gazsi. Prod: Objektiv.
In the Sign of the Scorpion. Dir: Péter Gárdos. Hunnia.

TOP TEN GROSSING FILMS IN HUNGARY: 1990

	Admissions
Look Who's Talking	1,033,000
Ghostbusters 2	654,000
See No Evil, Hear No Evil	645,000
Tango and Cash	618,000
The Gods Must Be Crazy 2	617,000
Back to the Future, Part III	603,000
She's out of Control	578,000
Honey, I Shrunk the Kids	542,000
Total Recall	542,000
My Stepmother Is an Alien	520,000

Hand and Glove. Dir: Francisko Gózon. Prod: Objektiv.
Goldberg Variations. Dir: Ferenc Grunwalsky. Prod: MIT.
Three Sisters. Dir: Andor Lukáts. Prod: Hunnia.
Mermaid. Script: János Matuz, József. Pacskovszky. Dir: József Pacskovszky. Players: Teréz Rudolf, Tibor Szervet. Prod: Objektiv.
Je t'aime. Dir: András Salamon. Prod: Hunnia/Monday Atelier.
Merciless Times. Dir: Sándor Sára. Prod: Objektiv/Budapest.
Sweet Emma, Darling Böbe. Dir: István Szabó. Prod: Objektiv.
Junk Movie. Dir: György Szomjas, Ferenc Grunwalsky. Players: Agi Szirtes. Prod: Budapest.
Holidaymakers. Dir: Can Togay. Prod: Hunnia/Objektiv.

Facts and Figures: 1990

Seventeen features (about the same as in 1989), 12 documentaries and one animated film (Tibor Hernádi's *Dragon and Slippers/Sárkány és papucs*) were released during the year. Cinema attendances continued to fall, to 35.7 million from 45.8 million in 1989 – down by a dramatic 22%, more than twice the previous year's rate of fall.

But the biggest bombshell of all was the decline in Hungarian films' share of attendances – down by 70%, to 1.8 million from 6.2 million. (see the top ten lists for individual attendance figures.) The number of cinemas also fell, to 822 35mm houses (down by 11%) and 781 16mm houses (down by 38%). Videotheques plummeted to 59, from 234 the previous year.

DEREK ELLEY has been associated with IFG for more than 19 years. He is known as a specialist in Hungarian and East Asian cinema, and is author of The Epic Film: Myth and History (1984) and consultant editor of The Variety Movie Guide and Chronicle of the Movies both 1991). A regular contributor to weekly Variety, he is currently completing A Handbook of Chinese Cinema.

Useful Addresses

(some changes are due simply to the recent name changes of streets)

Hunnia Film Studio
Róna utca 174 H–1145
Budapest
Tel: 251–6269
Telex: 226860
Fax: 251–6269

Béla Balázs Studio
Pasaréti út. 122
H-1026 Budapest
Tel: 176-7988
Fax: 176-7988

Hungarofilm
(*film import, production services, festivals*)
Báthori utca 10
H-1054 Budapest
Tel: 112-5425, 132-8724, 111-0020
Telex: 225768
Fax: 153-1850

CineMagyar
(*foreign sales*)
Báthori utca 10 H-1054
Budapest
Tel: 153-1317
Telex: 225768
Fax: 153-1317

Reflex Film
Tel: 201-2567
Fax: 201-2567

Fórum Film Studio
(*documentaries*)
Könyves Kálmán körüt 13-15
H-1097 Budapest
Tel: 134-3745

Novofilm
(*services, production*)
Mészáros utca 18
H-1016 Budapest
Tel: 175-0858
Fax: 175-2764

Dialóg Film Studio
(*same address & telex*)
Tel: 251-5069
Fax: 251-3168

Budapest Film Studio
(*same address & telex*)
Tel: 251-8568
Fax: 251-0478

Objektiv Film Studio
(*same address and telex*)
Tel: 251-7269
Fax: 251-2896

Mozgókép Innovációs Társulás & Alapítvány (MIT)
(*Same address & telex*)
Tel: 251-7369
Fax: 251-7369

Pannonia Film Studio
(*animation*)
Vörös Hadserg útja 64
H-1021 Budapest
Tel: 176-7091
Telex: 226823

Hungarian Film Institute and Film Archive
Népstadion út. 97
H-1143 Budapest
Tel: 142-9599

Still from Zoltán Kamondi's *Paths of Death and Angels*

ICELAND

by Gísli Einarsson

Icelandic feature film-making has been in a slump for the past few years after the boom of 1980–1984. The once fiercely loyal domestic market can no longer support local films due to a glut of foreign fare on video, TV and satellite transmissions. Foreign financing is vital and few Icelandic films are made without it, but it is hard to come by and there are few takers outside the Nordic and European film funds.

The Icelandic film industry is now starving for funds but on the other hand is high on qualified manpower. Directors' ranks have swelled due to an influx of young talent schooled abroad, but scarcity of feature work has led to local film-makers increasingly taking two national stations.

Currently only one to three feature films premiere yearly with two releases in 1990: **Paper Peter** and **Rust** (formerly *Baddi's Garage*).

Paper Peter is a children's film, the first made in ten years for the cinema here. Paper Peter is a life-size doll with a mind of his own and a versatile paper body to match. He was created by a respected children's author Herdis Egilsdóttir and debuted in a stage musical fifteen years ago. After featuring in books and shorts he appears on the silver screen in a film scripted and directed by seasoned Ari Kristinnsson. Ari has shot numerous Icelandic films including *White Whales*, *Magnus* and *Pastoral Life*. *Paper Peter* is his directing debut and was originally set to be an 8-part TV series, but the project was expanded to include theatrical release. The production company Hrif has made numerous TV programmes, including two *Paper Peter* shorts and is involved in the

upcoming film **Children of Nature**, with Ari once again behind the camera.

Rust is based on a popular stage play, *Baddi's Garage*, and features the Icelandic film debut of two film-makers who have found success abroad: Lárus Ýmir Óskarsson in Sweden and Sigurjón Sighvatson in Hollywood.

Producer Sigurjón Sighvatson became a household name in Iceland after the success of David Lynch's film *Wild at Heart* and the cult TV series *Twin Peaks* which were both inhouse projects at Propaganda Films, a company owned by Sigurjón and American partner Steve Golin in Hollywood.

Sighvatson left a promising musical career in Iceland for Hollywood in 1979 and five years later founded Propaganda Films with Golin. Their company has been remarkably successful in the commercial and music-video business and produces low-budget films regularly. Sigurjón and Golin have co-produced several feature films including *The Blue Iguana* and *Kill Me Again*.

Three Films Set for 1991

1991 has (at time of writing) yet to see a new film but three are set for year-end release: **Children of Nature** (*Börn náttúrannar*) is a down-to-earth fable about a farmer who gives up his farm for a retirement home. There he meets an elderly woman and together they decide to visit the place where they grew up. This is director Friðrik Þor Friðriksson's second feature after *White Whales* and the rock documentary *Rock in Reykjavík*.

Iceland, first-time film-maker Greenland

Scene from *Paper Peter*

and the Faeroe Islands in its second outing are collaborating on a three-part anthology film. Guðny Ragnarsdóttir (*Christianity under the Glacier*) directs the Icelandic part **Siggi and the Stallion**.

Much awaited, **The White Viking** is a $7 million epic, set in Iceland and Norway at the turn of the last millennium when religions clashed. A 7-hour television series (airing in 1992) and a feature film were shot simultaneously in a partnership between five Scandinavian TV-stations. Icelander and Viking-epic veteran Hrafn Gunnlaugson (*When the Raven Flies, Shadow of the Raven*) directs from an original script by himself and Englishman Jonathan Rumbold. The tale is fictitious but based on historical events and tells of the young lovers Askur and Embla brutally separated when King Olaf of Norway forced Christianity upon the pagan Vikings. To save his bride Askur must journey to Iceland as a Christian missionary.

Gains and Losses

The French and Icelandic governments signed a cultural exchange agreement when French President Mitterand visited Iceland. First project in the pipeline is a feature film by Kristín Jóhannesdóttir (**On Earth as in Heaven**). Kristín's script tells the story of a young peasant girl who in 1936 witnesses the legendary shipwreck of French research vessel "Pourquoi Pas" leaving a sole survivor. Kristín's controversial 1984 film, *Rainbow's End*, is still an object of heated debate.

1990 saw two important film projects officially discontinued. Hilmar Oddson's *Meffi* and Agúst Guðmundsson's Viking-epic, *The Hammer and the Cross*, have been shelved.

Against all odds young Icelandic filmmakers are turning to short films. Notable talents including Sigrún Harðardóttir whose 40-minute short **The Juniper Tree** won first prize at a women's festival in Montreal, Margarét Rún Guðmundsdóttir whose controversial **Stop Whining, Herman**, was made in Germany, Marteinn St. Þórsson, whose **Toy Soldiers** was the first novice film sold to national television, and Sigurbjörn Aðalsteinsson whose 5-minute **Dog Feelings** won at the No Budget Festival in Hamburg.

Ticket Sales Increase in Capital

Audiences that once flocked in tens of thousands to Icelandic films are decidedly less patriotic in recent times. They prefer to embrace American fare (see list), especially the teenage public. Local films have not benefited from the slight rise in cinema attendance,which had been declining for decades. *Paper Peter* performed tolerably with 18,000 admissions but *Rust* fell short of expectations with approximately 11,000 admissions. In the capital Reykjavík (pop. 100,000) six cinemas with a total of 19 screens showed 155 films to the tune of 1.2 million admissions in 1989. In 1990 the screen count reached all time high 23, when the University Theatre added four.

GISLI EINARSSON was born in Iceland in 1968, raised in Chicago, Paris, Copenhagen and Reykjavík. Star Wars made him a filmgoer, Blade Runner a devotee. He writes film criticism for the daily newspaper DV and will be studying psychology at the University of Iceland.

ICELANDIC FILMS

A survey of the Icelandic Cinema between 1979 and 1989 with excerpts from 24 films.

Available on VHS from:
THE ICELANDIC FILM FUND
Laugavegur 24, P.O.Box 320
121 Reykjavik, Iceland
Tel.: 354-1-623580
Telefax: 354-1-627171

Rust
(Ryö)

Script: Ólafur Haukur Símonarson, based on his play, *Baddi's Garage*. Director: Lárus Ýmir Óskarsson. Photography: Göran Nilsson. Music: Vim Mertens, Egill Ólafsson. Players: Bessi Bjarnason, Sigurður Sigurjónsson, Egill Ólafsson, Christine Carr, Stéfán Jónsson, Þórhallur Sigurðsson. Produced by Garage Films.

Rust is probably one of the best made Icelandic films, technically, that is. The story, however, leaves much to be desired. In a desolate auto-workshop a rather dysfunctional household is presided over by the dominating patriarch, Baddi. Suddenly an old friend shows up and the stage is set for a psychological game of chess, with a tragedy waiting in the wings.

Low on plot, the film aims for mood and subtlety but simply does not deliver what it promises. Stories about weird country families are fast becoming an Icelandic film

staple. Here the characters are not fleshed out and the story, while ironic at first becomes predictable. Themes explored are not brought to interesting (if any) conclusions. A handful of excellent actors, with Sigurður Sigurjónsson outstanding, have nowhere to to and enough time to get there. Their performances manage to keep the film together for quite a while. Production values, however, are seamless and film has a constant solid look, still too rare in Icelandic films.

Gísli Einarsson

Forthcoming Films

Börn náttúrunnar (Children of Nature). Script: Einar Már Guðmundsson, Friðrik Þór Friðrikson. Dir: Friðrik Þór. Phot: Ari Kristinnson. Players: Gísli Halldórsson, Sigriður Haglín, Egill Ólafsson, Tinna Gunnlaugsdóttir, Baldvin Halldórsson, Rúrik Haraldsson, Bruno Ganz). Prod: Max Film (Berlin) Metro Film (Oslo).
Hvíti Víkingurinn (The White Viking). Script: Hrafn Gunnlaugsson, Jonathan Rumbold. Dir: Hrafn. Phot: Tony Forsberg. Players: Maria Bonnevie, Gottskálkur D. Sigurðsson, Egill Ólafsson, Þorsteinn Hannesson, Helgi Skúlason. Prod: Filmeffekt A/s, Norway.
Siggi og folinn (Siggi and the Stallion). Script: Guðný Halldórsdóttir. Dir: Kristín Pálsdóttir. Prod: Thumall.
A jörðu svo sem á himni (On Earth as in Heaven). Script and Dir: Kristín Jóhannesdóttir.
Ingaló á grænum sjó (Ingaló at Sea). Script and Dir: Asdís Thoroddsen.
Jólatréð okkar (Our Christmas Trees). Script and Dir: Sigurður Örn Brynjólfsson. *Animated.*
Sodoma, Reykjavik. Script and Dir: Óskar Jónsson.
Birds of Paradise. Script: Lars Bill Lundholm. Dir: Lárus Ýmir Óskarsson. Prod: Sigurjón Sighvatson.
Fjalla Eyvindur and Halla. Script: Lárus Ýmir Óskarsson & Þórunn Valdimarsdóttir. Dir: Lárus Ýmir. Prod: Sigurjón Sighvatson.
King Jörundur. Script: Ragnar Arnalds. Dir: Guðný Halldórsdóttir. Prod: Halldór Thorgersson.

Egill Ólafsson and Christine Carr in *Rust*

Useful Addresses

The Icelandic Film Fund
Chairman: Ragnar Arnalds
Director: Thorsteinn Jónsson
Laugavegur 24
121 Reykjavík
Tel: (1) 623580
Fax: (1) 623068

The Association of Icelandic Film Producers
Chairman: Ágúst Gudmundsson
Laugavegur 120
P.O. Box 7103
107 Reykjavík

Icelandic Film Sales
Hafnarstraeti 19
101 Reykjavík
Tel: (1) 17270

Association of Film Distributors in Iceland
Chairman: Fridbert Pálsson
Háskólabíó
Hagatorg
107 Reykjavík
Tel: (1) 611212
Fax: (1) 27135

The Icelandic Film-Makers' Association
Chairman: Eiríkur Thorsteinsson
Laugavegur 24
P.O. Box 320
121 Reykjavík

The Ministry of Culture and Education
Hverfisgötu 4–6
101 Reykjavík
Tel: (1) 25000
Fax: (1) 623068

INDIA

by Uma da Cunha

1990–91 was a climactic time for India, with the tragedy of Rajiv Gandhi, tumultuous mid-year elections, and the *rupee's* sharp devaluation. Cinema could not fail to be affected. The art cinema stoically faced the most serious setbacks of its precarious existence. The mainstream cinema is alive and possibly well, despite the blows and arrows.

Living up to its India-rubber reputation, the industry bounced back and made more films in 1990 than it has since 1940, the year films were first censored. Of feature films, **948** were made, an astonishing increase of 167 films over the previous year. The production boom persists unabated.

Hindi films maintained second position with 200 films as against 148 the previous year. South Indian languages dominated with Telugu leading: 204 films (96 the previous year); Tamil 194 films (152); Malayalam 126 (75), Kannada 81 (50), Bengali 50 (9 films the previous year, a marked increase), Gujarati 14 (30 the previous year – the decrease caused mainly by constant curfews and local unrest, Marathi 25 (13), Oriya 13 (2), Punjabi 7 (4), Assamese 8 (10), Bhojpuri 5 (none made the previous year), Manipuri 2 (3), English 4 (7), Rajasthani 5 (1), Tulu 1, Urdu 4 (none the previous year). Indian Languages used in films rose to 36 and other language remakes of an original hit continued to be a safe bet – with South Indian films more often in the lead.

One plausible explanation for the sharp production rise is the injection of new money and the seduction of big profits. Cash is being siphoned into movies mainly by the new-rich trader in India and abroad.

The trader, unlike the former (often suspect) financiers, has an unequalled grasp of business opportunities. The younger scions of established families or new entrants are coping better with swiftly modernising technology and high risk financing that films need today.

Teenage Starlet Boom

The current formula for script and production aims at quick returns at lower risk and cost. Star power (with its crippling effect on a film's budget) is being replaced by "new face", teenaged lead pairs. The storyline concentrates on young lovers overcoming family opposition and dated taboos.

The film that triggered the change, Sooraj Bharjatiya's **I Fell in Love** (*Maine Pyar Kiya*), cautiously made and cleverly distributed, has remained on top for the third year. It is being continuously re-released in new, improved fashion. Its music sells beyond all belief as audio cassettes. Its stars are hot property. The male lead, Salman Khan, is rated today as second to Amitabh Bachchan. The female lead, Bhagyashree, who retired into matrimony is staging a comeback with her husband attempting to co-star. The box-office hit of the first half of 1991, **Betrayal** (*Sanam Bewafa*), stars Salman Khan again in a tear-strewn story of young lovers separated by warring clans.

Another surprise hit was **Young Love** (*Ashiqui*), made by Mahesh Bhatt, the undaunted propagator of urbane movie *masala*. The film is about a divorced mother, her pop-singer son, his orphan girlfriend (turned fashion model). and those who oppose their union. The film catapulted its young hero

Pakistani actress Zeba Bhaktiar and Indian actor Rza Murad in Randhir Kapoor's *Henna*

Rahul Roy into stardom. The course of true love has never run so profitably.

Finally, the real magic in the 1990's movie lies in its lyrics and songs. If the songs click, the movie sings. Not surprisingly, spin-offs stemming from the music and the open-sesame marvels being unfolded by the video and cable market, make movies a worthwhile investment. Example: the Amitabh Bachchan starrer **Hum** had a runaway hit song called "Joomma Chumma." So hummable was this song that Amitabh Bachchan mounted a live stage show around it to a capacity audience at London's Wembley Stadium, taped the show and blew it up to 35mm and released it theatrically in India and elsewhere.

Conclusion: musical chairs, with attached cash registers, is India's latest movie game.

The audio- and videocassettes of a film are a huge side business. 75% of the annual overall audio cassette market of 217 million cassettes concerns film music, which sells at 10,000 a day. Seven thousand video-cassettes of Kapoor's **Henna** (the film Raj Kapoor was working on when he died) were sold in Pakistan in the first week of its release. **Henna** registered a successful opening run in India on release in mid-1991. The film is a breakthrough in that it bonds the two countries romatically in its narrative, and has as its lovely heroine the Pakistani actress Zeba Bhaktiar.

Scope for Spin-offs

With over 30 million TV sets, 10 million VCR's, 4 million homes linked by cable, and satellite dishes open to the sky, the scope for spin-offs is enormous. India has an estimated 25,000 dish antennae. Although cable has only 5.5% of the 90 million TV viewers, the percentage is increasing – and advertising revenue is being diverted towards it.

Cable may soon sideline Doordarshan, India's sole and government-run TV network. When Doordarshan was noncommittal about showing Ramanand Sagar's video series *Krishna*, Shemaroo, a leading video company, decided to release the series on a profit-sharing basis and cable has grabbed it. Predictably, a fierce battle is on over segregating cable and video rights.

Cable TV is all set. CNN and SKY Channel have already entered Indian homes in major metro towns. Towards end-1991, BBC Television World Service and Hutchisons, in Hong Kong, will add to all-day home viewing. Already, videocassette magazines are multiplying, providing all manner of news, information and specialised items.

The art cinema is in deep trouble. Entertainment from video, cable and TV is luring viewers and directors away. A chronic lack of finance and distribution is sapping its roots. Festival show-casing and foreign recognition is on the wane. No Indian film has competed in Cannes and Berlin in recent years. India's festival entries rarely make the critical impact they used to.

On home ground, art films generate little excitement. One-time TV screening, often the only opportunity of financial return, gets low ratings. Video shops tend to bypass them. Cable too will give them short shrift. Their future has never seemed less promising.

The final blow came during the 1990 National Awards – the highest honour bestowed by government on cinematic achievement. The awards carry prestige, cash prizes and distribution aids that are a tremendous cachet and attraction. This year the awards swung sharply in favour of big names and big-budget films. The move was seen by the art cinema as a political attempt at downgrading it.

Hemen Choudhury in Jahnu Barua's *Firingoti*

To save the situation, film-makers banded together all over the country to form "The Forum for Better Cinema" with centres in Bombay (headed by Shyam Benegal), Calcutta and Thiruvananthapuram (Kerala). The Forum began in earnest to evolve practical ways by which its films could seek a wider following, opportunities for commercial distribution and, above, all, a supportive government. The Forum also aimed at ties abroad for festival publicity and export opportunities.

1991 promises more cinema of quality than the previous year. Satyajit Ray's new film **Family Reunion** (*Sakha Prasanka*) was telecast on May 2, his seventieth birthday. K. Bikram Singh's finely detailed academic study **Satyajit Ray Perspectives** was also telecast at this time. The film has been invited to the Sydney, Montréal and Leipzig festivals and has been purchased by Japanese television.

By June, Ray had already completed his latest feature **The Visitor** (*Agantuk*), scheduled for a special screening in Venice. His son Sandip Ray is steadily branching out on his own. His next feature, **Target**, will commence soon with Ray writing the music. Gautam Ghose is at work on his new feature, **Boatman of River Padma**, set in Bengal and Bangladesh. Budhadeb Dasgupta, Nabyendu Chowdhury and Utpalendu Chakravarty are busy completing their new features.

Benegal Back at the Helm
In Bombay, Shyam Benegal is back at work on feature films. He has two films on hand, one of them marking his first feature to be financed by NFDC. Ketan Mehta has embarked on an ambitious version of **Madame Bovary**, undaunted at learning that he follows hard upon Chabrol, Schlöndorff and a recent Russian filmed version of the same novel. Jahnu Barua's new film **The Sparks** (*Phiringoti*) is being edited. G.V. Iyer has launched his second Sanskrit epic, **Bhagwat Gita**. Pradip Kishen's **Electric Moon**, funded by Channel Four, will be ready by September. Much depends on its success if Channel Four is to extend its support of English-language films made in India.

Among recently completed films, Sai Paranjpe's **The Uprooted** (*Disha*) will compete in Montréal festival and Narsing Rao's **Men of Clay** (*Mati Manishulu*) in Moscow. The first film **A Rare Solution** (*Adi Mimansulu*) by noted cameraman A.K. Bir in the Oriya language has elicited high praise. Kerala now has to cope with the tragic loss of two major film-makers, Aravindan and Padmarajan, both felled by a heart-attack.

Earlier tentative moves at private funding have virtually disappeared. NFDC, Doordarshan and local State grants, individually or as co-producers, are the means available for financing the Indian-language art film. But distribution and exhibition remain root problems that are not being tackled decisively.

NFDC has released two of its films in major Bombay theatres, Govind Nihalani's **Drishti** and Kumar Shahani's **Kasbah**. This initiative banks on star value. Dimple Kapadia and Shekhar Kapoor star in the former, and Shatrughan Sinha in the latter. Ironically, the art cinema is turning to stars, when the mainstream is turning away from them.

A hopeful move by NFDC involves agreements in which the British Film Institute will receive Indian feature films for release and the Museum of Modern Art in New York will get over a dozen Indian films for non-commercial circulation.

In 1990, foreign imports numbered 118, of which 77 were imported from the USA, with *Pretty Woman* an outstanding hit. Foreign films shot in India included Roland Joffé's *City of Joy* which battled through many shooting problems, delays and controversy before it finally got done. A smaller effort was an Italian TV serial *The Mysteries of the Dark Jungle* starring Kabir Bedi and directed by Kevin Conner.

Actor Victor Bannerji, the first star to enter politics from Bengal – joined the election battle – and lost. Ex-star Rajesh Khanna fought a pitched war with a political tiger in Delhi – and almost won.

In the South, ex-movie star Jayalalitha won hands down and is now Chief Minister of Tamil Nadu State. At least in this sense, the stars seem to be favouring us.

New and Forthcoming films

Agantuk (The Visitor). Lang: Bengali. Story, Script, Music, Direction: Satyajit Ray. Phot: Barun Raha. Players: Utpal Dutt, Deepankar De, Mamata Shankar, Bikrim Bhattacharya, Dhritiman Chatterji, Rabi Ghosh. Prod: NFDC. *Anila lives with her husband Sudhendra Brose and her young son Satyaki in Calcutta. Out of the blue, an uncle of whom she has no memory invites himself to their house. He is Manomohan Mitra, who had left India in his teens and has returned after being away 35 years. In his week-long stay as their guest, he reveals his beliefs, his philosophy, his attitude to life spent largely with Indian tribes in America. Whether he is the uncle remains a mystery until the very end.* **Mahaprithivi (World Within, World Without)** Lang: Bengali. Script and Dir: Mrinal Sen. Story: Anjan Dutt. Phot: Shashi Anand. Music: B.V. Karanth/Chandan Roy Chowdhury. Players: Soumitra Chatterjee, Victor Bannerjee, Anjan Dutt, Abhijeet Mukherjee, Aparna Sen, Gita Sen. Prod: G.G. Films (P) Ltd. *It is four* *days prior to the historic German unification. In a Calcutta backstreet, the body of an old woman is found hanging inside a locked room. Her bereaved family delve into her diary to seek reasons for her suicide – and are led to events that, coincidentally, take place four days later.*

Suraj ka Satva Ghoda (Seventh Horse of the Sun's Chariot). Lang: Hindi. Script: Shama Zaidi. Story: Dr Dharamvir Gharati. Dir: Shyam Benegal. Phot: Jehangir Chowdhury. Music: Vanraj Bhatia. Players: Newcomers in the process of being selected. Prod: NFDC. *A comedy that attempts to define adolescent love through a series of romantic episodes, which in each case-study, takes its own course leading to an examination of something completely different.*

Untitled. Lang: Hindi. Script: Shama Zaidi, Sunil Shanbagh. Dir: Shyam Benegal. Phot: V.K. Murthy. Music: Vanraj Bhatia. Players: Kulbushan Kharbandha, Om Puri, Shabana Azmi. Prod: Funded by individual contributions from a fishermen's co-operative. *Based on the exemplary work of Pandurang Sastri over the past 35 years, in which a farming village and a fishing village are in a continuum of transformation using self-esteem and self-worth, and not necessarily self-interest. as the instruments to wield social change. In accordance with a favourite Benegal practice, the film's title will be selected as it nears completion through an open competition among the production team.*

Maya Memsahib. Lang: Hindi. Script: Ketan Mehta Sudarshan Yashish Chandra, adapted from Flaubert's Madame Bovary. Dir: Ketah Mehta. Phot: Anoop. Music Ravi Mageshkar. Lyrics: Gulzar. Players: Deepa Sahi, Raj Babbar, Farrouque Shaikh, Paresh Rawal, Om Puri. Prod: NFDC/Channel Four. *A structural investigation flitting between the past and the present of a happening, which in turn becomes an investigation into the mind of a lady named Maya.*

Tahader Katha (Their Story). Script and Dir: Buddhadeb Dasgupta. Story: Kamal Mazumdar. Lead Player: Soumitra Chatterjee. *A study of a middle-aged man who nurtures a dream, a vision of a new, just and genuinely free India. The man becomes an object of ridicule and suspicion, till eventually, he is consigned to a mental institution.*

Aadi Mimansa (A Rare Solution). Lang: Oriya/Hindi. Script, Phot and Dir: A.K. Bir. Music: Bhavdeet Jaipurwali. Players: Lalatendu Rath, Mohan Gokhale, Neena Gupta, Bijainee Misra, Gloria Mahanty. Prod: NFDC. *This first film by leading cameraman A.K. Bir deals with a Hindi-speaking Brahmin family (headed by Aarakhit Acharya) and a non-Brahmin Oriya family (headed by Kshetrapal Das) living as close-knit, cordial neighbours in a divided house in Orissa. Their common well is located in one half, while an open drainway leads from one half and out the other. Idle talk stressing the superiority of one caste makes the open drain a focus of discontent. An almost irreparable feud breaks out between the two families.*

Dharavi (Island). Lang: Hindi. Dir: Sudhir Mishra. Phot: Rajesh Joshi. Players: Om Puri, Shabana Azmi, Raghubir Yadhav, Virendra Saxena. Prod: NFDC/Doordarshan. *"Dharavi" is the largest slum in Asia. The film follows the lives of a family who came to Bombay to make money. They find themselves hounded by the dehumanising process concomitant with slum life.*

Naseem (The Morning Breeze). Lang: Urdu. Dir and Story: Saeed Akhtar Mirza. Script: Saeed Akhtar Mirza/Ashok Misra. Phot: Viorendra Saini. Music: Sharang Dev. Leading Players: to be decided. Prod: NFDC-Doordarshan. *This film, like Mirza's films to date, is preoccupied with the reality of today in Bombay. A sixteen-year-old Muslim girl tries to live like a typical teenager but her religious and cultural milieu will not permit it. Though she sees a more gracious and liberal past through the eyes of her grandfather, she herself becomes a tragedy of the history that he represents. The film is set in Bombay with brief flashbacks of a past lived in Agra.*

Target. Lang: Hindi. Script and Dir: Sandip Ray. Story: Prafulla Roy. Music: Satyajit Ray. Phot: Barun Raha. Players: Shabana Azmi, Om Puri, Mohan Agashe. Prod: NFDC/Doordarshan. *The film deals with bonded labour and untouchability, tinged with a little romance and intrigue.*

Bhagwat Gita. Lang: Sanskrit. Script and Dir: G.V. Iyer. Phot: Madhu Ambat. Music: Dr. Balamurali Krishna. Players: Gopi Manohar, G.V. Ragavendra, Prof. Govinda Rao, Neena Gupta. Prod: NFDC. *The director's second film in the ancient classical language of Sanskrit. The first was his celebrated Adi Shankaracharya. The film will interpret the philosophical contents of the Gita while making the narrative theme and its beliefs relevant to our times.*

Prasab (Deliverance). Bengali language. Script, Music and Dir: Utpalendu Chakravarty. Phot: Pantu Nag. Players: Srila Mazumdar, Arjun Chakraborty, Goutam Chakraborty, Satarupa Sanyal, Subroto Chatterjee. Prod: Srijan. *Political activists Samiran and his wife Pritha are arrested, and in jail Pritha gives birth to a son. Samiran is sentenced to life imprisonment. Pritha and son are given shelter by Samiran's friend Amal, who in time falls in love with her. Samiran advises Pritha to marry Amal since his future is bleak. Pritha decides on her own to leave Amal. When Samiran is released under a new political regime, his search for Pritha and his realisation of social change comes full circle.*

Padama Nadir Manjhi (Boatman of River Padma). Lang: Bengali. Script, Phot, Music, Dir: Gautam Ghose. Story: Manik Bannerji. Players: Utpal Dutt, Mamata Shankar, Humayun Faridi. Prod: Govt. of West Bengal/Govt. of Bangladesh. *The film is about a fisherman's quest to fulfil his impossible dream.*

Vasthuhara (The Dispossessed). Script and Dir: G. Aravindan. Story: C.V. Sreeraman. Phot: Sunny Joseph. Music: Salil Chowdhury. Players: Mohanlal, Neelanjona Mitra, Neena Gupta, Padmini, Shobhana. Prod. Ravindranath. *A story with political analogies which examines physical and emotional displacement. The narrative switches from Kerala to Calcutta and briefly, the Andaman Islands. This was Aravindan's last feature film before his untimely death.*

Aparna Sen in Mrinal Sen's *Mahaprithivi*

UMA DA CUNHA is based in Bombay and has acted in a promotional and executive capacity on several Indian films.

INDONESIA

by Frank Segers

Set against a backdrop of an overheated national economy with an overburdened infrastructure trying to catch up, Indonesian cinema over the last year has taken several interesting turns both on the commercial and artistic fronts. Commercially, Indonesia is becoming ever more attractive to the U.S. film majors still facing formidable market barriers and rampant video piracy. Artistically, the best of Indonesia cinema is attracting relatively new world attention thanks to government efforts working with private business interests.

In terms of film content in 1990, the usual mix of action–adventure, light drama and comedy ruled the screens. The big attractions are the ever-popular siren, Meriam Bellina, and actor Rano Karno, recipients of best acting Citra awards at the Indonesia Film Festival, held each year since 1973 in a different provincial capital, allowing local audiences to pay homage to the stars. They received yet another opportunity to view all of Bellina's charms in late August, 1991, with the release of **I Love You** (*Saat Kukatakan*), an out-and-out weepie, another genre popular with audiences.

As the nation tries to modernise roads

and telephone lines – the latter are very spotty in Indonesia even in the capital Jakarta – so too are theatre owners making an effort to spruce things up. More and more theatres are being built or renovated. Multiplexing, still in its infancy, is a trend. With a population of 182.6-million, making Indonesia the world's fifth largest country in that category, it finds itself vastly underscreened with some 2,300 cinemas (about 10% in Jakarta) serving an archipelago nation of 13,000 islands spanning more than 5,000 km from West to East. Video has filled the breach to some degree, with titles too often reaching far-flung markets in pirated forms. The American majors through the Motion Picture Export Assn. of America have put pressure on General Suharto's government to crack down. The video piracy situation is still bad, but the government is finally taking action.

Indonesia is one of the most economically stable countries in Asia's southern tier; the 1989–90 growth rate registered a healthy 6.7% advance, higher than originally projected. This performance has not been lost on either the U.S.A., which is trying to penetrate the market, nor Japan. Indonesia's biggest trade partner, Japan received nearly half of Indonesia's total exports in 1989. Just before the Gulf War, Japan sent a film delegation to Jakarta trying to drum up future film trade.

Major Event in New York
Indonesia has been doing a bit of foreign tubthumping itself. A "Cinema of Indonesia" event was staged in late April and early May at two venues in New York City, one the Museum of Modern Art. For a national cinema that has barely obtained notice on the world scene – it wasn't until 1989 that Indonesia's first feature was selected for showing at the Cannes Film Festival – the bifurcated event was truly remarkable. A total of 15 features was screened including director Eros Djarot's highly regarded 1988 outing, **Woman of Courage** (*Tjoet Nja' Dhien*), starring Indonesia's most accomplished actress, Christine Hakim, as an ageing, near-blind freedom fighter battling the Dutch at the turn of the century in the jungles of Sumatra, and actor Slamet (*continued on page 186*)

IRAN

by Jamal Omid

Midway through 1991, evidence points to high dividends for government policy in terms of the cultural aspects and structural growth of the cinema in Iran. However, the 1990 forecasts of an impending crisis in the film industry are turning into a disconcerting reality.

Official policy-makers concede that good box-office receipts for only 20% of last year's productions are hardly enough to guarantee or stabilise a sound economic trend. Consequently they are searching for practical ways of effecting a balance between cultural and economic priorities in Iranian cinema. By now the Iranian cinema has gained reasonable international status, and the majority of reputable festivals include Iranian entries. Only last year 230 Iranian pictures were screened at 78 festivals, while many other invitations could not be complied with.

Apart from attempts to enhance the cultural side of the production process, and improving movie theatres themselves, the

Still from Varuzh Karim-Masihi's *The Last Act*

photo: Mitra Mahasseni

authorities have been trying since last year to revise some of their policies and procedures, and to create a certain economic balance by various means such as increasing ticket prices.

But the continual increase in production costs have made it difficult and almost impossible to reach any simple, quick and practicable solutions to the crisis. The problem is compounded by the fact that economic trends are leading to the imposition of a higher official rate of foreign exchange (which had been kept considerably lower than the unofficial free market rate as a means of subsidising key industries). For the film industry that will mean an almost ten-fold increase in the cost of imported items such as raw stock and equipment and an inevitable crisis.

It would seem that a crash programme is needed to avert the full paralysing effect of this situation. For one thing, the creative powers of professional film-makers in the private sector should be given freer rein by the abolitions of the screenplay and screening commissions and with the objective of fostering belief in a healthy atmosphere of mutual understandings. This would have an enormous effect on creating incentives for artists and technicians to tap their resources of creativity in bringing about a new wave of artistic dynamism in the film industry, even if it means that the authorities will have to condone a degree of commercialism.

The preservation of the traditional cultural values, however, which have brought about for the Iranian cinema its present world recognition and esteem, is as important today as it was before. At the same time the import and screening of foreign films which represent the same kind of values in a recreational format, in addition to the

Promoting Iranian Cinema All Over The World

PRODUCTION, PROMOTION, IMPORT, EXPORT, DISTRIBUTION, CO-PRODUCTION,

AND MUCH MORE....

 Farabi Cinema Foundation

NO. 55 SIE-TIR AVE. TEHRAN 11358/I.R. IRAN
TELEX: 214283FCF TEL 671010/678156
FAX. 678155

import of serious and artistic works, would do a great deal to promote movie attendance among the Iranian public. And finally, new sources of revenue for Iranian productions must be created. On the local level this would mean the construction of new theatres in different parts of the country according to population density. Such a programme, together with the legal and official measures which the authorities could take to curb the inflation, would enable the film industry to weather the present crisis.

Entertaining and Thoughtful
In spite of the economic difficulties, the Iranian productions of the preceding year – presented at the 9th Fajr International Film Festival – proved that the local industry continues to produce entertaining and thoughtful works of art, dealing with a refreshing variety of themes. As many as 17 films were first works, and these young directors reaped a majority of the prizes at the Fajr Festival in February 1991.

Twenty-nine films are now in production and buffs are looking forward, with great optimism, to see more novel ideas and themes treated in more artistically accomplished pictures at next February's event. In the meanwhile, it is to be hoped that the government's new policies will become effective in controlling the economic crisis, and ensuring the preservation of the prestige and esteem the Iranian cinema has gained abroad.

Varuzh Karim Masihi

Recent Films

The Last Act. Script and Dir: Varuzh Karim-Masihi. Phot: Asghar Rafi'ie Jam. Editing: V. Karim-Masihi. Music: Babak Bayat. Players: Farimah Farjami, Dariush Arjomand, Jamshid Hashempoor, Saeed Poorsamimi. Prod: Cadre Film.
The Last Act promises the emergence of a new talent in Iranian cinema. In his first feature, Varuzh

Karim-Masihi shows that, except in rare moments, he is in total command of his medium in recounting a tale of the disintegration of an aristocratic family. A brother and sister, whose family wealth has been inherited by a woman, hire a group of itinerant players to stage a macabre scenario to frighten the heiress out of her wits. The Last Act reaped the greatest number of awards at the 9th Fajr International Film Festival and introduced its creator as a new director of great promise in Iranian cinema.
The Bride. Script: Alireza Davudnezhad, B. Afkhami. Dir: Behruz Afkhami. Phot: Nemet Haghighi. Editing: M. R. Moini. Music: Babak Bayat. Players: Abolfazl Poorarab, Niki Karimi, Abbas Amiri, Roghayeh Chehrehazad. Prod: Mahab Film.
This is another debut feature by a young director who is undoubtedly among the most promising discoveries of 1991. Working on the basis of a rather familiar story line (a newly-wed couple encounter an unexpected incident, argue, and separate), Behruz Afkhami has created a well-structured, suspenseful picture with the ease and assurance of an experienced professional.
Shadow of Imagination. Script: Masud Jafari Jozani. Dir: Hossien Dalir. Phot: Homayun Pievar. Editing: Davud Yusefian. Music: Freydun Shahbazian. Players: Ezzatollah Entezami, Hamid Jebeli, Hossein Panahi, Jalal Moghaddam. Prod: Simia Film.
Hossein Dalir's first directorial venture is a comedy of social interactions which presents the efforts of a

TOP TEN GROSSING FILMS IN IRAN: 1990

	Rentals ($U.S.)
Courtship	597,000
Dolls' Thief	583,000
Mother	434,000
Hamoon	224,500
Patal	307,000
Savalan	290,000
Last Flight	225,500
Fifth of June Flight	224,000
Death of the Leopard	213,000
Kakoli	210,000

young provincial writer trying to find a place among the Capital's intellectuals. Contrasting the world of imagination with the exigencies of daily life, the film runs the gamut of love, mysticism and sociology, and could actually have been a much more successful work, if it had managed to effect a smooth passage through such a very complex synthesis.

Time of Love. Script and Dir: Mohsen Makhmalbaf. Phot: Mahmud Kalari. Editing: M. Makhmalbaf. Players: Shiva Gerde, Abdorahman Yalmai, Aken Tunc, Khosroshahi. Prod: Khaneh Film Sabz.

Mohsen Makhmalbaf's last picture created a great controversy among those critics who liked the film and those who didn't. Makhmalbaf, who is much more prolific as a writer than as a director, has very personal views on philosophy and social psychology, and the new outlook he presents in each of his films always provoke conflicting responses. With this fresh look at the subject of love, he has once again set off a seemingly interminable chain of arguments.

Apartment No. 13. Script and Dir: Yadollah Samadi. Phot: Hassan Gholizadeh. Editing: Hossein Zandbaf. Music: Farhad Fakharddini. Players: Alireza Khamseh, Jamshid Esmaikhani, Naser Laghai, Sirus Ghorjestani. Prod: Y. Samadi.

With his special gift for situation comedy, and his unique satiric approach, Yadollah Samadi presents here an interesting collection of social types, inhabitants in an apartment complex which serves as a metaphor for the larger community. His critical examination of the idiosyncracies and behaviour pat-

terns of the lodgers highlights some hilariously absurd situations.

The Sergeant. Dir: Masud Kimia'ie. Script: Kambuzia Partovi, M. Kimia'ie. Phot: Mahmud Kalari. Editing: M. Kimia'ie. Music: Giti Pashai. Players: Ahmad Najafi, Golchehreh Sajjadieh, Saeed Pirdoost. Prod: A. Najafi (Cadre Film).

Masud Kimia'ie, whose previous film The Snake Fang aroused great public and critical interest as a competition entry at 1991 Berlin Festival, has always been telling tales of human loneliness, and of people suffering in forgotten corners of life. In his latest picture Kimia'ie is engrossed with the struggles of a former army sergeant to retrieve his piece of land from a local tyrant. The other dominating figure in the film is the sergeant's wife who is preparing to send her ailing mother (a Russian émigré) back to the Soviet Union after the opening of the frontiers. The film's bitter and despairing tone is relieved only by the presence of the sergeant's son, a ray of hope for the future.

Two Features with One Ticket. Script and Dir: Dariush Farhang. Phot: Alireza Zarrindast. Editing: Abbas Ganjavi. Music: Babak Bayat. Players: Mehdi Hashemi, D. Farhang, Afsaneh Bayegan, Atila Yasayai, Shahla Riahi. Prod: Farhang, Moayeri and Iranian Centre for Film Industry Services.

In his second feature (after The Spell) Dariush Farhang exhibits, in the overall structure and the content, his fascination and preoccupation with the medium of film. While The Spell was partly inspired by Edgar Allan Poe and Roger Corman, Two

Still from Dariyoush Farhang's *Two Features with One Ticket*

Features with one Ticket (which focusses on the problems of a director making his debut film) is an overt tribute to François Truffaut's Day for Night, and is on the whole a successful experiment.

In the Alleys of Love. Dir: Khosro Sinai. Script: group work. Phot: Ali Loghmani. Editing: K. Sinai, A. Loghmani. Music: K. Sinai. Players: Mehdi Ahmadi, Behnaz Rudani, Ali Galehdari, Reza Pezhuhi. Prod: Centre for Development of Experimental Film-Making.

The Iranian "official selection" at the 1991 Cannes Film Festival is an unusual blend of narrative and documentary cinema. A young Abadani returns to his home town after the war, and wanders through the deserted streets reminiscing about his childhood days and friends. The film presents a charming and beautiful synthesis of the reality of the present day with dreams and fantasies of the past in a harmonious and unified overall structure.

Glass Eye. Script and Dir: Hossien Ghasemi Jami. Phot: Mohsen Zolanvar. Players: Alireza Es'haghi, Javad Hashemi, Asghar Nagizadeh.

Love and Death. Script and Dir: Mohammad Reza Alami. Phot: Ahmad Reza Panahi, Hassan Etemadi. Players: Jamshid Hashempoor, Changiz Vosughi, Soraya Gol-Mohammadi.

Lucifer. Script and Dir: Ahmad-Reza Darvish. Phot: Turaj Mansuri. Players: Khosro Shakibai, Esmail Soltanian, Hadi Marzban.

On the Altar of Love. Script and Dir: Kamal Tabrizi. Photo: Mohammad Reza Sharifi. Players: Mahmud Bigham, Amir Yazdani, Hossein Yari.

The Bride of Halabcheh. Dir: Hassan Karbakhsh. Script: Mehdi Calhor. Phot: Alireza Zarrindast. Players: Parivash Nazarieh, Valiyollah Momeni, Atash Taghipoor.

Nights on Zayandeh Rud. Script and Dir: Mohsen Makhmalbaf. Phot: Alireza Zarrindast. Players: Manuchehr Esmaili, Mozhgan Naderi, Mehrdad Farid.

Chasing the Shadows. Dir: Ali Shah-Hatami. Script: Reza Mottaghian. Phot: Mohammad Darmanesh. Players: Jafar Dehghan, Gholamreza Akbari, Javad Hashemi.

The Dream of Marriage. Script: A. Hashemi,

Still from *In the Alleys of Love*

Freydun Jeirani. Dir: Asghar Hashemi. Phot: Gholamreza Azadi. Players: Mehdi Fathi, Bizhan Emkanian. Akbar Abdi.

Fire under Ashes. Script and Dir: Habib Kavosh. Phot: Bergruni Mardiros Baghusian. Players: Adib Ghadoreh, Ali Akbar Bahadori, Donya Jamalpoor.

Galan. Script and Dir: Amir Ghavidel. Phot: Jamshid Alvandi. Players: Behzad Javanbakhsh, Jamshid Mashayekhi, Fatemeh Noori, Jalal Moghadam.

Gozal. Script and Dir: Mohammad Ali Sajjadi. Phot: Alireza Zarrindast. Players: Mehdi Miami Firuz Behjat-Mohammadi, Pardis Afkari.

The Possessed. Script and Dir: Rasul Mollagholipoor. Phot: Azim Javanruh. Players: Masud Kramati, Parastu Golestani, Reza Khandan.

Renault, Tehran 29. Script: Khosro Dehghan. Dir: Siamak Shayeghi. Phot: Mohsen Zolanvar. Players: Farzaneh Kaboli, Hossein Sarshar, Parviz Poorhosseini.

Search in the Island. Script: M. Sabbaghzadeh, Asghar Abdollahi. Dir: Mehdi Sabbaghzadeh. Phot: Hassan Gholizadeh. Players:

Khosro Shakibai, Mohammad-Ali Keshavarz, Hassan Rezai, Fariba Kosari.

As Clouds in Spring. Script: S. Amirsoleimani, Mohammad Rahmanian. Dir: Saeed Amirsoleimani. Phot: Dariush Ayari. Players: Saeed Rad, Jamshid Mashayekhi, Kamand Amirsoleimaini, Farzaneh Kaboli.

The Extraordinary Journey. Script: A. Davudi, Iraj Karimi. Dir: Abolhassan Davudi. Phot: Maziar Partov. Players: Akbar Abdi, Azita Hajian, Mohammad Sheikhzadeh.

For Everything. Script and Dir: Rajab Mohammadin. Phot: Ata-Ollah Hayati. Players: Elisa Johari, Granaz Musavi, Belghis Rabihavi.

The Legend of Ah. Script and Dir: Tahmineh Milani. Phot: Reza Banki. Players: Jahangir Almasi, Mahshid Afsharzadeh, Yarta Yaran.

The Story of That Happy Man. Script and Dir: Reza Heidarnezhad. Phot: Hassan Puya. Players: Mahmud Jafari, Fathali Oveisi, Niku Kharadmand.

Silence. Script: A.S. Hosseini, Javad Kahnamui. Dir: Ali Sajjadi Hosseini. Phot: Alireza Taghikhani. Players: Naser Hashemi, Javad Hashemi, Gholamreza Framarzian.

You Whom I Did Not Know. Script and Dir: Mohammad Ebrahim Soltanifar. Phot: Sfandiar Shahidi, Nemat Haghighi, Hassan Soltani. Players: Saeed Soltanifar, Hassan Salem, Mahsa Karimi.

The Call of the Sea. Script and Dir: Rahman Rezai. Phot: Bahman Zanuzi. Players: Ahmad Eshraghi, Mohammad Poorhassan, Akram Mohammadi.

City of Ashes. Script and Dir: Hassan Hedayat. Phot: Hassan Puya. Players: Majid Mozaffari, Mehnaz Ansarian, Ali Shoaie.

The Herald. Script: Alaedin Rahimi, Masumeh Taghipoor. Dir: Samuel Khachikian. Phot: Jamshid Alvandi. Players: Parviz Poorhossieni, Hossien Yaryar, Nersi Gorgia.

Producers/ Distributors

Tehran Group of United Cinemas
Barbad Alley
Lalehzar Street
Tehran.
Tel: 314795

Hedayat Film
25 Loghman Adham Street
Jomhuri Junction
Vali-e Asr Ave.
Tehran.
Tel: 3851962

**Laleh Film Production and
Distribution Co-operative**
72 Lalehzar Street
Tehran.
Tel: 3852954

Iran Film Co-operative
7th of Tir Sq.
Tehran.
Tel: 824432

Novin Film
15 Jomhuri Ave.
Tehran.
Tel: 6403697

Khaneh Film Iran
Tavakol Building
Jomhuri Ave.
Tehran.
Tel: 671247

Arman Film
26 Razi Street
Jomhuri Ave.
Tehran.
Tel: 675418

**Iranmilad Film Production
and Distribution**
186 Shiraz Street
Bahar Ave.
Tehran.
Tel: 755674

Roshan Film
97 Arbab Jamshid Alley
Kushk Street
Tehran.
Tel: 3852975

Film-Makers' Co-operative
No. 7, Ghaffari Alley,
Bahar Mastian St.
7th of Tir Sq.

Tehran
Tel: 830676

Sepahan Cinema Company
126 Razi Street
Jomhuri Ave.
Tehran.
Tel: 676268

Mahab Film
No. 91, 7th of Tir Sq.
Tehran.
Tel: 837547 – 4408635

**Milad Film Production and
Distribution**
224 Iranshahar Street
Karimkhan Ave.
Tehran.
Tel: 828319

Pakhshiran Company
8 Somayeh Street
Bahar Ave.
Tehran.
Tel: 824052

**Fajr Film Production and
Distribution**
7 Saadi Ave.
Tehran
Tel: 391580

Farabi Cinema Foundation
55 Sie-Tir Ave.
Tehran.
Tel: 671010

**Cinematic Affairs of
Janbazan Foundation**
Vali-e Asr Junction
Beheshti Ave.
Tehran.
Tel: 623536

**Arts Bureau of the
Organization for the
Propagation of Islamic
Thought**
213 Somayeh Street
Tehran.
Tel: 820023–9

**Islamic Republic of Iran
Broadcasting**
Jaam-e Jam
Vali-Asr Ave.
Tehran.
Tel: 832527

Purika Film
119 Forsat Street
Taleghani Ave.
Tehran.
Tel: 828442

**Shiraz Film Production and
Distribution**
1/56 Neaufle-Le Château
Street
Tehran. Tel: 677952

**Co-operative of Art
Perspective**
Air France Building
Enghelab Ave.
Tehran.
Tel: 672340

**Hamrah Film Production
and Distribution**
No. 31, Mehrdad
St. Motahari Ave.
Tehran.
Tel: 832140

Cadre Film
No. 39, Nilufar Alley, Apadana
St.
Beheshti Ave.
Tehran.
Tel: 866110–865392

Sina Film
No. 401, Intersection of Shiraz
St.
Shariati Ave.
Tehran.
Tel: 762047

Useful Addresses

Arts Bureau
Intersection of Somayeh &
Hafez

Tehran.
Tel: 820654

**Cinematographic Affairs
Centre for the Intellectual
Development of Children
and Young Adults**
Motahari Ave. No. 37
Jam St.
Tehran.
Tel: 836065–7

Farabi Cinema Foundation
55 Sie-Tir Ave.
Tehran.
Tel: 671010.
Telex: 214283 FCF IR.
Fax: 678155

**Mostazafan and Janbazan
Cinema Foundation**
343 Shadid Beheshti Ave.
Tehran.
Tel: 632057–627536/5
Telex: 213427

**Department of Photography
and Film Production,
Ministry of Culture and
Islamic Guidance**
Baharestan Sq.
Tehran.
Tel: 391333

IRELAND

by Michael Dwyer

In 1990, for the first time in Irish cinema history, an Irish film – *The Field* – outpaced all the competition in a strongly U.S.-dominated market to become the box-office champion of the year. Although substantially funded by Granada in Britain, the film is Irish in every other respect – in its subject matter and its setting; the entire crew is Irish and only two of the principal cast came from abroad.

Hot on the heels of the Pearson–Sheridan team's Oscar success with *My Left Foot*, their second film, **The Field**, opened in Dublin amid a blaze of publicity in September 1990, attracting lengthy queues, day and night, continuing for months afterwards. The film also attracted an older audience which had not been to the cinema for decades, and with the keen interest of the country's large young cinema-conscious audience, it was still playing in Dublin eleven months after it opened.

As ever, precise box-office figures are not made available on the Irish market, but a reliable estimate puts *The Field* close to a net take at close on £1 million – comfortably ahead of the other big 1990 hits such as *Ghost, Look Who's Talking* and *Pretty Woman*.

By contrast, *My Left Foot*, for all its critical acclaim in Ireland and internationally, failed to make the national top ten box-office chart in 1989. However, there was a very significant revival of interest in that film with the announcement of its five Oscar nominations (and later, two wins). A similar pattern developed in February 1991 when Richard Harris received an Oscar nomination as best actor for *The Field* – his first since *This Sporting Life* in 1963.

Their success has led to Pearson and Sheridan signing a two-picture deal with Universal Pictures; individually, Sheridan scripted *Into the West*, a contemporary Irish comedy–drama to be directed by the Austrian, Robert Dornhelm (*Echo Park, Requiem for Dominic*) for the Irish company, Little Bird Films, while Pearson is planning a movie of the critically acclaimed new Brian Friel play, *Dancing at Lughnasa*, first staged at the Abbey in Dublin, before transferring to London and Broadway.

The Irish director, Neil Jordan, released his sixth film in ten years when **The Miracle** opened in the late spring of 1991; despite a very enthusiastic response at the Berlin and Dublin festivals and excellent reviews from the Irish media, the film failed to take off at the box-office – perhaps because its delicate (and well-publicised) theme of incest proved too difficult for audiences to handle.

Prolific as ever, Jordan is proceeding with plans for *When a Man Loves a Woman*, his ironically titled story of a terrorist unwittingly falling in love with a transvestite, and with his plans for a necessarily high-budget picture of the revolutionary hero, Michael Collins, who also is the subject of proposed films by Kevin Costner and Michael Cimino.

The most recent attendance figures at Irish cinemas, for the year 1989, showed the highest percentage increase of all the European Community countries – up by 16.7% to 17.5 million admissions. That figure is certain to be surpassed when the 1990 figures are established and again when the 1991 figures are counted.

Multiplexes Arise

Part of the upswing in Irish attendances can be attributed to the arrival of the multiplexes. Observing a large gap in the populous outer suburban Dublin area, United Cinemas International (UCI) opened a 12-screen complex in November 1990, which has been very successful, followed by ten screens in the north of the city in August 1991. With one third of the country's population, Dublin now accounts for more than half the national box-office.

Leading commercial successes in the first half of 1991 have been *The Silence of the Lambs*, *Dances with Wolves*, *Three Men and a Little Lady*, *Misery*, *Kindergarten Cop*, *Sleeping with the Enemy* and *The Doors*. Leading the art-house successes have been *Cyrano de Bergerac*, *An Angel at My Table* and *The Hairdresser's Husband*.

However, such is the crowded market in Irish cinema exhibition that many movies – such as *Mo'Better Blues*, *The Two Jakes*, *Men Don't Leave* and John Boorman's *Where the Heart Is* – failed to receive the most minimal release. Boorman, an Irish resident for 20 years, was the subject of a retrospective tribute in April 1991, as part of Dublin's celebrations as European City of Culture. In September 1990, the elder statesman of Irish cinema, Liam O'Leary – archivist, actor, producer, author and former *International Film Guide* correspondent – was saluted at a reception and with an exhibition of his work.

Foreign-language films suffered most as the commercial cinema recovered: in the period, January 1990–June 1991, a mere 17 of the 224 new releases in Dublin were in a language other than English. Yet the huge attendances attracted by foreign-language films at the three Irish film festivals makes it clear that there is a market for them and that it is seriously neglected.

Censorship fees, based on the length of a movie and averaging £800 per film, are prohibitive for the art-house market and take no account of the potential audience of a film. For example, the cost of having *Cyrano de Bergerac* censored, and it only played Dublin, was close to the total cost of putting the two widely released and very successful *Look Who's Talking* movies through the censor.

Then again, the Irish government never has been notable for an enlightened attitude towards any aspect of film. A significant statistic is this: the Irish government spends more annually on film censorship than on film production – even though censorship is well and truly relaxed, with no films of note being banned or cut, and the censor more preoccupied with questions of certification than anything else.

The Cork Film Festival, in October 1990, was one of the most successful to date, opening and closing on French movies – *Nikita* and *Cyrano de Bergerac*, respectively

– and showcasing the work of the American independent film-maker, Su Friedrich.

Scola in Town

The first major event in the City of Culture year, the Dublin Film Festival was opened by the country's new President, Mary Robinson, in February 1991 and featured a strong European flavour with retrospectives of Ettore Scola, who attended, and the German films of Fritz Lang, and as many as 12 new French features on the programme. Guests included directors Patrice Leconte, Stephen Frears, George Sluizer, Whit Stillman, Michel Deville, Hal Hartley and Philip Ridley.

The country's youngest festival, in Galway, had its third and most well-attended event to date in July 1991 when the main theme was Women in Film. Guests included the Irish actress, Maureen O'Hara, attending the 40th anniversary screening of *The Quiet Man*, actress Marianne Sagerbrecht, and directors Peter Chelsom, Nancy Kelly, Sue Clayton, and Bettina Wilhelm whose film, *All of Me*, won the audience prize.

After *The Field*, no film made in Ireland attracted more attention than Alan Parker's movie of the Irish author, Roddy Doyle's novel, **The Commitments**, a comedy of an Irish soul band formed in a Dublin working-class area. Parker and his team conducted extensive, much reported auditions for the film and he gave the 12 leading roles to Irish players, most of whom had never acted before. Twentieth Century Fox, who distribute the film in Ireland, are hoping to break all records with *The Commitments*.

Then there is Ron Howard's as yet untitled picture of Irish emigrants to the U.S.A. in the late Nineteenth Century, with Tom Cruise and Nicole Kidman in the lead, which had massive media coverage in Ireland, well before the production arrived in Dublin from its Montana set in August. And there has been the success story of

Thaddeus O'Sullivan's Irish feature, *December Bride* (reviewed in the 1990 IFG), which broke the box-office record at Dublin's leading art-house, The Light House, and won two prizes, including the Special Jury award, at the 1990 European Film Awards. And the success of Bill Whelan's initiative, Irish Film Orchestras, which has succeeded in attracting many international production companies to Dublin to record their musical scores.

Against all the odds, film-makers and film people in Ireland persist. Somehow, some of them get things done.

The Field

Script and Direction: Jim Sheridan. Photography: Jack Conroy. Editing: J. Patrick Duffner. Music: Elmer Bernstein. Production Design: Frank Conway. Players: Richard Harris, John Hurt, Sean Bean, Tom Berenger, Brenda Fricker. Produced by Ferndale Films for Granada Films, in association with Sovereign Pictures. 110 mins.

Reunited with his key crew members from *My Left Foot*, Jim Sheridan impressively lives up to the promise he displayed on that debut film, and he builds on it with his remarkable work on *The Field*. Working from his own screenplay, liberally adapted from the popular Irish stage play by John B. Keane, Sheridan demonstrates a firm narrative assurance and broadly extends his considerable cinematic skills.

Set in a fictitious Irish village in the 1930's, the film features Richard Harris in a towering, Oscar-nominated comeback performance as The Bull McCabe, an ageing tenant farmer wholly obsessed with the land and its position in his history and tradition. The field he rents provides him with an all-consuming interest in life, substituting for his marriage, during which, in all the previous 18 years, he has neither spoken to nor slept with his wife (Brenda Fricker), and

Richard Harris in *The Field*

a comfort to him in a life which lost all its joy with the death of his first son at the age of "13 years, six months and 24 days," a statistic which haunts him.

He is outraged when the field is put up for auction and sold to a returning Irish-American (Tom Berenger) who intends to cover the field with concrete and build it into a highway. The snowballing events which stem from the subsequent conflict have serious, far-reaching and tragic consequences: the more the Bull attempts to exert his control, the more he loses control over the land and over himself, and the greater his personal loss accrues.

Like another recent rural drama, *Jean de Florette*, Jim Sheridan's film of *The Field* is a powerful picture of the pain and suffering which ensues when a newcomer tries to wrest land from rigidly-rooted men who have spent their lives on that land and will stop at nothing to keep it for themselves.

For all its references to *Jean de Florette*, to *King Lear* and, extensively, to the western genre, Sheridan's film is shaped and crafted with such conviction and strength that it can stand very firmly on the weight of its own achievement. It builds with a slow, simmering power, charged by a series of superbly staged set-pieces, and crowned by the complete, complex and deeply immersed central performance by Richard Harris.

Michael Dwyer

MICHAEL DWYER is Film Correspondent of The Irish Times *and the producer–presenter of the RTE Television series,* Freeze Frame. *He co-founded the Dublin Film Festival in 1985 and acted as its Programme Director until 1991.*

The Miracle

Script and Direction: Neil Jordan. Photography: Philippe Rousselot. Editing: Joke Van Wijk. Music: Anne Dudley. Production Design: Gemma Jackson. Players: Beverly D'Angelo, Donal McCann, Niall Byrne, Lorraine Pilkington. Produced by Palace Pictures/ Promenade. 97 mins.

Beverly d'Angelo and Niall Byrne in *The Miracle*

Charming, colourful and confidently unconventional, *The Miracle* is an irresistible concoction from the fertile imagination of its prolific writer–director, Neil Jordan, who is back on home ground in more ways than one for his most sure-footed and accomplished movie since *Mona Lisa*.

Summertime in Bray, a seaside town outside Dublin, is the setting for this seductive story detailing the exploits of two young dreamers, Jimmy and Rose, 15-year-old friends indolently passing the long days as they play on words and devise elaborate imaginary scenarios for the various characters they observe on the promenade.

Confidently played by natural newcomers Niall Byrne and Lorraine Pilkington, Jimmy and Rose live in what one of them calls "that twilight zone – too friendly to be lovers, too close to be friends," although Rose is not as sexually indifferent to Jimmy as he is to her.

However, Jimmy soon becomes obsessed with a mysterious American woman (Beverly D'Angelo), an actress in town to perform in a tatty musical version of *Destry Rides Again*, and his sexual attraction towards her rapidly grows. Jimmy finds himself in too deep before he discovers that the American has been in Dublin before, where she met his father Sam (Donal McCann), now an alcoholic musician. Finally, Jimmy realises that the object of his desire is his mother who, Sam told him, had died a long time ago.

Alternately deeply touching and immensely entertaining, *The Miracle* sensitively and sympathetically observes its characters and follows them to the resolution of their problems as best this can be achieved under the circumstances.

When the narrative comes to the crunch, to confronting the difficult theme of incest, Jordan responds with a carefully measured and delicate approach. His film rewards the willing suspension of disbelief, but for all its most fantastical elements, it is rooted in reality, often unpleasantly so for young Jimmy, the romantic young dreamer forced to face up to the harsh facts of life in the adult world. The result is a heady, captivating experience infused by Jordan and his fine cast with wit, warmth and tenderness.

Michael Dwyer

Recent and Forthcoming Films

The Commitments. Script: Dick Clement and Ian La Fresnais, and Roddy Doyle. Dir: Alan Parker. Phot: Gale Tattersall. Players: Robert Arkins, Andrew Strong, Maria Doyle, Johnny Murphy. Prod: Beacon Communications.
Hear My Song. Script: Peter Chelsom and Adrian Dunbar. Dir: Peter Chelsom. Phot: Sue Gibson. Players: Ned Beatty, Adrian Dunbar, Shirley Anne Field, Tara Fitzgerald. Prod: Limelight.
Into the West. Script: Jim Sheridan. Dir: Robert Dorhelm. Phot/Players: To be announced. Prod: Little Bird Films.
The Playboys. Script: Shane Connaughton, Kerry Crabbe. Dir: Gilles MacKinnon. Phot: Jack Conroy. Players: Albert Finney, Aidan

Quinn, Robin Wright, Milo O'Shea. Prod: Green Umbrella Films.
The Railway Station Man. Script: Shelagh Delaney. Dir: Michael Whyte. Phot: Bruno de Keyser. Players: Julie Christie, Donald Sutherland. Prod: BBC/Turner Organisation.
Rock-A-Doodle. Script: David N. Weiss. Dir: Don Bluth. *Animated feature*. Voices: Glen Campbell, Sandy Duncan, Christopher Plummer, Ellen Greene. Prod: Sullivan Bluth Studios.
Thumbelina. Dir: Don Bluth. *Animated feature*.

Voices: John Hurt, Jodi Benson, Carol Channing, Gary Imhoff. Prod: Sullivan Bluth Studios.
A Troll in Central Park. Script: Stu Krieger. Dir: Don Bluth. *Animated feature*. Voices: Dom De Luise, Hayley Mills, Jonathan Pryce, Cloris Leachman. Prod: Sullivan Bluth Studios.
Far and Away. Script: Bob Dolman. Dir: Ron Howard. Phot: Mikael Salomon. Players: Tom Cruise, Nicole Kidman, Robert Prosky, Barbara Babcock. Prod: Imagine Films.

Producers

Little Bird Productions
122 Lower Baggot Street
Dublin 2
Tel: 614245
Fax: 600351

Mirror Films
44 Nassau Street
Dublin 2
Tel: 6795202
Fax: 6794842

Murakami Wolf
Bell House
Montague Street
Dublin 2
Tel: 783199
Fax: 783696

Pearson Productions
4 Harcourt Terrace
Dublin 2
Tel: 768890
Fax: 768874

Sullivan Bluth Studios (Ireland)
Phoenix House
Conyngham Road
Dublin 8
Tel: 6795099
Fax: 6795397

Tara Productions
Transit House
Sir John Rogerson Quay
Dublin 2

Tel: 713827
Fax: 715126

Windmill Lane Productions
4 Windmill Lane
Dublin 2
Tel: 713444
Fax: 718413

Yellow Asylum Films
6 Montague Street
Dublin 2
Tel: 781016
Fax: 781269

Distributors

Abbey Films
35 Upper Abbey Street
Dublin 1
Tel: 723922
Fax: 723687

Columbia TriStar Films
Merchant's Court
24 Merchant's Quay
Dublin 8
Tel: 6798234
Fax: 6798237

Twentieth Century Fox
5 Upper O'Connell Street
Dublin 1
Tel: 743068
Fax: 743069

Warner Bros
Russell House

Stokes Place
St Stephen's Green
Dublin 2
Tel: 784000
Fax: 784572

United International Pictures
D'Olier Chambers
D'Olier Street
Dublin 2
Tel: 6792433
Fax: 6798801

Useful Addresses

The Arts Council
70 Merrion Square
Dublin 2
Tel: 611840
Fax: 760436

Film Makers Ireland
20 Fitzwilliam Square
Dublin 2
Tel: 614399
Fax: 611397

Irish Film Institute
6 Eustace Street
Dublin 2
Tel: 6795744

Irish Film and Television Guild
c/o Royal Marine Hotel
Dun Laoghaire
Co Dublin
Tel: 2803050

ISRAEL
by Dan Fainaru

On a purely business level, the last year has been one of the most successful the Israeli film industry has ever had. Pathé Entertainment brought in no less than three major productions, including the already released *Not without My Daughter*. Menahem Golan's 21st Century added two of its own and three independent international features starring, respectively, Faye Dunaway, Peter O'Toole and Dolph Lundgren were completed here, also one ABC Movie of the Week and one French production, *Pour Sacha*. Services for all these productions earned $22 million, the second best year in the history of the local industry, an amazing performance considering the Gulf War period when all activities ground to a standstill.

As far as the Israeli film is concerned, however, the situation was pretty disastrous. Official statistics were bad enough, but the facts behind them are even worse. On paper, eight new Israeli films were released in the course of the last 12 months, a dramatic drop from the 15–16 titles a year the local industry has averaged in the last decade. Going through the titles, however, one soon discovers that Noam Yavor's **Point of View** (previously known as *War Shepherds*) has been around for almost three years before its belated and not very welcome release. **Streets of Yesterday** hardly qualifies as an Israeli production, being, as it is, an English-speaking picture with an international cost (Britisher Paul McGann plays the lead), financed by Channel Four and shot mostly in Berlin a couple of years before its brief release at the Tel Aviv Cinémathèque: while both *The Appointed* (shown last year in Cannes) and *Laura*

Adler's Last Love Affair (unveiled in the Venice 1990 competition), date from the previous year.

The reasons for this dearth of product are all too obvious to enumerate. To begin with, the Gulf crisis, which, as far as this part of the world is concerned, started in August 1990, long before General Schwarzkopf launched his ultimatum. The reluctance to enter a high risk investment, such as an Israeli film, at this particular time is pretty understandable, while the constant political strife, the massive immigration and the concern with the future security of the nation required concentration of State funds for more pressing purposes.

New Film Academy
Among several attempts made last year to breathe some life and encourage the industry, was the inauguration of an Israeli Film Academy, started with the blessing and support of various authorities such as the Israeli Film Center (Ministry of Industry and Commerce), the Fund for the Promotion of Quality Films and the Israeli Film Institute (both under the Ministry of Education and Culture), also the Producers Association, the various Artists Unions, the Critics Associations, the archives, etc. A bit of a rushed job, it left many of the partners uncomfortable. They went ahead in November 1990 with an Oscar-type distribution of prizes, before they had agreed on the statutes necessary for such a distribution. It is still not clear who will finally belong to this academy, what its regulations are going to be, and some observers wonder whether anything will be settled before the next ceremony.

In any case, the big winner for last year, with six out of the ten available prizes, was **Look Out** (*Shuru*), a sleeper made on a shoe-string budget which overnight became a cult movie and is still doing brisk business at the box-office, some six months after its initial release. A local comedy made by a young man fresh out of the Film Department of the Tel Aviv University, Sabi Gabison's picture sends up with a vengeance the freakish fringes of Tel Aviv's nightlife. Just as it was establishing its reputation as the hit of the season, war erupted, missiles started raining on Israel, and cinemas closed for six consecutive weeks. Any other film's career would have been ruined under the circumstances, but not *Shuru*. Back on the screens, it went on performing as if nothing had happened to hamper its style.

If *Shuru*'s appeal worked mainly for city audiences, Yehuda Barkan's latest soap, **The Day We Met**, fared much better in out-of-town locations. It's all about a hell-raising trucker who discovers his long-lost love and the daughter she has borne him twenty years ago, and takes place mostly in an Army camp, while the hero is going through his reserve service. Barkan, his own producer, is for the time being, the only bankable film star in the country, keeping up a regular string of productions. His next, **Skipper III**, his fourth feature film in the last three years, is already in the can, to be released soon.

Another film-maker who manages to work regularly is Uri Barbash. *One of Us*, his previous movie, may have generated less business than expected but it was still the top money maker in 1989. **Where Eagles Fly**, the story of a macho crop-dusting pilot who collapses physically and emotionally as the result of a brain tumour, didn't do as well, but the film's producers, Doron Eran and Arnon Tzadok (a top actor who decided to try his hand at producing) are already completing Barbash's next, **After the War**.

Much has been expected of Haim Buzaglos' **A Time for Cherries**, after the warm

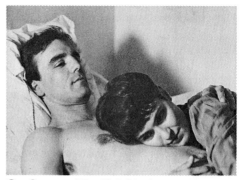
Guy Garner and Eva Hadad in *American Citizen*

critical reception of his previous *Bogus Marriage*, but his new effort turns out to be pretty much of a disappointment. Short on story and long on preaching, its tale of a muddled relationship between an Israeli advertising executive on duty during the Lebanon War and an aggressive female American TV correspondent, never really makes much sense. The film has its moments, to be sure, but they never come together in a satisfactory manner.

Buzaglo's film, however, does mark a return to politically motivated cinema, which threatened to go out of fashion. At least one other picture, **Cup Final** by Eran Riklis, already in the can but as yet unreleased, goes back to the Lebanon War and tackles the Arab Israeli conflict, in the context of a soccer match.

Fears Dispelled
In any case, as these lines are being written, things are looking up again for Israeli film-makers. The euphoria following the Desert Storm has generated new hopes and several projects have already been launched or are about to be completed. Fears that incoming productions would be reluctant to come back have been dispelled as Claude Lelouch has already finished shooting his next film here, distinguished cinematographer Vilmos Zsigmond returned to complete his first directorial effort, an Israeli-Hungarian co-

production with Liv Ullmann and Michael York entitled *The Prodigal Father*, and more projects are on their way. The combined resources of the Fund for the Promotion of Quality Films and the Israeli Television, when they agree to join forces, are sufficient now to cover up to 60% of the budget of an average production, more than ever before. It is encouraging, but judging by precedents, anything more than cautious optimism would be out of place in this much troubled area where every political breeze affects the state of the industry.

Distribution

With cinemas practically closed down for six weeks altogether, from mid-January until the end of February 1991 (they did open earlier but with so many security restrictions and the missile threat constantly present, attendance was symbolical at best), exhibition naturally suffered the severest blow. Stabilised in the last couple of years at approximately 1 million admissions per month, it was showing promising signs of doing even better by the end of 1990. Once theatres reopened, in March, the pace was picked up again, but unless several major blockbusters emerge before the end of 1991, there will be a 10% drop in the annual revenue. In the meantime, more multiplexes are opening, mostly in shopping malls, the latest marketing rage in the country.

If the number of screens is increasing (some 210, at present time), the number of seats they offer (89,000) is less than half the 182,000 available in 1970, and they are now concentrated in fewer hands than ever. Two circuits, the Globus Group (50 screens) and Israeli Theaters Forum Film (44 screens), each has its own distribution house, and any independent distributor who wishes to secure decent exposure for his products, has to have his own outlets, or else.

With the decision of Warner Bros. to move its products from independent Ephraim Gilad to the Globus Group organisation and with Orion joining the Columbia-TriStar stable, all American majors, with one exception, are now handled by two firms only. Globus Group has MGM-UA, Paramount and Universal (all under the UIP banner), as well as Pathé and Cannon, with Warner to be handled separately but from GG premises. A.D. Matalon keeps the Columbia, Tri-Star and 20th Century-Fox catalogues, adding Orion and Carolco. The exception is Disney-Touchstone, back to Forum Films, its home for over thirty years prior to the brief, but very successful, WB interlude with Gilad.

Shuru
(Look Out)

Script: Savi Gabison. Jonathan Aroch, Yohanun Raviv. Direction: Savi Gabison. Photography: Yoav Kosh. Editing: Tali Halter. Art Direction: Shmuel Muoz. Music: Lior Tevet. Players: Moshe Ibgi, Sharon Brandon Hacohen, Sinai Peter, Keren Mor, Shmuel Edelman, Ahuva Keren, Albert Iluz, Nathan Zohavi, Ezra Kafri. Produced by Jonathan Aroch and Yohanan Raviv for Rosy Productions. 85 mins.

Shuru, last year's top box-office hit, is a comedy of manners, offering an ironical portrait of Tel Aviv's night life and of the characters mooning around its pubs, a gallery of self-styled pseudo intellectuals who never stop chasing the latest cultural fashions. The script uses as its centerpiece a hapless visionary (Moshe Ibgi), whom nobody takes seriously but who sincerely believes he can help all the misguided innocent and not-so-innocent characters wandering listlessly through the Tel Aviv nights. Cabison takes him through a myriad of fragmented episodes, confronting him with a vast selection of fashionable freaks, be it art dealers with sex problems, TV producers suffering from acute loneliness, pretty women complexed by slight physical deficiencies, sadomasochistic university lecturers and so on. All through the film, a taxi driver drops in and out on the proceedings, observing this nocturnal human fauna with a condescending eye. Modest and rather amateurish, *Shuru* does not really qualify as a screwball comedy, but it has its moments: Ibgi trying to pay off his taxi fare by offering the driver (Albert Iluz) a chance to absue him, the camera tilting up vertically along a typical Tel Aviv house, to catch a variety of family feuds, a kibbutz chorus disconsolately chasing its bus through empty Tel Aviv streets. Cabison may have a flair for comedy, but he still lacks the discipline to write and direct one coherently from beginning to end. He also has the disconcerting tendency to put himself above his characters, and if he doesn't take them seriously, why should the audience?

Dan Fainaru

Derekh Hanesher (Where Eagles Fly)

Script: Assi Dayan, Benny Barbush, based on Assi Dayan and Naftali Alter's story. Direction: Uri Barbush. Photography: Amnon Salomon. Editing: Tova Asher. Art Direction: Eva Gronowitz Azoulal, Yonni Kroll. Music: Ilan Virtzberg. Players: Eli Danker, Nurith Galron, Giddi Gov, Ishai Golan, Gideon Shemer, Irith Gidron, Miri Fahian. Produced by Doron Eran and Arnon Tzadok for Doron Eran Productions.

Daniel (Eli Danker), a former maverick fighter pilot, flies a crop-dusting old crate for a living but misses no chance to display his acrobatic control over his antiquated machine. Happily married to Maya (Nurith Calron), a gymnastics teacher, he expects his teenage son, Tom, to follow the tradition and become a Fearless Flier, just like the father. But Tom (Ishai Golan) is a curly headed, long-haired, artistically inclined boy, who plays the guitar and wishes to be a

Moshe Ibgi and Abraham Pelta in *Shuru*

member of an Army Entertainment Group. His strong-willed mother understands and fully supports him, but for Daniel this is the ultimate insult. No fighter worth his salt will accept a sissy for his son.

Before this crisis is resolved, a second, much graver one erupts. Daniel's severe headaches are diagnosed as a malignant brain tumour. He tries to handle it like a man, or at least the notion he has of manhood. He attempts to bluff it away by excesses of authoritarian displays, refuses to share the tragic news with his family until it is too late, and then runs away and hides, because he cannot bear the idea of becoming a doomed and helpless physical wreck, and have his overpowering image tarnished by terminal disease.

This can easily qualify as a typical Uri Barbash picture, focusing yet again on the Israeli male as a macho type with a brilliant military record, who functions perfectly in the most difficult situations, as long as professional wits and personal courage are tested, but fails miserably once he has to face intimate relationships. At the same time, it attempts to mark the changing of the guard in Israeli society, from the old, adventurous, but rather immature generation of warriors to a younger generation, loss belligerent, more sensitive, but as determined and as qualified as the older one. That, at least, is what the last sequence of the film seems to indicate. Professionally directed and well shot, acted with much determination by Nurith Galron, a singer with no previous acting experience, and Giddy Gov, as the sympathetic friend of the family, the picture emerges as a melodrama whose characters are too slight to draw audiences, and insufficiently explored to show more than the intention of a statement.

Dan Fainaru

Scene from *A Time for Cherries*

Onath ha 'Duvdevanim (A Time for Cherries)

Script: Haim Buzaglo, Hirsch Goodman. Direction: Haim Buzaglo. Photography: Oren Shmukler. Editing: Era Lapid. Music: Adi Renert. Players: Gil Frank, Idith Tepperson, Sasson Gabai, Zachi Noi, Avi Gilor, Eli Yutzpan. Produced by Rikki Shelach, Avraham Godalia, Huguette Elhadad Azron for Contact Productions, 103 mins.

Haim Buzaglo's tendency to juggle too many balls in the air has already played some dirty tricks on his first feature film, *Bogus Marriage*, and literally sabotages his second one. Trying to run along several parallel plot lines, he loses the thread of each individual one and ends up with a picture overflowing with unrealised good intentions. This time, it's about Israelis, who are going about their daily business trying to ignore the fate awaiting them, fooling around with the latest gadgets, producing the fanciest commercials, dressed in the latest fashions, until they are dispatched to be killed on the battlefield, for no good reason at all.

Gil Frank plays an advertising mastermind obsessed with the premonition of his own death, who builds an entire publicity campaign on this theme. At the same time, he is called up for his reserve service (the plot takes place during the Lebanon War in 1982), sent across the border to Lebanon and watches death striking down friends and foes indiscriminately, which only enforces his obsession. He has an affair with a tough American TV lady reporter, who believes the expression on Frank's face makes it "The Face of this War," the perfect product to sell American audiences, as the image of the Middle East conflict in a nutshell. There are also various reflections on the advertising world and its moral standards, and lots of fashionable interior designs of the kind one would expect a successful executive in the advertising business to live. Buzaglo also indulges in flights of fantasy, leaving the basically realistic narrative to embark, once in a while, in allegorical fancies, culminating in the grand finale when Israeli soldiers return to their own territory in a jeep decorated with huge doves' wings, to the accompaniment of Orff's *Carmina Burana*, symbolising a joyous celebration of life.

Production-wise, this is a definite improvement on Buzaglo's earlier effort, the image is richer in every respect and every detail in it is polished. But as a story teller, he lacks the dexterity to handle all the various ingredients he is using in a satisfactory manner. Frank's acting register is sadly limited. Tepperson lucks the mad sparkle she had turned on in *Bogus Marriage*, and only Sasson Gabai, as Frank's bosom friend manages to add a third dimension to his character.

Dan Fainaru

Recent and Forthcoming Films

Me 'Ever Layam (Over the Sea). Script: Haim Marin. Dir: Yankul Goldwasser. Phot: David Gurfinkel. Players: Aric Mosconn, Dafna Rochter, Mili Avital, Uri Alter, Sinai Peter, Motti Gil'adi. Yair Lapid, Yossi Graber. Prod: Marck Rosenbaum and Ronnie Akerman for Transfax & Yarkon Productions.

Hashkedia Porakhat (La Femme du Déserteur). Script and Dir. Michal Bat Adam. Phot: Fabio Conversi. Players: Fanny Ardant, Sharon Alexander, Daniel Napolitano, Giddi Cov, Aviva Gor, Shafrira Zakkai, Hilel Ne'eman, Shmuel Viloini, Nicole Cassel, Alona Kimchi. Prod: Marek Rosenbaum for M.I.M.H. (Tel Aviv), Jacques Kirchner for Maud Films (Paris).

Ezrakh Amerikni (An American Citizen). Eytan Green. Phot: Danny Schneur. Players: Guy Garner, Icho Avital, Baruch David, Eva Hadad, Rofi Adir, Danny Roth, Haim Banai. Prod: Marek Rosenbaum for Transfax Productions.

Gmar Gavia (Cup Final). Script: Eyal Halfon, based on an idea by Eran Riklis. Dir. Eran Riklis. Phot: Amnon Salomon. Players: Moshe Ivgi, Mukhammad Bakri, Salim Dau, Bassam Zuamut, Yussef Abu Warda, Suheil Hadud, Gassan Abbass, Sharon Alexander, Johnny Arbid, Sami Samir. Prod: Michael Sharfatein for Local Productions.

HaMilkhama She'Akhorei (The War After). Script: Benny Barbash. Dir. Uri Barbash. Phot: Amnon Salomon. Players: Assi Dayan, Rivka Neuman. Neta Moran, Hana Maron. Prod: Doron Eran and Arnon Tzadok for Doron Eran Productions.

Abba Ganuv 3 (The Skipper 3). Script: Shlomo Mashiach, Haim Marin. Dir. Zyeloth Monahemi. Phot: Amnon Zelayet. Players: Yehuda Barkan, Ben Zion, Irith Sheleg, Goula Noni, Heli Goldenborg, Uri Shumir, Zarab Varianian, Rolf Brin. Prod: Yohuda Darkan for Re'ee Films.

DAN FAINARU is an Israeli film critic and journalist who has written regularly for "Variety", and has been correspondent for I.F.G. for several years. He is a familiar face at the world's major and minor festivals alike.

Distributors

Globus Group (*UIP, MGM Pathe, Cannon, Warner*)
10 Glinkson St
Tel Aviv
Tel: 972–3–200221
Fax: 972 3 283187

A.D. Matalon & Co.
(*Columbia, Tri Star, 20th Century-Fox, Orion, Carolco*)
15, Hess St.
Tel Aviv
Tel: 972 3–29625, 296251
Fax: 972–3 292977

Forum Films
11, Pinsker St.
Tel Aviv
Tel: 972–3 293105
Fax: 972–3 280313

Shapira Films
34, Allenby St.

Tel Aviv
Tel: 972–3–5102530
Fax: 972–3–5101370

Golfand Films
34, Allenby St.,
Tel Aviv
Tel: 972–3–657010
Fax: 972–3–657994

Seven Stars (*Rank, Sovereign*)
8, Pinsker St.
Tel Aviv
Tel: 972–3–296314
Fax: 972–3–281397

Shani Films
Dizengoff Center
Tel Aviv
Tel: 972–3—5288282
Fax: 972–3–204749

Cinema Paris
106, Hayarkon St.,
Tel Aviv

Tel: 972–3–222282
Fax: 972–3–240815

Erez Films
32, Allenby St.
Tel Aviv
Tel: 972–3–658654
Fax: 972–3–659874

Nachshon Films
22, Harakevet St.
Tel Aviv
Tel: 972–3–5660015
Fax: 972–3–615112

Shoval Films
32, Allenby St.
Tel Aviv
Tel: 972–3–659288
Fax: 972–3–659289

Tamuz Films
5, Pinsker St.
Tel Aviv
Tel: 972–3–201512

Useful Address

Israel Film Institute
7 Rothschild Blvd
Tel Aviv
Tel: (972) 3–656293

Israel Film & TV Producers
Association
Attn: Katriel Schory
26 Ruppin Street
Tel Aviv 63457
Tel: (972) 3–226116
Fax: (972) 3–235821

Israel Film Centre
Ministry of Industry & Trade
P.O. Box 299
94190 Jerusalem
Tel: (972) 2–750433, 750297
Fax: (972) 2–245110

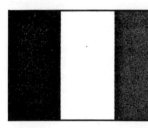

ITALY

by Lorenzo Codelli

Once again in the 1990–91 season the amount of national releases decreased to around 60 features (–25%), and their share of the home box-office went down to 18.1% of the gross. The Ente Gestione Cinema has estimated that the country spent 800 billion *lire* to import motion pictures, whereas exports brought in just 100 billion *lire*. Among the Top Ten list the only Italian hits that could exceed one million attendances were two cheap farces: **Vacanze di Natale 90** by Enrico Oldrini, which exploited the archaic formula of a bunch of TV-comedians enjoying their Christmas holidays; and **Le comiche** by Neri Parenti, with Paolo Villaggio and Renato Pozzetto sweating to emulate some old slapstick tricks, without Mack Sennett's tempo or style.

Then attracting fewer than 900,000 patrons was Carlo Verdone's usual Christmas comic package, **Stasera a casa di Alice**. The daily exploits of a group of Sicilian lawless boys in Marco Risi's **Ragazzi fuori** brought in almost 700,000 ticket-buyers; his follow-up to *Meri per sempre* (1989) was splendidly shot in an American actioner idiom, while his social criticism sounded this time a little too emphatic. Paolo Villaggio's endless Gogolian

saga **Fantozzi alla riscossa** appealed to nearly 650,000 customers. Maurizio Nichetti's **Volere volare** drew around 500,000, mostly adolescent spectators thanks to its Roger Rabbit elements. And Tinto Brass's slice of highbrow pornography, **Paprika**, lured 630,000 to the box-office before slipping into the video stores.

All the other Italian pictures have earned but a few hundred thousand in attendance, or even more limited audiences. Everybody was chatting for instance about **Il portaborse**, because of its vehement attack against political corruption in the Socialist party; but it opened too late in the spring to become a huge hit. And Daniele Luchetti's and Nanni Moretti's opus was even shown free during the campaign for the referendum at which masses voted unanimously for electoral reform. No network agreed to support this film and Moretti financed it off his own bat with added French money. In a more allegoric way, Gabriele Salvatores' **Mediterraneo** could also appear as a political rejection of today's dubious practices. Telling the abstract story of a patrol of Italian soldiers abandoned for years in a heavenly Mediterranean island near the end of the last war, Salvatores tries to imagine an unpolluted, alternative evolution for his nation. Too bad that he pasted on an epilogue showing his characters made-up like old men, as grotesque as those in Bertolucci's **1900**.

Mannerist and Repetitive

The so-called neo-Neorealist efforts, with the single exception of Marco Risi, were quickly becoming mannerist and repetitive. **Ultrà** by Ricky Tognazzi – dedicated to his father Ugo, the great actor who suddenly passed away last winter – wallowed in slang and populist clichés to describe soccer violence. The distinct touch of playwright Umberto Marino shone through two adaptations from his works: **La stazione**, the directing debut of Sergio Rubini (Fellini's alter-ego in *Intervista*), and **Italia Germania 4 a 3** by Andrea Barzini. One might suppose that these lively but visually modest one-room plays sound fashionable especially because they are so unexpensive to produce. Marino, incidentally, now has several personal projects in the making.

As a *kammerspiel* originally written for the screen, Francesca Archibugi's **Verso sera** successfully demonstrated that movies need to be born as movies. Similarly Daniele Luchetti's **La settimana della sfinge** was a freewheeling, space-exploring summer trip, not trapped in the ideological armour of his later *Il portaborse* (that was due to screenwriters Sandro Petraglia and Stefano Rulli, well-established authors of that popular TV-series *The Octopus*). Both these films display some of the best artistic qualities of the younger breed of Italian directors, without being burdened by their usual tendency towards over-explicitness. Silvio Soldini's **L'aria serena dell'ovest**, on the otherhand, was an attempt almost to forget dialogue and describe an intricate web of psychological and erotic relationships through mobile camerawork.

Comeback for Emmer

A nice surprise was the comeback to feature directing of Luciano Emmer, the under-

rated master of 1950's social comedies, who had been devoting himself to commercials for the past thirty years. His **Basta! Adesso tocca a noi** was an updating of his minor classic *Terza liceo* (1953), and an affectionate portrayal of some ideal schoolboys apparently untouched by commonplace vices. Pupi Avati's very ambitious **Bix** diligently recreated the fabulous era of jazzman *maudit*, Bix Beiderbecke. One of Avati's favourite actors, Carlo Delle Piane, was the genial star of **Condomino** by Felice Farina, a well-made sitcom about a struggling community in a huge building. Disappointingly dull and pretentious, Marco Bellocchio's **La condanna**, focusing on a rape trial, was partly galvanised by French actress Claire Nebout's profound grace.

Among the intriguing works by newcomers – those getting at least a limited commercial release – we should note Alessandro D'Alatri's **Americano rosso**, a provincial imbroglio nostalgically evoking the Fascist era; Davide Ferrario's nihilist black thriller **La fine della notte**; Christian De Sica's – Vittorio's son – broad sketch on obesity, entitled **Faccione**; and Antonio Monda's **Dicembre**, the sombre psychoanalytical study of a lonely child.

The glorious past of Italian movies was illustrated by various publications: *Costumisti e scenografi del cinema italiano* by Ste-

---

Silvio Orlando in Luchetti's *Il portaborse*

fano Masi, a second megatome from La Lanterna Magica Institute of L'Aquila; *Dizionario del cinema italiano; i film 1945–1959*, the first in a series of filmographies from Gremese Editore of Rome; in-depth filmographies were offered in *1918* by Vittorio Martinelli (a special issue of *Bianco e Nero* magazine) and in *Archivio del cinema italiano: il cinema muto 1905–1931* by Aldo Bernardini (ANICA/Ministry of Show Business). Methodological tools to rediscover the nitrate age were offered by Paolo Cherchi Usai's *Una passione infiammabile* (Utet, Turin); while director Alberto Lattuada collected some of his original stories and remembrances in *L'occhio di Dioniso* (La Casa Usher, Florence).

La casa del sorriso (House of Smiles)

Script: Marco Ferreri, Liliana Betti, Antonio Marino. Direction: Marco Ferreri. Photography: Franco Di Giacomo. Music: Bruno Guarnera, Henri Aguel. Editing: Dominique B. Martin. Art direction: Marco Ferreri. Players: Ingrid Thulin, Dado Ruspoli, Vincenzo Cannavale, Francesca Antonelli, Caterina Casini, Maria Mercader, Nuccia Fumo, Nunzia Fumo. Produced by Giovanna Romagnoli and Augusto Caminito for Titanus Distribuzione, Scena International. 95 mins.

La carne (The Flesh)

Script: Marco Ferreri, Liliana Betti, with the co-operation of Paolo Costella, Massimo Bucchi. Direction: Marco Ferreri. Photography: Ennio Guarnieri. Editing: Ruggero Mastroianni. Art direction: Sergio Canevari. Costumes: Nicoletta Ercole. Players: Francesca Dellera, Sergio Castellitto, Philippe Léotard, Farid Chopel, Petra Reinhardt, Gudrun Gundlach. Produced by Giuseppe Auriemma for M.M.D. 90 mins.

That almost forgotten iconoclast Marco Ferreri, following a prolonged series of uneven pictures, has made a blustering comback with *La casa del sorriso* and *La carne*, presented back to back at the Berlin Festival (Golden Bear) and at the Cannes Festival (no awards, even if it was by far the best Italian movie around). Is he just re-heating his old themes for the 1990's? Or is he again in the mood to distil a striking vision of impending disaster?

His inner dialectics have indeed sobered his creative urge, because *La casa del sorriso* shows the subversive serenity of a seasoned *savant* talking about the possible happiness of old age. Two characters, one crazy blonde (Ingrid Thulin in an enthusiastic performance) and a stiff old gentleman, fall in love in a gloomy asylum for the elderly. Their "scandalous" romance is observed and frequently disturbed by the other not-so-frolicsome guests. The two lovers part at the end, but a sunny destiny seems to be waiting for them anyway.

More caustic and aggressive, *La carne* is an apologue about the contemporary shift of sexual satisfaction towards plain physical greed, or cannibalism. A cabaret singer finds a gorgeous vagrant girl one evening; he brings her to his beach house and becomes a passive object for her libido. His Catholic upbringing still troubles his apparently "modern" mind, and when the girl decides to go off on her own, he kills her and starts religiously devouring her body in small pieces. As in *Dillinger Is Dead*, Ferreri underlines the plot's symbolic pauses, the untold truths and frustrations of the male "victim." No boring or pretentious messages weaken this bristling movie, which is played like a Feydeau *pas-de-deux* by the most self-mocking stars of the new generation, Francesca Dellera and Sergio Castellitto.

Lorenzo Codelli

Recent Films

L'africana (The African). Script and Dir: Margarethe von Trotta. Phot: Tonino Delli Colli. Players: Barbara Sukowa, Stefania Sandrelli, Samy Frey. Prod: Scena Group (Rome); Bioskopfilm (Munich); Rachel Productions (Paris). *Drama.*

Americano rosso (Red American). Script: Enzo Monteleone from Gino Pugnetti's novel. Dir: Alessandro D'Alatri. Phot: Alessio Gelsini. Players: Fabrizio Bentivoglio, Burt Young, Valeria Milillo. Prod: Videa, Rai 3. *Drama.*

L'aria serena dell'ovest (The Clear Air of the West). Script: Silvio Soldini, Roberto Tiraboschi. Dir: Silvio Soldini. Phot: Luca Bigazzi. Players: Fabrizio Bentivoglio, Antonella Fattori. Prod: Monogatari (Milan)/Pic Film, SSR-RTSI (Switzerland). *Drama.*

Atto di dolore (Act of Contrition). Script: Pasquale Squitieri, Sergio, Bianchi. Dir: Pasquale Squitieri. Phot: Romano Albani. Players: Claudia Cardinale, Bruno Cremer, Giulia Boschi. Prod: Vidi, Istituto Luce-Italnoleggio, Rai 2. *Drama.*

Basta! Adesso tocca a noi (Enough! Now It's Our Turn). Script: Luciano Emmer, David Emmer, Paolo Taggi. Dir: Luciano Emmer. Phot: Adriano Tagliavia. Players: David Emmer, Gianluca Angelini. Prod: Emmer Production. *Comedy.*

Bix. Script: Pupi Avati, Antonio Avati, Lino Patruno. Dir: Pupi Avati. Phot: Pasquale Rachini. Players: Bryant Weeks, Ray Edelstine, Julia Ewing. Prod: Duea Film, Union P.N., Rai 1. *Musical drama.*

Le comiche (The Comedies). Script: Leo Benvenuti, Piero De Bernardi, Alessandro Bencivenni, Domenico Saverni, Neri Parenti. Dir: Neri Parenti. Phot: Roberto Gerardi. Players: Paolo Villaggio, Renato Pozzetto. Prod: Penta Film Communications, Alto Verbano. *Farce.*

La condanna (The Sentence). Script: Massimo Fagioli, Marco Bellocchio. Dir: Marco Bellocchio. Phot: Beppe Lanci. Players: Claire Nebout, Vittorio Mezzogiorno. Prod: Cineuropa '92, Istituto Luce-Italnoleggio, Rai 2 (Rome)/Banfilm (Paris)/Cactus Film (Zürich). *Drama.*

Condominio (Condominium). Script: Paolo Virzì, Felice Farina, Francesco Bruni, Gianluca Greco. Dir: Felice Farina. Phot: Carlo Cerchio. Players: Carlo Delle Piane, Ciccio Ingrassia, Ottavia Piccolo. Prod: Cooperativa Imagine. *Drama.*

Dicembre (December). Script and Dir: Antonio Monda. Phot: Tonino Nardi. Players: Pamela Villoresi, Alessandro Haber. Prod: Ager 3, Istituto Luce-Italnoleggio, Rai 1. *Drama.*

I divertimenti della vita privata (Private Life Amusements). Script: Gérard Brach, Jackye Fryszman, Cristina Comencini. Dir: Cristina Comencini. Players: Delphine Forest, Christian Malavoy, Vittorio Gassman. Prod: Titanus, Solaris (Rome)/Cinemax (Paris). *Comedy.*

Fantozzi alla riscossa (Fantozzi's Revenge). Script: Leo Benvenuti, Piero De Bernardi, Alessandro Bencivenni, Domenico Saverni, Neri Parenti, Paolo Villaggio. Dir: Neri Parenti. Phot: Sandro D'Eva. Players: Paolo Villaggio, Milena Vukotic. Prod: Cecchi Gori Group Tiger, Maura International Film. *Farce.*

Faccione (Big Face). Script: Filippo Ascione, Liliana Betti, Christian De Sica. Dir: Christian De Sica. Phot: Sergio Salvati. Players: Nadia Rinaldi, Paco Reconti. Prod: Video Holding. *Comedy.*

La fine della notte (The End of the Night). Script and Dir: Davide Ferrario. Phot: Robert Schaefer. Players: Claudio Bigagli, Dario Parisini. Prod: Pagnoni Film. *Drama.*

In nome del popolo sovrano (In the Name of the Sovereign People). Script and Dir: Luigi Magni. Phot: Beppe Lanci. Players: Nino Manfredi, Alberto Sordi, Elena Sofia Ricci. Prod: Erre Produzioni, Rai 2. *Comedy.*

Italia Germania 4 a 3 (Italy-Germany: 4 to 3). Script: Andrea Barzini, Umberto Marino, from Marino's play. Dir: Andrea Barzini. Players: Fabrizio Bentivoglio, Massimo Ghini, Nancy Brilli. Prod: Rai 2. *Comedy.*

Matilda. Script: Graziano Diana, Antonio Fiore, Stefano Masi. Dir: Antonietta De Lillo, Giorgio Magliulo. Phot: Giorgio Magliulo. Players: Silvio Orlando, Carla Benedetti. Prod: Angio Film, So.Co.F.I.mm. Partecipazioni spa. *Comedy.*

Mediterraneo (Mediterranean). Script: Enzo Monteleone. Dir: Gabriele Salvatores. Phot: Italo Petriccione. Players: Diego Abatantuono, Claudio Bigagli, Giuseppe Cederna. Prod: Penta Film, A.M.A. Film. *Drama.*

Miliardi (Billions). Script: Carlo Vanzina, Enrico Vanzina, from Renzo Barbieri's novel. Dir: Carlo Vanzina. Phot: Luigi Kuveiller. Players: Carol Alt, Lauren Hutton, Billy Zane. Prod:

Cecchi Gori Group Tiger, International Video 80. *Drama.*

Paprika. Script: Tinto Brass, Bernardino Zapponi. Dir: Tinto Brass. Phot: Silvano Ippoliti. Players: Debora Caprioglio, Martine Brochard. Prod: Scena Group. *Drama.*

Il portaborse (The Factotum). Script: Sandro Petraglia, Stefano Rulli, Daniele Luchetti, from a story by Franco Bernini, Angelo Pasquini. Dir: Daniele Luchetti. Phot: Alessandro Pesci. Players: Nanni Moretti, Silvio Orlando. Prod: Sacher Film, Eidoscope Productions (Rome)/ Banfilm, Pyramide Production, Ciné 5, Canal Plus (Paris). *Drama.*

Ragazzi fuori (Boys Out). Script: Marco Risi, Aurelio Grimaldi. Dir: Marco Risi. Phot: Mauro Marchetti. Players: Francesco Benigno, Alessandro Di Sanzo, Roberto Mariano. Prod: Numero Uno International, Rai 2. *Drama.*

La setta (The Sect). Script: Dario Argento, Giovanni Romoli, Michele Soavi. Dir: Michele Soavi. Phot: Raffaele Mertes. Players: Kelly Curtis, Herbert Lom. Prod: A.D.C., Pentafilm. *Horror.*

La settimana della sfinge (The Sphynx' Week). Script: Daniele Luchetti, Franco Bernini, Angelo Pasquini. Dir: Daniele Luchetti. Phot: Tonino Nardi. Players: Margherita Buy, Paolo Hendel, Silvio Orlando. Prod: Erre Produzioni. *Comedy.*

Stasera a casa di Alice (This Evening at Alice's). Script: Leo Benvenuti, Piero De Bernardi, Carlo Verdone, Filippo Ascione. Dir: Carlo Verdone. Phot: Danilo Desideri. Players: Carlo Verdone, Sergio Castellitto, Ornella Muti. Prod: Cecchi Gori Group Tiger, Penta Film. *Comedy.*

La stazione (The Station). Script: Umberto Marino, Filippo Ascione, Sergio Rubini, from Marino's play. Dir: Sergio Rubini. Phot: Alessio Gelsini. Players: Sergio Rubini, Margherita Buy. Prod: Fandango S.r.l. *Drama.*

Tolgo il disturbo (I Won't Disturb You). Script: Dino Risi, Enrico Oldoini, Bernardino Zapponi. Dir: Dino Risi. Phot: Blasco Giurato. Players: Vittorio Gassman, Dominique Sanda, Elliot Gould. Prod: International Dean Film, Starlet Cinematografica. *Drama.*

Tracce di vita amorosa (Traces of Love Life). Script: Peter Del Monte, Giuseppe Manfridi, Alessandra Vanzi. Phot: Alessandro Pesci. Players: Walter Chiari, Valeria Golino, Stefania Sandrelli, Massimo Dapporto. Prod: Aura Film, Rai 1. *Drama.*

Ultrà. Script: Graziano Diana, Simona Izzo, Giuseppe Manfridi. Dir: Ricky Tognazzi. Phot: Alessio Gelsini. Players: Claudio Amendola, Ricky Memphis. Prod: Numero Uno International. *Drama.*

Vacanze di Natale 90 (Christmas Holidays '90). Script: Enrico Oldoini, Franco Ferrini. Dir: Enrico Oldoini. Phot: Sergio Salvati. Players: Diego Abatantuono, Christian De Sica, Massimo Boldi. Prod: Filmauro. *Farce.*

Verso sera (Sometime Tonight). Script: Francesca Archibugi, Gloria Malatesta, Claudia Sbarigia. Dir: Francesca Archibugi. Phot: Paolo Carnera. Players: Marcello Mastroianni, Sandrine Bonnaire, Zoe Incrocci. Prod: Ellepi Film, Rai 1 (Rome)/Paradis Films (Paris). *Drama.*

Il viaggio di Capitan Fracassa (Captain Fracassa's Journey). Script: Ettore Scola, Furio Scarpelli, from Théophile Gauthier's novel. Dir: Ettore Scola. Phot: Luciano Tovoli. Players: Massimo Troisi, Ornella Muti, Vincent Perez. Prod: Cecchi Gori Group Tiger, Studio EL, Massfilm (Rome)/Gaumont (Paris). *Drama.*

Volere volare (To Wish To Fly). Script and Dir: Maurizio Nichetti, Guido Manuli. Phot: Mario Battistoni. Players: Maurizio Nichetti, Angela Finocchiaro. Prod: Bamù srl Cinema e TV, Pentafilm. *Comedy.*

JAPAN

by Frank Segers

1990 was the year that Japan entrenched itself as the world's premier source of new entertainment finance via a series of moves as bold as they were controversial. In late 1990, Matsushita Electric Industrial Co. put the finishing touches on its $6.1-billion takeover of MCA Inc., the Hollywood entertainment giant that includes Universal Pictures – one of America's most established studios – among its holdings. This after Sony Corp.'s $4.6-billion takeover in the autumn of 1989 of Columbia Pictures.

The Matsushita buyout set off widespread concern in Hollywood that the Japanese were "taking over" one of America's most productive and financially fruitful export industries. It was also one of a number of less spectacular Japanese initiatives that tell without doubt that the acquisition of Western software – principally films from the U.S. and Europe – is big business and underway in earnest.

In July, a consortium of big business interests – two key banks, the giant Seibu Saison department store conglomerate, a major trading company and all tethered by a unit of NHK, Japan's powerful public broadcaster – formed Media International Corp. The fledgling concern (known as MICO) lost no time in undertaking substantial foreign investments. By presstime MICO worked up various agreements with Viacom of the U.S., Germany's public broadcaster ZDF and America's ABC–TV in the U.S. (for a two-hour drama, *U Boat*) and in the U.K., with foreign sales agency Majestic Films International – the company that made a significant investment in Kevin Costner's *Dances with Wolves*, and sold the film with great success internationally.

There was also a $10-million investment in actor Sean Penn's film, *The Indian Runner*, which played to successful response at the Director's Fortnight section in Cannes. At least ten other MICO deals are in the works, including potential arrangements with Hollywood producer Thom Mount and Italy's RAI. In all, MICO says it plans to invest more than $100 million in various projects in 1991, a prospect that has more than one hungry producer salivating.

In April, a new pay-tv satellite operation, Japan Satellite Broadcasting, went on line.

Still from *Kodayu – Dreams of Russia*, with Marina Vlady and Ken Ogata

photo: Daiei Co.

What he sees beyond his desperation DREAMS OF RUSSIA

KODAYU

- Executive producer YASUYOSHI TOKUMA

- Director JUNYA SATO

- Starring KEN OGATA/TOSHIYUKI NISHIDA MARINA VLADY/OLEG YANKOVSKII

- Based on a novel by YASUSHI INOUE
- Screenplay TATSUO NOGAMI FUMIO KONAMI/JUNYA SATO

- A Product of DAIEI CO., LTD./DENTSU INC.

- Co-produced by TOYO SUISAN KAISHA., LTD. TOPPAN PRINTING CO., LTD.

- With cooperation of TOKUMA SHOTEN PUBLISHING CO., LTD. DAIEI EIZO FILM INC. LENFILM STUDIO

 DAIEI CO., LTD. 1-18-21 Shimbashi, Minato-ku, Tokyo 105 Tel:03(3508)2631, Fax:03(3508)2030, Telex:J25983DIF

Myriad technical problems including a satellite fade out dogged the startup. But to both domestic and foreign film suppliers, the JSB launch was welcome indeed. JSB heavily programmes feature films, most imported from the U.S. Deals with several major studios are in the can, others are coming. JSB says it also plans to link up with key European film suppliers. With at least $40 million to spend this year on acquisitions, the stakes for producers are invitingly high.

Multiplexes Erected

Cultural cross-fertilisation cropped up on the film exhibition front as well. Time Warner Inc. of the U.S. and Japan's Nichii Inc./Mycal Group worked out an agreement to erect multiscreen complexes – some 30, each with from six to twelve screens, are envisioned – in Japan. The theory is that modern multiplexes spurred film attendance in the U.K., Germany and Australia, and should do likewise in Japan. If so, good news. A peek at the film statistics chart at the end of this section tells a gloomy tale. The number of theatres has dipped to a new low (1,836 in 1990) while attendance languishes. The American majors operating in Japan put the blame on the scarcity of first-class new theatres. Now the theory will be put to a test. It appears that the Japanese majors – or at least one of the big three, Toho – is getting the message. On July 6, the Japanese company opened a spanking new, four-screen complex in Tokyo's Shibuya area. Question: will these new theatres result in higher attendance? Only time will tell.

Time will also tell about the efficacy of the Japanese moves in Hollywood. The push is driven by two factors, the Americans' ability to come up with films of worldwide marketability and the Japanese need for "software" to fill the programming needs brought on by High Definition Television developments, satellite broadcasting and, of course, all those new theatres that are being planned. As independent American producer, Edward Pressman – who recently signed a co-production deal with Japan's Ascii Pictures – put it, "we (in Hollywood) are in a capital intensive business, and they (the Japanese) have the capital." The corollary to this is that the Japanese lack the means and/or the ability to produce exportable films on their own. In all of 1990, for example, Japanese producers sold slightly more than $12.5 million worth of feature films – in toto – on world markets outside Japan. By sharp contrast, just one American distributor (United International Pictures) realised half that amount in film rentals in just one month, May, by releasing in Japan a handful of features.

Japan's Hollywood studio moves may be canny investments in "software" at the production source. Or, as one American executive (Jeffrey Katzenberg, chairman of Walt Disney Studios) put it, the Sony–Columbia, Matsushita–MCA takeovers may not be marriages made in heaven. Sure enough, Katzenberg himself showed up in Tokyo in early June, and downplayed his querulousness. The occasion was a Walt Disney Film Festival sponsored by Fujisankei Communications, Japan's largest media conglomerate and no mean domestic film producer as well. Fujisankei, in the spirit of the times, has made a number of coventures in the U.S. and in Europe, and who knows if Disney itself might eventually become involved in some sort of co-venture with Fujisankei.

Domestically, the film industry at press-time is gearing up – or is it bracing itself? – for the fourth Tokyo International Film Festival, Sept. 27–Oct. 6. The event has been held biennially since 1985, and so far has been regarded as a duty rather than occasion for rejoicing by the Japanese film establishment. That may soon change since one longtime member of the establishment – media conglomerateur Yasuyoshi Tokuma, no mean film producer in his own right – has taken over as festival director.

Tokuma, renowned for his political connections and clout, succeeds Tatsuro Ishida, who died of cancer last year at the age of 72. Ishida spent virtually his entire career at Fujisankei and thus was regarded as essentially a "non-film" man despite the fact that Fuji TV, a Fujisankei unit, is probably Japan's most successful film producer.

Tokuma, a man of confidence given to occasional verbal bravado on the subject of Japan's position in the film production world, has wasted no time in making his mark. The Tokyo Festival will henceforth be an annual event. This is an idea that Ishida had unsuccessfully pushed against film industry apathy. TIFF will be held as usual in Tokyo's Shibuya area, and also as usual, will cost a bundle. Tokuma projects an expenditure of some $6–$7 million. Opening pic this year was director Yoji Yamada's latest non-*Tora-san* series outing **Son** (*Musuko*), toplining veteran actor Rentaro Mikuni – and the closer is expected to be Wim Wenders *Until the End of the World*, which, suitably enough, was made possible in part via Japanese funding. As if he isn't busy enough, Tokuma is currently embroiled in producing director Junya Sato's *Dreams of Russia*, a Russo-Japanese co-venture with a cast that includes actor Ken Ogata and Soviet actress Marina Vlady. The result should turn up in 1992 at the Cannes Festival.

This year's Japan Academy Award ceremonies were dominated by Masahiro Shinoda's **The Boyhood** (*Shonen Jidai*), which won "best film" and a citation for Shinoda as best director. A fine showing from a veteran Japanese director whose work these days turns on the theme of individual feelings in conflict with societal duties. A special "chairman's award" went to the late Shochiku-bred actress, Mieko Takamine, who made her debut at the studio in 1936, at the age of 18. Her work comprises leading roles in some 185 films. The Foreign Film Importer–Distributor Association (Gaihaikyo) "superior" citation was granted to France Eigasha, the concern run by Hayao and Kazuko Kawakita Shibata, also known as the Shibata Organisation.

Only Two from Sweden

In all there were 465 foreign films released in Japan in 1990, down 57 titles from 1989. U.S. pictures accounted for 248; 51 from France, 39 from Italy, 32 from the U.K., 13 from Hongkong and eight each from Germany, U.S.S.R. and Australia. Just two titles came from Sweden, a situation that the Swedish Film Institute is not especially happy with. SFI's general manager Willmar Andersson was spotted in Tokyo in early 1991 pitching for more distribution opportunities.

One of the 1990's most heartening developments on the domestic scene was the emergence of the Argo Project, an exhibitor-producer collective producing independent features for minority audiences. As Japan's film attendance has diminished – to about one-tenth the size of the early 1950's audiences – conditions for independent producers of specialist domestic product have become ever more arduous. Hopeful signs recently have been the development of Argo as a force in the art-house field. It has made eight films – most notably, **The Cherry Orchard** (*Sakura No Sono*), the story of a girls' high school drama society as it prepared a production of the Chekhov play of the same title. The pic, produced by Yutaka Okada's feisty New Century Producers Organisation, won the 1990 best film award from *Kinema Junpo*, the highly respected film journal. Argo has opened two 180-seat theatres, one in Tokyo, the other in Osaka, to guarantee its output at least initial playtime. Of the eight Argo projects, two have been hits (one is *The Cherry Orchard*) and have gone on to broader commercial runs. Altogether, good news.

Meanwhile, back at the three major studios: Shochiku Co. reshuffled its organisation, named Toru Okuyama president and broadened the production responsibilities of his son, Kazuyoshi; Toei Co. renamed its foreign film import operation Toei Astro Inc., keeping Josho Suzuki as head of the operation; and Toho Co, has embarked on production of the latest *Godzilla* movie. The $11 million outing, which went before the cameras in early June as *Godzilla Vs. King Ghidora*, describes the two big monsters battling it out against a backdrop of newly built government buildings in Tokyo's Shinjuku district. This will be the 18th in the *Godzilla* series, proving that like much in the Japanese film world, *plus ça change...*

FRANK SEGERS writes for Variety and specialises in Far Eastern entertainment issues.

Rentaro Mikuni and Masatoshi Nagase in *My Son*, directed for Shochiku by Yoji Yamada

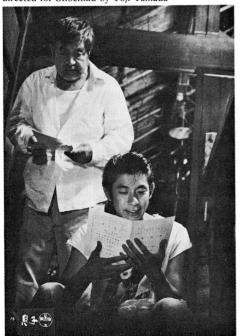

Statistics

Figures for the period, January-December 1990, with previous year's figures in brackets.

Number of cinemas:

total	1,836	(1,912)
for domestic films only	600	(630)
for foreign films exclusively	735	(755)
for both categories	501	(527)

Not counted in the totals are drive-in theatres and video theatres, small (generally 100-seat) venues playing films and other programming transferred to videotape. Statistics in these two categories are:

video theatres	37	(31)
drive-ins	16	(14)

Number of films:

total	704	(777)
domestic films	239	(255)
foreign films	465	(522)

Box-office:

annual attendance 145,522,000 (143,573,000)
gross theatre receipts 171,269 million yen (166,681 million yen)
average admission fee (without tax) 1,177 yen (1,161 yen)

TOP TEN GROSSING FILMS IN JAPAN: 1990

	Rentals (yen)
Back to the Future, Part II	5,530,000,000
Heaven and Earth	5,050,000,000
Back to the Future, Part III	4,750,000,000
Die Hard 2	3,200,000,000
Ghost	2,800,000,000
A Tale of Tasmania	2,520,000,000
Doraemon	1,910,000,000
Batman	1,910,000,000
Inamura June	1,830,000,000
Ghostbusters 2	1,750,000,000

Useful Addresses

Ascii Pictures Corp.
5F, No. 12 Mori Bldg.
1–17–3 Toranomon
Minato-ku
Tokyo

Assn. for the Diffusion of Japanese Films Abroad (UniJapan Film)
Ginza 5–9–13
Tokyo
Tel: (03) 572–5106

Cine Saison
Asako Kyobasi Bldg. 2F
6–13 Kyobashi, 1–Chome
Chuo-ku
Tokyo

Channel Communications
5th Fl., Osakaya Bldg.
3–1–9 Mita
Minato-ku
Tokyo

Comstock Ltd.
Akasaka Omotemachi Bldg.
4–18–19 Akasaka
Minato-ku
Tokyo

Daiei Co. Ltd.

1–18–21 Shimbashi
Minato-ku
Tokyo

Gaga Communications
Kanda Bldg.
2–7–17 Hamamatsu-cho
Minato-ku
Tokyo

Kuzui Enterprises
Jingumae-Otowa Heights 201
5–503 Jingumae
Shibuya-ku
Tokyo

Japan Cinema Associates
LSP Hanzomon 513
1–5–4 Kojimachi
Chiyoda-ku
Tokyo

Japan Audio Visual Network
Wako 32 Bldg.
2–11–10 Tsukiji
Chuo-ku
Tokyo

Japan Film Library Council
Ginza-Hata Bldg.
4–5, 4-chome, Ginza
Chuo-ku
Tokyo

Japan Satellite Broadcasting
1–19–10 Toranomon
Minato-ku
Tokyo

Media International Corp.
2–14–5 Akasaka
Minato-ku
Tokyo

Mitsubishi Corp.
6–3 Marunouchi
2–Chome
Chiyoda-ku
Tokyo

New Century Producers Co.
Kyodo Bldg. 313
4–3–1 Akasaka
Minato-ku
Tokyo

New Select Co.
Nakamura Bldg.
5–9–13 Ginza
Chuo-ku
Tokyo

Nikkatsu Corp.
28–12 Hongo, 3-chome
Bunyo-ku
Tokyo

Nippon Herald Films
No. 1 Shimbashi Ekimae Bldg.
20–15, 2-chome, Shimbashi
Minato-ku
Tokyo
Fax: (03) 574–6760

Shibata Organization
(France Eigasha)
2–10–8 Ginza
Chuo-ku
Tokyo
Fax: (03) 535–3656

Shochiku Co.
13–5 Tsukiji 1-chome
Chuo-ku
Tokyo

Shochiku-Fuji Co.
13–5 Tsukiji, 1-chome
Chuo-ku
Tokyo

Toei Co.
2–17, 3-chome, Ginza
Chuo-ku
Tokyo

Toho International Co.
Hibiya Park Bldg.
8–1, Yurakucho, 1-chome
Chiyoda-ku
Tokyo

Toho-Towa Co.
6–4, Ginza, 2-chome
Chuo-ku
Tokyo

Tohokushinsha Film Co.
17–7 Akasaka, 4-chome
Minato-ku
Tokyo

Voyager Entertainment Inc.
Imperial Roppongi Annex
5–16–3 Roppongi
Minato-ku
Tokyo

SOUTH KOREA

by Frank Segers

Those that view art as the by-product of adversity, perceived or real, can take heart from the 1990 experience of the South Korean film industry. Stunned in 1988 when the major Hollywood studios set up shop in Seoul and began direct distribution of popular American features – thereby posing an unprecedented economic threat – the South Korean industry took a series of bold, steps to assure that domestic films would not be lost in the artistic and commercial shuffle.

In 1990 and into early 1991, the government stepped up its support of film-making both administratively and in direct assistance. Some 30 domestic films played in Korean theatres last year, almost double the national average. Many of the new titles came from name directors who combined artistic ambition with commercial success. Signs emerged that perhaps the vaunted and feared American "domination" at the expense of domestic films was exaggerated. Action films from Hongkong appeared to be in retreat.

"Korean film-makers once again realised that the introduction of simple yet genuinely Korean stories was the only way to compete with many of the foreign films that centred on violence and science fiction produced with enormous expense," wrote critic Park Pyong-shik, who also dubbed 1990 as "the year of the takeoff."

There's no question that the American studio presence is firmly established. United International Pictures, the overseas distribution partnership of Paramount Pictures, Universal Pictures and MGM/UA, along with Twentieth Century Fox, are fixtures. Other Hollywood studios are either contemplating or have actually set up direct distribution arrangements of their own.

Direct distribution are the operative words. Before 1988, American distributors were forced to channel films to Korean audiences via a cozy network of Korean distributors, who paid outright for the distribution rights and then kept all the subsequent film rentals upon playoff. UIP sparked a virulent protest that took on nasty, even violent, nationalistic proportions when it challenged the status quo in the fall of 1988, by directly releasing Paramount's *Fatal Attraction*.

The brouhaha subsided amid positive signs that Korean cinema is far hardier than many in the Seoul film establishment originally gave it credit for being. It helps to have support from the top, and the government provided just that in 1990 when it split the Ministry of Culture from the former Ministry of Culture and Information. By so isolating its cultural function, the Ministry appeared to shift its focus from controlling the film business to fostering it. Modern equipment was imported. Production facilities were renovated. Pre-production assistance was offered and prize money was arranged for those responsible for quality films.

New Studio Complex

The Motion Picture Promotion Corp., the government's 18-year-old, non-profit film promotion unit, is building a four-stage studio complex in a mountainous valley that is an hour-and-a-half's drive from downtown Seoul. The compound, costing some 7 billion *won* (U.S.$9.5 million), will accommodate four buildings for film shooting, recording and editing facilities, a film library and a huge open set designed by Kim Won. Completion of the entire complex is projected in four years, although the Promotion Corp. says the site will be ready for actual lensing by the end of 1992. Some 700 representatives of the film industry plus Culture Minister Lee O-young turned out for groundbreaking ceremonies on April 17, 1991.

The government earlier declared 1991 to be "The Year of Cinema and Plays." According to its own statements, the government plans to encourage co-production with other countries "in joint ventures," the establishment of a production investment fund open to individual private investors, talent searches and training programmes for behind-the-camera personnel and some form of financial help to local cinemas in the way of advertising and publicity support. There's even talk – inevitably – of a national film festival.

Most importantly there is now an abundance of directorial talent making films that paying customers actually want to see. Many of the titles explore material familiar to Korean audiences, the pain of a divided Korea, for example, or historical films. There is also a fair sampling of modern social issues – the plight of a female rape victim, for instance. Films treat topics close to people's lives in a refreshingly realistic manner.

Heading the list of Korea's top 10 commercial releases in 1990 was a Tae Hung Production of director Im Kwon Taek's **The General's Son** (*Jang Kuni Adul*), a fast-clipped melodrama about a muscular youth who joins a Korean gang and takes on the dreaded Japanese yakuza battling for control of Chongno Street. Im is no hack action director. At 55, he is probably Korean's best known helmer abroad, the equivalent of, say, a Bergman in Sweden and a Fellini in Italy. *General's Son*, in addition to being a commercial success, was greeted with enthusiasm by national critics.

Im is best known abroad for his *Come, Come to a Higher Place*, which won for Kang Soo Yeon a best actress citation at the Moscow Festival in 1989.

The fixation with the North–South division found expression in the second most popular film, **Namboogun** (North Korea's Southern Army) from the decidedly independent director Jeong Ji-young. Set in 1950, the film tells of a North Korean war correspondent's experiences in the South as a member of a North Korean partisan group. In between skirmishes with South Korean forces, the protagonist falls in love with a South Korean nurse. Things end, as expected, on a bittersweet note.

Grand Bell Awards

The Korean equivalent of the Hollywood Oscars is the Promotion Corp.'s Grand Bell Awards. In 1990, Ye Film's **Because You Are a Woman** (*Yojaranun Iyumanuro*) took the "best film" second prize in the Grand Bells, and also won principals Won Mi-Kyung and Lee Young-Ha respective best actress and actor awards. *Woman* is a harrowing, outright feminist plea of sympathy for an attempted rape victim debased by governmental authorities and the judicial system. A tough drama in a nation that often favours softcore fare of sometimes roisterous explicitness.

The grand prizewinner in the 29th Grand Bell ceremonies was roughly speaking the Korean cinematic version of J.D. Salinger's *Catcher in the Rye* – from director Kwak Ji-Kyun, a 36-year-old graduate of the Seoul Arts College who has directed two other films (*Broken Heart* and *So Long Since Then*) since 1989. Kwak is young enough to be personally conversant with the subject matter of **Portrait of a Young Man**, a rite-of-passage saga starring film and TV personality Chong Po-sok. The scenario was based on novelist Yi Munyol's bestseller of the same title, which tells of college-age youths growing up in Korea's turbulent

(*continued on page 303*)

LUXEMBOURG
by Jean-Pierre Thilges

The large amounts of tax-shelter monies stuffed down the throats of (mostly) foreign producers by the Luxembourg Government over the last two years have had quite an impact on the development of film production. Location shooting for American, Canadian, French and German television series took a sharp upturn, creating havoc in several parts of the country as local authorities learned to deal with the numerous film crews haunting Luxembourg's medieval castles, its quiet villages and its busy cities.

As a matter of fact, things got so out of hand at one time, that the decision was taken to cut back on location permits and to favour indoor shooting as far as possible. Which is something of a contradiction, as the country does not have any studio facilities as yet. At least two projects for film-and-TV studios were under review at press time, with both Canadian and local investors trying to get their construction on the road. While foreign producers seemed eager to take advantage of the current tax laws, they showed a lot less enthusiasm when it came to hiring local talent – a tendency for using Luxembourg companies merely as a mailbox front seemed obvious with some projects.

Three Steps to Heaven?
While the likes of Christopher Lee, Patrick McNee, Morgan Fairchild, Sam Waterston, Dominique Sanda, Jean-Pierre Cassel, Alexandra Stewart, Mariangela Melato, Charles Aznavour, Mario Adorf, Judd Nelson, John Savage, Sally Kirkland and Richard Jordan came to Luxembourg over the last twelve months to star in a good half-dozen TV and film projects, and while some

of the country's technicians were given the opportunity to work on the sets of these productions (as assistants, line producers or location scouts) the output of indigenous films almost came to a halt.

Although 1990–91 must be considered a transition period for Luxembourg's filmmakers (several ambitious projects are in the pipeline), it was a bit of a shame that only one feature film made it to the big screen. Andy Bausch, whose new film **Three Steps to Heaven** started production in the autumn of 1991, was literally devoured by German television, for whom Bausch directed two productions back to back, *Ex und Hopp*, starring Mario Adorf and shot in Luxembourg, plus *Switch*, starring Gudrun Landgrebe, Otto Sander, Hark Bohm and shot in Berlin.

Wartime Saga
The only Luxembourgish feature to hit the cinemas during the last year was Samsa Film's **Schacko Klak**, directed by Paul Kieffer and Frank Hoffmann, from a screenplay by Frank Feitler, based on Roger Manderscheids' bestselling novel. Shot on the occasion of the 150th Anniversary of Luxembourg's independence, the film retells the sombre years of Nazi occupation in a small village, as seen through the innocent eyes of an adolescent boy, Chrëscht Knapp, who is robbed of his childhood years by the War. While Roger Manderscheid's epic book is closer to the spirit of Günther Grass' *The Tin Drum*, the film adaptation (initially planned as a 4 hour miniseries and subsequently cut down to a 90-minute-feature for budget reasons) has a more down-to-earth approach as it

chooses to retail only a few episodes rather than the whole book.

As a 35mm feature (the first ever in Luxembourg) budgeted at roughly $800,000 (30 million Francs), *Schacko Klak* looks great on the screen, even if monetary limitations are visible at times. This is, no less, a period recreation and while the costumes and sets seem right, the crowd and army scenes wear thin at times. One stunning moment, though, shows a turtle with a Luxembourg flag (prohibited during wartime) on its back running for cover as German soldiers are goosestepping past. The intimate scale of the story-telling and the natural interacting of non-pro children actors (Claude Wagner, Shirin Fabeck) and pro adults (André Jung, Paul Groisch, etc.) turn *Schacko Klak* into a sensitive period piece which makes it more than a mere curiosity to watch for at film festivals. As a matter of fact, it should fare well as a children's film in foreign markets not put off by the fact that the local dialect will have to be subtitled.

Not surprisingly, after a successful home run in the cinemas, the feature was sold to several TV stations (including Germany's ZDF and some Scandinavian countries) and has since been selected for the Moscow Film Festival, the Montréal Festival, the Europa Cinema event in Viareggio, and the London Film Festival.

Still from the Samsa production of *Schacko Klak*

Film Fund Money . . .

The Luxembourg Film Fund has paid out production aid monies for the second time in 1991 ($800,000 per annum), thus trying to give incentive to new projects. The fund favours indigenous productions, but – although its possibilities are rather limited – it also tries to assist Luxembourgish investors with European co-productions. At presstime, the following fund-supported projects were in different stages of development: *Wedding Night (Hochzeitsnacht)*, a feature directed by Paul Cruchten, produced by Videopress, principal photography completed; *Ladies Choice (Dammentour)* a feature directed by Paul Scheuer, produced by AFO Films; *Spooky Firetooth (Flitze Feuerzahn)*, a Luxembourg/German animated miniseries co-produced by Paul Thiltges for Samsa Films at Luxembourg's cartoon-studio 352 Productions, pilot episode completed; *The Seven Deadly Sins (Les 7 Péchés Capitaux)*, a feature film in seven episodes directed by six different directors, including Luxembourg's Geneviève Mersch, a Luxembourg-Belgian co-production between Samsa Films and Les Grands Films Belges, principal photography started; *Anna-Anna*, a Swiss/German/Luxembourg (Samsa) co-production of a children's film directed by Grethy Klay, principal photography started. The Luxembourg Film Fund is also supporting several scriptwriting projects.

Considering that ten years ago Luxembourg had never ever produced a feature film of its own, this lineup of coming attractions looks indeed quite attractive. The Government aid was more than welcome and is showing promising results. With the film-making gaining momentum from year to year, a substantial increase in funding money would be adequate, as international acclaim for the tiny Luxembourgish feature films seems to be growing from year to year.

With a bit of an effort thrown in by everyone, the country's fledgling audio-visual industry could well be ready in time for the big challenge of the Common Market in 1993: the Astra satellites are currently crowding the skies, RTL/CLT's star shines bright, international film and TV producers stampede the country, local directors are picking up steam and the exhibition business contemplates a great future, as the Utopia cinema-group is finalising plans for its 14 screen/3,500 seat "Utopolis" multiplex.

JEAN-PIERRE THILGES earns a living in banking; as a film critic, he has been fighting for the survival of the art of cinema in Luxembourg since 1972; a witness to the birth of the ongoing Luxembourg film boom, he has run his own cinema multiplex together with equally filmstruck friends since 1989; and was recently appointed to the board of governors of the "Fonds d'Aide à l'Audiovisuel".

Useful Addresses

AFO Films A.S.B.L.
18, rue Principale
L–9360 Brandenbourg
Gr. Duchy of Luxembourg
Tel: (352) 9 07 16

Centre National de l'Audiovisuel
5, route de Zoufftgen
L–3598 Dudelange
Gr. Duchy of Luxembourg
Tel: (352) 52 24 24 1
Fax: (352) 52 06 65

Samsa Films S.A.
1, rue de Nassau
L–2213 Luxembourg
Gr. Duchy of Luxembourg

Service des Medias et de l'Audio-Visuel
5, rue Large
L–1917 Luxembourg
Gr. Duchy of Luxembourg
Tel: 47 87 22
Fax: 47 56 62

352 Productions
30, rue des Bruyères
L–1274 Howald
Gr. Duchy of Luxembourg
Tel: (352) 49 28 07

Videopress S.A.
P.O. Box 1421
L–1014 Luxembourg
Gr. Duchy of Luxembourg
Tel: (352) 40 30 30 37
Fax: (352) 40 30 30 33

MALAYSIA

by Baharudin A. Latif

At the recently concluded Malaysian Film Festival, **The Heart Is Not a Crystal** took the main awards for Best Film, Director, Stars and Script, a rare, but well-deserved string of triumphs that surprisingly received popular endorsement by the public (which, however, had stayed away during the film's screening run). Its critical success, although indicating that the future may not be all Badul's, can hardly be expected to effect any overall changes, either in public taste towards films or executive predilection for the types of products they should invest in.

An adverse effect had always held true as some past winners learnt. It was therefore quite enlightening (even scandalous) for Erma Fatima in accepting her Best Actress award to remark for the benefit of producers present that her future price was negotiable!

Phenomenon, a light-weight but most heart-wrenching sudsy story of an English girl racked with a terminal disease seeking a traditional cure or living out her last days in Malaysia, topped the list of hits for the 1990–91 season. It was trailed by **Isabella**, another women's tear-jerker. Incidentally, both films featured the same popular song, "Isabella," by rock group Search, a factor decidedly responsible for their success.

Two other films, **Brother** and **Driving School**, essentially dramatic slush with liberal helpings of slapstick, garnered enough box-office returns to be termed hits. However, A.R. Badul, the toothy comedian who reigned as the box-office champion for over ten years and whose every film inexplicably had the Midas touch, finally made a flop. And **Colours of the Heart** was a *resounding* flop. Directors should stick their forte, and serious drama can never be

Badul's cup of tea. The noted comedy director Hafsham trespassed into John Carpenter territory with his suspense drama **The Hidden** way back in 1987 and got his fingers singed.

Hardly Heartening

The new crop of films for the 1991–92 season is hardly heartening with the conspicuous absence of respected film-makers Kamarul Ariffin and Rahim Razali but nonetheless varied enough to ensure all-round entertainment for all groups. **The Shadow of Death**, a cops-and-robbers actioner about an elite drug-busting squad, is the first to reach the one-million *ringgit* jackpot.

An upcoming film expected to do excellent business in view of the mass appeal of *Bayangan Maut* and buffs' seemingly insatiable yen for action flicks is **Operation Crime Prevention**, yet another adventure pitting duty-beholden law officers against hard-core criminals. **Innocence Untarnished** is set in the same mould. It remains

Erma Fatima, winner of the Best Actress award at the ninth Malaysian Film Festival

Erma Fatima and Raja Azura in the dramatic comedy, *Riang Tirana*

to be seen whether films depicting macho heroes demonstrating various martial arts forms can sustain their magical hold on audiences. If they can, then one can predict a sombre future for serious films and directors like Kamarul and Rahim who will continue to maintain a low profile.

However, there are two new films which should give hope to the more discerning picture-goers. Leading the pack is **Night Star**, dwelling on the seedy side of the metropolitan life and the directorial debut of London International Film School alumnus Adman Salleh. At least the film has strong box-office power in Eman Manan, Fauziah Ahmad Daud and recent awardee Erma Fatimah, all darlings of the discriminating fans.

Erma seems to be omnipresent this year. She also stars in **Fantasia**, Aziz M. Osman's much-awaited follow-up film to his success, *Phenomenon*. Aziz recently won major RTM television awards for his two-parter *Scoop*. He is presently doing a drama for a Japanese company.

FINAS, the National Film Development Corporation, imposed a ruling requiring all major cinemas to screen local films for seven consecutive days, while three days is the limit for sub-key cinemas. The dates and times of screening are fixed by FINAS. The full benefits of this ruling, if any, may take some time to sink in but in the mean-

time, everybody is hoping that local films will have another bumper harvest this year.

Meanwhile, across the causeway, the Singapore government is stealthily grooming a film industry that it hopes to become as lucrative as Hongkong's once 1997 sets in. Already, seven films intended for international markets are underway.

Fantasia

Direction: Aziz M. Osman. Producer and Script: Zain Mahmud. Photography: Jamal Maarif. Music: Azman Abu Hassan and Ross Ariffin. Editing: Ibrahim Ahmad. Players: Erma Fatima, Faizal Hussein, Mustapha Kamal, Melissa Saila, Kuza, Shah Rahman, M. Osman. Produced by Teletrade Sdn. Bhd. 108 mins.

Fantasia, Aziz M. Osman's eagerly-awaited film after his ultra-successful *Phenomenon*, is about innocence violated and the victim's relentless hauntings across the ages for appeasement. To Oriental minds steeped in the mysticisms of the East, films depicting murder, rape and spectral hauntings spiced with a liberal dash of religion and immortality cannot fail to arouse interest and at the same time ignite controversy.

Already, the film has "upset" the Film Censorship Board. After reviewing it three times and referring the film to the Islamic Centre, word has just come that the Board has seen it fit to "protect" the delicate Malay psyche from exposure to blasphemous materials. This decision is likely to have a strong influence on creative filmmaking in the country now that film-goers' maturity and receptivity to other than "routine" films has been denied access to *Fantasia*.

For a young director of 29, Aziz has set himself a herculean task in infusing elements of popular fiction with contemporary and religious overtones into a mythological tale of revenge. The literate and absorbing script by Zain Mahmud, who also wrote *Phenomenon*, no doubt assisted him a lot.

Rising from bit player to superstar, Yusof Haslam now stars in, writes, produces and directs his own company's products

Under Aziz's direction, characters are sharply etched. Erma Fatima (1990's Best Actress winner) plays a reporter who unwillingly becomes the pawn in a deadly duel of survival between spirits. Newcomer Kuza as the proverbial sacrificial virgin forever dressed in white to signify purity and Mustapha Kamal, garbed in Dracula-like black to symbolise evil, provide the heart of the conflict and the film's highlights. Watching *Fantasia* reminds one of the early 1970's and the macabre adventures of *The Night Stalker* on television, where Darren McGavin encountered free-lancing zombies, vampires and various denizens of the fourth dimension on his assignments.

Baharudin A. Latif

Recent and Forthcoming Films

Riang Tirana (Gay Tirana). Script: Osman Abadi. Dir: Arief Karmahani. Phot: Jamal Maarif. Players: Erma Fatima, Badrul Muhayat, Karen Iskandar, Azhar Sulaiman, Raja Azura, Romzie Johari. Prod: Fuego Enterprises.
Bayangan maut (The Shadow of Death). Script and Dir: Yusof Haslam. Phot: Badaruddin Hj. Azmi. Players: Noor Kumalasari, Yusof Haslam, Sabree Fadzill, Ella, A Galak, A Rahim, Sidi Oraza, Salley Yaacob. Prod: Skop Productions.
Warna-warna hati (Colours of the Heart). Script: M. Jamil. Dir: A.R. Badul. Phot: Johan Ibrahim. Players: Sarimah, Nor Albaniah, Zu

Ghairi, Siti Rohani Wahid, Karim Latif. Prod: MJSR Productions.
Sejati (Forbidden Love). Script and Dir: Norhan Mahmud. Phot: Abu Taib. Players: Jamal Abdillah, Raja Ema, Acappan, Latif Ibrahim, Noraini Hashim, Lily Rahman. Prod: S.V. Productions.
Konstabel Mamat (Constable Mamat). Script and Dir: Z. Lokman. Phot: Raja Idris. Players: Salleh Yaacob, Ziela Jalil, Kuza, Hamid Gurkha, Sidi Oraza, Latif Ibrahim, Rosnah Mat Aris. Prod: Perkasa Films.
Bintang Malam (Night Star). Script: Anuar Idris. Dir: Adman Salleh. Phot: Zainal Othman. Players: Eman Manan, Fauziah Ahmad Daud, Erma Fatima, Shaharuddin Thamby, Sidek Hussein, Zarina Zainuddin. Prod: Nizarman Productions.
Suci dalam debut (Innocence Untarnished). Script and Dir: Zulkiflee M. Osman. Phot: Badaruddin Hj. Azmi. Players: Sidi Oraza, Julia Rais, Iklim, Khairul Anwar, Aziz Singah. Prod: Aarti Films.
Nadia (Nadia). Script and Dir: Abdul Rahman Adam. Phot: Jamal Maarif. Players: Hani Mohsein Hanafi, Julia Rais, Susan Lankester, Normah Damanhuri, Sophia Jane Hashim. Prod: Filmeast Productions.
Memori (Memories). Script: Jamil Sulong. Dir: Rosnani Jamil. Phot: Johan Ibrahim. Players: Shahrul Kamal, Fauziah Ahmad Daud, Dato' Jins Shamsuddin, Rosnani Jamil, Fatimah Yassin. Prod: RJ Productions.
Wanita bertudung hitam (Woman in the Black Veil). Script, Dir and Phot: Mahadi J. Murat. Players: Ramona Rahman, Abdul Jalil Hamid, Kuna Mahmud June, Imuda, Kartina Aziz, Zami Ismail. Prod: Teknik Suria Productions.
Juara (The Champ). Script and Dir: Yusof Kelana. Phot: Omar Ismail. Players: Malek Noor, Sidi Oraza, Ira Faridah, A. Rahim, A. Galak, Latif Ibrahim. Prod: M.E. Communications.
OSJ (Operation Crime Prevention). Script and Dir: Eddie Pak. Phot: Ngai Thai. Players: Mustapha Kamal, Sabree Fadzil, Nancie Foo, Wendy Wong, Nor Albaniah, Hani Mohsein Hanafi. Prod: Cinefame.
Kelisa (The Deadly Fish). Script: Anuar Idris. Dir: Ahmad Ibrahim and Rahim Jailani. Players: Mahiza Bakri, Jacinta Lee, Ruzaidi Abdul Rahman, Malek Noor. Prod: NR Productions.

TOP TEN GROSSING FILMS IN MALAYSIA: 1990

Rentals ($M)

God of Gamblers II*
All for the Winner*
Front Page*
Teenage Mutant Ninja Turtles*
Pantyhose Hero*
Skinny Tiger Fatty Fragon*
Shanghai Shanghai*
Tango and Cash
Ghost
Fenomena (Malaysian)

List includes Hongkong productions

Harry Boy. Script: Julie Dahlan. Dir: A.R. Badul. Phot: Mohamed Amin Noordin. Players: Ziela Jalil, Badrul Muhayat, Sophia Jane Hashim, Norlida Ahmad, Julie Dahlan, Romzie Johari. Prod: JD Productions.
Syakila (Syakila). Script: A. Wahid Nasir. Dir: Baharuddin Hj. Azmi. Phot: Indera Che Muda. Players: Wan Aishah, Rahim Maarof, Kuza, Yusof Haslam, Hisham Ahmad Tajuddin, Shaharuddin Thamby, Rashidah Jaafar. Prod: SJ Productions.

BAHARUDIN A. LATIF is currently attached to FINAS, The National Film Development Corporation, as Assistant Director of Publications and Public Affairs. He has written more than 2,000 articles for international and local magazines and newspapers and penned documentary scripts.

Useful Addresses

FINAS (*The National Film Development Corporation Malaysia*)
Studio Merdeka Complex
Lot 1661, 8th Mile, Hulu
Kelang
68000 Ampang
Selangor D.E.
Tel: (03) 408–5722
Fax: (03) 407–5216

PPFM (*Association of Malaysian Film Producers*)
Studio Panca Delima
Lot 1045, 7½ miles, Jalan
Hulu Kelang
68000 Ampang
Selangor D.E.
Tel: (03) 408–1522

Seniman (*Artistes Association of Malaysia*)
Studio Merdeka Complex
Lot 1661, 8th Mile, Hulu
Kelang
68000 Ampang
Selangor D.E.
Tel: (03) 409–0008

Producers/ Distributors (West Malaysia)

Skop Productions Sdn. Bhd.
10B Jalan Pahang Barat
Off Jalan Pahang
53000 Kuala Lumpur
Tel: (03) 423–9425

53000 Kuala Lumpur
Tel: (03) 421–8911

Cinefame Sdn. Bhd.
Suite 8.4–8.6, 8th Floor
Menara Aik Hua
Changkat Raja Chulan
50200 Kuala Lumpur
Tel: (03) 230–5678
Fax: (03) 232–2003

Teletrade Sdn. Bhd.
1A, Jalan SS21/56B
Damansara Utama
47400 Petaling Jaya
Tel: (03) 719–9755/719–9746
Fax: (03) 719–9782

Fuego Productions Sdn. Bhd.
22, 2nd Floor, Jalan 1/82B
Bangsar Utama

59000 Kuala Lumpur
Tel: (03) 232–7850
Fax: (03) 232–8340

Nizarman Sdn. Bhd.
64, Jalan Burhanuddin Helmi
Taman Tun Dr. Ismail
60000 Kuala Lumpur
Tel: (03) 718–9766/718–9988
Fax: (03) 717–3192

(*continued on page 282*)

MEXICO

by Tomás Pérez Turrent and Gillian Turner

Film production in Mexico diminished in 1990, following the same tendency of 1989 and after the record number of 112 films made in 1988. In 1990 a total of only 72 films was produced. However, in contrast to previous years the production is remarkable for the amount of interesting, original and filmically rich films completed.

Mexican cinema had been absent from the major film festivals for some time (the only exception being San Sebastian, where traditionally at least one Mexican film is always present). However, in 1991 the Berlin Film Festival where no Mexican film had been present since 1977 (with the exception of *Frida* by Paul Leduc in 1986) invited eleven Mexican films: one to compete officially, the others in parallel sections. In Cannes, where the last Mexican film to be shown in any of the important sections dates from 1976, in 1991 one was included in "Un Certain Regard," another in "La Quinzaine des Réalisateurs."

The interest and quality of 1990's film production was amply demonstrated at the Guadalajara Film Festival this year. This is a festival showing only national film produc-

tion, held in the month of March and now in its sixth year. Never had the local public shown so much interest in the festival, nor had the films exhibited been of such a high quality. It is interesting to note that the fourteen films presented come from various sources. Traditionally state-produced cinema alone takes the risk of quality before commercialism. Some of the films shown in Guadalajara are co-productions with the state, but there are all sorts of new alternatives including new independent producers with new ideas, co-operative societies, groups of film-makers, film schools, etc.

Production methods are also more varied. After his experiment with *Intimacy in a Bathroom*, Jaime Humberto Hermosillo again films with a minimum of resources: two actors only, shooting in one room with the camera showing only one fixed point of view. The film is called **Homework** (*La tarea*) and is a repetition of what he had made on video in 1988 with the same title, the same story and the same methods. This first video version is exploited successfully in video clubs. The present film version is

25 minutes longer, with better performances from the actors and with a more meticulous production. In contrast, Nicolas Echevarria in making his film **Cabeza de Vaca** has used multinational production support, indispensable for any project in Mexico surpassing a cost of $500,000 dollars. Other film-makers have formed their own companies to co-produce with the state, thus keeping control over their work. The results of this are several new films now in the final process stages: **Only with your Partner** (*Solo con tu pareja*) by the newcomer Alfonso Cuaron (TriStar has already shown an interest in acquiring this film), **Bandits** (*Bandidos*) by Luis Estrada, **Danzon** by Maria Novaro, and several others.

In 1989 **Red Dawn** (*Rojo amanecer*) was made in most absolute secrecy. The film narrates for the first time on screen the student massacre of 1968. Once the film was finished its release was delayed by the censor but its scriptwriter, Xavier Robles, and the Society of Writers, managed to get the ban lifted (three small cuts notwithstanding) and the film has been shown for several months with great success among the public. Using this kind of theme is another possible method for keeping national cinema alive.

Exhibition Upheavals

While the state, following the present economics policy, has put on sale its exhibition company, Operadora de Teatros (approximately 200 film theatres all over the country), cinemas are still closing down not only in the provinces but now in Mexico City itself where the traditional movie theatres for two or three thousand spectators are being converted into three or four smaller cinemas. In spite of the low value of money and the ridiculous price of the ticket maintained by law at $2,500 pesos (US$0.80), film exhibition is still an attractive business (owners make money on concessions), while distributors such as Columbia Pictures (independently of whether any of its films are among the ten most profitable of the year) and the national Videocine usually achieve the best box-office profits because of the number of theatres allotted to them.

The novelty in Mexico now is that the creation of video theatres is being talked of by the huge television monopoly Televisa (and its affiliates Videovisa, Videocine, Videoteatro), using High Definition. Many people in the film business fear that this will deal the final blow to film exhibition as we know it. Videocine is already the most important distributor in Mexico, handling not only the most successful national films – with the aid of TV advertising, fundamental in the success of any film, taken care of by Televisa – but since February, 1991 it also manages the release of Warner titles. It is believed that very soon Televisa and its affiliates will soon be running the largest film monopoly in Mexico. This is a possibility which may open up new perspectives for film-makers.

Cabeza de Vaca

Script: Nicolas Echevarria, Guillermo Sheridan. Director: Nicolas Echevarria. Photography: Guillermo Navarro. Music: Mario Lavista. Editing: Rafael Castanedo. Players: Juan Diego, Daniel Jimenez Cacho, Carlos Castañon, Roberto Sosa, Jose Flores, Farnesio Bernal. Produced by Rafael Cruz, Berta Navarro, Jorge Sanchez, Julio Solorzano for Producciones Iguana, IMCINE, Fondo de Fomento a la Calidad Cinematografica, Cooperativa Jose Revueltas (Mexico) Televisión Española S.A., Fundación del Quinto Centenario (Spain) Channel Four (U.K.) Rock Films (U.S.A.).

After struggling for five years, the experienced documentarist Nicolas Echevarria has completed his first fiction film, thanks to a multinational production. He narrates the journey on foot of Alvar Nuñez Cabeza de

Still from Nicolas Echevarria's *Cabeza de Vaca*

important than the visible reality. An audacious cinematographic form and the excellent work of the photographer, the editor and the composer of the music, all add depth to this outstanding film.

Tomás Pérez Turrent

Rojo amanecer
(Red Dawn)

Script: Xavier Robles, Guadalupe Ortega. Direction: Jorge Fons. Photography: Miguel Garzón. Editing: Sigfrido García, Jr. Music: Karen and Eduardo Roel. Players: Hector Bonilla, María Rojo, Bruno Bichir, Demian Bichir, Jorge Fegan, Eduardo Palomo, Ademar Arau, Paloma Robles, Carlos Cardán. Produced by Hector Bonilla, Valentín Trujillo for Cinematográfica Sol.

Vaca, from Florida to Northeast Mexico, embarked upon in 1527. The expedition begins at sea. The ships sink, the troops are slaughtered by the Indians and only a few conquerors survive, including Cabeza de Vaca. Echevarria recreates the physical and spiritual journey of a man who, defeated at first by a hostile and foreign reality, slowly begins to integrate, reaching an understanding of it, making it his own. His experience is above all mystical, a true process of initiation. The director takes advantage of his experiences as a documentarist to create an authentic portrait of the indigenous world, in which the mind and its transformations, the imaginary, the invisible, and the magic are all elements more

This is the first film to be made about the massacre at Tlatelolco, on October 2, 1968. Three months after the beginning of a student movement in Mexico similar to those occurring all over the world that year, with the Olympic Games about to begin, the government decided to suppress the protests once and for all by sending in the army

TOP TEN GROSSING FILMS IN MEXICO: 1990

	Rentals (million pesos)
La risa en vacaciones	8,450
Pretty Woman	6,900
Home Alone	6,750
Gremlins 2	6,200
Tango and Cash	5,500
Dick Tracy	4,650
Dios se lo pague	4,420
Back to the Future II	4,400
Ghost	4,000
Rojo amanecer	3,300

Scene from *La leyenda de una mascara*

to disperse violently those attending a demonstration in the Square called "De las Tres Culturas" in Tlatelolco, Mexico City. The result was a hundred or so dead, an unknown number of casualties and a thousand arrested. *Rojo Amanecer* narrates these events. Its release has been achieved after having been delayed for a year by government authorities. The film is the result of a good script and a good production idea. All the action occurs in the interior of an apartment belonging to a family made up of three generations: the grandfather who was a soldier, the father who is a civil servant, and his children either in school or at the university. Thus the filming could be undertaken discreetly and on a low budget. The action begins at daybreak on October 2 and ends at daybreak on October 3. Emphasis is placed on what occurs within the family and without, although the violence in the square outside is perceived not through images so much as by way of the soundtrack; until that violence breaks all bounds and erupts with dramatic consequences.

Tomás Pérez Turrent

La leyenda de una mascara (The Legend of a Mask)

Script and Direction: José Buil. Photography: Henner Hofmann. Music: Oscar Reynoso. Editing: Sigfrido García, Jr. Art Direction: Patricia Eguia, Alfonso Morales. Players: Hector Bonilla, Hector Ortega, María Rojo, Gina Morett, Pedro Armendariz, Damián Alcazar, Fernando Rubio. Produced by Conacine/Imcine.

In this, his first full-length film, José Buil used a structure similar to that of *Citizen Kane*: on the death of a famous masked wrestler whose identity has been jealously hidden, a reporter is given the job of finding out who was behind the mask, what is the "Rosebud" of the famous Masked Angel. He collects statements from all those who were close to the hero. The film is like a jigsaw puzzle, its construction neither chronological nor linear. Buil uses a series of stereotypes: the alcoholic reporter, the ignorant film producer, and above all the masked wrestler in person made myth by the mask itself, the comic strip and the silver screen. *The Legend of a Mask* mixes humorously diverse types and movie conventions, and offers an ironic reflection on myths created by popular culture, power and the Mexican fascination for the mask *per se* (the origins of which can be traced to pre-Hispanic times); the possibilities of a national super-hero confronting transnational merchandising.

Tomás Pérez Turrent

Pueblo de madera (Lumber Town)

Script: Juan Antonio de la Riva, Francisco Sánchez. Direction: Juan Antonio de la Riva. Photography: Leoncio Villarías. Music: Antonio Avitia. Editing: Oscar Figueroa. Art Direction: Patricia Eguia. Players: Alonso Echánove, Gabriela Roel, Ignacio Guadalupe, Mario Almada, Angélica Aragón, José Carlos Ruiz. Produced by Conacite ll/lmcine, Televisión Española, S.A.

For his third film, Juan Antonio de la Riva returns to his native soil, the lumber town San Miguel de Cruces where in 1983 he made *Wandering Lives* (*Vidas Errantes*), and portrays a world without future whose inhabitants live, dream, make love, cheat, rob, plan to leave but never manage to. The women try to find a mate, while the men are condemned to work at the sawmill, the only work source available. Meanwhile, television supplants the movies, habitually the only place where the dwellers of this town could liberate their dreams.

De la Riva paints an affectionate and generous portrait of this tiny, futureless universe, and chooses for his purpose a structure similar to a fresco: a dozen characters all of similar importance who take on typical attitudes; two of them, both adolescents, are used as a narrative vehicle. All this permits a mural-type portrait of a real town, and at the same time is symbolic of Mexican provincial life in general.

Tomás Pérez Turrent

TOMÁS PÉREZ TURRENT has published several books on the cinema since 1963. He has also written numerous film scripts. He is a graduate of UNAM (National Autonomous University of Mexico) in Philosophy.

Recent and Forthcoming Films

Emboscada (Ambush). Script: Hernando Name, Carlos Valdemar. Dir: Hernando Name. Phot: Alberto Arellanos. Players: Fernando Almada, Mario Almada, Eric del Castillo, Norma Herrera, Manuel Capetillo, Blanca Rosa Torres. Prod: Carlos Vasallo, Cinematográfica del Prado, Alianza Cinematográfica Mexicana.
El extensionista (Extensionist). Script: Victor Ugalde, Fernando Pérez Gavilán, based on the stage play by Felipe Santander. Dir: Fernando Pérez Gavilan. Phot: Arturo de la Rosa. Players: José Carlos Ruiz, Ernesto Gómez Cruz, Caludia Guzmán, Sergio Jiménez, Eduardo Palomo, Manuel Ojeda. Prod: Fernando Pérez Gavilán.
Los pasos de Ana (Ana's Journey) Script: José Buil. Dir: Marysa Sistach. Phot: Emanuel Tacamba. Players: Guadalupe Sánchez, Emilio Echevarria, Roberto Cobo, Valdiri Durand, Pia Buil. Prod: Canario Rojo, Feeling, Tragaluz, IMCINE.
Retorno a aztlan-in Necuepaliztli in Aztlan (Return to Aztlan). Script and Dir: Juan Mora Catlett. Phot: Tony Kuhn. Players: Rodrigo Puebla, Rafael Cortés, Amado Sumaya, Socorro Avelar, Soledad Ruiz. Prod: Producciones Volcán, S.A., Cooperativa José Revueltas, DGAC-

UNAM, Fondo de Fomento a la Calidad Cinematográfica, IMCINE.
La tarea (Homework). Script and Dir: Jaime Humberto Hermosillo. Phot: Tony Kuhn. Players: Maria Rojo, José Alonso. Prod: Manuel Barbachano Ponce, Clasa Films.

Scene from *La Tarea*, directed by Jaime Humberto Hermosillo

Useful Addresses

Direccion General de Cinematografia
Avenida México-Coyoacán 389
03330, México D.F.
Tel: 688 8914, 604 1449
Fax: 688 4211

Direccion General de Actividades Cinematograficas (UNAM)
San Ildefonso 43, Centro
06020 México D.F.
Fax: 702 4503
Telex: 1777429 UNAME FILMOTECA

Estudios Churubusco-Azteca
Atletas 2, Col. Country Club
04220 México D.F.
Tel: 549–3060 to 65
Fax: 549 2195, 549 0761

Estudios America
Calzada de Tlalpan 2818
04460 México, D.F.
Tel: 254 8761, 677 8099, 677 8122

Compañia Operadora de Teatros (COTSA)
Av. Universidad 1330
03100 México D.F.
Tel: 534 8280
Fax: 524 8777

Instituto Mexicano de Cinematografia (IMCINE)
Atletas 2
04220 México D.F.
Tel: 689 6650, 689 3035, 689 6500
Fax: 689 1989; 549 0931

Sociedad General de Escritores de Mexico Sa De Ip.
José Maria Velazco 59
03900 México D.F.
Tel: 593 3566, 593 6017, 593 6976
Fax: 593 6017

Distributors

Arte Cinema de Mexico
Zacatecas 97, Col. Roma
06700 México, D.F.
Tel: 564 2133, 564 3476, 574 0828

Cine en el Mundo
Atletas 2
04220 México D.F.
Tel: 549 3060

Columbia Pictures de Mexico, S.A.
Ejército Nacional 343
11520 México D.F.
Fax: 203 4070

Leaders Films
Tonalá 63. Col. Roma
06700 México D.F.
Tel: 533 6855, 533 6856

Macondo Cine Video
Vicente Garcia Torres 120
04100 México D.F.
Tel: 549 7225
Fax: 549 1380

Peliculas Nacionales, S.A. de cv.
Av. División del norte 2462, 50 piso
03300 México D.F.
Tel: 688 7089, 688 7161, 688 7277
Fax: 688 7017

Twentieth Century-Fox
Querétaro 65–80 piso
06700 México D.F.
Tel: 574 5135, 574 6150, 574 3320

United International Pictures
Newton 256–70 piso
11520 México D.F.
Tel: 250 6905, 545 1618

Videocine
Fernández Leal 43
04100 México D.F.
Tel: 554 1915
Fax: 554 4332

Zafra Cine Difusion
Van Dyck 57
03910 México, D.F.
Tel: 598 3639

Producers

Asociacion de Productores de Peliculas
División del Norte 2462–80 piso
03300 México D.F.
Tel: 688 7378
Fax: 688 7251

Amaranta Films
Vicente Garcia Torres 120
04100 México D.F.
Tel: 549 1380
Fax: 549 1380

Cinematografica Tabasco, S.A.
Condor 240
01010 México D.F.
Tel: 593 1589

Producciones Raul de Anda, S.A.
Av. División del norte 2462–40 piso
03300 México D.F.
Tel: 688 7014, 688 7800

Producciones Rosas Priego, S.A.
Av. División del norte 2462–40 piso
03300 México D.F.
Tel: 688 7022

Clasa Films-Manuel Barbachano Ponce
Atletas 2
04220 México D.F.
Tel: 544 5002
Fax: 637 3159

Casablanca Films
Atletas 2
04220 México D.F.
Tel: 549 0185, 689 8912
Fax: 689 6460

Cinematografica Filmex, S.A.
Av. División del Norte 2462–60 piso
0300 México D.F.

NETHERLANDS
by Pieter van Lierop

Changes are afoot and those changes had better be drastic, because the present situation of Dutch film is far from flourishing. In 1990, cinema attendances fell back by 6.1% to a new low of 14,635,998 tickets sold. This means that since 1980, the number of cinema visits has halved to an average of less than once a year per head of the population. That is the lowest figure in the whole of Europe. Dutch government support to the national film industry is also the lowest in Europe: 40 dollar cents per head of the population. In a similarly small country for film like Denmark, five times as much assistance is provided.

There are more saddening figures. There wasn't a single Dutch film among the twenty with highest attendance figures in 1990 (which together earned 62% of the takings). It was calculated in 1986 that the Dutch TV organisations only spent about 1 thousandth of their total budget on participation in Dutch film productions. The installation of two special funds (a co-production fund and one to encourage culture) made it possible to generate an extra 10 million guilders. This sum may have been raised through the TV companies, but it was not from the TV companies themselves. Reports on 1990 make it clear that the broadcasting companies have become frighteningly unwilling to participate in the production of experimental, documentary, animation and short films. These are precisely the disciplines entrusted to the Film Fund with its 5,380,000 guilder budget from the Ministry

of Cultural Affairs. This fund can in exceptional cases provide a grant of up to a million guilders (about US$ 500,000). Then there is the Production Fund, which is expected to use its budget of 7,073,000 guilders only to provide grants to productions deemed commercially viable and which can provide up to 60% of the costs of 800,000 guilders.

The Ministry of Cultural Affairs is now thinking of combining the two funds. In addition, a kind of "studio" should become operational where young talent can develop further. The minister, Hedy D'Ancona, also cherishes the idea of providing some of the grants in retrospect, dependent on factors such as audience response or success at foreign festivals. About these and other issues, she wrote a film white paper in early 1991 to which she expected reactions from all corners of the Dutch film world. These could then be incorporated in the final policy correction. So far the reactions indicate that few support the idea of the two funds merging. But almost all parties agree that ideas on restructuring make little sense unless substantially more government money is made available for film, while TV companies should also be obliged to invest more in film productions.

Marianne Basler in *Eline Vere*

Smart Producers

Of all the producers, Kees Kasander and Denis Wigman are the least sensitive to the way the politics of film operate in Holland. This duo focuses on projects with co-producers in many countries. In this way, they have made more films in co-operation with the British director Peter Greenaway (whose *Prospero's Books* was shot entirely in the Netherlands) and the Argentine Alejandro Agresti. The latter's **Luba** (shot in an improvised Dutch studio) is something of a disappointment after his two previous masterpieces. *Luba* is about a political refugee who, in an indeterminate country and an indeterminate time, spends a night in the company of a prostitute with whom he falls in love. The meagre substance and laborious English dialogues are in stark contrast with the fantastic photography and marvellous sets. Art direction is by Jan Roelfs and Ben van Os, two Dutchmen who are starting to acquire an international reputation and were nominated for a Felix in 1990.

Among the full-blooded Dutch productions which certainly deserve international attention are the films **Vigour** (*Kracht*), by Frouke Fokkema (making her directing debut) and **The Indecent Woman** (*De Onfatsoenlijke Vrouw*) by Ben Verbong, which are reviewed separately. Another interesting work is **Oh Boy!**, a comedy salute to the American masters of slapstick shot by Orlow Seunke entirely in the studio. Seunke himself plays the lead as a Buster Keaton lookalike. *Oh Boy!* comes from the stables of producers Laurens Geels and Dick Maas who, despite the general malaise, have presented three new films and in

1991 they opened a studio of their own in the polder landscape near Almere (30 minutes from Schiphol or Amsterdam) bearing the name the First Floor Film Factory. This is a complex with two spacious studios, a back-lot more than two hectares (12 acres) in size and numerous facilities among the most modern in Europe. Geels and Maas want to use the Factory for their own films, but also make it available for other productions.

First Floor Features produced **The Last Island**, a feature which was nevertheless shot in its entirety on the island of Tobago. Using a classic outline – an airplane crashes and a handful of survivors discovers that the rest of the world has been destroyed by a nuclear bomb – Marleen Gorris tells a feminist fable. Driven by jealousy, religious fervour and assertiveness, the men come into conflict with each other and only the women – stronger and more practical – are able to endure the adventure and guarantee the survival of the human race. While the story line of *The Last Island* can certainly be criticised, it is impossible to avoid the conclusion that Gorris has performed an impressive technical feat. The production value of the film is first class. Ronald Beer made **My Blue Heaven**, set in the 1950's and focusing on East Indian immigrants who want to open a restaurant and are initially frustrated by the racist boss of a snack bar. It is a sympathetic film with a hint of *My Beautiful Laundrette*.

Dutch racism forty years ago is also the main theme of the very picturesque **Ava & Gabriel**, shot on the Dutch Caribbean island of Curaçao and made by Felix de Rooij and Norman de Palm. They provide a Romeo and Juliet cameo as a painter from Surinam falls in love with an Antillean schoolteacher who was really already betrothed to a Dutch policeman. He causes even more of a stir by painting in a church a black Madonna for which his beloved had been the model. *Ava & Gabriel* won the Special Jury Award at the 1990 Dutch Film Days.

As an international co-production orchestrated from Holland, **Eline Vere** is certainly the most impressive achievement of 1991. Matthijs van Heijningen chose the Belgian Harry Kümel to direct this classic novel by the Dutch writer Louis Couperus. It is a psychological drama set a century ago in The Hague and Brussels. Eline (played by the Swiss actress Marianne Basler) is a girl from the upper middle-class. She would appear to have everything to guarantee happiness. She is passionate, beautiful, rich and young. But following three unrequited loves and in the suffocating awkwardness of her surroundings, she is eventually driven to death. In the cast, Basler receives excellent support from Michael York, Aurore Clément, Monique van de Ven and Thom Hoffman among others. The reconstruction of the period is monumental. The only weakness is that the drama lacks sufficient subtlety. This objection will probably be removed when Eline Vere appears in a longer version as a mini series for television.

Minimal Movies Strike Again

The low-budget film corner was again dominated in the last twelve months by Pim de la Parra and his friends, specialised in what they call "minimal movies." These are feature films made for minimal sums (sometimes less than 100,000 guilders) and shot in minimal time: sometimes in twelve days, sometimes even in six. They are striking for their humour and spontaneity. De la Parra was on form as a director in **Let the Music Dance**, about a composer commissioned to write the European anthem, but continually kept from his work by lovers and bailiffs. The best "minimal movie" was made by Paul Ruven, a promising young director who has just completed his courses at the film academy, but only after he already had two feature films to his name. The latest is called **How to Survive a Broken Heart** and is set among drop-outs of various nationalities living near the port of Amsterdam. Erik de Bruyn plays the lead; a melancholy young man who earns money in "chicken" races. He has to drive along a certain stretch of dual carriageway on the wrong side of the road while the underworld places bets on the outcome. Erik doesn't really care about the outcome, because he has lost his girl.

Another intriguing film, also shot in black-and-white, is **Passengers** (*Passagiars*), directed by Ben van Lieshout. More an impression than a story, it is about two couples who take off because they can't settle down in the polder new towns. No less depressing is **Death by Guilt** (*In Naam der wer*), a semi-documentary by Barbara den Uyl, who investigates the notorious death in police custody in 1986 of Hans Kok. This 26-year-old junkie was arrested with a group of 22 other anarchist Amsterdam squatters during a violent police eviction. Kok was found dead in his cell next day. The official cause of death was an overdose of methadon. Barbara den Uyl ascertains in her reconstruction that the Amsterdam police also bear responsibility for Kok's death.

The most effective Dutch contribution to the 1991 Rotterdam Film Festival was Peter Delpeut's piece **Lyrical Nitrate**, a pleasurable compilation of film fragments from the years 1905–1915, mostly sections of melodrama along with old opera footage. The resulting film aims to pay homage to the pioneering days of the film medium.

Also worthy of note are the short films *Baito* (by Peter Dop) and *Viaduc* (by Danniel Danniel). The Rotterdam Film Festival, where both the FIPRESCI and Dutch critics crowned the Soviet film-maker Sokurov, drew 6% less visitors in 1991, resulting in a drop in receipts from 425,000 to 400,000 guilders. This was not surprising as the festival coincided with the most tense days of Operation Desert Storm. Marco Müller left for the Locarno Festival and passed on his directorship to Dutchman Emile Fallaux.

The Dutch Film Days in Utrecht (always

Patricia Hayes and Shelagh McLeod in Marleen Gorris's *The Last Island*

the last week in September) had a glorious tenth edition with a broader programme and an increase in ticket sales from 24,786 in 1989 to 40,127 in 1990. Less glorious were the shortfall on the budget and the mediocre level of the programme, in which the Cinema Militans lecture by Alexei German was a high point. The national film prizes, the Golden Calves, were distributed as follows. Best film: **Evenings** (*De Avonden*) directed by Rudolf van den Berg for producers René Solleveld and Peter Weijdeveld. Special Jury Prize: *Ava & Gabriel* by Felix de Rooij and Norman de Palm. Best director: Frouke Fokkema for *Vigour* (*Kracht*). Best actor: Thom Hoffman for *Evenings*. Best actress: Monique van de Ven for *Romeo*. Best documentary: *Gold Fever* by Joost Kraanen. Best short: *Schrödinger's Cat* by Paulo Pistolesi. Music (oeuvre prize); Loek Dikker. Culture Prize: Jos Stelling as founder of the festival. And Film Critics' Prize: Rita Horst, first-time director of *Romeo*.

Among the better documentaries a special mention is deserved by Olivier Koning's **São Paulo, SP**. A vivid portrait of an energetic metropolis.

Pieter van Lierop

Anneke Blok, the main actress in *Vigour*

Kracht
(Vigour)

Script and director: Frouke Fokkema. Photography: Theo Bierkens. Players: Theu Boermans, Anneke Blok, Dave van Dinther. Produced by Mattheijs van Heijningen for Sigma Film Productions and Trust Toneel.

Frouke Fokkema's debut as film-maker is the very distinctive and morbid country drama, *Vigour*, in which farming life is freed from all arcadian myths. Before Fokkema developed into a prominent playwright, she had studied agriculture and spent years on farms in the Pyrenees, Vosges, in Norway, Russia, Israel and the southern province of the Netherlands where *Vigour* is set: Limburg. Everywhere she saw the same things: people struggling on the brink of poverty, living in isolation in narrow-minded communities with extremely high suicide figures.

Fokkema's film opens picturesquely and dramatically. It is winter and the rolling hills evoke an atmosphere of death and decay. On an age old farmstead, a woman has died of a brain tumour. The funeral procession gets stuck in the mud and is too late reaching the church, where another funeral has already started. Farmer Bert takes his dead wife back home and cremates her body in the stove.

The story then moves on several months. During a visit to an agricultural show, widower Bert attracts the attention of a young woman called Rose, an artist who has had her fill of city life. She becomes obsessed by Bert and later visits him in his muddy hills. A relationship develops, overshadowed by the objections of Bert's relatives and memories of his dead wife. Rose has obviously overestimated her ability to adapt, her romantic expectations are disappointed and she is nauseated by the lack of culture and coarse code of behaviour on the farm. She hangs herself in a barn and is eaten by the pigs. The film ends where it started, in a graveyard.

What makes *Vigour* so fascinating is the uncompromising way in which Fokkema bundles her themes in powerful and dramatic scenes. It is a pity that the intrigue is not unravelled as convincingly as it was formulated. Where Theu Boermans gives perfect shape to the farmer and other villagers are portrayed true to life by professional and amateur actors, Anneke Blok's role as big-city artist is dubious. The turnabout from naive romantic expectations to sudden disillusionment ending in suicide is not made convincing enough. The weakness of the film does not detract from the fact that *Vigour* certainly earned its awards at the Dutch Film Days (a Golden Calf for the best director) and at the Women's Film Festival at Créteil.

Pieter van Lierop

PIETER VAN LIEROP was appointed film editor of the Utrechts Nieuwsblad in 1974, also serving the twelve daily papers of the Netherlands Press Association (GPU) as a correspondent. He has been correspondent of the International Film Guide since 1981.

José Way in *The Indecent Woman*

De onfatsoenlijke vrouw (The Indecent Woman)

Script: Marianna Dikker, Jean van der Velde, Peter Märthesheimer, Pea Frölich and Ben Verbong. Director: Ben Verbong. Photography: Lex Wertwijn. Players: José Way, Huub Stapel, Coen van Vrijberge de Coningh, Marieke van Leeuwen, Theo de Groot. Produced by Chris Brouwer and Haig Balian for Movies Film Productions.

Ben Verbong's *The Indecent Woman* is about the desire for lust; about lust versus love and the fable that these things can be kept strictly separate. Verbong introduces us to Emilia, a violinist. She is an affluent, young and attractive woman (José Way) and apparently happily married to Charles (Coen van Vrijberge de Coningh), a prison psychiatrist. Such a singular profession can only be intended to indicate the Emilia's ties to this man involve an element of mental enslavement. During a concert in the prison just one glance exchanged with a prisoner is enough to shock Emilia into discovering an unbridled desire for sex for sex's sake; for more lust than her husband has to offer. That same day she meets the fanciful seducer Leon. With him, Emilia is willing to lose herself in "indecency" to the wonderful music of Nicola Piovani.

We don't find out exactly who Leon is. Emilia says it herself: "It's not about him but about me." That is also what Ben Verbong makes so interesting about his film. The director stylises out everything of direct relevance to the behaviour and psychological development of his heroine.

While *The Indecent Woman* allows José Way, in an excellent debut role, and the perfect Huub Stapel to play an imaginative and erotic game of cat and mouse evocative of *9½ Weeks*, Ben Verbong manages to

TOP TEN GROSSING FILMS IN THE NETHERLANDS: 1990

	Admissions
Look Who's Talking	1,300,229
Pretty Woman	968,502
Ghost	713,607
Koko Flanel	704,988
Total Recall	490,530
She's out of Control	369,865
Another 48 Hours	354,814
Back to the Future, Part III	338,809
Die Hard 2	317,952
The War of the Roses	304,338

make the opposite of a one-dimensional voyeuristic film. No peeping-tom camera in search of piquant details, but a Jacques Deray-like atmospheric approach to eroticism which is often more emphatically present in the dialogue than in the pictures. This while Lex Wertwijn's sensitive photography makes the eroticism more palpable through rhythm and the use of colour than in impudent anatomical close-ups.

The film might have been more powerful if it had been made slightly more intense and provocative. On the other hand, such a slightly-more-indecent approach may have made the difference between a beauty and a flop.

Pieter van Lierop

Recent and Forthcoming Films

Last Island. Script and Dir: Marleen Gorris. Phot: Marc Felperlaan. Players: Paul Freeman, Shelagh McLeod, Patricia Hayes, Kenneth Colley, Mark Hembrow, Marc Berman, Ian Tracey. Prod: Laurens Geels and Dick Maas for First Floor Features.
Alissa in Concert. Script and Dir: Erik van Zuylen. Phot: Alejandro Agresti. Players: Frances-Marie Uitti, Michael Matthews, Pim Lambeau, Johan Leysen. Prod: Kees Kasander and Denis Wigman for Allarts.

Ava & Gabriel. Script: Norman de Palm. Dir: Felix de Rooy. Phot: Ernest Dickerson. Players: Nashaira Desbarida, Cliff San-A-Jong, Geert de Jong, Rina Penso, Ana Muskus, Theu Boermans, Dolf de Vries. Prod: Norman de Palm for Cosmic Illusion Productions.
Luba. Script, Dir and Phot: Alejandro Agresti. Players: Elio Marchi, Bozena Lasota, Viveca Lindfors, Adrian Brine, Michael Matthews, Alex van der Wyck. Prod: Kees Kasander and Denis Wigman for Allarts.
My Blue Heaven. Script and Dir: Ronald Beer, Phot: Marc Felperlaan. Players: Bo Bojoh, Ruud De Wolff, Angelique Corneille, Leen Jongewaard, Ivon Pelasula, Koen Wauters, Edda Barends. Prod: Laurens Geels and Dick Maas for First Floor Features.
The Phenix Mystery. Script and Dir: Leonard Retel Helmrich. Phot: Jan Wich. Players: Luc Boyer, Liz Snoyink, Manouk van der Meulen, Rutger Weemhoff, Gerrit Brokx. Prod: Fransjoris de Graaf for Phoenix Films.
Let the Music Dance. Script and Dir: Pim de la Parra. Phot: Jan Wich. Players: Boudewijn de Groot, Bonnie Williams, Marc Hazewinkel. Prod: Sherman de Jesus for Minimal Movies Europe.
How to Survive a Broken Heart. Script: Paul Ruven, Pim de la Parra, P.J. Vernu. Dir: Paul Ruven. Phot: Jan Wich. Players: Bonnie Williams, Eric de Bruyn, Alejandro Agresti, Jim Cook, Isabella van Rooy. Prod: Pim de la Parra for Minimal Movies International.
Eline Vere. Script: Jan Blokker and Patrick

Pesnot, based on the novel by Louis Couperus. Dir: Harry Kümel. Phot: Eduard van der Enden. Players: Marianne Basler, Monique van de Ven, Thom Hoffman, Johan Leysen, Aurore Clément, Michael York, Paul Anrieu, Joop Admiraal. Prod: Matthijs van Heijningen for Sigma Film Productions.

Oh Boy! Script and Dir: Orlow Seunke. Phot: Marc Felperlaan. Players: Orlow Seunke, Kees van Kooten, Jim van der Wouden, Monique Smets, Peer Mascini, Steffen Kroon. Prod: Laurens Geels and Dick Maas for First Floor Features.

De Provincie. Script: Hugo Heinen, based on a novel by Jan Brokken. Dir: Jan Bosdriesz. Phot: Jules van der Steenhoven. Players: Thom Hoffman, Pierre Bokma, Gijs Scholten van Aschat, Tamar van den Dop, Peter Oosthoek, Gerard Thoolen. Prod: Frans Rasker for Horizon Film Productions.

In Naam Der Wet (Death By Guilt). Script and Dir: Barbara den Uyl. Phot: Frans Bromet. Players: Martijn Oversteegen, Ed van Thijn, Henk Kersting. Prod: Leen van den Berg for Van der Hoop Filmproducties.

Producers

Added Films Holland BV
Herenstraat 64A
1406 PH Bussum
Tel: (2159) 35908
Fax: (2159) 388808

Allarts BV
Sarphatistraat 117
1018 GB Amsterdam
Tel: (20) 6384866
Telefax: (20) 6207254

Annette Apon Prods.
Binnenkant 24–III
1011 BH Amsterdam
Tel: (20) 6267856

Black Tulip Films
Postbus 72
2050 AB Overveen
Tel: (23) 272637
Fax: (23) 247912

Cannon City Prods. BV
De Lairessestraat 111–115
1075 HH Amsterdam
Tel: (20) 5751751
Fax: (20) 6622085

Casa Film
Prinsengracht 151
1015 DR Amsterdam
Tel: (20) 6265550

Castor Films
Hoofdstraat 94

9968 AG Pieterburen
Tel: (5952) 422
Fax: (5952) 446

Cinété Film Prods.
Elisabeth Wolffstraat 45
1053 TR Amsterdam
Tel: (20) 6167719
Fax: (20) 6891954

Cine Ventura
Allard Piersonstraat 6
1053 ZZ Amsterdam
Tel: (20) 6837439

Cine/Vista BV
Prinses Marielaan 8
3743 JA Baarn
Tel: (2154) 23720
Fax: (2154) 23736

Commercial Artists
Leeuwenwerf 77
1018 KA Amsterdam
Tel: (20) 6271045
Fax: (20) 6271045

Cosmic Illusion Prods.
P.O. Box 11582
1001 GN Amsterdam
Tel: (20) 6237234
Fax: (20) 6247922

Nico Crama Films
Stevinstraat 261
2587 EJ Den Haag
Tel: (70) 3544964

Creative Projects

Bogaardslaan 45
7339 AL Ugchelen
Tel: (55) 334902
Fax: (55) 334902
Telex: 20010

Roy Dames Film-productions
Sumatrastraat 225 d
1092 PH Amsterdam
Tel: (20) 6925479
Fax: (20) 6658423

Stichting DD Film Prods.
Entrepôtdok 66
1018 AD Amsterdam
Tel: (20) 6381327
Fax: (20) 6209857

Dessafilms B.V.
Oudezijds Voorburgwal 219
1012 EX Amsterdam
Tel: (20) 6250093/6245602

Cilia van Dijk
Ged. Voldersgracht 20
2011 WD Haarlem
Tel: (23) 314273
Fax; (23) 314273

Ecco Films
P.O. Box 53223
1007 RE Amsterdam
Tel: (20) 6239457

First Amsterdam Film Association
Eddy Wijngaarde/Leon de Winter

Leliegracht 25
1016 GR Amsterdam
Tel: (20) 6265613
Fax: (20) 6228753

First Floor Features
P.O. Box 53221
1007 RE Amsterdam
Tel: (20) 6647471
Fax: (20) 6794040
Telex: 12027 basic nl

Fly by Night Film Prod.
Spuistraat 40
1012 TT Amsterdam
Tel: (20) 6222200
Fax: (20) 6382004

Frank Fehmers Prods. BV
Prins Hendrikkade 161 b
1011 TB Amsterdam
Tel: (20) 6238766/6235863
Fax: (20) 6246262
Telex: 11802 Inter

Filmwerk
Vasteland 447
3011 BJ Rotterdam
Tel: (10) 4116385

Grace Films BV
Van Eeghenstraat 109
1071 EZ Amsterdam
Tel: (20) 6753671
Fax: (20) 6753671

Bert Haanstra Films BV
Verlengde Engweg 5
1251 GM Laren (NH)
Tel: (2153) 82428
Fax: (2153) 82428

**Holland Animation
Foundation**
Stevinstraat 261
2587 EJ Den Haag
Tel: (70) 3544964

Horizon Film Prods. BV
Nieuwe Keizersgracht 58
1018 DT Amsterdam
Tel: (20) 6258817
Fax: (20) 6200226

**Roeland Kerbosch Film
Prods. BV**
Keizersgracht 678
1017 ET Amsterdam
Tel: (20) 6230390
Fax: (20) 6279879

Linden Film BV
Chopinstraat 25
1077 GM Amsterdam
Tel: (20) 6793128
Fax: (20) 6797209

Lucid Eye Productions
Prinseneiland 91
1013 LM Amsterdam
Tel: (20) 6230354

**Filmproduktie 'De
Maatschap'**
Nieuwe Uilenburgerstr. 110
1011 LX Amsterdam
Tel: (20) 6234628
• Fax: (20) 6253729

Olga Madsen BV
Marnixstraat 356
1016 XV Amsterdam
Tel: (20) 6266295

Stichting Meatball
Oranjestraat 3
2514 JB Den Haag
Tel: (70) 3646915
Fax: (70) 3562282

Meerkat Productions
P.O. Box 160
4330 AD Middelburg
Tel: (1180) 14454
Fax: (1180) 24069

**MGS Film Amsterdam BV
Golden Egg Film**
Singel 64
1015 AC Amsterdam
Tel: (20) 6231593/6629960
Fax: (20) 6243181
Telex: 41275 MayD NL

Molenwiek Film Productions
Tuinstraat 64–66
1015 PG Amsterdam

Tel: (20) 6248805
Fax: (20) 6386384 ext. 0005

Moskito Film
Oostelijke Handelskade 12
1019 BM Amsterdam
Tel: (20) 6381924

**Movies Film Productions bv
BV**
Prinsengracht 546
1017 KK Amsterdam
Tel: (20) 6275636
Fax: (20) 6252981

Open Studio Productions
Herengracht 156
1016 BN Amsterdam
Tel: (20) 6223661
Fax: (20) 6275090

Oranda Films B.V.
De Lairessestraat 111–115
1075 HH Amsterdam
Tel: (20) 65751751
Fax: (20) 6622085

Rolf Orthel Film Prods.
Lauriergracht 123 II
1016 RK Amsterdam
Tel: (20) 6220255
Fax: (20) 6261885

Praxino Pictures BV
Keizersgracht 60
1015 CS Amsterdam
Tel: (20) 6266355
Fax: (20) 6201059
Telex: 16183 Euroc NL

Pretty Pictures
Stadhouderskade 104 III
1073 AX Amsterdam
Tel: (20) 6730297
Fax: (20) 6892635

Fons Rademakers Prods. BV
Prinsengracht 685
1017 JT Amsterdam
Tel: (20) 6221298

Red Dog Productions
Valeriusstraat 111

1075 ER Amsterdam
Tel: (20) 6625747

Riverside Pictures
P.O. Box 190
1430 AD Aalsmeer
Tel: (2977) 54452/51711
Fax: (2977) 45016

Rotterdam Film City Life Foundation
Provenierssingel 33
3033 EG Rotterdam
Tel: (10) 4658565
Fax: (10) 4658392
Telex: 26401 intx nl, Ref nl
1098 City Life

Scorpio Verstappen Films BV
P.O. Box 245
1000 AE Amsterdam
Tel: (20) 6225552

Shooting Star Filmcompany B.V.
Singel 395
1012 WN Amsterdam
Tel: (20) 6247272
Fax: (20) 6258533

Sigma Film Productions B.V.
Bolensteinweg 3
3603 CP Maarssen
Tel: (3465) 70430/70341
Fax: (3465) 69764

Sol Film Prods. v.o.f.
P.O. Box 1032
4801 BA Breda
Tel: (76) 220080
Fax: (76) 229359

Spectrum Film
Kloveniersburg 46
1011 JX Amsterdam
Tel: (20) 6241921

Van de Staak Film Prods.
Jacob Oliepad 2
1013 DP Amsterdam
Tel: (20) 6260634

Staccato Films
De Ruyterweg 37
1057 JV Amsterdam
Tel: (20) 6168641/6831555
Fax: (20) 6892929

Jos Stelling Film Prods. BV
Springweg 50–52
3511 VS Utrecht
Tel: (30) 313789
Fax: (30) 310968

Studio Nieuwe Gronden
Van Hallstraat 52
1051 HH Amsterdam
Tel: (20) 6867837
Fax: (20) 6824367
Telex: 12682 sngfp

Theorema Films
Van Hallstraat 52
1051 HH Amsterdam
Tel: (20) 6881843
Fax: (20) 6863574

Three Lines Productions BV
Soesterdijkerstraatweg 58
1213 XD Hilversum
Tel: (35) 833815
Fax: (35) 857696

Topaz Pictures
St. Antoniesbreestraat 69
1011 HB Amsterdam
Tel: (20) 6226345
Fax: (20) 6242536

United Dutch Film Company
Singel 440
1017 AV Amsterdam
Tel: (20) 6273631
Fax: (20) 6249277

Jan Vrijman Cineproductie
Vondelstraat 51
1054 GJ Amsterdam
Tel: (20) 6187943/6124423
Fax: (20) 6854491

Yuca Film
P.O. Box 1379
1000 BJ Amsterdam

Tel: (20) 6270274
Fax: (20) 6380149

Zigzag Film BV
W.G. Plein 467
1054 SH Amsterdam
Tel: (20) 6168911
Fax: (20) 6853716

Distributors

Actueel Film BV
Co Bremanlaan 29
1251 HT Laren (NH)
Tel: (2153) 89830

Stichting Animated People
Ged. Voldersgracht 20
2011 WD Haarlem
Tel: (23) 314273

Argus Film BV
P.O. Box 18269
1001 ZD Amsterdam
Tel: (20) 6254585
Fax: (20) 6268978
Telex: 11084 argus nl

Cannon City Film Distribution BV
De Lairessestraat 111–115
1075 HH Amsterdam
Tel: (20) 5751751
Fax: (20) 6622085

Cannon Nova Film BV
De Lairessestraat 111–115
1075 HH Amsterdam
Tel: (20) 5751751
Fax: (20) 6622085

Cannon Tuschinski Film Distribution BV
De Lairessestraat 111–115
1075 HH Amsterdam
Tel: (20) 5751751
Fax: (20) 6622085

C.N.R. Film & Video
Amstellandlaan 78
1382 CH Weesp

Columbia/Tri-Star Films (Holland) BV
P.O. Box 533
1000 AM Amsterdam
Tel: (20) 5737655
Fax: (20) 5737656

Concorde Film
Lange Voorhout 335
2514 EC Den Haag
Tel: (70) 3605810/3924571
Fax: (70) 3604925
Telex: 34568 cofil nl

Cor Koppies Filmdistribution BV
P.O. Box 75242
1070 AE Amsterdam
Tel: (20) 6767841
Fax: (20) 6714968

Express Film
Heemraadschapslaan 13
1181 TZ Amstelveen
Tel: (20) 6412331

Film Entertainment Group BV
Edisonlaan 160
7316 JR Apeldoorn
Tel: (55) 213355
Fax: (55) 213394

Filmtrust BV
Molenkade 57A
1115 AC Duivendrecht
Tel: (20) 6957719/6955503
Fax: (20) 6956625

Gofilex Film BV
P.O. Box 334
3430 AH Nieuwegein
Tel: (3402) 70922
Fax: (3402) 70283

Hafbo BV
P.O. Box 424
3740 AK Baarn
Tel: (2154) 13213
Fax: (2154) 13213

Holland Film Releasing BV
De Lairessestraat 111–115

1075 HH Amsterdam
Tel: (20) 5751751
Fax: (20) 6622085

Hungry Eye Pictures BV
Prinsengracht 652
1017 KE Amsterdam
Tel: (20) 6223187
Fax: (20) 6268978
Telex: 39495

Vereniging Onderlinge Studenten Steun "Kriterion"
Roeterstraat 170
1018 WE Amsterdam
Tel: (20) 6231709

Melior Films BV
Steynlaan 8
1217 JS Hilversum
Tel: (35) 45542
Fax: (35) 235906

Meteor Film BV
Prinsengracht 546
1017 KK Amsterdam
Tel: (20) 6233858
Fax: (20) 6252981

Motion Picture Group BV
Beijersweg 18
1093 KR Amsterdam
Tel: (20) 6684866
Fax: (20) 6682467

The Movies BV
Haarlemmerdijk 161
1013 KH Amsterdam
Tel: (20) 6245790
Fax: (20) 6206758

BV Netherlands Fox Film Corp.
De Lairessestraat 111–115
1075 HH Amsterdam
Tel: (20) 5751751
Fax: (20) 6622085

NIS Film Distribution Holland
Anna Paulownastraat 76
2518 BJ Den Haag
Tel: 31 (70) 3564205

Fax: 31 (70) 3564681
Telex: 33159

Profile Films BV
Beijersweg 18
1093 KR Amsterdam
Tel: (20) 6929440

UIP United International Pictures (Netherlands) BV
Willemsparkweg 112
1071 HN Amsterdam
Tel: (20) 6622991
Fax: (20) 6623240

Verenigde Nederlandsche Filmcompagnie BV
't Witte Huys
Singel 440
1017 AV Amsterdam
Tel: (20) 6273631
Fax: (20) 6249277

Warner Bros (Holland) BV
De Boelelaan 16–III
1083 HJ Amsterdam
Tel: (20) 5411211
Fax: (20) 6449001

Cinemien
Entrepôtdok 66
1018 AD Amsterdam
Tel: (20) 6279501/628152/6258357
Fax: (20) 6209857

International Art Film
Rieks Hadders
Vondelpark 3
1071 AA Amsterdam
Tel: (20) 5891400
Fax: (20) 6833401

Useful Addresses

Nederlandse Bond van Bioscoop en Filmondernemingen *(The Netherlands Cinematographic Assn.) Sections: feature film producers; distributors; exhibitors*

Jan Luykenstraat 2
1071 CM Amsterdam
Tel: (20) 6799261
Fax: (20) 6750398

GNS
*(The Filmmakers' Society of the
Netherlands)*
P.O. Box 581
1000 AN Amsterdam
Tel: (20) 6200920
Fax: (20) 6268233

VAP
*(United Audiovisual Production
Companies)*
p/a H.A.F. Wennink
's-Gravelandseweg 131
1217 ES Hilversum
Tel: (35) 238677
Fax: (35) 238674

**Associatie van Nederlandse
Filmtheaters**
*(Association of Dutch Film
Theatres)*
Prinsengracht 770
1017 LE Amsterdam
Tel: (20) 6267602
Fax: (20) 6275923

KNF
(Circle of Dutch Film Critics)
Snelliuslaan 78
1222 TG Hilversum
Tel: (35) 856115

NBF
*(The Association for Film-and
Television-makers)*

Donker Curtiusstraat 7–414
1051 JL Amsterdam
Tel: (20) 6881670
Fax: (20) 6865661

NVPI
*(Dutch Association of Phonogram
and Videogram Producers)*
Albertus Perkstraat 36
1217 NT Hilversum
Tel: (35) 40951
Fax: (35) 41954
Telex: 73564 nvpi nl

**Ministry of Welfare, Health
and Cultural Affairs**
*(Department of International
Affairs)*
P.O. Box 5406
2280 HK Rijswijk
Tel: (70) 3405737/3405745
Fax: (70) 3407340

**Netherlands Information
Service**
NIS/RVD
Anna Paulownastraat 76
2518 BJ Den Haag
Tel: 31 (70) 3564205
Fax: 31 (70) 3564681
Telex: 33159

Dutch Film Fund
Jan Luykenstraat 2
1071 CM Amsterdam
Tel: (20) 6647838
Fax: (20) 6750398

Holland Animation Assn.
Ged. Voldersgracht 20
2011 WD Haarlem
Tel: (23) 314273
Fax: (23) 314273

Holland Film Promotion
Herengracht 164
1016 BP Amsterdam
Tel: (20) 6240091
Fax: (20) 6386389

Production Fund
Jan Luykenstraat 2
1071 CM Amsterdam
Tel: (20) 6799261
Fax: (20) 6750398

**SEKAM (Associated with
AGICOA)**
*(Foundation for the exploitation of
Cable-television rights)*
P.O. Box 75048
1070 AA Amsterdam
Tel: (20) 6799261
Fax: (20) 6750398

VEVAM
*(Association for the exploitation of
copyright in Audiovisual Material)*
P.O. Box 581
1000 AN Amsterdam
Tel: (20) 6200920
Fax: (20) 6268233

NEW ZEALAND

by Mike Nicolaidi

Like the country itself, the New Zealand theatrical movie business is looking down the barrel.

Given extraordinarily difficult economic times, which have cast 10% of the 3.5 million population into the ranks of registered unemployed, competition for the leisure dollar is intense. Turmoil within the cinema industry is at a peak as exhibitors and distributors seek to adjust and, belatedly, restructure facilities and operations in an economic climate likely to remain perverse and unpredictable.

Box-office revenues dived $12\frac{1}{2}\%$ in the 1990 calendar year to a low of $NZ 31.5 million ($NZ 34 million in 1987). Admissions fell 20% to 5.7 million (8.5 million in 1987). The cause according to Timothy Ord, chairman, Motion Picture Distributors Assn (NZ)., was threefold: the introduction of competitive television in New Zealand, a moribund economy, and a lack of multiplex facilities.

The first six months of 1991 offered little relief. Yet, for the optimists, a few glimmerings began to shred the gloom.

Ord has predicted that audience levels will lift 40% if multiplex development – nation-wide – becomes a reality. The country's first genuine plex, a six-screen facility in the heart of the university city of Palmerston North, opened in August 1990, and has shown what can happen. In its first weeks of business it surpassed revenue takings from cinemas in two larger cities. Within ten months, the Palmerston North region had become the country's top moviegoing centre with per capita attendance running at 4.5 annually compared with the national average of 1.7.

In mid-1991 an independent operator opened a triplex in a shopping centre in Christchurch, creating a new if smaller facility for that city. Construction is underway on a $NZ 6 million, six-screen plex, in south Auckland, which will be open in time for the 1991 Christmas trade.

Hoyts, one of the two major chains in the country, has added two additional screens to its downtown triplex in Wellington.

Given this evidence, multiplex development could be about to flower, on the assumption that a depressed property market – and the construction business generally – rises from the current harsh economic bedrock.

Resisting Monopoly

Another positive sign is that the grip on the cinema market by the country's two dominant chains may be loosening.

The Pacer Kerridge group has been in financial difficulties for more than two years with a consortium of banks virtually running the operation over the last 12 months. In

Alison Routledge and Philip Gordon in John Day's *The Returning*

late 1990 Hoyts, the other major player, sought to merge both companies' cinema interests. However the application was turned down by the Commerce Commission on the grounds that a merged identity could be dominant in the market in terms of both exhibiting and distributing films.

This decision has been appealed, but was not be heard in Auckland High Court until the end of 1991. Meantime, the Commission's rejection opened the way for another major entrant to the market – Australian's Village Roadshow. The company has 21% market share for cinema attendance in Australia (compared with Hoyts' 31%) and has an active policy on multiplex construction. The company has been cleared by the Commission to acquire Pacer Kerridge's cinema operations.

The thumbs-down on Hoyts' bid was welcomed by major distributors (like UPI and Warners) and independent cinema operators, an increasing number of whom are developing significant art house markets for a wide variety of North American and European product.

Several of these operators are looking at distribution as well, and have begun picking up films at the American Film Market and Cannes. Two of them, Kelly Rogers of Auckland's Bridgeway, and Mark Gooder, Charley Gray's Pictures, were both active in seeking French product at Cannes. Both seek to persuade offshore suppliers that it is in the suppliers' best interests to sell New Zealand direct rather than tie-up Kiwi rights in some Australasian (Australia and New Zealand) package.

New Burst of Funding

Although the production of local feature films continues to be tenuous, a surprising sum of more than $NZ 200 million will have been invested in film and TV production during 1991. The line-up of new features due to be completed by mid-1992 appears particularly strong.

What this new burst of production re-flects is the continuing importance of State funding to the entertainment industries.

Whether the situation will change with the new National Party government, elected to power October 1990, remains a moot point. In the first year of its three-year term it proved more market-orientated than its Labour predecessor and, to the alarm of most broadcasters and film and TV production houses, scrapped all foreign investment restrictions in local television and radio thus opening the door to 100% offshore ownership of these industries.

As matters stood at the end of the June 1991 ·financial year, the government remained far and away the main provider of funds for local film and TV production. Its principal hand-maidens are: State-owned enterprise Television New Zealand (the only profit-making broadcaster in New Zealand or Australia) and its subsidiaries, South Pacific Pictures and Avalon; the TV licence fee collection agency, the Broadcasting Commission (also known as "NZ On Air"); and the N.Z. Film Commission, these days financed almost two thirds by State lottery profits.

Important new entrants into feature film production are South Pacific Pictures and NZ On Air. SPP produced Ian Mune's new film, **The End of the Golden Weather**, which was financed by NZ on Air and the Film Commission.

The most significant new player, however, is the other Wellington-based TVNZ subsidiary, Avalon, which two years ago absorbed the State-owned National Film Unit studios and laboratory. It has an equity investment in Barry Barclay's **Te Rua**, and co-produced **Chunuk Bair**, a low-budget First World War film about the Gallipoli campaign, with Auckland's Daybreak Pictures.

Reg Russ, Avalon's managing director, wants the Avalon production facility, which can service all phases of feature film-making to final print, to be involved in some six productions a year. During the latter half

Still from *Moonrise*

of 1991 the company was expected to be involved in at least three new local features, and a N.Z. – Australian co-production, **Secrets**, produced by Victorian International Pictures, of Melbourne Australia.

Film Commission to the Fore

But the Film Commission remains the predominant force in developing and financing local feature films. While it continues to have little luck opening up avenues of private investment, it has embarked on a $NZ 2 million scheme aimed at achieving a greater range of product and strengthening the infrastructure of local film production companies. The scheme, dubbed Super-Pods, also seeks to give the recipient companies more autonomy in the development of projects.

After its big success locally and offshore with Jane Campion's *An Angel at My Table*, the Commission approved major investment in a strong package of director-driven features.

These included new films by Peter Jackson (*Bad Taste*, *Meet the Feebles*) and David Blyth, a N.Z. director (*Red Blooded American Girl*) who also works in the U.S. Two other projects are from the successful production partnership of Bridget Ikin (*An Angel at My Table*) and John Maynard (Campion's *Sweetie*, and Vincent Ward's *The Navigator*).

All films are geared for completion early 1992.

Ikin's production, **Crush**, is the first feature of Alison Maclean, whose short film *Kitchen Sink* premiered at the 1991 Sundance Film Festival. She was one of six directing fellows selected for Sundance Institute's 11th Filmmakers Lab in June.

The Maynard production is **The Footstep Man**, the second feature by a leading N.Z. cinematographer Leon Narbey.

Campion was expected to begin shooting

her third feature, a probable French-Australian-New Zealand co-production, on N.Z. locations, late 1991. Vincent Ward was in post-production on his new film, **Map of the Human Heart**, another co-production involving four countries, at year's end.

The two new feature releases in 1991, John Day's **The Returning**, and Barclay's **Te Rua**, were disappointing. Day's first feature looked good but lacked structural coherence of storyline. *Te Rua*, a N.Z.-German coproduction, had difficulty meshing a local ethnic community background with the more readily accessible genre of international action adventure.

A museum break-in in *HVII 7 – 7A*
photo: Andrzej Nowakowzki

MIKE NICOLAIDI, writer and freelance journalist, was New Zealand correspondent for Variety from 1978 to 1991. He has had a close involvement with the N.Z. film industry since the early 1970's when moves first began to establish a N.Z. Film Commission. He has been a political and foreign correspondent for various N.Z. news media.

Recent and Forthcoming Films

The End of the Golden Weather. Script: Ian Mune, Bruce Mason. Dir: Ian Mune. Phot: Alun Bollinger. Players: Stephen Fulford, Stephen Papps, Paul Gittens, Gabrielle Hammond, Ray Henwood. Prod: South Pacific Pictures.
Te Rua. Script: Barry Barclay. Dir: Barry Barclay. Phot: Rory O'Shea, Warrick Attewell. Players: Wi Kuki Kaa, Peter Kaa, Stuart Devenie, Donna Akersten. Prod: Pacific Films Productions.
The Returning. Script: Arthur Baysting, John Day. Dir: John Day. Phot: Kevin Hayward. Players: Phillip Gordon, Alison Routledge, Max Cullen, Jim Moriarty. Prod: Echo Pictures.
Chunuk Bair. Script: Grant Hindin Miller. Dir: Dale Bradley. Phot: Warrick Attewell. Players: Robert Powell, K J Wilson, Darryl Beattie, Tim Bray, Jed Brophy. Prod: Daybreak Pictures/Avalon.
Moonrise. Script: Michael Heath. Dir: David Blyth. Phot: Kevin Hawyard. Players: Al Lewis, Justin Glocke, Milan Borich, Pat Evison, Noel Appleby. Prod: Tucker Productions.
Brain Dead. Script: Fran Walsh, Stephens Sinclair, Peter Jackson. Dir: Peter Jackson. Phot: Murray Milne. Players: Tim Balme, Liz Moody, Dana Penalver, Ian Watkin. Prod: Wingnut Films.
Crush. Script: Alison Maclean, Anne Kennedy. Dir: Alison Maclean. Phot: Dion Beebe. Players: Maria Gay Harden, Caitlin Bossley, Donogh Rees, William Zappa. Prod: Hibiscus Films.
The Footstep Man. Script: Leon Narbey, Martin Edmond. Dir: Leon Narbey. Phot: Alan Guilford. Players: Steven Grives, Rosie Jones, Jennifer Ward-Lealand, Michael Hurst, Sarah Smuts-Kennedy. Prod: John Maynard Productions.
Secrets. Script: Jan Sardi. Dir: Michael Pattinson. Phot: David Connell. Players: Danii Minogue, Beth Campion, Malcolm Kennard, Willa O'Neill, Noah Taylor. Prod: Victorian International Pictures/Avalon-NFU Studios.

Useful Addresses

N.Z. Film Commission
36 Allen Street
Wellington
Tel: (04) 859 754
Fax: (04) 849 719

Avalon
PO Box 31–444
Lower Hutt
Tel: (04) 619–0600
Fax: (04) 674 411

South Pacific Pictures
56 Anzac Rd
Brown's Bay
Auckland
Tel: (09) 479 3000
Fax: (09) 479 3007

NZ On Air
54–56 Cambridge Tce
Wellington
Tel: (04) 829 524
Fax: (04) 829 543

Daybreak Pictures
280 Parnell Rd
Auckland
Tel: (09) 776 793
Fax: (09) 394 001

Endeavour Entertainment Ltd
46–56 Brown Street
Auckland
Tel: (09) 781 900
Fax: (09) 781 905

Film Facilities Ltd
26 Wright Street
Wellington
Tel: (04) 844 192
Fax: (04) 843 774

Gibson Group
119 Taranaki Street
Wellington
Tel: (04) 847 789
Fax: (04) 844 727

Hibiscus Films
PO Box 1852
Auckland
Tel: (09) 309 83 88
Fax: (09) 734 722

Hoyts Corp. Holdings (NZ)
103–107 Hobson Street
Auckland
Tel: (09) 303 2739
Fax: (09) 370 011

Independent Producers & Directors Guild
PO Box 9116
Wellington
Tel: (04) 854 344

Isambard
118 Asquith Avenue
Auckland
Tel: (09) 897 772
Fax: (09) 897 755

Midnight Film Productions
41 Tasman Street
Wellington
Tel: (04) 846 911
Fax: (04) 854 256

Pacer Kerridge Corp
44 Khyber Pass Road
Auckland
Tel: (09) 797 003
Fax: (09) 370 041

Pacific Film Productions
PO Box 2040
Wellington
Tel: (04) 872 191
Fax: (04) 878 298

Pinflicks
1 Oak Park Avenue
Wellington
Tel: (04) 844 496
Fax: (04) 851 807

The Bridgeway
122 Queen Street
Northcote
Auckland
Tel: (09) 418 3308
Fax: (09) 418 4183

UIP
crn Wyndham/Albert Streets
Auckland
Tel: (09) 796 269
Fax: (09) 796 271

Warner Bros (NZ)
5 Hopetoun Street
Auckland
Tel: (09) 775 223
Fax: (09) 392 795

Charley Grays Pictures
43 Sentinel Road
Auckland
Tel: (09) 360 0278
Fax: (09) 360 1337

NORWAY

by Trond Olav Svendsen

The Norwegian film production normally consists of 5–7 feature films per year, yet represents remarkable diversity and has a very respectable share of theatre box-office. Since the mid-1980's in particular Norwegian features have been a vital phenomenon in the cultural life of the small nation. Artistic and commercial progress was highlighted by the international success of *The Pathfinder* (1987), and several other films have done very well with home audiences.

Producing films in a small country remains difficult. Tax shelter financing came to an end in 1988, and all Norwegian films require government support. Norwegian politicians are not moviegoers, however, and in 1989 the right-wing government reacted to the success of the Norwegian film community in a particularly unwelcome and even ignorant way – by slashing 30% off the subsidising coin.

In addition to this, the Norsk Film

Still from *Herman*

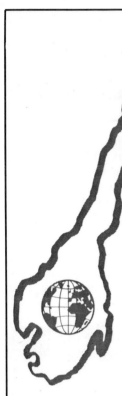

Company, cornerstone in Norwegian film production, lurched into trouble, mostly because the company anticipated a second national TV-channel too early. This second channel will, however, come, and hopefully acquire its programming through commissioned productions from the whole film-making community. Esben Højlund Carlsen, a Danish film director and media executive, was last year appointed the new head of the company, and has reportedly harvested a large selection of script and script ideas to be selectively considered as next year's features.

Still from Martin Asphaug's *Svampe*

Despite hardships, Norwegian feature films as premiered during the season of 1990–91 can be described as nothing less than a burst of creativity, even if as always they proved to be an uneven lot. After a very good autumn, with home product generating much enthusiasm from both audiences and critics, the winter gave rise to some discontent.

First to be premiered (August) was **Twice Upon A Time** (*Smykketyven*) by well-known veteran director Anja Breien, in many ways an accomplished piece of moviemaking. Swedish actor Sven Wollter is excellent as a man who loves and is loved by several women, but eventually frustrates them because he is not able to bring his whole self into the various relationships. His character is a theatrical set-designer by profession, and the film takes place partially behind the stage of a theatre, but apart from a few entertaining scenes Breien does not exploit this milieu for what it is worth. The film is both elegant and formally assured to a point, then becomes unsure and a little bogged down by its slightly pretentious use of symbols. Still, the film shows Anja Breien to be Norway's most capable director in many ways. As a film-maker she is now at a level of maturity that surely will result in great things in the future.

Death at Oslo Central (*Døden på Oslo S.*), with its sympathetic teenage detectives solving a mystery among the drug addicts of downtown Oslo, was a resounding commercial success, and the director, Eva Isaksen, whose second feature this is, received the Norwegian Critics' Award. The story, if not outstandingly original, is told with a fair degree of effectiveness. The cinematography (by talented Philip Øgaard), with its forbidding urban vistas and putrid colours, wrap the proceedings in an impressive, if slightly too fashionable, gloom. The film has many small points to make about being a youngster in a modern city environment, and about being a parent, too. It also seems to offer critical comment on the moral state of the nation's capital itself. Perhaps not all of it will travel well, but the home audience certainly loved it.

Parents Well Portrayed

It has been the rule in Norwegian films throughout the 1980's to portray children as victims of unthinking, selfish parents, and having the older generation representing everything that is old and tired in the world. *Death at Oslo Central* avoids this populism towards the young, and give charming, eccentric portraits of the parents. A similar fresh view is also offered by Erik Gustavson, the director of *Herman*. **Herman** is Gustavson's second feature, and in this account of a small family, set in Oslo in the early 1960's, he happily suggests that parents most often are willing to share their offspring's problems. The central character,

TOP TEN GROSSING FILMS IN NORWAY: 1990

	Admissions
Pretty Woman	482,413
Look Who's Talking	367,380
Death at Oslo Central (Norwegian)	270,276
Dead Poets Society	223,803
Born on the Fourth of July	220,591
The Hunt for Red October	170,635
Viva Villaveien! (Norwegian)	157,679
Bird on a Wire	157,409
Home Alone	130,748
Gremlins 2	129,510

12-year-old Herman, loses his hair because of a rare disease, and Gustavson treats the subject both with distance and warmth. Technically the film is very well done. The images (by cinematographer Kjell Vassdal) shine, though the air of perfection about them perhaps add a certain coolness to parts of the picture.

Oddvar Einarson, former prize-winner at the Venice festival with X, presented the impressive **Rising Tide** (*Havet stiger*), a film *not* situated anywhere near the ocean, but in a circular abandoned factory in Poland. The film is a poetic story of a small "post-apocalyptic" community, very well acted by mostly Polish actors and exquisitely shot by expert cinematographer Svein Krøvel. Perhaps dramatically somewhat unsatisfactory, the film did not catch on with audiences.

Hopeful eyes were directed towards **Seagulls** (*Måker*), the story of a shipping agent and his family on the Norwegian seaboard at the turn of the century. At the helm was Vibeke Løkkeberg who in 1981 made an impact both at home and abroad with her second feature *The Betrayal*. Seagulls, however, was a disappointment. For Løkkeberg the 1980's have been a bumpy road indeed. Her third feature, *The Wild One* (*Hud*), was a high-strung drama centred pessimistically on a woman trapped between the incestuous advances of her stepfather and the mindless materialism of her merchant skipper husband, all set in a romanticised west coast landscape of a hundred years ago. Despite the good looks of *Seagulls*, the film seems distinctly underbudgeted with its lack of momentum and pretty, but static pictures. A heavy burden of turn-of-the-century theatricals such as bankruptcies, fatal lung conditions and so on rest uneasily atop it.

Espen Thorstenson brought some relief to the situation with his simple and unassuming children's picture **Beyond the Seven Seas** (*Bak sju hav*). This small film, co-directed with Pakistani theatre and film director Saeed Anjum, tells the story of a young Pakistani boy moving with his family from Pakistan to Norway. The film is a bit empty – a stronger and more coherent plot would be welcome – but there are genuine poetic touches and a few insights into the situation of one of Norway's immigrant minorities. Thorstenson, who went to film school in Paris in the 1960's, has directed only sporadically. But he seems to keep a memory of the impact of the French New Wave – there is something in the film's stylistic straightforwardness that reminds one of Truffaut or Rohmer.

Finally, the international commercial success of **Shipwrecked** (*Håkon Håkonsen*) again made heroes of *Pathfinder*-director Nils Gaup and his shrewd producer, Johan

Jacobsen of Filmkameratene. The film originates in a story for the young, published by a Norwegian civil servant in the 1860's, who spiked this marine tale with exotic characters and dangerous incidents. The international success of the film comes at an important juncture. Norwegian film-talent is scrambling for what little funds there can be found, *Shipwrecked* proves that Nordic tales can arouse world-wide interest.

Peter Snickars and Juha Muie in Leidulv Risan's *The Long Road Home*

Recent and Forthcoming Films

Smykketyvan (Twice Upon a Time). Script: Anja Breien and Carl Martin Borgen. Dir: Anja Breien. Phot: Philip Øgaard. Players: Sven Wollter, Kjersti Holman, Ghita Nørby. Prod: Norsk Film (Gunnar Svensrud).

Døden på Oslo S (Death at Oslo Central). Script: Axel Helstenius, based on a novel by Ingvar Ambjørnsen. Dir: Eva Isaksen. Phot: Philip Øgaard. Players: Håvard Bakke, Tommy Karlsen, Helle Figenschow. Prod: Norsk Film (Harald Ohrvik).

Herman. Script: Lars Saabye Christensen. Dir: Erik Gustavson. Phot: Kjell Vassdal. Players: Anders Danielsen Lie, Bjørn Floberg, Elisabeth Sand, Harald Heide-Steen jr., Jarl Kulle, Linn Aronsen. Prod: Filmeffekt (Dag Alveberg).

Håkon Håkonsen (Shipwrecked). Script: Nils Gaup, Bob Foss, Greg Dinner, Nick Thiel. Dir: Nils Gaup. Phot: Erling Thurmann-Andersen. Players: Stian Smestad, Gabriel Byrne, Trond Peter Stamsø Munch, Louisa Haigh. Prod: Filmkameratene (Johan Jacobsen).

Lucifer – sensommer gult/sort (Summer's Ending). Script and Dir: Roar Skolmen. Phot: Svein Krøvel. Players: Bjørn Andresen, Anniken Krogstad, Jan Clemens, Astrid Folstad. Prod: Atomfilm (Odd G. Iversen).

Svampe. Script: Elisabeth Young. Dir: Martin Asphaug. Phot: Philip Øgaard. Players: Martin Bliksrud, Espen Skjønberg, Karl Sundby, Brit Elisabeth Haagensli. Prod: Filmeffekt (Dag Alveberg).

Havet stiger (Rising tide). Script and Dir: Oddvar Einarson. Phot: Svein Krøvel. Players: Gard Eidsvold, Petronella Barker, Darota Stalinska, Marek Walczewski. Prod: Oslo Film (Aamund Johannessen).

Måker (Seagulls). Script and Dir: Vibeke Løkkeberg. Phot: Paul Rene Roestad. Players: Vibeke Løkkeberg, Helge Jordal, Tonje Kleivdal Kristiansen, Marie Kleivdal Kristiansen, Elisabeth Grannemann, Klaus Hagerup. Prod: The Norway Film Development Co (Terje Kristiansen).

Mange flagg – ingen grenser (Many Flags – No Borders). *Feature-length documentary*. Script and Dir: Kikki Engelbrektson. Phot: Rolf Larsen. Prod: Norsk Filmstudio and NKK (National Broadcasting Corp.)

For dagene er onde (For the Days Are Evil). Script: Eldar Einarson based on a novel by Anne Karin Elstad. Dir: Eldar Einarson. Phot: Bjørn Jegerstedt. Players: Anne Krigsvoll, Pål Skjønberg, Bjørn Sundquist. Prod: Norsk Film (Hilde Berg).

Bak sju hav (Beyond the Seven Seas). Script and Dir: Espen Thorstensson. Phot: Halvor Næss. Players: Sajid Hussain, Jafar Malik, Rubina J. Rana. Prod: Aprilfilm.

Bricken (The Buick). Script and Dir: Hans Otto Nicolayssen. Phot: Kjell Vassdal. Players: Anne Marie Ottersen, Helge Jordal, Lasse Lindtner. Prod: Motlys (Sigve Endresen).

Frida – med hjertet i hånden (Frida – The Art of Loving). Script: Torun Lian. Dir: Berit Nesheim. Players: Maria Kvalheim, Helge Jordal, Ellen Horn. Prod: Teamfilm.

Den lange veien hjem (The Long Road Home). Script: Leidulv Risan and Arthur Johansen. Dir: Leidulv Risan. Phot: Harald Paalgard. Players: Anniken von der Lippe, Peter Snickars, Bjørn Sundquist, Solfrid Heier. Prod: Norsk Film (Elin Erichsen).

Den hvite viking (The White Viking). Script and Dir: Hrafn Gunnlaugsson. Players: Maria Bonnevie, Gottskalk Sigurdarson. Egill Olafsson. Prod: Filmeffekt (Dag Alveberg).
Kvitebjørn Kong Valemon (The Polar Bear King). Script: Erik Borge, based on a Norwegian folk tale. Dir: Ola Solum. Phot: Philip Øgaard. Players: Maria Bonnevie, Tobias Hoesl, Jack Fjeldstad. Prod: Northern Lights.
Lakki. Script and Dir: Sven Wam. Prod: Mefistofilm.
Det perfekte mord (The Perfect Murder).

Script: Morten Barth. Dir: Eva Isaksen. Phot: Philip Øgaard. Prod: MovieMakers (Petter Bøe).
Giftige løgner (Lethal Lies). Dir: Martin Asphaug. Players: Håvard Bakke, Tommy Karlsen, Helle Figenschow. Prod: Filmkameratene.
Stella Polaris. Dir: Knut Erik Jensen. Prod: Oslo Film.
Koloss (Colossus). Dir: Witold Leszczynski and Håkon Sandøy. Prod: Irisfilm, Regionalfilm Perspektywa (Poland).

Useful Addresses

Norwegian Cinema and Film Foundation
Stortingsgt. 16
N–0161 Oslo 1
Tel: (2) 42 89 49

Norwegian Film Institute
Grev Wedels Plass 1
N–0105 Oslo 1
Tel: (2) 42 87 40
Fax: (2) 33 22 77

National Association of Municipal Cinemas
Stortingsgt. 16
N–0161 Oslo 1
Tel: (2) 33 05 30
Fax: (2) 42 89 49

Norwegian Film Distribution Association
Nedre Vollgt. 9
N–0158 Oslo 1 ·
Tel: (2) 42 48 44
Fax: (2) 42 30 93

(continued from page 251)

SJ Film Productions Sdn. Bhd.
94, Jalan Maarof
Bangsar Park
59000 Kuala Lumpur
Tel: (03) 256–2236

JD Productions Sdn. Bhd.
Panca Delima Studio
1045, 7½ Miles, Jalan Hulu Kelang
68000 Ampang
Selangor Darul Ehsan
Tel: (03) 408–7622

Aarti Film Sdn. Bhd.
198A, Jalan Tun Shambanthan
50470 Kuala Lumpur
Tel: (03) 238–0059
Fax: (03) 238–0054

NR Productions Sdn. Bhd.

Panca Delima Studio
Lot 1045, Batu 7½, Jalan Hulu Kelang
68000 Ampang
Selangor Darul Ehsan
Tel: (03) 407–7587

Salon Films (M) Sdn. Bhd.
2B, Jalan Gurney
54000 Kuala Lumpur
Tel: (03) 293–7482/293–9794/293–7502
Fax: (03) k293–1728

Sunny Film Productions Sdn. Bhd.
60b, Faber Plaza, Jalan Desa Bakti
Taman Desa Bakti
58100 Kuala Lumpur
Tel: (03) 781–3881
Fax: (03) 781–4724

M.E. Communications Sdn. Bhd.
No. 10B, Jalan Pahang Barat
Off Jalan Pahang

Filmeast Productions
3A, Jalan Sena 3/13A
40006 Shah Alam
Selangor Darul Ehsan
Tel: (03) 550–3926

Montage Distributions Sdn. Bhd.
2C (3rd Floor), Jalan Pandan 3/6A
Pandan Jaya
55100 Kuala Lumpur
Tel: (03) 983–2981/983–2982
Fax: (03) 238–2599

PAKISTAN

by Aijaz Gul

With every passing day of the month, there has been a drop in the film business nationwide. The civil unrest in Sind, the Gulf War, bomb explosions in the theatres, a rise in petrol prices, high entertainment tax, CNN transmissions plus TV screenings of feature films every day, could be cited as the major reasons for this decline. Of course the real reason could be the mediocrity and stagnation of film direction, themes and presentation.

If figures alone were significant for the trends, the first five months of 1991 cast heavy clouds over everything. Almost thirty Punjabi and Urdu films released during January–May this year have performed below expectations. Director Hassan Askari's **Blade** (*Gandasa*), Jan Mohammad's **International Spy** (*Almi jasoos*), and Masood Butt's **Cobra** (*Nag devta*), were all big productions with bankable names, foreign locations and huge sets. Their lukewarm response at the box-office left a lot to be desired for everyone. As for their creative and critical worth, there is literally nothing to comment about.

During 1990, 84 features were produced (37 Punjabi, 23 Pushto, 21 Urdu, 3 Sindhi). Director Hussnain's **Enemy** (*Insaniat key dushman*) was the biggest grosser of the year, filling the air with vengeance and explosives, raucous dialogue and sexual innuendos. With Nadeem, Anjuman, Sultan Rahi, Neeli and Izhar Qazi in the leading roles, the film perpetuates the myth of superstars who are now ageing heroes and bulky heroines. The myth was exploded during the latter half of the year with director Javaid Fazil's **Vantage** (*Bulandi*) and Altaf Hussain's **Jewel** (*Nagina*),

introducing four new artists. Both the films played well at the box-office, leading their new faces of Reema, Shan and Madiha Shah into overnight stardom. Probably Nazaral Islam's **Culprits** (*Kaley chor*) was the only meaningful film of 1991. The good news was that the film is still playing in many parts of the country, ridiculing the corruption of law and the courts.

Sweet Songs and Explicit Romance

As for trends, vengeance and vendetta, which ruled the screen for fifteen years, began to slip for the first time in the face of increasing annoyance from the audience. This was to be replaced with sweet songs and explicit romance. *Jewel* and **Thief of Hearts** (*Hussan da chor*), directed by Altaf Hussain, cashed in on the new trend. *Thief of Hearts*, for instance, is the story of rags to riches. A poor boy from a village falls for a popular film actress in the city, taking up a job with her, and finally becoming a bigger star than her ideal. The film brings out all the backlot mess of the studios, including the bloody fights and brawls between the director and the actors.

The censor was lenient for film-makers who went by the books. **Bride for a Night** (*Dulhan ek rat ki*) made it back after fifteen years with two additional musical numbers featuring tarty Musarrat Shaheen. Her other soft porno movie *Haseena Atom Bomb*, did not do well. Musarrat Shaheen, now fallen from the box-office grace, was ready to disrobe in a last desperate effort to retain popularity. Similarly, ageing Babra Sharif (*Miss Cleopatra*) and Salma Agha (*Number One*) tried to seduce the audience with their physical charms, but their careers were

Neeli and Sultan Rahi in *Culprits*

private concerns can import feature films and film stock directly rather than through the National Film Development Corporation. However, many importers continued to import films via the National Film Development Corporation, thereby paying a certain fee as a service charge but remaining free of the hassles of import and clearance from the various agencies. A reissue of *Samson and Delilah* played well along with *The Punisher* and *Red Scorpion*. NAFDEC organised a Polish Film Festival in three major cities to warm crowds. A film festival of seven Iranian films was held nationwide in 1991.

AIJAZ GUL went to Aitchison College, Lahore for his early education. He earned his A.B. and M.A. in Cinema from UCLA. Now Head of Export and Film Promotion, National Film Development Corporation Limited. He also runs the Shabistan Cinema in Rawalpindi.

Shan and Nadira in *Thief of Hearts*

pretty much at an end. Anjuman also started performing sexy rain songs and one of her flops, *Shadmani*, was taken off the screen by force by the censor authorities when banned segments were shown. With a new Islamic bill passed by the assembly, the tarts and rain songs could be in real trouble.

Like everywhere else the superstars are white elephants who may be dying but their precious trunks are pretty much in demand. Ageing Sultan Rahi continued to raise hell in almost every Punjabi film. Nadeem, Anjuman, Javaid Sheikh, Neeli and others may be signing new contracts but today the real superstars are the new faces like Reema, Shan and Madiha Shah. There were no new discoveries as directors. Masood Butt, Jan Mohammad, Altaf Hussain, Hassan Askari and Javaid Fazil were the bankable names.

Film import has been liberalised and now

Recent and Forthcoming Films

Sarkata Insan (Beheaded Man). Script: Iqbal Rizvi. Dir: Saeed Rizvi. Players: Babra Sharif, Ghulma Mohiuddin, Izhar Qazi.
Dirandagi (Vicious). Script: Ijaz Arman. Dir: M. Maqbool. Phot: Waqar Bokhari. Players: Neeli, Reema, Ajab Gul, Javaid Sheikh.
Hussan da chor (Thief of Hearts). Script: Bashir Niaz. Dir: Altaf Hussain. Phot: Pervaiz. Players: Nadira, Shan, Afzal.

Zid (Obstinacy). Script: Syed Noor. Dir: Javaid Fazil. Phot: Saleem Butt. Players: Nadeem, Babra Sharif, Ghulam Mohiuddin.
Kaley chor (Culprits). Script: Nasir Adeeb. Dir: Nazaral Islam. Phot: Waqar Bokhari. Players: Sultan Rahi, Neeli, Javaid Sheikh.
Bulandi (Vantage). Script: Syed Noor. Dir: Mohammad Javaid Fazil. Phot: Kamran Mirza. Players: Nadeem, Shan, Reema, Afzal, Sameena Pirzada.

Useful Addresses

National Film Development Corporation
56–F, Blue Area
P.O. Box 1204
Islamabad 44000
Tel: 821154, 823148
Fax: 81723

Ministry of Culture
No. 13–K
Al-Markaz
F.7/2
Islamabad
Tel: 829972, 825991, 825990
Fax: 81723

Central Board of Film Censors
Street No. 55
F–6/4
Islamabad
Tel: 824939, 826211

Pakistan Film Producers Association
Regal Cinema Building
Sharahe Quaid-e-Azam
Lahore
Tel: 3322094
and
16–D, Bambino Chambers
Garden Road
Karachi 3
Tel: 729497

Pakistan Film Distributors Association
Sheikh Chambers (2nd Floor)
Near Light House Cinema
M.A. Jinnah Road
Karachi
Tel: 216378
and
Qayyum Jan Building
11, Royal Park
Lahore
Tel: 223324

Pakistan Film Exhibitors Association
Lyrie Cinema Building
Garden Road
Karachi 3
Tel: 727764
and
Prince Cinema Building
Mahmood Ghaznavi Road
Lahore
Tel: 227047, 52119

Eveready Pictures
18, Mawlai Mansion
M.A. Jinnah Road
Karachi
Tel: 215293, 215273

Evernew Pictures
2, Abbot Road
Lahore
Tel: 52088, 58563

Shama Parvana Pictures
Royal Park
Lahore
Tel: 222284

Chandani Films
Bari Studios
Multan Road
Lahore
Tel: 430014, 444932

Minerva Pictures
6, Asif Building
McLeod Road
Lahore
Tel: 222479, 322114

Mandiviwala Entertainment
Nishat Cinema Building
M.A. Jinnah Road
Karachi
Tel: 710535, 710884
Telex: 23323 HAKIM PK

Saleem Aftab Corporation
1, Abbot Road
Lahore
Tel: 222781

PERU
by Paul Lenti

The fifth annual National Short-Film Festival (Festival Nacional de Cortometrajes) was held June 13–16, 1991 at the auditorium of the Museo de Arte de Lima. Sponsored by the Asociación de Cineastas del Perú, the event was held under the auspices of the Banco Latino.

Because of guerrilla terrorist attacks on tourists, tourism has dropped considerably to Cuzco and Machu Pichu. In order to counteract this, the local government in Cuzco sponsored an international film festival (Muestra Internacional de Cine de Cuzco), also in June 1991. Although more of a showcase of national and international works, plans are to make the event an official annual film festival in the future.

Also, from November 3–13, the groups TV Cultura and IPAL sponsored the second Latin American Women's Video Festival (II Festival Latinoamericano de Video Dirigido por Mujeres) in Lima. Featuring a workshop in "Directing Actors for Videomakers" and the seminar "The Image of Latin American Women in Videos Directed by Women," the festival offered a broad selection of video works in the capital

at El Cinematógrafo and the Asociación de Video de Lima, and at the Villa el Salvador in Barrios. Attending the gathering were videomakers from Argentina, Bolivia, Brazil, Cuba, Chile, Ecuador, Mexico, Peru and Uruguay.

Recent and Forthcoming Films

Alias La Gringa. Script: José Watanabe, José María Salcedo, Alberto Durant. Dir: Alberto Durant. Phot: Mario García Joya. Players: Germán González, Elsa Olivero, Gonzalo de Miguel, Orlando Sacha, Juan Manuel Ochoa, Ramón García. Prod: Perfo Studio. 92 mins.

Caidos del Cielo (Fallen from the Sky). Script: Francisco Lombardi, Gerardo Herrero, Giovanna Pollarolo, Augusto Cabada. Dir: Francisco Lombardi. Phot: José Luis López Linares. Players: Gustavo Buevo, Diana Quijano, Leontina Antonina, Carlos Gassols, David Zúñiga, Edward Centeno, Delfina Paredes, Oscar Vega. Prod: Inca Films, in co-production with Tornasol Films and Televisión Española (TVE). 127 mins.

La Manzanita del Diablo (The Devil's Little Apple). Script: Federico García, Guillermo Guedes. Dir: Federico García. Phot: Rodolfo López. Players: Tania Helfgott, Antonio Arrue, Diana Quijano, Ricardo Tosso, Pablo Fernández. Prod: Pilar Roca, Cinematográfica Kuntur, in co-production with the Cuban Film Institute (ICAIC). 85 mins.

Danny. Script: Pedro Mateu-Gelabert, Cady Abarca. Dir: Cady Abarca. Phot and Editing: Gianfranco Annichini. Players: Daniel Ercilla, Juan Manuel Ochoa. Prod: Abarca Films. 18 mins.

Ni con Dios Ni con el Diablo (Neither with God nor the Devil). Script, Dir and Phot: Nilo Pereira del Mar. Players: Marino León, Patty

Still from Cady Abarca's *Danny*

Cabrera, Eduardo Cesti, Ivonne Frayssinet, Diana Escobar, Reinaldo Arenas. Prod: URPI Prods. Cinematográficas (Peru), in co-production with JBA (France) and Channel Four (UK). 90 mins.
Juliana. Script: René Weber, Oswaldo Carpio, Stefán Kaspar, Fernando Espinoza, Alejandro Legaspi. Dir: Fernando Espinoza and Alejandro Legaspi. Phot: Dany Gavidia. Players: Rosa Isabel Morfino, Julio Vega, Guillermo Esqueche, Edward Centeno, David Zúñiga. Prod: Grupo Chaski. 97 mins.

Useful Addresses

Asociación de Cineastas del Perú
Diez Canseco 552–1
Miraflores
Lima
Tel: 46–6953/41–6725

Producciones Inca Films
Independencia 559
Miraflores
Lima 18
Tel: 47–4367

Grupo Chaski
León Velarde 1064
Casilla de Correo 11099
Lima 14
Tel: 71–8199/71–1032
Fax: 71–1870

Perfo Studio
Av. Arequipa 4130, Of. 706
Lima 18
Tel: 45–8249
Fax: 44–0660

Películas del Pacífico
Conquistadores 1020, 4to piso G
San Isidro
Lima
Fax: 42–3572

Cinematográfica Kuntur
Av. Tacna 411, Of. 22
Lima 1
Tel: 28–2309
Fax: 40–5812

PHILIPPINES
by Agustin Sotto

The untimely death of Lino Brocka in a car accident on May 22, 1991 stunned the Philippine public and was front-page headlines for a week. It was considered a big blow to the progressive sector of society and left a leadership void in the film industry. His funeral was accorded an adulation reserved only for heroes and thousands walked miles to escort his remains to its final resting place. His wake attracted both friend and foe alike with Mrs. Imelda Marcos sending a wreath of orchids.

The hard-hitting director was known for his outspoken views on a variety of subjects – especially censorhip and human rights. He did not consider himself to be a political person and did not subscribe to any ideology. However, he rallied and fought according to his gut feelings and because the situation was usually too critical to ignore.

In the last years of his life, he expressed his disappointment with the Aquino administration which, he felt, had betrayed the aims of the EDSA revolution. Although he worked largely on commercial films, he stirred the conscience of the masses through a new genre – the political melodrama.

Although more commercial in treatment, *Get out of the Mud, Destroy Everything* and *The Other Side of Everything*, are peppered with caricatures of political figures and exposes of the deteriorating moral order. The last film has a TV commentator whose scruples are compromised by her affair with

Adrian Ramirez ponders on his cultural identity in *Dreaming Filipinos*

a mayor, a naïve TV reporter who thinks that the press is immune from political death squads, steamy sex scenes, and a satire on fundamentalists trying to preach the word of God to convicts.

At the time of his death, Brocka was preparing a sequel to *Fight for Us* – **Miserere Nobis** on the political realities of the post-Marcos era.

Two other important directors belonging to another generation died within weeks of each other. Lamberto Avellana, national artist for film and theatre, died of a heart attack at the age of 76. He directed over seventy films – among them, *Child of Sorrow*, on the problems of readjustment faced by a Korean war veteran and which won Best Film at the 1956 Asian Film Festival, *Badjao*, on the clashes of two Moro tribes, *Song of the Race* on feudalism in the countryside, and *Portrait of an Artist as Filipino* on the loss of the Spanish heritage due to the war.

Ramon Estella also left behind a legacy of important works – *Buenavista, Last Request* and *The Desperate One*. However, he left Manila in the 1960's to settle in Puerto Rico, then New York. He also directed several films in Malaysia with P. Ramlee in the 1950's.

String of Blockbusters

Other than these dire news, the film industry registered its best showing at the box-office with a string of super blockbusters. **Whoever you are** proved to be a phenomenal. It was shown in a hundred theatres on Valentine's Day and grossed over $2 million in a week. It starred Sharon Cuneta and new action star Robin Padilla in a story of an heiress-singer who is hunted down by her killer stepfather.

Another big box-office hit was **Pido Dida**, the first picture by Kris Aquino, daughter of the president. She was astutely paired with comedian Rene Requiestas whose toothless grin never fails win crowds. However, their second picture, **Pido Dida 2**, only did fairly at the box-office.

Despite this fine showing, the 1990 output dipped to a low 138 features. This was ascribed to the inability of independent producers to get important stars and viable playdates for their films. Only three studios dominate the film industry – Seiko, Viva and Regal.

Among the year's outstanding films is Chito Rono's **Is It a Sin to Worship You**, a *Fatal Attraction* type of movie with an outstanding performance by Vivian Velez. The film richly explores the psychology of a women obsessed with a married man and is more sympathetic to her plight.

Laurice Guillen's **When the Heavens Pass Judgement** is a feudal saga of love and revenge spanning two generations. It is adapted from a Komiks novel – meaning it is full of cliffhanger situations and star-crossed lovers. But the film is expertly directed and photographed, its passions under control and presented with such sensitivity that the overwrought episodes become credible.

Carlitos Siguion-Reyna's **Will Wait for You in Heaven** is a commendable adaption of *Wuthering Heights*. Shot in the northern Philippine islands of Batanes, the setting is breathtakingly photographed and many of the dramatic twists are handled with restraint.

Gil Portes **Andrea** heralds the return of Nora Aunor in top form. She is brilliant as the guerrilla mother who must leave behind her child because of circumstances. Gina Alajar is also impressive as the friend who adopts the child.

Two non-mainstream works also deserve mention. Critic Emmanuel Reye's **Dreaming Filipinos** is a 52-minute discourse on the colonial mentality of most Filipinos. The green card syndrome, the magnetic pull of western consumer goods, and the repudiation of the native culture are analysed in this documentary. It has been selected for showing at the 1991 Toronto Film Festival.

Lito Tiongson's **A Piece of Land** looks at the effects of an agrarian incident a generation later. A landlord is hacked to death by his aggrieved tenant for his brutish, arrogant ways. The film observes both past and present with the recent massacre of farmers in a rally as framework. Shot in 16mm, this 25 minute film is impressive for the tightness of storytelling.

POLAND

by Wanda Wertenstein

Early in 1991 the Committee for Cinema presented their programme of reform in the system of Polish film production. In 1990 fundamental changes were effected in film distribution and exhibition. The former monopolistic State organisation for distribution was divided into seven local State companies dealing independently in buying, renting and selling video rights of foreign films or distributing some Polish films and running State-owned cinemas. A growing number of cinemas was allowed to pass into private hands. Private distributors (with Polish or mixed Polish and foreign capital) are

HIGH CLASS FILMS FOR HIGH CLASS AUDIENCE

Fundacja Sztuki Filmowej
Film Art Foundation

ul. Krakowskie Przedmieście 21/23, 00-071 Warszawa, Poland.
Tel: (+48-22) 26 14 09, Fax: (+48-2) 635 2001

Founded in May 1990 to promote art cinema.

— distribution – exhibition – production
— organization of film events
— film education
— publishing of trade magazines "KINO"
    and "Filmowy Serwis Prasowy"

Młodzieżowa Akademia Filmowa
Youth Film Academy

ul. Marszałkowska 28, 00-576 Warszawa, Poland.
Tel: (+48-22) 21 78 28

Film education programme for young people.

— 40,000 participants
— 30 divisions all over Poland
— own TV programme

Warszawski Festiwal Filmowy
Warsaw Film Festival

October 9-19, 1992

— since 1985
— annual
— international
— non-competitive
— mostly for features

P.O.Box 816, ul. Krakowskie Przedmieście 21/23,
00-950 Warszawa 1, Poland.
Tel: (+48-22) 26 14 09, Fax: (+48-2) 635 2001,
Tlx: 812508 kokin pl

already heading the market with ITI Ltd (Warners) being the strongest in quality and quantity.

While Film Polski is still active in the export of Polish, and import of foreign, films it is no longer a monopoly. Video shops and renters have grown like mushrooms throughout the country and a special Association, RAPID, has been created to fight copyright piracy. The irony is that the illegal video market, which deserves such enormous praise for breaking censorship under the Communist regime, is almost a criminal danger today. Abolishing censorship (in June 1990) and allowing private and foreign distributors to operate in the country resulted in a flood of American films – some very good but many just cheap trash. But it can be considered symbolic that – for the first time since the war – an Oscar-winning film, *Dances with Wolves*, opened in Poland only a few weeks after the Hollywood ceremony.

As every good development can have negative sides, so the sad result is that Polish films almost completely disappeared from Polish screens. Even such a fine and important film as Marczewski's **Escape from the Liberty Cinema** had only a short run, not to speak of Wajda's **Korczak**. Audiences consist mostly of teenagers and young people bent on fun, sensation and thrill; but unpredictable as it can be it made Weir's *Dead Poets Society* one of the greatest box-office successes of 1990–91. Naturally, with Poland's huge economic problems of transforming a State-controlled system to a free market, one demanding enormous sacrifice from the people, the families' money availability fell drastically and most of the older population stay at home and limit themselves to watching films on TV.

Even if private production companies can be created and operate, the bulk of national film production is in the hands of Film Studios (once called Film Units or Film Groups like the famous TOR or Wajda's X which was dissolved under martial law).

Hanna Dumowska in *Femina*

The Studios are independent but not private. They are no longer fully financed by the State as they were under the old system. They can receive State subsidies for a given film project amounting to 70% of its budget, also a project development subsidy; they can get their money from home distribution (which is practically zero), from selling their films abroad (for which they don't have to use the once obligatory services of Film Polski), from selling production facilities and services to foreign productions shooting in Poland; and finally, they can enter into co-production deals with foreign producers or distributors in order to help finance their own films, like Wajda's *Korczak*, Marczewski's *Escape from the Liberty Cinema* and Kieślowski's *The Double Life of Veronica*.

And that is where the new system of funding national film production enters: two agencies were created for the purpose by the Committee for Cinema, a Project Development Agency (otherwise called Script Agency) and a Production Agency. The first is based on the philosophy that enough money never went to encourage, develop and and provide film scripts in reasonable proportion to the number of films produced. In principle the Agency

Anna Romantowska in Feliks Falk's *End of the Game*

must grant money to projects backed by a producer and approved by a number of independent professionals; in justified cases the Agency can also give an eight-months grant to the writer on the basis of a presented treatment. The Production Agency grants up to 70% of production costs of a film on the basis of its budget, eventual co-producer participation, a promised or signed distribution deal. The newly established company Film Garantie Pologne (a joint venture with the French insurance company AGF) is the first film completion bond company in post-communist Europe which will offer such completion guarantee if demanded by an investor (State or private, Polish or foreign).

Further plans include a third Agency – the Agency for Distribution of Polish films – which will be able to fund up to 50% of the distributor's expenses on publicity and production of the film's prints. This Agency should begin to function before the end of 1991.

Not to overlook – in the attempts to rationalise the economic system of Polish cinema – its cultural aspects the Film Art Foundation (directed by the splendid organiser of the Warsaw Film Weeks, Roman Gutek) is preparing to revive the network of arthouses, as well as taking over a Film Academy in Warsaw, giving 40 thousand children from 143 schools the chance to receive proper film education.

Production up towards 30 Features

In spite of the really grave financial difficulties films *are* being made and the 1991 output should be about thirty. Still unsolved and dramatic are the problems of the big studios (Łódź primarily but also Wroclaw and Warsaw) with their antiquated equipment and obsolete organisation, as well as those of the Warsaw Documentary and the Łódź Educational Film Studios.

Of the 1990–91 films only a few deserve attention. In the changed political situation film-makers seem somewhat lost, unable to find interesting stories, universal themes or simply good contemporary human interest subjects.

Krzysztof Zanussi's **Life for a Life** – the story of Saint Maximilian Kolbe's death in a hunger cell in Auschwitz after having offered himself to die for a condemned man, father of a family – was a sad disappointment with its rather flat story and all-too careful direction. Of course, it is an almost impossible task to show in a film the spirituality of a saint who was a real, authentic man of our times, even if he died nearly fifty years ago. Maybe the trouble lies in the honourable attempt to remain strictly faithful to the known facts. By far the best Polish film of the 1990–91 season was Wojciech Marczewski's story of remorse and repentance of a Communist activist, a censor, the film **Escape from the Liberty Cinema**, which could be seen at the 1991 Cannes Festival.

Piotr Mikucki's first feature **Crossed Lines**, a delicate story of matrimonial complications, was much better received in Berlin and in Cannes than by Warsaw critics. In **Only This Forest** Jan Łomnicki brings us back again to the times of Nazi occupation showing a simple old woman smuggling out of the Warsaw ghetto the young daughter of a once affluent and beautiful woman for whom she used to work as servant and washerwoman. The family jewels she carries hidden in her clothes will help the child to find shelter in a village.

The film gives an honest and fair picture of Polish attitudes to the Jewish tragedy – those who like the old woman try to help and those who treat their fate as a chance to blackmail them. The film is beautifully acted by the veteran actress Ryszarda Hain, funny and pathetic at the same time, and the child is deeply moving in her full consciousness of inevitable death. The film ends with a fine sequence in the forest where they are halted by a German who realises their situation. . .

Not fully satisfactory is Piotr Szulkin's sensuous **Femina**, but it is extremely interesting and completely different from his futuristic parables.

The new film by Feliks Falk, **The End of the Game**, is a well-told and entertaining story of a young ambitious woman running for parliament and her lover, a mathematician working for a big magazine. The young intellectual loses his love and his money while the woman who nearly manages to cure herself of her kleptomania pursues her electoral campaign to a triumphant conclusion.

Finally, the fact that in the recent and forthcoming production eight films are debut features may be read as a rather optimistic sign.

Zbigniew Zamachowski and Janusz Gajos in *Escape from the Liberty Cinema*

WANDA WERTENSTEIN is a critic and translator who has rendered into Polish many major books about the cinema. She is a member of the staff of the monthly film magazine Kino.

Podwojne życie Weronki (The Double Life of Veronica)

Script: Krzysztof Kieślowski and Krzysztof Piesiewicz. Direction: Krzysztof Kieślowski. Photography: Slawomir Idziak. Editing: Jacques Witta. Music: Zbigniew Preisner. Production Design: Patrice Mercier. Players: Irène Jacob, Philippe Volter, Halina Gryglaszewska, Wladyslaw Kowalski, Sandrine Dumas, Claude Duneton. Produced by Leonardo de la Fuente for Sideral Productions/Le Studio Canal + (Paris)/TOR Production (Warsaw). 92 mins.

Audacious in concept, meticulous yet inspired in execution, *The Double Life of Veronica* finally establishes Kieślowski as a creative director with few peers in European cinema. Ten years after we featured him as a "Director of the Year" in IFG, and four years after *A Short Film about Killing* inaugurated his momentous *Decalogue*, the Polish master has found in Paris a romantic flair, a flamboyant daring of expression, and a richly talented actress in Irène Jacob (who he had glimpsed in Malle's *Au revoir les enfants*).

From the opening close-ups of Veronica singing in the rain, Kieślowski seizes the curiosity of his audience. What animates Veronica with such an overwhelming passion? Who is the "double" she sees among a busload of French tourists, just as a demonstration gets under way in a square in Krakow? What is the mysterious ailment to which she succumbs at the moment of her triumph as a classical singer? Veronica's death so early in the film shocks us as fiercely as Janet Leigh's murder in *Psycho*, and her spirit lingers on through the identical body of her French double, Véronique – a woman born on the same day as her Polish

Irène Jacob in Kieślowski's *The Double Life of Veronica*

counterpart, and blessed with the same pro-digious, sublime voice. Kieślowski does not promulgate a simplistic theory of reincarnation. Instead he charts two parallel lives, Siamese twins only vaguely aware of the "other"s existence. He persuades us that people can communicate through sheer intensity of thought and feeling, and he bathes this enigma in a marvellous wash of music and imagery. Where *The Decalogue* looks coarse and murky, *The Double Life of Veronica* boasts a refulgence and soaring assurance, reminding us that, in the greatest cinema, form can transcend content and burnish the most tantalising of conceits.

Peter Cowie

Recent and Forthcoming Films

Cynga. Script and Dir.: Leszek Wosiewicz, from J. Drewnowski's novel *The Land of Happy Pains*. Phot: Krzysztof Ptak. Players: Ewa Dałkowska, Henryk Bista, Tomasz Łysiak, Władysław Kowalski. Prod: TOR Film Studio.

Dziecko Szcześcia (Born with a Silver Spoon). Script: Sławomir Kryński and M. Murzyński, M. Orzechowski, D. Romanowski, J. Sobierajski, Maria Szajer. Dir: Sławomir Kyński. Phot: Tomasz Wert. Players: Ewa Gawryluk, Marek Cichucki, Monika Bolibrzuch and Piotr Walczewski. Prod: KADR Film studio.

Edelman. Script and Dir.: Bohdan Kowalik. Phot: Jolanta Dylewska. *A documentary feature with Hanna Krall, Jacek Kuroń, Adam Michnik, Simon Wiesenthal and others*. Prod: TOR Film Studio.

Femina. Script: Krystyna Kofta from her own novel. Dir: Piotr Szulkin. Phot: Dariusz Kuc. Players: Hanna Dumowska, Ewa Salacka, Marcin Troński, Krzysztof Bauman. Prod: PERSPEKTYWA Film Studio.

Głuchy Telefon (Crossed Lines). Script: Barbara Fatyga and Piotr Mikucki. Dir: Piotr Mikucki. Phot: Pawel Edelman. Players: Hanna Mikuć, Katarzyna Latawiec, Maciej Orłoś, Waldemar Kownacki. Prod: TOR Film Studio.
In Flagranti. Script and Dir: Wojtek Bierdroń. Phot: Dariusz Panas. Players: Małgorzata Foremniak-Jedruszczak, Bogusław Linda, Ewa Skibińska, Zdzisław Wardejn. Prod: Karol Irzykowski Film Studio.
Jeszcze tylko ten las (Only This Forest). Script Anna Strońska from her own novel. Dir: Jan Łomnicki. Phot: Artur Radźko. Players: Ryszarda Hanin, Joanna Friedman, Marek Bargełowski, Marzena Trybala. Prod: KADR Film Studio.
Kanalia (Rat). Script and Dir: Tomasz Wiszniewski. Phot: Tomasz Wert. Players: Henryk Bista, Adam Ferency, Boguslaw Linda, Piotr Siwkiewicz, Joanna Trzepiecińska, Zbigniew Zamachowski. Prod: ZODIAK Film Studio, PLEOGRAF Ltd, State Film, Drama and Television School.
Koniec Gry (End of the Game). Script: Feliks Falk and Maciej Karpiński. Dir: Feliks Falk. Phot: Dariusz Kuc. Players: Anna Romantowska, Jan Brunow, Piotr Cieślak, Maria Trafankowska, Jerzy Zass. Prod: PERSPEKTYWA Film Studio.
Kroll. Script and Dir: Władysław Pasikowski. Phot: Pawel Edelman. Players: Alicja Jachiewicz, Cezary Pazura, Bogusław Linda, Olaf Lubaszenko. Prod: Film Studio ZEBRA.
Latajace Machiny kontra Pan Samochodzik (Flying Machines Against Mister Motorcar). Script and Dir: Janusz Kidawa. Phot: Tomasz Tarasin. Players: Piotr Krukowski, Jaś Strumiłło, Krystyna Feldman, Joanna Jędryka, Witold Prykosz. Prod: Film Studio PROFIL.
Nad rzeka Ktorej niema (By the River That Doesn't Exist). Script and Dir: Andrzej Barański based on a book by Stanisław Czycz. Phot: Ryszard Lenczewski. Players: Miroslaw Baka, Adrianna Biedrzyńska, Marek Bukowski, Tomasz Hudziec. Andrzej Masztlaerz, Joanna Trzepiecińska. Prod: OKO Film Studio and Polish Television.
Niech żyje milosc (Long Live Love). Script: Michał Arabudzki. Dir: Ryszard Ber. Phot: Przemysław Skwirczyński. Players: Katarzyna Walter, Marek Probosz, Jerzy Bończak, Bronisław Pawlik, Marcin Troński. Prod: OKO Film Studio.

Odjazd (Departure). Script and Dir: Magdalena and Piotr Łazarkiewicz. Phot: Jarosław Zamojda. Players: Teresa Budzisz-Krzyżanowska, Henryk Bista, Maria Ciunelis, Krzysztof Janczas, Grażyna Jędras, Wojciech Siemion, Halina Winiarska. Prod: ZODIAK Film Studio/WDR (Germany).
Panny i wdowy (Maidens and Widows). Script: Maria Nurowska from her own novel. Dir: Janusz Zaorski. Phot: Witold Adamek. Players: Maja Komorowska, Katarzyna Figura, Piotr Machalica, Joanna Szczepkowska, Joanna Trzepiecińska. Prod: DOM Film Studio.
Papierowe małżeństwo (Paper Marriage). Script: Marek Kreutz and Krzysztof Lang. Dir: Krzysztof Lang. Phot: Grzegorz Kędzierski. Players: Gary Kemp, Joanna Trzepiecińska. Prod: ZODIAK Film Studio/Mark Forstater Prod. Ltd. (London)
Obywatel Świata (Citizen of the World). Script and Dir: Roland Rowiński. Phot: Jarosław Zamojda. Players: Adrianna Biedrzyńska, Jan Frycz. Prod: PERSPEKTYWA Film Studio.
Podróż z zaczarowanym ołówkiem (Travel with the Magical Pencil). Script: Sławomir Grabowski, Adam Ochocki. Dir: Andrzej Piliczewski. Phot: Grzegorz Swietlikowski, Wacław Fedak. Prod: Film Studio SEMAFOR (Łódz)/ODRA-FILM (Wrocław).
Ptak (Bird). Script and Dir: Jacek Gąsiorowski. Phot: Witold Adamek. Players: Maria Gładkowska, Zbigniew Zamachowski. Prod: PERSPEKTYWA Film Studio. A Polish-French co-production.
Rozmowy Kontrolowane (Controlled Talks). Script: Stanisław Tym. Dir: Sylwester Chęciński. Phot: Jerzy Stawicki. Player: Stanisław Tym. Prod: ZODIAK Film Studio.
Rosja dzisiejsza (Russia Today). Script and Dir: Krzysztof Zanussi. Phot: Sławomir Idzia, Jarosław Zamojda. *Documentary feature with, among others, Boris Yeltsin.* Prod: TOR Films Studio.
Siwa legenda (Grey Legend). Script: Wladimir Matviyev, Sergei Bulyga, Dir: Bohdan Poręba. Phot: Jacek Stachlewski. Players: Ivars Kalnins, Lembid Ufsyek, Alla Murina, Genadij Garbug, Artur Gandrabura, Iwona Pawlak, Leon Niemczyk, Józef Fryźlewicz, Maria Probosz. Film Studio PROFIL/KINOTRUST (Belorussian Branch).
Szwedzi w Warszawie (Swedes in Warsaw). Script and Dir: Wlodzimierz Golaszewski, based

on Walery Przyborowski's novel. Phot: Henryk Janas. Players. Bożena Dykiel, Piotr Fronczewski, Bogdan Ferenc, Ryszard Pietruski, Eugeniusz Priwieziencew, Anna Seniuk. Prod: Film Studio PROFIL.

Tajemnica puszczy (The Secret of a Wild Forest). Script and Dir: Andrzej Barszczyński. Phot: Tomasz Tarasin. Players: Rafał Zwierz, Karolina Lutczyn, Gustaw Lutkiewicz, Ryszard Kotys. Prod: Film Studio PROFIL.

Thirty Door Key – Klucz do drzwi 30. Script and Dir: Joseph Kay, Laad Yorrick, Jerzy Skolimowski. "Ferdydurke" from Witold Gombrowicz's novel. Phot: Witold Adamek. Players: Iain Glen, Crispin Glover, Judith Godreche, Fabienne Babe, Robert Stephens, Tadeusz Łomnicki. Prod: Million Frames (Warsaw)/ CINEA (Paris).

Trzy dni bez wyroku (Three Days Without a Sentence). Script: Czesław Białaczyński, Wojciech Wójcik. Dir: Wojciech Wójcik. Phot: Krzysztof Tusiewicz. Players: Artur Zmijewski, Jerzy Bończak, Edward Lubaszenko, Witold Pyrkosz, Lucyna Zabawa. Prod: Film Studio OKO.

Usłyszcie mòj krzyk (Hear My Cry). Script and Dir: Maciej J. Drygas. Phot: Stanisław Sliskowski. *Documentary tracing the story of a man who burnt himself in protest against the the invasion of Czechoslovakia in 1968.* Prod: Film Group LOGOS (Educational Film Studio in Łódź)/ ZODIAK Film Studio (Warsaw).

VIP. Script and Dir: Juliusz Machulski. Phot: Janusz Gauer. Players: Liza Machulska, Paul Barge, Wojciech Malajkat, Jan Peszek, Tomasz Mędrzak, Krzysztof Majchrzak, Beata Tyszkiewicz, Bogusław Sobczul. Prod: Film Studio ZEBRA (Warsaw)/High Speed FILMS (Paris).

Korczak. Script: Agnieszka Holland. Dir: Andrzej Wajda. Phot: Robby Müller. Art dir: Allan Starski. Mus: Wojciech Killar. Players: Wojciech Pszoniak, Ewa Dałkowska, Teresa Budzisz Krzyżanowska, Marzena Trybała, Zbigniew Zamachowski, Aleksander Bardini. Prod: Film Studio PERSPEKTYWA, Regina Ziegler Productions, Erato Film, ZDF, BBC Films.

Ucieczka z kina wolnosc (Escape from the Liberty Cinema). Script and Dir: Wojciech Marczewski. Phot: Jerzy Zieliński. Players: Janusz Gajos, Zbigniew Zamachowski, Teresa Marczewska, Piotr Fronczewski, Władysław Kowalski. Prod: Film Studio TOR and Crone Productions A/S.

Producers

Film Studio DOM
(dir: Janusz Zaorski),
Puławska 61
00975 Warsaw
Tel: (22) 455065

Film Studio KADR
(dir: Jerzy Kawalerowicz),
Puławska 61
00975 Warsaw
Tel: (22) 454923

Film Studio OKO
(dir: Tadeusz Chmielewski),
Puławska 61
00975 Warsaw
Tel: (22) 455581

Film Studio PERSPEKTYWA
(dir: Janusz Morgenstern),
Puławska 61
00975 Warsaw
Tel: (22) 455494

Film Studio PROFIL
(dir: Bohdan Poręba),
Puławska 61
00975 Warsaw
Tel: (22) 454986.

Film Studio TOR
(dir: Krzysztof Zanussi),
Puławska 61
00975 Warsaw
Tel and Fax: (22) 455303

Film Studio ZEBRA
(dir: Juliusz Machulski),
Puławska 61
00975 Warsaw
Tel: (22) 455484

Film Studio ZODIAK

(dir: Jerzy Hoffman),
Puławska 61
00975 Warsaw
Tel: (22) 452047

Karol Irzykowski Studio
(dir: Jacek Skalski),
Mazowiecka 11
00052 Warsaw
Tel: (22) 276653

MM Potocka Productions Ltd,
Zwycięzców 8/1
03941 Warsaw
Tel and Fax: (22) 175965

Pleograf Ltd.
Orla 6/40
Hanna Barbera Poland Ltd,
Domaniewska 39A
02672 Warsaw
Tel: (22) 489539

ELGAZ
Północna 9 A
81029 Gdynia
Tel: (58) 237021
Fax: (58) 237858

Distributors

IFDF ODRA – FILM
Bogusławskiego 14
Wrocław

IFDF Silesja-Film
Plebiscytowa 36
Katowice
Tel: (832) 510522

IFDF Art-Film
Batorego 3
Szczecin
Tel: (91) 533574

IFDF MAX
Jagiellońska 26
03719 Warsaw
Tel: (22) 194261, 190481

IFDF Helios Film
Rysy 6
Łódź
Tel: (42) 782796

IFDF Neptun Film
Piwna 22
08958 Gdansk
Tel: (58) 314876

IFDF Apollo Film
Smoleńsk 2
Kraków
Tel: (12) 228366

Film Polski
Mazowiecka 6/8
00048 Warsaw
Tel: (22) 268455

ITI Co Ltd
Wernyhory 14/2
02727 Warsaw
Tel: (22) 433488
Fax: (22) 434532

Aminapol
Pl. Piłsudskiego 9
00078 Warsaw
Tel: (22) 264078

Syrena Entertainment Group
Mazowiecka 115
00950 Warsaw
Tel: (22) 200301 ext. 390, 391
Fax: (22) 268563

Oskar Ltd
Tamka 4
Warsaw

Opal Ltd
Szkolna 2
Warsaw
Tel: (22) 261427

Eurocom
Smocza 1
Warsaw
Tel: (22) 382533

Useful Addresses

Association of Polish Film Makers
Krakowskie Przedmieście 21/23
00071 Warszawa
Tel: (22) 276785
Fax: (22) 276233

Polish Screen Writers Guild
same address

Rapid (*Association Against Copyright Theft*)
Ksawerów 23 A
02656 Warsaw
Tel and Fax: (22) 486163

PORTUGAL

by Peter Besas

Though its film-making tradition goes back to 1896, Portugal produces only three or four films each year due to limited financing sources and small audiences.

Over the past five years theatrical attendance has been on the decline, although a number of suburban multiplexes have sprung into existence, as hardtops in the centres of big cities such as Lisbon and Porto have tended to close. Scheduled to open was a new 7-plex in Lisbon, jointly owned by Warner Bros and local banner Lusomundo.

Financing from the government-run Portuguese Film Institute for local product remains modest. The Institute is now also providing some seed money for screenplays. Young directors trying to get a start now tend to turn more to State-run television (RTP). Some observers are hoping the advent of two private channels in 1992 will provide more incentives. The most active producers such as Paulo Branco and Antonio-Pedro Vasconcellos are involved in co-productions with other countries, making their films more financially viable.

Thus Vasconcellos produced **Lieutenant Lorena** (*Aqui d'el rei*) with a French company, which will be released as both a feature and a TV series.

Among other notable titles were **Mr. Ventura** (*O Senhor Ventura*), directed by Jose Fonseca e Costa, and Luis Filipe Rocha's **Love and Toes** (*Amor e dedinhos dos pes*) both of which were partly financed by investors from Macao. The former also received under-the-line help from China.

The grand old man of Portuguese cinema, Manoel de Oliveira, continues to make one feature a year. In 1991 it was **Divina Comedia**, produced by Paulo Branco's Atlanta/Madragos banner, a social comedy set in modern Portugal; Oliveira was also prepping an updated version of *Madame Bovary*, to be set in modern Porto, based on a story by Agustina Bessa Lufs.

Portugal plays host to various film festivals. Due to be expanded in 1992 is the Fantasporto festival in the city of Porto, which will feature a competitive new directors section in addition to its traditional sci-fi competing section. Also still going strong is the film festival in Troia, on a peninsula dedicated to tourism, opposite the city of Setubal, south of Lisbon. Troia tends to screen a mixed bag of films. Oldest event is the Figueira da Foz festival, located at a seaside resort north of Lisbon, dedicated mostly to art house films.

PETER BESAS has lived in Madrid since the mid-1960's and is chief of Variety's bureau there. He has written various books, including a history of Spanish cinema.

Producers/ Distributors

Atlanta/Madragoa Films
Avenida D. Carlos
1, 72–D3
Lisbon 1200
Tel: 674841/674723

Filmargem
Rua Padre Antonio Vieira 17
Lisbon 1000
Tel: 692–571

Films Castello Lópes
Praça Marqués de Pombal 6
Lisbon 1288
Tel: 563–366

Lisboa Films
Praça Bernardino Machado
Lisbon 1700
Tel: 759–1063

Filmes Luso Mundo
Praça de Alegria 22
Lisbon 1200
Tel: 370–964

Opus Filmes
Rua de Oliveira ao Carmo 24
Lisbon 1200
Tel: 373010

Prole Films
Rua dos Lusiadas
112–3 dto
Lisbon 1300

Tel: 363–6979/648028
Fax: 363–7290

Useful Addresses

Portuguese Film Institute
Rua San Pedro de Alcántara 45
Lisbon 1200
Tel: (3511) 346–7395
Fax: (3511) 372–777

Uniportugal
Avda. Duque de Loulé 79
Lisbon 1000
Tel: 520339

PUERTO RICO

by José Artemio Torres

Film-making in Puerto Rico, in all areas, was very slow during the second half of 1990 and the first of 1991. There was no local feature film production and nobody came from abroad to shoot here. Only one video documentary, and a poor one, was released: Sonia Fritz's **Visa for a Dream**, about Dominican women immigrants. Two dramatic shorts were produced in English and although they have shown at festivals abroad, they haven't been shown in Puerto Rico. The first, entitled **The Bell**, is based on a Puerto Rican legend and was directed by Puerto Rican Noel Quiñones. The second is called **A Story of Old San Juan** and was written and directed by American Kevin McLeary.

Even the area of TV commercials production suffered from the economic recession that hovered over the island during this period. Also, some advertising agencies moved to countries like Venezuela, Chile and Brazil looking for lower production costs. TV drama came down to near zero: no soap operas, no one-day dramas, only a couple of mini-series.

One major TV event, the showing of **On the Surface of the Skin**, was a disappointment. The one-hour film, shot on 35mm and directed by Marcos Zurinaga, was sponsored by the government's Commission of Women Affairs. Its theme of women's abuse suffer from didacticism and over-simplification of the characters' feelings and motivations.

Still, there are many projects on the drawing boards and a few documentaries in the post-production stage. This means that next year will be a busier one on the exhibition front. This confirms a pattern of film production in Puerto Rico: projects take a long time to get made and there will be noteworthy releases only in odd years.

TOP TEN GROSSING FILMS IN PUERTO RICO: 1990

	Rentals ($U.S.)
Teenage Mutant Ninja Turtles	1,000,000
Robocop 2	850,000
Gremlins 2	800,000
Total Recall	800,000
Die Hard 2	700,000
Back to the Future, Part III	700,000
Home Alone (until Dec. 31)	680,000
Ghost	600,000
Tango and Cash	540,000
Problem Child	500,000

ROMANIA

by Manuela Cernat

In the immediate aftermath of the 1989 revolution, Romanian film-makers went on hunger strike to free the national film industry from the bureaucratic grasp of the Culture Ministry. Nowadays they seem to regret that hasty and passionate move. The new set-up proposed last February by the Provisional Committee and enthusiastically endorsed last May by the General Assembly of the newly-created Film Union, proved to be very shabby indeed.

In early summer 1991, a general strike of the film industry, including the cinemas which closed for 24 hours (unprecedented in their 85 year history), challenged Dan Piţa's mismanagement as President of the National Cinema Centre and the absence of a Cinema Law to protect the national film industry under the new circumstances of a free market. While attendance figures drop drastically, and state support stays at a symbolical level, there is little hope for the future, as the budget of a single project has escalated ten times since the revolution, and the Buftea Production Centre alone needs 400,000 *lei* per year.

Old crumbling cinemas with outdated sound equipment and a poor repertory – even the films from our neighbouring countries to the east must be paid in hard currency, while the prices required by our former western partners grow prohibitive, and the huge TV and video challenge – are the reasons why in the future Romania's national production can count no longer on refunds from admissions. In these transitional years from the state monopoly to the private industry, subsidies from the government are just not on. Yet, in tune with its policy of obvious lack of interest in all cultural matters, the present regime hardly seems eager to support this cause. Up there somebody doesn't like movies.

Long-awaited Documentary
The Senate, the Parliament and even President Iliescu keep promoting Stere Gulea's full-length documentary **University Square–Romania** (*Piaţa Universităţii– Romania*), by protesting angrily against the release of this poignant cinematic statement on a most controversial political issue: the April–June 1990 anti-communist University Square Movement that entered the Guinness Book of Records as the longest non-stop street demonstration of the century (53 days and nights).

Produced by Lucian Pintilie under the prestigious banner of the Ministry of Culture, in a sort of defiant gesture against the hitherto ponderous, hesitant and conformist National Cinema Centre, Stere Gulea's film recalls the magic atmosphere and the deep political significance of those extraordinary days of hope, solidarity and peaceful rejection of the neo-communist threat, which were to end in the nightmarish and savage so-called "Events of June 13–15," when the miners were called to Bucharest to clear up the University Square . . .

The opening night, scheduled deliberately on the very anniversary day of the start of the "Square Movement" in a theatre two blocks away from the Square, gave way to stormy events inside and outside the hall. A few minutes after the screening, the violent clashes between the police and the "squarists" just witnessed in the documentary were to be unexpectedly re-enacted in reality. Emerging from a film that exorcised a dramatic mass-experience, the audience saw, a few yards away in the Square, students being beaten again by the *scutieri* (ruthless, well-shielded cops). Spontaneously, everybody in the area, journalists, film-makers or just filmgoers, formed a huge column and marched towards the Square, where, once again they were to be charged and brutally beaten.

After such a "smashing" opening, one can easily guess why in its first week of release, Gulea's movie had already attracted 70,000 entries, a record never envisaged for a documentary!

The more aggressively the producer and the director were attacked by Romanian TV, at peak viewing hours, the more successful proved their achievement, each screening providing a fascinating "political happening."

Warned publicly by President Iliescu that he would be "placed under penal investigation" for having falsified the soundtrack of a sequence that reveals his personal involvement and responsibility in "the June events", Stere Gulea was also threatened with the suppression of the film, while the Minister of Culture, Andrei Pleşu, was repeatedly and vehemently interrupted in the Parliament, on behalf of the ruling Party, F.S.N. (Front of National Salvation), to account "for having spent the money of the people" on such a "destabilizing film."

Finally, in a bitter TV statement, Culture Minister Pleşu hoped that such interference with freedom of expression does not reflect the standpoint of the majority of the Chambers elected last year to rule the country in its way towards democracy, or else the 1989 revolution was useless and its martyrs had died for nothing.

Film Monopoly Splits
Romania's small but highly productive Anima-Film Studio is the first one to escape from the bureaucratic grasp of the State Monopoly. Founded in 1965 and providing ever since some 80% of the total amount of foreign currency earned each year from the foreign sales of the entire national film production, Anima-Film covers a wide range of techniques, from cartoons and cut-outs to puppets, claymation, painting in front of the camera, pixillation, etc, the outstanding creative wit and poetry of its artists being generously rewarded all around the world with prizes at the main Festivals.

Releasing 65 shorts per year and 3–4 long features every two years, it is the only branch of the domestic industry with a chance of staying afloat in the post-revolutionary turmoil that keeps paralysing the activity of the other studios. Tired of the hesitant back and forth moves of the National Cinema Centre appointed in 1990, and keen to acquire the autonomous status of a limited corporation, in order to start a new life, based on free market economic and production bases, Anima-Film broke away from the old system by daringly entering a joint venture with the Spanish Dale Multibrook Ltd. Company, backed by a multinational group. The Romanians will contribute their Studio, their craft and work, while the foreign partners will introduce much-needed modern technology and basic lab facilities.

Among the initial projects of the young company, are, as one might guess, some features to be ready in time for the Barcelona Olympic Games.

MANUELA CERNAT is a Romanian film critic and historian who has written various books, some of which, like her study of war movies, have been translated into other languages. She has also taught in the United States.

SINGAPORE
by Fred Marshall

The Singapore Economic Development Board's new package for film companies offers various benefits and initiatives in support of the local industry. Among these is a 5 to 10 year "tax holiday" to qualified companies that produce films on a long-term basis in Singapore, as well as a waiver of withholding tax on income for foreign stars and creative talents in the film industry.

The launch of the multi-million dollar Tang Dynasty Village and the Tuas Television World has also given local film-making a shot in the arm. The Tang Dynasty Village movie-theme park in Jurong will contain three motion picture studios with state-of-the-art facilities for local and foreign productions. In addition, on its 12-hectare site, life in the golden age of China's Seventh Century will be re-created on what is Asia's largest historical and cultural theme park.

Opening next year, Tuas Television World, organised by the Singapore Broadcasting Corporation, will be one of the world's largest television backlots. There will be eight distinct sets, five of which will re-create aspects of Old Singapore such as Malay kampongs, Little India, and Chinatown; the early commercial district; Peranakan, Chinese and Western bungalows as well as the neighbourhood of the Singapore River.

Movie Impact, the first Hongkong film company to set up a base in Singapore, has met with success with its first made-in Singapore production, *The Last Blood*. Plans are already under way for more films. Hongkong producer Eric Tsan has announced plans to make two films here at a total cost of US$5 million. Depending on the success of this initial venture, he hopes to shoot three films a year from now on in Singapore. The first, starring Alan Tam, began shooting in May 1991 and the second, to star Andy Lau, rolled in July.

New Censorship System Sought
The Singapore Board of Film Censors is introducing a classification system for films instead of the "one size fits all" method. Rama Meyappan, Chairman of the Board, told a local newspaper that views on the feasibility of such a system are being solicited from distributors, exhibitors, members of the film appeals committee, the film advisory committee and other bodies. "We will have to look into which system would be suitable, the problems of enforcing it, and what would be the public's expectations. I can't tell how long this will take," he said, "but it is under way."

The recent success of the Singapore Film Festival has attracted several major personalities to the city in recent years. Visitors to the 1990 event included Joan Chen, Lino Brocka and Richard Chen (directors), Alan Tam (actor), and Eric Tsang (producer).

Useful Addresses

Tang Dynasty Village
Motion Picture Division
10 Mount Faber
Singapore 0409
Tel: 271–6111
Fax: 271–6100

Tuas Television World
Singapore Broadcasting Corp
Caldecott Hill
Andrew Road
Singapore 1129
Tel: 256–0401
Fax: 253–8808

**Ministry of Information and
the Arts**
#36–00 PSA Building
460 Alexandra Road
Singapore 0511
Tel: 279–9707
Fax: 279–9784

Yarra Films Ptd Ltd
13 Mohammed Sultan Road
Singapore 0923
Tel: 235–2122
Fax: 733–3278

Movie Impact (S) Pte Ltd
16B Lorong Ampas
GS Building
Singapore 1232
Tel: 255–3136
Fax: 253–3668

Joan Chen, a visitor to the Singapore Film Festival

(continued from page 243)
post-Civil War period. Critics hailed the film for spirited performances by a young cast and director Kwak's cinematic feeling for landscapes as counterpoints to a young man's journey into adulthood. In all, *Portrait* won eight Grand Bells citations in 1991, including best director award for Kwak. The film was produced by veteran commercial producer Lee Taewon, marking an interesting commingling of art and commerce and the emergence of a directorial talent notably worth watching.

Korean cinema was much in evidence on the international festival circuit over the last year or so. Director Shin Sung-soo's depiction of alienation amid rampant materialism – *The Rooster*, denoting the metaphor of the protagonist as a rooster confined in a chicken coop – competed in competition at the Montréal Film Festival. Park Kwang-soo's *They, Like Us* played the Three Continents Festival in Nantes, France, and at the Berlin Festival. Jang Seonwoo's *Lovers in Woomukbaemi* was screened out of competition at the Karlovy Vary Festival.

Two film-related events underscore cosmic ideological shifts in terms of South Korea and the Communist world. For a month beginning in late August, 1990, Korean Film Weeks were observed in Moscow and other cities, introducing eight domestic titles to the Soviets and paving the way for increased film exchanges between the nations. More notably, screenings of North Korean films started in the South, and the first North–South Film Festival was held in New York – the first exchange of its kind in 45 years of territorial division.

SOUTH AFRICA
by Martin Botha

Between 1980 and 1990 approximately 566 full-length features were made in South Africa. The local commercial cinema was made possible by means of tax concessions and 130 films have been made in this way since 1984. The majority of these films are rather poor imitations of American genre movies. Recent examples are *American Kickboxer*, *The Rutanga Tapes*, *Act of Piracy*, *African Express*, *Odd Ball Hall*, *Chameleon* and *American Ninja 4*. Towards the final years of the 1980's, this industry has come to an end with the shift from tax incentives to a governmental subsidy system based on box-office income. This has placed film-making within the commercial inudustry in the hands of a few established companies who are interested in only making safe, formula films such as Franz Marx's *Agter Elke Man*, based on a popular television series, the musical *Ipi Tombi* and a film about the life of Emily Hobhouse, *That Englishwoman*.

Censorship, distribution problems, a lack of support from local film critics, and general funding limitations have *not* prevented a few directors from producing some remarkable indigenous films within the commercial industry and especially in the independent, "alternative" industry that has experienced a revival since the mid-1980's.

The watershed years were between 1985 and 1987. Independent film-maker Johan Blignaunt's Afrikaans film *Mamza* portrayed the aspirations and frustrations of the so-called "coloureds" in a *cinéma vérité manner*. In the mainstream industry Katinka Heyns's *Fiela's Child*, Gray Hofmeyr's *Jock of the Bushveld*, and Robert Davies's *Saturday Night at the Palace* explored the socio-political aspects and myths of South African

society. John Smallcombe's *An African Dream* and Frans Nel's *'n Wêreld Sonder Grense* (*A World without Borders*), a moving portrayal of the border war, added themes and indigenous images to this mosaic of the South African reality.

Oliver Schmitz's **Mapantsula** became a landmark film, a contemporary account of a township gangster who inadvertently becomes involved in a complex triangle of politics, self-interest and genuine compassion. It was made in 1988 while the country suffered under the state of emergency, but was for the first time released on the general circuit in South Africa during 1991 after years of censorship problems.

The talented young director Darrell Roodt made a trilogy of films about racial conflicts within rural settings: *A Place of Weeping*, *The Stick* and *Jobman*. **The Stick**, also released during 1991 in South Africa after a long battle with the local censors, was selected to open the Montreal Film Festival in 1988. The film is a harrowing examination of the dehumanising effect of war on seven soldiers who set out on a "search and destroy" mission in a neighbouring northern state. At the time of writing, **Jobman** has still not been released on the main circuit. This human drama explores how fear and violence in a community, caused by someone who is an outcast, destroy attempts at communication and understanding. Roodt was awarded the Standard Bank Award in 1991 for the Best Young Filmmaker in this country. He is working on two new projects, an Afrikaans film *Na die geliefde land*, and *Lightning Bird*. He is only 28 and has directed five films.

Local audiences, however, seem not to

relish these socially conscious movies. Instead of supporting Francis Gerard's moving *A Private Life* and Helena Nogueira's *Quest for Love* with their love stories set against the apartheid state, or Manie van Rensburg's *The Fourth Reich* and *The Native Who Caused All The Trouble*, they flocked to see light comedies such as *Tolla is Tops* and Leon Schuster's *Oh Schucks . . . Here Comes U.N.T.A.G.*

Disappointment for Reich

The failure of **The Fourth Reich** at the box office was a shock for the local industry. This impressive saga of Afrikaner nationalism during the early 1940's cost some R16 million, raised mostly through the tax incentive scheme. The film opened with 20 prints, highly favourable reviews and a saturated media. Van Rensburg won the best director award at the South African Awards ceremony. One explanation is that the main distributors, Ster-Kinekor and Nu-Metro, only cater for a small proportion of the local population. Although Ster-Kinekor and Nu-Metro respectively owned 232 and 106 cinemas and drive-ins by January 1991, these luxury complexes are basically in the cities. The cinema outlets to which blacks in the townships have easy access are virtually non-existent. Cinemas may be multi-racial, but outside the cities there are no substantial distribution chains to ensure that the majority of the South African population gets to see these local movies.

It is thus remarkable that fine films are produced in this country, if one considers the fact that local films have to be seen by a minimum number of local viewers before subsidy is paid. Gray Hofmeyr's **Lambarene**, about the life of Dr. Albert Schweitzer (played by Malcolm McDowell) in the rainforest of Gabon in West Africa, is one such quality production. It was the 1990 recipient of the AA Life/M-Net Vita Award for Best South African Film and is visually splendid. Terence Ryan's **Hold My Hand, I'm Dying** portrays the socio-political

Malcolm McDowell as Schweitzer in *Lambarene*
photo: Ster-Kinekor

changes in Zimbabwe during the 1960's. Although technically well made, it gives a rather sinister image to the liberation struggle.

On the independent side, Elaine Proctor's **On the Wire** has broken thematic ground as it deals brilliantly with the troubled psyches of South African Defence Force soldiers who have committed atrocities on the border and in Angola, and have failed to adapt to "normal" life inside South Africa. David Wicht's **Windprints** depicts the story of a young liberal Afrikaner cameraman who gets involved in the hunt for a renegade Nama who has killed a number of farm labourers over a period of two years. The film, set against harsh Namibian landscapes, was screened on the main circuit as part of a focus on local films.

The frustrations and aspirations of people in the townships: Johan Blignaut's *Mamza*

Still from Manie van Rensburg's *The Native Who Caused All the Trouble*

Another of these is Jean Delbeke's *The Schoolmaster*, an exploration of South African society during the birth of apartheid in 1948. The film, although visually impressive, suffers from a rather stereotyped depiction of poor, rural Afrikaners.

Documentaries and Shorts

The independent industry not only includes full-length features, but also documentaries and short fiction films. During the 1980's at least three outstanding full-length documentaries were made, portraying the destruction of indigenous cultures due to colonialism and apartheid legislation. These films are Paul Myburgh's *People of the Great Sandface*, Mark Newman's *The Two Rivers* and Jurgen Schadeberg's rich portrait of the 1950's, *Have You Seen Drum, Recently?* Myburgh and Schadeberg's films were screened for the first time on local TV during 1990–91.

At the *Weekly Mail* Film Festival of 1990, co-hosted by the *Weekly Mail* newspaper and the Film and Allied Workers Organisation (FAWO), a collection of rare films on South Africa found in archives around the world, examples of resistance cinema never seen publicly in this country, as well as twenty films by independent South African film-makers and over 20 short films in a short film competition were screened. Features such as Neil Sonnekus's *A.W.O.L.* and Chris Curling's *Dark City* attempted to break new ground. Sonnekus's film, although flawed, depicts the psychological effects of military life on a young man, while Curling's thriller portrays the killing of a councillor during township unrest. Aldo Lee and Lance Gewer's *Sacrifice* won the short film competition. It concerns an Afrikaans family in the process of disintegration.

Censorship remains a problem for independent directors: Andrew Worsdale's innovative satire on white paranoia, *Shotdown*, remains banned in this country. Cedric Sundstrom's *The Shadowed Mind*, a visually splendid thriller about murder in a mental institution, was banned for screening at the *Weekly Mail* Festival. The theme of the festival was "transitions" and South Africa, as well as the local film industry, are in a phase of transition. FAWO worked during 1991 on a possible model for a future, non-racial industry. Johan Blignaunt's corporate venture, Showdata, a computerised on-line information service on all aspects of the South African film industry, became an important facilitator in this transitional period within the industry. The future will tell if independent South African cinema will repeat the revival of the late 1980's, but the potential surely is there.

DR. MARTIN BOTHA is a film and TV researcher at the Human Sciences Research Council. He has been involved in media research for the past five years, and is author of a book on independent film-making in South Africa during the 1980's.

One of the best South African films in recent years: Manie van Rensburg's *The Fourth Reich*

The Fourth Reich

Script: Malcolm Kohll. Direction: Manie van Rensburg. Photography: Dewald Aukema. Editing: Nena Olwage. Music: Louis van Rensburg. Production Design: Mark Wilby. Players: Marius Weyers, Ryno Hattingh, Grethe Fox, Percy Sieff, Elize Cawood, Pierre Knoessen, Marcel van Heerden, Louis van Niekerk. Produced by David Selvan for Zastron Films. Aprox 200 mins.

A two and a half hours version of *The Fourth Reich* was released in this country during 1990, but the director's cut running approximately three hours is the real thing. Based on the book "Operation Weissdorn" by Hans Strydom, the film deals with the true story of two Afrikaners during the Second World War. The one was Robey Leibbrandt (Ryno Hattingh), an Olympic boxer who hated the British and the South African government's involvement with the Allies in World War Two and hoped to install a Nazi regime in South Africa. The other was a young police captain, Jan Taillard (Marius Weyers), picked by Genl. Jan Smuts to stop Leibbrandt.

The film has received 14 nominations for the 1989–1990 AA Life/M-Net Vita Film Awards, an indication of the film's artistry regarding direction, acting, cinematography, script, editing, sound, art direction and music score. It is a complex account of the subversive violence of an extremist right-wing Afrikaner group who plotted to overthrow the government with rather uneasy parallels with recent reports of right-wing threats in contemporary South Africa.

As the saga unfolds with its startling images of secret blood oaths within this extremist organisation, Van Rensburg brilliantly explores his well-known themes of betrayal, the outcast, communication problems (in this case between Taillard and his wife), as well as Afrikaner nationalism. It is also one of the major local films to make the great South African landscapes into an integral part of the narrative structure and visually the film is hauntingly beautiful, shot by Dewald Aukema who has won the AA Life Vita award for his cinematography.

Martin Botha

Profile of a Director:
MANIE VAN RENSBURG

Manie van Rensburg is the most prominent director in South Africa over the past decade. His work can be described as critical chronicles of the psyche of the Afrikaner in a contemporary or historic situation (especially the period from the 1920's to the 1940's) that includes the following themes: the way of life of, and motivation for, individuals living on the "edge" of society, loneliness and communication problems between people. His work can be divided into three periods: the Afrikaans films of 1971 to 1975, the television films and series from 1976 to 1987, and from 1988 onwards, a shift towards the international film scene with *The Native Who Caused All the Trouble*, *The Fourth Reich* and *Taxi to Soweto*.

His major films are set within the 1930's and 1940's, exploring Afrikaner nationalism and the struggle of Afrikaner farmers to retain their land in the four hours drama *Verspeelde Lente* (*Lost Springtime*) and the drama *Die Perdesmous* (*The Horse Trader*). These movies critically portray authentic historic events, drawing in culture, class and rural-urban conflicts. The existence of South Africa's segregationist race policies (in particular the 1913 Land Act) and the harmful effects it had on blacks since the 1930's, are satirically portrayed in *The Native Who Caused All the Trouble*. The conflict of value systems (Western Colonial versus African Traditional) is brilliantly explored in the movie.

The revival of Afrikaner nationalism during 1939 to 1948 is the subject of Van Rensburg's best films, *Heroes* and *The Fourth Reich*, both over three hours in length. The destructive part played by a rightwing organisation, the "Ossewabrandwag" and its military wing, is critically examined in both films. These films give a rich portrait of a complex socio-political situation during the stormy times of the Second World War.

In contrast, Van Rensburg's latest film is a comedy. *Taxi to Soweto* sets out to walk the tricky line of balancing sentiment and humour. It concerns a bored, over-pampered, rich, urban Afrikaans woman, her workaholic husband and a street-sharp taxi driver, whose lives entwine in the realities of Soweto. With this movie Van Rensburg departs from his period dramas to explore the psyche of the contemporary Afrikaner within the rapid changing South Africa.

Recent and Forthcoming Films

Act of Piracy. Script: Hal Reed. Dir: John "Bud" Cardos. Phot: Vincent Cox. Players: Belinda Bauer, Ray Scharkey. Prod: Igo Kantor, Hal Reed.
Agter Elke Man (Behind Every Man). Script & Dir: Franz Marx. Phot: Dave Aenmey. Players: Steve Hofmeyr, Dulsie van den Bergh. Prod: Leisureco & FMF.
American Kickboxer. Script: Emil Kolbe. Dir: Frans Nel. Phot: Paul Morkel. Players: John Barret, Keith Vitali, Terry Norton. Prod: Cine-Clic Productions.
American Ninja 4: The Annihilation. Script: David Geeves. Dir: Cedric Sundstrom. Phot: Joseph Wein. Players: Michael Dudikoff, David Bradley. Prod: Nu Metro Productions.
A.W.O.L. Script: Neil Sonnekus, Roy Macgregor. Dir: Neil Sonnekus. Phot: Roy Macgregor. Players: Danny Keogh, Joanna Weinberg, Sean Higg. Prod: Johan Blignaut.
Chameleon. Script & Dir: Michael MacCarthy. Phot: James Robb. Players: Michael Nouri, Lee van Cleef. Prod: Edgar Bold.
Dark City. Script: David Lan. Dir: Chris Curling. Phot: Dick Pope. Players: Sello Maake Ka-Ngube, Vusi Dibakwane. Prod: Celestia Fox.
Ipi Tombi. Script: Bima Stagg. Dir: Koos Roets. Phot: James Robb. Players: Henry Cele, O'Neil Johnson. Prod: Tommie Meyer Films.
Lambarene. Script: Michael Potts. Dir: Gray Hofmeyr. Phot: Buster Reynolds. Players: Malcolm McDowell, Susan Strasberg, Helen Jessop. Prod: Egar Bold.
Die Nag van die Negentiende (The Night of the Nineteenth). Script: P.G. du Plessis. Dir:

Koos Roets. Phot: James Robb. Players: Embeth Davidtz, Adam Botha, Pieter Hough. Prod: Movieworld Ltd.

Oh Schucks ... Here Comes U.N.T.A.G. Script: Paul Slabolepszy. Dir: David Lister. Phot: James Robb. Players: Leon Schuster, Bill Flynn. Prod: Toron International.

On the Wire. Script & Dir: Elaine Proctor. Players: Michael O'Brien, Aletta Bezuidenhout, Gys de Villiers.

The Schoolmaster. Script, Dir & Phot: Jean Delbeke. Players: Elsa Fourie, Danny Keogh, Lida Botha. Prod: Jean Delbeke.

The Sheltering Desert. Script: Roderick Mann. Dir: Regardt van den Bergh. Phot: Jiri Tirl. Players: Jason Connery, Rupert Graves. Prod: Mirabib Films.

Tolla is Tops. Script, Dir & Phot: Elmo de Witt. Players: Hermann Visser, Elmo de Witt, Tolla van der Merwe. Prod: Elmo de Witt Films.

Vanessa – Déjà Vu. Script: Robert van der Coolwijk. Dir: Laurens Barnard. Phot: Marc Bower. Players: Joe Stewardson, Nian Hamilton, Morton Swayne. Prod: Laubar Production.

South African Film Awards 1990 (AA Life/ M-NET)

Best Film: *Lambarene.*
Best Performance by a Lead Actor: Marius Weyers (*The Fourth Reich*).
Best Performance by a Lead Actress: Elsa Fourie (*The Schoolmaster*).
Best Performance in a Supporting Role (male): Danny Keogh (*The Schoolmaster*) and Ian Roberts (*The Fourth Reich*).
Best Performance in a Supporting Role (female): Lida Botha (*The Schoolmaster*) and Helen Jessop (*Lambarene*).
Best Direction: Manie van Rensburg (*The Fourth Reich*).
Best Script: Jean Delbeke (*The Schoolmaster*).
Best Original Music Score: Zane Cronjé (*Lambarene*).
Best Sound: Brian Frost, Sid Knowles, Henry Prentice (*Lambarene*).
Best Art Direction: Michael Philips (*Lambarene*).
Best Editing: Maggie Vaughan (*The Schoolmaster*).
Best Cinematography: Dewald Aukema (*The Fourth Reich*).

Useful Address

Showdata
Johan Blignaut
11 Frost Ave
Auckland Park 2092,
Johannesburg.
Tel: (27–11) 482–1382
Fax: (27–11) 726–1422
(On-line information service on all aspects of the South African film industry, i.e. production companies, distributors, directors, screenwriters, players, etc. The largest of its nature in the southern hemisphere, it includes information on approximately 4,000 personalities in the industry.)

Communication problems between human beings in the world of Manie van Rensburg. Scene from *The Native Who Caused All the Trouble*

CINE ESPAÑOL PARA EL MUNDO · SPANISH CINEMA FOR THE WORLD

The
SPANISH FILM INSTITUTE

MINISTERIO DE CULTURA
Instituto de Cine (ICAA)

is proud to have helped promote films from Spain at leading international film festivals throughout 1991

Among competing films were:

BERLIN   "Amantes" (Lovers) by Vicente Aranda

MOSCOW   "Don Juan en los Infiernos" (Don Juan in Hell) by Gonzalo Suárez

MONTREAL   "La Viuda del Capitán Estrada" (Captain Estrada's Widow) by José Luis Cuerda

VENICE   "Chatarra" (Scrap Metal) by Félix Rotaeta

SAN SEBASTIAN   "La Noche Más Larga" (The Longest Night) by José Luis García Sánchez

"Alas de Mariposa" (Butterfly Wings) by Juanma Bajo Ulloa

"Los Papeles de Aspern" (The Aspern Papers) by Jordi Cadena

SPAIN

by Peter Besas

1992 is Spain's great year in the spotlight. Barcelona will play host to the Olympics; Seville is the site of the world's fair to commemorate the 500th anniversary of the discovery of America; and Madrid will be designated as official culture capital of Europe.

Although there will certainly be lots of glitz and activity, Spain's film industry isn't expected to cull much advantage from it. Thus far, one of the strongest supports for local producers was the money funnelled into feature production by the State-run TV network, Televisión Española (RTVE). But due to cut-throat competition from new regional and private channels around the country, RTVE has lost half its audience and about half its ad revenue. Chances are,

for 1992, local producers will not be able to count upon support from RTVE, which, in many cases, constituted between 30%– 50% of production costs.

The Spanish industry, however, is no newcomer to crises, and the level of production (41 features in 1990) can be expected to be maintained. Indeed, several new financing groups, mainly with an eye to the Spanish TV market, have emerged and announced production slates of from three to five films a year. Among these are IDEA (Iberoamericana Derechos Audio), Cartel, and ESICMA.

Various Spanish films performed well at the box-office in 1990, pushing their market share up from 7.69% the previous year to 11.09%. The 1991 results will probably be

Carmen Maura and Antonio Resines in *Como ser mujer y no morir en el intento*

IBEROAMERICANA FILMS

IBEROAMERICANA FILMS • Velázquez, 12 - 28001 Madrid. SPAIN • Tels.: (91) 431 42 46 · 431 42 73 • Telex: 45753 CINE E • Fax: 435 59 94

THE BEST OF SPANISH CINEMA :

ALMODOVAR
   BARDEM
      BIGAS LUNA
         BUNUEL
            CHAVARRI
               COLOMO
                  FERNAN GOMEZ
                     GARCIA BERLANGA
                        SAURA
                           SUAREZ
                              TRUEBA

... and many others in our 300 hundred-title catalogue!

Jorge Sant, director Vicente Aranda, and Maribel Verdú in *Amantes*

comparable, thanks to some local hits, mainly from Spain's leading producer, Iberoamericana Films.

Spain's best-known *wunderkind*, Pedro Almodóvar, was expected to release his new film, **High Heels** (*Tacones Lejanos*), in the fall. Produced by his El Deseo company, the film features Victoria Abril and Miguel Bosé and has already been picked up by Warner Bros. for release in the States.

Proving to be one of Spain's top films in 1991, and expected to run off with a good number of Goya awards, is **Lovers** (*Amantes*), directed by Vicente Aranda, produced by Pedro Costa. The film, brilliantly photographed by José Luis Alcaine, toplines Victoria Abril and Maribel Verdú in a memorable *mano a mano*. The story is set in Spain's postwar period in a small village and with a triangle plot, between two women who vie for the love of a callow youth, played by Jorge Sanz.

Aranda superbly builds up the tension, as the three enact their tragic village drama. Victoria Abril is already well known by those who keep tabs on Spanish cinema talent; the discovery here is pretty young Maribel Verdú who out-performs even the accomplished Abril.

Not released yet at press time, but expected to be an eye-opener is Gonzalo Suarez's **Don Juan in Hell** (*Don Juan en Los Infiernos*) with Fernando Guillén, Mario Pardo and Charo López. The film was Spain's official entry at the Moscow Film Festival.

Explicit and Kinky

The big succès de scandale in 1991 was Bigas Luna's **The Ages of Lulu** (*Las edades de Lulú*) probably one of the most explicit and kinky films ever made in Spain, with Italo actress Francesca Neri topcast. The story was negligible, but the sex element potent.

EL DESEO S.A. PRESENTS

A FILM BY ALMODOVAR

On the day of his death
Manuel was visited by three women.
He made love with one of them,
he argued tensely with another,
and the third one found him dead...

Victoria ABRIL
Marisa PAREDES
Miguel BOSÉ

An EL DESEO S.A. - CIBY 2000
Production

tacones lejanos

(HIGH HEELS)

Costume designer JOSE Mª COSSIO
Make-up GREGORIO ROS
Hair JESUS MONCUSI
Sound JEAN PAUL MUGEL
Art director PIERRE THEVENET
Editor JOSE SALCEDO
Director of photography ALFREDO MAYO
Music composed by RYUICHI SAKAMOTO
Songs by LUZ CASAL
Production manager ESTHER GARCIA
Associate producer ENRIQUE POSNER
Executive producer AGUSTIN ALMODOVAR
Written and directed by
Pedro ALMODOVAR

DOLBY STEREO
IN SELECTED THEATRES

Fernando Guillén in *Don Juan en los infiernos*

On the lighter side was **How To Be a Woman and Not Die Trying** (*Como ser mujer y no morir en el intento*) with Carmen Maura as the long-suffering and ultimately rebellious housewife, and Antonio Resines as the husband. The film takes the couple through a stormy year of marital relations. Though it lacks the punch of American women's lib films, it nonetheless was a crowd pleaser in Spain. The script was by Carmen Rico Godoy and direction by Ana Belén, heretofore better known as an actress and singer.

In Cataluña (Barcelona), the most successful film of the year was Rosa Vergès's **Boom Boom**, a droll comedy with Viktor Lazlo and Sergi Mateu about an attractive lady dentist and a shoe shop owner who live in the same building. While each pursues his and her own unhappy love affairs, and interact with common contacts, they never meet until one day imbibing bloody marys at a fiesta.

Among other films that surfaced during the past year on Spanish screens were Antoni Ribas's biopic **Dalí** covering the artist's early years; **The White Dove** (*La blanca paloma*) anent Basque terrorist problems, directed by Juan Miñón; **Don Juan My Dear Ghost** (*Don Juan mi querido fantasma*) by Antonio Mercero, a spoof on the Don Juan legend; **Against the Wind** (*Contra el Viento*), a rambling tale of incest, directed by Francisco Periñán; and the naval drama **Alone with You** (*A solas contigo*), directed by Eduardo Campoy, with Victoria Abril and Imanol Arias.

Made in Barcelona was the animated feature **Sparks of the Catalan Swords** (*Despertaferro*), directed by Jordi Amorós:

Latino Bar, an idiosyncractic, no-dialogue film by Paul Leduc, was a Catalan co-production with Latin America.

In the Hopper

A number of important films were in the hopper at press time. *Beltenbros* marks the return of femme helmer Pilar Miró. The film was partly shot in England and Poland, as well as Spain, and features Patsy Kensit, Geraldine James and José Luis Gómez. Also *El Rey Pasmado*, a co-production with companies in Paris and Lisbon set in seventeenth-century Spain, with Gabino Diego, Juan Diego and Laura del Sol in this period drama. Ready for a fall release is *Veil of Dreams*, a Tesauro Films co-production with Roger Corman, directed by Hervé Hachuel. Topcast in the psychodrama are Maryan d'Abo, Cliff de Young and Shary Shuttuck.

As for Carlos Saura, Spain's veteran prestige director is preparing a one-hour TV special called *Goya*, which focuses on the painter's final days of exile in Bordeaux.

On the more commercial tack, producer/director Juan Piquer completed *Cthulhu Mansion* based on the H.P. Lovecraft story. Topcast in the film, partly shot in Czechoslovakia, are Frank Finlay, Marcia Layton, and Melanie Shatner.

Francesca Neri being "had" by two extras in *Las edades de Lulú*, released through Iberoamericana Films

But the most popular Spanish films usually are local boulevard comedies that never make it to festivals or screens abroad. Last year the topgrossing film in Spain was **Aquí huele a muerto** with popular comic duo Martes y Trece, followed closely by Almodóvar's **Tie Me Up, Tie Me Down**. Placing third was **Yo soy esa**, with the voluptuous Isabel Pantoja belting out a dozen songs.

PETER BESAS has lived in Madrid since the mid-1960's and is chief of Variety's bureau there. He has written various books, including a history of Spanish cinema.

Producers

Iberoamericana Films
Velázquez 12
Madrid 28001
Tel: 4314246
Fax: 4355994

José Frade P.C.
Gran Via 70
Madrid 28013
Tel: 2487144
Fax: 2485415

El Deseo S.A.
Ruiz Perelló 15
Madrid 28028

Tel: 2550285
Fax: 3557467

Multivideo S.A.
Luna 15
Madrid 28004
Tel: 5229347
Fax: 5328695

Figaro Films
Consejo de Ciento
Barcelona 08007
Tel: 3235654
Fax: 3237596

Jet Films
Manuel Montilla 1
Madrid 28016
Tel: 2506200
Fax: 4578874

Elías Querejeta
Maestro Lasalle 21
28006 Madrid
Tel: 2592322
Fax: 4579696

Opalo Films
Consell de Cent 303
Barcelona 08007

CATALONIA is a country of six million inhabitants. Our film production consists of an average of 15-20 feature films per year. In its production Barcelona has technical film and video infraestructure of
- film studios and video editing
- processing laboratories
- sound, dubbing and subtitling laboratories

In the video sectors the production, design and technical services companies have an advanced technology which covers all video-engineering possibilities from HB production to video-animation, etc. Morover there is The Sitges International Fantasy Film Festival known the world over which is held in October.

If Barcelona is known, among other reasons, for the Olympic Games 1992, discover Catalunya as a partner in TV production. We have projects ready to become reality, however you are welcome as possible co-producers in order to carry them out.
We also have feature films and TV production to sell.

If you need any more information about our TV and cinema production, production companies and our professionals, contact the CATALAN FILMS & TV booth at the following markets: Berlin European Film Market, MIP-TV, Cannes Film Market, MIFA, MIPCOM and MIFED, or write to our head office in Barcelona.

HEAD OFFICE
Diputació, 279-283
08007 Barcelona
Ph: (3) 317 35 85
Tx: 53916 TRPW E (ATT.
GENERALITAT/CODE 836)
Fax: (3) 301 22 47

USEFUL ADDRESSES
SITGES INTERNATIONAL FANTASY
FILM FESTIVAL
Diputació, 279-283
08007 BARCELONA
Ph: (3) 317 35 85
Fax: (3) 301 22 47

AGRUPACIÓ CATALANA DE
PRODUCTORS CINEMATOGRÀFICS
Castanyer, 31 Baixos
08022 BARCELONA
Ph: (3) 212 55 08
Fax: (3) 418 69 84

ASSOCIACIÓ CATALANA DE CRÍTICS
I ESCRIPTORS DE CINEMA
Valencia, 248
08007 BARCELONA
Ph: (3) 215 94 79

ACEVIP (ASSOCIACIÓ CATALANA
D'EMPRESARIS DE VIDEO
INDUSTRIAL I PROFESSIONAL)
Rambla de Catalunya, 54
08007 Barcelona
Ph: (3) 216 02 49
Fax: (3) 215 61 57

ANDICCA (ASSOCIACIÓ NACIONAL DE
DISTRIBUIDORS CINEMATOGRÀFICS
DE CATALUNYA)
Rambla de Catalunya, 47 1°.
08007 BARCELONA
Ph: (3) 301 57 40

ASSOCIACIÓ PROFESSIONAL DE DIRECTORS
DE CINEMA DE CATALUNYA
Mestre Nicolau, 19
08021 BARCELONA
Ph: (3) 201 30 22

TV3 TELEVISIÓ DE CATALUNYA
Jacint Verdaguer s/n.
08970 SANT JOAN DESPÍ (Barcelona)
Ph: (3) 473 03 33
Tx: 97990 TVCT E
Fax: (3) 473 15 63

Generalitat de Catalunya
Departament de Cultura

TOP TEN GROSSING FILMS IN SPAIN: 1990

	Rentals ($U.S.)
Pretty Woman	12,097,000
Dead Poets Society	9,453,000
Total Recall	8,075,000
Ghost	7,969,000
Look Who's Talking	7,938,000
Tango and Cash	6,627,000
Die Hard 2	5,977,000
Gremlins 2	5,922,000
Born on the Fourth of July	5,884,000
Aqui huele a muerto	4,827,000

Tel: 2549506
Fax: 2546781

Cartel
Orense 33
Madrid 28020
Tel: 5970772
Fax: 5970766

Ion Producciones
Av. Alfonso XIII, 62
Madrid 28016
Tel: 4166580
Fax: 5191305

Tesauro Films
José Abascal 44
Madrid 28003
Tel: 4429288
Fax: 4419232

Distributors

United International Pictures
Plaza del Callao 4
Madrid 28013
Tel: 5227261

Warner Bros/Columbia
Manuel Montilla 1
Madrid 28016
Tel: 2506200

Lauren Films
Balmes 73
Barcelona 08007
(*In Madrid*: Tetuán 29
Madrid 28013)
Tel: 3235400 (Barcelona)
5218285 (Madrid)

Araba Films
San Prudencio 13
Vitoria 01005
Tel: 140126

C.B. Films
Diagonal 407
Barcelona 08008
Tel: 2179354

Iberoamericana Films
Velázquez 12
Madrid 28001
Tel: 4314246
Fax: 4353994

Musidora Films
Princesa 5
Madrid 28008
Tel: 2487233

Manuel Salvador/20th Century-Fox
Callao 4
Madrid 28013
Tel: 5329320

Prime Films
Clara del Rey 17
Madrid 28002
Tel: 5190181

Recordvisión
Córcega 372
Barcelona 08037
Tel: 2073556
Fax: 2584740

Alta Films
Martin de los Heros 12
Madrid 28008
Tel: 5422702

Alas Films
Maestro Guerrero 2

Madrid 28008
Tel: 2476585

Ivex Films
Pasco San Gervasio 16
Barcelona 08022
Tel: 4184858

Golem Distribution S.A.
Avda. de Bayona 52
Pamplona 31008
Tel: (948) 260243

Surf Films
Zurbano 74
Madrid 28010
Tel: 4422944

San Marcos 40
Madrid 28004
Tel: 532–5089

Fedicine (Distributors'
Association)
Velázquez 10
Madrid 28001
Tel: 2769511

Federación de Exhibidores
(Exhibitors' Association)
Velázquez 10
Madrid 28001
Tel: 2762774

Basque Film Producers
Association
República Argentina 2
San Sebastian 20004
Tel: 422944
Fax: 428782

Quinto Centenario
Avda. Reyes Católicos 4
Madrid 28040
Tel: 5931992

Academia de las Artes y las
Ciencas Cinematograficas de
España
General Oraa 68
Madrid 28006
Tel: 5633341

Useful Addresses

Spanish Culture Ministry
(Film Institute)

Servei de Cine Catalan
Diputación 279
Barcelona 08007
Tel: 3173585

SRI LANKA
by Amarnath Jayatilaka

The year 1990 marked a restabilisation in the film exhibition sector after the disturbances it experienced in the latter part of the 1980's owing to terrorism. Moreover the ill-effects of one decade of misrule of the affairs at the National Film Corporation was completely dispelled by the sound financial management initiated by the new administration, headed by its Chairman, W.J. Fernando.

Many of the films released during last year and the first four months of 1991 were box-office hits. Many of the producers succeeded in recouping their investment, which in itself is an achievement as well as an inducement to continue in production. This apparent revival at the box-office has clearly boosted the Sinhala film industry.

While dozens of films are currently under production, over thirty are lined up for release.

The off-beat film **Under the Bridge** (*Palama Yata*) which was selected for showing at the Hawaii International festival and in competition for the Best of Asian Cinema at the Singapore International Festival became the biggest record-breaking film of recent times.

There are now indications that to entertain the people, a film need not be replete with total fantasy and absurdities. The audience now wants even the glossy unrealistic pot-boilers to display some aspects of the reality around them. Although not an outstanding creative film, *Under the Bridge* is an epoch-making event as it proved again the possiblity of commercial success for really good cinematic creations. One of the major reasons for the success of such an unconventional film is the chance a producer has of getting his film released in an island-wide 12 Centre special circuit where priority release is given to artistic films. This is perhaps one of the most successful experiments carried out by a state sector film corporation anywhere in the world. The film distribution system operated by the NFC is a uniquely worthwhile system that Sri Lanka adopted for the promotion of good cinema. It is highly praised by most of the Third World film experts and needs to be emulated in developing countries.

Veena Jayakody in *Surabidena*

Black-and-White in Comeback

The year 1980 marked the production of colour movies on a regular basis. Thereafter, the production of colour films steadily grew in number until it reached a peak in 1989. During that year all twelve films released were in colour. 1990 marked a strong re-entry of black-and-white films into the theatre circuits. Thus of the twenty films released in 1990, eight were in black-and-white. Most of the colour films were developed and printed in Hongkong owing to the absence of a colour lab in Sri Lanka.

Apart from the traditional import of thirty Tamil films a year from India, 1990 was also notable for the return of Hindi films. Even though the films were reissues most of the old Hindi hits released ran for 100 days – which is considered an important achievement for a film released in a single theatre or in one of the five circuits in Sri Lanka – where distribution is scheduled by the NFC. The stalemate created by the dispute between the private importers and NFC with regard to the import of major American movies which prevented the release of any such film for the last two years, continued up to May 1991. However in March 1991, the government announced the complete liberalisation of foreign film imports under its new privatisation policy. It is expected that the MPEAA movies will gain release in the near future.

President Involved

The most significant event of the year under review has been the personal interest the President of Sri Lanka, Ranasinghe Premadasa, has shown in the development of the National Film Industry. Mr Premadasa being a novelist, poet and a connoisseur of the arts, called a meeting of all the representative members of trade bodies for a discussion in August 1990 to ascertain the programme of work needed for the growth of this important medium of art and entertainment.

Prior to this, the President had released 10 million *rupees* to save the collapse of the NFC, as it was about to close owing to the corrupt practices of the previous administration. Today in Sri Lanka, the existence of the NFC is a vital factor not only for the progress of a national cinema, but also for the mere survival of its film industry.

Among the many decisions taken at the meeting convened by the President the following programmes have already been implanted:

(1) To have uniform admission tickets printed by the NFC.

(2) The allocation of one of the best cinemas in Colombo for the release of titles selected under the Priority Release Scheme for quality films.
(3) To grant tax-benefits and loan facilities for the rehabilitation of many theatres affected by the riots and also to construct new ones.
(4) To grant financial assistance for five high-quality, creative films per year.
(5) To update and rehabilitate the Color Film Lab and to equip and modernise the NFC Film Studio. The President has already released 30 million *rupees* from government funds for this purpose. It is expected that the studio will be ready before the end of 1991, which is an essential need in the film industry.

A few months prior to this meeting, the president had appointed D.B. Nihalsinghe, the leading film-maker and former CEO of the Film Corporation, as Advisor to the NFC. Admired for his many innovative programmes and able administration of the Film Corporation during its first five years from its inception in 1972, his appointment was naturally hailed by the industry. He will be expected to reorganise the entire film industry on a sound footing and devise ways and means of not only uplifting the technical and business side of the film industry but also the development of the art and technique of film production, appreciation and other areas of film culture as defined in the objectives of the Film Corporation act.

New and Forthcoming Films

Sthree (Woman). Script. Prasanna Vithanage. Prod and Dir: Malini Fonseka. Players: Malini Fonseka and Lucky Dias.
Kulageya (Sweet Home). Thissa Abeysekera. Dir: H.D. Premaratna. Phot: Suminda Weerasinghe. Players: Sriyani Amerasena, Lucky Dias.
Sisila Giniganee (Fire on Ice). Script and Dir: Prasanna Vithanage. Phot: Suminda Weerasinghe. Players: Sanath Gunatilaka, Sabitha and Veena. Prod: Sanath Gunatilaka.
Surabidena (Sacred Cow). Script and Dir: Chandaratne Mapitigama. Players: Ravindra Randeniya, Anoja and Veena.
Awaragira (West End). Script: Tony Ranasinghe. Dir: Lester James Peries. Phot: Donald Karunaratne. Players: Swarna Mallawarachchi, Tony Ranasinghe. Prod: Dilman Jayaratna.
Meeharaka (Buffalo). Script and Dir: I.N. Hewawasam. Phot: Suminda Weersinghe. Players: Swarna Mallawarchchi, Linton Semage.

AMARNATH JAYATILAKA is a film historian and an award-winning film director. He is now planning his first English-language film entitled The Yellow Robe. He is the founder-Vice President of AmeriLanka Entertainment in Hollywood, where he lives periodically each year.

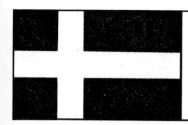

SWEDEN
by Peter Cowie

All the Nordic countries twisted and turned in the grip of recession during 1990–91. In Sweden, the slump in company profits and the alarming rise in inflation prompted an ailing Social Democratic government to apply for membership of the European Community. The giant among Swedish film concerns, AB Svensk Filmindustri, reported a loss of 56 million *kroner*. Attendances slumped by 20% in 1990, to 15,300,329 compared with the previous year's 19,205,236. Gross box-office receipts fell by 14.5% (although at $8.60 a ticket, going to the movies in Sweden is certainly not cheap). Most of those missing customers were probably watching films in the comfort of their own homes, courtesy of the ever-increasing range of satellite and terrestrial TV channels serving the Nordic region.

Surgery was required in the face of this malaise, and in February 1991 the Swedish Film Institute announced a package of redundancies and budget cuts to cope with the relentless decline in revenue from both box-office receipts and the video sector. The department that suffered the most in this operation was Willmar Andersson's distribution arm, which had brought to Swedish audiences literally hundreds of high-quality foreign films that would otherwise not have enjoyed release in the Nordic area.

Production levels remain buoyant, with around a dozen Swedish features in the works at any one time, plus a further four or five co-productions with other Nordic countries.

Quality not quantity remains the nub of the problem, however. Swedish films attract neither audiences at home (the much-praised *Guardian Angel* sold just 34,496 tickets in Sweden) nor rave reviews at festivals. Movie buffs have come to terms with the retirement of Ingmar Bergman; more baffling is the absence of a new generation to supplant the Widerbergs, Troells, Sjömans, and Gredes of this world. Finland has yielded the Kaurismäkis, Denmark has Lars von Trier, but Sweden's younger talents (Carl Gustaf Nykvist, Boman Oscarsson, Agneta Fagerström-Olsson, and Stig Larsson) are not yet firing on all cylinders.

Stina Ekblad in *The Rabbit Man*

Excess of Worthiness

Kjell Grede's **Good Evening, Mr. Wallenberg** (*God afton, herr Wallenberg*) enjoyed selection for the Competition at the Berlin Festival, but never seemed to catch fire. This tribute to Raoul Wallenberg, the Swedish diplomat who rescued thousands of Jews in Budapest before vanishing into the Soviet Union at the end of the Second World War, proceeds at a leaden pace, while the usually reliable lead actor, Stellan Skarsgård, seems miscast as Wallenberg. Indeed, one of the abiding flaws of the Swedish cinema manifests itself in Grede's film. One cannot fault the technique or the ensemble performances, but the production as a whole suffers from an excess of worthiness at the expense of flesh-and-blood drama.

Stig Larsson's **The Rabbit Man** (*Kaninmannen*) would work best as a TV movie, and perhaps lacks the power to grip a spectator on the big screen. But there are many effective scenes in this psychological thriller, which advances carefully towards its exposure of a rapist whose father is a popular TV reporter. Carl Gustaf Nykvist has not yet fulfilled the promise of his excellent debut, *The Women on the Roof*, and **Shining Weapon** (*Blankt vapen*) does not exude the mystery and sexual allure that, on paper, it ought to do. Just as his first feature concerned two women, so Nykvist's new film revolves around the relationship between two men, who indulge their desire for adventure by stealing to order. The star of *The Women of the Roof*, Helena Bergström, gives a convincing performance in Colin Nutley's **Black Jack** (*Black Jack*), with its vigorous images of people coming together in Sweden's weekend dance-halls.

Stefan Jarl, the documentarist, has shifted gears with **Good People** (*Goda människor*), the story of a boy's kinship with his father in the lush countryside of Skåne, Sweden's southernmost province. Admirers

Stellan Skarsgård and Katharina Thalbach in *Good Evening, Mr. Wallenberg*

of Jarl may conclude, however, that like Ken Loach he is happiest when making documentaries with a fictional twinge than when embarking on fiction with a documentary tone.

For many years now, the future has always seemed brighter than the present in Swedish cinema. So the new season holds much promise with Daniel Bergman conjuring up his father's vanished youth in **Sunday Children** (*Söndagsbarn*), from a script by Ingmar himself, Sven Nykvist directing some of the country's most distinguished actors in **The Ox** (*Oxen*), and Jan Troell investigating a controversial double-murder in **Il Capitano, A Swedish Requiem** (*Il Capitano – ett svenskt rekviem*). Most ambitious of all imminent releases is the Danish director Bille August's **Best Intentions** (*Den goda viljan*), a kind of spiritual sequel to *Fanny and Alexander* scripted by Ingmar Bergman and inspired by the early years of his parents' relationship.

Recent and Forthcoming Films

Black Jack (Black Jack). Script: Colin Nutley, Johanna Hald, Catti Edfaldt, Kjell Sundstedt. Dir: Colin Nutley. Phot: Jörgen Persson. Players: Helena Bergström, Jan Mybrand, Jo-

hannes Brost, Ing-Marie Carlsson, Reine Brynolfsson. Prod: Svensk Filmindustri, FilmTeknik.
Bulan (The Bump). Script, Dir and Edit: Karsten Wedel. Phot: Mischa Gavrjusjov. Players: Thomas von Brömssen, Nora Plau, Henrik Holmberg, Lars Brandeby, Per Oscarsson. Prod: Filmstallet for Exat, Swedish Film Institute.
Macken (The Gas Station). Script and Dir: Claes Eriksson. Phot: Dan Myhrman. Players: Anders Eriksson, Jan Rippe, Kerstin Granlund, Hans Alfredson. Prod: Svensk Filmindustri, Kulturtuben, FilmTeknik.
Goda människor (Good people). Script and Dir: Stefan Jarl. Phot: Per Kallberg. Players: Ernst Günther, Viggo Lundberg, Hesse Overgaard, Axel Danielsson. Prod: Stefan Jarl Filmproduktion, Swedish Film Institute, FilmTeknik, Filmfotograferna, LO, LRF.
Hjälten (The Hero). Script and Dir: Agneta Fågerström-Olsson. Phot: John Olsson. Players: Lena Carlsson, Helge Jordal, Marianne Mörk, Ulf Friberg. Prod: Swedish Film Institute,

Max Vitali in *Subterranean Secrets*, directed by Clas Lindberg

Svensk Filmindustri, Swedish Television/TV2.
Honungsvargar (Honey Wolves). Script: Christina Olofson, Annika Thor based on the novel by Sun Axelsson. Dir: Christina Olofson. Phot: Lisa Hagstrand. Players: Maria Grip, Johan Rabeus, Nicolas Chagrin, Agneta Ekmanner. Prod: Belladonnafilm for the Swedish Film Institute, Sandrews, Swedish Television/TV2.
Kurt Olsson. Script: Lasse Brandeby, Håkan Wennberg. Dir: Håkan Wennberg. Phot: Folke Johansson. Players: Lasse Brandeby, Hans Wiktorsson, Anki Rahlskog, Ulla Skoog. Prod: Svensk Filmindustri.
Hemligheten (The Secret). Script: Ralf Karlsson, Ulla-Carin Nyquist. Dir: Ralf Karlsson. Phot: Peter Kruse. Players: Carl-Gustaf Lindstedt, Sif Ruud, Susanna Björklund, Peter Öberg. Prod: Drakfilm for Sandrews.
Den hemliga vännen (The Secret Friend). Script and Dir: Marie-Louise Ekman. Phot: Tomas Boman. Players: Ernst Hugo Järegård, Margareta Krook, Gösta Ekman, Carl Billquist. Prod: Paris förlag, through Sonet Media.
Blankt vapen (Shining Weapon). Script: Carl Gustaf Nykvist, Lasse Summanen. Dir: Carl Gustaf Nykvist. Phot: Ulf Brantås. Players: Boman Oscarsson, Reine Brynolfsson, Maria Grip, Ing-Marie Carlsson, Harriet Andersson. Prod: Swedish Film Institute, Svensk Filmindustri, Swedish Television/Channel 1, Film-Teknik.
Simon Small. Script and Dir: Staffan Götestam, based on a children's novel by Astrid Lindgren. Phot: Rolf Lindström. Players: Oscar Löfkvist, Jonathan Lindoff, Britta Pettersson. Prod: Svensk Filmindustri, Swedish Television/Channel 1, Astrid Lindgrens värld.
Tåg till himlen (Train to Heaven). Script and Dir: Torgny Anderberg. Phot: Tony Forsberg. Players: Carlos Lopez, James Coburn, Teodor de la Torre, Hugo Alvarez. Prod: Filmstallet, Exat (Sweden)/Condor Film, Cinemateca Ecuador (Ecuador), through Jane Balfour Films.
Werther. Script: Håkan Alexandersson, Johann Peckerman, Tomas Norström, from the novel by Goethe. Phot: Christer Strandell. Players: Gert Fylking, Ulrika Hansson, Peter Kneip, Ellen Lamm. Prod: Meyer-ateljéerna, Swedish Film Institute.
Il Capitano – ett svenskt rekviem (Il Capitano, a Swedish Requiem). Script: Per Olov Enquist, Jan Troell, Göran Setterberg. Dir: Jan Troell. Phot: Jan Troell. Players: Maria He-

iskanen, Antti Reini. Prod: Panfilm for Four Seasons Venture Capital, FilmTeknik, Swedish Film Institute, Bold Productions.
Freud flyttar hemifrån (Freud Leaves Home). Script: Marianne Goldman. Dir: Susanne Bier. Phot: Erik Zappon. Players: Gunilla Röör, Ghita Nørby, Palle Granditsky, Philip Zandén. Prod: Omega Film and Television.
Operation Striptease (Operation Striptease) Script and Dir: Jonas Cornell. Phot: Erling Thurmann-Andersen. Players: Philip Zandén Marie Richardson, Frej Lindqvist, Agneta Ekmanner. Prod: Sonet, Swedish Film Institute, TV4, through Sonet Media.
Oxen (The Ox). Script: Sven Nykvist, Lasse Summanen. Dir: Sven Nykvist. Phot: Sven Nykvist. Players: Stellan Skarsgård, Ewa Fröling, Liv Ullmann, Max von Sydow, Erland Josephson, Helge Jordal. Prod: Sweetland (U.S.A.)/ Sandrews, Swedish Film Institute (Sweden)/ Nordisk Film (Denmark).
Underjordens hemlighet (Underground Secret). Script and Dir: Clas Lindberg. Phot: Andra Lasmanis. Players: Kristina Törnquist, Gösta Ekman, Gunnel Fred, Veiron Holmberg. Prod: Sandrews, Swedish Film Institute, Swedish Television/Channel 1, FilmTeknik.

Documentaries from Sweden

Four new documentaries of note have been added to the repertoire of the Swedish Institute's library of films available on 16mm and videocassette. Stefan Jarl's **Good People** (see comments in main article above) will provide foreign audiences with an offbeat look at life in the Swedish rural areas. Jarl's latest work, **Javna, a Reindeer Herdsman in the Year 2000**, runs for just 30 minutes and tells the story of a twelve-year-old Sami boy, who speculates on his future in the wake of the Chernobyl disaster.

PeA Holmquist, Suzanne Khardalian and Jim Downing have combined to make **Come On Gaby!**, about a small boy who arrives in Sweden as a refugee from the fighting in Lebanon. This fierce documentary was named "Best Youth Film of 1990" in Sweden.

A new study of the legendary Swedish warship that sank in Stockholm harbour during the 17th century is available also from the Swedish Institute. Entitled **Vasa – 1628**, it follows the salvaging and restoration of the Vasa from the day she was found, in 1956, to the opening of the new museum surrounding her, in 1990.

Readers should write to the Swedish Institute's Film department at P.O. Box 7434, S–103 91 Stockholm.

Scene from Stefan Jarl's *Good People*

PETER COWIE founded International Film Guide in 1963. He is European Publishing Director of Variety, and author of various books on film, including a history of Nordic Cinema, and biographies of Ingmar Bergman and Francis Coppola.

Producers

Athena Film
Hjortstigen 3
S–181–43 Lidingö
Tel: (8) 765-7–10

Bold Productions AB
P.O. Box 125
S–230–22 Smygehamn
Tel: (410) 243–11

Boomerangfilm
Artillerigatan 83
S–115–30 Stockholm
Tel: (8) 664–64–01

Cinema Art Productions
Danderyds Krog
S–182–36 Danderyd
Tel: (8) 753–10–40
Fax: (8) 753–49–21

Devkino
P.O. Box 43–73
S–100–72 Stockholm
Tel: (8) 19–31–89

Drakfilm Prod. AB
Skånegatan 61
S–116 37 Stockholm
Tel: (8) 44 90 35.

Eden Film
S Brobänken Hus 30
S–111–49 Stockholm
Tel: (8) 20–94–03

Facta & Fiction AB
Tantogatan 49
S–117 42 Stockholm
Tel: (8) 669–0975

FilmLance Int. AB
Gävlegatan 12A
S–113–30 Stockholm
Tel: (8) 728 8689.

Hagafilm AB
St Paulsgatan 34
S–116–48 Stockholm
Tel: (8) 58–44–46

Hinden HB
Humlegårdsgatan 13
S–114–46 Stockholm
Tel: (8) 663–12–10

MovieMakers Sweden AB
Djursholmsvägen 35
S–183–50 Taby
Tel: (8) 756–85–40

Nordisk Tonefilm International AB
Kungsklippan 7

S–112–25 Stockholm
Tel: (8) 54–20–65
Fax: (8) 54–46–67

Omega Film AB
Oxenstiernsgatan 33
S–113–27 Stockholm
Tel: (8) 662–0390
Fax: (8) 663–3313

Pan Film AB
Magasin 3
Frihamnen
S–115–56 Stockholm
Tel: (8) 660 1480

Pennfilm
Bruksvägen 9B
Hököpinge
S–235–00 Vellinge
Tel: (40) 46–67–84

Public Motion Picture AB
P.O. Box 1147
S–171–23 Solna
Tel: (8) 735 4745.

Sandrew Film & Teater AB
P.O. Box 5612
S–114–86 Stockholm
Tel: (8) 23–47–00
Fax: (8) 10–38–50

Sonet Media AB
P.O. Box 20–105
Tel: (8) 764–77–00
Fax: (8) 29–90–91

Spice Filmproduction AB
Banérgatan 55
S–115–26 Stockholm
Tel: (8) 663–5–55

AB SF-Produktion
S–117–88 Stockholm
Tel: (8) 58–75–00
Fax: (8) 669–37–78

Street Movies AB
Reimersholmsgatan 57, nb
S–117 40 Stockholm
Tel: (8) 58 40 61

Swedish Film Institute
P.O. Box 27–126
S–102–52 Stockholm
Tel: (8) 665–11–00
Fax: (8) 661–18–20

Viking Film AB
Humlegårdsgatan 22
S–114–46 Stockholm
Tel: (8) 661–33–10
Fax: (8) 662–55–77

Distributors

Columbia Film AB
P.O. Box 9501
S–102–74 Stockholm
Tel: (8) 58–11–40
Fax: (8) 84–12–04

Walt Disney Sweden AB
P.O. Box 9503
S–102–74 Stockholm
Tel: (8) 58–10–50

Esselte Video AB
P.O. Box 9006
S–102–71 Stockholm
Tel: (8) 772–25–00
Fax: (8) 666–90–98

Folkets Bio
P.O. Box 2068
S–103–12 Stockholm
Tel: (8) 20–30–59

Plånborg Film AB
P.O. Box 4083
S–182–2 Enebyberg
Tel: (8) 758–04–30
Fax: (8) 768–72–76

Polfilm
Norrtullsgatan 29
S–113–27 Stockholm
Tel: (8) 34–22–92
also
Östra Rönneholmsvägen 4
S–211–47 Malmö
Tel: (40) 12–40–44

Sandrew Film & Teater AB
P.O. Box 5612
S–114–86 Stockholm
Tel: (8) 23–47–00
Fax: (8) 10–38–50

Sonet Film AB
P.O. Box 20–105
S–161–20 Bromma

Tel: (8) 764–77–00
Fax: (8) 29–90–91

Succéfilm AB
Klippvägen 3
S–181–31 Lidingö
Tel: (8) 765–26–10
Fax: (8) 767–61–40

AB Svensk Filmindustri
S–117–88 Stockholm
Tel: (8) 58–75–00
Fax: (8) 668–50–70

Swedish Film Institute
P.O. Box 27–126
' S–102–52 Stockholm
Tel: (8) 665–11–00
Fax: (8) 661–18–20

Triangelfilm
P.O. Box 17156
S–200–10 Malmö
Tel: (40) 12–55–47

United Artists AB
P.O. Box 9502
S–102–74 Stockholm
Tel: (8) 58–10–40

**United International
Pictures AB**
P.O. Box 9502
S–102–74 Stockholm
Tel: (8) 58–10–40
Fax: (8) 84–38–70

Warner Bros Sweden AB
P.O. Box 9503
S–102–74 Stockholm
Tel: (8) 58–10–50

SWITZERLAND
by Christoph Egger

1991 was the year in which the Swiss film industry enjoyed its greatest international success to date: Xavier Koller received an Oscar for **Journey of Hope** (*Reise der Hoffnung*) in the best foreign-language film category – the first time a Swiss film has ever won. It is the poignant story of a Kurdish couple whose small son freezes to death in the snow during their illegal attempt to cross the border into Switzerland. The plot reflects an incident which took place at the Splügen Pass in October 1988. It follows a tradition in Swiss film-making which has repeatedly earned international acclaim for its humanitarian aspect. In 1946 *Marie-Louise* brought Leopold Lindtberg an Oscar for his screenplay, as did Fred Zinnemann's *The Search* in 1949. In 1982 *The Boat Is Full* (*Das Boot ist voll*) by Markus Imhoof was also nominated for an Oscar.

Unfortunately this success is not reflected in the general state of Swiss film-making – at least not where feature films are concerned. Markus Imhoof's latest work, **The Mountain** (*Der Berg*), is based on a play by Thomas Hürlimann. The story unfolds inside a mountain cabin where an Alpine guide competes with the resident warden for his wife and job. The film remains an uncertain mixture of psychological naturalism and aesthetic stylisation. Even the younger generation shows signs of talent but nothing of any outstanding quality. **Forever and Eternity** (*Immer und Ewig*) by Samir (the Zürich based author of *Morlove* and *Filou*) is interesting mainly because of its formal experimentation in the use of video. Thomas Imbach's first full-length film, **Restlessness**, successfully demonstrates how form can exceed content. Anka Schmid presented **Behind closed Doors** (*Hinter verschlossenen Türen*) as her graduation piece at the Berlin Academy of Film and Television, which promises well for the future. **Al Gatun** is a work of veiled beauty and puzzling mystery which was directed by Kali in Bergell.

After numerous technical hassles, both Gertrud Pinkus' **Anna Göldin – Last Witch** (*Anna Göldin – Letzte Hexe*) and Véronique Goël's **Perfect Life** finally emerged. Paul Muret has completed her first feature film, **Nothing but Lies** (*Rein que des mensonges*). The following films are all ready for screening: Léa Pool's **The Wild Lady** (*La demoiselle sauvage*), Francis Reusser's **Jacques & Françoise**, Leo Kaneman's **Pierre qui brule**, Alain Bloch's **Niklaus et Sammy** as well as **Days of Doubt** by Bernhard Giger. Nicolas Hayek recently made **Family Express** with Peter Fonda in a co-production with the Italian media mogul, Silvio Berlusconi.

Markus Fischer is busy with **Brandnacht** after making several thrillers for television with varying artistic success. Heinz Bütler has finished shooting **Holozän**. Alain Tanner has just finished his latest work, **The Man Who Lost His Shadow** (*L'homme qui a perdu son ombre*); Claude Goretta is working on **Guillaume T. – La fouine** and Daniel Schmid, who was unable to finance *Der Tee der drei alten Damen*, is now working on **Out of Season** (*Hors Saison*). **Land of the Shadows** (*Land der Schatten*) is the title of Kurt Gloor's project about Carl Jung's early years in Zurich, which will concentrate on his relationship with Freud. Dani Levy has made **Fool's Paradise** in New York and Nino

Jacusso's **The Nice Invitation** (*Die schöne Einladung*) has just been shot in southern Italy. Cameraman Renato Berta and comedian Dimitri are working on a project called **Capo stazione Molinari**.

Influential Documentaries
The helplessness which seems to have affected the subject matter of several feature films is fortunately not evident in the documentaries. The past year has without doubt been a climax for this type of film. Well-known documentary writers have made a comeback with influential works. *Seriat* by Urs Graf and Marlies Graf Dätwyler is the intensive result of a year long fascination with the lifestyle of a Turkish family in Switzerland. *Chronique Paysanne* by Jacqueline Veuve is a poetic evocation of peasant life in the Freiburg Alps. *Männer im Ring* by Erich Langjar records the historic annual assembly in Appenzell where women also received the right to vote in cantonal elections. Both the personal and the general aspects are well expressed in contrast to *Palaver, Palaver* by Alexander J. Seiler. The latter's documentary about the abolition of the Swiss army hardly probes beneath the surface.

For years Richard Dindo has been working on *Arthur Rimbaud, Une biographie*; and it has now developed into a beautifully detailed and unusual film. Matthias Knauer has also been working on a biography – portraying the German computer pioneer in *Konrad Zuse* – as has Friedrich Kappeler with *Adolf Dietrich*, a very empathetic portrait of the eminent naïve painter from eastern Switzerland. *Chartres* by Heinz Bütler will also be a portrayal of the musician Paul Giger, who performs his own composition in the cathedral. It is noteworthy that several productions no longer have a direct connection with

Necmettikn Çobanoglu in Xavier Koller's Academy Award-winning *Journey of Hope*

Switzerland. *Terra prometida* by Peter von Gunten expands on *Terra roubada* (1980), which outlined the development of a reservoir project in Brazil. *Traumzeit* by Franz Reichle looks to continue the considerations explored in *Lynz* (1990) about the relationship between man and nature by focussing on the people of Siberia. Mike Wildholz examines similar questions in his new portrayal of the famous Swiss animal-catcher *Peter Ryhiner* from the 1950's. Using the example of the Antarctic in *The Congress of Penguins (Der Kongress der Pinguine)* Hans-Ulrich Schlumpf combines documentary and fiction to produce a film in the style of a parable, examining the relationship between progress and the destruction of the earth's basic wealth.

Celebrating 700 years

Two co-productions are taking place for the 700th anniversary of the Swiss Confederation. Freddy Buache has invited 14 filmmakers each to make a half-hour study of Switzerland's film heritage for *Le film du cinéma suisse*, and Claude Richardet has persuaded 11 writers to participate in *Visages suisses*, short portrayals of "representative" Swiss citizens. The change in the management of the Swiss Film Centre has gone smoothly: after four years of highly successful work, Alfredo Knuchel was able to hand over to his successor, Yvonne Lenzlinger, at the beginning of the year.

CHRISTOPH EGGER is responsible for cinema in the media section of the Neue Zürcher Zeitung, for which he has been writing since 1978. He is also a member of the Swiss Jury for quality awards.

SWISS FILM BIZ
by Bruno Loher

In view of the European integration process, the Swiss film economy began a rapid re-structuring and consolidation programme during 1990. Despite the fact that until now Switzerland is not an EEC member, there is a desire to take an active part in all initiatives and programmes for film production and distribution organised by the European Community and the Council of Europe. Since the EEC already had arrangements with various media institutions (EuroAim, efdo, Eave, Babel), Switzerland also became a member of the European Script Fund. The pressure to join an integrated media programme is increasing within the film world.

Several films were completed during 1990 with support from Eurimages, a Council of Europe project. Christian Zeender, director of film at the Swiss Federal Office of Culture was elected as president of the "Film Committee" in Strasbourg this year. Zeender sees the Committee's most pressing task as the creation of a standard-ised contract for future co-productions. This should ease the relationship between those member states of the Council of Europe who hope to work together in the future, but have not yet signed bilateral contracts. Such an agreement is all import-ant for Swiss film production, since even today a large number of the big feature films are made in co-production with other coun-tries.

State Projects

Swiss film-making depends largely on state support due to the differences in language and culture, the confined borders, and the general lack of interest in funding. State film promotion has recently taken on a wider role and gone beyond film production alone. Along with assistance for scripts came help for promotion, training and this year, for the first time, for distribution of culturally valuable films. This will be a necessary and useful asset to the support of the equally subsidised film festival and Swiss Film Centre. In view of such expan-sion the money available is still relatively little, although the amount has trebled over the last decade to ten million Swiss Francs.

For the first time since the state has supported film projects with outright grants, not only did the total number of applications decrease (by 3.5% to 352), but also the number of production grants awarded (by 6.3% to 119). After the steady increase during the mid-1980's, when applications doubled in certain years, some circles have been debating the possibility of Swiss pro-duction capacity being exhausted. Many of the grants offered by the state, which totalled SFr 6.5 million and covered 34 projects, had not actually been paid out by the end of 1990. This was because the remaining finances proved to be increasingly difficult, especially for big budget films, and state assistance is only awarded when the finance is secure. The dwindling interest from private inves-tors is hitting the larger projects hardest, where institutional aid is not nearly enough.

In 1990 concrete steps were finally taken to modify film regulations which date back to 1962, to accommodate the changing technical and economic factors. It is not only the Swiss film business that needs up-to-date and clearly defined boundaries to develop. However the long-awaited reversion has not come about effortlessly: first of all the film industry, which had many conflicting opinions, had to reach an overall agreement with regard to the expected re-forms. Then the outline plans had to be brought into line with European develop-ment and international commitments within the framework of GATT and the OECD. The basic tendency has been towards greater freedom, especially for the cultural aspect of film distribution, which is a re-quirement of State intervention.

Until now only Swiss citizens were allowed to distribute films or own cinemas on Swiss territory. Foreign capital was also banned from the film market, and every distributor was only entitled to import and distribute a limited amount of films according to an annual quota. The Swiss agencies dependent on the American leaders (UIP, Warner Bros., 20th Century-Fox) were regarded as something of an exception, despite the guaranteed so-called "Freedom of choice towards other countries," but they are still required to show evidence of their ownership. The recent draft from the Swiss Ministry of the Interior revising film law now proposes to abolish these requirements for distributor and cinema owners to be Swiss citizens as well as the import quota.

The proposed law aims at preventing monopolies and trusts, which limit the scope of the film market. A licence for distributors and exhibitors will only be granted to a distributor who does not exceed a certain share of the market (between 10% and 30% is proposed). In order to guarantee the diversity of cinema programming, no distributor may have total control over any single cinema. In order to achieve this, the licence is only granted to cinema owners who show films from more than one distributor (maximum 66% per distributor).

Exhibitors and Distributors

The use of films by distributors and cinema owners is controlled by the "Film Market Regulation," an agreement dating back to 1935. Members of the two associations, the Swiss Distributors' Association (Schweizer Filmverleiher Verband – SFV) and the Swiss Exhibitors' Association (Schweizer Kino Verband – SKV) are under obligation only to distribute to or be supplied by members of the respective associations. After many years of discussion the existing "Film Market Regulation" was finally revised at the third attempt. An additional clause about the priority supply to provincial

Mathias Gnädninger and Peter Simonischek in Imhoof's *The Mountain*

cinemas (the so-called "Lex Marti") was written in. Once an agreement had been reached, both associations went a step further and in the autumn of 1990 the common holding association Procinema was founded. Members of the SFV and SKV automatically belong to this. At the inaugural meeting at Procinema, in a somewhat questionable move, the founder and long-time president of the Swiss Distributors' Association, Marc Wehrlin, was eased out; despite the fact that he is a personality much admired in the Swiss film business for his competence and foresight.

Continuing the trend of the last few years, attendances declined during 1990 by almost one million, which consequently affected sales. The takings were 1.2% down on the previous year and amounted to SFr 146 million. The number of film titles also decreased by 5.2% and totalled 1,852, while the number of showings remained about the same as the previous year at 347,516. With growth rates in town centres of over 20%, 1991 looks set to be a successful year. 10.9 million (76.07% compared to an increase of 4.95% in 1989) bought tickets to watch U.S. productions, which accounted for the nineteen most successful films of the year. France came second in the rankings with 1.4 million and 10% of the market (a decrease of 3%) followed by Italy. In 1989 the Federal Republic of Germany came fourth but lost 3% this year and dropped to sixth place. Switzerland came in at fourth place with 409,933 (plus 0.5%) visitors, although the increasing number of co-productions often make a cut-off point impossible.

There are a number of question marks over these statistics, since the statistical film year runs from January 1 to December 31 in Switzerland, while for other purposes it works on a twelve month period from July 1 to June 30. This means that films that are released over Christmas (the high season) are included in these statistics, but the figures are hardly worthy of any comment. This applies in particular to Rolf Lyssy's *Leo Sonnyboy*, first released in 1989 with over 100,000 viewers and *Journey of Hope*, released in 1990 with 76,826 viewers. They are the most popular Swiss films, but each was released shortly before Christmas.

Although the Swiss Distributors' Association has more than twenty members, only ten of these are currently active and altogether achieved a turnover in 1990 of a little less than SFr 58 million. For the first time in years Warner Bros had the highest turnover of all film distributors, with their 27% share of the total pushing U.I.P.'s share of 23% into second place. 20th Century-Fox came some way behind with 11% and the first independent Swiss distributors appeared in fourth and fifth places. Ringier's Monopol Pathé was fourth with a turnover of SFr 6.7 million amounting to 10.5% of the total, and Rialto Film was fifth with 8.8% has Jürg M. Judin as its Chief Executive Officer. Amongst the remaining active distributors are Sadfi with 3.5%, Mascotte with 3% and Alpha Films, Columbus and Filmcooperative each with approximately 2%. Apart from Judin's activities, it is noteworthy that amongst the other independent distributors the merger of Orion and Carolco with Columbia put a stop to their output deal with Monopol Pathé. This probably resulted in the independent distributor Monopol Pathé losing more than a quarter of its expected turnover. There were also changes at Indie Columbus, where Rudolf Hoch retains his position as president, but the management of the company is now in the hands of Alfi Sinniger, co-producer of *Journey of Hope*.

A Partnership Between Judin and Reinhart

The unlikely partnership between Jürg M. Judin and Georg Reinhart, which surprised many of those involved in Swiss filmmaking when it was announced in February 1990, was either a result of Judin's business ambitions or Reinhart's cultural aspirations. "It was never any secret that I'm open to new ideas, and Jürg just happened to come along," commented Reinhart on the origins of their co-operation. One result of this "openness" is that Reinhart now has a 49% share in Screen AG, with Judin owning the remaining 51%. A decisive factor in Judin's search for a partner came in the spring of 1990 when the Hellstern Brothers offered an 8.8% share in Rialto-Film AG, Switzerland's second largest independent distribution company.

Statements from Judin maintain that he may well have been able to finance Rialto with the help of the bank, but he was spared the difficulties that would doubtless have been involved in such a venture by the intervention of Reinhart. Today their Screen AG has a 75% share in the Swiss company, Indie (the remaining 25% belong to Martin Hellstern) and they have undertaken this year to improve the structure of their somewhat unwieldy conglomerate network. Screen AG, which was founded in 1986 as a means of financing Judin's first cinema, will in future serve as holding company for the various other activities such as worldwide sales (Metropolis Film Sales AG), distribution (Rialto-Film AG) and several cinema operations (seven theatres in total) which will soon include Switzerland's first multiplex, planned for Zurich.

Georg Reinhart, a member of the wealthy Swiss industrial family which owns the Volkart company in Winterthur, took an active role in the Swiss film scene when he became involved in founding a production company in 1976. Limbo Film AG went on four years later to produce Markus Imhoof's *The Boat Is Full* (*Das Boot ist voll*) which was nominated for an Oscar. Reinhart still owns a third of the company, with the other two thirds being divided between Luciano Gloor and Thérèse Scherer. Limbo proved to be a stepping stone for Reinhart towards forming a whole series of other production companies such as Xanadu Film AG in 1981, Pierre Grise Production in Paris in 1987, Balthazar Piel Inc. in New York in 1988 and Metropolis Filmproduktion in Berlin in 1989 – all these companies form part of the Lunix company. In addition Reinhart is also involved with companies in the music business, grouped together under Almarginal AG, and with various publising concerns such as Amman Verlag AG and Parkett/Der Alltag. Reinhart is currently in the process of restructuring this empire and is coordinating his varied business interests under the holding company SCAT AG, by means of which he will also maintain his involvement in Screen AG.

Judin's won foreign interests may well also have been a deciding factor during his search for a partner, along with the financial opportunities which Reinhart has opened up for him. Following his meteoric progress from being a mere cinema owner to becoming Switzerland's youngest distributor at 27, Judin the whizz kid is once more reflecting upon the European Empire that he longs to establish. He makes reference with some pride to his business deals which are reaching their conclusion with the British company, Electric Pictures, in which Screen AG will soon have a 50% share. This "majority theory" is according to Judin "the only sensible system" and he comments that it is really only a question of funding well-run companies which could one day act as partners in other companies. This confirms what Reinhart is attempting to encapsulate in the term, Synergies. The two are united in the belief that Screen's main aim is "to acquire globally and to utilise locally." This, they believe, is the only way to survive the highly ambitious European audio-visual market in the future.

Recent and Forthcoming Films

Niklaus et Sammy. Script: Efrem Camérin, Michéle Letellier. Dir: Alain Bloch. Phot: Claude Egger. Prod: Yves Peyrot, Slotint (Genève)/MOD-Films (Paris)/Avista (München).

Holožan (Holocene). Script: Heinz Bütler, Manfred Eicher, in collaboration with Max Frisch. Dir: Heinz Bütler. Phot: Giorgos Arvanitis. Prod: Al Castello (Arzo)/EMC Records (München)/RTSI.

Tage des Zweifels (Days of Doubt). Script and Dir: Bernhard Giger. Phot: Martin Fuhrer. Prod: Theres Scherer-Kollbrunner, Limbo Film AG (Zürich).

Guillaume T.-La fouine. Script: Claude Goretta, Muriel Théodori, Efrem Camérin. Dir: Claude Goretta. Phot: Bernhard Zitzerman. Prod: Jena-Marc Henchoz, Les Productions J.M.H. (Lausanne)/Odessa Film (Paris)/Bioskop (München).

Perfect Life. Script and Dir: Véronique Goël. Phot: Jürg Hassler, Stephen Dwoskin. Prod: Scherzo films (Genève).

Family Express. Script: Carlo Mandelli, G. Nicolas Hayek. Dir: G. Nicolas Hayek. Phot: Dominique Brenguier. Prod: Hayek Film AG (Zürich)/Sesame Films SA (Paris)/Silvio Berlusconi Communications (Milano).

Al Gatun. Script and Dir: Kali. Phot: Rainer Klausmann, Beat Presser. Prod: Roma Fasciati (Basel)/RTSI.

Pierre qui brûle (Burning Stone). Script: Léo Kaneman, John Gutwirth, Berhnard Tremège, Claude Muret. Dir: Léo Kaneman. Phot: Denis Jutzeler. Prod: André Martin, Artimage (Genève)/Alizes Films (Paris)/Mafilm Europa (Budapest).

Schmetterlingsschatten (Butterfly's Shadow). Script and Dir: Anne Kasper Spoerri. Phot: Edwin Horak. Prod: Anne Kasper Spoerri (Oetwill). *Dokumentary-Feature.*

Fool's Paradise. Script: Maria Schrader, Dani

TOP TEN GROSSING FILMS IN SWITZERLAND: 1990

	Admissions
Pretty Woman	721,262
Look Who's Talking	561,853
Dead Poets Society	541,842
Ghost	328,587
Born on the Fourth of July	309,008
The Little Mermaid	286,067
The War of the Roses	285,188
Back to the Future, Part III	260,875
Back to the Future, Part II	243,982

Levy. Dir: Dani Levy. Phot: Carl Friedrich Koschnick. Prod: Luna Film GmbH (Berlin)/Fama Film AG (Bern).

Rien que des mensonges. Script: Paule Muret, Jean-Françoise Goyet. Dir: Paule Muret. Phot: Renato Berta. Prod: Ruth Waldburger, Vega Film AG (Zürich)/Arena Films (Paris).

Jacques & Françoise. Script and Dir: Francis Reusser. Phot: Joël David. Prod: Jean-Marc Henchoz, Les Productions J.M.H. (Lausanne)/Les Films du Phare (Paris).

Hors Saison (Between Seasons). Script: Daniel Schmid, Martin Suter. Dir: Daniel Schmid. Phot: Renato Berta. Prod: Marcel Hoehn, T & C Film AG (Zürich)/Metropolis Filmproduktion (Berlin)/Pierre Grise Productions (Paris).

Sprung aus den Wolken (Dive from the Clouds). Script: Stefan Schwietert, Nancy Rivas. Dir: Stefan Schwietert. Phot: Arthur Ahrweiler. Prod: DFFB (Berlin)/Neapel Film (Berlin)/DRS.

L'Homme qui a perdu son ombre. Script and Dir: Alain Tanner. Phot: José Luis Gomez Linares. Prod: Gerardo Herrero, Tornasol Films (Madrid)/Filmograph (Genève)/Gemini Films (Paris).

Producers

Al Castello SA
CH–6864 Arzo
Tel: (91) 46–85–43
Fax: (91) 46–31–65

Artimage
3, Rue Beau-Site
PO Box 117
CH–1211 Genève 18
Tel: (22) 44–85–89
Fax: (22) 45–07–89
Telex: 415 867

Balsli Res & Cie
Hauptstrasse 33
CH–2560 Nidau
Tel: (32) 51–75–10
Fax: (32) 51–13–87

CAB Productions SA
Rue du Port-Franc 17
CH–1003 Lausanne
Tel: (21) 312–80–56
Fax: (21) 312–80–64

Cactus Film AG
PO Box 299
CH–8021 Zürich
Tel: (1) 272–87–11
Fax: (1) 271–26–16

Arthur Cohn
Gellertstr. 18
CH–4052 Basel
Tel: (61) 312–12–42
Fax: (61) 312–07–17

Catpics AG
Theaterstrasse 10
Postfache
CH–8024 Zürich
Tel: (1) 262–42–22
Fax: (1) 262–45–14

Ciné-Manufacture
2, chemin de la Chocolatière
CH–1030 Bussigny-Lausanne
Tel: (21) 701 24 31
Fax: (21) 701 24 15

Condor Productions AG
Restelbergstr. 107
PO Box 782
CH–8044 Zürich
Tel: (1) 361–9612
Fax: (1) 361–95–75

The Film Department of PRO HELVETIA Arts Council of Switzerland

promotes Swiss cinema. We arrange and coordinate seasons, retrospectives and other special film events around the world. We specialize in bilateral exchange with film archives, universities, arthouses, ministries of culture, etc.

Hirschengraben 22, P.O. Box, CH-8024 Zurich
Phone: ++41 (1) 251 96 00, Fax: ++41 (1) 251 96 06, Telex: 817599

Elite-Film AG
Molkenstr. 21
CH–8026 Zürich
Tel: (1) 242–8822
Fax: (1) 241–2123

Fama Film Ag
Balthasarstr. 11
CH–3027 Bern
Tel: (31) 56–44–10
Fax: (31) 56–64–04

Filmkollektiv Zürich AG
Turnerstr. 26
CH–8006 Zürich
Tel: (1) 362–4644

Hubschmid Edi AG
Filmproduktion
Zimmergasse 8
CH–8008 Zürich
Tel: (1) 252–27–27
Fax: (1) 251–92–05

Limbo Film AG
PO Box 258
Josefstrasse 106
CH–8031 Zürich
Tel: (1) 271–8881
Fax: (1) 271–3350

Praesens–Film AG
PO Box 322
CH–8034 Zürich
Tel: (1) 55–38–32
Fax: (1) 55–37–93

Strada Films
11, Rue de Conseil-Général

CH–1205 Geneva
Tel: (22) 29–35–10
Telex: 429157
Fax: (22) 20–41–14

Slotint SA
11, rue de la Fontaine
PO Box 766
CH–1211 Genève 3
Tel: (22) 21 59 58
Fax: (22) 20 59 21

T & C Film AG
Seestr. 41A
CH–8002 Zürich
Tel: (1) 202–3622
Telex: 817–639 tc
Fax: (1) 202–30–05

Vega Film AG
Carmenstr. 25
CH–8032 Zürich
Tel: (1) 252–6000
Fax: (1) 252–66–35

Les Productions J.M.H. SA
Ch–1000 Lausanne 9
Tel: (21) 312–99–33
Fax: (21) 312–99–34

Pic Film SA
Via G. Lepori 16
CH–6900 Lugano-Massagno
Tel: (91) 5638–71
Fax: (91) 56–38–72

Jacques Sandoz Film
Productions SA
20, rue Micheli-du-Crest
CH–1205 Genève

Tel: (22) 20–46–36
Fax: (22) 20–46–49

Thelma Film AG
Josefstrasse 106
PO Box 258
CH–8031 Zürich
Tel: (1) 271–88–81
Fax: (1) 271–33–50

Bernard Lang AG
Kirchgasse 26
CH–8001 Zürich
Tel: (1) 252–6444
Fax: (1) 252–77–29

Dschoint Ventschr AG
CH–8003 Zürich
Tel: (1) 462–86–83
Fax: (1) 462–86–21

Distributors

Alpha Film SA
4, place du Cirque
PO Box 233
CH–1211 Genève 11
Tel: (22) 28–02–12
Fax: (22) 781–06–76

Citel Films Distribution SA
6 rue du Prince
CH–1204 Geneva
Tel: (22) 21–93–22
Telex: 421241
Fax: (22) 21–93–15

Columbus Films
Steinstr. 21

CH–8036 Zürich
Tel: (1) 462–7366
Telex: 813322
Fax: (1) 462–01–12

Elite Film AG
Molkenstrasse 21
CH–8026 Zürich
Tel: (1) 242–8822
Fax: (1) 241–21–23
Telex: 812381

Filmcooperative ZH
PO Box 172
CH–8031 Zürich
Tel: (1) 271–8800
Telex: 817565
Fax: (1) 271–80–38

Monopole Pathé Films SA
PO Box 299
Neugasse 6
CH–8031 Zürich
Tel: (1) 271–1003
Fax: (1) 271–5643
Telex: 823104

Regina Films SA
4 rue de Rive
CH–1204 Geneva
Tel: (22) 28–81–36
Telex: 429465
Fax: (22) 20–04–76

Rialto Film Ag *(including Neue Cactus, Rex, Monopol)*
PO Box 347
Münchhaldenstr. 10
Ch–8034 Zürich
Tel: (1) 55–38–31
Fax: (1) 55–64–21

Sadfi Films SA
8, rue de Hesse
PO Box
CH–1211 Geneva
Tel: (22) 21–77–67
Telex: 428657
Fax: (22) 781–31–19

Septima Film SA
13, rue Louis Favre
PO Box 67

CH–1211 Geneva 7
Tel: (22) 34–97–80

Idéal Film SA
PO Box 162
CH–1003 Lausanne 3
Tel: (21) 312–99–33
Fax: (21) 312–99–34

Impérial Film SA
3, rue Sismond
CH–120 Geneva
Tel: (22) 732–18–30
Fax: (22) 738–78–82

Look now!
PO Box 3172
CH–8031 Zürich
Tel: (1) 272–03–60

Trigon–Film, Filmverleih Dritte Welt
Rösmattstrasse 6
CH–4118 Rodersdorf
Tel: (61) 75–15–15

Twentieth Century-Fox Film Corp
PO Box 33
CH–1211 Geneva 26
Tel: (22) 43–33–15
Fax: (22) 43–92–55
Telex: 428689

United International Pictures (Schweiz) GmbH
Signaustr. 6, PO Box 295
CH–8032 Zürich
Tel: (1) 383–85–50
Fax: (1) 383–61–12
Telex: 816462

Warner Bros. Inc.
Studerweg 3
Postfach
CH–8802 Kilchberg
Tel: (1) 715–50–11
Fax: (1) 715–34–51
Telex: 812480

Useful Addresses

Swiss Film Center
Münstergasse 18

CH–8001 Zürich
Tel: (1) 261–28–60
Fax: (1) 262–11–32
Telex: 817 226
Lausanne Office
33, rue St-Laurent
CH–1003 Lausanne
Tel: (21) 311–03–23
Fax: (21) 311–03–25

Federal Office of Culture
Film Department
Hallwylstrasse 15
PO Box
CH–3000 Bern 6
Tel: (31) 61–92–71
Fax: (31) 61–92–73

Pro Helvetia
Arts Council of Switzerland
Film Department
Hirschengraben 22
CH–8024 Zürich
Tel: (1) 251–96–00
Fax: (1) 251–96–06

Swiss Association for Feature and Documentary Film
(Association of Film Producers)
Effingerst. 4a
Ch–3011 Bern
Tel: (31) 26–08–38
Fax: (31) 26–14–77

Swiss Association of Industrial Film and Audiovision
c/o U. Silberschmidt
Weinbergstrasse 31
CH–8006 Zürich
Fax: (1) 262–29–96
(no phone).

Procinema
Swiss Association of Cinema and Motion Pictures Distribution
Effingerstrasse 11
PO Box 8175
CH–3001 Bern
Tel: (31) 25–50–77/25–27–32
Fax: (31) 26–03–73

SYRIA

by Rafik Atassi

For the second year running, a government film has been hindered by official censorship. The first was **Stars of Midday** by Osama Mohammed, which was produced in 1989 and won numerous prizes at festivals in Valencia, Carthage, and Nantes, and was screened in Tokyo and Montréal. It was selected to open the Damascus Film Festival in November 1989, but has still not been released to the public. The film deals with life and social traditions in the coastal mountains of Syria. It exposes the human relations among local peasants and illiterate women in a way that brings to mind the work of Italian and Latin-American realist directors, but at the same time preserves its own identity and special atmosphere.

The second film that faced the same censorship hassles was made this year and is entitled **The Moss**. Like its predecessor, it is the first feature by its director, Rimon Botross, and like the previous film too, it describes social conditions in the region where the director grew up. Botross recreates memories and fragments of his family life in the central town of Hama and its surroundings. He criticises fiercely certain forgotten rituals such as the death penalty for young girls accused of committing the "sin" of adultery, girls who were executed at the hands of a brother or a very close relative.

The real problem, however, does not lie in banning a film or reforming it, which is not something unique to Syrian cinema. It is essentially the fact that both films were produced by the National Film Organisation, a government body that reports to the Ministry of Culture which, in turn, has the right of censorship over all films shown in Syria, whether domestic or imported!

Two other features were shot in Syria last year, with largely private funds. The well-known comedian Dureid Lahham, who had previously presented two controversial pictures, *The Borders* and *The Report*, made **Kafroun**, based on a script by Rafik Sabban. This film has nothing to do with either politics or social criticism. It examines the wonderful world of childhood and how to treat the young with love and confidence. Lahham chooses the simplest of forms in which to convey his thoughts and ideas, using clever songs, well-written and composed so as to make them easy for kids to memorise and repeat, in addition to subtle camerawork and appealing scenery.

Kafroun (the name of a village) proved a hit at the box-office for eight months in Damascus and all other Syrian cities. It was chosen for the opening of the First Cairo International Film festival for Children, and was screened in several regional and international film events.

Recent Films

Al-Tahaleb (The Moss). Script and Dir: Rimon Botros. Players: Mouna Wasef, Ayman Zeidan, Adnan Barakat, Samir Hakim. Prod: National Film Organisation.
Kafroun. Script: Rafik Sabban. Dir: Dureid Lahham. Players: Dureid Lahham, Madlene Tabar, Samia Jazairi, Husam Tahseen. Prod: Nader Atassi.
City Foxes. Script and Dir: Mohammad Chaheen. Players: Naji Jabr, Sabah Salem, Leila Awad, leila Jabr. Prod: Walid Trabulsi.

TAIWAN

by Derek Elley

With no standard-bearing work from Hou Hsiao-hsien during the 1990–91 season, Taiwan cinema almost dropped off the international map. It is now a very different story to the mid-1980's, when New Taiwan Cinema was touring the international circuit and the island was hitting the headlines with names like Hou, Edward Yang and a host of other thirtysomething colleagues who seemed to be changing the face of its industry.

The break-up of the New Wave was natural and to be expected, and most of the movies had made little impact at the local box-office (or in neighbouring Hongkong). But its ebb has left Taiwan cinema even more noticeably exposed to Hongkong product, which still swamps the local market and accounts for most of the Chinese-language money-spinners. In a similar way that the U.K. industry can hardly compete with U.S. product, Taiwan movies have little market within other East Asian countries (partly because they are in the Mandarin dialect, partly because they are simply not as slick or well-made as Hongkong films) and cannot recoup their costs simply at home. This limits budgets, which in turn limits their chances.

The only film to break out of this catch-22 in 1990 was **A Home Too Far** (*Yi yü* – literally, *A Foreign Land*), a pacey action adventure set in China and Burma during the 1950's and directed by Chu Yen-p'ing, who has been grinding out popular local fare for years. In fact co-produced by Hongkong-based Impact Films, it went on to do well at the Hongkong box-office in late 1990, mostly due to the presence of local star Andy Lau (only in for part of the action) than its true story of a stranded KMT army unit which sets up camp in the wilds of northern Burma until forced by international pressure to disband. Solidly directed, and with a cast comprising Taiwan's K'o Chün-hsiung, T'o Tsung-hua and Yen Feng-chiao, former Mainland Chinese star Siqin Gaowa (now a Swiss resident), and Hongkong's Ku Feng, it in fact differed little from Taiwan's earlier flag-wavers of the 1970's, despite an injection of political cynicism at the end.

But despite the apparent lack of international profile, Taiwan money has been active in several pictures not officially perceived as such. Hou himself spent most of 1990 working as associate producer on Zhang Yimou's **Raise the Red Lantern** (see China section), produced by Ch'iu Fu-sheng through a Hongkong subsidiary of his video/production company Era International (a convenience to save face on both sides of the Taiwan Strait). Ch'iu is also producing Hou's next picture, **In the Hands of a Puppetmaster**, a documentary biopic of the veteran Li T'ien-lu who has played in many of Hou's previous movies.

Taiwan money was also behind Yim Ho's **Red Dust**, funded by Taiwan producer Hsü Feng (former swordswoman in action movies like King Hu's *A Touch of Zen*) through a Hongkong subsidiary of her Tomson Films. (The movie swept the Golden Horse Awards in late 1990.) And, just as it was behind Ann Hui's *Song of the Exile*, Taiwan money was also responsible for Hui's subsequent **My American Grandson** (*Shanghai chia-ch'i*), a wistful melodrama set in the Mainland city between a retired old man (Wu Ma) and his 12-year-old grandson from America (hot Taiwan child actor Huang K'un-hsüan). Scriptwriter was again Taiwan's prolific Wu Nien-chen, and the pair have since gone on to make **Zodiac Killers** for Hongkong's Golden Harvest, with Andy Lau and Cherie Chung in a true story of a Mainland Chinese girl who committed suicide while studying in Japan.

Hongkong still provides a useful international window for Taiwan money, given the latter territory's relatively poor production facilities, lack of international know-how, and political restrictions on using Mainland stars. So important have Mainland locations become to Taiwan film-makers looking for a fresh angle that the producer of *My American Grandson* even bowed to Mainland pressure to delete a couple of small scenes that seemed to show China in a less-than-glowing light (see China section). The implied threat was that he may never be allowed to use Mainland locations again.

Blurred Boundaries

In some respect the political boundaries between Hongkong, Taiwan and China are blurring all the time, leading perhaps to a day when Chinese cinema will no longer be stretched across three territories. But Taiwan's recent liberalisation, despite much publicity, has still left the ruling KMT effectively calling the shots – even when Robert Wise's *The Sand Pebbles* (1966) was finally shown in Taiwan in December 1990, it was cut by 20 minutes and put out on TV, much to the annoyance of Wise himself who was actually attending the Golden Horse Awards in Taipei at the time. Wise went on record as saying that the movie (of which the Yangtze scenes were shot in Taiwan) had already suffered script cuts at the time of production.

Present government restrictions are that, although travel and film-making is allowed in China, Mainland stars or co-finance stars cannot be used. Hence, the use of

Lu Hsiao-fen and Cora Miao in Richard Chen's *Autumn Moon*

Hongkong subsidiaries. This situation even led, in summer 1991, to the curious solution of making two versions of *God of Gamblers II* (a Taiwan one with local songstress Fang Chi-wei as the female lead, and an international one with Gong Li); but as of early July, Gong Li was still grounded in China by a government smarting over the *Judou* affair (see China section).

The Mainland craze has led to directors like Ch'en K'un-hou, Wang T'ung and Sylvia Chang all expressing interest in filming the works of writer Shen Congwen; to veteran Li Hsing attending a Taiwan cinema seminar in Peking in 1990; and to the boldest Taiwan production of 1990, Richard Chen's **Autumn Moon** (*Mingyüeh chi-shih yüan*).

Adapted by Chen himself from an 1985 novel by authoress Hua Yen, **Autumn Moon** is an unblinking, stylised look at the break-up of a woman's seemingly happy marriage and her search for a way to cope with her new life. The trail leads from Taipei to Singapore to Shaanxi province in China, sometimes accompanied by her more free-wheeling younger sister (Lu Hsiao-fen). It is a film made with uncompromising rigour but great beauty, very different to Chen's previous *Spring Swallow* (1989), with an undercurrent of black humour, and a stunning performance by Hongkong's Cora Miao in the lead role.

(The Cantonese-speaking actress coached herself in Mandarin specially for the film, which was shot direct-sound.) Made on a comfortable budget of NT$20.6 million, with post-production work in Japan, it is a work that puts Chen on a par with directors like Hou Hsiao-hsien and Edward Yang – and deserves equal international exposure (its world premiere was at the London festival in November 1990).

Meanwhile, the KMT-funded Central Motion Picture Corporation (CMPC), after floundering around for several years under Lin Teng-fei with no clear policy on production, has appointed a new head in Chiang Feng-ch'i, a former Government Information Office cinema dept officer, and a new deputy in former Film Library head Hsü Li-kung. The result so far has been two new productions that started shooting in April 1991, one by New Waver K'o Yi-cheng and another, from a novel by Hongkong romantic authoress Yik Su, by fellow New Waver Wan Jen of *Ah Fei* and *Super Citizen* fame. CMPC also has a 25% stake in Edward Yang's new production (see below).

Dynamic Chang

After giving birth to a son in August 1990 amid much publicity (saying she intended neither to marry nor to reveal the name of the father), Sylvia Chang, now mostly based in Hongkong, has since thrown her energies into a variety of projects behind the camera, including a script about a Mainland woman and westernised Hongkong man to star Gong Li and George Lam. In the event this did not transpire, but Chang's long-planned project **Mother** (*Mu-ch'in*), about a mother and two daughters, may finally go before the cameras in late 1991: like her earlier *Passion*, it will be scripted and directed by her, and she will also star alongside actresses Yeh Feng and Josephine Siu.

As of summer 1991 Edward Yang, who has not produced a movie since *The Terroriser* (1986), was finally finishing A

Brighter Summer Day (*Ku-ling chieh shao-nien sha-jen shih-chien*) after over a year of on-off shooting occasioned by the principals being free during school holidays. Based on a true event in Taipei during the 1960's, the film, whose title literally means *Incident of a Juvenile Murder on Ku Ling Street*, has already attracted Japanese interest in buying world rights and, despite missing Cannes because it was not ready, is expected to be a major event of late 1991. As his small but powerful body of work attests, Yang is a perfectionist who would rather not make movies at all if he cannot do them his own way (he has edited a comic book collection in the time since *The Terroriser* and has made his latest film through his own company, Yang & Gang). In the current state of the Taiwan industry it is the perfect situation in which to be.

DEREK ELLEY has been associated with IFG for more than 19 years. He is known as a specialist in Hungarian and East Asian cinema, and is author of the The Epic Film: Myth and History (1984) and consultant editor of The Variety Movie Guide and Chronicle of the Movies (both 1991). A regular contributor to weekly Variety, he is currently completing A Handbook of Chinese Cinema.

Recent and Forthcoming Films

Hsi-meng jen-sheng (In the Hands of a Puppetmaster). Script: Wu Nien-chen, Chu T'ien-wen. Dir: Hou Hsiao-hsien. Prod: Era International.

Ku-ling chieh shao-nien sha-jen shih-chien (A Brighter Summer Day). Dir: Edward Yang. Prod: Yang & Gang/CMPC.

Hsiung-ti, t'ou-k'o huai-le. Dir: Richard Chen.

Yen-chih. Dir: Wan Jen, from the novel by Yik Su. Players: Jeanette Lin Tsui, Tseng Chiang, Su Ming-ming, Wu P'ei-yü, Ch'en Chun-sheng. Prod: CMPC.

Wa-wa. Script: Hsiao Yeh. Dir: K'o Yi-cheng. Players T'u Shan-ni, Huang Hsiang-yün. Prod: CMPC.

A-ying. Dir: Ch'iu Kang-chien.

TOP TEN LOCAL* FILMS IN TAIWAN: 1990

God of Gamblers*
A Chinese Ghost Story II*
A Home Too Far
No Risk, No Gain (Casino Raiders – The Sequel)*
Kung Fu vs. Acrobatic*
All for the Winner*
Swordsman*
Kinmen Soldiers
The Legend of Ah Hsiu Lo*
The Fortune Code*

List includes Hongkong productions

The 26th Golden Horse Awards (1990)

The 26th Golden Horse Awards, announced on December 15, 1990 were:
Best Film: *Red Dust*.*
Best Director: Yim Ho (*Red Dust*).*
Best Original Script: Wu Nien-chen (*Song of the Exile*).
Best Adapted Script: Hsiao Yeh (*Curses of the Knife*).
Best Actor: Leung Kar-fai (*Farewell China*).*
Best Actress: Lin Ch'ing-hsia (*Red Dust*).*
Best Supporting Actor: Jacky Cheung (*Swordsman*).*
Best Supporting Actress: Maggie Cheung (*Red Dust*).*
Best Photography: Poon Hang-seng (*Red Dust*).*
Best Art Direction: Edith Cheung, Jessinta Lau (*Red Dust*).*
Best Costume Design: Edith Cheung (*Red Dust*).*
Best Editing: Kam Ma (*Farewell China*).*
Best Sound: Sam Sing-tak (*Farewell China*).*
Best Music: Sih Chieh-yung (*Red Dust*).*
Best Song: James Wong (*Swordsman*).*

* Hongkong production

Useful Addresses

Government Information Office
Dept. of Motion Picture Affairs
15/F, 17 Hua Chang Street
Taipei
Tel: 331–8390, 331–8351
Telex: 11636 inform

Film Library
4/F, 7 Ching Tao East Road
Taipei
Tel: 392–4243, 392–3540
Fax: 392–6359
Telex: 11636 inform

Central Motion Picture Corporation
P.O. Box 475
116 Han Chung Street
Taipei
Tel: 371–5191

Taiwan Film Culture Company
292 Min Sheng Road
Wu Feng
Taichung
Taiwan
Tel: 311–1202 (Taipei office)
Telex: 311–1021 (Taipei office)

Cos Group
7/F, 144 Chung Hua Road, Sec. 1
Taipei
Tel: 383–1360
Fax: 371–9686

Era International
5/F, 46 Pa Te Road, Sec. 1
Taipei
Tel: 397–1122
Fax: 397–2205
Telex: 13057 erapro

THAILAND
by Fred Marshall

Thai cinema as such means little to serious film buffs and, in the international marketplace, few of its writers, directors and artists are known. It may stay like this for a further ten or twenty years as the country does not try to promote or develop its cultural horizons.

There are, of course, formula pictures like *Gold, Boonchu,* and *The Monk* (see below). There are also many good actors and actresses, but Thai is a difficult language and an isolated culture. Among established directors are Prince Chatri Yukhol, Phoemphol Cheyaroon, Cherd Songsri (who won a top prize at Nantes in 1981), Bandit Ritikol, Ethana Mukdansit, and Toranon Srichuq. The principal production companies are Apex, Poonsab, Five Star, and Saha Mongkol. A budget rarely climbs beyond $150,000 for a colour feature, and this sum can be recouped from exhibition within the country. Stars earn a living from TV commercials and other small-screen appearances. Censorship is reasonable, apart from sex scenes, which have to be carefully planned by directors and producers in order not to offend local sensibilities.

Some 500 Western feature films are imported into Thailand each year. All must be dubbed into Thai, usually via the import companies like Apex.

Chinese films are now the main competitor of Thai movies. They are brought into the country in negative form rather than as one-off prints. Taxes are less than those on Western imports, so the Chinese distributors are in a better position to bring in more titles and capture a major slice of the market.

Current New Wave

Thoranong Srichua and Phoemphol Cheyaroon are two of the most exciting Thai directors in the current new wave. Cheyaroon established his reputation with *The Red Bamboo* and *Temple Bells,* and Srichua with *Opium Warlord* and *Kampuchea.* Both recently switched to making erotic films and challenging the censors into a reaction. "Most Thais are hypocrites," says Thoranong. They don't want to accept the truth. Rejecting erotic films means that we are rejecting today's society.

Recent Films

Tawipop. Script and Dir: Cherd Songsri, based on a story by Thomayantee. Costumes: Channeepa Jedsomma. Players: Chadchai Plengpanich, Chancheera Joojang. *Romantic fantasy with ghost story elements.*

Luangta (The Monk, Part III). Script and Dir: Phoemphol Cheyaroon. Prod: Five Star. *Two intertwined stories involving a young girl and a monk whose faith in Buddhism is undermined.*

Song for Chao Phaya. Script, Dir and Edit: Prince Chatri Yukol. Music: Surachai Chantimatorn: Prod: Prommitr International. *Story about three river workers, one of whom quits the routine to seek fame as a film star in Bangkok.*

Tell Them We're Number One. Script: Udom Udomroj, Thongkao Makarmpom. Dir: Udom Udomroj. Phot: Panya Nimcharoenpong. Music: Charmrat Savataporn. Prod: Thai Entertainment Co. *Film about a young kid that has echoes of My Life as a Dog.*

Devil War. Dir: Kitti Daskorn. Players: Bin Banluerit, Kitti Daskorn. *Drama about a U.S. war veteran who has fled to Thailand and creates his own brand of mayhem.*

UNITED KINGDOM
by Mark Le Fanu

The longest-running story of 1990–91 was whether anything would emerge out of the "Downing Street initiative" set up by Mrs Thatcher in June 1990 to find ways of making Great Britain, if possible, a central player in European film-making. Everyone agrees there is a long path to travel: the United Kingdom has one of the least subsidised film sectors – and lowest feature film outputs – on the continent, though by the same token most people agree the country possesses excellent studios, technicians, artists and directors. The question is how to organise these advantages better, and cut through the malaise that has affected British film-making since the collapse of Goldcrest in the mid-1980's.

Two "working parties" were set up, one charged with looking into fiscal incentives that might be introduced to attract investors, the other with examining the organisation of the industry itself — in the broadest sense, the balance between producers, distributors, exhibitors and the television networks, querying how they can work better together mutually, to the profit of the industry as a whole.

The "fiscal" working party, consulting with the Treasury, delivered its report very rapidly, in September 1990. There were three main proposals, of which the most important was the suggestion to establish a film investment fund of £100 million by offering special tax breaks to investors, somewhat along the lines of the French Soficas (Sociétés pour le financement de l'industrie cinématographique et audio-visuelle). This fund in turn would be administered by a quasi-official body such as British Screen, and used to seed British film projects. How this might be done was worked out in some detail.

However, once it was presented, the report failed at the key hurdle to attract government approval. In his first budget, delivered in March 1991, the new Chancellor of the Exchequer Norman Lamont rejected the proposals outright, at the same time claiming to offer an "open door" to any revised or alternative proposals that the working party cared to come up with.

At this point the temptation for many of those involved was withdrawal. Instead they bravely hid their disappointment and re-entered negotiations, feeling perhaps it was worth giving one last effort. Part of the problem they faced was that the government (or rather, the head of government) had changed since their deliberations first got under way. If Mrs Thatcher was a convert to the belief that it was possible to establish Great Britain as a centre for European film-making, there have been few signs that her successor John Major shares this vision.

Intractable Quarrels

So, back to square one with fiscal reform, though something may yet be salvaged from the wreckage. Meanwhile, the other working party has not been faring well either, bogged down by seemingly intractable quarrels between the different sectors of the industry and their different representatives. Essentially, the producers want the successful exhibitors and distributors (in effect, the Hollywood majors) who do well by releasing their films here, to be forced somehow to redirect a portion of their profits into the

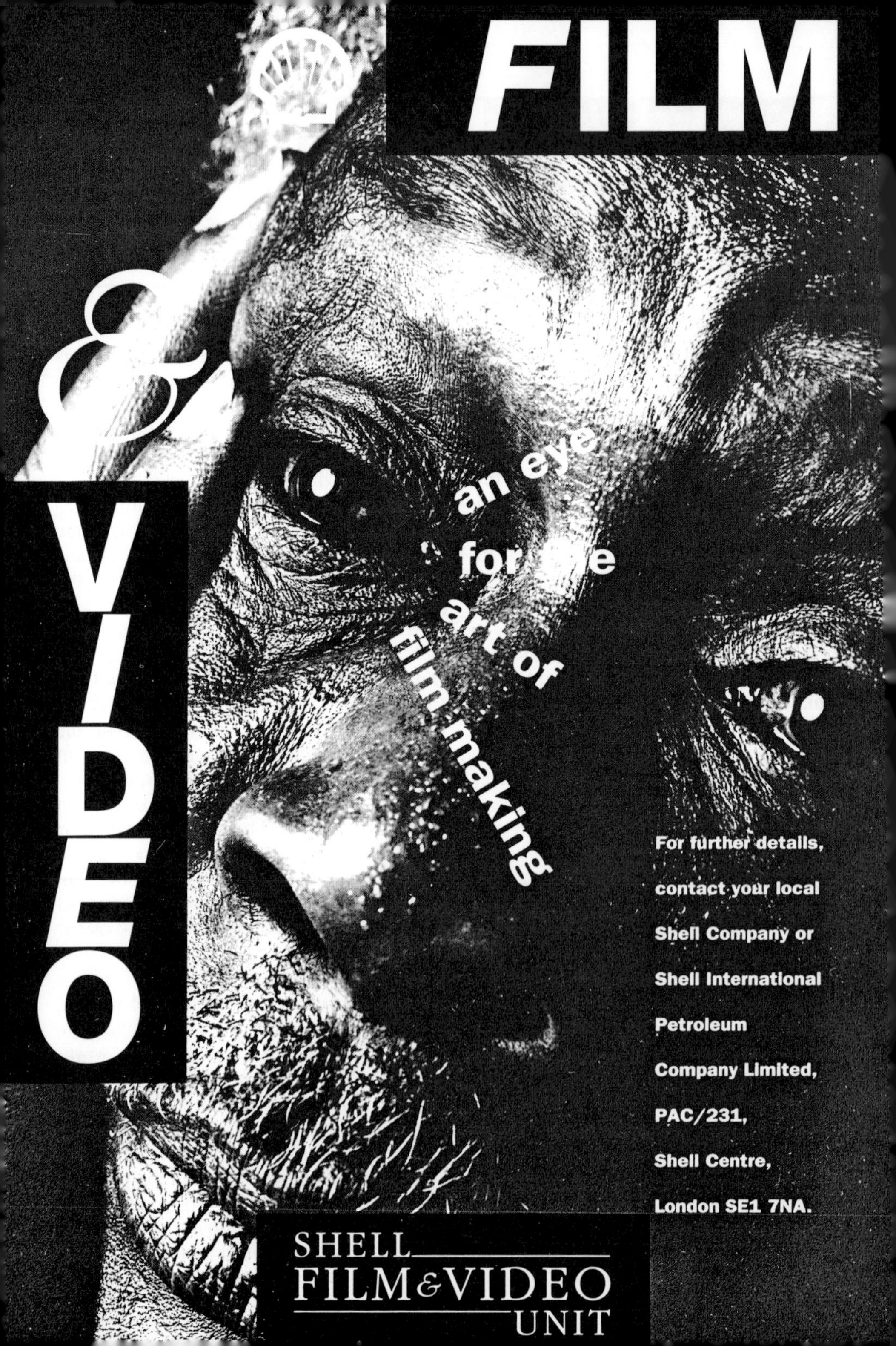

FILM

&

VIDEO

an eye
for the
art of
film making

For further details,
contact your local
Shell Company or
Shell International
Petroleum
Company Limited,
PAC/231,
Shell Centre,
London SE1 7NA.

SHELL
FILM&VIDEO
UNIT

native film industry. Not surprisingly, the exhibitors and distributors are opposed to this. The government, without Mrs Thatcher at the helm, seems reluctant to *force* the exhibitors and distributors by any of the levies, quotas or "cultural disapproval" by which France, for instance, succeeds in curbing the overweening financial might of Hollywood.

At the time of going to press the report of this second, "industry structure," working party is as far as ever from being delivered. Lord Hesketh, a sympathetic films minister (he had invested in movies himself) was promoted to higher office in June 1991, to be succeeded by Lord Reay, an unknown quantity. Few observers seem to be very confident that anything substantial will come out of the year's deliberations. Even the celebrated £5 million fillip which Mrs Thatcher delivered immediately last year to be used on co-productions with Europe, has been diluted by the subsequent insistence of the government that one third of it (£1.3 million) be used over a three year period to part-fund the British subscription to Eurimages, the Council of Europe initiative for European production and distribution. (The U.K. is not yet a member of this organisation, despite having played a prominent part in devising the scheme in the mid-1980's.)

All this means that the British film industry remains – compared to European equivalents – grimly underfunded. It is harder than ever to find a British film of any ambition that is wholly backed by British resources: Michael Palin's **American Friends** (Prominent Pictures), shot in 1990, and funded by the BBC and British Screen, being perhaps a rare exception to this general rule. All the films shot in the first half of 1991 were in one way or another co-productions with foreign partners. This may be no bad thing in itself, but it is worrying in its indication of the timidity of British film finance (although paradoxically some of the best international financiers,

such as John Heyman, Jake Eberts, Frans Timmermans and Julian Melzack, continue to use London as a base).

Television and Film

Television involvement with British film, a vital interface, had mixed fortunes during the year. On the one hand, in the independent sector, the ITV companies were retrenching in the vital lead-up period to the new commercial franchises, granted by competitive tender in October 1991. All of them were eager to demonstrate to the regulatory body, the ITC, that they ran a sharp commercial organisation. The logic of this was: no extravagant investment in cinema. Yet despite this necessary prudence, the film arms of Granada, Central, Anglia and London Weekend Television moved ahead tentatively (boldly in Granada's case) in announcing new slates of films.

Meanwhile, the BBC, after floating various plans to found an independent film arm of its own in conjunction with different parties including the merchant bankers Guinness Mahon, surprised everyone by finally opting for a development deal with American producer Arnon Milchan of Regency International, giving the organisation access to the funds he possesses through his production partnership – worth $600 million – with Warner Brothers, French TV chain Canal Plus and German financiers Skriba and Deyhle. Existing head of drama department Mark Shivas is to head the operation which, if successful, will conduct a lot of talent at present locked into television out into mainstream feature making. (Smaller films emerging from the development fund will be wholly produced by the BBC, larger ones assimilated into Milchan's list, the BBC continuing to maintain strong creative presence on all projects.)

By this bold manoeuvre, which taps directly into both the European and the American audiovisual market, the BBC would seem to have stolen a march on its rival Channel Four, until now film's best ally in TV, but currently in a period of retrenchment following the retirement of its legendary drama head David Rose, to be replaced by David Aukin, a tough and independent man of the theatre, still in the process of stamping his personal authority on the "Film on Four" slot. Will he be able to keep up the tradition that resulted in films like *My Beautiful Laundrette, Wish You Were Here, Prick Up Your Ears*, and *Mona Lisa*? Time alone will tell. Aukin has a budget of £11 million a year to play with.

Exhibition

The exhibition sector continued its healthy improvement of recent years. If 1990 just failed to breach the magic 100 million mark for admissions, the first quarter of 1991 brought in the best figures for 11 years. Audited figures for cinemas taking advertising came to 28,987,252 for the three months January, February, March. Calculating another 2.2 million for cinemas that do not take advertising (such as the successful National Amusements multiplex chain) the extrapolated figure for 1991 is set to exceed the 100 million mark with ease. A number of strong Hollywood films – *Dances with Wolves, Misery, The Silence of the Lambs* among them – tempted potential audiences, including an increasing percentage of women and older people, out of the comfort of their sitting rooms.

The growth of the multiplexes, reported in this section last year, continued to be vital, bringing in a far wider spectrum of audiences than the habitually-targeted 16–25 age group. Whereas in 1989 the multiplexes accounted for 25% of the audience figures, in 1990 that figure was up to 43% (out of a total of 97.6 million cinema visits) and the figure was still rising in 1991, if less steeply. A word of caution however was issued from retiring secretary of the Cinema Advertising Association Bob Wittenbach: "I think multiplexes have succeeded in bringing cinemas to the suburbs and in getting families to go. But there is no doubt that if the multiplexes are getting close to taking half the total cinema audiences, then there will be some casualties among the non-multiplex theatres." That said, the increase in screens is encouraging: 1,509 for 1990 against 1989's 1,236 (up 7.16 per cent), with 70 more added in the first quarter of 1991.

Production

In an era of increasing co-productions, the confusion about what is, and what is not, a "British film" continues to be taxing. How many U.K. films were made in the year 1990–91? According to which statistics one trusts the figure varies between 27 and 52. Taking into account some productions that are in essence only television programmes, the sensible figure would seem to lie between 35 and 40. Yet anomalies remain striking as between films that are culturally British (but financed by outsiders) and, conversely, films – like the two Jeremy Thomas-produced projects **Everybody Wins** and **The Sheltering Sky** – which, although produced from the U.K., have a cosmopolitan or largely American content. Zeffirelli's version of **Hamlet** with Mel Gibson and Glenn Close was backed by American producer Dyson Lovell of Icon Films. Similarly Tom Stoppard's **Rosencrantz and Guildenstern Are Dead** (his first shot as a director) is credited to an American production company Brandenberg International. Yet in either case, and despite American stars in major roles, could any subject be more British? And where do we locate a film like the psychological thriller **The Comfort of Strangers**, an adaptation of the novel by British author Ian McEwan, set in Venice, with a mainly British cast, directed by American Paul Schrader (incidentally, his best film in years)?

Then, too, the emergence of a strong wave of films with Irish subject matter poses similar problems of classification. Three of

Tim Roth and Gary Oldman in *Rosencrantz and Guildenstern Are Dead*

the best new "Irish" film that followed, in 1990–91, in the wake of the Oscar winner **My Left Foot** – Neil Jordan's **The Miracle** (Palace), Jim Sheridan's **The Field** (Granada) and Thaddeus O'Sullivan's **December Bride** (Film Four, CTE, British Screen) – were backed either exclusively or mainly by U.K. companies. An addition to these mild confusions of identity were the two films to emerge from the recently set up Spectator label, *The Assassin of the Tsar* and *Lost in Siberia*, both of them English-language, English-financed films shot in the Soviet Union by Russian directors.

Indeed Soviet and East European based film-making seems for the time being to be something of a trend: Christopher Young

Films is currently shooting an adaptation of Virgina Woolf's famous novel *Orlando* in Soviet central Asia (Sally Potter directing); Mark Forstater Productions is engaged on two Polish co-productions (**The Touch** and **Paper Marriage**); while Ian Sellar, who strikingly debuted last year with *Venus Peter*, departed to Czechoslovakia to shoot a second film, **Prague**, with an international cast including Sandrine Bonnaire and Bruno Ganz.

Better perhaps to take it for granted that definitions of the "British film" will be liberal. Peter Greenaway's long-awaited **Prospero's Books** (French and Dutch financing, Japanese post-production) failed to make it in time for Cannes, being tied up by complicated HDTV techniques. Instead it was selected for the competition in Venice.

Other long-time British stalwarts came up with interesting – if occasionally flawed – movies. After the boring political propaganda of last year's *Hidden Agenda*, for example, Ken Loach reassured his many admirers with a first rate intimate tragicomedy **Riff-Raff**, set in the rough and ready milieu of the building trade. Another strongly personal film – hailed by many (though not by this reviewer, who found it strident and self-indulgent) – was Derek Jarman's **The Garden**, a sort of lyrical-Tarkovskian-elegiac mediation on death and England, filmed near the director's country cottage at Dungeness. Jarman has subsequently filmed an updated version of Christopher Marlowe's celebrated blank verse drama **Edward II**, in conjunction with the BBC.

Yet a third fine British director, Mike Leigh, capped last year's dislocating *High Hopes* with an equally tender and richly observed comedy **Life Is Sweet**. After years of being anchored in television he seems at last freer to move out into the larger medium, backed by an enlightened producer, Simon Channing-Williams of Thin Man Films.

While still on the subject of well-known British faces it is sad to report, after the recent loss of Michael Powell, the deaths of a further two much-loved figures: Sir David Lean was struck down in the midst of preparations to film the great Conrad novel *Nostromo*; while June 1991 saw the death from cancer of the Scot Bill Douglas, whose long-meditated trilogy (*My Childhood*, *My Ain Folk* and *My Way Home*) achieved a deserved fame far in excess of its modest shoe-string origins at the BFI.

Meanwhile, Terence Davies, the director of another famous BFI-backed trilogy, found himself able to make a start on a much delayed project **The Long Day Closes**, the autobiographical successor to *Distant Voices, Still Lives*, shot from April to June 1991 at the Rotherhithe headquarters of Sands Films, a marvellous studio-archive-workshop constructed in an old warehouse by the Thames, and run by married film-makers Christine Edzard and Richard Goodwin, who last year followed up their epic Dickens adaptation *Little Dorritt* with another Victorian costume piece, **The Fool**, based this time on the life of the famous Victorian friend of the poor, Henry Mayhew.

Both Ends of the Social Spectrum

More "social realism," but of a different sort, came in the form of a gritty prison drama, **Silent Scream**, directed by David Hayman, which sympathetically attempted to enter the head of a life-imprisoned murderer of exceptional imagination who eventually destroyed himself by drugs. The complex stylisation of Scottish working class life was a feature, too, of David Leland's new film **The Big Man**, about a modern bare-knuckle boxer – a follow up feature to Leland's delightful and widely liked *Wish You Were Here*, though very different in tone. While formally bold (with a musical score by Ennio Morricone, it parodied certain aspects of the Spaghetti Western), some critics felt the film to be an artistic falling-off from his previous work.

At the opposite end of the social spectrum, the novels of E.M. Forster continue to be a rich source of cinematic ideas. After *Maurice*, *A Passage to India* and *A Room with a View*, the two remaining works of fiction by this long-lived (he died at 90) but not very prolific writer have been brought to the screen. Charles Sturridge, who directed the famous television adaptation of Evelyn Waugh's *Brideshead Revisited* in 1981 opted for the light Italian comedy **Where Angels Fear to Tread**; while the Merchant-Ivory team embarked on the weightier and deeper novel **Howards End**.

A hostile article in the newly revamped film magazine *Sight and Sound* heaved a sigh of relief that there were no more bargains to option from that particular stately home, though the same article failed to make any useful discriminations between what, from this particular group of films, was thoughtful and artistic and what merely fashionable and parasitic. The journalist seemed to think that all rummaging in the past was dubious; but if so, he would have missed the charm of one of the quietest film surprises of the year, Michael Palin's **American Friends**, as visually pleasurable as any of the Forster/Waugh-Henry James adaptations, yet sharing with those masters a finally sardonic view of the possibility of human happiness.

Finally, two films about black experience in modern Britain. Isaac Julien's **Young Soul Rebels** was greeted sympathetically in Cannes where it was shown in the Critics Fortnight section; less noticed, though highly regarded by many, was **Smack and Thistle**, a small budget television feature supported by Channel Four and directed by Tunde Ikoli.

Michael Palin in *American Friends*

American Friends

Script: Michael Palin, Tristram Powell. Direction: Tristram Powell. Photography: Andrew Bonham-Carter. Editing: Dennis McTaggart. Design: Andrew McAlpine. Players: Michael Palin, Trini Alvarado, Connie Booth, Bryan Pringle, Alfred Molina. Produced by British Screen/BBC. 95 mins.

The BBC/British Screen-backed film *American Friends* speaks well for the corporation's new policy of interest in commercial cinema. Directed by Tristram Powell, a past distinguished exponent of BBC small-screen drama, and ravishingly photographed by Philip Bonham-Carter with excellent use of deep-focus compositions in the outdoor Alpine scenes, the film sits confidently on the big screen with no sense of strain or inflation. The moving spirit behind it is the film's main star, Michael Palin, who wrote the script based on a true incident in the life of one of his ancestors, an Oxford don who in the 1860's renounced compulsory celibacy in order to marry a pretty Irish–American cousin on whom he subsequently fathered seven children. Unlike a number of films based on "real-life" incidents, this one is unaffected by bogus naturalism and communicates a subtle moral delicacy. The genre is romantic comedy with a happy ending, but in the desolation and disappointment of the girl's handsome mother (beautifully played by Connie Booth) the film retains a sense of the real restraints of society operating in a world that favours men's aspirations at the expense of women's. Trini Alvarado, an American newcomer playing the young transatlantic visitor, gives a very touching performance, convincing the viewer of the psychological appropriateness of what, on the surface, is/was surely an unlikely love alliance. A modest, intelligent film that fits happily into the tradition of Merchant Ivory adaptations of Henry James and E.M. Forster (*The Europeans, A Room with a View, Maurice*), *American Friends* scores over these filmic predecessors by being an original work of the imagination rather than a mere literary adaptation. The film possesses a fresh simple integrity that will surely win admirers.

Mark Le Fanu

Rosencrantz and Guildenstern Are Dead

Script and Direction: Tom Stoppard. Photography: Peter Biziou. Editing: Nicolas Gaster. Design: Vaughan Edwards. Players: Gary Oldman, Tim Roth, Richard Dreyfuss, Iain Glen, Joanna Roth, Donald Sumpter, Ian Richardson. Produced by Brandenburg International. 118 mins.

Tom Stoppard's adaptation of the play that brought him to fame in the mid-1960's won the Golden Lion Award for best film at Venice. This might be surprising in view of the fact that its author is a first time film director. One sees however that the skills acquired in writing screenplays for such diverse modern cineastes as Losey (*A Romantic Englishwoman*), Preminger (*The Human Factor*), Fassbinder (*Despair*), Spielberg (*Empire of the Sun*) and Schepisi (*The Russia House*) have rubbed off on Stoppard well. *Rosencrantz and Guildenstern Are Dead* is a real film rather than an exercise in photographed theatre. Its distinction lies in the subtle layers of reality it builds up through recourse to, firstly, the play-within-a-play (the travelling players giving their version of *The Murder of Gonzago*), but beyond that, to what can only be described as play-within-play-within-play (and even play-within-play-within-play-within-play) as, watching from behind the actors, we watch the actors themselves rehearse the action to be performed using puppets and mime-show for assistance. One is taken back to those vertiginous leaps of ontology that are a feature of the films of Orson Welles or Jean Renoir, where fantasy and reality – the world of the theatre and the "real" world of time, death and suffering – exist side by side, interlocked. Maybe this makes it sound too fancy, but Stoppard is a fancy artist in the best sense. The test of the film's quality is its ability to weave an underlying seriousness out of its brilliant surface of wordplay. A seriousness about death (as the film's title implies): what it is, what it

Tim Roth in *Rosencrantz and Guildenstern Are Dead*

must feel like, and how – though it may be juggled with – it shan't be gainsaid. The last time there was metaphysical wit and imagination of this order was Bergman's *Seventh Seal*. Gary Oldman and Tim Roth are finely cast as the hapless emissaries; Richard Dreyfuss is marvellously energetic as the chief player; and Iain Glen, in the scenes he shares with the protagonists, makes a surprisingly plausible and effective Hamlet.

Mark Le Fanu

Life Is Sweet

Script and Direction: Mike Leigh. Photography: Dick Pope. Editing: Jon Gregory. Design: Alison Chitty. Players: Alison Steadman, Jim Broadbent, Claire Skinner, Jane Horrocks, Stephen Rea, Timothy Spall. Produced by Thin Man/British Screen/Film Four International. 103 mins.

Mike Leigh Films have always been difficult to judge in terms of optimism and pessimism. On one level you could say his lower middle class characters are the most benighted of lost souls, cast adrift in life with no real education, no culture and no system of inherited beliefs to sustain them. On the other hand, though most of the things they do are embarrassingly inept, they are always human and ultimately touching. So it is here, in Mike Leigh's latest film for the cinema (for many years he worked happily in television). The line-up includes vulgar and brassy mother (marvellous Alison Steadman) with a hugely irritating false laugh; her husband, a bearded Walter Mitty-style chef whose one dream is to get out of organised employment and set up a caravan selling snacks on his own; two awkward red-headed daughters, one of them – delicate, bourgeois, sensitive – a plumber by occupation, the other a truculent drop-out in rebellion against convention, but secretly a victim of anorexia who gorges herself in nightime feasts of chocolate bars which she then sicks up in the wastepaper basket. Add to the menagerie a friend of the family played by Timothy Spall, a small-time businessman in the process of opening a ludicrously pretentious restaurant (the "Regret Rien") and one has the ingredients for vintage social comedy. As with *High Hopes*, Leigh's previous film, some critics found sections of the work over-the-top and caricatured: for example, Timothy Spall's disgusting first night menu, lovingly detailed ("brains in chocolate sauce on a bed of parsley"). Yet maybe it is better to see such episodes as licenced energetic exaggeration in the tradition of the old masters of farce like Ben Jonson (and more recently, like Bill Forsyth). At any rate they are made up for by places elsewhere in the film where restraint and understatement are in evidence. For example, Leigh knows just how much to show of the life of the plumber daughter: an oblique scene or two of her at work and then relaxing in the pub, a few remarks to her sister over the Sunday lunch, a glimpse of her in bed reading a travel brochure about America give us everything we need to have to make the girl touching and complicated. People accuse Leigh of condescending to his characters, but it's far from the truth. He's on the side of vulnerability and awkwardness.

Mark Le Fanu

Emer McCourt and Robert Carlyle in *Riff Raff*
photo: Paul Chedlow

Riff Raff

Script: Bill Jesse. Direction: Ken Loach. Photography: Barry Ackroyd. Editing: Jonathan Morris. Design: Martin Johnson. Players: Robert Carlyle, Emer McCourt, Jimmy Coleman, George Moss, Ricky Tomlinson, David Finch.

Riff Raff is one of Ken Loach's best films for years, a highly original and disconcerting work of art. It was well-received by foreign critics at Cannes, though the British viewer somewhat marvels that the work's most striking characteristic – its rich polyphony of accents, dialects and customs – could genuinely be communicated in its fullness to non-native speakers. In a film with just the right amount of plot and no more, the real focus of interest accrues round the vigorous liveliness of the conversations and quarrels of the film's main characters, a group of labourers working on a London building site – men drawn by unemployment from every part of the country, from Glasgow, Liverpool, Sheffield and Ireland, and rubbing shoulders, here, with the native South London blacks, with whom however, there is no real sense of solidarity. The film paints these characters "warts and all," delineating weaknesses as well as working-class integrities. Though Loach and his writer, the late Bill Jesse (who worked for many years on building sites himself) have sympathies that are plainly "left-wing", or anti-Thatcherite, the drama to its credit avoids slick temptations to load the ideological dice. *Riff-Raff* is not in the least a work of facile propaganda. The characters whom Loach chooses to examine in close up – particularly a slim Glaswegian and his Irish singer girl friend – are treated with great psychological subtlety and sympathy. You feel that the director has observed everything first hand from life, that he has abandoned easy presuppositions and prejudices. Comedy and something grimmer are finely modulated in subtle shiftings of tone. The film in the end, like all Loach's work, is pessimistic. But the characters are full of life and intelligence.

Mark Le Fanu

MARK LE FANU is a senior reporter on the Financial Times fortnightly newsletter Screen Finance. *He is the author of a book on Tarkovsky and of a forthcoming study of Mizoguchi.*

Producers

Allied Vision
360 Oxford Street
London W1N 9HA
Tel: (71) 409 1984
Fax: (71) 493 4286

British Film Institute Production
29 Rathbone Street
London W1P 1AJ
Tel: (71) 636 5587
Fax: (71) 580 9456

British Lion
Pinewood Studios
Iver Heath
Bucks. SL0 ONH
Tel: (753) 651 700
Fax: (753) 656 844

Enigma Productions
13–15 Queens Gate Place
Mews
London SW7 5BG
Tel: (71) 581 0238
Fax: (71) 584 1799

Euston Films
365 Euston Road
London NW1 3AR
Tel: (71) 387 0911
Fax: (71) 388 2122

Flamingo Pictures
47 Lonsdale Square
London N1 1EW
Tel: (71) 607 9958
Fax: (71) 609 7669

Mark Forstater Productions
8A Trebeck Street
London W1Y 7RL
Tel: (71) 408 0733
Fax: (71) 499 8772

Goldcrest Films and Television
36/44 Brewer Street
London W1R 3HP
Tel: (71) 437 8696
Fax: (71) 437 4448

Greenpoint Films
5A Noel Street
London W1V 3RB
Tel: (71) 437 6492
Fax: (71) 437 0644

HandMade Films
26 Cadogan Square
London SW1X 0JP
Tel: (71) 584 8345
Fax: (71) 584 7338

Initial Films and Television
10–16 Rathbone Street
London W1P 1AH
Tel: (71) 637 8251
Fax: (71) 637 9024

Little Bird
91 Regent Street
London W1R 7TA
Tel: (71) 434 1131

Euan Lloyd Productions
Pinewood Studios

Iver Heath
Bucks. SL0 0NH
Tel: (753) 651 700
Fax: (753) 656 844

Merchant Ivory Productions
46 Lexington Street
London W1P 3LH
Tel: (71) 437 1200

NFH
37 Ovington Square
London SW3 1LJ
Tel: (71) 584 7561
Fax: (71) 589 1863

Palace Productions
16–17 Wardour Mews
London W1V 3FF
Tel: (71) 734 7060

Portobello Productions Ltd.
52 Tavistock Road
London W11 1AW
Tel: (71) 379 5566
Fax: (71) 379 5599

Prominent Features
68A Delancey Street
London NW1 7RY
Tel: (71) 284 0242
Fax: (71) 284 1004

Recorded Picture Company
8–12 Broadwick Street
London W1V 1FH
Tel: (71) 439 0607

Red Rooster Films
11–13 Macklin Street
London WC2B 5NH
Tel: (71) 405 8147
Fax: (71) 831 0679

Sands Films
119 Rotherhithe Street
London SE16 4NF
Tel: (71) 231 2209
Fax: (71) 231 2119

Michael White
13 Duke Street
London SW1 6DB
Tel: (71) 839 3971
Fax: (71) 839 3836

Working Title
10 Livonoa Street
London W1V 3PH
Tel: (71) 439 2424
Fax: (71) 911 6150

Zenith Productions
43–45 Dorset Street
London W1H 4AB
Tel: (71) 224 2440
Fax: (71) 224 3194

Distributors

Majors

**United International
Pictures (U.I.P.)**
Mortimer House
37–41 Mortimer Street
London W1A 2JL
Tel: (71) 636 1655
Fax: (71) 636 4118

Warner Brothers
135 Wardour Street
London W1V 4AP
Tel: (71) 734 8400
Fax: (71) 437 2950

**Columbia/TriStar Film
Distributors**
19–23 Wells Street

London W1P 3FP
Tel: (71) 436 5720
Fax: (71) 528 8980

Twentieth Century Fox
20th Century House
31–32 Soho Square
London W1V 6AP
Tel: (71) 437 7766
Fax: (71) 437 1625

Rank Film Distributors
127 Wardour Street
London W1V 4AD
Tel: (71) 437 9020
Fax: (71) 434 3689

Independents

Artificial Eye Film Co.
211 Camden High Street
London NW1 7BT
Tel: (71) 267 6036
Fax: (71) 267 6499

Blue Dolphin Films
15 Old Compton Street
London W1V 6JR
Tel: (71) 439 9511
Fax: (71) 287 0370

British Film Institute
21 Stephen Street
London W1P 1PL
Tel: (71) 255 1444
Fax: (71) 436 7950

Contemporary Films
24 Southwood Lawn Road
London N6 5SF
Tel: (81) 340 5715
Fax: (81) 348 1238

Curzon Film Distributors
38 Curzon Street
London W1Y 8EX
Tel: (71) 465 0565
Fax: (71) 499 2018

Electric Pictures
22 Carol Street
London NW1 0HU

Tel: (71) 284 0524
Fax: (71) 284 0476

**Entertainment Film
Distributors**
27 Soho Square
London W1V 5SL
Tel: (71) 439 1606
Fax: (71) 734 2483

First Independent Films
69 New Oxford Street
London WC1A 1DG
Tel: (71) 528 7767
Fax: (71) 528 7770/1/2

Guild Film Distribution
Kent House
14–17 Market Place
Great Titchfield Street
London W1N 8AR
Tel: (71) 323 5151

Hobo Film Enterprises
9 St. Martins Court
London WC2N 4AJ
Tel: (71) 895 0328
Fax: (71) 895 0329

ICA Projects
12 Carlton House Terrace
London SW1Y 5AH
Tel: (71) 930 0493
Fax: (71) 873 0051

Mainline Pictures
37 Museum Street
London WC1A 1LP
Tel: (71) 242 5523
Fax: (71) 430 0170

Medusa Pictures
Regal Chambers
51 Bancroft
Hitchin
Herts. SG5 1LL
Tel: (462) 421 818
Fax: (462) 420 393

Oasis
155 Oxford Street
London W1R 1TB
(continued on page 393)

TOP TEN GROSSING FILMS IN U.K.: 1990

	Rentals (£)
Ghost	19,161,000
Pretty Woman	12,068,000
Look Who's Talking	10,381,000
Honey, I Shrunk the Kids	9,395,000
Total Recall	8,580,000
Ghostbusters 2	8,491,000
Back to the Future, Part III	8,007,000
Back to the Future, Part II	7,675,000
Gremlins 2	7,419,000
When Harry met Sally	7,000,000

Still from a graduation film, *Visiting Hours*, at the London International Film School

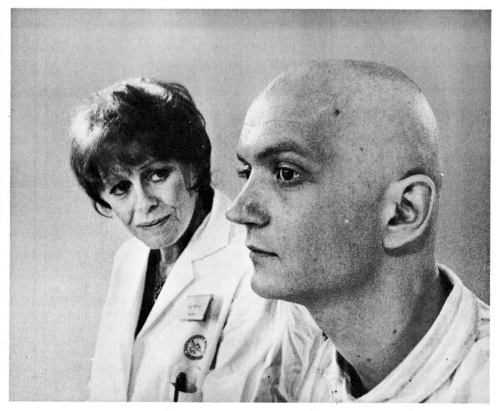

U.S.A.

by William Wolf

The most striking phenomenon on the American film scene has been the dramatic upsurge in black-oriented film-making, a breakthrough for ethnic movies unlike anything since the "blacksploitation" action films of the 1970's. Spike Lee, whose own film *Jungle Fever* was a hot topic at the Cannes Film Festival, noted that a total of 19 black films was due by the end of 1991.

Lee himself was credited by those following in his footsteps for opening the door. True, unlike the mature theme of interracial love in Lee's ambitious **Jungle Fever**, traditional action involving drug gang warfare was the mainstay of the violent **New Jack City**, which grossed nearly $44 million in its first eleven weeks of release and was directed by Mario Van Peebles, whose father Melvin Van Peebles paved the way for black films in the 1970's.

Other films about ghetto life seriously tackled themes of survival. **Boyz N The Hood**, a stunning writer-director debut by 23–year-old John Singleton, dramatised the struggle of coming of age in violence-ridden South Central Los Angeles. Pent-up anguish and rage was realistically depicted in another powerful first feature, **Straight Out of Brooklyn**, written and directed by 19-year-old Matty Rich. A lighter mood, nonetheless serious in overtone, characterised funny, tough, and streetwise **Hangin' with the Homeboys**, depicting the life of blacks and Hispanics in New York's South Bronx. Brimming with new talent, the film was a remarkable writer-director turn for Joseph B. Vasquez. Bill Duke's **A Rage in Harlem** mixed action and comedy. Significantly, many of the

black films were released by major companies.

The year also saw independent film-makers continue stubbornly to persist in their determination to beat the odds. Certainly there are role models in the saga of Joel and Ethan Coen, whose rise from independent newcomers with *Blood Simple* culminated at the 1991 Cannes Film festival with winning the Palme d'Or for **Barton Fink**, a satire of 1941 Hollywood. The film also earned Cannes awards for best direction, and star John Turturro won for best actor.

Among current independents Hal Hartley showed immense talent with **Trust**, a quirky film about values; Henry Jaglom's entertaining **Eating**, constructed around a group of women talking about the relationship of food to their lives, hit upon a volatile, involving subject; Texas filmmaker Richard Linklater's **Slacker** was a

Cuba Gooding Jr., Larry Fishburne, and Ice Cube in *Boyz N the Hood*

hymn to a new generation of neo-beatniks; Todd Haynes's **Poison**, inspired by Jean Genet's writings, aroused the ire of the censor-minded upset by a portion dealing with prison homosexuality, and Jennie Livingston garnered acclaim for her unusual documentary **Paris Is Burning**, focusing on the bizarre world of drag balls in Harlem.

Costner's Triumph

In the mainstream the major attention-grabber was the surprising coup scored by Kevin Costner's **Dances with Wolves**. Defying the wisdom that Westerns were passé, Costner, directing for the first time and, also starring in his own film, dared make a Western that was three-hours long and at times even used the Sioux language Lakota with subtitles. He was scoffed at but *Wolves*, released by Orion, grossed more than $170 million by June, 1991. It won seven Oscars, including for best picture and

Kevin Costner in *Dances with Wolves*

best direction, although there were rumblings of dissent from those who thought that Martin Scorsese's searing mob saga **GoodFellas** was artistically superior.

A major surprise was the emergence as a huge hit of **Home Alone**, a formula-type

Andy Garcia and Talia Shire in *The Godfather Part III*

photo: Emilio Lari

comedy about a boy whose parents forgot to take him on vacation. Although **Ghost**, about a slain husband who comes back to solve his murder, led at the box office at the close of 1990, by February, 1991, **Home Alone** had amassed $215 million, surpassing *Ghost's* $213 million, and continued to zoom in the charts to $274 million by mid-June, 1991.

Another big hit was **The Silence of the Lambs**, Jonathan Demme's Hitchcock-like thriller with Jodie Foster riveting as an F.B.I. agent who enlists a brilliant psychopathic murderer (Anthony Hopkins in a chilling performance) to help catch a serial killer of women. **The Grifters**, about low-life con artists and directed by Stephen Frears, was particularly effective, with Anjelica Huston in top acting form and Annette Bening proving that she is a major talent on the rise.

Other noteworthy films among the eclectic output included Woody Allen's **Alice**, a funny and touching tale of a bored wife, delightfully played by Mia Farrow; Robert Altman's **Vincent and Theo**, about the relationship between artist Vincent Van Gogh and his brother; Alan Rudolph's **Mortal Thoughts**, with Demi Moore and Glenne Headly excelling as women involved in the murder of a brute, convincingly played by Bruce Willis; and Francis Ford

Coppola's **The Godfather Part III**, passable considering there was no compelling artistic reason for a sequel.

Irwin Winkler's **Guilty by Suspicion**, enhanced by a fine Robert De Niro performance, dealt with the Hollywood blacklist; De Niro was also strong, along with Robin Williams, in Penny Marshall's **Awakenings**, dramatising the revitalisation of catatonic patients by a dedicated doctor. Oliver Stone's **The Doors** starred Val Kilmer in a *tour de force* as the late rock star Jim Morrison; and Jeremy Irons won the best actor Oscar for playing controversial Klaus von Bulow in Barbet Schroeder's **Reversal of Fortune**.

Kathy Bates took the best actress Oscar for her portrayal of the menacing nurse in Rob Reiner's **Misery**. Other good performances included Mel Gibson showing he could play *Hamlet* convincingly in Franco Zeffirelli's production, Joanne Woodward co-starring with husband Paul Newman in **Mr. & Mrs. Bridge**, Cher as the free-spirited mother in Richard Benjamin's **Mermaids**; Vanessa Redgrave memorable in a bloody fistfight with Keith Carradine in the otherwise disappointing **The Ballad of the Sad Café**, directed by Simon Callow.

Feminist Hit

Susan Sarandon and Geena Davis teamed charismatically in Ridley Scott's rip-roaring **Thelma & Louise**, an enormously entertaining and popular buddy picture adventure with a feminist agenda, a kind of *Bonnie and Clyde/Butch Cassidy and the Sundance Kid* of the 1990's. Mel Brooks served up his brand of outrageous comedy in **Life Stinks**, with Brooks casting himself as a mean rich man who tries to survive on skid row to win a bet. Albert Brooks, with charming assistance from Meryl Streep, amusingly examined life after death in **Defending Your Life**. Billy Crystal had some of the funniest gag lines of the year in **City Slickers**, directed by Ron Underwood. Bill Murray tickled funnybones as a compulsive patient

Wesley Snipes and Annabella Sciorra in Spike Lee's *Jungle Fever*

harrassing Richard Dreyfuss as his psychiatrist in **What About Bob?**. And Sylvester Stallone did better than expected trying his hand at comedy in **Oscar**.

Madonna again demonstrated her show business and promotion savvy in the documentary **Truth or Dare**. Warner Bros. released **Rover Dangerfield**, built around a cartoon character fashioned after comedian Rodney Dangerfield, and with the other majors all having animated projects on tap, a comeback for the genre was indicated.

Susan Sarandon and Geena Davis in *Thelma and Louise*

The studios indulged in their usual quest for blockbusters in their 1991 summer release schedules, the most promising of which (box-office-wise) loomed as *Robin Hood: Prince of Thieves*, starring Kevin Costner, and *Terminator 2: Judgment Day*, with Arnold Schwarzenegger. There were also *The Naked Gun 2½: The Smell of Fear*, and **V.I.** *Warshawski*, featuring Kathleen Turner as a private eye. *Backdraft*, a look at the dangerous job of firefighting, was long on action but short in the script department. The expensive *Hudson Hawk*, heavy on action and starring Bruce Willis, was roundly trounced by critics.

To mark the 50th anniversary of its release, the seminal *Citizen Kane* was given a fresh go-around. The 1960 epic *Spartacus* was restored and re-released, including material previously deleted as too raunchy for its time. John Cassavetes' impressive *Opening Night*, made in 1978, but never achieving wide commercial distribution, finally was released, thanks to Castle Hill.

The motion picture industry abandoned its long-criticised X rating in favour of an NC–17 (no children under 17). Diehards scorned it as the X in disguise, but for the most part it was accepted as a rating that distinguished serious films from the stigma of pornography that the X has carried in the public mind. The first film bearing the NC–17 tag was Philip Kaufman's candid **Henry & June**, exploring the relationship between author Henry Miller and the women in his life.

Highlights of other industry news were the purchase of MCA Inc., including Universal Pictures, by Matsushita of Japan; the shakeup at Paramount Communications, where Stanley R. Jaffe was appointed corporate president and Brandon Tartikoff was named chairman of Paramount Pictures; Disney chairman Jeffrey Katzenberg's widely faxed internal memo criticizing runaway budgets; the continuing build-up of Creative Artists Agency honcho Michael Ovitz's reputation as the most powerful man in Hollywood; and the seven-month boycott of New York as a location by the major studios until an agreement was finally reached providing union concessions.

Barton Fink

Script: Ethan Coen, Joel Coen. Direction: Joel Coen. Photography: Roger Deakins. Editing: Roderick Jaymes. Music: Carter Burwell. Production Design: Dennis Gassner. Players: John Turturro, John Goodman, Judy Davis, Michael Lerner, John Mahoney. Produced by Ethan Coen, Graham Place, Ben Barenholtz for Circle Films. A 20th Century Fox release. 116 mins.

Barton Fink is the most intriguing and bizarre of the four feature films made by the Coen Brothers, outdoing and even synthesising the wildly disparate elements of the

John Turturro and John Goodman in *Barton Fink*

first three. If the Coens' tendency to the excessive and outlandish is still in evidence here it is more in the service of its quirky narrative. A provocatively unsettling film, *Barton Fink* seems paradoxically to be both pitilessly cold and deeply felt.

The 1930's storyline follows the odyssey of an Odetsian type playwright, Barton Fink, who reluctantly journeys to Hollywood to earn money that will provide the leisure time for more serious work. The plot moves similarly to such plays as *Once in a Lifetime* and *City of Angels*, with the protagonist encountering glib, fast-talking studio bosses with past formulas for success. Midway, however, the story takes a peculiarly macabre turn. Even before then the Gothic direction of the narrative is suggested by the dilapidated hotel Fink chooses to reside in, making the Overlook Hotel of *The Shining* seem more like a benign seaside resort. Never seen from the outside, Dennis Gassner's production design is a crumbling setting of perpetually peeling wallpaper. As

Fink struggles with the improbable assignment of a Wallace Beery wrestling film, rarely has a writer's isolation been so intensely captured on film as Roger Deakins' camera moves from all sorts of bizarre angles and lingers on disquieting details. As Fink, John Turturro, sporting an eccentric pompadour, displays the temperaments of both a repressed introvert and an idealistic mad scientist.

In both the studio and hotel scenes the characters are caught in a jangle of miscommunication and missed opportunities to communicate, while surface appearances often prove unreliable. In the end, it is not clear if the scenario Fink writes, inspired by his mad experiences, is really as great as he believes it is, or if it is, whether anyone will ever know it. A number of high-toned films have speculated about the relationship between art and reality but the Coens here express considerable doubts that either can be properly appreciated.

Fred Lombardi

Alice

Script and Direction: Woody Allen. Photography: Carlo Di Palma. Editing: Susan Morse. Production Design: Santo Loquasto. Players: Mia Farrow, Joe Mantegna, Keye Luke, William Hurt, Cybill Shepherd, Alec Baldwin. Produced by Robert Greenhut for Jack Rollins and Charles H. Joffe. An Orion release. 100 mins.

Mia Farrow in Woody Allen's *Alice*

Woody Allen continues his growth as a film-maker, and Mia Farrow, his leading lady on screen and in life, further expands her range to take advantage of the opportunities her mentor lavishes upon her. In *Alice* Allen deftly mixes romance and comedy with fantasy, and spices his brew with barbed social comment about wasted lives versus commitment. Farrow, playing an unfulfilled upper middle-class Manhattan wife and mother, dominated by a boorish, chauvinist husband (William Hurt), is more radiant than ever. She is also touching as she yearns for something more meaningful, as well as delightfully amusing in scenes that enabled her to display a heightened flair for deadpan comedy. The combination, abetted by a colourful cast of characters entertainingly played, is terrific fun.

A highlight is the performance of Keye Luke, veteran Number One Son of the old *Charlie Chan* movies, who died shortly after *Alice* was released. Luke niftily steals scenes in portraying a wizard at mixing drug potions that sporadically loosen Alice's libido, resulting in mood swings that utterly bewilder Joe Mantegna as the musician with whom she becomes involved. Alice's idol is Mother Theresa, and her ultimate decision to find happiness working with the poor may not be totally convincing, but it does succeed in making a statement.

As usual, Allen more than does visual justice to New York. Carlo Di Palma's photography is splendid, particularly in the Chinatown sequences. Allen keeps sharpening his ability to delve more deeply into character and subject matter while still regaling audiences with his unique humour, all served with technical perfection and mature judgment. His films, however, still must fight their way in a marketplace increasingly dominated by the blockbuster mentality. That's all the more reason for treasuring and enjoying them.

William Wolf

Eating

Script and Direction: Henry Jaglom. Photography: Hanania Baer. Editing: Michelle Hart, Mary Pritchard. Players: Nelly Alard, Lisa Richards, Frances Bergen, Marlena Giovi, Marina Gregory, Gwen Welles, Mary Crosby, Elizabeth Kemp, Rachelle Carson. Produced by Judith Wolinsky. From Rainbow Releasing. 110 mins.

Devouring a hearty meal is recommended for anybody with guilt feelings about food before seeing *Eating*, Henry Jaglom's entertaining and provocative meditation on woman's battle to stay thin in accordance with society's notion of attractiveness. The unique movie should have universal appeal, although in non-English speaking countries subtitling needs will be extensive. As with

The feisty cast of *Eating*

most Jaglom films, conversation is the essence.

The director assembled an appealing, fascinating group of 38 actresses, explored their experiences in dieting, bingeing, and coming to terms with food in relation to their lives, and after working out his script based on what he learned, structured his film around women gathered for a three-tier birthday party. One is turning 30, another 40, and a third 50. The catalyst is Martine (Nelly Alard), a visiting Frenchwoman making a documentary about behaviour in Southern California.

Anguish, jealousies, assorted anxieties, and deep-seated fears about relationships burst to the surface as the women bare their souls. Some of it is hilarious, some of it painfully revealing, and although there's a bit of repetition that might be trimmed, the overall effect is enjoyable and thought-provoking. Jaglom obviously sympathises with his subjects, and the actresses are riveting, even when only doing relatively small turns. Gwen Welles is outstanding as the jealous, neurotic spoiler. Alard is a striking beauty. Frances Bergen (Candice Bergen's mother) gives a tender performance as a representative of her more compliant generation. But the entire contingent merits applause. Jaglom, one of America's most iconoclastic directors, is in top form here.

William Wolf

Trust

Script and Direction: Hal Hartley. Photography: Mike Spiller. Editing: Nick Gomez, Kate Sanford. Music: Phil Reed. Production Design; Daniel Ouellette. Players: Adrienne Shelly, Martin Donovan, Merritt Nelson, John MacKay. Produced by Bruce Weiss. A Fine Line Features release. 90 mins.

Hal Hartley could turn out to be one of the most creative among new American directors. Following his earlier acclaimed *The Unbelievable Truth*, he again reveals his individuality with *Trust*, an odd love story between characters rebelling against family and society. For openers Adrienne Shelly as Maria, a high school girl who becomes pregnant, has angry words with her father, who drops dead moments after she leaves the house. And that's before the credits. Maria meets her soul mate in Martin Donovan as Matthew, who can't hold jobs that require him to cast aside principles and who is beaten down by his domineering father.

They develop a trust in each other and take on the world, at least as it exists in suburban Long Island, peopled by a colourful supporting cast. Family life is stripped naked, and nothing in the business world makes moral sense. Shelly is poignant in her role, and Donovan, who is interestingly handsome, has tremendous screen

Maria Coughlin and Matthew Slaughter in *Trust*

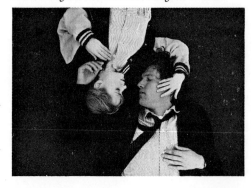

presence with all the makings of a striking leading man.

Hartley's gifts lie in writing sharp, irreverent dialogue, placing his characters in situations with potential for satirising society, and filming his story with angles, visual choices, and colour contrasts that underscore his sceptical view of the world around him. He succeeds in dramatising a quest for better values in a manner that is entertaining, funny, touching, and different. *Trust* revives some of the free-wheeling spirit that typified the French New Wave, but is thoroughly American in contemporary tone and content.

William Wolf

Straight Out of Brooklyn

Script and Direction: Matty Rich. Photography: John Rosnell. Editing: Jack Haigis. Music: Harold Wheeler. Players: George T. Odom, Ann D. Sanders, Lawrence Gilliard Jr., Mark Maline, Reana E. Drummond, Barbara Sanon. Produced by Rich in association with American Playhouse. Associate producer: Allen Black. Executive Producers: Lindsay Law, Ira Deutchman. A Samuel Goldwyn release. 91 mins.

At 19, Matty Rich makes a remarkable debut with *Straight Out of Brooklyn*, a gritty and passionate cry of despair for the plight of blacks attempting to break free of Brooklyn ghetto life and realise some of America's promise. The outcome of the plot is predictable and Rich may accomplish more polished films in the future, but the honesty of the outrage expressed resonates with raw power that makes his first feature stand tall and communicates much about today's crime problem in the United States.

Lawrence Gilliard Jr. as Dennis Brown is headstrong and restless as a youth who sees a robbery of a local drug dealer as the only way to break loose from his dead-end environment. His girlfriend, convincingly portrayed by Reana E. Drummond, has

more sense and wants no part of him if he resorts to crime. But Dennis grows increasingly desperate and impatient as he recoils at what society has done to his father, a man trying to earn an honest living but wracked by booze and frustration, and to his battered mother.

Straight Out of Brooklyn contains unforgettable scenes of domestic violence. George T. Odom is a powerful father, who takes his frustrations out on his wife, whom he beats with mounting frequency in confrontations that are wrenching. Anne D. Sanders plays the woman with such skill that one understands her lingering love for her husband despite her outer scars and inner pain. Rich, who plays a supporting role, thrives on realism, yet endows the film with a sense of underlying poetry. Experiencing it is a bit like it was seeing John Cassavetes's *Shadows* for the first time.

William Wolf

WILLIAM WOLF is a noted American film critic and journalist whose work has appeared in Cue, New York Magazine, Gannett publications, and elsewhere. He teaches at New York University and is the author of Landmark Films: The Cinema and Our Century.

Recent and Forthcoming Films

(Some 1991 films are not represented because they appeared on last year's chart.)

The Addams Family. Script: Larry Wilson, Caroline Thompson, Paul Rudnick. Dir: Barry Sonnenfeld. Phot: Owen Roizman, Gale Tattersall. Players: Anjelica Huston, Raul Julia, Christopher Lloyd, Christina Ricci. Prod: Orion/Paramount.
Across the Tracks. Script and Dir: Sandy Tung. Phot: Michael Delahoussaye. Players: Rick Schroder, Brad Pitt, David Anthony Marshall, Carrie Snodgress. Prod: Academy Entertainment.
Afraid of the Dark. Script and Dir: Mark

Peploe. Phot: Bruno de Keyzer. Players: Fanny Ardant, James Fox, Paul McGann, Clare Holman. Prod: New Line/Fine Line Films.

An American Tail: Fievel Goes West. Script: Flint Dille from a story by Charles Swenson. Dir: Phil Nibbelink, Simon Wells. Voices: John Cleese, Dom DeLuise, Philip Glasser, Cathy Cavadini, Amy Irving, James Stewart. Prod: Universal.

Another You. Script: Ziggy Steinberg. Dir: Maurice Philips. Phot: Vic Kemper. Players: Gene Wilder, Richard Pryor, Mercedes Ruehl. Prod: Tri-Star.

Article 99. Script: Ron Cutler. Dir: Howard Deutch. Phot: Richard Bowen. Players: Ray Liotta, Kiefer Sutherland, Forest Whitaker, Kathy Baker, John Mahoney. Prod: Orion.

Back in the USSR. Script: Lindsay Smith. Dir: Deran Sarafian. Players: Frank Whaley, Natalia Negoda, Roman Polanski. Prod: Fox.

Backdraft. Script: Gregory Widen. Dir: Ron Howard. Phot: Mikael Salomon. Players: Kurt Russell, William Baldwin, Robert De Niro, Donald Sutherland. Prod: Universal.

The Ballad of the Sad Café. Script: Michael Hirst from Carson McCullers' novel and Edward Albee's play. Dir: Simon Callow. Phot: Walter Lassally. Players: Vanessa Redgrave, Keith Carradine, Cork Hubbert, Rod Steiger. Prod: Angelika Films.

Basic Instinct. Script: Joe Eszterhas. Dir: Paul Verhoeven. Phot: Jan de Bont. Players: Michael Douglas, Sharon Stone, George Dzundza. Prod: Tri-Star.

Beauty and the Beast. (*Animated*) Script: Linda Woolverton. Dir: Kirk Wise, Gary Trousdale. Voices: Angela Lansbury, Jerry Orbach. Prod: Buena Vista.

Beethoven. Script: Edmond Dantes, Amy Holden Jones. Dir: Brian Levant. Players: Charles Grodin, Bonnie Hunt, Dean Jones. Prod: Universal.

Bill and Ted's Bogus Journey. Script: Chris Matheson, Ed Solomon. Dir: Pete Hewitt. Phot: Oliver Wood. Players: Keanu Reeves, Alex Winter, George Carlin. Prod: Orion.

Billy Bathgate. Script: Tom Stoppard from E.L. Doctorow's novel. Dir: Robert Benton. Phot: Nestor Almendros. Players: Dustin Hoffman, Bruce Willis, Nicole Kidman, Loren Dean, Steven Hill. Prod: Touchstone/Buena Vista.

Bingo! Script: Jim Strain. Dir: Matthew

Robbins. Phot: Mark Freborn. Players: Cindy Williams, David Rasche, Robert Steinmiller Jr. Prod: Tri-Star.

Blame It on the Bellboy. Script and Dir: Mark Herman. Phot: Andrew Dunn. Players: Dudley Moore, Bryan Brown, Richard Griffiths. Prod: Buena Vista.

Blood and Concrete. Script: Richard La Brie, Jeffrey Reiner. Dir: Reiner. Phot: Declan Quinn. Players: Billy Zane, Jennifer Beals, James Le Gros. Prod: IRS Media.

Blood in the Face. (*Documentary*) Dir: Anne Bohlen, Kevin Rafferty, James Ridgeway. Phot: Rafferty, Sandi Sissel. Prod: First Run Features/ Right Thinking production.

Blue Sky. Script: Rama Lurie Stagner, Arlene Sarner, Jerry Leichtling. Dir: Tony Richardson. Phot: Steve Yaconelli. Players: Jessica Lange, Tommy Lee Jones, Powers Booth. Prod: Orion.

Body Parts. Script: Eric Red, Norman Snider, Larry Gross. Dir: Red. Players: Jeff Fahey, Brad Dourif, Lindsay Duncan. Prod: Paramount.

Born to Ride. Script: Michael Pardridge, Janice Hickey. Dir: Graham Baker. Players: John Stamos, John Stockwell. Prod: Warner Bros.

Boyz N the Hood. Script and Dir: John Singleton. Phot: Charles Mills. Players: Larry Fishburne, Ice Cube, Cuba Gooding Jr., Nia Long, Morris Chestnut. Prod: Columbia/New Deal.

Bright Angel. Script: Richard Ford. Dir: Michael Fields. Phot: Elliot Davis. Players: Dermot Mulroney, Lili Taylor, Sam Shepard, Valerie Perrine. Prod: Hemdale.

Bugsy Siegel. Script: James Toback. Dir: Barry Levinson. Phot: Allen Daviau. Players: Warren Beatty, Annette Bening, Harvey Keitel, Joe Mantegna, Ben Kingsley, Elliot Gould. Prod: Tri-Star.

The Butcher's Wife. Script: Ezra Litwak, Marjorie Schwartz. Dir: Terry Hughes. Phot: Frank Tidy. Players: Demi Moore, Jeff Daniels, George Dzundza, Frances McDormand, Margaret Colin, Mary Steenburgen. Prod: Paramount.

Cape Fear. Script: Wesley Strick based on 1962 movie and John D. MacDonald's novel "The Executioners". Dir: Martin Scorsese. Phot: Freddie Francis. Players: Robert De Niro, Nick Nolte, Jessica Lange, Joe Don Baker, Juliette Lewis. Prod: Universal.

Child's Play 3. Script: Don Mancini. Dir: Jack Bender. Phot: John Leonetti. Players: Justin

TOP TEN GROSSING FILMS IN U.S.A. AND CANADA: 1990

	Rentals ($U.S.)
Ghost	94,000,000
Pretty Woman	81,900,000
Home Alone	80,000,000
Die Hard 2	66,500,000
Total Recall	65,000,000
Teenage Mutant Ninja Turtles	62,000,000
Dick Tracy	59,500,000
The Hunt for Red October	58,500,000
Driving Miss Daisy	49,500,000
Back to the Future, Part III	48,950,000

Whalin, Perrey Reeves. Prod: Universal.

China Moon. Script: Roy Carlson. Dir: John Bailey. Phot: Willy Kurant. Players: Ed Harris, Madeleine Stowe, Benicio Del Toro. Prod: Orion.

City of Hope. Script and Dir: John Sayles. Phot: Robert Richardson. Players: Vincent Spano, Joe Morton, Tony LoBianco, Anthony John Denison, Barbara Williams, Sayles. Prod: Samuel Goldwyn Co.

City of Joy. Script: Mark Medoff. Dir: Roland Joffé. Phot: Peter Biziou. Players: Patrick Swayze. Prod: Tri-Star.

City Slickers. Script: Lowell Ganz, Babaloo Mandel. Dir: Ron Underwood. Phot: Dean Semler. Players: Billy Crystal, Daniel Stern, Bruno Kirby, Patricia Wettig, Jack Palance. Prod: Columbia.

Clifford. Script: Bobby Von Hays, Jay Dee Rock. Dir: Paul Flaherty. Phot: John A. Alonzo. Players: Martin Short, Charles Grodin, Mary Steenburgen, Dabney Coleman. Prod: Orion.

Closet Land. Script and Dir: Radha Bharadwaj. Phot: Bill Pope. Players: Madeleine Stowe, Alan Rickman. Prod: Universal.

The Comfort of Strangers. Script: Harold Pinter from Ian McEwan's novel. Dir: Paul Schrader. Phot: Dante Spinotti. Players: Christopher Walken, Rupert Everett, Natasha Richardson, Helen Mirren. Prod: Sovereign Pictures/Reteitalia/Skouras(U.S.)

The Commitments. Script: Richard Clement, Ian LaFrenais from Roddy Doyle novel. Dir: Alan Parker. Phot: Gale Tattersall. Players: Robert Arkins, Angeline Ball, Johnny Murphy, Andrew Strong. Prod: Fox (U.S. & U.K. only)/ Sovereign Pictures.

Company Business. Script and Dir: Nicholas Meyer. Phot: Gerry Fisher. Players: Gene Hackman, Mikhail Baryshnikov. Prod: MGM/ Pathe.

Cool as Ice. Script: David Stenn. Dir: David Kellogg. Players: Vanilla Ice, Kristin Minter, Michael Gross, Candy Clark. Prod: Universal.

Criminals. Script: Charles Shyer, Nancy Meyers based on the 1960 film *Crimen*. Dir: Eugene Levy. Phot: Giuseppe Rotunno. Players: John Candy, Jim Belushi, Cybill Shepherd, Sean Young, Ornella Muti, Richard Lewis, Giancarlo Giannini. Prod: De Laurentiis Communications/MGM/Pathé.

Crisscross. Script: Scott Sommer. Dir and

Billy Crystal (centre), with Bruno Kirkby and Daniel Stern in *City Slickers*

Meryl Streep and Albert Brooks in *Defending Your Life*

Phot: Chris Menges. Players: Goldie Hawn, Arliss Howard, David Arnott, James Gammon, Keith Carradine. Prod: MGM/Pathé.

Curly Sue. Script and Dir: John Hughes. Phot: Jeff Kimball. Players: James Belushi, Kelly Lynch. Prod: Warner Bros.

The Dark Wind. Script: Neil Jimenez, Eric Bergren, Mark Horowitz. Dir: Errol Morris. Phot: Stefen Czapsky. Players: Lou Diamond Philips, Fred Ward, Gary Farmer. Prod: Seven Arts (U.S. only)/Int'l Distrib: Carolco.

Dead Again. Script: Scott Frank. Dir: Kenneth Branagh. Phot: Matthew F. Leonetti. Players: Branagh, Emma Thompson, Derek Jacobi, Andy Garcia, Hanna Schygulla. Prod: Paramount.

Defending Your Life. Script and Dir: Albert Brooks. Phot: Allen Daviay. Players: Albert Brooks, Meryl Streep, Rip Torn, Lee Grant. Prod: Warner Bros./Geffen Film Co.

Dice Rules. Script: Andrew Dice Clay, Lenny Shulman. Dir: Jay Dubin. Phot: Michael Negrin. Players: Clay, Eddie Griffin, Sylvia Harman. Prod: Seven Arts.

Diplomatic Immunity. Script: Randall Frakes, Jim Trombetta, Richard Donn. Dir: Peter Maris. Phot: Gerald B. Wolfe. Players: Bruce Boxleitner, Billy Drago. Prod: Fries Entertainment.

Doc Hollywood. Script: Jeffrey Price, Daniel Pine, Peter Seamon. Dir: Michael Caton-Jones. Phot: Michael Chapman. Players: Michael J. Fox, Bridget Fonda. Prod: Warner Bros.

The Doctor. Script: Robert Caswell. Dir: Randa Haines. Phot: John Seale. Players: William Hurt, Christine Lahti, Elizabeth Perkins, Adam Arkin, Mandy Patinkin. Prod: Touchstone/Buena Vista.

Dogfight. Script: Bob Comfort. Dir: Nancy Savoca. Phot: Bobby Bukowski. Players: River Phoenix, Lili Taylor, Holly Near. Prod: Warner Bros.

Don't Tell Mom the Babysitter's Dead. Script: Neil Landau, Tara Ison. Dir: Stephen Herek. Phot: Tim Suhrstedt. Players: Christina Applegate, Joanna Cassidy, John Getz. Prod: Warner Bros.

The Doors. Script: J. Randall Johnson, Oliver Stone. Dir: Stone. Phot: Robert Richardson. Players: Val Kilmer, Meg Ryan, Kevin Dillon, Kyle MacLachlan, Kathleen Quinlan. Prod: Tri-Star.

Dutch. John Hughes. Dir: Peter Faiman. Phot: Chuck Minsky. Players: Ed O'Neill, JoBeth Williams. Prod: Fox.

Dying Young. Script: Richard Friedenberg. Dir: Joel Schumacher. Phot: Juan Ruiz Anchia. Players: Julia Roberts, Campbell Scott, Vincent D'Onfrio, Coleen Dewhurst, Ellen Burstyn. Prod: Fox.

Eyes of an Angel. Script: Robert Stitzel. Dir: Robert Harmon. Phot: Theo Van Sande. Players: John Travolta. Prod: Triumph Releasing.

Father of the Bride. Script: Nancy Meyers, Charles Shyer based on Frances Goodrich, Albert Hackett's 1950 script from Edward Streeter's novel. Dir: Shyer. Players: Steve Martin, Diane Keaton, Martin Short. Prod: Buena Vista.

Ferngully: The Last Rainforest. (*Animated*) Script: Jim Cox from stories by Diana Young. Dir: Bill Kroyer. Prod: Fox.

Fires Within. Script: Cynthia Cidre. Dir: Gillian Armstrong. Phot: David Gribble. Players: Greta Scacchi, Jimmy Smits, Vincent Philip D'Onofrio. Prod: Pathé/MGM.

The Fisher King. Script: Richard La Gravenese. Dir: Terry Gilliam. Phot: Roger Pratt. Players: Robin Williams, Jeff Bridges, Amanda Plummer, Mercedes Ruehl. Prod: Tri-Star.

For the Boys. Script: Marshall Brickman, Neal Jimenez, Lindy Laub. Dir: Mark Rydell. Phot: Stephen Goldblatt. Players: Bette Midler, James Caan, George Segal, Norman Fell, Melissa Manchester. Prod: Fox.

Forever Activists (*Documentary*). Script: Yasha Aginsky, Phil Cousineau, Judith Montell. Dir: Montell. Phot: T. Robin Hirsh. Prod: Tara Releasing.

Frankie and Johnny. Script: Terrence McNally from his play "Frankie and Johnny in the Clair de Lune." Dir: Garry Marshall. Phot: Dante Spinotti. Players: Al Pacino, Michelle Pfeiffer, Hector Elizondo, Kate Nelligan. Prod: Paramount.

Freejack. Script: Geoff Murphy, Steve Pressfield, Dan Gilroy. Dir: Murphy. Phot: Amir Mokri. Players: Emilio Estevez, Anthony Hopkins, Mick Jagger, Rene Russo. Prod: Warner Bros. (U.S. Distrib)/Morgan Creek (Int'l).

Fried Green Tomatoes at the Whistle Stop Cafe. Script: Fannie Flagg, Jon Avnet. Dir: Jon Avnet. Players: Kathy Bates, Jessica Tandy, Mary Stuart Masterson, Louise Parker, Cicely Tyson. Prod: Universal.

FX 2: The Art of Deadly Illusion. Script: Bill Condon. Dir: Richard Franklin. Phot: Victor J. Kemper. Players: Bryan Brown, Brian Dennehy, Rachel Ticotin, Joanna Gleason, Philip Bosco. Prod: Orion.

The Gladiator. Script: Nicholas Kazan, Lyle Kessler. Dir: Rowdy Herrington. Phot: Tak Fujimoto. Players: James Marshall, Cara Buono, Brian Dennehy, Robert Loggia, Ossie Davis. Prod: Columbia.

Go Natalie. Script: Pamela Gibson, Nelson George. Dir: Kevin Hooks. Phot: Zoltan David. Players: Halle Berry, Joseph C. Philips. Prod: Warner Bros.

Grand Canyon. Script: Lawrence Kasdan, Meg Kasdan. Dir: Lawrence Kasdan. Phot: Owen Roizman. Players: Danny Glover, Kevin Kline, Steve Martin, Mary McDonnell, Mary Louise Parker, Alfred Woodard. Prod: Fox.

Guilty by Suspicion. Script and Dir: Irwin Winkler. Phot: Michael Ballhaus. Players: Robert De Niro, Annette Bening, George Wendt, Sam Wanamaker, Martin Scorsese. Prod: Warner Bros.

The Hand that Rocks the Cradle. Script: Amanda Silver. Dir: Curtis Hanson. Phot: Robert Elswit. Players: Rebecca DeMornay, Annabella Sciorra, Ernie Hudson, Matt McCoy. Prod: Interscope/Buena Vista.

Hangin' with the Homeboys. Script and Dir: Joseph P. Vasquez. Phot: Anghel Decca. Players: Doug E. Doug, Mario Joyner, John Leguizamo, Nestor Serrano. Prod: New Line.

Hard Promises. Script: Julie Selbo. Dir: Martin Davidson. Phot: Andrzej Bartkowiak. Players: Sissy Spacek, William Peterson, Brian Kerwin, Mare Winningham. Prod: Columbia (U.S.)/Int'l: Vision Int'l.

The Hard Way. Script: Daniel Pyne, Lem Dobbs. Dir: John Badham. Phot: Don McAlpine. Players: Michael J. Fox, James Woods, Stephen Lang, Annabella Sciorra. Prod: Universal.

Harley Davidson and the Marlboro Man. Script: Don Michael Paul. Dir: Simon Wincer. Phot: David Eggby. Players: Mickey Rourke, Don Johnson, Robert Ginty, Chelsea Field. Prod: MGM/Pathé.

He Said, She Said. Script: Brian Hohfield. Dir: Ken Kwapis ("He Said"), Marisa Silver ("She Said"). Phot: Stephen H. Burum. Players: Kevin Bacon, Elizabeth Perkins. Prod: Paramount.

Homicide. Script and Dir: David Mamet. Phot: Roger Deakins. Players: Joe Mantegna, William H. Macy, Natalija Nogulich. Prod: Triumph Releasing.

Hook. Script: Jim V. Hart, Malia Scotch Marmo, Nick Castle Jr. from the James Barrie play and story, "Peter Pan." Dir: Steven Spielberg. Phot: Dean Cundey. Players: Dustin Hoffman, Robin Williams, Julia Roberts, Bob Hoskins, Maggie Smith. Prod: Tri-Star.

Hot Shots. Script: Jim Abrahams, Pat Proft. Dir: Jim Abrahams. Phot: Bill Butler. Players: Charlie Sheen, Lloyd Bridges, Valeria Golino, Cary Elwes. Prod: Fox.

House Party 2. Script: Rusty Cundieff. Dir: Paris Barclay. Players: Kid n' Play. Prod: New Line Cinema.

Hudson Hawk. Script: Steven de Souza, Daniel Waters, from Bruce Willis Story. Dir: Michael Lehmann. Phot: Dante Spinotti. Players: Bruce Willis, Danny Aiello, Andi MacDowell, James Coburn. Prod: Tri-Star.

Impromptu. Script: Sarah Kernochan. Dir: James Lapine. Phot: Bruno De Keyzer. Players: Judy Davis, Hugh Grant, Mandy Patinkin Bernadette Peters, Julian Sands, Emma Thompson, Anna Massey. Prod: Hemdale (U.S. only)/Sovereign Pictures.

The Indian Runner. Script and Dir: Sean Penn. Phot: Anthony B. Richmond. Players: David Morse, Viggo Mortense, Valeria Gollino. Prod: Univ. (U.S. only)/Columbia Tri-Star.

The Inner Circle. Script: Andrei Konchalovsky, Anatoly Usov. Dir: Konchalovsky. Phot: Ennio Guarnieri. Players: Tom Hulce, Lolita Davidovich, Bob Hoskins. Prod: Columbia.

Iron Maze. Script: Tim Metcalfe. Dir Hiroaki Yoshida. Phot: Morio Saegusa. Players: Bridget Fonda, Jeff Fahey, J.T. Walsh, Hiro Murakami. Prod: Edward Pressman Prods./Castle Hill.

Jack the Bear. Script: Steve Zallian. Dir: Marshall Herskovitz. Phot: Fred Murphy. Players: Danny DeVito. Prod: Fox.

JFK. Script: Oliver Stone, Zachary Sklar from "On the Trail of the Assassins" by Jim Garrison, and "Crossfire" by Jim Marrs. Dir: Stone. Phot: Robert Richardson. Players: Kevin Costner, Gary Oldman, Tommy Lee Jones, Sissy Spacek, Kevin Bacon, Sally Kirkland, Michael Rooker, Angela Lansbury, Jack Lemmon. Prod: Warner Bros.

Jungle Fever. Script and Dir: Spike Lee. Phot: Ernest Dickerson. Players: Wesley Snipes, Annabella Sciorra, Lee, Ossie Davis, Ruby Dee, Samuel I. Jackson, John Turturro. Prod: Universal.

King Ralph. Script: David Ward from on the novel, "Headlong", by Emlyn Williams. Dir: Ward. Phot: Kenneth MacMillan. Players: John Goodman, Peter O'Toole, John Hurt, Camille Coduri. Prod: Universal.

A Kiss Before Dying. Script: James Dearden from novel by Ira Levin. Dir: James Dearden. Phot: Mike Southon. Players: Matt Dillon, Sean Young, Max von Sydow, James Russo. Prod: Universal.

Kiss Me a Killer. Script: Christopher Wooden, Marcus DeLeon. Dir: DeLeon. Phot: Nancy Schrieber. Players: Julie Carmen, Robert Beltran, Guy Boyd. Prod: Concorde.

Lame Ducks. Script: Pat Proft. Dir: Dennis Dugan. Phot: David M. Walsh. Players: John Turturro, Mel Smith, Bob Nelson, Nancy Marchand. Prod: Paramount.

L.A. Story. Script: Steve Martin. Dir: Mick Jackson. Phot: Andrew Dunn. Players: Martin, Victoria Tennant, Richard E. Grant, Marilu Henner, Sarah Jessica Parker. Prod: Tri-Star.

The Last Boy Scout. Script: Shane Black. Dir: Tony Scott. Players: Bruce Willis, Damon Wayans. Prod: Warner Bros.

Late for Dinner. Script: Mark Andrus. Dir: W.D. Richter. Phot: Peter Sova. Players: Brian Wimmer, Peter Berg, Marcia Gay Harden, Colleen Flynn, Peter Gallagher. Prod: Columbia.

Leaving Normal. Script: Edward J. Solomon. Dir: Edward Zwick. Phot: Ralph Detler Bode. Players: Christine Lahti, Meg Tilly, Patrika Darbo, Lenny Von Dohlen. Prod: Universal.

Life Stinks. Script: Mel Brooks, Ron Clark, Rudy De Luca, Steve Haberman. Dir: Brooks. Phot: Steven Poster. Players: Brooks, Lesley Ann Warren, Jeffrey Tambor, Stuart Pankin. Prod: MGM/Pathé.

Little Man Tate. Script: A. Scott Frank. Dir: Jodie Foster. Phot: Mike Southon. Players: Jodie Foster, Dianne Wiest, Adam Hann-Byrd, Harry Connick Jr. Prod: Orion.

Livin' Large (The Tapes of Dexter Jackson). Script: Bill Payne, Fred Johnson. Dir: Michael Schultz. Phot: Peter Lyons Collister. Players: T.C. Carson, Blanche Baker, Lisa Arrindell. Prod: Samuel Goldwyn Co.

Love Field. Script: Don Roos. Dir: Jonathan Kaplan. Phot: Ralf D. Bode. Players: Michelle Pfeiffer, Dennis Haysbert, Brian Kerwin. Prod: Orion.

Love Potion No. 9. Script and Dir: Dale Launer. Phot: William Wages. Players: Tate Donovan, Sandra Bullock. Prod: Fox.

The Mambo Kings. Script: Cynthia Cidre. Dir: Arnold Glimcher. Phot: Michael Ballhaus. Players: Armand Assante, Antonio Banderas, Maruschka Detmers, Cathy Moriarty, Celia Cruz, Tito Puentes. Prod: Warner Bros./New Regency.

Man in the Moon. Script: Jenny Wingfield. Dir: Robert Mulligan. Phot: Freddie Francis. Players: Sam Waterston, Tess Harper, Gail Strickland. Prod: MGM/Pathe.

Married to It. Script: Janet Kovalcik. Dir: Arthur Hiller. Phot: Victor J. Kemper. Players: Beau Bridges, Stockard Channing, Robert Sean Leonard, Mary Stuart Masterson, Cybill Shepherd, Ron Silver. Prod: Orion.

Meeting Venus. Script: Michael Hirst, István Szabó. Dir: Szabó. Phot: Lajos Koltai. Players: Glenn Close, Niels Arestrup, Erland Josephson. Prod: Warner Bros.

Memoirs of an Invisible Man. Script: William Goldman, Robert Collector, Dana Olsen. Dir: John Carpenter. Phot: William A. Fraker. Players: Chevy Chase, Daryl Hannah, Sam Neill. Prod: Warner Bros.

Men of Respect. Script and Dir: William Reilly. Phot: Bobby Bukowski. Players: John Turturro, Katherine Borowitz, Dennis Farina, Peter Boyle, Rod Steiger. Prod: Columbia.

The Mrs. Script: Mary Agnes Donoghue. Dir: Damian Harris. Phot: Jack N. Green. Players: Goldie Hawn, John Heard, Ashley Peldon,

Wesley Snipes threatens Allen Payne in *New Jack City*

Robin Bartlett, Amy Wright. Prod: Buena Vista.
Mississippi Masala. Script: Sooni
Taraporeavala. Dir: Mira Nair. Phot: Ed
Lachman. Players: Denzel Washington, Sarita
Choudhury, Roshan Seth. Prod: Cinecom.
Mobsters. Script Nicholas Kazan, Michael
Mahern. Dir: Michael Karbelnikoff. Players:
Christian Slater, Patrick Dempsey, Richard
Grieco, Costas Mandylor, F. Murray Abraham.
Prod: Universal.
Mom and Dad Save the World. Script: Ed
Solomon, Chris Matheson. Dir: Greg Beeman.
Phot: Jacques Haitkin. Players: Jon Lovitz, Teri
Garr, Jeffrey Jones, Thalmus Rasulala, Eric Idle.
Prod: Warner Bros.
My Girl. Script: Laurice Elehwany, Barbara
Benedek. Dir: Howard Zieff. Phot: Paul Elliott.
Players: Dan Aykroyd, Jamie Lee Curtis,
Macaulay Culkin, Ann Chlumsky. Prod:
Columbia.
My Own Private Idaho. Script and Dir: Gus
Van Sant. Phot: Eric Alan Edwards, John
Campbell. Players: River Phoenix, Keanu
Reeves. Prod: New Line/Fine Line Films.
My Cousin Vinny. Script: Dale Launer. Dir:
Jonathan Lynn. Phot: Peter Deming. Players: Joe
Pesci, Ralph Macchio, Mitchell Whitfield,
Marisa Tomei, Fred Gwynne. Prod: Fox.
Mystery Date. Script: Parker Bennett, Terry
Runte. Dir: Jonathan Wacks. Phot: Oliver Wood.
Players: Ethan Hawke, Teri Polo, Brian
McNamara. Prod: Orion.
The Naked Gun II½: The Smell of Fear.
Script: David Zucker, Pat Proft. Dir: David
Zucker. Phot: Robert Stevens. Players: Leslie
Nielsen, Priscilla Presley, George Kennedy, O.J.
Simpson, Margery Ross. Prod: Paramount.

Naked Lunch. Script and Dir: David
Cronenberg from William Burroughs' novel.
Phot: Peter Suschitzky. Players: Peter Weller,
Judy Davis, Julian Sands, Roy Scheider,
Monique Mercure. Prod: Jeremy Thomas/Fox.
Necessary Roughness. Script: Rick Natkin,
David Fuller. Dir: Stan Dragoti. Phot: Peter
Stein. Players: Scott Bakula, Robert Loggia.
Prod: Paramount.
New Jack City. Script: Thomas Lee Wright,
Barry Michael Cooper. Dir: Mario Van Peebles.
Phot: Francis Kenny. Players: Wesley Snipes,
Ice T, Van Peebles, Allen Payne, Judd Nelson.
Prod: Warner Bros.
Newsies. Script: Bob Tzudiker, Noni White,
David Fallon, Tom Rickman. Dir: Kenny
Ortega. Phot: Andrew Laszlo. Players: Christian
Bale, David Moscow, Luke Edwards, Ele Keats,
Robert Duvall, Ann-Margret. Prod: Buena Vista.
Noises Off. Script: Marty Kaplan from the
Michael Frayn play. Dir: Peter Bogdanovich.
Phot: Tim Suhrstedt. Players: Carol Burnett,
Michael Caine, Denholm Elliott, Julie Hagerty,
Mark Linn-Baker, Marilu Henner. Prod: Buena
Vista.
One Good Cop. Script and Dir: Heywood
Gould. Phot: Ralf Bode. Players: Michael
Keaton, Rene Russo, Anthony LaPaglia, Kevin
Conway. Prod: Warner Bros.
Only the Lonely. Script and Dir: Chris
Columbus. Phot: Julio Macat. Players: John
Candy, Maureen O'Hara, Ally Sheedy, Kevin
Dunn, Bert Remsen, Anthony Quinn. Prod: Fox.
Oscar. Script: Michael Barrie, Jim Mullholland
from the play by Claude Magnier. Dir: John
Landis. Phot: Mac Ahlberg. Players: Sylvester
Stallone, Ornella Muti, Peter Riegart, Tim
Curry, Don Ameche. Prod: Buena Vista/
Touchstone.
Other People's Money. Script: Alvin Sargent
from the Jerry Sterner play. Dir: Norman
Jewison. Phot: Haskell Wexler. Players: Danny
DeVito, Gregory Peck, Penelope Ann Miller,
Piper Laurie, Dean Jones. Prod: Warner Bros.
Out for Justice. Script: David Lee Henry. Dir:
John Flynn. Phot: Ric Waite. Players: Steven
Seagal, William Forsythe, Jerry Orbach. Prod:
Warner Bros.
Paradise. Script and Dir: Mary Agnes
Donoghue based on Jean-Loup Hubert's 1987
film "Le Grand Chemin." Players: Don Johnson,
Melanie Griffith, Elijah Woods. Prod: Buena
Vista.

Robin Givens in *A Rage in Harlem*

Paris is Burning. (*Documentary*) Dir: Jennie Livingstone. Phot: Paul Gibson, Maryse Alberti. Prod: Off White Prods.

Peltier. (*Documentary*) Dir: Michael Apted. Prod: Seven Arts.

The People Under the Stairs. Script and Dir: Wes Craven. Players: Brandon Adams, Everett McGill, Wendy Robie. Prod: Alive Films/ Universal.

Point Break. Script: W. Peter Ilif, Rick King. Dir: Kathryn Bigelow. Phot: Donald Peterman. Players: Patrick Swayze, Keanu Reeves, Gary Busey, Lori Petty. Prod: Fox.

Poison. Script: Todd Haynes, inspired by writings of Jean Genet. Dir: Haynes. Phot Maryse Alberti (color), Barry Ellsworth (b&w). Players: Edith Meeks, Larry Maxwell, Scott Renderer. Prod: Zeitgeist Films.

Prelude to a Kiss. Script: Craig Lucas from his play. Dir: Norman René. Phot: Stefan Czapsky. Players: Alec Baldwin, Meg Ryan, Patty Duke, Ned Beatty, Kathy Bates. Prod: Fox.

Prince of Tides. Script: Becky Johnston, Pat Conry, Barbara Streisand from Conroy's novel. Dir: Streisand. Phot: Stephen Goldblatt. Players: Streisand, Nick Nolte, Blythe Danner, Kate Nelligan, Melinda Dillon. Prod: Columbia.

Pure Luck. Script: Herschel Weingrod, Timothy Harris based on film "La Chèvre." Dir: Nadia Tass. Players: Martin Short, Danny Glover, Shelia Kelley, Scott Wilson, Harry Shearer, Sam Wanamaker. Prod: Universal.

Radio Flyer. Script: David Mickey Evans. Dir: Richard Donner. Phot: Laszlo Kovacs. Players. Elijah Woods, Joseph Mazello, Lorraine Bracco, John Heard. Prod: Columbia.

A Rage in Harlem. Script: John Toles-Bey, Bobby Crawford from the novel by Chester Himes. Dir: Bill Duke. Phot: Toyomichi Kurita. Players: Forest Whitaker, Gregory Hines, Robin Givens, Zakes Mokae, Danny Glover. Prod: Miramax.

Rambling Rose. Script: Calder Willingham. Dir: Martha Coolidge. Phot: Johnny Jensen. Players: Laura Dern, Diane Ladd, Lukas Haas, Robert Duvall, John Heard. Prod: Seven Arts/ Int'l Distrib: Carolco.

Regarding Henry. Script: Jeffrey Abrams. Dir: Mike Nichols. Phot: Giuseppe Rotunno. Players: Harrison Ford, Annette Bening, Bill Nunn, Mikki Allen. Prod: Paramount.

Return to the Blue Lagoon. Script: Leslie Stevens. Dir: William A. Graham. Phot: Robert Steadman. Players: Milla Jovovich, Brian Krause, Lisa Pelikan. Prod: Columbia.

Ricochet. Script: Steven DeSouza. Dir: Russell Mulcahy. Phot: Peter Levy. Players: Denzel Washington, John Lithgow, Kevin Pollack, Lindsay Wagner. Prod: Warner Bros./HBO.

Roadside Prophets. Script and Dir: Abbe Wool. Phot: Tom Richmond. Players: Adam Horovitz, John Doe, David Carradine, Timothy Leary, Arlo Guthrie, John Cusack. Prod: New Line/Fine Line.

Robin Hood: Prince of Thieves. Script: Pen Densham, John Watson. Dir: Kevin Reynolds. Phot: Doug Milsome. Players: Kevin Costner, Morgan Freeman, Mary Elizabeth Mastrantonio, Christian Slater, Alan Rickman. Prod: Warner Bros.

The Rocketeer. Script: Danny Bilson, Paul de Meo, William Dear. Dir: Joe Johnston. Phot: Hiro Narita. Players: Bill Campbell, Jennifer Connelly, Alan Arkin, Timothy Dalton, Paul Sorvino. Prod: Buena Vista.

Rush. Script: Peter Dexter: Dir: Lili Fini Zanuck. Phot: Kenneth MacMillan. Players: Jennifer Jason Leigh, Jason Patric, Sam Elliot, Max Perlich, Gregg Allman. Prod: MGM/ Pathé.

The Search for Intelligent Life in the Universe. (*Documentary*) Script: Jane Wagner. Dir: John Bailey. Phot: Bailey. Cast: Lily Tomlin. Prod: Orion Classics.

Sex, Drugs, Rock and Roll. Script: Eric Bogosian, based on his one-man show. Dir: John McNaughton. Phot: Ernest Dickerson. Player: Bogosian. Prod: Avenue Pictures.

Shadows and Fog. Script and Dir: Woody Allen. Phot: Carlo Di Palma. Players: Woody

Allen, Mia Farrow, Madonna, John Malkovich, Jodie Foster, Kathy Baker, John Cusack, Lily Tomlin. Prod: Orion.

Shattered. Script: Wolfgang Petersen, Andrew Birkin from Richard Neely's novel "The Plastic Nightmare." Dir: Peterson. Phot: Laszlo Kovacs. Players: Tom Berenger, Bob Hoskins, Greta Scacchi, Corbin Bernsen, Joanne Whalley-Kilmer. Prod: MGM/Pathé.

Shining Through. Script and Dir: David Seltzer. Phot: Jan de Bont. Players: Michael Douglas, Melanie Griffiths, Liam Neeson, John Gielgud. Prod: Fox.

Shipwrecked (Norwegian title: Håkon Håkonsen). Script: Nils Gaup, Bob Foss, Greg Dinner, Nick Thiel. Dir: Gaup. Phot: Erling Thurmann-Andersen. Players: Stian Smedstad, Gabriel Byrne, Louisa Haigh. Prod: Buena Vista.

Showdown in Little Tokyo. Script: Jonathan Lemkin. Dir: Mark L. Lester. Phot: Mark Irwin. Players: Dolph Lundgren, Brandon Lee. Prod: Warner Bros.

Shout. Script: Joe Gayton. Dir: Jeffrey Hornady. Players: Jamie Walters, Richard Jordan, Heather Graham, John Travolta. Prod: Universal.

The Silence of the Lambs. Script: Ted Tally from the Thomas Harris novel. Dir: Jonathan Demme. Phot: Tak Fujimoto. Players: Jodie Foster, Anthony Hopkins, Scott Glenn, Ted Levine. Prod: Orion.

Singles. Script and Dir: Cameron Crowe. Phot: Ueli Steigner. Players: Bridget Fonda, Campbell Scott, Krya Sedgwick, Matt Dillon. Prod: Warner Bros.

Slacker. Script and Dir: Richard Linklater. Phot: Lee Daniel. Players: Linklater, non-pros. Prod: Orion Classics.

Sleeping with the Enemy. Script: Ronald Bass from the novel by Nancy Price. Dir: Joseph Ruben. Phot: John W. Lindley. Players: Julia Roberts, Patrick Bergin, Kevin Anderson. Prod: Fox.

Soapdish. Script: Robert Harling, Andrew Bergman. Dir: Michael Hoffman. Phot: Ueli Steiger. Players: Sally Field, Kevin Kline, Robert Downey Jr., Cathy Moriarty, Whoopi Goldberg. Prod: Paramount.

Something to do with the Wall. (*Documentary*) Script, Dir and Phot: Marilyn Levine, Ross McElwee. Prod: First Run Features.

Star Trek VI – The Undiscovered Country. Script: Nicholas Meyer, Denny Martin Flynn.

Dir: Nicholas Meyer. Players: William Shatner, Leonard Nimoy, DeForest Kelley, David Warner. Prod: Paramount.

Step Kids. Script: Frank Mugavero. Dir: Joan Micklin Silver. Phot: Players: Griffin Dunne, Margaret Whitton, David Straithairn, Ben Savage. Prod: New line.

Stepping Out. Script: Richard Harris. Dir: Lewis Gilbert. Phot: Alan Hume. Players: Liza Minnelli, Ellen Greene, Bill Irwin, Jane Krakowski, Andrea Martin, Julie Walters, Shelley Winters. Prod: Paramount.

Stone Cold. Script: Walter Doniger. Dir: Craig R. Baxley. Phot: Alexander Gruszynski. Players: Brian Bosworth, Lance Henriksen, William Forsythe. Prod: Columbia.

Storyville. Script and Dir: Mark Frost. Players: James Spader, Jason Robards. Prod: Fox.

The Super. Script: Sam Simon, Nora Ephron. Dir: Rod Daniel. Phot: Bruce Surtees. Players: Joe Pesci, Vincent Gardenia, Ruben Blades. Prod: Fox.

Switch. Script and Dir: Blake Edwards. Phot: Dick Bush. Players: Ellen Barkin, Jimmy Smits, JoBeth Williams, Lorraine Bracco. Prod: Warner Bros./HBO.

Talent for the Game. Script: David Himmelstein, Tom Donnelly, Larry Ferguson. Dir: Robert M. Young. Phot: Curtis Clark. Players: Edward James Olmos, Lorraine Bracco. Prod: Paramount.

Terminator 2: Judgment Day. Script: James Cameron, William Wisher. Dir: Cameron. Phot: Adam Greenberg. Players: Arnold Schwarzenegger, Linda Hamilton. Prod: Tri-Star.

Thelma and Louise. Script: Callie Khouri. Dir: Ridley Scott. Phot: Adrian Biddle. Players: Susan Sarandon, Geena Davis, Harvey Keitel, Michael Madsen. Prod: MGM/Pathé.

This is My Life. Script: Nora Ephron, Delia Ephron from Meg Wolitzer's novel. Dir: Nora Ephron. Phot: Robert M. Stevens. Players: Julie Kavner, Samantha Mathis, Dan Aykroyd. Prod: Fox.

Time Bomb. Script and Dir: Avi Nesher. Players: Tracy Scoggins, Michael Biehn, Patsy Kensit, Robert Culp. Prod: MGM/Pathé.

Toy Soldiers. Script: David Keoppe, Daniel Petrie. Dir: Petrie. Phot: Thomas Burstyn. Players: Sean Austin, Will Wheaton, Louis Gossett Jr. Prod: Tri-Star.

True Identity. Script: Andy Breckman. Dir: Charles Lane. Phot: Tom Ackerman. Players:

Lenny Henry, Anne Marie Johnson, Frank Langella. Prod: Buena Vista.

Truth or Dare: In Bed with Madonna. (*Documentary*). Dir: Alex Keshishian. Prod: Miramax/ Propaganda Films.

29th Street. Script and Dir: George Gallo Jr. Phot: Steven Fierberg. Players: Danny Aiello, Anthony LaPaglia, Frank Pesce, Lainie Kazan, Robert Forster. Prod: Fox.

The Unborn. Script: Henry Dominic. Dir: Rodman Flender. Phot: Wally Pfister. Players: Brooke Adams. Jeff Hayenga, James Karen. Prod: Califilm.

The Vagrant. Script: Richard Jeffries. Dir: Chris Wales. Phot: Jack Wallner. Players: Marshall Bell, Bill Paxton, Michael Ironside, Mitzi Kapture, Colleen Camp. Prod: MGM/ Pathé.

V.I. Warshawski. Script: Edward Taylor, David Aaron Cohen, Nick Dhiel. Dir: Jeff Kanew. Phot: Jan Kiesser. Players: Kathleen Turner, Charles Durning, Jay O. Sanders. Prod: Buena Vista.

Welcome to Buzzsaw. Script: Daniel Goldin. Joshua Goldin. Dir: Francis Verber. Players: Matthew Broderick, Jeffrey Jones, Heidi King. Prod: Universal.

What About Bob? Script: Tom Schulman, Alvin Sargent, Laura Ziskin. Dir: Frank Oz. Phot: Michael Ballhaus. Players: Bill Murray, Richard Dreyfuss, Julie Hagerty. Prod: Buena Vista.

White Fang. Script: Jeanne Rosenberg, Nick Thiel, David Fallon from the Jack London novel. Dir: Randal Kleiser. Phot: Tony Pierce-Roberts. Players: Klaus Maria Brandauer, Ethan Hawke, Seymour Cassel. Prod: Buena Vista.

Whore. Script: Ken Russell, Deborah Dalton from the play "Bondage" by David Hines. Phot: Amir Mokri. Players: Theresa Russell, Benjamin Morton, Antonio Fargas, Sanjay. Prod: Trimark.

Wild Hearts Can't be Broken. Script: Matt Williams, Oley Sassone. Dir: Steve Miner. Phot: Daryn Okada. Players: Gabrielle Anwar, Michael Schoeffing, Cliff Robertson. Prod: Buena Vista.

Year of the Gun. Script: David Ambrose from the book by Michael Mewshaw. Dir: John Frankenheimer. Phot: Blasco Giurato. Players: Andrew McCarthy, Valeria Golino, Sharon Stone, John Pankow, Mattia Sbagia, Lou Castel. Prod: Edward Pressman Prods./Initial Films/ Triumpn Releasing.

Producers

Alive Enterprises
8912 Burton Way
Beverly Hills
California 90211
Tel: (213) 247 7800
Fax: (213) 247 7823

Amblin Entertainment
Building 477 First floor
100 Universal City Plaza
Universal City
California 91608
Tel: (818) 777 4600

Carolco Pictures
8800 Sunset Boulevard
Los Angeles
California 90069
Tel: (213) 850 8800
Fax: (213) 657 1629

Castle Rock Pictures
335 North Maple Drive
Suite 135
Beverly Hills
California 90210
Tel: (213) 285 2300
Fax: (213) 285 2345

Sony Pictures
Columbia Plaza
Burbank
California 91505
Tel: (818) 954 6000
Fax: (818) 954 4141

TriStar Pictures
(*A Columbia Pictures Entertainment Company with same address as Sony*)
Tel: (213) 280 7700

Concorde Pictures
8721 Sunset Boulevard
Los Angeles
California 90069
Tel: (213) 820 6733
Fax: (213) 207 6816

Dino De Laurentiis Communications
8670 Wilshire Boulevard
Beverly Hills
California 90211
Tel: (213) 289 6100
Fax: (213) 855 0562

Walt Disney Company
(*Walt Disney Pictures, Touchstone Pictures, Hollywood Pictures all released through Buena Vista*)

500 Buena Vista Street
Burbank
California 91521
Tel: (818) 560 1000
Fax: (818) 560 1930

Hemdale
7966 Beverly Boulevard
Los Angeles
California 90048
Tel: (213) 966 3700
Fax: (213) 651 3107

Imagine
1925 Century Park East
Suite #2300
Los Angeles
California 90067
Tel: (213) 277 1665
Fax: (213) 785 0107

Interscope
10900 Wiltshire Boulevard
Suite 1400
Los Angeles
California 90024
Tel: (213) 208 8525
Fax: (213) 208 1197

Largo Entertainment
10201 West Pico Boulevard
Bldg. 86, Room 206
Los Angeles
California 90035
Tel: (213) 203 3600
Fax: (213) 203 4133

Lorimar Television
(*A Warners Co. producing TV films that are sometimes released theatrically abroad*)
300 South Lorimar Place
Burbank
California 91505
Tel: (818) 954 6000

Lucasfilm
P.O. Box 20009
San Rafael
California 94912
Tel: (415) 662 1800

MGM/Pathé

Communications Company
640 South San Vicente Blvd.
Los Angeles
California 90048
Tel: (213) 658 2100
Fax: (213) 658 2111

Morgan Creek Productions
1875 Century Park East
Los Angeles
California 90067
Tel: (213) 284 8884
Fax: (213) 282 8794

New Line Cinema
116 North Robertson Blvd.
Los Angeles
California 90048
Tel: (213) 854 5811
Fax: (213) 854 1824

New Regency Films Inc.
4000 Warner Boulevard
Producers Building 66
Burbank
California 91522
Tel: (818) 954 3044
Fax: (818) 954 3295

Orion Pictures
1325 Avenue of the Americas
New York, N.Y. 10019
Tel: (212) 956 3800
Fax: (212) 956 9499

Paramount Pictures
5555 Melrose Avenue
Hollywood
California 90038
Tel: (213) 468 5000
Fax: (213) 468 5555

PentAmerica
11111 Santa Monica Boulevard
Suite 1100
Los Angeles
California 90025
Tel: (213) 473 5199
Fax: (213) 477 5879

Edward R. Pressman Film Corporation
445 North Bedford Drive

Penthouse
Beverly Hills
California 90210
Tel: (213) 271 8383
Fax: (213) 271 9497

Twentieth Century Fox
10201 West Pico Boulevard
Los Angeles
California 90035
Tel: (213) 277 2211

Universal Pictures
100 Universal City Plaza
Universal City
California 91608
Tel: (818) 777 1000
Fax: (818) 777 6431

Viacom
(*produces television films that are released theatrically abroad*)
1515 Broadway
New York, N.Y. 10036
Tel: (212) 258 6000

Warner Bros.
4000 Warner Boulevard
Burbank
California 91522
Tel: (818) 954 6000
Fax: (818) 954 2464

Distributors

Angelika Films
110 Greene Street
Suite 1102
New York, N.Y. 10012
Tel: (212) 274 1990
Fax: (212) 966 4957

Avenue Pictures
12100 Wilshire Boulevard
Los Angeles
California 90025
Tel: (213) 442 2200
Fax: (213) 207 1753

Buena Vista
See production listing for Disney

Castle Hill Productions
1414 Avenue of the Americas
New York, N.Y. 10019
Tel: (212) 888 0080
Fax: (212) 644 0956

Cinecom
850 Third Avenue
14th Floor
New York, N.Y. 10022
Tel: (212) 319 5000
Fax: (212) 371 1845

Columbia
See production listing

Tri-Star
See production listing

Triumph Releasing Corp.
(*A Columbia Pictures Co.*)
Tri-Star Building
Suite 30459
Culver City
California 90232
Tel: (213) 882 1177

Concorde Pictures
See production listing

Fries Entertainment
6922 Hollywood Boulevard
Hollywood
California 90028
Tel: (213) 466 2266
Fax: (213) 466 9407

Samuel Goldwyn Company
10203 Santa Monica Boulevard
Los Angeles
California 90067
Tel: (213) 552 2255
Fax: (213) 284 8493

Hemdale
See production listing

International Film Exchange
201 West 52nd Street
New York, N.Y. 10019
Tel: (212) 582 4318
Fax: (212) 956 2257

MGM/Pathé
11111 Santa Monica Boulevard
Los Angeles
California 90025
Tel: (213) 444 1500
Fax: (213) 479 7641

Miramax
375 Greenwich Street
New York, N.Y. 10013
Tel: (212) 941 3800
Fax: (212) 941 3949

New Line
*See production listing for
California operations*
Also:
575 Eighth Avenue
New York, N.Y. 10018
Tel: (212) 239 8880
Fax: (212) 239 9104

Fine Line
(*A New Line Co.*)
1500 Broadway
Suite 2011
New York, N.Y. 10036
Tel: (212) 221 2410
Fax: (212) 221 2415

Seven Arts
(*New Line distributor for Carolco
Pictures*)
Same listing as New Line

New Yorker Films
16 W. 61st Street
New York, N.Y. 10023
Tel: (212) 247 6110
Fax: (212) 307 7855

Orion Classics
See production listing for Orion

Orion Pictures
See production listing

Paramount
See production listing

Skouras Pictures
1040 North Las Palmas

Avenue
Hollywood
California 90038
Tel: (213) 467 3000
Fax: (213) 467 0740

Universal Pictures
See production listing

Warner Bros.
See production listing

Useful Addresses

**Academy of Motion Picture
Arts and Sciences**
8949 Wiltshire Boulevard
Beverly Hills
California 90211
Tel: (213) 278 8990

American Film Institute
John F. Kennedy Center for
the Performing Arts
Washington D.C. 20566
Tel: (202) 828 4000
Fax: (202) 659 1970
West Coast Branch:
2021 N. Western Avenue
Los Angeles
California 90027

Directors Guild of America
7920 Sunset Boulevard
Hollywood
California 90046
Tel: (213) 289 2000

Independent Feature Project
132 W. 21st Street
New York, N.Y. 10011
Tel: (212) 243 7777

**Independent Feature
Project/West**
5550 Wilshire Boulevard
Suite 204
Los Angeles,
California 90036
Tel: (213) 937 4379
Fax: (213) 937 4038

Motion Picture Association of America (MPAA)
1133 Avenue of the Americas
New York, N.Y. 10036
Tel: (212) 840 6161

Motion Picture Export Association of America
Same as MPAA

National Association of Theatre Owners (NATO)
116 North Robertson Blvd.
Suite F
Los Angeles
California 90048
Tel: (213) 652 1093
Fax: (213) 657 4758

U.S.S.R.

by Forrest S. Ciesol

By mid-1990 it appeared that Soviet cinema was taking the international film festival world by storm. In Berlin, the Silver Bear went to Kira Muratova's **Asthenic Syndrome** and a Jury Prize to **The Guard**. Three months later, in Cannes, the Best Director prize was awarded to Pavel Lounguine for **Taxi Blues**, a Jury Prize to **Mother**, the Caméra d'Or to **Freeze, Die and Revive**, and International Critics Prize to **Swan Lake – the Zone**. Additional prestigious festival awards followed, making 1990 a tough if not impossible act to follow.

Few outstanding films surfaced in 1991. Except for a Silver Bear (Berlin) to **Satan**, and the Grand Prix of the Moscow International Film Festival to **Spotted Dog Running along the Seashore**, Soviet cinema fared poorly on the international festival scene. The year (apart from the coup!) will be remembered more as a year of "process" than for outstanding "product."

Made possible only a few years ago, the restructuring of the Soviet film industry is proceeding with remarkable speed, outpacing any other sector of the economy. The once monopolistic, vertically integrated, government-controlled industry is in the midst of a convulsive, chaotic period of transition in which traditional methods of financing, production, distribution, and ex-hibition are changing simultaneously. In fits and starts, the industry is struggling to reinvent itself in the western mode. Nevertheless, the Soviet industry is swiftly integrating into the world of film-making community and market and, with some promising early results, is rebuilding its obsolete infrastructure.

Where monolithic studios once controlled all film production, numerous co-operatives and independent production companies have blossomed. These new companies now rent the state-owned facilities and equipment. Consequently, annual film production has soared to a record high of 350–450 films, financed by banks and other cash-heavy concerns. This huge increase in production – largely forgettable quickies – begs the question: where will all of these films play commercially at a time when Soviet screens are clogged with American and foreign product? One film director, whose film was scheduled to open mid-July in Moscow, complained that "we're running out of venues to see Soviet films. Right now in Moscow I know of only four theatres that are showing Russian films. All we have now is American movies."

The ironic, if lamentable domination of Soviet screens by foreign films has raised the spectre of import quotas being imposed

Scene from *A Spotted Dog Running on the Edge of the Sea*

to preserve screen time for domestic productions. It is unlikely that any such quota system would produce the desired impact. Further, quality American product may be impossible to obtain for the forseeable future given the embargo placed on sales to the Soviet Union by the Motion Picture Producers Association in response to the flagrant piracy (unlicensed theatrical, video and television exhibition) which the Soviet government has done little to curb. Americans substantially boycotted the Moscow Film Festival to bring this issue to the forefront but, as one might suspect, the piracy situation, bolstered by neither legislation nor enforcement mechamisms, will not be resolved soon.

International Co-productions

Co-productions and joint venture companies are swiftly changing the face of Soviet cinema. A nearly impossible dream just a few years ago, co-productions are now streaming into the international marketplace. And not just from the large studios in Moscow (Mosfilm) and Leningrad (Lenfilm), but even from the republic studios in the Ukraine, Georgia, Uzbekistan and Turkmenia. The far-reaching consequences of the increasing number of international co-productions will not be known for several years, but the production of 1991 provide some revealing previews of what Soviet cinema made for an international audience will look like.

The Russian Republic

Mosfilm

The two highest profile Soviet films of 1991 – both official selections for the Cannes Film Festival – were co-productions of London-based Spectator Entertainment International with Mosfilm Studios. **The Tsar's Assassin** and **Lost in Siberia** are glossy, big budget ($6–7 million; large by Soviet standards) technically superior films. Clearly made for international audiences, both films feature prominent British actors in the lead roles and were made or are available in English or Russian language versions.

In Alexander Mitta's **Lost in Siberia**, Anthony Andrews stars as a British archaeologist who, in 1945, is excavating an area in Persia that the Russian army wants for a gunnery range. He is kidnapped, falsely convicted in Moscow as a spy, and sent to a Siberian prison camp. The film chronicles his day to day travails – not speaking Russian to begin with – in the camp, including an aborted escape and his struggle to stay alive and maintain some semblance of human dignity. Not as thoroughly grim as the subject matter might suggest, the film offers convincing scenes of genuine human warmth and ironic contrast to the extreme inhumanity of the camp. Much of the film is shot in English, but authenticity is preserved by subtitling Russian-language secenes.

Made in identical Russian and English language versions, *The Tsar's Assassin* probes one of the dark mysteries of modern Russian history: the killing of Tsar Nicholas II and the royal family. Directed by Karen Shakhnazarov (*Zero City*), the film features perennially popular actor Malcolm McDowell as a haggard Russian schizophrenic who, in a series of flashbacks, attempts to convince a psychiatrist that he singlehandedly killed the tsar in 1918.

A co-production between French producer Serge Silberman and Mosfilm Studios descended like something of a UFO on the Official Competition in Cannes. Directed by Rustam Khamdanov, **Anna Karamazova** stars veteran French actress Jeanne Moreau as a woman released from a prison camp into a much changed world. Unlike the British co-prods, this has no sleek, conventional plot structure, but instead is an extended exercise in avant-garde cinema in which Moreau takes part in, or observes, several unrelated and absurd encounters. However tedious and unfathomable the narrative, masterful art direction, lighting and cinematography combine for a film of stunning visual beauty.

One of the most pleasant discoveries of the year was Viacheslav Krishtofovich's Mosfil comedy **Adam's Rib**, the story of three generations of Russian women living under one roof: the catatonic, bed-ridden grandmother, the rebellious teenage daughter and the divorced mother (a smashing performance from Inna Churikova) who wails that her life is being ruined and the best years of her life are being stolen by the other two. The predictable love-hate fireworks are confined to the family's claustrophobic apartment, but an excellent script, acting and a delightful touch of magic realism make this one of the year's best films.

Yevgeny Tsymbal's (*Defense Counsel Sedov*) first feature film **The Tale of the Unextinguished Moon** represented the U.S.S.R. in competition at the Montreal World Film Festival. The film is based on a short story by writer Boris Pilnyak who was himself vilified and eventually eliminated by Stalin. The thinly veiled and highly suggestive story tells of a famous Russian

Anthony Andrews in *Lost in Siberia*

Malcolm McDowell in *Assassin of the Tsar*

combat General (i.e. Mikhail Frunze) who is recalled to Moscow by "Number One" or "The Unbending Man" (Stalin) and forced to undergo necessary surgery from which he knows he will not recover. Tsymbal polished the script during an internship at the Sundance Institute.

The Stalin era will certainly provide material for many more years of films. For example, though it scarcely has been seen at home or abroad, poet Yevgeny Yevtushenko made his second feature film **Stalin's Funeral** based on his own childhood remembrances of that era.

Veteran Mosfilm director Vadim Abdrashitov, one of the most consistently inventive and provocative Russian intellectual directors, followed his 1989 triumph **The Servant** with the less enthusiastically received **Armavir**, the name of a famous boat that sunk in the Black Sea. Sergei Solovyov completed **The House under the Starry Sky**, the third film in his absurdist trilogy which began with **Assa** and **Black Rose Stands for Sorrow, Red Rose Stands for Love**. Arguably the best film of the three, Solovyov's rigorous absurdity will challenge even the most adventurous festival audiences.

Lenfilm Studios

Lenfilm Studios (Leningrad) provide an interesting example of the changing mode of Soviet film production. While Lenfilm still produce films under its own banner, the studio has in the last two years become home to 16 financially independent production companies (called "studios") largely made up of former Lenfilm employees.

Victor Aristov's **Satan**, awarded the 1991 Berlin Silver Bear (special jury prize), is a chilling drama about a young man who matter-of-factly murders the 10-year-old daughter of his lover and then, as if a kidnapper, anonymously demands a hard-currency ransom. The killer demonstrates a variety of other sociopathic behaviour in this visually and narratively grim film which aspires to, but ultimately lacks, the philosophical constructs of similar material which has been handled with aplomb by Polish director Kieślowski and others.

Two young directors who won international acclaim in 1990 made follow-up films at Lenfilm Studios. Alexander Rogozhikin (*The Guard*: Berlin Silver Bear) made **Third Planet**, a less tightly structured, less realised film that presents a parable for the perestroika era. A man enters a remote, mystical "zone" in a desperate search for a (possibly imaginary) healer to cure his terminally ill daughter. His perilous, perhaps irresponsibly planned journey brings disaster upon himself and the residents of the zone.

Nijole Adomenaite (*Coma*) made her first feature film **The House Built on Sand**, a highly stylised though ultimately unaffecting rendering of a story by Tatyana Tolstaya concerning a wealthy family that takes in a simple, luckless dressmaker and proceeds to play a tragic, cruel joke by sending her a long series of fictitious love letters from an unknown admirer.

Lenfilm also completed an international co-production with England, the U.S.A and Canada, the Eighteenth-century drama **Young Catherine** with Michael Anderson directing an international all star cast. Next year, Lenfilm will make a big-budget U.S. co-production of **Gunga Din**.

Elsewhere in the Russian Republic
Popular on the international festival circuit, **Spotted Dog Running along the Seashore** provides a fascinating glimpse – for audiences tolerant of the slow pace – of the primitive, often pagan life of the Nivkh people living on the northern coast of Sakhalin Island in the North Pacific. Though loosely based on a short story by Chinghiz Aitmatov, the film leans heavily toward an artful ethnographic documentary. Directed by Karen Gevorkain, this co-production between Dovzhenko studios and German film and TV sources, recounts a 10-year old boy's first seal-hunting trip with his granfather, father and uncle. Their boat becomes lost in an unrelenting fog and mounting hunger and thirst produce a series of tragedies. The film was unanimously awarded the Grand Prize at the Moscow International Film Festival.

Still from Yermek Shinarbaev's *Revenge*

Kazakhstan

The Kazakh new wave of young filmmakers, heralded in 1988 by Rachid Nugmanov's international hit *The Needle*, and a string of refreshingly offbeat, low-budget features, continues with remarkable diversity. Young first-time directors continue to be nurtured and to make consistently provocative new films unlike those being made anywhere else in the U.S.S.R. Many of the directors who established the Kazakh new wave are now making their follow-up features, laying to rest any suspicions that the new wave was just a flash in the pan.

An Official Selection in Cannes, Yermek Shinarbaev's **Revenge** (aka *The Reed Flute*) begins with an ominous prologue set in ancient Korea and jumps forward to the Soviet far east in 1915 where a peasant's young daughter is brutally murdered. The girl's father begins a lifelong search for the killer, but when he finds him in China, is unable to take his revenge. On his deathbed, he passes the vow of revenge to his son who continues to search for the killer. Presented in seven chapters with several interrelated stories and viewpoints, the film becomes an engaging philosophical exploration of violence and revenge as the enemies of beauty and poetry. Now planning his fourth feature, Shinarbaev is a major talent to watch.

After three years in production, Ardak Amirkulov completed his first feature film. Nearly three hours long, **The Fall of Otrar** is an epic period drama that tells the story of a city in Kazakhstan that was destroyed by Genghis Khan during the Thirteenth Century. Scripted by Alexei Gherman, the film is a sharp allegory for the political and social climate in Russia just before Hitler's 1941 invasion.

Abai Karpikov's (*Little Fish in Love*) second feature film **Blown Kiss** is again filled with the quirkiness and oddball surrealism that first endeared him to festival audiences. The film recounts the tale of a nurse whose predictable, normal life is turned upside down by her sexual encounters with a young racecar driver who is admitted to the hospital. Her life takes a downward turn when the young man is released... and disappears.

Woman Between Two Brothers is a startling first feature from 25 year-old director Amir Karakulov. This spare story of two brothers and the shift in their relationship when the older brother's girlfriend moves in with them is a rigorous, minimal deconstructive exercise reminiscent of Bresson. The slow pace, highly stylised atmosphere and non-motive acting make this a true work of "art" cinema that will undoubtedly travel to many festivals. However limited the audience, this is nevertheless a stunning debut for so young a director.

Central Asian Republics

Throughout the Soviet Union in 1991 the most interesting work came from young, first or second-time directors. Financially, these are difficult times for the smaller output of Central Asia, which have a traditionally small output that does not sell well beyond its republican borders. Two new films will bring international attention to the little unknown Tadzhikfilm Studios in Dushanbe. **Brother** by Bakhtiar Khudonazarov is a black-and-white film (owing a heavy debt to Italian neo-realism) about a teenage boy who begrudgingly, yet always lovingly, cares for his little brother. Together, they take a broken-down train to visit their estranged father. The train links all of the small, remote villages in this impoverished region of Tadzhikistan, and on their journey, the two boys encounter many delightful eccentric characters and strange occurrences.

Mairam Yusupova previously has directed thirteen documentaries. Her first feature film, **The Time of Yellow Grass**, is a splendidly photographed evocation of the timeless, traditional life in the remote Pamir mountains. The deliberately paced, simple story tells what happens in a small village when two shepherds discover an unidentified dead body. The history and customs of these people have ill-prepared them for such an untoward occurrence.

At the Uzbekfilm Studios in Tashkent – the home of a modern, popular narrative cinema with strong social themes – 1991 was a year of inactivity by established directors. Private "studios" or independent production companies have flourished in this city of two million inhabitants (fourth largest in Soviet Union) and have been cranking out a steady stream of mafia thrillers and action films.

Samir Abbasov (son of director Shukhara Abbasov – *Little Man in a Big War*) made a strong debut with the low-budget **Meeting in Samarra**, a nightmarish, black-and-white avant-garde feature which sustains itself surprisingly well over its length. The winter of 1991 promises the completion of new follow-up features by two young Uzbek directors: Dzhakangir Faiziyev (*Siz Kim Siz*, a 1990 festival circuit hit) and Yuri Sabitov (*Scarred by Kandahar*) as well as a first feature by Zufakir Moussakov whose diploma featurette **Soldier's Fairytale** revealed a significant talent.

Useful Adresses

Union of Soviet Film-makers
(*Federation of Republican Unions*)
13 Vasilievsjkaya ul.
123825 Moscow
Telex: 411939 ECRAN
Fax: (7095) 200–4284

State Committee of the U.S.S.R for Cinematography (GOSKINO)
International Relations

Department
Maly Gnezdikovsky per. 7
103877 Moscow
Telex: 411417
Fax: (7095) 229–6433

American-Soviet Film Intitiative
6922 Hollywood Blvd.
Suite 318
Los Angeles, CA 90028
Telephone: (213) 469–2703

Cine-Eye Magazine
(*Kino-Glaz*)
Khrzizanovsky ul. 14
cor. 2
117218 Moscow
Telex: 411237

Sovexportfilm
14 Kalashny per.
Moscow 103869
Fax: 200 1256
Telex: 411 143

FOCUS ON THE BALTIC REPUBLICS

Estonia

The "Singing Revolution" of 1988 started by the cultural intelligentsia to protest against the Soviet occupation of Estonia was quick, triumphant and very optimistic. The national blue black and white flag which in the past was absolutely banned, was hoisted as a symbol atop Toompea in the spring of 1989. Estonia was the first of the Soviet republics to allow the formation of new parties other then the Communist Party. Today Estonia is slowly changing its ways to catch up to other western European countries. Although inflation is constantly rising due to shortages, the republic is trying to follow the path of economic reform and privatisation in order to achieve economic independence from Moscow.

Although the arts in general are changing the basic socialist mentality is still intact. Overtly politically motivated films are being replaced with American adventure and action movies as well as old French melodramas. As many as 250 foreign films are making their way to Estonia each year. Unfortunately distribution is still very centralised and the making of alternative films hasn't yet developed. The lack of hard currency makes the buying of foreign films very expensive. The films that *do* finally reach Estonia are mostly of the erotic or violent kind that first pass through Moscow where Russian subtitles are added.

In 1991 wages doubled in comparison to 1990 but clothes doubled in price as well while food items quadrupled. Thus the average person has to think twice before spending money on cultural entertainment. In 1990 movie attendances reached only 10.5 million whereas in the years between 1960–1970 20 million people went annually to the cinema (current population is 1.6 million).

The first Estonian to own a camera was Johannes Pääsuke who took pictures of his surroundings. In 1914 he staged and filmed the first movie, a satirical farce called *A Bear Hunt in Pärnumaa*. During the Estonian independent years between 1920–1940, documentaries were made by a company called Estonian Culture Films, and directed by Konstain Märska. Features were not made due to their enormous costs and most films were imported from Hollywood or Germany.

After the Second World War filmmaking was propagandist in tone. Not until the 1960's did there appear films that were more geared to a general public, even if the virtues of socialism were still the main themes. The more notable directors that graduted in Moscow but made films in Estonia include Juri Müür, Grigori Kromanow, Leida Laius, Kaljo Kiisk and Arvo Kruusement. To Grigori Kromanov goes the honour of having made one of Estonian's best films **The Last Relic** (*Viimine Reliikvia*, 1969), which has been distrubuted around the world. Kaljo Kiisk and Leida Laius have also achieved a high reputation. Kiisk is interested how people interact in society (**Madness**, 1968) as well as human

Sulev Luik and Maria Klenskaja in Jüri Sillart's *Awakening*, which won the top prize at the Espoo Festival in 1990

conflicts and the creative side of human personality as in **Nipernaadi** (1983). Leida Laius has devoted her long film and stage career into probing of the female psyche. In her films the woman is the dominant character while the man is cast in the weaker role (**The Werewolf**, 1968; **Ukuaru**, 1973; **The Stolen Meeting**, 1989). Arvo Kruusement has made into films some of Estonia's classic novels (**Spring**, 1969 and **Fall**, 1990).

New Generation Appears

In 1979–1980 the new generation of Estonian directors appeared, who made films that were supposed to make the audience think. Most of them graduated from the Soviet Film Institute or the Moscow Director's School. They include Olav Neuland, Peeter Simm, Arvo Iho, Valentin Kuik, Peeter Urbla, Helle Murdmaa, Jüri Sillart, Sulev Keedus, Jaan Kolberg, and Aare Tilk. The 1979 Olav Neuland film **Nest of Winds** showed the life of a farmer between the Nazi and Soviet occupations of Estonia. Peeter Simm's tragi-comical film **The Ideal Landscape** (*Ideaalmaastik*, 1980) showed how a young man was forced into becoming a suppressor of his society through his job as a commissar on a collective farm in 1950.

After Laius and Iho made **Keep Smiling** in 1985 which tracked the lives of society's outsiders in a teenage camp, the newspapers openly discussed the merits of socialism and its effects on society. In 1987 Arvo Iho shot **The Observer** (*Vaatleja*) which was a film about the love between an Estonian man and a middle-aged Russian woman. The young director Jaan Kolberg has attempted to use symbolism and allegory in his adventure film **This Lost Way** (*See Kadunud Tee*, 1990). Sulev Keedus' **The Only Sunday** (*Ainus Pühapaev*, 1990) tried to show the conflicts of two brothers in the Stalin era in an emphatic style.

The biggest problem young directors face is the enormous costs and the lack of financing available. The average cost of shooting a film is 1 million roubles which in the past few years has increased by 250%. Although there are 15 film studios in Tallinn, Tallinnfilms makes about 3–4 feature films a year while Estonia Telefilm makes 1–2 features annually. Most of the techonology and raw material comes from the Soviet Union; Arriflex BL cameras and Nagras are also used, however. Tallinnfilm receives state subsidies as well as bank loans in order to produce its films.

The animated films of Priit Pärn, R. Raamat, and A. Paistik have won acclaim at many festivals, of course, and recognition for feature films is also on the way (**The Awakening** took top prize at the Espoo International Film Festival in 1990).

Estonian film-making has just recently freed itself from the centralised grasp of Moscow and the censorship laws have been cast aside. Estonian society is trying to become more capitalistic and as such film-makers are trying to learn and cope in a new and unexplored environment.

Jaan Ruus

Recent and Forthcoming Films

Äratus (The Awakening). Script: Rein Saluri. Dir: Jüri Sillart. Phot: Mait Mäekivi. Players: Tõnu Kark, Sulev Luik, Kaljo Kiisk, Maria Klenskaja. Prod: Tallinfilm Studios. *Jüri Sillart, one of the best cinematographers in Estonia, made his directorial debut with this film, which is about the mass deportations of 1949 and shows how good and evil become polarised. This conflict is shown through the struggle between the KGB and the Church, state and society. Visually the film's emphasis is put on symbolism.*

Inimene keda polnud (The Man Who Never Was). Script: Toomas Raudam. Dir: Peeter Simm. Phot: Ago Ruus. Players: Katri Horma, Andres Lepik, Tõnu Raadik, Sulev Luik. Prod: Tallinfilm Studios. *Director Peeter Simm has always been interested in how young people grow and become part of society. This film takes place between 1939 and 1949. The story is about a female radio actor who falls in love with a confident and vibrant radio reporter. The woman changes just as society*

changes during the turbulent decade. The film is extremely subtle and touches upon deeply sensitive and emotional times.
Ainult hulludele ehk halastajaõde (Only for Crazies). Script: Marina Septunova. Dir: Arvo Iho. Phot: Ago Ruus. Players: Margarita Terehhova, Mihkel Smeljanski, Hendrik Toompere, Lembit Ulfsak, Vija Artmane, Maria Avdjuško, Hendrik Toompere, Katrin Kohv, Ines Aru. Prod: Tallinnfilm Studios. *Borrowing the title from Hermann Hesse's Steppenwolf, Arvo Iho asks the question: can love cure all and if so do you have to be insane to believe in it? Arvo Iho has tried to understand the female spirit and its sufferings that the male dominated society has overlooked. The setting of the film is a small banal town where the main character who is a nurse in a town hospital, tries to answer the film's main question about charity.*

Margareta Terehhova and Hendrik Toompere in *Only for Crazies*, directed by Arvo Iho

Varastatud kohtumine (Stolen Rendez-vous). Script: Maria Zvereva. Dir: Leida Laius. Phot: Jüri Sillart. Players: Maria Klenskaja, Andres Kangur, Kaie Mihkelson, Lembit Peterson. *Drama.*
Ainus pühapäev (Only Sunday). Script: Veiko Jürisson. Dir: Sulev Keedus. Phot: Tõnis Lepik. Players: Elmo Nüganen, Kadri Ots, Erik Ruus. Prod: Tallinnfilm Studios. *Drama.*
See kadunud tee (This Last Path). Script and Dir: Jaan Kolberg. Phot: Rein Kotov. Players: Tarmo Koidla, Ants Ander, Diana Kokla, Raine Loo, Kiiri Tamm, Ene Rämmeld, Lembit Ulfsak, Luule Komissarov. Prod: Tallinnfilm Studios. *Comedy drama mixed with symbolism.*
Rahu tänav (Peace Avenue). Script: Toomas Kall. Dir: Roman Baskin. Phot: Ago Ruus. Players: Mikk Mikiver, Katrin Karisma, Jüri Järvet. Prod: Tallinnfilm Studios. *Intellectual drama.*
Armastuse lahinguväljad (Battlefield of Love). Script and Dir: Valentin Kuik. Phot: Ago Ruus. *Psychological drama.*
Võõrad inimesed (Strangers). Script: Maria Zvereva. Dir: Tõnis Kask. Phot: Enn Putnik. Players: Kaljo Kiisk, Raivo Trass, Ain Lutsep, Hendrik Toompere Jr. *Social drama.*
Noorelt õpitud (Taught Young). Script: Rein Saluri. Dir: Jüri Sillart. Phot: Mait Mäekivi. *Historical drama.*
Surmatants (Death Dance). Dir: Tõnu Virve. *Drama about the middle-ages.* Prod: Freyja Film.
Riigivanem (State Elder). Script and Dir: Mark Soosaar. *Historical documentary.*

Draakoni aasta (The Year of Dragon). Script, Dir and Phot: Andres Sööt. *Witty documentary about the absurdity of perestroika.*
Põgenemine (The Fleeing). Script: Jaak Lõhmus. Dir and Phot: Andres Sööt. *Historical documentary about emigration in 1944.*
Hitler & Stalin 1939. Script: Aigar Vahemetsa. Dir: Olva Neuland. *Montage film about two dictators.*
Kommunismi õppetunnid (Five Lesons about Communism). Script: Aigar Vahemetsa and Olav Neuland. Dir: Olav Neuland. *5-part montage film based on chronicles.*
Eine murul (Breakfast on the Grass). Script and Dir: Priit Pärn. *Animation.*
Hotell E (The Hotel E). Script and Dir: Priit Pärn. *Animation.*

Estonian Producers

Tallinnfilm
Harju 9
200105 Tallinn
Tel: (0142) 44 20 88
Fax: (0142) 44 37 61
Telex: 173213 KINO SU

Eesti Telefilm
Faehlmanni 12
200100 Tallinn
Tel: (0142) 43 46 50/43 41 57
Fax: (0142) 43 41 55
Telex: 173271 RADIO SU

Eesti Raklaamfilm
Raekoja plats 16

200001 Tallinn
Tel: (0142) 44 93 65
Fax: (0142) 44 43 41

Estofilm
Leningradi mnt 47
200107 Tallinn
Tel: (0142) 21 16 18

Eesti Kultuurfilm
Välja 29
200006 Tallinn
Tel: (0142) 55 28 58

Stuudio B
Sakala 3
200001 Tallinn
Tel: (0142) 69 13 74
Fax: (0142) 69 13 74

Freyja Film
Uus 3
200001 Tallinn
Tel: (0142) 60 27 95

ERF Video SP Maurum
Vana-Posti 2
200001 Tallinn
Tel: (0142) 44 14 20
Fax: (0142) 44 50 05

Telex: 173248 MURF SU

Eesti Video
Tartu mnt 4
200090 Tallinn
Tel: (0142) 43 13 59/43 27 77
Fax: (0142) 42 60 57
Telex: 173185 VIDEO SU

Eesti Infofilm
Pirita tee 76
200103 Tallinn
Tel: (0142) 42 18 08
Fax: (0142) 42 18 08
Telex: 173180 EIF SU

Estonian Distributors
Medium
Narva mnt 63
Tel: (0142) 42 57 10/42 59 30
Fax: (0142) 42 72 51

Useful Addresses

Ministry of Foreign Affairs
Lossi plats 1 A
200100 Tallinn
Tel: (0142) 44 32 66

Minstry of Cultural Affairs
Suur-Karja 23
200001 Tallinn
Tel: (0142) 44 50 77
Fax: (0142) 44 09 63

Estonian Filmmakers' Union
Uus Tänav 3
200101 Tallinn
Tel: (0142) 44 53 37
Fax: (0142) 60 14 23
Telex: 173213 KINO SU

Estonian Federation of Film
Societies
Sakala 3/16
200001 Tallinn
Tel: (0142) 44 15 12
Fax: (0142) 42 70 81

Pärnu International Visual
Anthropology Festival
P.O. Box 150 203600 Pärnu
Tel: (0144) 43 869
Telex: 173134 ESTO SU

Latvia

The origins of Latvian film-making can be traced back to 1910, when mainly chronicles and cultural films were made. The first Latvian silent movie, **Lācplēsis**, was made in 1929. Starting with 1940 film-making in Latvia took a radically reverse turn, becoming a mirror of the existing Socialist ideology.

During the past thirty years in this small (2.7 mil. people) country, a considerable production base has been developed. Riga Film Studios has produced about ten feature films a year recently, dozens of documentaries, educational and industrial films, as well as puppet films and animated cartoons.

The entire production system in Latvia has undergone major changes since April 1990. Now at the top of it there is the Latvian Film Corporation, Latvijas Kino, which will eventually be transformed into the Latvian Film Institute. The corporation includes three feature film studios, a documentary and animation studio as well as two advertisement studios. Apart from that there is a production service factory within the corporation. Independently from this system there exist Riga Videocentre, an Association of Film Clubs, the Latvian Film-makers' Union and a number of newly established, independent production companies.

Documentaries Make Big Impact

During the last decade the widest international acclaim among Latvian film productions has been gained by documentaries. Worldwide recognition has been given to the directors **Herz Frank** and **Juris Podnieks**, whose film **Is It Easy To Be Young?** (1987) was shown in most European countries and recently his series **Soviets** (1990), a film about the dramatic processes of "perestroika" in the crumbling U.S.S.R., made for British TV, was shown by many broadcasting companies throughout the whole world; and Ivars Seletskis, whose **Crossroad Street** was awarded the European Film Prize as the best documentary of 1990.

At the beginning of 1991 several documentaries were made about the dramatic situation in the Baltic states and the fight for restoration of their legitimate independence. Two Latvian directors, Andris Slapiņš and Gvido Zvaigzne, were gunned down while filming these events. However, the footage taken by them and their colleagues was aired by TV companies throughout the world.

Recent changes have also affected the production of feature films in Latvia. Yet, as usual, exact dates and years do not matter greatly. Two of the most impressive productions that have marked the turning point are **The Days of Man** (*Dni cheloveka*) and **Eve's Paradise Garden** (*Ievas paradīzes dārzs*), produced in 1989 and 1990. The mysterious and entangled love story between the beautiful flautist Eve and the illusionist Tom, played against the background of events in the pre-war independent Latvia State in 1939, is full of emotions and visions.

The Days of Man deals with Infanteev, who because of his mother's bossiness towards him in his young days has failed to love a woman who does not correspond to his "social level," so he cannot recover his balance even by middle age. Almost acutely real and fancied images of those two women

Dita Krenberga and Alvis Hermanis in *Eve's Paradise Garden*

keep hunting him all his life.

An important part in both these films is played by the visual imagery, the mood created by the skilful camerawork (in both cases) of Dāvis Sīmanis, one of the most experienced and masterful Latvian cinematographers. The whole visual set of **Eve's Paradise Garden** is a series of lush and elaborate paintings, while the prevalence of gloomy, bluish colouring in **The Days of Man** creates the feeling of doom and loneliness.

Riga Film Studios is famous in the Soviet Union for its police and detective films. The newly established company DEKRIM has tried to live up to this standard by producing **Depression** (*Depresija*), a psychological police film about depression not only as the mental hazard of an individual but of society as a whole and the evil it brings with it.

There are also good traditions in making children's films in Latvia. Some have earned international recognition at several film festivals, **Sprīdītis** by Gunāris Piesis.

Still from the first Latvian feature-length animated film, *Ness & Nessy*

His new production, **Maija and Paija** (*Maija un Paija*), based on a popular Latvian classic children's play by Anna Brigadere, was recently released.

The most important event for Latvian animators as well as numerous film fans in Latvia this year has been the release of the first feature-length animated, ecological fairy tale **Ness and Nessy** (*Ness un Nesija*), directed by Roze Stiebra and Ansis Bērziņš.

Now, as Latvia gathers its strength to develop its freedom and find a way out of its economic crisis, the old financial resources are exhausted and the future of Latvian film-making is in serious danger. The coming two or three years will show whether the creative and spritual potential of Latvian directors is strong enough to overcome these economical problems and retain film-making as a part of the national culture.

Dace Andžāne

Recent and Forthcoming Films

Features:

Dvēseles aizvējā (Sheltered Souls). Script: Valeryy Todorovskyy. Dir: Andris Rozenbergs. Phot: Miks Zvirbulis. Players: Valentina Telichkina, Girts Jakovlevs, Vladimir Menshove. Prod: Trīs.

Cilvēka bērns (The Child of Man). Script and Dir: Jānis Streičs. Phot: Harijs Kukels. Players: Andris Rudzinskis, Signe Dundure, Akvelīna Līvmane, Jānis Paukštello, Romualds Ancāns. Prod: TRīS.

Maija un Paija (Maija and Paija). Script: Lija Brīdaka. Dir: Gunārs Piesis. Phot: Mātiņš Kleins. Players: Elīna Silina, Ieva Saviča, Lilita

Ozolina, Hermanis Tihonovs, Elza Radzina, Inga Aizbalte. Prod: TRīS.

Mazās kaislības (Small Passions). Script: Andra Neiburga. Dir: Olegs Rozenbergs. Phot: Andris Seleckis. Players: Indra Brike, Rēzija Kalnina, Ingrīda Kilšauskaite, Vera Singajevska, Zane Eglīte, Sindija Rimša, Raimonds Bartašēvics, Andris Makovskis. Prod: ALKO.

Mērnieku laiki (The Time of the Land Surveyors). Script: Alvis Lapinš, based on the novel by Reinis & Matīss Kaudzītes. Dir: Varis Brasla. Phot: Alvis Mengots. Players: Voldemārs Zandbergs, Elita Dobulāne, Girts Jakovlevs, Mārtinš Vērdinš, Jānis Reinis, Juris Lisners and others. Prod: ALKO.

Rokenrols Baltijā (Rock'n'roll in the Baltics). Script and Dir: Igors Linga & Aigars Grauba. Phot: Andris Damburs. With groups: "Bix", "Foje", "UTV" (Lithuania); "Roovel Oobik", "Just knud Qvikstad", "Ultima Tuule" (Estonia); "Arhīvs", "Juans Mēness", "Linga", "Tango", "Ingus & Edīte" (Latvia). Prod: Latrek-film.

Sala (The Island). Script: Alexandra Sazonova. Dir: Una Celma. Phot: Uldis Millers. Players: Povilas Budzis, Sulev Luik, Ulle Kaljuste, Ingrīda Grass, Olga Mashnaya, Zigfrīds Muktupvels, Mārtinš, Vilsons and others. Prod: Laterk-film.

Simts jūdzes pa upi (A Hundred Miles Down the River). Script: Alexander Yurovsky, based on the novel by Alexander Grīns. Dir: Ēriks Lācis. Phot: Dāvis Sīmanis. Prod: ALKO.

Suns, kurš prata dziedāt (The Dog Who Could Sing). Script: Antolyy Kozak, based on the stories by Jack London. Dir: Ada Neretniece. Phot: Harijs Kukels. Players: Yuryy Chervotkin, Regīna Razuma, Andray Ilyin. Prod: ALKO.

Valsis mūža garumā (Waltzing through Life). Script: Dagnija Zigmonte. Dir: Dzidra Ritenberga. Phot: Gvido Skulte. Players: Astrīda Kairiša, Baiba Broka, Ints Jurjāns, Indra Brike, Anna Eižvertina, Juris Plavinš, Uva Seglina, Dainis Porgants and others. Prod: ALKO.

Vilkaču mantiniece (Heiress of the Werewolves). Script: Gunārs Cilinskis, based on the novel by Ilona Leimane. Dir: Gunārs Cilinskis, Phot: Miks Zvirbulis. Players: Zane Jančevska, Andreas Dvinianinov, Marga Tetere, Ēvalds Valters, Dace Everss, Gunārs Cliniskis, Antra Liedskalnina, Juris Strenga, Jānis Paukštell. Prod: ALKO.

Zirneklis (Spider). Script: Vladimirs Kaijaks.

Dir: Vasilyy Mass. Phot. Gvido Skulte. Prod: DEKRIM.

Documentaries:

Es esmu latvietis (I Am Latvian). Script: Imants Ziedonis, Ansis Epners. Dir: Ansis Epners. Phot: Kalvis Zalcmanis. Prod: Riga Documentary film Studios. 139 mins.

Latvijas prezidents (The President of Latvia). Script and Dir: Arvīds Krievs. Phot: Dāvis Sīmanis & Voldemārs Jemeljanovs. Prod: KAUPO S.I.A. 52 mins.

Saules pilsēta.La cita del sole (The Sun City). Script: Ilmārs Latkovskis & Romulads Pipars. Dir: Romualds Pipars. Phot: Olegs Kotovičs. Prod: Riga Documentary Film Studios. 56 mins.

Zolitūde (Solitude). Script: Tālivaldis Margēvičs. Phot and Dir: Ivars Seletskis. Prod: Riga Documentary Film Studios. 72 mins.

Animation:

Avārijas brigāde (The Rescue Team), Script: Māris Putninš. Dir: Jānis Cimmermanis. Anim: Māris Putninš. Prod: Animation Studios DAUKA. 10 mins.

Dialogi (Dialogues). Script and Dir: Rauls Sēnbergs. Anim: Uldis Auliks. Prod: Animation Studios DAUKA. 10 mins.

Spēle ar dzīvību (Life at Stake). Script and Dir: Arnolds Burovs, based on the poetry by Alexander Caks. Anim: Gedimins Kotello. Prod: Animation Studios DAUKA. 10 mins.

Rezgalības (Mischiefs). Script: Jānis Cimmermanis & Pēteris Trups, based on the comic strips by W. Busch. Dir: Jānis Cimmermanis. Anim: Māris Putninš. Prod: Animation Studios DAUKA. 10 mins.

Latvian Producers

Film Studio ALKO
3, Šmerla iela
226037 Riga
Tel: 0132/529–930

Film Studio DEKRIM
3, Šmerla iela
226037 Riga
Tel: 0132/520–025

Animation Studio DAUKA
3, Šmerla iela

226037 Riga
Tel: 0132/529–071
Telex: 161151 SHAR SU

Documentary Film Studios
3, Šmerla iela
226037 Riga
Tel: 0132/529–860

Film Studio KAUPO S.I.A.
3, Šmerla iela
226037 Riga
Tel: 0132/520–628; 551–234
Fax: 0132/520–701
Telex: 161116 SVT SU

**Advertisement Studio
LATREK-FILM**
3, Šmerla iela
226037 Riga
Tel: 0132/529–929

**Advertisement Studio
ORIENT**
3, Šmerla iela
226037 Riga
Tel: 0132/520–682

R. Pipars Production
15, Keguma iela, apt. 6
226006 Riga
Tel: 0132/529–805; 210–022
Fax: 0132/331–920 Riga Post
Latvia for N.725

Film Studio TRīS
3, Šmerla iela
226037 Riga
Tel: 0132/520–506; 529–977.

Distributor

MIRIGREM
3, Šmerla iela
226037 Riga
Tel: 0132/520–638; 520–840.

Useful Addresses

**European Documentary
Film Symposiums**
Contact: Latvian Film-makers
Union
85, Brīvbas iela
226250 Riga PDP
Tel: 0132/277–142

Fax: 0132/297–279
Telex: 161128

**International Centre for
New Cinema**
Peitavas str.4
P.O. Box 88
226047 Riga
Tel: 0132/210–114; 221–620
Fax: 0132/229–403
Telex: 161137 ARS SU

**The Latvian Film
Corporation**
(Latvijas Kino)
3, Šmerla iela
226037 Riga
Tel: 0132/520–411; 551–234
Fax: 0132/520–701
Telex: 161116 SVT SU.

Riga Video Centre
Mārstalu Str. 12
P.O. Box 541
226047 Riga
Tel: 0132/212–132
Fax: 0132/229–403
Telex: 161137 ARS SU.

Lithuania

No basis for a national cinema was created under the independent Republic of Lithuania (the years 1918–1940). Film production was limited to newsreels, documentaries, animated (puppet) films, as well as occasional feature films by individual enthusiasts.

In 1945, when Lithuania was reincorporated into the Soviet Union, it was given an ambiguous chance to develop the film industry. The Lithuanian Film Studio was established, and several pseudo-Lithuanian feature films, such as *Maryte* (1947) and *Dawn at the River Nemunas* (1953) were made by the Mosfilm and Lenfilm Studios.

Young people from Lithuania were offered the opportunity to study at the Cinema Institute in Moscow. Since 1956, feature films have been produced by Lithuanian artists on their own, although film financing, just like the system of film distribution, was strictly centralised. Therefore until recently it was impossible to produce a film from a script not approved by Moscow.

Despite difficult conditions, the Lithuanian film industry managed during the so-called Khrushchev thaw of the 1960's, to draw attention to itself thanks to high professional standards, originality and striving to show, if only by means of allusion, the dramatic history of the country and the problems it was facing. The novelette film *The Living Heroes* (1960, Dir. M. Giedrys, B. Bratkauskas, A. Žebriūnas and V. Žalakevicius) was awarded a prize at the Karlovy Vary Festival, and *The Last Day of the Holidays* (1964, dir. A. Žebriūnas) received prizes at the Locarno Festival and the Cannes Youth Film Festival. Vytautas Žalakevičius proved to be a gifted artist with his films *Adomas Wants To Be a Man* (1959), *The Chronicle of a Single Day* (1963) and *Nobody Wanted to Die* (1965). Žalakevicius then went to work at the Mosfilm Studio. *The Stairway to Heaven* (1966), dir. Raimondas Vabalas, was probably the most straightforward film of the period. It depicted the postwar Resistance movement in Lithuania, enabling the spectator to understand how the Lithuanian nation was forcefully divided. A more recent film *The Feelings* (1968, dir. A. Dausa and A. Grikevičius) met the disapproval of Soviet censors, although it received a warm welcome and was awarded a prize when it finally reached the San Remo Festival in 1975.

Darius Kazlauskas in *The Serpent's Look*

Fits and Starts

During the following two decades, as a result of inadequate production opportunities and the ever-growing ideological pressure, the Lithuanian film industry developed painfully, by fits and starts. The production rate, however, grew. If previously 1 to 2 feature films had been produced annually, the number grew to 5 to 6 during this period, including films made for TV. Documentaries (15 to 20 films a year) were rather favourably received, and so were the animated cartoons revived in mid-1980's.

The initial stage of Lithuanian filmmaking was marked by a tendency towards gloomy, ponderous psychological drama on the one hand, and poetical sketches represented by the films of directors like A. Žebruīnas and A. Araminas on the other.

During the more recent period attempts were made to widen the range of genres and to create Lithuanian detective film (*Near the Boundary*, 1973, dir. R. Vabalas), historical film (*Herkus Mantas*, 1972, dir. M. Giedrys) and musical (*The Devil's Bride*, 1974, dir. A. Žebriūnas). The most interesting plans, however, fell foul of centalised management. Great harm has been done to Lithuanian cinema by Moscow's so-called "social orders" from the central TV of the Soviet Union, which on the pretext of the western aspects of Lithuania and non-Russian appearance of Lithuanian actors used to order screen versions of works by such Western authors as Jack London, Theodore Dreiser, G.K. Chesterton, Irwin Shaw and O'Henry.

Recently several producers of a younger generation have proved to be quite skilled, and more original films have been made which are not readily ascribable to a particular film genre. **Yesterday and Ever** (1984), directed by Gytis Lukšas, who drew attention to himself with his subtle film novelettes as far back as the 1970's, intertwines folklore, music, feature and television films. This film, shot on the eve of the Lithuanian national revival, deeply impressed all kinds of audiences, stimulating the spirit of national solidarity. **To the Memory of the Day Passed** (1989), the debut of Šarūnas Bartas, a young director, which occupies a place somewhere between a feature film and a documentary, can be best described as a philosophical novelette. Jonas Vaitkus, one of the most famous producers of the present-day Lithuanian Drama Theatre, deliberately makes use of theatrical influences. His films, **The Zodiac of M.K. Čiurlionis** (1984), **Don Juan** (1988), based on Mozart's opera, **Waking Up** (1989) and **A Thrush, a Green Bird** (1990), impress with their associations between cinema and theatre, abstract plastics and music.

Algimantas Puipa has been fruitfully producing traditional films. His best works, such as the poetically stylised **The Devil's Seed** (1979), **The Woman and Her Four Men** (1983), **The Eternal Light** (1988) and **The Ticket to Taj Mahal** (1990), blending humour and bitterness, analyse the past and the more recent history of Lit-

huania. Films by A. Puipa have not yet reached the world's commercial markets, but they are often shown at various international film festivals. **The Eternal Light** took the Grand Prix at the San Remo Festival in 1990. At present A. Puipa is making an impressionistic film about the eccentrics of the Lithuanian countryside. His previous film **The Ticket to Taj Majal** was financed by the Kazakhstan Film Studio, which is paradoxical, since the problems dealt with in the film are purely Lithuanian.

Since March 11, 1990 . . .

The old cinema structures in Lithuania have broken down, and new ones are still in the process of gestation and so the time that has passed since the declaration of Lithuanian independence (March 11, 1990), has been a period of great trials. The Lithuanian Film Studio has broken up into several independent studios (including those for documentaries and animated cartoons), new film companies are being set up, which face such problems as those of financing and profitability hitherto unheard of. The government of the Lithuanian Republic offers to support documentaries and animated cartoons, as well as to create film-making opportunities for some of the young people now studying film-making in Tbilisi, in the Republic of Georgia, and Vilnius.

Saulius Macaitis

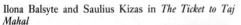

Ilona Balsyte and Saulius Kizas in *The Ticket to Taj Mahal*

Recent and Forthcoming Films

The Serpent's Look. Script: Saulius Tomas Kondrotas. Dir: Gytis Lukšas. Players: Darius Kazluskas, Vytautas Petkevičius, Algirdas Surna, Gediminas Karka, Eglė Gabrėnaitė. Prod: ARS. *A philosophical tale about evil in human beings. The action takes place in the picturesque surroundings of Nineteenth-century Lithuania.*
The Ticket to Taj Mahal. Script: Rimantas Šavelis, Dir: Algimantas Puipa. Players: Saulius Kizas, Ilona Balsytė, Nijolė Narmonaitė, Kostas

Smoriginas, Povilas Stankus. Prod: KATARSIS. *A peasant recoils from the Stalin terror raging in postwar Lithuania.*

The Children from Hotel America. Script: Maciej Dryg, Dir: Raimundas Banionis. Players: Augustas Šavelis, Gabija Jaraminaitė, Jurga Kaščiukaitė, Gediminas Karka, Linas Paugis. Prod: LKS. *A new Lithuanian generation, protesting against attempts to take away personal freedom, is maturing in Kaunas.*

A Thrush, a Green Bird. Script: Sigitas Geda and Jonas Vaitkus. Dir: Jonas Vaitkus. Music: Osvaldas Balakauskas. Players: Povilas Budrys, Virginija Kelmelyte. Prod: ARS. *A metaphorical musical about the tragedy that befell the Lithuanian people.*

At Sunset. Script and Dir: Šarūnas Bartas. Players: Yekaterina Golubeva, Rima Latypova, Arūnas Sakalauskas, Audrius Stonys, Vaclovas Bartkevičius. Prod: KINEMA. *A story of lonely young people, taking place in the surroundings of decaying Koenigsberg.*

Useful Addresses

Lithuanian Film Studio
Nemencines 4
232016 Vilnius
Tel: (0122) 76 34 44,
(0122) 76 42 54
Fax: (0122) 22 74 74
Telex: 261168 MUZA SU.

Ministry of Culture and Education
Volano 2/7
232691 Vilnius
Tel: 61 94 86, 61 60 05
Fax: 623120
Telex: 261168 MUZA SU

Lithuanian Film-makers' Union
Kalvariju 1
232005 Vilnius
Tel: 73 12 04, 73 12 11

(*continued from page 356*)

Tel: (71) 734 7470
Fax: (71) 734 7477

The Other Cinema
79 Wardour Street
London W1V 3TH
Tel: (71) 734 8508

Premier Releasing
Room 522
Premier House
77 Oxford Street
Tel: (71) 493 0440

Virgin Vision
Atlantic House
1 Rockley Road
London W14 0DL
Tel: (81) 746 2122
Fax: (81) 967 1360/1

Useful Addresses

British Academy of Film and Television Arts

(BAFTA)
195 Piccadilly
London W1V 9LG
Tel: (71) 734 0022
Fax: (71) 734 1792

British Board of Film Classification (BBFC)
3 Soho Square
London W1V 5DE
Tel: (71) 439 7961
Fax: (71) 287 0141

British Actors Equity
8 Harley Street
London W1N 2AB
Tel: (71) 636 6367
Fax: (71) 580 0970

British Screen
38–39 Oxford Street
London W1R 1RE
Tel: (71) 434 0291
Fax: (71) 434 9933

Cinematograph Exhibitors' Association (CEA)

72–73 Dean Street
London W1V 6HQ
Tel: (71) 734 9551
Fax: (71) 734 6147

Directors' Guild of Great Britain
Lyndhurst Road
London NW3 5NG
Tel: (71) 734 7470
Fax: (71) 734 7477

Independent Programme Producers' Association (IPPA)
50–51 Berwick Street
Lodnon W1A 4RD
Tel: (71) 439 7034
Fax: (71) 494 2700

The Producers' Association
162–170 Wardour Street
London W1V 4LA
Tel: (71) 437 7700
Faxs: (71) 734 4564

VENEZUELA
by Paul Lenti

Venezuelan film-makers saw signs of a recovering economy when the country received a major boost following Iraq's invasion of Kuwait, which sent world oil prices soaring. With international demand up, the government created a special offshore fund for excess oil earnings, which by the end of the Gulf War had grown to US $1.2 billion. Film-makers hope that this influx of capital, coupled with more available cash as a result of the government's restructuring of the foreign debt, will allow them to recapture the heyday of the mid-1980's, when annual national production was up to almost 20 features.

Burdened with a US $29 billion foreign debt (due to the oil glut of the 1980's) – Latin America's fourth highest – the country has been forced to devalue the *bolivar* drastically over the past eight years (from 4.3 to about 58 x US $1). This has taken its toll on national film-makers, who must depend heavily on imports of equipment. In addition, the preferential exchange rate – where distributors paid foreign remittances at a lower ratio – was dissolved in 1989, making distributors more selective with new films they bring into the country.

Beside the boost in oil revenues, the government had undertaken various measures to turn the economy around and diversify production. Venezuela's Gross National Product growth for first quarter of 1991 saw an increase to 10.5%, compared to only 0.5% for the first quarter of 1990, reversing the severe depression of 1989 which sent rioters into the streets of the capital, leaving around 300 dead. According to the planning ministry, the year's overall growth for 1991 is expected to come in at 7%. Inflation has also fallen from a record 81% in 1989 to only 35% in 1990, which remained stable last year. And, in December 1990, the government signed an agreement slashing the debt service on foreign loans virtually in half – using 30-year bonds – which means more available cash. Under this new agreement, Venezuela will also receive US$1.2 billion in fresh loans.

Restructuring and Consolidating

Over the past two years, the state production agency Foncine (Fondo De Fomento Cinematográfico de Venezuela) has developed a blueprint for restructuring and consolidating domestic cinema into a national industry. It has also taken a leading role in unifying Latin cinema through legislation to establish a Latin America common market for films and ease of co-production restrictions between Spanish-speaking countries. To achieve this, Foncine hosted the Conference of Ibero-American Cinema Authorities (Conferencia de Autoridades Cinematográfica Iberoamericana) in July 1991, which brought together representatives from 13 countries, with Canada, Martinique and Chile acting as observers.

The C.A.C.I. is a continuation of the Foro Iberoamericano de Integración Cinematográfica (Ibero-American Cinema Integration Forum), held in Caracas in November 1989. The purpose of both meetings was to develop strategies unifying production and distribution measures throughout Latin America in an effort to amplify natural markets of films in Spanish and Portuguese speaking countries. Also, protectionist measures found in some national legislations currently impede co-production with other Latin countries. Documents establishing a common market – in which Latino films pass freely between signatory countries – and promoting co-production between nations were signed by representatives from a dozen countries. (At the 1991 Cartagena Film Festival in March, Venezuela further signed a co-production agreement with Colombia and Mexico to spark such collaborative works.) And through the Mecla (Mercado de Cine Latinoamericano), Venezuela and other Latin American film bodies have been able to attend the major world film markets collectively to sell film and video product.

Marau Robelo (left) stars in *Joligud* (phonetic spelling for Hollywood!), directed by Maracaibo-based Augusto Pradelli

As for business at home, Foncine president Julio Sosa Pietri notes Venezuela is attempting to recapture a steady level of film production, which had fallen drastically in recent years. Plans to create a National Film Institute, as part of a major National Cinema Law, are currently before Congress and by press time were awaiting national debate. The preliminary document – Ante-Proyecto de Ley de Cinematografía Nacional – was introduced in June at the Congreso de la República by Chamber of Deputies president Luis Enrique Oberto, representing various film-related entities that included the Venezuelan Chamber of Feature-Film Products (CAVEPROL); the Venezuelan Association of Film Writers (ANAC); the Radio, TV and Cinema Workers Union; the Venezuelan Chamber of the Film and Video Industry; and Foncine.

The National Film Law is an attempt to consolidate the various film-related companies into an industry. It is composed of four main points:

1. To establish the state's acknowledgement of a responsibility for domestic production as an expression of national culture. This would give the government the responsibility to protect all sectors of the industry: production, distribution and exhibition.

2. To stabilise the diverse sectors of the industry – laboratories, distributors, publicity, exhibitors, etc. – which is important for the economic growth of the industry as a whole.

3. To create a National Film Institute, one in which Foncine could be incorporated into its production section. The institute would supervise and co-ordinate all film-related activity. It would also promote Venezuelan locations for foreign companies and attract co-productions with Venezuelan companies. (If a foreign company currently wishes to film in Venezuela, it must arrange everything through a multitude of people. A central office could reduce this to one person.)

4. To overhaul the tax structure concerning film. Through the creation of tax shelters, the private sector could be attracted to invest in production. Also, a new 10% tax on ticket sales could go to finance production. (This figure is similar to the exisiting 6.6% Foncine tax, but it would be shifted from the distributor to the consumer.) Municipal taxes on cinemas could be eliminated and duties levied on professional film-related imports could be reclassified and lowered.

Also, Swedish-born film-maker Solveig Hoogesteijn – maker of the acclaimed 1987 film *Macu, the Policeman's Wife* – was elected to head the film writers' association ANAC in May for the period 1991–93. Among future plans, she announced the association would push for passage of the national film law, work on making ANAC a self-financing group, promote national cinema both at home and abroad, enforce film/video-related copyright laws, participate in the production and marketing of domestic short films, and create an information bank of international film buyers and production companies.

Supportive Audiences

In contrast to most Latin American countries, Venezuelan film-goers have always supported their cinema. For example, while distributors released only 17 national features in 1985 (representing a mere 4% of all films distributed in the country), these movies managed to capture 17% of the gross revenues. Yet, Venezuela's relatively small population makes it virtually impossible for producers to recuperate investment with the national territory alone. According to Sosa Pietri, a national film must attract more than 1,000,000 people at domestic box-offices to break even, something which has been achieved by only two films in the last decade: *Macu, the Policeman's Wife* and *Homicidal Guilt*.

After the several-year lull in domestic production, Venezuelan film-makers have been busy with new projects – the majority in co-production with other countries. Ten new features were finished in 1990 and are currently in exhibition or awaiting national release. These are **Señora Bolero**, by Marilda Vera; **Rio Negro**, by Atahualpa Lichy; **Flaming Knives** (*Cuchillos de Fuego*), by Román Chalbaud; **Caracas Contact** (*Contacto en Caracas*), by Phillipe Toledano; **Tender is the Night** (*Tierna La noche*), by Leo Henriquez; **The Other Illusion** (*La otra ilusión*), by Roque Zambrano; **Hollywood** (*Joligud*), by Augusto Pradelli; **Among Blows and Boleros** (*Entre Golpes y Boleros*), by John Dickinson; **Jericó**, by Luis Alberto Lamata, and **The Bruzual Case** (*El caso Bruzual*), by Henry Ramos.

Last year eight further national films were produced or finished postproduction, including: **Terra Nova**, written and directed by Calógero Salvo and produced by Producciones Terra Nova, in co-production with the Italian company Cinelife S.R.L.; the Spanish Television (TVE) co-productions **Shoot To Kill** (*Disparen a Matar*), directed by Carlos Ozpúrua, **Heart in Shadows** (*Corazón en Tinieblas*) and **End of the Round** (*Fin de Round*); the French Venezuelan co-production **Full Moon** (*Luna Llena*), directed by Ana Cristina Henriquez; **Pounding on My Door** (*Golpes a mi puerta*), directed by Alejandro Saduna, a co-production with Argentina and England's Channel Four; **The Crystal Mountain** (*La Montaña de Cristal*), directed by Joaquin Cortez in co-production with the U.S. and Spain; and **A Dream in the Abyss** (*Un sueño en el abismo*), a first film by Oscar Lucién.

Also filmed in Venezuela in 1990–91 was the international feature **Latino Bar**, written and directed by Mexican director Paul Leduc, known for the 1985 biographical film *Frida*. The film is a co-production between the Film Department of the Universidad de los Andes (ULA), the Cuban Film Institute ICAIC and TVE.

Terra Nova

Script and Direction: Calógero Salvo. Photography: Giuseppe Tinelli. Editing: Mauro Bonanni. Music: José Vinicio Adames. Art Direction: Tania Manela. Players: Marisa Laurito, Antonio Banderas, Mini Lazo, Patrick Bauchau, Massimo Bonetti, Nathalia Martínez. Produced by Producciones Terra Nova, in co-production with the Italian company Cinelife S.R.L. 100 mins.

The second feature film by Cológero Salvo, *Terra Nova* is set in a rural Venezuelan town

Marisa Laurito and Mimi Lazo in *Terra Nova*

in the 1950's, and finds impetus in the friendship between two women, Rosetta, the matriarch of a humble Italian immigrant family, and Noemi, an aristocratic local landowner. This small personal story achieves an intensity within its handling of the themes of change and self-acceptance.

Filmed in both Italian and Spanish, the film's title refers to the new land, which offers those from the Old World an opportunity to find a better life. Haunted by the past, the immigrants are torn between returning to Italy or staying in the New World. All of the main characters find themselves at a turning point in their lives.

Actress Marison Laurito's earthy portrayal of Rosetta is reminiscent of Anna Magnani and her screen presence always maintains interest. The friendship with Noemi emerges as the two women come to represent two sources of power (family and society), becoming a metaphor for the challenges of self-acceptance and the consequences of self discovery that affect the other characters.

The small-town life is ably recreated and Salvo keeps the focus where it belongs, firmly on the characters. Also featured in the film is Spanish actor Antonio Banderas (a Pedro Almodóvar favourite) as the Italian son.

Paul Lenti

Jericó

Script and Direction: Luis Alberto Lamata. Photography: Andrés Agusti. Editing and Sound: Mario Nazoa. Music: Federico Gaitorno. Art Direction: Aureliano Alfonzo. Players: Cosme Cortázar, Francis Nueda, Alexander Milic, Doris Diaz. Produced by Thalia Producciones and Foncine. 90 mins.

Luis Alberto Lamata makes an impressive debut with his first feature film *Jericó*, which, coupled with next year's 500th anniversary of the discovery of America, should generate international interest through its revisionist view of the Spanish conquest of the New World, seen through the eyes of a Dominican friar. Its sensitive pro-Indian stance finds a parallel in such recent international ventures as Mexico's *Cabeza de Vaca* and the Oscar-winning *Dances with Wolves*.

The story chronicles the experiences of Fr. Santiago (Cosme Cortázar), who accompanies a group of Spanish *conquistadors* to the jungles of South America to bring God to the people. Instead of bringing about spiritual conversion, he is the one who is changed when confronted with egregious greed, meaningless slaughter and cannibalism among the "civilised" Spaniards. Later, when he is taken prisoner by indigenous people and lives among them, he encounters further challenges, including

Cosme Cortázar in *Jericó*, directed by Luis Alberto Lamata

contemplation of murder and temptations of the flesh among scantily clad villagers.

His faith is tried at every turn: his first attempt to say Mass finds the Indians at first curious before ignoring him completely. He is forcefully inducted into a cocaine ceremony, later shedding his habits and becoming a member of the tribe before he is eventually "rescued" by the Spaniards.

The film is fascinating both as an anthropological study and in its portrayal of the nobility of the Indians in comparison with the brutality of the Spaniards. Technically, the film is also stunning and Andrés Agusti's rich camerawork layers the movie in a patina that serves to recreate this lost world teeming with life.

Paul Lenti

PAUL LENTI is a freelance journalist specialising in Latin American cinema. In addition to working eight years as a film critic for The Mexico City News and eight years with the trade publication Variety, he more recently co-ordinated the film section of the 1990 and 1991 New York Festival Latino.

Recent and Forthcoming Films

Río Negro. Script: Atahualpa Lichy, Antonio Laneta, Joaquín González, Eduardo de Gregorio. Dir: Atahualpa Lichy. Phot: Mario Garcia Joya. Editing: Jacqueline Meppiel. Music: José Maria Vitier, Rafael Salazar, Sergio Vitier. Players: Angela Molina, Frank Ramírez, Daniel Alvarado, Javier Zapata. Prod: Yavita Films, Flack Film. 117 mins.

Cuchillos de Fuego (Flaming Knives). Script: Román Chalbaud, David Suárez, based on Chalbaud's play *Todo bicho de uña*. Dir: Román Chalbaud. Phot: José Maria Hermo. Music: Federico Ruiz. Players: Miguel Angel Landa, Marisela Berti, Gabriel Fernández, Javier Zapata. Prod: A Gente de Cine, in co-production with TVE (Spain). 93 mins.

Joligud (Hollywood). Script: Augusto Pradelli, Consuelo González, based on the book *Crónicas de el Saladillo* by Rutilio Ortega. Dir: Augusto Pradelli. Phot and Editing: Ricardo Rubio. Music: Daniel Castro. Players: Marau Robelo,

Fátima Colina, Vidal Figueroa, Gustavo Hidalgo, Héctor Peña, Juana Rivero. Prod: Kromática Producciones Audiovisuales. 90 mins.

Latino Bar. Script: Paul Leduc, José Joaquín Blanco, based on *Santa* by Federico Gamboa. Dir: Paul Leduc. Phot: José María Civit. Editing: Marisa Aguinaga. Music: Joan Albert Amargos. Players: Dolores Pedro, Roberto Sosa. Prod: ULA in co-production with the Cuban Film Institute (ICAIC). 80 mins.

Contacto en Caracas (Caracas Contact). Script: Philippe Madral. Dir: Philippe Toledano. Phot: Johnny Semeco. Editing: José Alcalde. Music: Miguel Angel Fuster. Players: Philippe Caroit, Ruddy Rodríguez, Pierre Dux, Herriete Lesser, Miguel Angel Landa. Prod: Producciones Tango Bravo, in co-production with the French company Les Films du Sabre. 90 mins.

Entre golpes y boleros (Between Blows and Boleros). Script: Rafael Alvarado. Dir: John Dickinson. Phot: Césare Jaworski. Editing: Luisa de la Villa, Carlos Briceño. Music: Eduardo Valls. Players: María Alejandra Martín, Vladimir Torres, William Mujica, Marcos Moreno. Prod: ULA and Foncine, in co-production with Channel Four (UK). 93 mins.

El Caso Bruzual (The Bruzual Case). Script: Germán Aponte, Ana Llorente, Manuel Manzano. Dir: Henry Romos. Phot: Jimmy Nasser. Editing: Cacho Briceño. Players: Corina Azopardo, Javier Vidal, Alberto Sunshine, Zamira Segura, Elias Martinello. Prod: Consuelo Delgado, Henry Ramos. 100 mins.

Señora Bolero. Script: Marilda Vera, Milagros Rodríguez, David Suárez. Dir: Marilda Vera. Phot: Hernán Toro. Music: Carlos Moréan. Players: Carlota Soca, Héctor Mayerston, Marcelo Romo. Prod: Cinematografía Macuto. 93 mins.

Tierna es la noche (Tender Is The Night). Script, Dir and Editing: Leonardo Henríquez. Phot: Césare Jaworski. Music: José Vinicio Adames. Players: Víctor Cuica, Constanza Giner, Diego Risquez. Prod: Producciones Post Meridian. 93 mins.

Sherlock Holmes en Caracas. Script and Dir: Juan Fresán. Phot: Ricardo Younis. Editing: José Garrido. Players: Juan Manuel Montesinos, Charles Ramos, Mirtha Chiana Uno, Antonio Ruiz. Prod: Big Ben Producciones. 90 mins.

Useful Addresses

Foncine (*Fondo de Fomento Cinematográfico de Venezuela*)
Edificio Centro Colgate, piso 2
Ala Sur.
Oficina 2.B. Los Ruices
Caracas 1071
Tel: (58–2) 238–1775, 238–1564
Fax: (58–2) 239–4786

Dirección de la Industria Cinematográfica
Av. Libertador
Edificio Nuevo
Centro Chacoa
Caracas
Tel: 32–4045

Ateneo de Caracas
Apdo. 662
Caracas 1010
Tel: 573–4622
Telex: 29316 ATENA VC

VIETNAM
by Fred Marshall

Pity the Vietnamese film-makers. For years they were obliged to tailor their work to attract government approval. And now that the government is allowing them relatively more artistic freedom, they are having difficulty finding theatres in which to screen their films. Ironically, the open-door policy which widened their artistic boundaries is also threatening to bankrupt their industry. The resultant flood of smuggled foreign videos is drawing audiences out of theatres into sidewalk cafés.

In the past, distributors received state subsidies, making it easier to show creative Vietnamese films. But official funding has recently been halved. A Vietnamese film can cost up to $20,000 for a single copy with distribution costs. The result is that it is hard to find a cinema showing a domestic film.

Directors admit that they still lack world-class equipment, and are far too dependent on Eastern European countries for raw materials. According to Vietnamese and foreign film critics, the pacing of local films is typically slow, more influenced by French than Russian styles and the subject matter is often psychological, exploring the suffering and moral dilemmas related to war and poverty and, occasionally, the corruption of government officials.

French co-productions dominated the scene in Vietnam this year, with three productions, budgeted at around $50 million, coming here to be shot on location, among them Pierre Schoendoerffer's *Dien Bien Phu*, Jean-Jacques Annaud's *L'amant*, and the spectacular *Indochina*, starring Catherine Deneuve. *L'amant* is based on the novel by Marguerite Duras, and is set in Saigon, among the rice paddies of Vietnam, where the author spent several years.

Schoendoerffer fought at Dien Bien Phu himself, and is using Donald Pleasence, as an American journalist, as a kind of filter for the traumatic experiences of the garrison at Dien Bien Phu. With a budget of $18 million, the director had to scout private collections for old tanks and aircraft.

In Hanoi, many trading companies appear to be flourishing, importing films from Hongkong and Taiwan. Subtitling is not necessary, and prints are easily obtained. With Western product out of reach financially, and domestic cinema going through hard times, the public has been occupied with Cantonese police and action adventures.

YUGOSLAVIA
by Maja Vlahović

When, last July, a long row of marines in white uniforms cheered or booed the films shown during the Yugoslav Film Festival in Pula, many people felt sorry for them. For they were among the rare visitors to the once crowded Roman Arena and they were freezing – the summer was unusually rainy. This time, as they take their seats (and they will – Pula is a garrison town) they are likely to be booed themselves. For the Western part of the country (Slovenia, Croatia) they represent the Yugoslav Army – the only weapon the Eastern Republic of Serbia still has for preserving Yugoslavia as it is. On the other hand, this concept of deliverance is indeed a narrow one: the 38-year-old Festival is about to cede its "Yugoslav" prefix to the nationalistic ambitions of the local Croatian regime. The Arena will host half a dozen American blockbusters, while "selected domestic films" will be shown in the Festival Hall, according to the new Godfather of the manifestation – the deputy Minister of Culture of Croatia.

What film-makers as well as politics-makers seem to forget is that politics need to be exorcised quickly from the films and from the Festival. For the last 45 years the measure of the quality of films was never the attendance in theatres, but rather the mood of the rulers (Tito, above all – the great movie fan himself, the lifelong patron of the Pula Festival). Last year, Goran Paskaljević withdrew his **Time of Miracles** from the Festival, because a member of his crew, a Serbian living in Croatia, was assaulted by "unknown perpetrators." Later, this pretentious, clumsily directed work became the Yugoslav candidate for both the Oscar and the Felix awards. (Strangely enough,

Paskaljević is the president of the Yugoslav Association of Film-makers.) it dwells on a worldwide trend of films inspired by the life of Jesus, only set in the times of the beginning of the Communist rule during the Second World War. It rehabilitates the religion vs. Communism struggle – an act of blasphemy when the project was conceived, but a perfectly fashionable approach by the time it hit the screens.

Bahrudin Bata Čengić, one of the ostracised auteurs of the "film noir" in the 1960's, finally masterminded his spendid return, using an all-Yugoslav crew, cast and money to render his version of the Communist Resistance movement. His expansive, beautifully shot **Unhearing Powder** owes his magnificence to Čengić's massive talent. His occasional stylistic anachronism is due to the fact that the production dinosaur once reserved for the "film red," but put out of business by the decline of Communism, couldn't but beget an out-of-date "film noir."

The darker the outlook for the country, the bigger projects the industry launches. Rajko Grlić's seventh feature **Čaruga** was finally shot thanks to the commercial success of a gastronomic video on Istrian cookery. This film, based on a true story of a pre-war bandit, a combination of Robin Hood and Bolshevik degenerate, boasts ten thousand extras, over fifty locations, even many original props from the 1920's. When first planned, it was supposed to be a homage to young Grlić's favourite adventure films like *The Thief of Bagdad*. Once the complicated financing was assembled and an all-Yugoslav cast in place, Grlić's fellow directors in Croatia begun disputing the choice of the topic – asking why should the Croatian motion picture industry finance a story of a Serbian bandit harassing pre-war Croatia? When screened, the film painfully resembled reality: groups of armed civilians in fact patrol through areas of Croatia mostly inhabited by Serbians; vigilantes from both sides, Serbian as well as Croatian, defy the authorities and engage in constant clashes – calmed only by the prompt presence of the Yugoslav Army. This nostalgic trip to Grlić's childhood full of local tales was overburdened with numerous victims of present-day Charugas.

Project off the Shelf

Pursuing his dream to put the unappealing half of the entire ordinary people on screen, Srdjan Karanović interviewed two thousand girls for the role of **Virgina**, a girl disguised as a boy in a patriarchal Yugoslav family during the war. On the shelf for eight years, this screenplay won a Europe-oriented French award and an appropriate sum with which to launch the project. The crew spent six months at work, mostly in areas occupied by the vigilantes. Karanović is writing down every predicament the project went through during the eight years. Knowing his obsession with his own experiences, it is safe to predict that *Virgina* will engender yet another Karanović film.

The Slovenian production in general reached European technical standards, while offering two artistically important films. Karpo Godina's **Artificial Paradise** traces the roots of Fritz Lang's lifelong inspiration with films to his Army days in Slovenia, where he met a Yugoslav film pioneer named Karl Grossman. **To the End and Beyond** by Jure Pervanje, a light-hearted comedy about an unorthodox brigand, establishes the scriptwriter Nebojša Pajkić as the only relevant professional (in the Hollywood sense of the word) from the 1980's, promising to dominate production in the 1990's (if any production in Yugoslavia should continue to exist at all).

Birth of Jugoexport

This year brought many novelties into the film business. Avala Film, once the biggest production company in Serbia, equipped with huge studios on the leafy outskirts of Belgrade, now belongs to the trading corporation Jugoexport, a conglomerate quite disinterested in the fate of its newest outlet. The similar Croatian company, Jadran Film, famous for its services for numerous foreign films and TV series, seems to be abandoning domestic production altogether.

The first private distributor (once a leading video pirate in Belgrade) is also the first copyright owner successfully to protect his investment in court. His skilled sense for the market has brought him considerable gain in a racket where state-owned firms either passively follow the path set by the U.S. majors in direct distribution deals – or quit. Exclusive deals with Gaumont in films and with Carolco in the video business have become the ventures of the year. This example set by private entrepreneurs may eventually disillusion Yugoslav film-makers who still think that the poorest-ever attendance figures for practically all domestic films is just some kind of mistake. A town that, ten years ago, bragged about half a million visitors to a contemporary comedy, couldn't even atract 2,000 people to a comparable film this year. Similarly, the "heavier" topic, Zoran Maširević's story on life on the Yugoslav-Hungarian border during the War, entitled **The Border** (*Granica*), but with the world limit also in mind, attracted 2,500 film fans in Belgrade. The time for normal, non-political films has come in Yugoslavia. Nothing will ever be the same in Yugoslav cinema. There remains just one question: will it survive the political gamble in which the whole country is at stake or will

MAJA VLAHOVIĆ is a journalist and radio and TV host of cultural programmes in Yugoslavia, and has co-written a feature film in production, Sixteen and Three-quarters.

next year's report consist of six separate stories?

[Note: this report was filed prior to the outbreak of civil war in Yugoslavia]

Sveto mesto (The Holy Place)

Script and Direction: Dorde Kadijević. Photography: Aleksandar Petković, Music: Lazar Ristovski, Sets: Ranko Maskareli, Costumes: Mirjana Ostojić, Players: Dragan Jovanović, Branka Pujić, Aleksandar Berček, Mira Banjac, Danilo Lazović, Radoš Bajić, Maja Sabljić, Predrag Miletić, Produced by Magna Plus, Beograd/RTV BGD, Beograd.

A young deacon, Toma, is summoned to read holy texts during the final rites for Katarina, the late daughter of a notorious nobleman Zupanski. But Katarina seems very much alive, ravishing and unforgettable. Alas, love is her eternal curse which she enjoys bestowing on mortals. On the third night, the graveyard chapel becomes the arena for their final match.

Based on 19th century Russian prose, seasoned with Serbian mythology, the film offers many layers of surprisingly smooth metaphysics. While maintaining the viewer's interest in the powerful story, Kadijević in fact discusses elusive notions like life, death, love, evil, time, and space. His lucid use of the conventions of the horror genre transposed to Serbian mythology and orthodox religion reveals an ingenious insight into this specific culture. Shot in nineteen days, this meticulously devised film creates a whole new genre – Kadijević's own brand of horror. In it, suave, silky demons appear sad and lonely, while naive, benevolent simpletons infuriate Fate. Although Kadijević refuses to depict the actual reality around us, his film is saturated with the decline of Županski's civilisation, the inevitable lack of perspective for his heroes and the hollow authority of the faith. It is by far the best piece of work this year.

The most wondrous side to it is that representatives of both invariably opposed streams in movie criticism have been praising it.

Maja Vlahović

Plastični Isus (Plastic Jesus)

Script and Direction: Lazar Stojanović. Photography: Branko Perak. Sound: Bata Pivnički, Marko Rodić. Players: Tomislav Gotovac, Svetlana Gligorijević, Vukica Dilas, Kristina Pribićević, Živojin Gligorijević, Melanija Bugarinović, Mida Stevanović. Production by Centar TRZ, Beograd Akademija za film, pozorište, radio 1 TV, Beograd.

Plastic Jesus was finally shown in 1990, nineteen years after it was made. Contrary to other "undesirable" examples of "film noir," simply set aside from the public eye, this film was officially banned, confiscated and kept in the Archives of the Security Service, while its author, Lazar Stojanović, served three years in prison and was prevented from working for two decades. The vague public idea about the film during that time was that it was "somehow against Tito,' more precisely that it compared Tito and Hitler. Up until some three years ago, that notion was intolerable to most Yugoslavs. Nowadays, it is, more or less, a general attitude. But it turned out that there's much more to this film than just the unmasking of a dictator.

The ideological layers in *Plastic Jesus* are so complex that any attempt to decipher them must immediately be disputed. The narrative line, about an offbeat guy, a film director from Zagreb (Croatia), using sex to secure semi-permanent lodging in Belgrade (Serbia) is combined with a lot of archive material about self-centred figures like Tito, Hitler, and Mussolini, mixed with great care for cinematic values and a style influenced by American underground films, a little Godard and plenty of talent. The

Still from the recently unshelved *Plastic Jesus*

result is an amazingly modern piece of work, indebted of course to its post '68 context, but much wider in scope than any Makavejev or Žilnik work. Thus the case of a film school graduate, chosen to serve as a severe example to his internationally acclaimed (and therefore more immune) colleagues, acquires the proportions of a personal and a cultural tragedy.

Maja Vlahović

Recent and Forthcoming Films

Adam Ledolomac (Adam, The Icebreaker). Script: Duško Trifunović. Dir: Zlatko Lavanić. Phot: Karpo Godina. Players: Davor Dujmović, Mustafa Nadarević, Radmila Živković. Prod: Art Studio, Sarajevo.

Bel Epok (Belle Epoque). Script & Dir: Nikola Stojanović. Phot: Radoslav Vladić. Players: Davor Janjić, Vita Mavrić, Radmila Živković. Prod: TRZ Bosna.

Bolje od bekstva (Better than Escape). Script: Miroslav Lekić, Siniša Kovačević. Dir: Miroslav Lekić. Phot: Boris Gortinski. Players: Claire Beeckman, Žarko Laušević, Aleksandar Berček. Prod: FRZ Klapa 22, Beograd/Avala Film, Beograd/RTB/Magna Plus, Beograd.

Bračna putovanja (Marital Travels). Script: Jovan Marković, Ratko Orozović. Dir: Ratko Orozović. Phot: Dragan Resner. Players: Vicko Ruić, Velimir Živojinović, Spela Rozin. Prod: Forum, Sarajevo.

Čaruga (Charuga). Script: Ivan Kušan. Dir: Rajko Grlić. Players: Ivo Gregurević, Ena Begović, Petar Božović. Prod: Maestro Film, Zagreb/Viba Film, Ljubljana/HTV, Zagreb.

Divljač za odstrel (The Game To Be Killed). Script: Duško Rodev. Dir: Dimitrije Osmanli. Phot: Slobodan Stojkov. Players: Mirče Doneski, Katarina Kocevska, Kiro Popov, Vladimir Cvetljev. Prod: TV Skopje.

Dora (Dora). Script & Dir. Zvonimir Berković. Phot: Goran Trbuljak. Players: Alma Prica, Rade Serbedžija, Zdravka Krstulović. Prod: Croatia Film, Zagreb/HTV, Zagreb.

Dr No 2: Balkanska perestrojka (Dr No 2: A Balkan Perestroika). Script: Milan Šećerović, Vuk Babić. Dir: Vuk Babić. Phot: Mišo Samuilovski. Prod: Film I Ton, Beograd.

Duka Begović (Jukah Begovich). Script & Dir: Branko Schmidt. Phot: Goran Trbuljak. Players: Slobodan Ćustić, Asja Potoćnjak, Fabijan Šovagović. Prod: Zagreb Film, Zagreb/HTV, Zagreb.

Krhotine (Fragments). Script: Lada Kaštelan, Zrinko Ogresta. Dir: Zrinkr Ogresta. Phot: Davorin Gecl. Players: Filip Šovagović, Alma Prica, Slavko Juraga, Nada Subotić. Prod: Jadran Film, Zagreb/HTV, Zagreb.

Mala (Babe). Script: Radoslav Pavlović. Dir: Predrag Antonijević. Phot: Radoslav Vladić. Players: Mirjana Joković, Mirjana Karanović, Danilo Lazović. Prod: Beograd Film, Beograd.

Moj brat Aleksa (My Brother Aleksa). Script: Dorde Lebović, Josip Lešić. Dir: Aleksandar Jovdević. Phot: Mustafa Mustafić. Players: Branislav Lečić, Snežana Bogdanović, Alma Prica. Prod: Forum, Sarajevo/TV Sarajevo.

Noć u kući moje majke (A Night in My Mother's House). Script & Dir: Žarko Dragojević. Phot: Veselko Krčmar. Players: Igor Pervić, Zumreta Ibrahimović, Ljubiša Samardžić. Prod: Cinema design, Beograd.

Original falsifikata (Original Forgery). Script: Rade Radovanović. Dir: Dragan Kresoja. Phot: Predrag Popović. Players: Velimir Živojinović, Dragan Nikolić, Lazar Ristovski. Prod: Profil, Beograd/Avala Film, Beograd.

Praznik u Sarajevu (A Festive Day in Sarajevo). Idea: Hajrudin Krvavac. Script: Abdulah Sidran. Dir: Benjamin Fllipović. Phot: Tomislav Pinter. Players: Mustafa Nadarević, Slobodan Ćustić, Mirsad Tuka. Prod: Forum, Sarajevo.

Siva Zona (The Grey Zone). Dir: Snježana Tribuson. Prod: Marjan Film, Split.

Srčna dama (The Queen of Hearts). Script:

Jože Dolmark, Stojan Pelko. Dir: Boris Jurjaše-
vić. Phot: Zoran Hochstätter. Players: Svetozar
Cvetković, Ivana Kreft, Natalie Devaux. Prod:
E-MOTION FILM, Ljubljana/Viba Film,
Ljubljana.
Ukleti brod (The Cursed Ship). Script: Živko
Nikolić, Dragan Nikolić. Dir: Živko Nikolić.
Prod: Jugoslavija Film, Beograd/NHK, Tokio.
Virgina (Virgina). Script & Dir: Srdan Karano-
vić. Phot: Slobodan Trninić. Players: Miodrag
Krivokapić, Ina Gogalova, Marta Keler. Prod:
Centar Film, Beograd/Maestro Film, Zagreb/
Constellation Production, Paris/RTB, Beograd.
Istočno od Istoka (East of East) – *an omnibus*:
1. *Ružina osveta (The Vengeance of the Rose)*

Script & Dir: Aleš Kurt. Phot: Dušan Joksimo-
vić. Players: Slobodan Čustić, Saša Petrović,
Davor Dujmović. Prod: Film I Ton, Beograd/
Sutjeska Film, Sarajevo/TV Sarajevo.
2. *Raketa (A Rocket)*. Script: Ivana Momčilović.
Dir: Slobodan Skerlić. Phot: Dušan Joksimović.
Players: Bogdan Diklić, Enver Petrovci. Prod:
Film I Ton, Beograd/RTB, Beograd. 3. *Kroz
prašume Južne Amerike (Through the Jungles of
South America)*. Script & Dir: Marko Marinković.
Phot: Dušan Jokslmović. Players: Vladica Mi-
losavljević, Dušanka Stojanović, Dubravko Jo-
vanović. Prod: Film I Ton, Beograd/RTB,
Beograd.

Useful Addresses

Institut za Film
Cika Ljubina 15
11000 Beograd
Tel: (11) 62 51 31
Fax: (11) 62 41 31

Jadran Film
Oporovecka 12
41040 Zagreb

Tel: (41) 25 12 22
Fax: (41) 25 13 94

Avala Film
Kneza Viseslava 88
11000 Beograd
Tel: (11) 55 94 55
Fax: (11) 55 94 74

Maestro Film
P.O. Box 40
41020 Zagreb
Tel: (41) 52 30 11
Fax: (41) 52 42 43

Emotion Film
Kersnikova 4/IV
61000 Ljubljana
Tel: (61) 31 96 62

Guide to International Locations

As film production becomes increasingly cosmopolitan in its topography, the art of selecting (and marketing) locations is taking on considerable significance. We offer herewith a succinct guide to regions that welcome film and TV productions, and (for those responding to our questionnaire) details of climate, access, local union regulations etc. More general information may be obtained from the Association of Film Commissioners International, c/o Utah Film Commission, 324 South State Street, Suite 230, Salt Lake City, UT 84111.

AUSTRALIA
New South Wales

Diverse region encompassing the famous beaches and coastal areas of Australia, farming lands with vast sheep and cattle herds, desert regions (e.g. Broken Hill), vineyards, rain forests, open-cut-mines, and green-belt suburban areas. The capital, Sydney, has a population of 5 million.

Climate: average temperatures in Sydney in December through March are around 22 C; these drop to around 12 C in June and July. Snowfalls on the high mountains and plateau, June to August.

Access: Sydney airport (Mascot) is main entry point.

Labour Factors: actors covered by Actors Equity awards, and crews work under ATAEA Union awards (700 skilled freelance crew available in Sydney region).

Information: NSW Film and Television Office, Level 2, 10 Quay Street, Haymarket, Sydney, NSW 2000. Tel: (02) 281.8711. Fax: (02) 281.8710.

Western Australia

Enormous state comprising spectacular national parks, rugged coastlines, forests, farmlands, "ghost towns" from goldrush days, and superb coral reefs.

Climate: Perth, the capital, enjoys 250 days of sunshine each year. Rain in the cooler winter months (May through August) in north and south, but minimal precipitation inland.

Access: Perth is a major airport.

Labour Factors: Actors Equity and ATAEA both have branch offices in Perth. Heads of departments are permitted to enter Australia for a foreign production being shot there. All foreign technicians must be members of an equivalent union in his/her own country.

Recent Shoots: *Wind, Clowning Around.*

Information: Western Australian Film Council, Suite 8, 336 Churchill Avenue, Subiaco, Perth, Western Australia 6008. Tel: (09) 382.2500. Fax: (09) 381.2848.

AUSTRIA

Spectacular yet intimate Alpine country, with rolling wooded hills as well as mountain peaks, from the flat land of the Puszta with Europe's only steppe lake, to glacier lakes as well as architecturally attractive towns and quaint villages.

Climate: summer days can be hot, but summer evenings are always cool. Winter snow lasts from late December through March in the valleys, from November through May at about 6000 ft, and becomes permanent above 8500 ft.

Access: Vienna and Salzburg.

Labour Factors: obtain information from ORF (Austrian TV), individual film companies, or Cine Austria.

Recent Shoots: *Red Heat, The Hotel New Hampshire, The Sound of Music.*

Information: Cine Austria, Gabriele Hlooz-Pohl Margaretenstrasse 1, A–1040 Vienna. Tel: (0222) 25 71 13/14. Fax: (0222) 257.1315.

BAHAMAS

Information: Bahamas Film Promotion Bureau, P.O. Box N 3701, Nassau. Tel: (809) 326.0635. Fax: (809) 328.0945.

CANADA
Nova Scotia

Abundant in historical associations, both French and English. The province contains some 50 museums as well as numerous converted sites still in commercial, residential and recreational use. Spectacular shorelines.
Climate: moderate conditions due to proximity of the Atlantic. Summer highs around 25 C, winter lows −6 to −13 C.
Access: Halifax International Airport.
Labour Factors: union and non-union labour available.
Recent Shoots: Little Kidnappers, The Midday Sun, The Bruce Curtis Story.
Information: Film Nova Scotia, P.O. Box 2287, Stn M, Halifax, Nova Scotia B3J 3C8. Tel: (902) 422.3402. Fax: (902) 424.0563.

Other Regions

Information: Ontario Film Development Corporation, 81 Wellesley Street East, Toronto, Ontario M4Y 1H6. Toronto Film Liaison, 18th floor, East Tower, City Hall, Toronto, Ontario M5H 2N2. Montreal Film Commission, 425 Place Jacques Cartier, Suite 300, Montreal, Quebec H2Y 3B1.

COSTA RICA

Ideal mix of location backdrops: beaches, mountains, jungle, deserts, volanoes, rapids, waterfalls, and plantations.
Climate: sunshine 6 A.M. to 6 P.M. daily. Rains late May through late October, but only a few hours each day. No snow.
Access: flights originate from Miami, Mexico City, New York, Los Angeles, New Orleans, Houston.
Labour Factors: supporting actors and extras available at very reasonable rates. Cameras and sound equipment not available in Costa Rica.
Information: Costa Rican Film Commission, 9000 West Sunset, Suite 1000, Los Angeles, CA 90069. Tel: (213) 271.5858. Fax: (213) 273.5566.

GERMANY
Bavaria/Munich

Largest German federal state in the south, known for its monasteries, castles, lakes, mountains and the historic city of Munich.
Climate: winter with snowfall, hot summers, beautiful autumns.
Access: Munich int'l airport.
Labour Factors: about 20,000 skilled personnel in the region. Mostly union members.
Recent Shoots: Last Exit to Brooklyn, Seven Minutes, Abraham's Gold.
Information: Film Information Office, Türkenstrasse 93, D–8000 Munich 40, F.R.G. Tel: (89) 38 19 04 30–31. Fax: (89) 38 19 04 26.

GREECE

Exquisite scenery for a vast variety of locations, most easily accessible by a short flight from Athens.
Access: Athens is a major airport.
Climate: The Attica region (in which Athens is located), the Peloponnese and southern islands conform to typical Mediterranean climate, meaning it is sunny and warm from mid-April to mid-October. Attica has the least rainfall of the regions of Greece. Farther north and inland conforms more to a continental climate with cool to cold winters. Northern mountain ranges, some an easy three hour drive from Athens, are covered in snow for two to three months of the winter.
Labour factors: Cinematographers and technical personnel have a solid reputation for fast, efficient, high-quality work.
Information: Greek Film Centre, 10 Panepistimiou, 106 71 Athens, Greece. Tel: 363 4586. Telex: 222614 GFC GR. Fax: (301) 361 4336.

IRELAND

The Emerald Isle offers a mixture of the idyllic and the dramatic: small, unspoiled villages set against sweeping green pastures and rugged coastline.

Climate: variable conditions, contact SIPTU with specific requests.
Access: Dublin and Shannon international airports are main points of entry.
Labour Factors: contact SIPTU (see below).
Recent Shoots: *The Field, Playboys, An Irish Story*.
Information: SIPTU, 29/30 Parnell Square, Dublin 1, Ireland. (Film and Broadcasting Branch).

ISRAEL

Long Mediterranean coastline, religiously charged region of the Galilee, Jerusalem, Bethlehem, Nazareth etc.
Climate: no rain from mid-April to mid-October, and a California style diet of sunshine for most areas.
Access: Tel Aviv, Jerusalem, Haifa etc.
Labour Factors: most manpower is non-union and multi lingual.
Recent Shoots: Iron Eagle, Delta Force 3, Rambo III.
Information: Ministry of Industry and Trade, P.O. Box 299, 94190 Jerusalem. Tel: (02) 210433, 210297. Fax: (02) 245110.

LUXEMBOURG

Mini-scale European nation with medieval towns, castles, and natural forests.
Climate: up to 200 hours of sunshine between March and September. Some snow in winter.
Access: Luxembourg int'l airport.
Labour Factors: non-union crews, limited selection of other types of film personnel.
Recent Shoots: The Saint, Dracula (the series), local feature films.

NEW ZEALAND

Information: Avalon Television Centre/National Film Unit, PO Box 31–444, Lower Hutt. Tel: (4) 6190.600. Fax: (4) 674.411. Contact: Marketing Director.

THAILAND

Information: Thailand Film Promotion Center, 599 Bumrung Muang Road, Bangkok 10100. Tel: (662) 223.4690. Fax: (662) 223.2568.

UNITED KINGDOM
England

A wide range of scenic locations throughout the country, emcompassing urban inner-cities, rolling countryside, national forests and national heritage. Many of the major cities (e.g. Liverpool, Birmingham) now have their own Film Office to deal with more specific inqiries.
Climate: unpredictable, but generally mild during summer and autumn months.
Access: Main international airports are Manchester, Birmingham and London (Heathrow and Gatwick). Other cities and areas easily accessible.
Labour Factors: actors covered by British Actors Equity, crews covered by BECTU/EETPU.
Recent Shoots: Robin Hood: Prince of Thieves, American Friends, The Garden, Riff-Raff.
Information: U.K. Film Commission, 31 West Heath Avenue, Golders Green, London NW11 7QJ, England.

Scotland

A rich, diverse country boasting some of the most spectacular countryside in Europe. Vast landscapes and seascapes, historical towns and castles, all within a relatively small geographical area.
Climate: as diverse as the scenery itself, with some snow cover on the Northern high ground during the winter months, with mild and moderate conditions during the long summer days.
Access: Glasgow and Edinburgh have international airports, ease of access to other points in Scotland.
Labour Factors: technicians must be BECTU members (an amalgam of BETA and ACCT), electricians EETPU members.
Recent Shoots: Hamlet, Venus Peter, Lorna Doone, The Year of the Comet.
Information: Scottish Screen Locations, Film House, 88 Lothian Road, Edinburgh EH3 9BZ, Scotland.

Wales

Breathtaking hillside and valley views, deserted beaches, Victoriana and fairytale castle locations all within a ten mile radius of Cardiff, the U.K.'s second media city.
Climate: up to 6.7 hours of sun in summer, but only 2 hours per day in winter.
Access, ease of access from U.K., two hours from London.
Labour Factors: EQUITY/BECTU/EETPU (see England and Scotland).
Recent Shoots: Morphine and Dolly Mixtures, A Kiss Before Dying.
Information: Cardiff-Media City, 33–35 Cathedral Road, Cardiff, CF1 9HB, Wales.

U.S.A.

Alabama

Information: Alabama Film office, 340 North Hull Street, Montgomery, AL 36120. Tel: (205) 242.4195. Fax: (205) 265.5078.

Alaska

Information: Alaska Film Office, 3601 C Street, Suite 700, Anchorage, AK 99503. Tel: (907) 562.4183. Fax: (907) 563.3575.

Arizona

Anyone familiar with John Ford's westerns will recognise one of Arizona's finest locations – Monument Valley. In addition, the state boasts the Grand Canyon, Montezuma's Castle, Sunset Crater, Sedona, and several national monuments.
Climate: the warm dry desert climate of the far West and Southwest portions of Arizona result in high temperatures, low humidity and sparse rainfall. An annual average of more than 200 clear days.
Access: Phoenix and Tucson.
Labour Factors: both union and non-union labour available (see Arizona Productions Services Directory).

Recent Shoots: Midnight Run, Back to the Future III, Young Guns II, Rambo III.
Information: Arizona Film Commission, 1700 West Washington Avenue, Phoenix, AZ 85007. Tel: (602) 542.5011. Fax: (602) 255.2146.

Arkansas

Information: Arkansas Motion Picture Development Office, 1 State Capitol Mall, Room 2C–200, Little Rock, AR 72201. Tel: (501) 682.7676. Fax: (501) 682.7691.

California

The world's most popular source of film locations. According to recent estimates, 60% of all U.S. films are shot in this state. Year-round sunshine, combined with mountain and desert landscapes as well as lush urban and coastal topography.
Climate: contact CFC with specific inquiries.
Access: dozens of major airports, with Los Angeles, San Francisco, and San Diego the favourite entry points.
Labour Factors: largest pool of union and non-union talent in the U.S.A. Permits for filming state-owned property are issued speedily and without undue formality.
Information: California Film Commission, 6922 Hollywood Boulevard, Suite 600, Hollywood, CA 90028. Tel: (213) 736.2465. Fax: (213) 736.3159.

Colorado

Information: Colorado Film Commission, Lisa Gilford, Director, 1625 Broadway, Suite 1975, Denver, Colorado 80202. Tel: (303) 572.5444. Fax: (303) 572 5099.

Connecticut

Enjoys four distinct seasons: a cool, colourful spring; a warm, green summer; an autumn filled with dazzling foliage; and a snow-covered winter. Connecticut is famed for its colonial villages, river valleys, and English-style rolling hills.
Climate: few extremes, and the relatively mild

weather is interrupted on average by only 12 days of temperatures above 90 F. Frosts occur from mid-October to mid-April.

Access: Bradley International Airport, 20 mins north of Hartford.

Labour Factors: all covered in the "Connecticut Production Manual," available on request.

Recent Shoots: *Jacknife, Mystic Pizza, Stanley & Iris, Other People's Money, Scenes from a Mall.*

Information: Connecticut Film Commission, 865 Brook Street, Rocky Hill, CT 06067. Tel: (203) 258.4301. Fax: (203) 563.4877.

Delaware

Information: Delaware Development Office, 99 Kings Highway, Dover, DE 19903. Tel: (302) 736.4271.

District of Columbia

Information: Mayor's Office of MP/TV, 1111 E Street Northwest, Suite 700, Washington, DC 20004. Tel: (202) 727.6600.

Florida

Sunshine state featuring marine locations (Gulf of Mexico, Atlantic seaboard), tranquil rivers and lakes, the exotic Everglades, as well as the urban charisma of Miami.

Climate: probably the best in the world for filming purposes, although temperatures soar during the summer months.

Labour Factors: producers can choose union, non-union or mixed crew at negotiated wages and benefits.

Recent shoots: over 17,000 TV commercials, almost 50 major features and TV projects.

Information: Motion Picture & Television Bureau, Division of Economic Development, 101 East Gaines Street, Tallahassee, Florida 32399–2000. Tel: (904) 487.1100. Fax: (904) 487.3014.

Georgia

Mountains, beaches, coastal islands, swamps, and undulating hills. Period towns, metropolitan areas and historical cities also located within the state.

Climate: quite mild winters, but quite high precipitation (dry periods occur mainly during the late summer and early autumn).

Access: primary hub is Atlanta, the world's second busiest airport.

Labour Factors: Georgia is a right-to-work state so both union and non-union technical talent are available. It is also a permit-free state.

Recent Shoots: *Driving Miss Daisy*, *Glory*, *Career Opportunities*, *Robocop 3*, *Free Jack*.

Information: Georgia Film and Videotape Office, 285 Peachtree Center Avenue, Marquis Two Tower, Suite 1000, Atlanta, GA 30303. Tel: (404) 656.3591. Fax: (404) 651.9063.

Hawaii

An exceptionally benevolent climate, and lush, exotic landscapes have made Hawaii one of the world's most popular film locations. Sandy beaches, steep ocean cliffs, volcanic terrain, and rain forests – all scattered over a comparatively small spread of islands.

Climate: the persistent pattern is a combination of cooling trade winds and equable temperatures throughout the year. Enormous range of rainfall, with the windward side of the islands being generally wetter then the leeward.

Access: Honolulu, Oahu.

Labour Factors: information available from local branches of IATSE, Screen Actors Guild, Screen Extras Guild etc.

Recent Shoots: *Father Damien*, *Wind*, *Picture Bride*.

Information: Film Industry Branch, P.O. Box 2359, Honolulu, Hawaii 96804. Tel: (808) 548.4535. Fax: (808) 548.2189.

Idaho

Information: Idaho Film Bureau, 700 West State Street, Boise, ID 83720. Tel: (208) 334.2470. Fax: (208) 334.2631.

Illinois

Information: Illinois Film Office, 100 West Randolph, Suite 3–400, Chicago, IL 60601. Tel: (312) 814.3600. Fax: (312) 814.6732.

Indiana

Information: Indiana Film Commission, Department of Commerce, 1 North Capitol, Indianapolis, IN 46204. Tel: (317) 232.8829. Fax (317) 232.4146.

Iowa

Information: Iowa Film Office, Department of Economic Development, 200 East Grand Avenue, Des Moines, IA 50309. Tel: (515) 242.4757. Fax: (515) 242.4859.

Kansas

Information: Kansas Film Commission, 400 West 8th Street, Topeka, KS 66603. Tel: (913) 296.4927. Fax: (913) 296.5055.

Kentucky

Information: Kentucky Film Commission, Berry Hill Mansion, Frankfort, KY 40601. Tel: (502) 564.3456. Fax: (502) 564.7588.

Louisana

Information: Louisiana Film Commission, P.O. Box 94361, Baton Rouge, LA 70804. Tel: (504) 342.8150.

Maine

Picturesque villages, rugged coastlines, and verdant countryside attest to Maine's New England heritage.

Climate: 83% of Maine days are sunny, although it is very much a four-season state.

Access: Bangor and Portland int'l airports.

Labour Factors: union, non-union, and mixed crews available in ample numbers.

Recent Shoots: *Stephen King's Graveyard Shift*, *Sarah, Plain and Tall*, *Signs of Life*.

Information: Maine Film Office, Station 59, 189 State Street, Augusta, ME 04333. Tel: (207) 289.5710. Fax: (207) 289.2861.

Maryland

Information: Maryland Film Commission, 217 East Redwood, Baltimore, MD 21202. Tel: (301) 333.6633. Fax: (301) 333.6643.

Massachusetts

The original New England imagery distinguishes Massachusetts, with elegant Boston only 3 hours distance from any location in the state. Wetlands, farmlands, coastlines, of every type and description, and everywhere the Pilgrim memories.

Climate: more than 50% chance of sunshine on every day of the year in Boston. Temperatures can climb to 100 F in the summer and dip as cold as –10 F in December and January.

Access: Boston's Logan Airport the main entry point (fog can be a problem in winter).

Labour Factors: many productions hire as much as 90% of their labour within the state. In 1989 and 1990 local labour crewed up to three full-scale motion picture projects shooting concurrently with local production.

Recent Shoots: *Mermaids, Glory, Once Around, Unsolved Mysteries*.

Information: Massachusetts Film Office, The Transportation Building, 10 Park Plaza, Suite 2310, Boston, MA 02116. Tel: (617) 973.8800. Fax: (617) 973.8810.

Michigan

Information: Michigan Film Office, P.O. Box 30107, Lansing, MI 48909. Tel: (517) 373.3456. Fax: (517) 373.3872.

Minnesota

Information: Minnesota Film Board, 401 North 3rd Street, Suite 460, Minneapolis, MN 55401. Tel: (612) 332.6493.

Mississippi

Information: Mississippi Film Office, 1200 Walter Sillers Building, Box 849, Jackson, MS 39205. Tel: (601) 359.3297. Fax: (601) 359.2832.

Missouri

Information: Missouri Film Commission, P.O. Box 118, Jefferson City, MO 65102. Tel: (314) 751.9050. Fax: (314) 634.5472.

Montana

Information: Montana Film Commission, 1424 Ninth Avenue, Helena, MT 59620. Tel: (406) 444.2654. Fax: (406) 444.2808.

Nebraska

Nebraska's geography features rolling hills, flat prairies, lakes and rivers, bluffs and rock formations and the vast Sandhills and Pine Ridge areas. Especially noted for its pioneer and agricultural heritage (Pony Express and Oregon Trail sites, for example).

Climate: well-defined seasons. Everything from spring blossoms, to sultry summers, to colourful autumns and blustery winters.

Access: Lincoln and Omaha have the state's largest airports.

Labour Factors: ample creative, technical, and support personnel available through the Film Office. Nebraska is a right-to-work state.

Recent Shoots: *Terms of Endearment, Home Fires Burning, The Indian Runner, O Pioneers!*

Information: Nebraska Film Office, P.O. Box 95143, Lincoln, NE 68509–4666. Tel: (402) 471.2593. Fax: (402) 471.3778.

Nevada

Information: Motion Picture & Television Development, McCarran International Airport, 2nd floor, Las Vegas, NV 89158. Tel: (702) 486.7150. Fax: (702) 486.7155.

New Jersey

New Jersey is by no means merely the backdoor to New York. There is the Victorian resort of Cape May, the Great Gorge ski resort area, Atlantic City, and the Meadowlands Sports Complex.

Climate: fairly even temperatures in the 70's F

throughout the summer months. New Jersey boasts few extremes of weather.

Access: Newark International Airport is expanding and increasing in importance with each passing year.

Labour Factors: skilled labour is readily available, and full details are included in the state's Production Services Directory.

Recent Shoots: *Presumed Innocent*, *She-Devil*, *Mortal Thoughts*, *A Kiss Before Dying*.

Information: New Jersey Motion Picture & Television Commission P.O. Box 47023, 153 Halsey Street, Newark, NJ 07101. Tel: (201) 648.6279. Fax: (201) 648.7350.

New Mexico

Topography ranges from the low desert to alpine mountains; there are state and national parks as well as historical sites, national forests, and wilderness areas. Wide diversity of architecture representing the Native American Indian, Spanish, and Anglo.

Climate: semi-arid with light precipitation, abundant sunshine and low relative humidity. 85% of New Mexico is over 4000 ft high.

Access: Albuquerque International Airport, centrally located in the state.

Labour Factors: large talent pool for print, commercial, TV and feature work. Film Commission publishes a business personnel directory.

Recent Shoots: *Twins*, *Indiana Jones and the Last Crusade*, *Lonesome Dove*, *Enid Is Sleeping*.

Information: New Mexico Film Commission, 1050 Old Pecos Trail, Santa Fe, NM 87503. Tel: (505) 827.7365. Fax: (505) 827.7369.

New York

Information: New York State Governor's Office for MP/TV Development, 1515 Broadway, New York, NY 10036. Tel: (212) 575.6570. Fax: (212) 840.7149.

North Carolina

Information: North Carolina Film Office, 430 North Salisbury Street, Raleigh, NC 27611. Tel: (919) 733.9900. Fax: (919) 733.0110.

North Dakota

Widely varied terrain across the state, with the Theodore Roosevelt National Park an outstanding location.

Climate: 2,800 hours of sunshine per year. Precipitation ranges from 13″ in the west to 20″ in the east. Generally low humidity.

Access: Bismarck, Fargo, Grand Forks and other cities.

Labour Factors: see Film and Video Services Directory, available through the Tourism Office (address below).

Recent Shoots: commercials and documentaries. No features.

Information: Tourism Promotion Division, Liberty Memorial Building, Bismarck, ND 58505. Tel: (701) 224.2525. Fax: (701) 223.3081.

Ohio

Information: Ohio Film Bureau, 77 South High Street, 28th floor, Columbus, OH 43266–0101. Tel: (614) 466.2284. Fax: (614) 644.1789.

Oklahoma

Information: Oklahoma Film Office, P.O. Box 26980, Oklahoma City, OK 72316–0980. Tel: (405) 841.5135. Fax: (405) 841.5199.

Oregon

Oregon has 400 miles of spectacular coastline on the Pacific, as well as 1,600 lakes, 4 mountain ranges, and Hell's Canyon, the deepest gorge in the world.

Climate: widely varied, with areas of minuscule rainfall and regions where wet weather is frequent. Sunshine also varies, with 20–25 days per month during the summer in most parts of the state.

Access: Portland int'l airport.

Labour Factors: both union and non-union personnel available.

Recent Shoots: *Drugstore Cowboy*, *Come See the Paradise*, *Breaking In*, *Kindergarten Cop*.

Information: Oregon Film Office, 775 Summer Street Northeast, Salem, OR 97310. Tel: (503) 373.1232. Fax: (503) 581.5115.

Pennsylvania

Information: Pennsylvania Film Bureau, Forum Building, Room 455, Harrisburg, PA 17120. Tel: (717) 783.3456. Fax: (717) 234.4560.

Puerto Rico

272 miles of beaches, 11 forest reserves, and Spanish Colonial relics in plenty.

Climate: Mostly sunny, with an average temperature of 77 F throughout the year.

Access: Luis Munoz Marin International Airport is the main point of entry.

Labour Factors: no unions that affect filming in Puerto Rico. Local talent is sufficient to supply an entire feature film production on location.

Recent Shoots: *Jacob's Ladder, Cat Chaser, Q & A, The Barry Seal Story, As The World Turns*.

Information: Puerto Rico Film Institute, P.O. Box 362350, San Juan, Puerto Rico 00936–2350. Tel: (809) 754 7110/758 474 (ext. 2250–2255). Fax: (809)764 1415.

Rhode Island

Information: Rhode Island Film Commission, 150 Benefit Street, Providence, RI 02903. Tel: (401) 277.3456. Fax: (401) 277.6046.

South Carolina

A state of three natural divisions: rolling mountains, unspoiled forests upstate; midlands region, more heavily populated; and the "Low Country" known for its subtropical beaches, marshes and historic cites and small towns. There are over 400,000 acres of lakes and some 45 State Parks in S.C.

Climate: 17.2 C (63 F) annual average temperature. Average of 11.41 daylight hours of sunshine/shooting time.

Access: Main air hubs are Columbia, Charleston, and the Greenville/Spartanburg area.

Labour Factors: S.C. is a right-to-work state and welcomes both union and non-union productions. Crews can be located within 24 hours by the Film Office.

Recent Shoots: *The Prince of Tides, Sleeping with the Enemy, Paradise*.

Information: South Carolina Film Office, P.O. Box 927, Columbia, SC 29201. Tel: (803) 737.0400. Fax: (803) 737.0418.

South Dakota

Information: South Dakota Film Commission, Capitol Lake Plaza, Pierre, SD 57501. Tel: (605) 773.3301. Fax: (605) 773.3256.

Tennessee

Information: Tennessee Film/Entertainment/Music Commission, 320 Sixth Avenue North, 7th floor, Nashville, TN 37219. Tel: (615) 741. 3456. Fax: (615) 741.5829.

Texas

Texas conatins two National Parks, a national seashore, 10 national wildlife refuges, four national forest, more than 100 State Parks, a biological preserve, and numerous historic sites and memorials.

Climate: sunshine throughout the state all-year round. Most years, winter only bites in January and February. Snow falls only in the High Plains.

Access: 1,276 airports function in Texas, with main hubs being Dallas-Fort Worth, Houston, San Antonio, Austin, and El Paso.

Labour Factors: Texas is a right-to-work state. The *Texas Production Manual* lists 653 individuals and companies providing film and video services.

Recent Shoots: *Dark Angel, Indiana Jones and the Last Crusade, Neurotic Cabaret*.

Information: Texas Film Commission, P.O. Box 12728, Austin, TX 78711. Tel: (512) 469.9111. Fax: (512) 473.2312.

Utah

No more spectacular state exists in the United States. Famed for its canyons, its exceptionally clear air, and its awesome buttes and outcrops.

Climate: mountain climate, with fine skiing at resorts like Park City, and scorching heat in the sandstone canyons.

Access: Salt Lake City, St. George (from Las Vegas).
Labour Factors: experienced union and non-union crew are available as well as skilled labour.
Recent Shoots: *Wait Until Spring, Bandini, Halloween V, Indiana Jones and the Last Crusade*.
Information: Utah Film Commission, 324 South State Street, Suite 230, Salt Lake City, UT 84111. Tel: (801) 538.8740. Fax: (801) 538.3396.

Virginia

Information: Virginia Film Office, P.O. Box 798, Richmond, Virginia 23206–0798. Tel: (804) 371.8204. Fax: (804) 786.1121.

Washington

Famous for the Cascade and Olympic mountain ranges, Seattle and its Space Needle, the ferry boats, the rain forests, and the rugged ocean coast. Plus mementoes of the Old West.
Climate: very little precipitation by comparison with regions at similar latitudes. There is plenty of sunshine during the summer months, and extended "sun breaks" during autumn and winter.
Access: Seattle is the major international airport.
Labour Factors: experienced pool of production personnel from cinematographers to property masters, plus fully-equipped sound stages, labs, and equipment,
Recent Shoots: *The Fabulous Baker Boys, Bird on a Wire, The Hunt for Red October, Twin Peaks*.
Information: Washington State Film & Video Office, 2001 Sixth Avenue, Suite 2700, Seattle, WA 98121. Tel: (206) 464.7148. Fax: (206) 464.7222.

West Virginia

Rich in Civil War and 19th century history. Harper's Ferry National Historical Park, New River Gorge National River, and Charleston, the state capital, are excellent locations.
Climate: four distinct seasonal changes.
Access: Charleston, Clarksburg, and Huntingdon.

Labour Factors: West Virginia publishes a production services directory on personnel, transportation, caterers, lodging etc.
Recent Shoots: *Matewan, Strangest Dreams*.
Information: West Virginia Film Industry Development Office, 2101 Washington Street E, Charleston, WV 25305. Tel: (304) 348.2286. Fax: (304) 348.0108.

Wisconsin

Known for its profusion of lakes (15,000+) and rivers, Wisconsin contains huge forests, prehistoric burial grounds, and a state capitol that resembles the one in Washington, D.C.
Climate: sunshine averages between 50% and 60% year round. Winter weather can begin in early November and last through to March, with most rivers and lakes in the north of the state frozen during this spell.
Access: Madison, Milwaukee, Green Bay.
Labour Factors: no special restrictions.
Information: Wisconsin Film Office, P.O. Box 7970, Madison WI 53707. Tel: (608) 267.3456. Fax: (608) 266.3403.

Wyoming

Contains some of the cinema's most memorable landmarks – Devil's Tower National Monument, Yellowstone and Grand Teton National Parks, Wind River Indian Reservation, South Pass City, Old Trail Town.
Climate: arid with four distinct seasons. Over 200 days of sunshine yearly. Snowfall heaviest in February and March.
Access: main hub cities are Cheyenne, Casper and Jackson.
Labour Factors: both union and non-union. Wyoming is a right-to-work state. Computer listing of talent and technicians throughout the state/region is available.
Recent Shoots: *Dances with Wolves*, Japanese documentary *The World Is Calling*, and not forgetting *Shane* and *Close Encounters of the Third Kind*.
Information: Wyoming Film Office, I–25 at College Drive, Cheyenne, WY 82002–0660. Tel: (307) 777.7777. Fax: (307) 777.6904.

TRIBUTE:
The Gothenburg Film Festival

The Gothenburg Film Festival is, in my opinion, one of the best things that has happened to film in Sweden in recent years. It has certainly been very heartening, both for me as a Swedish film critic and for the filmgoers in the city where I spend most of my time.

Gothenburg in January and February is a city which lies huddled up with its back to the rest of Sweden and its nose sticking out into the waters of the Skaggerak. Those familiar with the average temperature levels, windspeed and rainfall for this time of year will probably deem someone who praises an event which so flagrantly violates the norms of film festivals to be odd, if not downright eccentric.

It's something that I can understand. In principle, I agree with many of the other Swedish film critics that a really good film festival needs to have a plenitude of palms, a surfeit of sun and some fine films – and preferably in that order.

However, practice is more important than theory, so that I (and thousands of other Swedish film-lovers) have come to realise that the Gothenburg Film Festival is one of the best festivals in the world, and in these particular latitudes it is most definitely *the* very best. After all, when it comes down to it, it's the number of outstanding films, the vitality of the other activities and the participation of the general public which make a film festival. Now I am a fairly seasoned traveller, so you may believe me when I tell you that it is here that the Gothenburg Film Festival scores heavily over many of the festivals which are generally considered to be players in the first division, as it were.

The festival has yet to add waving palms and torrid heat to its attractions, but it has certainly affected the film climate: during the brief span of its existence it has been a major factor in transforming Gothenburg into the best town in Sweden as far as film is concerned. On average, each denizen of Gothenburg goes to the movies five times per annum, and with the passage of time the Gothenburgers have become more and more active and omnivorous film buffs. The festival has also become something of a dynamic force as far as film in Sweden is concerned, giving rise to activities and influencing policies which are having an ever-greater effect on the film situation in Sweden during the rest of the year.

Fifteenth Anniversary

To borrow a phrase which was once much used by the adherents of the New Wave in *Cahiers du Cinéma*, the Gothenburg Film Festival is "an axiom." This axiom is the basis of so much else in Sweden as far as film is concerned, that one might imagine that the festival shared that same brief span of eternity that has been allocated to the history of the entire Swedish Cinema. However, the year 1992 will be merely the

Klas Olofsson, Gunnar Carlsson, and Göran Bjelkendahl at the fourth Gothenburg Film Festival

Klaus Kinski, a guest at the first Gothenburg event

Andrej Smirnov at Gothenburg in 1989

Youssef Chahine and Tom Benson attending the second Gothenburg Film Festival

fifteenth anniversary. Indeed, the success of the festival was by no means guaranteed when it started and the doubters became ever more numerous and vocal the closer you got to Stockholm and the Swedish Film Institute.

It is doubtless the case in other countries where the population, mass media and cultural activities are concentrated in the capital, that anything which doesn't happen in, is described by or run by the capital and its inhabitants, can hardly be said to exist. In Gothenburg in the latter half of the 1970's however, two relatively young film enthusiasts. Göran Bjelkendal and Gunnar Carlsson, recognised that pitifully few of the multitude of marvellous films which they could see at international film festivals abroad were ever shown in Sweden. That was something they wanted to change. They wanted to organise at least one or two showings of these films in Sweden and preferably arrange for their distribution among Swedish cinemas, or, if all else failed, at least see to it that they were shown on national television. They thought they'd arrange a film festival in Gothenburg. They kept on saying this, while the people around them smiled condescendingly and the pundits shook their heads in disbelief: "A film festival? in Gothenburg?? They must be mad!" Nobody had ever heard of such a thing. Apparently the idea had simply never occurred to anybody before. Still, since they *were* mad, Bjelkendal and Carlsson persevered, and when the first Gothenburg Film Festival opened in 1979, the two of them were able to present a surprisingly sybaritic programme, although the number of screenings were few as yet and spread

The main venue, the Draken Cinema, for the Gothenburg Film Festival

over no more than a weekend or so.

The public response was so enthusiastic that in its second year the festival was one day longer, there were more films, and far more representatives from the industry and the mass-media attended. Film-makers with outstanding reputations, who were quite unknown in Sweden, came to add their lustre both to the occasion as a whole and to the screenings of their works. Among them was Youssef Chahine. When he left his home in Egypt it was 25 degrees and sunny, but the shock he doubtless felt at finding Sweden to be in the grip of winter was ameliorated by the warmth with which he was received by a delighted audience. Even after the festival had officially ended, extra screenings had to be arranged for the next day by public demand. The public got what they wanted, because giving the public what they want is the whole point of the Gothenburg Film Festival. As a result, delighted audiences have gaped at important films either neglected or waiting to be discovered, and people have turned up in such large numbers, (and with such evident interest) to see films which the TV and cinemas had largely ignored, that there has been a definite change in the sort of fare now offered on both the large and the small screen, and many films first shown at the festival have subsequently had a wider showing in the rest of Sweden.

Bertrand Tavernier attending the 1987 Gothenburg Festival

Audience Participation

The Gothenburg Film Festival has a cherished tradition of giving the public the opportunity to discuss a film with its creator, and audiences have leapt at this chance to participate. There is an immediate sense of dialogue, and from the well-filled auditorium can come an immediate response – or a distinct lack of one.

To return to the historical thread of our narrative: 33 films were screened at the third Gothenburg Film Festival to an audience that had once again doubled in size. Dennis Hopper turned up, not quite *Out of*

the Blue, and suddenly the Gothenburg Film Festival was no longer a matter which concerned merely Sweden's second city.

Since 1964, the Swedish Film Institute has bestowed an annual award known as "The Gold Bug" ("Guldbaggen" in Swedish). This insect is the Swedish equivalent of the Oscar, and the statuette's design is every bit as hideous as that of the American award. In 1981 the jury needed little persuasion to declare the Gothenburg Film Festival to be the winner one of the four Gold Bugs awarded that year. According to the citation: "The Gothenburg Film Festival has broadened the horizons of film in Sweden with enthusiasm and proficiency." This citation is even more appropriate

Teng Wenji and Zhow Li at the 1991 Gothenburg event

today when the festival offers around 300 screenings of approximately 100 feature films at five festival cinemas; when attendance figures continually break new records (68,000 tickets were sold at the fourteenth festival): when sideshows, seminars, guest visits and other activities proliferate; when one of national television's two channels has excellent in-depth reports on the festival almost every evening; and when the number of film critics from other Nordic countries who attend the festival will soon match the hordes of hacks who descend upon Gothenburg from all parts of Sweden.

Imposing Guest-List

Over the years I, my colleagues, and most important the general public, have been able to talk to Wim Wenders, Samuel Fuller, Med Hondo, Werner Herzog, Krzysztof Kieślowski and many other top film-makers from around the world. Many who came were subsequently discovered by filmgoers throughout Sweden: Scotland's Bill Forsyth, Pál Erdöss from Hungary, the Georgian Otar Iosselani, Bengal's Mrinal Sen, the Frenchman Patrice Leconte, and the Kaurismäki brothers from Finland – to mention but a few names from an imposing guest-list. The point being that at the Gothenburg Film Festival it is the film-maker who is centre stage, and this is something which critics in particular appreciate. This has been emphasised even more in recent years thanks to a popular event known as "Open Forum" which takes place every evening: directors, professional interviewers and ordinary members of the public have the chance to participate in in-depth discussions.

The main purpose of the Gothenburg Film Festival has been to safeguard the future of film in Sweden for an even broader public. We have begun to see some of the results of this policy, and several film-makers who are regularly featured at the festival have begun to find commercial outlets for their films, and for the first time, both Hou Hsiao-hsien and Emir Kusturica managed to find distributors for their works.

Gunnar Carlsson and his colleagues have also consciously striven to give contemporary films a personal and historical perspective. The festival has certainly been successful in this respect, and has screened several well-deserved and much appreciated retrospectives of Swedish and Nordic directors such as Vilgot Sjöman, Stig Björkman, Nils Malmros and Vibeke Løkkeberg. Unfortunately, their work is seldom seen nowadays, since the tradition of showing reruns at cinemas has all but died out.

Nordic Film Prize on Offer

From the very beginning the festival aimed to be a reflection of all corners of the film world. In recent years there have been more wide-ranging and thorough analyses of contemporary and national film cultures: there have been films from and about South Africa, Austrian film, Soviet film (several times and never unnecessarily!), and most recently France (11 films) and China (when several films received their first screening outside their country of origin). Nordic films and film-makers have been frequent and welcome visitors. This was important groundwork, since Nordic films have long been greeted with considerable (and often quite unjustified) scepticism by Swedish filmgoers. In recent years these ambitions have been strengthened in several ways: not only are there more films, but as part of the festival, the Gothenburg Post newspaper

Krzysztof Kieślowski visiting the Gothenburg Film Festival

The "Culture Boxing" contest at the Gothenburg Film Festival

Festival director Gunnar Carlsson greeting Mrinal Sen at Gothenburg in 1987

Fernando Rey and Vibeke Løkkeberg at Gothenburg in 1986

(GP) bestows the Nordic Film Prize, a sum of SEK 30,000 which is given to a deserving film-maker. In addition a jury composed of members of the public gives a smaller sum of money (donated by GP) to their favourite film among the many Nordic contributions.

There have been many other pleasant aspects to the festival in recent years. Of these, I would like to mention the seminars, which are often very stimulating. Most recently there were three international seminars which discussed the training which European film-makers receive, film concerts and "boxing matches" (which were much appreciated by the audience) between competent and loquacious combatants dealing with some pressing cultural question.

I don't want to make the list too long, so I'd like to conclude by touching on some sideshows or side-effects of the Gothenburg Film Festival. "The 90-minute 90s" is a Swedish relay race of short films at the rate of one new film annually. The aim of the series is to take the temperature of Sweden and the Swedes during the 1990's. Each new film is linked to its predecessors and the final result will be one long feature film. Everything is initially screened at the festival and then shown on TV. Roy Andersson, who had not made a feature film since *Giliap* in 1975 was first. 1992's rejoinder comes from Agneta Fågerström-Olsson, one of the best female directors in the country.

With contributions from both institutions, companies and private individuals, the Gothenburg Film Festival has invested SEK 100,000 in Sweden's largest ever script competition, which it has dubbed

Tony Huston, Louise Drake, and Fridrik Thór Fridriksson attending the Gothenburg Film Festival in 1988

"Script 92." Only original scripts may be submitted, and it is naturally hoped that "new and exciting Swedish scenarios" will be discovered. In the middle of the Fifteenth Gothenburg Film Festival, on February 10, 1992, the winner will be announced.

Cinematics is the name of the festival magazine, whose watchful editor is a gentleman by the name of Gunnar Bergdahl. It did not take long for it to become famous not only for its originality, (the most spectacular issue was circular and each one came enclosed in an old film canister), but also for its new ideas as far as the choice of articles and viewpoints is concerned. ·

Cinematics has also managed to issue the very first book about Stefan Jarl, who is one of the most prominent figures in Swedish documentary and socially-minded films. The book is called *Rebel in Reality* and is written by Mats Nilsson.

The Gothenburg Film Festival has established itself as a powerhouse in the world of Swedish film. The success of the festival has tempted other towns in Sweden, such as Umeå, Uppsala, Stockholm and Malmö to start their own festivals. This is perhaps a trifle confusing for foreign film-makers who don't know which Swedish film festival is the oldest, the biggest and the best. However, the Swedes know (though this doesn't mean that they belittle the value of the others or deny the need for them).

SVEN E. OLSSON

Sven E. Olsson, Mika Kaurismäki, and Marie-Louise Arvidsson at the 1987 Gothenburg gathering

Guide to Leading Festivals

Berlin

February 13–24, 1992

Berlin is generally recognised to be the most efficiently-organised of the world's major festivals, even if it is suffering from budget restrictions. The dramatic changes in Eastern Europe have added immense significance to the Berlinale, and the Film Market is prospering under Beki Probst. In addition to the competitive programme and information section, there is a Retrospective, screenings of all new German films, and of course the Forum of Young Cinema, directed by Ulrich Gregor, where many of the most imaginative films are screened. *Inquiries to*: Berlin International Film Festival, Budapester Strasse 50, 1000 Berlin 30. Tel: (30) 254890. Telex: 185255. Fax: (30) 25489249.

AWARDS 1991

Golden Bear (features): **House of Smiles** (Italy), Ferreri.

Silver Bear (Special Jury Prize); *(shared)* **The Judgement** (Italy), Bellocchio; **The Satan** (U.S.S.R.), Aristov.

Best Director: *(shared)* Ricky Tognazzi for **Ultra** (Italy); Jonathan Demme for **The Silence of the Lambs** (U.S.A.).

Best Actress: Victoria Abril for **Lovers** (Spain).

Best Actor: Maynard Eziashi for **Mr. Johnson** (U.K.).

Outstanding Single Achievement: Kevin Costner for **Dances with Wolves** (U.S.A.).

Golden Bear (shorts): **Six Point Nine** (U.S.A.), Bootzin.

FIPRESCI Prize: **Le petit criminel** (France), Doillon.

Cambridge

July 9–26, 1992

A film festival in this historic university town can call on considerable local and student interest, and now deserves ranking alongside London and Edinburgh as the best festival in the U.K. Now in its 16th year the event is non-competitive and screens both shorts and feature films often in the presence of directors and actors. *Inquiries to*: Tony Jones, Cambridge Film Festival, PO Box 17, Cambridge CB2 3PF, U.K. Tel: (223) 462666. Telex: 81574. Fax: (0223) 462555.

Cannes

May 7–18, 1992

Cannes remains the world's top festival, attracting the American studios and personalities as well as entries from the more obscure countries, although its avowed intention to move to October could be a disaster. Cannes includes three major sections: the Competition, the Directors' Fortnight, and the "Certain Regard" screenings. There is also the Critics' Week, and innumerable other useful screenings (e.g. the Australian, New Zealand and Scandinavian films). The great advantage of Cannes is that everyone of importance attends the event. *Inquiries to*: 71 rue du Faubourg Saint-Honoré, 75008 Paris, France. Tel: (1) 42 66 92 20. Telex: 650765. Fax: (1) 42 66 68 85. Marché International du Film: Fax: (1) 45 62 60 25.

AWARDS 1991

Palme d'Or: **Barton Fink** (U.S.A.), Coen.

Special Grand Prix du Jury: **La belle noiseuse** (France), Rivette.

Best Director: Joel and Ethan Coen for **Barton Fink** (U.S.A.).

Best Actor: John Turturro for **Barton Fink** (U.S.A.).

Best Actress: Irène Jacob for **The Double Life of Veronica** (Poland/France).

Best Supporting Performance: Samuel L. Jackson for **Jungle Fever** (U.S.A.).

Prix du Jury: *(shared)* **Europa** (Denmark/Germany), von Trier; **Hors la vie** (France), Bagdadi.

Caméra d'Or: **Toto the Hero** (Belgium), van Dormael.
FIPRESCI Awards: **The Double Life of Veronica** (Poland/France) Kieślowski *(official section)*; **Riff-Raff** (U.K.), Loach *(non-official section)*.

Clermont-Ferrand

January 31–February 8, 1992

The ideal destination for anyone who wants to explore around 200 of the best short films of the year, the volcanoes of the Auvergne, and the exquisite cuisine of the region. This competitive event has enhanced its reputation recently (38 countries in 1991) and has really displaced such former festivals as Tours and Lille. *Inquiries to:* Clermont-Ferrand Short Film Festival, 26 rue des Jacobins, 63000 Clermont-Ferrand, France. Tel: (33) 73 91 65 73. Fax: (33) 73 92 11 93.
MAIN AWARDS 1991
Days of Waiting (U.S.A.), Okazaki.

Den första kyssen (Sweden), Olsson.
Ilha das Flores (Brazil), Furtado.

Denver

October 1992

More than 85 film programmes from around the world make up the 15th Denver International Film Festival for eight days in October. New international features, documentaries, new American cinema and

15th Denver International Film Festival
October 15 - 22, 1992

ENQUIRIES TO:
Ron Henderson
Denver International Film Festival
P. O. Box 480044, Denver, CO 80248 USA

DENVER INTERNATIONAL
FILM·FESTIVAL   TELE: (303) 298 8223   FAX: (303) 298 0209

critic's programmes are screened and more than 40 directors are due to attend the event in Colorado's delightfully spacious and un-crowded capital. Denver is non-competitive, but presents two achievement awards. *Inquiries to*: DIFF, P.O. Box 480044, Denver, Colorado 80248, U.S.A. Tel: (303) 321 3456. Fax: (303) 298 0209.

Stichting Nederlandse Filmdagen, Hoogt 4, 3512 GW Utrecht, Holland. Tel: (31) 30 322684.

AWARDS 1990
Golden Calf (Best Film): **Evenings** (Netherlands), van den Berg.
Best Director: Frouke Fokkema for **Kracht**.
Best Actor: Thom Hoffman for **Evenings**.
Best Actress: Monique van de Ven for **Romeo**.
Special Jury Award: **Ava and Gabriel – A Love Story** (Caraçao), de Rooy.

Dutch Film Days
September 17–24, 1992

Now established as an important occasion during which the entire output of Dutch film-making may be assessed, in the attractive old town of Utrecht. All new Dutch features and shorts are screened and judged, and there is a Golden Calf award for the Best Film. A special programme is the Holland Film Meeting, the foreign section of the festival. Useful for festival directors, film buffs, distributors and critics, national and international. *Inquiries to*:

Edinburgh
August 15–30, 1992

One of the world's oldest film festivals now going through a period of adjustment and rejuvenation after director of eight years Jim Hickey stepped down following the 1988 event. British critic David Robinson took over the reigns in 1989 with virtually new staff, and is now succeeded by Penny Thomson. Emphasis on U.K. films and young directors, with particularly well-chosen retrospectives and seminars. *Inquiries to*:

12ᵉ Nederlandse Film Dagen

16 t/m 24 September 1992 Utrecht

Dutch Film Days

Annual screening of all new Dutch features, shorts, documentaries, animations and commercials.

Retrospectives, seminars, talkshows and the 'Cinema Militans-lecture'.

Grand Prix of the Dutch Cinema: the Golden Calf Awards.

Holland Film Meeting.

Please contact:
Dutch Film Days
Hoogt 4-10
3512 GW Utrecht
The Netherlands
Telephone 31 30 322684
Fax 31 30 313200

The Edinburgh International Film Festival, 88 Lothian Road, Edinburgh EH3 9BZ, Scotland. Tel: (31) 228 4051. Telex: 72166. Fax: (31) 229 5501.

Fajr International Film Festival

February 1–11, 1992

The Fajr festival has flourished as a competitive event and is now the leading Iranian film festival. Catering mainly for Iranian films, although screenings of international films are on the increase. The festival also plays host to foreign guests and industry figures. *Inquiries to*: Farhang Cinema, Dr. Shariati Ave., Gholhak, Tehran 19139, Iran. Tel: 265 086. Fax: 678 155.

Fantasporto

February 7–16, 1992

The Porto film festival specialises in science-fiction films, but in 1992 will be expanding to a second competitive section for young directors. Festival director Mario Dorminsky will also feature a retrospective of animation films from the 1980's, and another on Monty Python. Other sidebars include Jean-Claude Carrière's Buñuel films, another on Bertrand Tavernier, plus a retrospective of Dutch cinema. *Inquiries to*: Porto Film Festival, Rua Diogo Brandao 87, Porto 4000, Portugal. Tel: (3212) 320 759. Fax: (3212) 383 679.

FESTIVAL DES 3 CONTINENTS
NANTES 26 NOVEMBER- 3 DECEMBER 1991

ASIAN, AFRICAN, LATIN & BLACK AMERICAN CINEMATOGRAPHIES IN COMPETITIVE & NON COMPETITIVE SECTIONS

RETROSPECTIVE FROM ANDEAN CINEMA AND PANORAMA OF MALIAN CINEMA

Festival des 3 Continents

November 1992

This is the only annual competitive festival for films emerging solely from Africa, Asia, and black and Latin America. Since it began in 1979, the event has acquired international prestige as well as public following in the French town of Nantes. The retrospectives, devoted to such artists as Youssef Chahine, Nagisa Oshima, and Nelson Pereira dos Santos, are also significant. Essentially for those interested in both the culture and the society of the developing countries. In 1991 there were tributes to Andean Cinema, Lino Brocka, Satyajit Ray, and Seijun Suzuki. *Inquiries to*: Alain and Philippe Jalladeau, Director, Festival des 3 Continents, BP 3306, 44033 Nantes Cedex, France. Tel: (33) 40 69 74 14. Fax: (33) 40 73 55 22.

10th Fajr International Film Festival

TEHRAN 1—11 Feb. 1992

7TH INTERNATIONAL FESTIVAL OF FILMS FOR CHILDREN AND YOUNG ADULTS

ISFAHAN 6—12 Oct. 1991

Farhang Cinema,
Dr. Shariati Ave. Gholhak,
Tehran 19139 Iran

Tel.: 265086 - 267082
Telex: 214283 FCF IR
Fax: 678155

10°FESTIVAL INTERNAZIONALE CINEMA GIOVANI TORINO-ITALIA

10th TURIN INTERNATIONAL FILM FESTIVAL

NOVEMBER 13 - 21, 1992

OFFICIAL COMPETITION
Feature and short films

HORS CONCOURS SECTION

ITALIAN INDEPENDENTS

RETROSPECTIVE
American Independents of the Sixties

SPECIAL EVENTS

Recognized by the International Federation of Film Producers Associations

Festival Internazionale Cinema Giovani
Piazza San Carlo,161
10123 Torino, Italia
Phone (11) 5623309
Fax: (11) 5629796
Telex: 216803 FICG I

de Silva Associati

Festival de Genève

October 1992

Previously known as Stars de Demain, this festival dedicates itself to seeking out future talents in the film industry. A programme of seminars and debates led by professionals provide valuable contacts for younger, more inexperienced participants. *Inquiries to*: Promoguide SA, 2 rue Bovy-lysberg, Case postale 418, 1211 Geneva 11. Tel: (022) 21 54 66. Fax: (022) 21 98 62.

Festival International Nouveau Cinéma et de la Vidéo

October 1992

This long-established festival in Montréal seeks to discover and promote films of outstanding quality produced as an alternative to the conventions and commercialism of the established film industries. There is emphasis on the formal structure and experimental nature of filmmaking. Note the Québec Film and Video Market, held during the festival. *Inquiries to*: 3724 Boulevard Saint-Laurent, Montréal, Québec, Canada H2X 2V8. Telex: 5560074.

Festival Internazionale Cinema Giovani

November 13–21, 1992

This well-organised event takes place in Turin each autumn and focuses exclusively on films made by young directors. There is a competitive section for shorts, features and Italian independents, as well as a section for retrospectives. The festival aims to act as a forum where people discuss aspects of the film world reflecting youthful behaviour. *Inquiries to*: Festival Internazionale Cinema Giovani, Piazza San Carlo 161, 10123 Torino, Italy. Tel: (11) 547171. Telex: 216803. Fax: (11) 519796.

Filmfest München

June 27–July 4, 1992

Over the past nine years the Filmfest München has found its place among non-competitive festivals, with attendances of over 100,000. *Inquiries to*: Eberhard Hauff, Director, Internationale Münchner Filmwochen GmbH, Türkenstrasse 93, D–8000 Munich 40, Germany. Tel: (89) 3819040. Telex: 5214674. Fax: (89) 38190461.

Flanders-Ghent

October 9–19, 1992

The International Flanders Film Festival has been held in the Belgian city of Ghent for 18 years now, and takes as one of its main themes the use of Music in Film (with cash awards). Scores of new films receive their Belgian premiere in Ghent, and the event has proved both popular and efficiently organised. *Inquiries to*: International

Flanders Film Festival, 1104 Kortrijkse Steenweg, B–9051 Ghent, Belgium. Tel: (91) 21 89 46. Telex: 12750. Fax: (91) 21 90 74.

French Film Festival in Sarasota

November, 1992

Supported by the French film trade, this event has a quality programme selected by Molly Haskell, and serves as an admirable showcase for French cinema not just in Florida but also in the United States as a whole, for films screened here are often picked up for distribution. *Inquiries to*: French Film Festival, 5555 North Tamiami Trl, Sarasota, Florida 34243, U.S.A. Tel: (813) 351 9010.

Göteborg

January 31–February 9, 1992

A genuine success story. In a mere decade Göteborg has established itself as not only the best film festival in Norden but as one of the key events in Europe, with more than 70,000 eager and discriminating spectators who warm the cockles of a nervous director's heart with their spontaneous applause. Hotels and cinemas are close to one another. Swedish TV selects one film daily for simultaneous telecasting, a symbol of the prestige which the event carries in Sweden. *Inquiries to*: Göteborg Film Festival, PO Box 7079, S–402 32 Göteborg, Sweden. Tel: (31) 41 0546. Telex: 28674. Fax: (31) 410063.

Hongkong

April 10–25, 1992

The usual selection of Asian product is included among about 170 films on show at various venues in Kowloon and on Hongkong mainland. The festival has been recognised as a 'showcase' for Asian works and valuable for the West to discover the

April 10–25, 1992

Information:
Hong Kong International Film Festival,
Level 7, Administration Building,
Hong Kong Cultural Centre,
10 Salisbury Road, Tsim Sha Tsui,
Kowloon, Hong Kong.

Tel: (852) 7342900-6
Fax: (852) 3665206
Telex: 38484 USDHK HX
Cable: FESTUSD HX

The 16th Hong Kong International Film Festival

Presented by
the Urban Council, Hong Kong.

riches of Chinese cinema. *Inquiries to*: Senior Manager, Festivals Office, Urban Services Department, Level 7, Administration Building, Hongkong Cultural Centre, 10 Salisbury Road, Tsimshatsui, Kowloon, Hongkong. Tel: (852) 734 2900–6. Fax: (852) 3665206. Telex: 38484. USDHK HK. Cable: FESTUSD HX.

Imagfic

March–July, 1992

The Madrid International Film Festival is organising diverse film festivals for 1992, due to the designation of Madrid as cultural capital of Europe. From March 13–21, the festival will zero in on animated films; March 27–April 11 will be dedicated to European films. Then in May, there will be a retrospective of former Imagfic films, whilst June brings a retrospective of films made by "Europeans in America." The festival will end in July with eight outdoor concerts of film music. *Inquiries to*: Rita Sonlleva, Director, IMAGFIC, Gran Via 62–8, 28013 Madrid, Spain. Tel: 541 3721/241 5545. Telex: 42710. Fax: 341 5425495.

India

January, 1992

The International Film Festival of India (IFFI) is held each year (Bangalore in 1992) and is non-competitive (recognised by FIAPF). There is a substantial information section, and an annual focus on films from a particular geographical region or country (Asia, Africa or Latin America), foreign and Indian retrospectives, and a film market, as well as a most valuable panorama of the best Indian films of the year, subtitled in English. *Inquiries to*: Mrs. Deepak Sandhu, Director, Directorate of Film Festivals, Ministry of Information and Broadcasting, Government of India, 4th Floor, Lok Nayak Bhavan, Khan Market, New Delhi 110003,

■ IMAGFIC

● FESTIVAL INTERNACIONAL DE CINE DE MADRID

MARCH 13 - 21
Animated European Cinema

MARCH 27 -APRIL11
XIII INTERNATIONAL MADRID FILM FESTIVAL
Films produced from March 90 to March 92

Sections: Established Directors
New Directors
Fantastic Cinema
Europeans in America
Panorama

MAY Retrospective of European Cinema
JUNE Retrospective Europeans in America
JULY - AUGUST Music and Cinema

Imagfic	Tel 541-3721
Gran Via 62	541-5545
Madrid 28013, Spain	Fax 542-5495

Paul Schrader introducing *The Comfort of Strangers* at the Hof Film Days in Germany

India. Telex: (31) 62741 FEST IN. Cable: FILMOTSAV. Fax: (91) 11 694920. Tel: (91) 11 615953/4623430/692849/697167.

International Hofer Filmtage

October, 1992

Dubbed 'Home of Films' by Wim Wenders, Hof is famous for its thoughtful selection of some 40 features. Founded by the directors of the New German Cinema, Hof enjoys a high reputation among German film-makers and American cult figures like Roger Corman, Monte Hellman, John Sayles and Henry Jaglom, all of whom have attended retrospectives in their honour. The real applause should go to the peripatetic Heinz Badewitz, who had the idea for the festival 25 years ago. A screening in Hof can often result in a distribution deal. Director Paul Schrader was guest of honour at the 1990 event. *Inquiries to*: Postfach 1146, D–8670 Hof, F.R.G. or Heinz Badewitz, Lothstr. 28, D–8000 Munich 2, F.R.G. Tel: (89) 1297422. Fax: (89) 1236868. Telex: 5215637 FDA D

Istanbul

March 14–29, 1992

The International Istanbul Film Festival, recognised as a specialised competitive event by FIAPF, acts as a valuable showcase for distributors – not just Turkish. Attend-

Festival

OF FESTIVALS

TORONTO INTERNATIONAL FILM FESTIVAL

★ SEPTEMBER 10-19, 1992 ★

70 Carlton Street
Toronto, Ontario
Canada, M5B 1L7

Tel: (416) 967-7371 Fax: (416) 967-9477 Telex: 06-219724

ances reached 125,000 last year. The festival focuses on features dealing with arts (literature, music, cinema, dance, etc.) with other thematic sections such as Tributes, selections from World Festivals, A Country – A Cinema, and a panorama of the Turkish Cinema. *Inquiries to*: Vecdi Sayar/Hülya Uçansu, Yildiz Kültür ve Sanat Merkezi, Beşiktaş 80700, Istanbul, Turkey. Tel: (90–1) 161 32 94. Fax: (90–1) 161 88 23. Telex: 26 678.

AWARDS 1991
Golden Tulip: **Farendj** (France), Prenczina.
Special Jury Prize for Direction: Buddhadeb Dasgupta for **Tiger Man** (India).
Special Jury Prize for Acting: Luisa Perez Nieto for **Supporting Roles** (Cuba/Spain).
International Critics Prize: **Prishvin's Paper Eyes** (U.S.S.R.), Ogorodnikov; **Xenia** (Greece), Vivancos *(shared)*.
Best Turkish Film of the Year: **A Heart of Glass** (Turkey), Yaşar.

International Tournée of Animation

Now in production on its 24th annual programme, this feature-length touring showcase of international short animated films is exhibited in over 400 specialised theatres and art centres in the United States and Canada. Since 1985 the Tournée has been on the Top Ten list of the highest grossing speciality pictures. Typically the Tournée includes 15 to 20 film selections including each year's Academy Award-winner, the prizewinners from the major festivals, and the best new work of independent animators. *Inquiries to*: Terry Thoren, 2222 S. Barrington Avenue, Los Angeles, California 90064, U.S.A. Tel: (213) 473 6701. Telex: 247770. Fax: (213) 444 9850.

Karlovy Vary
July, 1992

Alternates with Moscow as the major competitive festival in Eastern Europe, with a strong emphasis on the latest Czechoslovakian features. *Inquiries to*: Ceskoslovensky Film, Jindriska 34, 110 00 Praha 1, Czechoslovakia. Tel: 236 5385–9. Telex 122259.

La Rochelle
July 2–12, 1992

Jean-Loup Passek builds a bright and enthusiastic bridge between past and future cinema with his popular and distinguished festival in this French resort, where only the superlative seafood may distract one from a wealth of restrospectives (always some discoveries among the silents), new features and thematic programmes. Passek coaxes many a director to his event, and 1991 guests included Peter Weir. Much more exciting than most competitive festivals! *Inquiries to*: Festival International du Film de La Rochelle, 28 Boulevard du Temple, 75011 Paris, France. Tel: (1) 43 57 61 24. Fax: (1) 48 06 40 22.

Locarno
August 7–17, 1992

Under its new director Marco Müller, Locarno will continue to be an extraordinary meeting-point for film-makers from around the world, in a location where new features may be viewed in a peaceful atmosphere. Locarno awards are much prized, and can often go to films unjustly ignored at the more glamorous festivals. Locarno now also offers visitors a useful chance to catch up on recent Swiss films. *Inquiries to*: Festival Internazionale del Film, Casella Postale, CH–6600 Locarno, Switzerland. Tel: (93) 31 02 32. Telex: 846565 FIFL. Fax: (93) 31 74 65.

London
November, 1992

The London Film Festival has now ranged

Jean Loup Passek and Peter Weir at the 19th Festival de La Rochelle, attended by more than 41,000 spectators
photo: Regis d'Audeville

XXᵉ FESTIVAL INTERNATIONAL DU FILM DE LA ROCHELLE

directed by jean-loup passek   **JULY 2nd - JULY 12th**

100 LONG FEATURES FILMS - 300 SCREENINGS - NON COMPETITIVE

3 MAIN SECTIONS

- Retrospectives devoted to the work of past filmmakers
- Tributes to contemporary directors, in their presence
- Le Monde tel qu'il est (The World as it Is), a selection of unreleased films from all over the world

for any information, please contact:

**Festival International du Film de La Rochelle
28, bd du Temple 75011 Paris
Phone: (1) 43 57 61 24 Fax: (1) 48 06 40 22**

out well beyond the National Film Theatre with screenings in various venues (including major West End screens) and around 170 films or so shown during the event, with a special section devoted to video productions. Directors are encouraged to discuss films with the audience. All programmes are open to the public, and the festival is FIAPF recognised. *Inquiries to*: National Film Theatre, South Bank, London SE1 8XT. Tel: (71) 928 3535. Telex: 929220. Fax: (71) 633 9323.

Los Angeles International Animation Celebration

Annually on October 31

This "festival of festivals" is a new concept for animation, and more than 400 films are showcased at the event. A panel of experts presents cash prizes and awards of more than $100,000 to the best in 15 categories. The festival is open to films in 16mm, 35mm, video (almost all standards),

completed since January 1989. There are also restrospectives and artist tributes. *Inquiries to*: Terry Thoren, Chairman, Expanded Entertainment, 2222 S. Barrington Avenue, Los Angeles, California 90064, U.S.A. Tel: (213) 473 6701. Telex: 247770 ANIM UR. Fax: (213) 444–9850.

Los Angeles European Community Film Festival

June 1992

AFI EuroFest takes place every June in Los Angeles, Washington, D.C., New York and Minneapolis. The best new films from each of the member countries of the European Community are shown with stars and filmmakers in attendance. Recent festivals have spotlighted films by Ermanno Olmi, Jacques Rivette, Margarethe von Trotta, Derek Jarman, Luigi Comencini, Mario Camus, and Reinhard Hauff. *Inquiries to*: American Film Institute, PO Box 27999, 2021 North Westrn Avenue, Los Angeles, California 90027, J.S.A. Tel: (213) 856 7707. Fax: (213) 462 4049.

Los Angeles International Film Festival

April, 1992

Continuing the tradition started by Filmex, this event is the largest of its kind in the United States, though only in its sixth year. Collaborating with over 30 film and arts organisations, the L.A. FilmFest is each year dedicated to different aspects of film-making (the producer, writer and cinematographer were honoured in the first three years). Over 200 feature films, shorts and documentaries from 45 countries are screened, with gala premieres, seminars, workshops and on-stage tributes. *Inquiries to*: AFI Festivals, 2021 N. Western Avenue, Los Angeles, CA 90027. Tel: (213) 856 7707. Fax: (213) 426 4049. Telex: 372 9910 FILM LSA.

Mannheim

November 2–7, 1992

One of the world's liveliest festivals, specialising for almost forty years in first features, long and short documentaries, featurettes and animation films. Known as "a fixed star for all Third World film-makers." The 1991 Prizes were the Mannheim Film Debut Prize of 25,000 Marks for the best feature film debut; the Josef von Sternberg Prize of 5,000 Marks for the most original film; and the SDR Documentary Film Prize of 10,000 Marks including an offer by the television company to purchase the broadcasting rights. *Inquiries to*: International Mannheim Film Festival, Collini-Center, Galerie, D–6800 Mannheim 1, Germany. Tel: (621) 10 29 43. Telex: 46 34 23. Fax: (621) 29 15 64.

Melbourne

June 6–21, 1992

Now flourishing again under the direction of Tait Brady, Melbourne is respected for the attention it gives to quality short films as well as to the major features of the year, culled from various countries and festivals around the world. *Inquiries to*: Melbourne International Film Festival, P.O. Box 12367, A'Beckett Street Post Office, Melbourne 3000, Australia. Tel: (3) 663 1395. Fax: (03) 662 1218. Telex: 152613.

AWARDS 1991

Grand Prix: **Sink or Swim** (U.S.A.), Friedrich.
Best Short Fiction Film; **Don't Be Afraid** (U.K.), Neubauer.
Best Animation Film: **Door** (U.K.), Anderson.
Best Documentary: *(shared)* **The Body Beautiful** (U.K.), Onwurah; **Hidden Faces** (U.K.), Longinotto/Hunt.
Best Experimental Film: **Relax** (U.K.), Newby.
Best Student Film: **The Sure Thing** (Australia), Perske.
Best Australian Film; **Luke's Party** by Ros Sultan and Tim Burns.

THE 15TH ANNUAL
MILL VALLEY FILM FESTIVAL
OCTOBER 1992

Eight Days of Movie Magic!

FOR INFORMATION
38 MILLER AVENUE #6 • MILL VALLEY
CALIFORNIA • 94941 USA
TEL: (415) 383-5256 FAX: (415) 383-8606
TLX: 282 696

MIFED (Milan)

October, 1992

Long established film market held in the expansive Milan Trade Fair, particularly well attended by the European buyers and sellers. Third (in calendar terms) of the year's big three film markets – preceded by the American Film Market and Cannes Film Festival – the atmosphere is all business, but Milan is still attractive, even in gloomy October. *Inquiries to*: E.A. Fiera Internazionale di Milano, Largo Domodossola 1, 20145 Milano, Italy. Tel: (02) 4997267–270. Telex: 331360. Fax: (02) 49977020.

Mill Valley

October, 1992

The Mill Valley Film Festival presents a wide variety of international programming that is shaped by a commitment to cultural and artistic excellence. This intimate event of unusually high calibre and dedication is set in a beautiful small town just north of San Francisco. The week-long, non-competitive festival includes the prestigious Videofest, as well as tributes, seminars and special events. *Inquiries to*: Mill Valley Film Festival, 38 Miller Avenue, Suite 6, Mill Valley, CA 94941, U.S.A. Tel: (415) 383 5256. Fax: (415) 383 8606.

Montpellier

October 25–November 3, 1991

Unusual event focusing on "Mediterranean" cinema, and awarding financial prizes for both features and shorts. Now in its 13th year, Montpellier also mounts a useful Information section. The 1991 programme ranged from Greece to Spain, with special tributes to Pupi Avati (Italy), Tengiz Abuladze (Georgia, U.S.S.R.) and Mohamed Khan (Egypt), and a retrospective dedicated to Roberto Rossellini. There is also an animated film section and a major symposium. *Inquiries to*: International Festival of Mediterranean Film, Hôtel des Festivals, 7 Bd Henri IV, Montpellier, France. Tel: (33) 67 04 29 39. Fax: (33) 67 04 29 41.

Montréal World Film Festival

August 1992

Serge Losique has established a major competitive festival in Montréal in late summer, and it is the only such event recognised by FIAPF in America. There are several categories, public attendance is extremely high, and the number of foreign personalities swells each year. Montréal is the ideal location for such an event, with its bilingual facilities and its proximity to all major North American outlets. *Inquiries to*: Serge Losique, World Film Festival, 1455 Boulevard de Maisonneuve Ouest, Montréal, Québec,

Jean-Pierre Léaud was on the jury at the Clermont-Ferrand Short Film festival in 1990
photo: Bruno Couderc

Canada H3G 1M8. Tel: (514) 848 3883. Telex: 05–25472. Fax: (514) 848 3886.

AWARDS 1990

Best Film: **Fallen from the Sky** (Peru), Lombardi.

Special Jury Award: (shared) **Funeral Ceremony** (Czechoslovakia), Sirovy; **Landscape with a Woman** (Yugoslavia), Matić.

Best Actor: (shared) Andres Pajares for **Ay, Carmela!** (Spain); Marcel Lebœuf for **Blizzard** (Canada).

Best Actress: Natalia Goundareva for **Dog Feast** (U.S.S.R.).

Best Director: Teng Wenji for **Ballad of the Yellow River** (China).

Best Screenplay: Joe Wiesenfeld for **Princes in Exile** (Canada).

Best Artistic Contribution: (shared) **Waltzing Regitze** (Denmark), Rostrup; **Mt. Aso's Passions** (Japan), Kumai.

FIPRESCI Prize: **Landscape with a Woman** (Yugoslavia), Matić.

13ᵉ FESTIVAL INTERNATIONAL
CINEMA MEDITERRANEEN MONTPELLIER
25 octobre - 3 novembre 1991
Festival International du Cinéma Méditerranéen
7, Bd Henri IV, 34000 Montpellier, France
Tél. (33) 67 04 29 39 / Fax : (33) 67 04 29 41

Best Short Film: **Feelings of Mountains and Water** (China), Wei.

Best First Film: (shared) **Time of the Servants** (Czechoslovakia), Pavlaskova; **Lost Spring** (France), Mazars.

New York
September–October, 1992

Back in the heady days of the 1960's, when Richard Roud and (especially) Amos Vogel pioneered the event, the NY Fest was a lodestone for film-makers like Truffaut and Godard. Now the sheen has dulled, and although attendances at Lincoln Center remain high, one feels that New York as a festival is uncertain of its own identity and forte. But a screening here can certainly help the cause of a foreign film as well as that of an American independent. *Inquiries to*: Film Society of Lincoln Center, 140 West 65th Street, New York, NY 10023, U.S.A.

Nordische Filmtage
November, 1992

This annual event held in the charming medieval town of Lübeck (north of Hamburg), throws a spotlight on the Scandinavian cinema exclusively, and enables members of the Nordic trade, critics, and other visitors to see the best of the new productions. *Inquiries to*: Nordische Filmtage, Postfach 1889, D–2400 Lübeck 1, Federal Republic of Germany. Tel: (451) 1224105. Fax: (451) 1221331.

Norwegian Film Festival
August 17–24, 1992

Held in the west coast port of Haugesund every summer, the Norwegian film festival has now become the country's major film event attended by many international visitors along with about 200 representatives from the Norwegian and Scandinavian film world. The festival is run by festival director

Gunnar Johan Løvvik and programme director is Nils Klevjer Aas. Honourable President is Liv Ullmann. The Norwegian 'Amanda Statuettes' are presented there. *Inquiries to*: PO Box 145, N–5501 Haugesund, Norway. Tel: (47) 4 728 144. Fax: (47) 4 721 347.

Nyon

October 1992

For over 20 years, Nyon has been a focus for the world's documentaries to aim at. There are awards for the best entries and an indispensable retrospective section as well as informative screenings, all under the diligent stewardship of Erika de Hadeln. *Inquiries to*: Festival International du Film Documentaire – Nyon, Case postale 98, CH–1260 Nyon, Switzerland. Fax: (41) 22 61 70 71.

Oberhausen

April 30–May 6, 1992

Oberhausen still has a just claim to be the world's premier short film festival. Not only is there a wider selection of shorts from all over the world (with special emphasis on productions from the Third World and Latin America in particular), but also an opportunity to attend the "Information Days" devoted to West German short films. *Inquiries to*: Westdeutsche Kurzfilmtage, Christian-Steger-Strasse 10, D–4200 Ob-

:rhausen 1, F.R.G. Tel: (208) 8252652. Telex: 856414. Fax: (208) 28159.

MAIN AWARDS 1991
The Comb (U.K.), Quay; **Ten Minutes before the Flight of Icarus** (Lithuania), Matelis; **House of Life** (Germany), Brillowska; **Laura – Translucid Women** (Cuba), Rodriguez; **The Uninvited Guest** (C.S.F.R.), Venclik; **Waiting for de Bil** (U.S.S.R.), Alenikov.

Odense

August, 1993

Denmark's only international short film festival invites unusual films with an original and imaginative sense of creative delight – the sort of delight to be found in the works of Hans Christian Andersen. All 16mm and 35mm films can participate. Maximum length 60 minutes running time. *Inquiries to*: Odense Film Festival, Vindegade 18, DK–5000 Odense C, Denmark. Tel: (45) 66 131372, ext. 4294. Fax: (45) 65 914318.

Pesaro

June, 1992

The "Mostra Internazionale del Nuovo Cinema" (Pesaro Film Festival) is particularly concerned with the work of new directors and emergent cinemas – in other words, with innovation at every level of the film world. For the past 27 years this Mediterranean resort has been the centre for some lively screenings and debates, and in recent seasons the festival has been devoted to a specific theme, country or culture. Pesaro also tries hard to arrange commercial distribution for films during the festival. *Inquiries to*: Mostra Internazionale del Nuovo Cinema, Via Yser 8, 00198 Roma, Italy. Fax: 884 0531.

Pordenone

October, 1992

Impeccably organised and meticulously researched tribute to the silent cinema, held

David Robinson preparing his exhibition of silent film music at Pordenone in 1990

each year in this small Italian town with love and devotion since 1982. In 1988 the festival screened 60 features and 30 shorts from the American 1910's and 1989 saw a rare programme of Russian and Soviet silents. Pordenone devoted its most recent edition to the work of the DeMille family, and met with even greater success than ever. *Inquiries to*: La Cineteca del Friuli, Via Osoppo 26, 33013 Gemona (UD), Italy. Tel: (0432) 980458. Fax: (0432) 970542.

Rotterdam

January 23–February 2, 1992

This is the 21st annual festival. Its aim is to create a focal point for directors, festival programme heads (Rotterdam being one of the earliest events of the season), and the Dutch public. There are no awards, but a distribution guarantee is given to the film regarded as best in a poll among critics and public. More than half the programme is

chosen from outside the United States and Europe. Rotterdam is an immediately friendly and informal festival where guests can talk to visiting directors and personalities in pleasant conditions. There is a "Cinemart" which functions as a co-production workshop. *Inquiries to* Rotterdam Film Festival, PO Box 21696, 3001 AR Rotterdam, Netherlands. Tel: (10) 4118080. Telex: 21378. Fax: (10) 4135132.

San Francisco
April, 1992

North America's oldest international film festival celebrates its 35th anniversary in 1992, but seems to grow younger and more audacious with each passing year. The Golden Gates Awards competition has expanded to include features made for TV, as well as documentaries and shorts. Peter Scarlet is the much respected and widely-travelled Artistic Director, and his team triumphed over the after-effects of the 1989 earthquake to achieve their most popular festival to date. *Inquiries to*: San Francisco International Film Festival, 1560 Fillmore Street, San Francisco, California 94115, U.S.A. Tel: (415) 567 4641. Telex: 6502816427. Fax: (415) 567 0432.

Sanremo
March, 1992

This distinguished event exists to promote original cinema in all its forms, and also organises admirable retrospectives. The Gran Premio carries a substantial cash award. *Inquiries to*: Nino Zucchelli, Director, Mostra Internazionale del Film d'Autore, Rotonda dei Mille 1, 24100 Bergamo, Italy. Fax: (035) 240816.

San Sebastian
September, 1992

Held in an elegant Basque seaside city, only

SAN SEBASTIAN

THE SEPTEMBER FESTIVAL

**SAN SEBASTIAN
INTERNATIONAL FILM
FESTIVAL**
Apartado de Correos, 397
Tel: 43-48 12 12, Fax: 43-28 59 79
Tx: 38145 FCSS E

**20080 SAN SEBASTIAN
SPAIN**

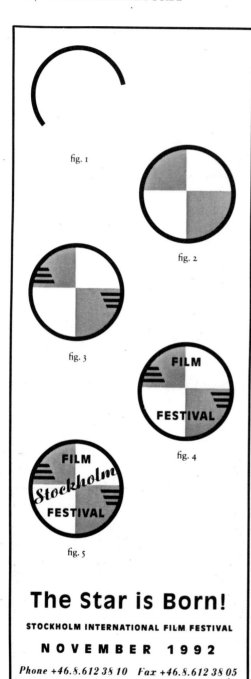

fig. 1

fig. 2

fig. 3

fig. 4

fig. 5

The Star is Born!

STOCKHOLM INTERNATIONAL FILM FESTIVAL

NOVEMBER 1992

Phone +46.8.612 38 10   Fax +46.8.612 38 05

20 kilometers from the French border, San Sebastian is still by far the most important film festival in Spain in terms of budget, glitter, sections, facilities, attendance, competition, partying and number of films. Key movers at the festival are Rudi Barnet, General Delegate, and festival Director Koldo Anasagasti. Among special sections in 1991 festival were a tribute to Richard Attenborough, another on Jesuits in cinema, one on pre-perestroika pictures, as well as the customary zabaltegi sidebar for new directors, and a section on documentaries. The city is known for its superb gastronomy, beautiful beaches and quaint streets. The festival usually attracts a number of international celebrities, as well as a wide selection of national and international press, talent, and buffs. *Inquiries to*: International Film Festival, PO Box 397, 20.080 San Sebastian, Spain. Tel: (43) 481–212. Telex: 38145. Fax: (43) 285979.

AWARDS 1990

Golden Shell (Best Feature): **Letters from Alou** (Spain) Armendáriz.

Silver Shell (Best Director): Joel Coen for **Miller's Crossing** (U.S.A.).

Special Jury Prize: **Red Daybreak** (Mexico), Fons.

Best Actress: Margherita Buy for **The Week of the Sphinx** (Italy).

Best Actor: Mulie Jarju for **Letters from Alou** (Spain).

Stockholm

November, 1992

This newcomer to the festival circuit offers a Competition for current feature films with new ideas, a survey of European cinema, a focus on American independents, and a Retrospective. Around 75 feature films have their Swedish premiere during the festival. Stockholm is at present the only northern European festival with a FIPRESCI Jury. *Inquiries to*: Stockholm International Film festival, P.O. Box 45015, S-104 30 Stockolm, Sweden. Tel: (46) (8) 612 3810. Fax: 46) (8) 612 3805.

AWARDS 1990

Bronze Horse for best film: **The Natural History of Parking Lots** (U.S.A.), Lewis.

FIPRESCI Prize: **The Reflecting Skin** (U.K.), Ridley, and **Outremer** (France), Rouan.

Sundance Film Festival

January 16–26, 1992

The Sundance Film Festival (formerly the United States Film Festival) is widely recognised as one of America's most respected exhibition events of American independent cinema. The dramatic and documentary films presented in the Independent Feature Film Competition each year are indicators of the current trends prevalent in American independent cinema. In addition, the Festival presents a number of international and American premieres, special retrospectives, and sidebars. *Inquiries to*: Sundance Film Festival, c/o Columbia Pictures, 10202 West Washington Boulevard, Culver City, CA 90232, U.S.A. Tel: (213) 204 2901. Fax: (213) 204 3901.

AWARDS 1991

Grand Jury Prize (features): **Poison** (U.S.A.), Haynes.

Grand Jury Prize (documentary): *(shared)* **American Dream** (U.S.A.), Kopple; **Paris is Burning** (U.S.A.), Livingston.

Film-Makers Trophy (features): **Privilege** (U.S.A.), Rainer.

Film-Makers Trophy (documentary): **American Dream** (U.S.A.), Kopple.

Best Cinematography: **Daughters of the Dust** (U.S.A.), Dash.

Waldo Salt Screenwriting Award: *(shared)* Joseph B. Vasquez for **Hangin' with the Homeboys**; Hal Hartley for **Trust**.

Sydney

June, 1992

Going into its 39th year, Sydney remains a broad-based non-competitive festival with a loyal public following and a good reputation internationally. Current line-up, under director Paul Byrnes, is about 170 films, of which about 60 are new features. Festival is competitive for short Australian films only, and the event is well patronised by local distributors. *Inquiries to*: Paul Byrnes, PO Box 225, Glebe, NSW 2037, Australia. Tel: (2) 660 3844. Fax: 692 8739. Telex: 75111.

Taipei

December, 1992

International Film Exhibition Taipei is run every year alongside Taiwan's Golden Horse Awards for offshore Chinese cinema, and is organised by the city's Film Library. *Inquiries to*: International Film Exhibition Taipei, Film Library, 4/F., 7 Ch'ingtao East Road, Taipei, Taiwan.

Tampere

March 4–7, 1992

The leading short film festival in Europe, an event that attracts entries from all over the world, especially Eastern Europe. The international competition consists of categories for documentaries, animation, and fiction and experimental films. In addition there is a full retrospective programme. *Inquiries to*: Tampere Film Festival, PO Box 305, SF–33101 Tampere, Finland. Tel: (358) 31 235681/30034. Fax: (358) 31 230121.

AWARDS 1991

Grand Prix: **On Christmas Day We Took Our Share of Liberty** (Romania), Catalina/Fernoaga/Mihalache.

Best Documentary Film: **To Shura** (U.S.S.R.), Lintrop.

Best Fiction Film: **The Dream in Fact** (Tadzhikistan), Hokdodov.

Best Animated Film: **Amentia** (U.S.S.R.), Ainutdinov.

Special Prize of the Jury: **The Russians Have Gone** (U.S.S.R.), Gutman.

Telluride

September 4–7, 1992

Over the past 18 years, this friendly gathering in a spectacular location in the mountains of Colorado has become one of the world's most influential festivals, with the town of Telluride virtually doubling in size as famous directors, players, and critics descend on the Sheridan Opera House and

15th

TYNESIDE INTERNATIONAL FILM FESTIVAL

AUTUMN 1992

TYNESIDE CINEMA
10 Pilgrim Street
Newcastle upon Tyne
England NE1 6QG

Tel: (091) 232 8289
Fax: (091) 221 0535

the other well-equipped theatres there. It is a formula that others have tried to emulate – and always fail, because the team of Bill and Stella Pence and Tom Luddy blend wit and wisdom and bathe the festival in a mood of discovery. *Inquiries to*: The National Film Preserve, PO Box B1156, Hanover, New Hampshire 03755, U.S.A. Tel: (603) 643 1255.

Toronto International Film Festival of Festivals

September, 1992

A rich diversity of world cinema is featured yearly with over 250 films in ten days during the Toronto International Film Festival. The event offers hundreds of films and film-makers, in a wide range of international programmes – Galas, Contemporary World Cinema, The Edge, First Cinema, Asian and Latin American Panoramas, Spotlight, Open Vault, Midnight Madness and Perspective Canada – to a large and eager audience. There is also a Sales Office and

Sissy Spacek and Gérard Depardieu enjoying that special Telluride atmosphere

an industry Trade Forum. *Inquiries to*: Festival of Festivals, 70 Carlton St. Toronto, Ontario, Canada M5B 1L7 Tel: (416) 967–7371. Fax: (416) 967–9477.

Tyneside International Film Festival

October, 1992

A lively Festival, fifteen years old in 1992, it established a reputation as a major British forum for new international independent cinema. Changing direction in the mid 1980's, it is now programmed on a non-competitive basis with a strong emphasis on European cinema. This has resulted in a regular Spanish Cinema Showcase, now in its seventh year, featuring new and retrospective work with visiting directors. Discussion and television events are also featured. *Inquiries to*: Tyneside International Film Festival, 10 Pilgrim Street, Newcastle upon Tyne, NE1 6QG, United Kingdom. Tel: (091) 232 8289. Fax: (091) 221 0535.

Uppsala

October, 1992

With a local audience of around 11,000 plus journalists, Uppsala is yet another Swedish event that covers both features and shorts. Awards to three titles annually. The festival composes its programmes so as to show how certain types of film-making are achieved, or how certain topics are handled. Note also the Children's section. *Inquiries to*: Uppsala Film Festival, PO Box 1746, S–751 47 Uppsala, Sweden. Tel: (18) 16 22 70. Fax: (18) 50 15 10. Telex: 76020.

Twenty-first Wellington Film Festival
Twenty-fourth Auckland International Film Festival
July 1992

Box 9544, Te Aro Wellington, Fax 64 4 801 7304, Phone 64 4 850 162
Courier address, 1st floor, 30 Courtenay Place, Wellington, New Zealand

Valladolid

October, 1992

Now firmly established as one of Spain's leading festivals, Valladolid offers an Official section with features and shorts in competition, special tributes, retrospectives and documentaries. In 1991, events included a tribute to U.S. film-maker Carl Reiner, another on Czech animator/director Jan Svankmajer and another on N.Y.U.'s Tisch School of the Arts. *Inquiries to*: Semana Internacional de Cine de Valladolid, Spain. Tel: (3483) 305700/77/88. Telex: 26304. Fax: (3483) 309835.

AWARDS 1990

Golden Sheaf: **Ju Dou** (China/Japan), Yimou.
Silver Sheaf: **An Angel at My Table** (New Zealand), Campion.
Best First Film: **Lie Still – Die – Revive** (U.S.S.R.), Kanevski.
Best Actress: Kerry Fox for **An Angel at My Table** (New Zealand).
Best Actor: Dirk Bogarde for **Daddy Nostalgie** (France).

11th Uppsala International
Short Film Festival
16 – 25 Oct '92
Films 60 minutes or less

Last day of entry: 1 August 1992

Contact:
Uppsala Film Festival, P.O.Box 1746, S–751 47 Uppsala, Sweden.
Tel +46–18 50 30 10, fax +46–18 50 15 10, telex 76020

Best Photography: Tonino Nardi for **Open Doors** (Italy).
Best Short Film: **A Day Will Come** (Romania), Moscu.

Vancouver

October, 1992

Now in its seventh year, this festival has grown into an event of some stature. About 85,000 people attend more than 200 screenings, and the Canadian city's natural beauty adds to the hospitality offered guests. Areas of special focus are Canada, the Pacific Rim, U.K. and the Soviet Union. Overlapping events include the Annual Trade Forum, the Screenwriter's Art, international section and special showcase events. *Inquiries to*: Alan Franey, 303–788 Beatty Street, Vancouver, B.C., V6B 2M1, Canada. Tel: (604) 685 0260/6. Telex: 045 08354. Fax: (604) 688 8221.

Venice

September, 1992

After Biraghi, the deluge? Who knows what could happen not just to the Mostra del Cinema but to the whole Biennale, the state-managed bureacracy on which it depends. It needs to be linked to revivification of the real film-market, renouncing to be an easy shop window for the major networks. In a country invaded by festivals, this oldest cultural establishment has to rethink its entire function. *Inquiries to*: La Biennale Cinema, Cà Giustinian, 30100

37th VALLADOLID INTL. FILM FESTIVAL

23/31 OCT.'92

P.O. BOX 646 ● Tel.: (34-83) 30 57 00 / 77 / 88
FAX: (34-83) 30 98 35 ● Telex: 26304 FONCAB E
47003 VALLADOLID-SPAIN

Venice, Italy. Tel: (41) 5200311. Telex: 410685.

AWARDS 1990

Golden Lion: **Rosencrantz and Guildenstern Are Dead** (U.S.A.), Stoppard.

Silver Lion (direction): Martin Scorsese for **Goodfellas** (U.S.A.).

Silver Lion (script): Helle Ryslinge for **Syrup** (Denmark).

Special Jury Award: **An Angel at My Table** (New Zealand), Campion.

Best Actor: Oleg Borisov for **The Sole Witness** (Bulgaria).

Best Actress: Gloria Munchmeyer for **The Moon in the Mirror** (Chile).

Best Photography: Mauro Marchetti for **Boys on the Outside** (Italy).

Best Editing: Dominique Auvray for **No Fear, No Die** (France).

Best Music: Valeri Milovanski for **The Sole Witness** (Bulgaria).

FIPRESCI Awards: **Mathilukal** (India), Gopalakrishnan; **The Station** (Italy), Rubini; **La Discrète** (France), Vincent.

Viennale

October 15–25, 1992

The International Vienna Film Festival has undergone a dramatic restructuring for the nineties under the joint directorship of Richard Pyrker and Werner Herzog. The new event hopes to incorporate artist/director tributes, and will spotlight films from a certain region or with a common theme. The programme will also seek to forge closer links with the former Eastern bloc countries now that Vienna is back at the geographical centre of Europe. *Inquiries*

to: Viennale, Uraniastrasse 1, 1010 Wien, Austria. Tel: (222) 75 32 84/5. Telex: 113985 FILMF.

Warsaw

October 9–19, 1992

Annual event showing the cream of quality films from all over the world, along with new Polish features, documentaries and shorts. Non-competitive, and now in its seventh year. *Inquiries to:* Warsaw Film Festival, P.O. Box 816, 00–950 Warsaw 1, Poland. Tel: (48) (22) 261409. Fax: (48) (2) 635 2001. Telex: 812508 Kokin pl.

Wellington

July, 1992

Attractive festival that twins with Auckland

Tom Stoppard presented *Rosencrantz and Guildenstern Are Dead* at the Valladolid International Film festival

in offering New Zealand's best festival showcase. *Inquiries to*: Wellington Film Festival, Box 9544, Te Aro, Wellington, New Zealand. Tel: (64) (4) 850162. Fax (64) (4) 8017304

Wine Country Film Festival

July, 1992

Set in the heart of Northern California's premium wine country, this event showcases new films, with special series of independent features and international films. Non-competitive, but an award is given each year to the film company of the year, acknowledging their commitment to independent films. Past winners include Hemdale, Orion Classics and Miramax. Not surprisingly, the festival also presents special events featuring the culinary arts and the finest of wines, as well as the related arts of dance, painting, photography and music to tie in with special screenings. *Inquiries to*: PO Box 303, Glen Ellen, CA 95442, U.S.A.

Worldfest–Houston

April 24–May 3, 1992

The Houston International Film Festival celebrates its 25th Anniversary this year, and now boasts a new film and video market. Worldfest–Houston is the largest film and video competition in the world in terms of the number of entries received (in 1991, over 3,200 entries from 47 countries). Festival director J. Hunter Todd now operates a new discovery festival programme which automatically enters all winners in more than 100 major international film festivals. They are then elegible for more than $2 million in cash awards. *Inquiries to*: P.O. Box 56566 Houston, Texas 77256. Tel: (713) 965 9955. Fax: (713) 965 9950. Telex: 317 876.

THE HOUSTON INTERNATIONAL FILM FESTIVAL
WORLDFEST 92! THE DISCOVERY FESTIVAL!

Houston WorldFest 92 offers you the the largest film and video competition in the world in terms of entries. We present a complete film/video market with a program book, plus competition and awards in 6 major categories: features, shorts, documentary, TV commercials, experimental/independent and TV production. Now WorldFest 92 offers you the world's richest award competition, with more than two million dollars in cash prizes through our Discovery Festival Program, where winners are submitted to the top 150 international festivals. No other festival or film market provides you so much!

FOR THE COMPLETE ENTRY & INFORMATION KIT, PLUS POSTER, CONTACT:
J. HUNTER TODD, CHAIRMAN & FOUNDER-WORLDFEST HOUSTON , P.O. BOX 56566, HOUSTON, TEXAS 77256
PHONE (713) 965-9955 FAX: (713) 965-9960 TELEX: 317-876 (WORLDFEST-HOU)

Other Festivals and Markets of Note

American Film and Video Festival, 920 Barnsdale Road, LaGrange Park, Illinois 60625, U.S.A. (*Formerly in New York, this is the definite round-up of documentaries and animated films in the States – June.*)

American Film Market, 10000 Washington Boulevard, Culver City, California 90232. (*Efficiently-run market primarily for English-language theatrical films. Buyers must be accredited – February.*)

American Independent Feature Film Market, 21 West 86th Street, New York, NY 10024. (*Showcase for independently produced American films – October.*)

Amiens, Marché International du Film, 36 rue de Noyon, 80000 Amiens, France. Telex: 140754. (*Film Market, with workshops and co-production finance deals being negotiated, plus competitive section – November.*)

BP Expo '92, Riverside Studios, Crisp Road, Hammersmith, London W6 9RL, U.K. Tel: (081) 741.2132. Fax: (081) 563.0336. (*Short films and video, seminars – February.*)

Belgrade, Sava Center, M. Popovica 9, 11070 Belgrade, Yugoslavia (*Cream of world cinema, exceptionally well attended and with its BESEF event recognised by FIAPF – January–February.*)

Bergamo Film Meeting, Via Pascoli 3, 24110 Bergamo, Italy. (*Useful gathering aimed at the specialist distributors interested in buying quality films for Italy – competitive cash prizes – July.*)

Biarritz Festival du Film Ibérique et Latino-American. Comité du tourisme et des fêtes, Cité administrative, 64200 Biarritz, France. (*Film in Spanish and Portuguese language from Europe and the Americas – September.*)

Birmingham Film and Television Festival, c/o Birmingham City Council, Dept. of Recreation and Community Services, Auchinleck House, Five Ways, Edgbaston, Birmingham B15 1DS, U.K Tel: (21) 4402543/4221. Fax: (21) 44(4372. (*Growing provincial festival – October–November.*)

British Industrial and Sponsored Film Festival, BISFA, 26 D'Arblay Street, London W1V 3FH. (*Annual presentation of awards to best sponsored documentaries produced in Britain – June.*)

Bristol Animation Festival, 41B Hornsey Lane Gardens, London N6 5NY, U.K. (*Retrospectives, new animated films, exhibitions seminars – October.*)

Brussels International Festival of Fantasy and Science Fiction Films, 144 avenue de la Reine, B–1210 Brussels, Belgium. (*Dedicated to the gruesome and outlandish – March.*)

Cairo International Film Festival, 17 Kasr El Nil Street, Cairo, Egypt. Tel: 3923562/3923962. Telex: 21781 CIFFUN. Fax: 3938979. (*Non-competitive, aimed at showing major international films not usually available at local cinemas. There is also a Children's film festival in Cairo – December.*)

Canadian Film Celebration, PO Box 2100, Station "M" (No. 300), Calgary, Alberta T2P 2M5, Canada. Tel: (403) 268 1370. Fax: (403) 233 8327. Telex: 038 27873. (*Exclusively for Canadian films, giving the public the chance to see and participate behind the scenes – March.*)

Cherbourg, Festival de Cinéma Franco-Britannique, Association Travelling, 1 rue du Fourdray, 50100 Cherbourg, France. (*Charming and enthusiastic small festival focusing on British film – October.*)

Chicago International Film Festival, 415 North Dearborn, Chicago, Illinois 60610, U.S.A. Telex: 936086. (*Oldest competitive event in the States – October.*)

Cine Espoo, PO Box 96, SF–02101 Espoo, Finland. Tel: (0) 446 599. Fax: (0) 446 458. (*New, partly competitive festival focusing on the Baltic and related countries – August.*)

Cleveland International Film Festival, 6200 SOM Center Road C20, Cleveland, Ohio 44139, U.S.A. Telex: 980131.

Film journalist Reinhard Pyrker (right), and film director Werner Herzog (right) are the new directors of the Viennale

photo: A Tuma

(Round-up of new and classic films from all major countries – April.)
Cork Film Festival, 38 MacCurtain Street, Cork, Ireland. (Annual competitive, for documentaries, animation, art films, fiction and sponsored shorts – October.)
Cracow, Festival Bureau, Pl. Zwyciestwa 9, PO Box 127, 00–950 Warsaw, Poland. (Poland's only international film festival and respected short film showcase – June.)
Dance on Camera, Dance Films Association Inc., 241 East 34th Street, New York, NY 10016, U.S.A. (16mm and video films on various aspects of dancing. Competitive – January.)
Dublin Film Festival, 1 Suffolk Street, Dublin 2, Eire. Tel: (001) 792937/792939. (Amicable Irish festival focusing on world cinema with special emphasis on Irish film – October–November.)
Europa Cinema, Via Giulia 66, 00186 Roma, Italy. (Successor to the Rimini festival, concentrating on European product, now down

near the heel of Italy at Bari – September.)
Festival du Film Strasbourg, L'Institut International des Droits de l'Homme, 1 quai Lezay-Marnesia, 67000 Strasbourg, France. (Concentrates on European films with a humane slant. Competitive – March.)
European Environmental Film Festival, 55 rue de Varenne, 75341 Paris Cedex 7. Telex: 201220. (Films and discussions about environmental issues – April.)
Festival dei Popoli, Friedensallee 7, D–2000 Hamburg 50, F.R.G. (Documentaries on social issues, films on history etc., in part competitive – November–December.)
Festival International de Créteil et du Val de Marne, Maison des Arts, Place Salvador Allende, 94000 Créteil, France. Tel: (1) 4980 9050. Fax: (1) 4399 0410. (Features, shorts, animated films all made by women, annual spotlight on an actress – April.)
Festival International du Film de Comédie, Place de la Gare 5, Ch–1800 Vevey, Switzerland. Tel: (021) 921 8282.

Fax: (021) 921 1065. (*Screenings of new and old films, as long as they are amusing – August.*)
Festival of Films and Photographs, No. 20, 19th Alley, Gandhi Ave., Tehran, Iran. Tel: 762 280. (*November.*)
Festival International du Film Nature, WWF-Genève, CP28, CH–1212 Grand-Lancy, Switzerland. (*Films on 16mm and Super 8, devoted to nature and the environment – November.*)
Festival International du Film sur l'Ecologie et l'Environment, AFIFEE, Domaine de Grammont, route de Mauguio, 3400 Montpellier, France. (*Films on ecology and natural resources – April.*)
Festival du Cinéma International en Abitibi-Témscamingue, 215 Avenue Mercier, Rouyn-Noranda, Québec J9X 5WB, Canada. Tel: (819) 762 6212. Fax: (819) 762 6762. (*Competitive for features and shorts held in northwestern Québec – October–November.*)
Festival Internacional de Cinema de Animacão ('Cinanima'), rue 62, No. 251–1/ Apart. 43, P–4500 Espinho. (*Animation.*)
Festival of Three Continents, c/o Oxfam Wereldwinkel, Gelmuntstraat 8, 8000 Bruges, Belgium. (*Small but dedicated Third World specialist event – March.*)
Figueira da Foz, rua Luis de Cameos 106, 2600 Vila Franca de Zira, Portugal. (*Competitive festival on the Portuguese coast – September.*)
Film Festival Cologne, Am Malzbüchel 6–8, D–5000 Cologne, Germany. (*European independent films, tributes and retrospectives – September.*)
Filmfest DC, PO Box 21396, Washington DC 20009, U.S.A. Tel: (202) 727 2396. Telex: 440 732. Fax: (202) 347 7342. (*Improving non-competitive American event, which focuses on innovative films and individual countries – April.*)
Florence Film Festival, c/o Assessorarto alla Cultura, Comune di Firenze, Diapartimento Arti Visive, Via Sant'Egidio 21, 50122 Florence, Italy. (*Review of independent cinema – features only – May–June.*)
Gay and Lesbian Film Festival, National Film Theatre, South Bank, London SE1 8XT. Tel: (71) 928 3535. Fax: (71) 633 9323. (*Films made by, or about, gays and lesbians – March.*)
Giffoni Film Festival, Piazza Umberto 1, 84095 Giffoni Valle Piana (Salerno), Italy. Tel: (89) 868544. Telex: 721585. (*Annual survey of films for youths and children – July–August.*)
Gijón, Cerinterfilm, Paseo de Begoña, 24 entlo, Gijón, Asturias, Spain. Tel: (85) 343 739. Fax: (85) 354152. Telex: 87443 FICG E. (*Concentrates on films for young people, with competitive and non-competitive sections – July.*)
Greek Film Festival (Thessaloniki), Valaoritou 9, Athens 106 71, Greece. Tel: 364 2129. Fax: 364 6544. (*Complete panorama of new Greek films – October.*)
Havana International Film Festival, ICAIC, Calle 23 No. 1155, Plaza de la Revolucion, Habana 4, Cuba. Tel: 3 4400/4711. Telex: 511 419 ICAIC. (*Excellent, immense Latin American festival with many celebrities on hand – December.*)
Hawaii International Film Festival, 1777 East-West Road, Honolulu, Hawaii 96848, U.S.A. Telex: 989171. Fax: (808) 944 7970. (*Aims to bring East and West together through film; all screenings free – November–December.*)
Hiroshima Animation Festival, 1–1 Nakajima-cho, Naka-hu, Hiroshima 730, Japan. (*Competitive event for animation – August 8–13, 1990.*)
Holland Animation Film Festival, Hoogt 4, 3512 GW Utrecht, Holland. (*Unique biannual competitive survey of applied animation.*)
Humboldt Film Festival, Humboldt State University (Theatre Arts), Arcata, California 95521. (*For student and independent films under 60 minutes, and on 16mm – May.*)
Iberoamerican Film Festival, Hotel Tartessos, Huelva, Spain. Tel: (55) 245

MONTREAL

AUGUST 27 – SEPTEMBER 7 1992

THE WORLD FILM FESTIVAL

The only competitive film festival in North America recognized by the International Federation of Film Producers Associations.

The World Film Festival offers:

- OFFICIAL COMPETITION
- HORS CONCOURS SECTION
- CINEMA OF A PARTICULAR COUNTRY HONORED EACH YEAR: SPAIN 1992
- LATIN AMERICAN CINEMA OF TODAY
- CINEMA OF TODAY AND TOMORROW (new trends) WITH A BIG PRIZE FOR THE FIRST FEATURE FILM
- PANORAMA CANADA
- T.V. FILMS
- TRIBUTES

The World Film Festival is the most attended festival in the Western hemisphere.

Offices:
MONTREAL WORLD FILM FESTIVAL
1455 de Maisonneuve West
Montreal, Canada H3G 1M8
Tel: (514) 848-3883
     (514) 933-9699
Telex: 05-25472 WOFILMFEST
Fax: (514) 848-3886

THE INTERNATIONAL FILM, TELEVISION AND VIDEO MARKET

An annual meeting place for producers, distributors, investors... in the most European city in North America.

Everything is within walking distance: hotels, offices for sellers, video rooms, theatres, press rooms and other facilities.

The International Film, Television and Video Market offers:

- ACCREDITATION ALLOWING ACCESS TO FACILITIES.

Offices:
INTERNATIONAL FILM, TELEVISION AND VIDEO MARKET
1455 de Maisonneuve West
Montreal, Canada H3G 1M8
Tel: (514) 933-4339
Telex: 05-25472 WOFILMFEST
Fax: (514) 848-3886

611. Fax: (55) 250 617. (*Survey of films from Latin America and the Spanish peninsula – December.*)

Indonesian Film Festival, National Film Council, Jalan Merdeka Barat no. 9, Jakarta, Indonesia. (*Colourful annual survey of Indonesian cinema – November.*)

International Children's Film Festival, Communal Cinema Oulu, Rantakatu 30, SF–90120 Oulu, Finland. (*Non-competitive annual event covering children's films, with retrospectives – November.*)

International Filmwochenende Würzburg, Filminitiative Würzberg, Gosbersteige 2, D–8700 Würzburg, F.R.G. Telex: 680070. (*Non-competitive event screening some 20–25 features, emphasis on dialogue between film-makers and audience – January.*)

Internationales Kinderfilmfestival im Frankfurt am Main, Kinder- und Jugendfilmzentrum in der Bundesrepublik Deutschland, Kuppelstein 34, D–5630 Remscheid 1, F.R.G. Tel: (2191) 794 233. Fax: (2191) 71810. (*New films for, or featuring, children, judged by children and professionals. Plenty for parents too – September.*)

International Roshad (Educational) Film Festival, No. 8, Semnan Alley, Bahar Ave., Tehran, Iran. Tel: 762 280. (*November.*)

International Film and TV Festival of New York, 5 West 37th Street, New York, NY 10018, U.S.A. (*Annual competitive survey of films and videotape productions, TV programmes, industrial and educational productions, TV and cinema commercials – November.*)

International Film School Festival, Münchner Filmwochen GmbH, Türkenstrasse 93, D–8000 Munich 40, Federal Republic of Germany. (*Highly regarded event that's a kind of 'Junior Championships' for film school students and graduates – November.*)

Isfahan International Festival of Films for Children and Young Adults, Farhang Cinema, Dr. Shariati Ave., Gholhak, Tehran 19139, Iran. Tel: 265086. Fax: 678155. Telex: 214283 FCFIR. (*November.*)

Jerusalem Film Festival, PO Box 8561, Jerusalem 91083, Israel. (*Broad spread of new films from throughout the world, retrospectives – June.*)

Kaleidoscope, PO Box 2260, S–103 16 Stockholm, Sweden. (*International Immigrant Film Festival, competitive – April.*)

Leipzig Festival, Chodowieckistr, 32, 1055 Berlin, Germany. Telex: 512455. (*Documentaries and animation. Competitive – November.*)

Lille International Festival of Short and Documentary Films, 26–34 rue Washington, 75008 Paris, France. (*Competitive for shorts, with additional panorama of recent French production in the field – March.*)

Miami Festival, Film Society of Miami, 7600 Red Road, Suite 307, Miami, Florida 33143, U.S.A. Tel: (305) 377 3456. Telex: 264047. (*Non-competitive, with emphasis on Hispanic cinema – February.*)

Midnight Sun Film Festival, PO Box 305, SF–33101 Tampere, Finland. Tel: (358) 31 235681/30034. Fax: (358) 31 230121. (*Long weekend for film lovers in the Midsummer beauty of Finland, and above the Arctic Circle! – June.*)

Mostra Internacionnais de Cinema & Video, NCV, Rua Eng. Ewbank Camera, 78 Bela Vista, CEP 90.420, Porto Alegre/ RS, Brazil. (*Films and videos from abroad as well as South American programmes – September.*)

Mostra Internacional de Cinema, Al. Lorena 937 cj., 302–1424, São Paulo, Brazil. Telex: (11) 25043. (*Non-competitive panorama of best films of year, plus critics and audience awards – October.*)

New Orleans Film and Video Festival, PO Box 70556, New Orleans, LA 70172, U.S.A. Tel: (504) 581 3420. (*October/ November.*)

New York International Home Video Market, Knowledge Industry Publications Inc., 701 Westchester Ave., White Plains, NY 10604, U.S.A. (*Showplace for video retailers, distributors, publishers, media buyers etc. – April.*)

Norwegian Short Film Festival, Storengveien 8b, N–1342 Jar, Norway. (*Local shorts in competition, plus selection of titles from other international festivals – held in Grimstad every June.*)
Österreichische Filmtage, Columbusgasse 2, A–110 Vienna, Austria. Tel: 604 0126. Fax: 602 0795. (*Annual survey of new Austrian features, documentaries, TV, avant-garde, and video productions – October.*)
Palm Springs International Film Festival, 401 South Pavilion Way, PO Box 1786, Palm Springs, CA 92263, U.S.A. Tel: (619) 322 8389. Fax: (619) 320 9834. (*Glamorous new festival spearheaded by Palm Springs' mayor Sonny Bono – January.*)
Piccadilly Film and Video Festival, 177 Piccadilly, London W1V 9LF, U.K. (*Growing festival focusing on off-beat, with stress on retrospectives – June.*)
Polish Film Festival, Piwna 22, PO Box Nr. 192, 80–831 Gdańsk, Poland. Telex: 0512153. (*15th edition of the festival focusing on Polish film – September.*)
Pula Festival, Festival jugoslavenskog igranog filma, Marka Laginje 5, 52000 Pula, Yugoslavia. (*Annual screening of all new Yugoslavian features – July.*)
Rencontres Internationales du Jeune Cinéma, 70 rue Faider, 1050 Brussels, Belgium. (*Accent on films for and by young people.*)
Restoration Festival, National Film Theatre, South Bank, London SE1 8XT. Tel: (71) 928 3535. Fax: (71) 633 9323. (*First of an annual, reciprocal event between the UCLA and National Film Theatre, a tribute to preservation and restoration of archive material – August.*)
Rivertown (Minneapolis/St. Paul) International Film Festival, University Film Society, Minnesota Film Center, 425 Ontario Street SE, Minneapolis, MN 55414. Tel: (612) 627 4431. (*Event built up over 26 years by the reliable Al Milgrom. Scores of unusual foreign films on display – April–May.*)
Rouen, Festival du Cinéma Nordique,

7th Umeå International Film Festival
September 18 - 23
Features, Documentaries, shorts, Silent Classics, Women Directors, Camera Obscura, Retrospectives. We screen anything good that runs through a projector, and more!!
P.O.Box 43, 901 02 Umeå, Sweden
Phone: +46 90 13 33 88, 13 33 56
Fax: +46 90 11 79 61

91 rue Crevier, 76000 Rouen, France. Tel: 35 98 28 46. Telex: 771444. (*Competitive festival of Nordic cinema, including retrospective and information sections – March.*)
San Juan Film Festival, Apartado 4543, San Juan, Puerto Rico 00905. Tel: (809) 721 5676. Telex: 383 9686. (*New festival focusing on the film and video harvest of the Caribbean countries – October.*)
Santa Barbara International Film Festival, 1216 State Street, Suite 201, Santa Barbara, CA 93101, U.S.A. Tel: (805) 963 4408. (*Non-competitive, usually focusing on a single country – March.*)
Seattle International Film Festival, 801 East Pine Street, Seattle, Washington 98122, U.S.A. (*Unusual Northwest Pacific coast event that has done a great deal to establish Dutch cinema in the States – May–June.*)
Settimana Cinematografica Internazionales di Verona, Via S. Giacomo Alla Pigna 6, 37121 Verona, Italy. Telex: 434339. (*Features, new and retrospective – June.*)
Short and Documentary Film Festival, Farhang Cinema, Dr. Shariati Ave., Gholhak, Tehran 19139, Iran. Tel: 265 086. Fax: 678 155. (*New Iranian event – July.*)
Singapore International Film Festival, 11 Keppel Hill, Singapore 0409. Telex: 38283. Fax: 2722069. (*Biannual non-competitive event showcasing international films – January.*)
Sitges Festival, Diputación 279, Barcelona

08007, Spain. Tel: (3) 317 3585/418 4858. (*Decades-old science fiction and fantasy film festival, competitive, usually attended by celebrities and directors, set in charming seaside town – October.*)

Solothurn Filmtage, Postfach 92, CH–4500 Solothurn, Switzerland. (*Screenings of all new Swiss films – January.*)

Taormina International Film Festival, Comitato 'Taormina Arts,' Palazzo Corvaja, Taormina, Sicily. Telex: (in Rome) 625673. (*Competitive and non-competitive event in Sicily with stress on films by new directors, plus retrospectives and discussions – July.*)

Tokyo International Film Festival, No. 3 Asano Building, 2–4–19 Ginza, Chuo-ku, Tokyo 104, Japan. Telex: 34548. Fax: 81–35636310. (*New mammoth event with competition and other sidebar events – September–October.*)

Troia Film Festival, 2901 Setúbal Codex, Portugal. Tel: (35165) 44121. Fax: (35165) 44123. (*Wide variety of categories in this competitive festival. Held in a Summer recreational area on the tip of a peninsula – June.*)

Umeå Film Festival, Box 43, S–901 02 Umeå, Sweden. Tel: (46) 90 33388. Telex: 540 84. Fax: (46) 90 117961. (*Busy festival featuring international panorama, films for children, and obscure films section – September.*)

USA Film Festival, PO Box 3105, Dallas, Texas 75275, U.S.A. (*Collection of new and old American movies – March.*)

Valencia: Mostra of Mediterranean Cinema, Plaza Arzobispo, 2 acc. B., Valencia 46003, Spain. Tel: (96) 392 1506. Fax: (96) 391 5156. Telex: 63427. (*Major tributes for films made in and around the Mediterranean – October.*)

Viareggio Mystery Festival, Via dei Coronari 44, 00186 Rome, Italy. (*A festival for all genres and media covered by the term "mystery" – June.*)

Women in Cinema, International Festival of Films made by Women, Lavalle 1578 9 "B", Buenos Aires, Argentina. Tel: 467 318. Fax: (54 11) 12559. (*April.*)

Women in Film Festival, 6464 Sunset Blvd., Suite 600, Los Angeles, California 90028, U.S.A. (*Dedicated to the improvement of women's image in film and TV. Various categories – October.*)

Zagreb Animation, Zagreb Film, Nova ves 18, 41000 Zagreb, Yugoslavia. Telex: 21790. (*Competitive festival in hospitable surroundings, concurrent market for animated films – June.*)

ANIMATION

by Theresa FitzGerald

Animation will be the predominant art form of the 21st Century – or so at least claimed the great Russian animator, Yuri Norstein, on a recent trip to London. He may well be right. Certainly the last few years have seen a world-wide explosion of animated images – especially on television, and particularly in the realms of advertising, title sequences, pop-promos and "youth" programmes.

Yet in terms of technique, animation seems to have hit something of a plateau. Overall quality may be higher than ever, but little recently has created the stir of a *Who Framed Roger Rabbit* (1988) or *Luxo Jr* (1986). The last year or so has been more a period of consolidation and structure-building than of artistic and technical innovation or excitement.

Features in particular, though prolific, have been generally uninspiring. Disney, promising a full-length feature a year, followed the somewhat glutinous **The Little Mermaid** with a better-than-anticipated adventure yarn, **The Rescuers Down Under**. The company has high hopes for its 30th feature, **Beauty and the Beast**, and for **Aladdin**, its 1992 release. Such an industrial pace, however, has irked Disney's workforce. There's particular resentment over new contracts binding animators to the studio for several years.

These days, of course, Disney no longer monopolises features. Plenty of other production companies are in on the act, but more certainly doesn't seem to mean better. **Felix the Cat: The Movie** probably buried the resourceful feline for good, while Hanna-Barbera's **Jetsons: The Movie** re-cycled their 1950's futuristic TV series flop to little advantage – a shame, if for no other reason than that the film features the final performance of lengendary voice-artist Mel Blanc.

Another contender for Least Ingenious Title award, the Canadian/French co-production **Barbar: The Movie**, mish-mashed styles and sentiments but had its exciting moments – which is more than can be said of Philippe Grimond's **Asterix and the Big Fight**. Jacques Colombat's 1991 Annecy prize-winner, **Robinson and Co**, fortunately restored faith in Gallic imagination with striking visuals and deft handling of its small cast.

Neither Swede Per Åhlin's version of *The Tempest*, **Voyage to Melonia**, nor Jannik Hastrup's Danish production, **War of the Birds**, quite threw off the shadow of Disney but both, particularly the latter, achieved some effective set-pieces. The Scandinavian scene in general is showing an encouragingly high level of activity, with several series and features in production: among them Flemming Quist Möller's *Hugo: The Jungle Animal* in Denmark, Åhlin's version of Offenbach, *Hoffmann's Eyes*, and Finnish company Franck Film's cross between 1,001 Nights and the Kalevala – *Sinbad: The Dream Quest*.

Lavish Colour and Startling Images

Katsuhiro Otomo's *Akira* finally spiked the patronising myth, widely held in the West, that Japan can make nothing but cheap production-line cartoons. The lavish colour and startling images are let down, however, by a routine, if complex, sci-fi plot taken from Otomo's own graphic novel. The Japanese/American co-production **Little Nemo**, directed by William Hurtz and

Masami Hata, also boasts superb production values but again suffers from a banal story, despite its origins in animation pioneer Winsor McCay's classic 1900's comic strip.

Perhaps the only real surprise among recent features was the universally-hailed **Alice**, Jan Svankmajer's disquieting reworking of Lewis Carroll, mixing models and live-action to stunning effect. Richard Williams's legendary and long-awaited **The Cobbler and the Thief**, after nearly a quarter-century in preparation, is currently slated for a Chistmas 1992 release. The project was finally taken in hand by Jake Eberts and Allied Filmmakers with distributors Majestic Films pre-selling worldwide, and Warner Bros taking the North American rights.

Off-screen drama was provided by ex-Disney animator Don Bluth's company Sullivan-Bluth. Both the disappointing 1989 feature **All Dogs Go to Heaven**, and **Rock-A-Doodle**, the tale of a rooster who quits the farmyard for a rock'n'roll career, went substantially over budget. Long-running artistic and financial disputes with backers Goldcrest came to a head early in 1991 with Goldcrest petitioning the Irish High Court to liquidate the company after it failed to repay a short-term loan. Matters were settled out of court, with Sullivan-Bluth paying an undisclosed sum and Goldcrest pulling out of its three-picture deal with the studio. Sullivan-Bluth, though, barely missed a beat, promptly starting work on their next two projects, **A Troll in Central Park** and **Thumbelina**, with support from European investors.

Creative Shorts

If features have hardly dazzled in the past few years, shorts have been as creatively diverse as ever. As so often recently Britain seems to have made much of the running both for quality and quantity. Channel Four's pioneering efforts have resulted in an extraordinary burst of work aimed at adults, such as Nick Park's quirky clay animations, **A Grand Day Out** and 1991 Oscar-winner, **Creature Comforts**, and Joanna Quinn's **Body Beautiful**, a delightful sequel to her raunchy 1986 hit, **Girls' Night Out**.

Out of the proliferating richness on offer it is also worth noting the Quay Brothers' obscure **The Comb ... From the Museums of Sleep**, the nightmare worlds of Andrew McEwan's **Toxic** and David Anderson's **Deadsy** and **Door**, Candy Guard's wry women's-eye views **Fatty Issues** and **The Wrong Type**, Emma Calder and Ged Haney's modern fairytale **The Drummer**, Karen Anne Kelly's award-winning **Egoli** and student Charlie Watson's mixed techniques meditation on Nicaragua, **Bluefields Express**. From a mass of children's animation Graham Ralph's **Spider in the Bath**, Dianne Jackson's **Grandpa** and **Father Christmas**, and Richard Ollive's enchanting **Night Visitors** particularly stand out.

Canadian animation may not be as prolific but its standards are equally high. Caroline Leaf returned to animation after a ten-year gap with the stunning scratched-on-film, **Entre deux sœurs**, which won best short film at Annecy. Wendy Tilby's charming paint-on-glass **Strings**, Pierre M. Trudeau's **Enfantillage**, about a child's reaction to a domestic quarrel, and Stephen McCallum's adaptation of the tragic fisherman's tale, **From Flores**, showed the National Film Board had lost none of its vigour. And Richard Condie's "study in foolishness," **The Apprentice**, and Marv Newland's erotic **Pink Komkommer** suggest the country's West Coast animators are also flourishing.

Flexible Computer Animation

Over the border in the States, computer animation took another small leap with John Lasseter's **Knicknack**, the tale of a lovelorn souvenir snowman, and Luxo Jr made a welcome return in **Surprise** and **Light &**

Cel from *War of the Birds*, from Per Holst Filmproduktion

Heavy with the help of Pixar colleague Andrew Stanton. Steve Goldberg's **Locomotion** illustrated just how flexible computer animation has become, even if its storyline was a little stiff.

Among traditional animators Bill Plympton's **Push Comes to Shove – 15 Ways to Deform Your Counterpart's Face** displayed a cynical quirkiness worthy of Eastern Europe, and Sheryl Marie Sardina's **Eternity** gave life's struggles a new twist. The big surprise, however, was the TV series, **The Simpsons**. Its tight scripts and jaundiced slant on American working-class life seem to have captured the world's imagination.

Animation from Africa, Latin America, and India rarely make much impact internationally, but the Zaire/Belgian co-production **The Toad Visiting His In-laws**, an adaptation of a Tetela folk-tale from Kibushi Ndjate Wooto, Flavia Alfinito's look at the life of a Brazilian housewife, **Leonora Down**, and Indian Arun Gongade's plea for peace, **Shanti** – all warmly received at Annecy – suggest a flowering of fresh talent.

The same cannot be said for Eastern Europe's animation scene. The recent political turmoil has upset all assumptions, financial no less than political. While some film-makers are still stuck in the old Cold War mode of gloomy parables about human self-destructiveness – Estonian Avo Païstik's **Silmus**, the Russian-Armenian Robert Sahaguian's **The Button** – others seem to be flailing around, uncertain how to come to terms with the new freedoms: Robert Turlo's anti-war **W.A.L.** from Poland, Svankmajer's disappointingly heavy-handed **The Death of Stalinism in Bohemia**.

Even so, good work is still being produced: Svankmajer's own brilliant **Darkness, Light, Darkness**, Pole Piotr Dumala's witty **Freedom of the Leg**, Hungarian Gábor Holoya's succinct **Western**, and from Russia Igor Kovalyov's strange **Hen, His Wife** and Hélène Gavrilko's **Girlfriend**, about a fisherman's affair with a fish. Also Russian, and irresistibly confident, was the puppet-animation winner of the Grand Prix at Annecy, **Grey Wolf and Little Red Riding Hood** from Garry Bardin.

Confidence in Western Europe

Confidence also seems to characterise much of current production in Western Europe. Germany's Christoph and Wolfgang Lauenstein won 1990's Oscar with their stark puppet tale of greed upsetting the **Balance**. And Switzerland is making an increasing impact with devilish tales like Gisèle and Ernest Ansorge's **Sabbat**, and Michel Duford's private-eye pastiche, **Real Puppets Don't Die**.

France has produced relatively few "per-

Cel from Gerrit van Dijk's *Janneke*

sonal" films in recent years, but Michel Ocelot's delicate silhouette cut-outs for his Hokusai-inspired tale, **Ciné Si: The Old Lady's Coat**, and the Fantôme studio's vivacious 3-D computer animation of La Fontaine, **Geometric Fables**, prove the French haven't lost their touch. And the intervention of TV stations such as La Sept and Canal Plus promises well for the future.

The Netherlands confirmed its strong reputation for idiosyncratic work with a raft of new productions, including the prolific Gerrit Van Dijk's paean to the life-force, **Janneke**, Paul Maggré's droll tale of a banana which loses its skin, **Van een banaan die zijn schil kwijt was**, and Ellen Meske's eleborate clay animation, **Capriccio**. The eclectic Paul Driessen, having exposed some family scandals in **Uncles and Aunts**, went on to explore the 70mm IMAX/OMNIMAX system with **Fly for a Day**.

The Italian veteran Bruno Bozzetto, recipient at Ottawa of a special award for his oeuvre, showed no lessening of vitality with his latest film, **Grasshoppers**, a sardonic comment on nature and human barbarism. Other Italian work seemed a touch subdued, although with **The Dance Floor** Simona Mulazzani and Gianluigi Toccafondo offered an elegant and painterly tribute to the era of Fred Astaire.

But in general, Western European animation feels hearteningly buoyant. A major factor in this has been the work of CARTOON, the European Association of Animation Film, part of the European Commission's MEDIA Programme. In its brief two-year existence CARTOON has spawned a plethora of imaginative schemes to assist European animation (and not just within the borders of the EEC), particularly by encouraging the smaller animation houses to form Studio Groupings. These enable them to share creative, technical and financial resources, making them competitive with the larger U.S. and Far Eastern studios. Besides providing contacts and in-

formation, CARTOON also gives practical financial help with pre-production and distribution costs.

One result of this is that countries which were hitherto mainly confined to servicing Disney or the larger European studios are beginning to establish their own distinct industries. Portugal, for instance, is embarking on its first independent feature, with several series and shorts in the pipeline, and Ireland's Sullivan-Bluth and Murakami-Wolf studios are being joined by small independent Animedia Teo.

Another direct outcome of the CARTOON initiative is the first truly pan-European animated feature, **Seven Deadly Sins**. Supervised by the irrepressible Gerrit van Dijk, whose idea it was originally, the film draws on the talents of nine different European countries, seven of them each responsible for a specific sin, with the co-producer and scriptwriter coming from the U.K. It is hoped that the film will be ready for release early in 1993, to celebrate the birth of the new Europe.

CARTOON's first Forum, designed to bring together animators and potential distributors and facilitate the deal-making process, was held in 1990 in Lanzarote and pronounced a conspicuous success. A second Forum took place in St Malo in France in September 1991 and was well attended. And a major new, specifically European award, the CARTOON d'Or, was offered for the first time in 1991, and won by Nick Park's ubiquitous *Creature Comforts*.

Though animators have seen too many promising initiatives trickle away into the sand not to retain an edge of scepticism, developments such as these bode well for the immediate future. The predominant feeling at Annecy, the year's premier animation festival, was one of quiet optimism, of film-makers consolidating current strengths in anticipation of the next notable breakthrough in technique. With only eight years to go, Norstein's prediction may yet be fulfilled even sooner than he thought.

THE LONDON
•INTERNATIONAL•
FILM SCHOOL

•Training film makers for over 30 years •
• Graduates now working worldwide •
• Located in Covent Garden in the heart of London •
• Recognised by A.C.T.T. •
• 16mm documentary & 35mm studio filming •
• Two year Diploma course in film making
commences three times a year: January, April, September •

**London International Film School, Department IG10, 24 Shelton Street, London WC2H 9HP
071-836 0826**

FILM SCHOOLS

AUSTRALIA

Australian Film, Television and Radio School, PO Box 126, North Ryde NSW 2113. The Australian national centre for professional training in film, television and radio production. The School conducts full-time training in both film and video, varying in length from 1 semester to 3 years. Also offered is a six-month full-time commercial radio course and a nation-wide programme of specialist short and part-time courses through its Industry Program.

The three year Bachelor of Arts course and the one and two semester extension courses offer specialisations in cinematography, directing, editing, production design, producing, scriptwriting and sound. There are no specific educational requirements for entry; however, places are limited. Applicants are judged on previous experience, commitment and attitude.

Applications close at end of June for the following year's courses. For course details and information contact the Student Centre on (02 805 6444.

AUSTRIA

Hochschule für Musik und darstellende Kunst, Abteilung für Film und Fernsehen, Metternichgasse 12, A-1030 Vienna, Director: Prof. Mag. Robert Schöfer.

BELGIUM

Koninklijke Academie voor Schone Kunsten – Gent, Academiestraat 2, B-9000 Gent. Director: Pierre Vlerick. Animation department: Director: Raoul Servais assisted by Jean Marie Demever, Dirk de Paepe, Rembrand Hoste as workshop teachers. The department focuses on the animated cartoon technique, although other animation techniques, such as puppet, pixillation and cut-out animation, are also taught.

Institut National des Arts du Spectacle et Techniques de diffusion (I.N.S.A.S., Rue Thérésienne, 8, 1000 Bruxelles-Belgium. Director: Jean-Pierre Casimir. 215 students and 120 staff. Tel: 02/511.92.86. Fax: 02/511.02.79. Four year course leading to a degree, concerned with all aspects of film/radio/television production. Three-year course giving more specialised instruction in photography, sound, writing or acting.

Institut des Arts de Diffusion, (I.A.D.), Rue des Wallons No. 77, B 1348 Louvain-la Neuve, Belgium. Chairman: Jean-Marie Delmée. 250 students and 100 staff. Four-year course in direction, production in film, television, radio and the theatre. Three-year course in photography, sound, editing and writing. Films made by students include features, documentaries and animated shorts.

Hoger Rijksinstituut voor Tonell en Cultuurspreiding (RITCS), 8, Theresiënstraat, 1000 Brussels. Dutch four-year course in film/radio/television/theatre.

BRAZIL

Escola Superior de Cinema, Faculdade São Paulo.

Escola Superior de Cinema, Pontificia Universidade Catolica, Av. Brasil 2033, Belo Horizonte, Minas Gerais.

Instituto de Arte e Communicação Social, Universidade Federal Fluminense, Rua Professor Lara Villela 126, 24.210 – Niterói, Rio de Janeiro.

CANADA

Sheridan College, Faculty of Visual Arts, 1430 Trafalgar Road, Oakville, Ontario, L6H 2L1, Canada. Dean: Scott Turner. The International Summer School of Animation is an intense three year diploma programme offered each year from the middle of May to the middle of August. Each fourteen week summer segment is equivalent to one College academic year. The summer programme covers the study of animation, drawing, design and basic production techniques. Studies examine both contemporary and traditional approaches to animation. Applicants must have two years post secondary art education or the equivalent in professional experience. Competence in English is also required.

York University, Faculty of Fine Arts, Film & Video Department, 4700 Keele Street, North York, Ontario M3J 1P3. Offers studies in Film,

Video, Screenwriting, and Theory over a 4-year Honours BA of BFA course. 2-year MFA.

Simon Fraser University, School for the Contemporary Arts, Burnaby, B.C. Canada V5A 1S6. Tel: (604) 291 3363. Fax: (604) 291 5907. The film programme consists of a blend of 16mm film and video productions, theory and analysis courses within an interdisciplinary context allowing contact with students in theatre, music and the visual arts. The programme focuses on the development of skills valuable to independent film-makers and appropriate to cinematic expression as an art form. Potential students can pursue either an interdisciplinary Fine and Performing Arts major programme with a concentration in film or a Film major programme both of which lead to a Bachelor of Arts degree. In addition, students may pursue a M.F.A. interdisciplinary degree specialising in an aspect of Film or Video production.

Emily Carr College of Art & Design, 1399 Johnston St., Vancouver, BC V6H 3R9. Animation, Video, Film.

Univ. of British Columbia, Film & T.V. Studies Programme, Dept., of Theatre, Vancouver, BC V6T 1W5. Film & TV Advanced and Comprehensive.

University of Alberta, Television & Film Institute, Box 60090, University of Alberta, Edmonton, Alberta T6G 2S4. Tel (403) 437–5171. During 1992 the Institute will conduct a series of seminars concentrating on writing for film and TV. Past instructors have included: Gerry Davis, Syd Field, Linda Seger and Danny Simon. Courses are designed for professionals or those aspiring to careers in the film industry. Top students are selected for a programme using computers to link them with top screenwriters, worldwide. As a companion programme, the TFI operates a computer bulletin board dedicated to both amateur and professional screen and TV writers internationally via (403) 487–7089.

Univ. of Regina, Regina, Sask S4S OA2. Film and Video.

Univ. of Manitoba, 447 University College, Winnipeg, Man R3T 2N2. Basic film-making.

Humber College, 205 Humber College Blvd, Rexdale, Ont M9W 5L7. Film, TV & A/V.

Queen's University, 160 Stuart St, Kingston, Ont K7L 3N6. Film Studies.

Ryerson Polytechnical Institute, 50 Gould St, Toronto, Ont M5B 1E8. Film and TV advanced and comprehensive.

Seneca College, 1750 Finch, E Toronto, Ont M2J 2X5. TV & Video.

Wilfrid Laurier University, Waterloo, Ont N2L 3C5. Production courses.

University of Windsor, Windsor, Ont N9B 3P4. Film, Radio, TV.

Concordia University, Production & Animation 1395 Dorchester Blvd W, Montréal, Qué H3G 2M5. Dept. of Cinema and Photography.

Niagara College, Welland Campus, PO Box 1005, Welland, Ont L3B 5S2. Film, TV & Radio.

CZECHOSLOVAKIA

FAMU Film and Television Faculty, Academy of Performing Arts, Smetanovo nábř. 2, CS 116 65 Prague 1. Tel: (42) 2 265623. Fax: (42) 2 268735. Dean: Josef Pecák. Film and TV departments: directing, script-writing, cinematography, production, editing, sound, cartoon animation. Photo department: still photography/art, commercial, journalistic photography. Regular day study in Czech language. Bachelor and Master Degree, 3 and 2 years. Programme 3F-FAMU for foreigners, in English, 1 to 2 years. Entrance examinations. Short courses at all departments in English. Special course at Still Photography department, 3 months to 2 years. Foreign nationals may apply direct to FAMU.

DENMARK

Danish Film School, Danish Film Institute, Store Søndervoldstr., DK-1419 Copenhagen K.

EGYPT

Egyptian Film Institute, City of Arts, Pyramids, Giza. Established 1959. Higher Studies. Sections devoted to Direction, Production, Editing and Photography. Dean: Dr. Shawki Ali Mohamed.

FINLAND

Taideteollinen korkeakoulu, elokuvataiteen laitos, University of Industrial Arts, Department of Cinema and TV, Pursimiehenkatu 29–31, SF-00150 Helsinki. Chief Instructors: Ywe Jalander, Raimo Paananen, Tove Idström. Approximately 60 students (14 per year), 6 full-time and 25 part-time staff. Qualifications for admission: matriculation exam and the admission course of one week. Foreign students admitted with knowledge of Finnish. Average duration of studies: five years. Main subjects: directing, camerawork, screenwriting, sound, editing, documentary, producing. Production on 16 and 35mm films plus videotape. Production facilities: professional film equipment and TV studio and photographic equipment.

FRANCE

Fondation Européenne des Métiers de L'Image et du Son (FEMIS), Palais de Tokyo, 2 rue de la Manutention, 75116 Paris. Chairman: Jean-Claude Carrière. Director: Jack Gajos.
Conservatoire Libre du Cinéma Français (C.L.C.F.), 16 rue de Delta, 75009 Paris.
Institut Supérieur de Cinéma, Radio et Télévision (I.S.C.R.T.), 65 Bd. Brune, 75014 Paris.

GERMANY

Deutsche Film- und Fernsehakademie Berlin GmbH, DFFB, Pommernallee 1, 1000 Berlin 19. Director: Prof. Dr. Thomas Koebner. Four year course dealing with theories of filmmaking, film-history, and all aspects of practical film and television production; script-writing, direction, camerawork, editing and special effects. Students make films and videos and are encouraged to gain experience in as wide a variety of techniques as possible.
Hochschule für Fernsehen und Film, Frankenthaler Strasse 23, D–8000 München 90. President: Prof. Dr. Helmut Oeller. Approx. 160 students, 50 staff. Four-year course providing instruction in the theory and practice of film and television. Facilities provide for work in 16 and 35mm as well as video equipment. Studies are free. Two-step admission process; ask for details in January each year. Studies begin each Autumn.
Hochschule für Film und Fernsehen "Konrad Wolf", Karl Marx Strasse 33/34, 0-1590 Potsdamm. Rector: Prof. Wolf-Dieter Panse.

HUNGARY

Szinház-es Filmmüvészeti Föisskola, Vas u. 2/c, 1088 Budapest. Rector: Dr. Jenö Simó. General Secretary: László Vadász.

INDIA

Film and Television Institute of India, Law College Road, Poona 411 004. Director: K.G. Varma. 97 students in Film wing. Experienced teaching staff. The Institute conducts three-year courses in (1) Film Direction, (2) Motion Picture Photography, (3) Sound Recording and Sound Engineering, (4) Film Editing (two year duration). All four courses include one year integrated training. The training in TV is in the nature of in-service training for employees of Doordarshan i.e. Television Authority of India.
Film and Television Institute of Tamil Nadu, Department of Information and Public Relations, Government of Tamil Nadu, Madras, Adyar, Madras–600 020.

ISRAEL

Department of Film and Television, Tel Aviv University, Tel Aviv. Offers a two track curriculum, one with emphasis on film and TV production, the other with film theory.

ITALY

Centro Sperimentale di Cinematografia (C.S.C.), Via Tuscolana 1524, Rome. Director: Ernesto G. Laura.
Instituto di Storia del Cinema e dello Spettacolo, Universitá di Torino Facoltá di Magistero, Via Sant'Ottavio 20, 10124 Torino. Comprises courses in the history and appreciation of cinema.

JAPAN

Nihon University College of Art, Asahigaoka 2–42, Nerimaku, Tokyo, 176. Head of Film Department: Professor Toru Otake.

NETHERLANDS

Nederlandse Film- en Televisie Academie, De Lairessestraat 142, 1075 HL Amsterdam. Managing Director: Henk Petiet. 150 students, 30 staff. Four years.

POLAND

Pańswowa Wysza Szkola Filmowa, Telwizyjna e Teatralna, im Leona Schillera, ul. Targowa 61/63, 90 323 Lódz. Tel: (42) 743943. Fax: (42) 743538.

ROMANIA

Institutul de Artă Teatrală şi Cinematografică "I.L. Caragiale", str. Matei Voievod nr. 75–77 sect. 2 cod 73226, Bucharest. Dean: Professor Dr. Ileana Berlogea.

SPAIN

University of Valladolid, Cátedra de Historia y Estética de la Cinematografica, Palacio de Sta. Cruz, Valladolid. Director: Sr. Dr. Francisco Javier de la Plaza. Diploma Course on Film Theory, History, and Criticism.

SWEDEN

Dramatiska Institutet (College of Theatre, Film, Radio and Television), Borgvägen, Box 27090, S–102 51 Stockholm. Head of School: Janos Hersko. Formed in 1970, the Institute is intended to provide instruction in production techniques for theatre, film, radio and television. A three year course (Theatre, Film and T.V.); a two year course (Radio); and a one year course providing insight into the various media and their production methods; and continuing and advanced education in the form of extension courses. The Institute is equipped with film and TV studios, 10 editing rooms for 8, 16 and 35mm, and 4 video editing rooms with S-VHS, 1 on-line editing room with M4, sound mixing studios and portable video equipment.

Department of Theatre and Cinema Arts, University of Stockholm, Filmhuset, Borgvägen 1–5, Box 27062, S–102 51 Stockholm. Stockholm University is the only university in Sweden offering both Theatre and Cinema. Tuition in Cinema Arts is provided for between 300–350 students, and the curriculum offers courses in the history of the cinema, film analysis and mass media studies.

TURKEY

Sinema-TV Enstitüsü Kişlaönü, Beşiktas, Istanbul. Director: Sam Sekeroğlu. Film and TV school offering applied and theoretical training.

U.K.

National Film and Television School, Station Road, Beaconsfield, Bucks. HP90 1LG. Tel: (0494) 671234. Fax: (0494) 674042. Director: Colin Young. Approximately 100 students. 15 full-time teaching staff complemented by a large number and variety of part-time tutors, all experienced professionals. Three year full-time course with the emphasis on creative production for the cinema and television, through practice and instruction, designed to equip graduates for employment in the industry. Admission is through open competition. The studios are fully equipped for 16mm films with some 35mm, and professional video facilities. The School operates a positive equal opportunities policy.

London International Film School, 24 Shelton Street, London WC2H 9HP. Principal: Martin M. Amstell. Two year Diploma Course to professional level recognised by the British Film Technicians' Union – A.C.T.T. On average, half each term is devoted to film production and half to practical and theoretical tuition. The School has two cinemas, two shooting stages with professional lighting equipment, two rehearsal stages and fifteen cutting rooms. Comprehensively equipped departments use Bolex, Arriflex and Panavision cameras, Nagra, Westrex and Perfectone recorders, Steenbeck and Moviola editing tables and U-matic Portapacks and editing suites. Productions are on 16mm and 35mm film and video tape. Tuition is by permanent and visiting professionals. Entrance requirements: a degree or an art or technical diploma. Lesser qualifications accepted in cases of special ability or experience. All applicants must submit examples of their work and be proficient in English. New courses start three times a year.

Middlesex Polytechnic, Faculty of Art and Design, Cat Hill, Barnet, Herts EN4 8HT. Tel: (081) 368 1299. Course Leader: David Furnham. MA in Video. This one year course (48 weeks, full-time) offers graduate students who already have considerable experience in low-band video production the opportunity to think creatively and critically about video production, to acquire detailed knowledge of professional practice in the television and video industries, to work as part of a team to produce a video tape of fully professional standard for a stated context. It also allows each student to produce, as an individual project, a fully developed script. This course replaces the previous Post-graduate Diploma.

Northern School of Film and Television, Leeds Polytechnic, Calverley Street, Leeds LS1 3HE, England. Tel: 532–832 600. MA/Postgraduate Diploma in Scriptwriting for Film and Television (Fiction). Staffed largely by working professional writers, this one year course covers writing for short and feature films, TV dramas and soap operas etc. Aims to help graduates set up a credible freelance practice. MA/Postgraduate Diploma in Film Production (Fiction). This one year practical course admits the students into one of six categories: direction, production, camera, art direction, editing or sound. Six short films are produced and may be screened by Yorkshire TV. Emphasis is on joint creativity under pressure. Based at Sheffield Polytechnic.

Polytechnic of Central London, School of Communication, 18/22 Riding House Street, London W1P 7PD. M.A. in Film and Television Studies: advanced level part-time course (evenings and weekends) concerned with theoretical aspects of film and TV. Modular credit transfer and accumulation scheme, with exemption for work previously done. Post-graduate Diploma normally awarded after two years (70 credits), M.A. after three years (120 credits, including research thesis). Modules offered: Authorship and Mise-en-Scène, Structuralism, Realism and Anti-Realism, The Film and TV Audience; Film, Culture and Society; Hollywood 1900–1950, British Cinema History, British TV Drama, The Documentary Tradition, Public Service Broadcasting, TV Genres and Gender, Psychoanalysis and Cinema, Third World Cinema, Soviet Cinema of the 1920s and 1930s, Production Studies, Issues in British Film Culture, Modernism and Postmodernism, Women and Film. No practical component. Course leader: Dr Robert E. Peck.

Royal College of Art, Department of Film and Television, Kensington Grove, London SW7 2EU. 30 students. Two year post-graduate course.

Bournemouth and Poole College of Art, Department of Photography, Film and Television, Wallisdown Road, Poole, Dorset BH12 5HH. B/Tec Higher National Diploma in Photography, Film & Television. Qualifications for admission are minimum age 18, with five G.C.S.E. passes, two of which must be a 'A' level, or appropriate B/Tec Diploma or satisfactory completion of a foundation course or approved commercial/industrial experience.

Bristol University, Department of Drama, Radio, Film and Television Studies, 29 Park Row, Bristol BS1 5LT. Director of Film Studies: John Adams. Undergraduate courses leading to BA in practical criticism, history, theory and practice of film and TV. Postgraduate: higher degree by dissertation leading to M.Litt and Ph.D.; Diploma in Film and Television, predominantly practical, provides an introduction to a wide range of technical skills, followed by production of films and TV programmes in the Department's studio and on location. Normally one year. Film production entirely on 16mm; video production on Betacam and U-matic; 4 colour-camera Studio; rostrum facilities.

Derbyshire College of Higher Education, Kedleston Road, Derby DE3 1GB. Director of Studies: John Fullerton. MA/Post-graduate Diploma in Film with Television Studies. Subject specialist course offered in the College's Modular Master's Scheme. Taught programme up to Postgraduate Diploma level; Master's Degree by Dissertation and supporting studies in film historiography and research methodology. Study supported by the Centre for Early Film plus range of materials in the Faculty Library.

University of East Anglia, School of English and American Studies, Norwich NR4 7TJ. Offers Film as a BA Hons Major in combination with English Studies, and as a BA Hons Minor in combination with other Arts subjects: also offers a taught MA in Film Studies, with a new option in Film Archive work based on collaboration with the East Anglian Film Archive. The MA is awarded 50% on individual dissertation. Students are also accepted for the research degrees of M.Phil and Ph.D. Staff: Charles Barr, Thomas Elsaesser, Andrew Higson (Archive work: David Cleveland).

Newport Film School, Faculty of Art and Design, Gwent College of Higher Education, Clarence Place, Newport, Gwent NP9 OUW. Film and Television Practice – A two-year H.N.D. practical course in film and video production with an opportunity to specialise in either live action, 2D or 3D animation techniques. Course director: Henry Lutman. Senior lecturers: Peter Turner and Cyril Moorhead.

Harrow College of the Polytechnic of Central London, Northwick Park, Harrow, HA1 3TP. Three-year full-time BA(Hons) in Contemporary Media Practice (formally BA-(Hons) in Photography Film & Video). The course offers an integrated approach combining theory and practice, and encouraging students to explore a range of media. Years one and two teach skills in photography, film (16mm and S–8), video (Umatic Hi-and Lo-band, and VHS), A-V and computer animation etc in the context of a wide-ranging core of theoretical studies. Year three students work on a self-initiated project which may be in any – or a combination of – media and includes a long contextual study.

University of Stirling, Film and Media Studies, Stirling FK9 4LA. Head of Department: Professor P.R. Schlesinger. Undergraduate Film and Media Studies is designed at Stirling to give a grounding in the theory and criticism of film, television, radio and the press together with some practical experience. Also offers Postgraduate studies in the same area.

West Surrey College of Art and Design, Falkner Road, Farnham, Surrey GU9 7DS. CNAA BA (Hons) in Photography. 3 years full time. Intake is 35. Course leader Peter Hall. CNAA BA (Hons) in Animation. 3 years full time. Course accredited by ACTT. Intake is 25. Course leader Roger Noake. CNAA BA (Hons. in Film & Video. 3 years full time. Course accredited by ACTT. Intake is 25. Course leader Claire Mussell. Entry requirements for each course in accordance with CNAA regulations.

URUGUAY

Escuela de Cinematografía, 18 de Julio 1265 p. 2, Montevideo. Director: Juan José Ravaioli.

U.S.A.

Information on the many thousands of U.S. film courses is contained in the *American Film Institute's Guide to College Courses in Film and Television* which can be ordered at Publications, The American Film Institute, 2021 North Western Avenue, Los Angeles, California 90027.

U.S.S.R.

Vsesoyuzni Gosudarstvenni Institut Kinematografi (VGIK) (All-Union State Institute of Cinematography), ulitsa Vilgelma Pika 3, Moscow 129226. Director: Vitali Nikolayevich Zzhdan. No. of students: 1,500. No. of instructors: 250. Length of courses: actors, economists – 4 years; cameraman – 4 years; writers, directors – 5 years; designers – 6 years. Specialisation is always taken into account during training. The various disciplines taught can be divided into three groups; socio-economic (e.g. philosophy – 140 hours), general knowledge (e.g. history of Fine Arts – 160 hours – history of theatre. Soviet and foreign literature), and

specialist instruction (e.g. for cameramen; 320 hours on operating, 110 on lighting). Practical work undertaken on all courses. The Institute has a training studio (with four stages totalling 1,000 sq. metres and 100 cameras of various types), an information department, its own textbooks, and teaching manuals, and also auxiliary instruction quarters for Soviet cinema, foreign cinema operating, direction, etc.

YUGOSLAVIA

Fakultet dramških umetnosti (pozorišta, filma, radija i televizije), Ho Si Minova 20, 11070 Beograd. Vladan Slijepčević. Four-year course equivalent to undergraduate level; specialisation in direction, production, photography, dramaturgy, acting or editing (as well as a fine *animation* and *special effects* division). Students make films on 8 and 16mm, and a final diploma film on 35mm.

From the March of Time episode, *T-Men in Action*. Stock footage from this classic series is available from Archive Film Productions in New York

FILM ARCHIVES
■ ■

ALBANIA
Arkivi Shtetöror i Filmit i Republikes Populor Socialiste të Shqipërisë, Rruga Alexandre Moisiu Nr–76, Tirana. Tel: 77–94/-51–6. Director: Abaz Hoxha. Stock: 5,000 film titles, 10,000 film stills, 1,025 posters.

ALGERIA
Cinémathèque Algerienne, rue Larbi-Ben-M'Hidi, Algiers. Tel: 638301. Telex: 67437. Director: Boudjemaa Kareche. Stock: 15,000 film titles, 30,000 film stills, 3,000 posters.

ARGENTINA
Cinemateca Argentina, Corrientes 2092, 2nd floor, 1045 Buenos Aires. Tel: (54–1) 953 3755/953 7163. Fax: 005413110562. Telex: 24569 SICVIL AR. Executive Director: Mrs. Paulina Fernandez Jurado. Established in 1949. Stock: 11,250 film titles, 5,600 books, collection of film periodicals, 340,000 film stills, 6,300 film posters. The collection of micro-filmed clippings holds 32,000 files on individual films, 18,000 on foreign film personalities, 7,000 on Argentine film personalities. The library is open to researchers and students. The Cinemateca operates two film theatres with daily screenings.

AUSTRALIA
National Film and Sound Archive, McCoy Circuit, Acton, Canberra A.C.T. 2601. Tel: (61–6) 2671711. Telex: AA 61930. Director: Graham Gilmour. Deputy Director: Ray Edmondson. Stock: 52,000 film and video titles, 315,000 stills, 8,500 scripts, 56,000 posters, 400,000 publicity items, 2,500 memorabilia items.
State Film Archives, Library and Information Service of Western Australia. Alexander Library Building, Perth Cultural Centre, Perth, WA 6,000. Tel: 427 3303. Film Archivist: Robin Faulkner. Stock: 1,800 film titles.

AUSTRIA
Österreichisches Filmarchiv, A–1010 Vienna, Rauhensteingasse 5, Film stores and theatre: Laxenburg, Altes Schloss. Tel: 5129936. Fax: 513 5330. President: Prof. Dr. Alfred Lehr. Director: Dr. Walter Fritz. Stock: 36,621 film titles, 8,800 books, 1,006 periodicals, 221,200 film stills, 5,130 photo negatives, 6,186 posters. Regular Summer exhibitions and retrospectives at Laxenburg, Altes Schloss.
*Österreichisches Filmmuseum, A–1010 Vienna, Augustinerstr. 1, Tel: 533 70 54–0. Fax: 533 70 56 25. Telex: 111768 fma. Directors: Peter Konlechner and Prof. Peter Kubelka. Stock: app. 10,000 film titles, and an extensive library. A non-profit institution, the Museum now has 15,000 members and holds daily screenings in its invisible cinema at the Albertina Gallery. The shows have created a hungry audience for cinema in spite of the unimaginative programming of Vienna's commercial cinemas. "One of the most active cinémathèques in Europe" (Der Spiegel).

BELGIUM
*Cinémathèque Royale, 23 rue Ravenstein, 1000 Brussels. Tel: 5134155. Telex: 23022. Stock: more than 45,000 film titles, 25,000 books, 200,000 film stills and a large collection of posters. Publishes useful catalogues and screens three sound and two silent films daily. A preserving archive, where films can only be consulted for research purposes.

BOLIVIA
Cinemateca Boliviana, Pichincha esq. Indaburo, s/n-Casilla 20271–La Paz. Tel: 325346. Director: Pedro Susz K. Stock: 5,850 film titles, 850 books, 8,200 film stills, 1,900 posters, 8,000 clippings. The Cinemateca operates one film theatre with daily screenings at 16.00 and 19.30 hours.

BRAZIL
Cinemateca Brasileira, Caixa Postal 12900, 04092 São Paulo. Tel: 5774448. Telex: 1153714. Director: Maria Rita Galvão. Stock: 30,000 film titles, 33,220 photos, 3,610 posters. Mainly concerned with Brazilian films, this

archive has laboratory facilities to preserve and restore films, and all the nitrate in the country is deposited here.

Cinemateca do Museu de Arte Moderna, Caixa Postal 44, CEP 20021, Rio de Janeiro, RJ. Tel: (021) 2102188. Telex: 21–22084 FTVR BR. Director: João Luiz Vieira. Stock: 10,000 film titles, 4,500 books, 2,570 periodicals, 75,000 film stills, 4,800 posters. Daily screenings are held in the archive's 185 seat theatre. The archive publishes a monthly bulletin, restores and preserves its collections and provides facilities for researchers.

BULGARIA
Bulgarska Nacionalna Filmoteka, ul. Gourko 36,1000 Sofia. Tel: 802749.

CANADA
National Archives of Canada, Moving Image and Sound Archives, 395 Wellington Street, Ottawa, Ontario K1A 0N3. Tel: (613) 9966009. Telex: 0533367. Director: Jana Vosikovska. Stock: 300,000 film, video and sound recording titles, 9,000 books, 1,060 periodicals, 600,000 stills, 7,000 posters. Title index of 500,000 films. Reference dossiers on 95,000 personalities, films and subjects. The collection concentrates on Canadian film and television production and oral history, but the Archives are building up an international collection and expanding facilities are available for researchers and students.

La Cinémathèque Québécoise., 335 boul. de Maisonneuve est, Montréal, Québec H2X 1K1. Tel: (514) 842 9763. Curator: Robert Daudelin. Stock: 23,000 film titles, 250,000 stills, 12,000 posters. The Cinémathèque specialises in preserving the work of animators and of Canadian film-makers and this collection is on show at thirteen screenings a week, together with other aspects of world cinema.

Conservatoire d'Art Cinématographique de Montréal, 1455 de Maisonneuve West, Montréal, Québec. Director: Serge Losique. Stock: 3,000 film titles, 1,000 books, 100 periodicals, 2,000 film stills.

CHILE
Cinemateca Chilena en al Exilio, Padre Xifré 3, oficin 111, Madrid 2, Spain. Director: Pedro Chaskel. Curator: Gaston Angelovici. The Cinemateca is continuing in exile the work of Chile's principal archive, the Cinemateca Universitaria.

Member of the Union de Cinematecas de América Latina.

CHINA
Cinémathèque Chinoise, 25B rue Xin Wai, Beijing. Tel: 2014316. Telex: 22195. Director: Xu Zhuang. Stock: 21,000 films, 11,000 stills.

COLOMBIA
Fundacion Patrimonio Filmico Colombiana, Carrera 13 No. 13–24 piso 9, Bogotá. Tel: 2815241–2836496. Executive Director: Claudia Triana de Vargas. Curator: Jorge Nieto. Documentation Centre: Jorge Caicedo. Stock: 40,000 reels of film and videotape, 222 museum apparatus, screening rooms for film and video. Books: 565 titles (700 volumes). Periodicals: 290. Posters: 305 titles (535 copies). Press books: 210. Press clippings: 6,000. Screenplays: 85 titles (90 volumes). Stills: 7,000. Other special collections, viewing and library service. FIAF observer.

CUBA
Cinemateca de Cuba, Calle 23 no. 1155, Vedado, Havana. Tel: 34719. Telex: 511419. Interim Director: Pastor Vega. Stock: 6,300 film titles, 110,500 film stills. Members of the Coordinated Latin American de Archivos de Imagenes en Movimiento (CLAIM).

CYPRUS
Kypriaki Tainiothiki, PO Box 5314, Nicosia. Curator: Panikkos Chrysanthou. Stock: 230 films.

CZECHOSLOVAKIA
Ceskoslovenský filmový ústav-filmový archiv, Malešická ul., CS–130 00 Praha 3. Tel: 894501. Fax: 261618. Curator: Vladimír Opěla. Stock: about 16,000 features, plus the same number of shorts and documentaries, incl. newsreels, 82,000 books, 12,000 periodicals 450,000 stills, 50,000 posters.

DENMARK
Det Danske Filmmuseum, Store Sondervoldstraede, DK–1419 Copenhagen K. Tel: 31576500. Telex: 31465. Fax: 31541312. Director: Ib Monty. Stock: 13,000 film titles, 42,000 books, 350 periodicals subscribed to, 1,800,000 film stills, 15,000 posters. 158-seat cinema used for three daily screenings for researchers and

students. The Museum also publishes a magazine "Kosmorama" and occasional leaflets and books on film.

ECUADOR

Cinemateca Nacional del Ecuador, Avenida 6 de Diciembre y Tarqui, Quito. Tel: 543748. Director: Ulises Estrella. Stock: 298 film titles, 3,600 film stills, 250 posters.

EGYPT

National Film Archive, c/o Egyptian Film Centre, City of Arts, Pyramids Road, Giza, Egypt. Tel: 854801/850897. Telex: 21863 EG-FICUN. Fax: 854701. Curator: Nagui Riad. Stock: 1,817 film titles, 700 film stills, 600 posters.

FINLAND

Suomen elokuva-arkisto, Pursimiehenkatu 29–31 A, P.O. Box 177, SF–00150 Helsinki. Tel: + 358.0.171417. Telex: 125960. Fax: + 358.0.171544. Director: Kaarle Stewen. Programmer: Antti Alanen. Stock: 8,000 feature film titles, 20,000 shorts and advertising film (spots), 6,000 videocassettes, 14,000 books, 132 magazines (currently subscribed), 7,000 dialogue lists and scripts, 320,000 different stills, 110,000 posters and 30,000 documentation files. The archive arranges regular screenings in Helsinki and seven other cities.

FRANCE

Cinémathèque Française, 29 rue de Colisée, 75008 Paris. President: Jean Rouch.
Cinémathèque de Toulouse, rue de Faubourg Bonnefoy 12, 31500 Toulouse, France. Tel: (33) 61 48 90 75. Fax: (33) 61 58 19 79. President/Curator: Guy-Claude Rochemont. Administrator/Deputy Curator: Jean-Paul Gorce. Stock: 16,503 films, 550,000 film stills, 41,200 posters, 38,000 reference dossiers on personalities, films and subjects, 80 periodical subscriptions, 700 complete periodical collections, 12,000 books, 600 scripts. A non-profit making organisation devoted to the preservation, restoration and exhibition of films, the Cinémathèque operates one film theatre with daily screenings. It collects whatever film is presented or deposited. It also has miscellaneous collections or objects related to film exhibition and exploitation. A journal, *"Archives"*, and a number of brochures and programme leaflets are regularly published. Research and viewing facilities are available at university level and by appointment.

Service des Archives de Film du Centre National de la Cinématographie, 7 bis rue Alexandre Turpault, 78390 Bois d'Arcy. Tel: 34602050. Curator: F. Schmitt. Stock: 97,000 film titles, 150,000 stills, 15,000 posters, 24,700 screenplays, 1,200 apparati. Founded in 1969. Film vaults capable of holding 1,200,000 reels of film, and laboratory for restoration of old films. Documentation department.

Cinémathèque Universitaire, UER d'Art de d'Archéologie, 3 rue Michelet, 75006 Paris.
Institut Lumière, 25 rue du Premier-Film, 69008 Lyon. Tel: 78.00.86.68. President: Bertrand Tavernier. Admirable institution that screens precious old films, organises exhibitions, preserves films, and publishes monographs.
Musée du Cinéma de Lyon, 69 rue Jean Jaurès, 69100 Villeurbanne. Tel: 8532769. Curator: Paul Génard. Stock: 1,600 film titles, 1,000 film stills, 50 posters.

GERMANY

Münchner Stadtmuseum/Filmmuseum, St.-Jakob-Platz 1, 8000 München 2. Tel: (49) 89 233 22348. Fax: (49) 89 2333931. Curator: Enno Patalas. A municipal archive devoted to the restoration of German classics and to the preservation of the New German Cinema.
Stiftung Deutsche Kinemathek, Pommernallee 1, 1000 Berlin 19. Tel: 30307234. Fax: 3029294. Director: Hans Helmut Prinzler. Stock: 8,000 film titles, 1,000,000 film stills, 15,000 posters, 60,000 film programmes, 10,000 scripts etc. The Kinemathek's library of books and periodicals is amalgamated with that of the Film-und-Fernsehakademie, in the same building.
Bundesarchiv-Filmarchiv, Hausvogteiplatz 3–4, –1080 Berlin. Tel: (37–2) 212 4324. *Also at:* Potsdamer Str. 1, POB 320, D– 5400 Koblenz. Tel: (49–261) 5050. President: Prof. Dr F.P. Kahlenberg. Stock: 120,000 film titles, including 100,000 documentary films and newsreels and 20,000 long film features, exclusively of German production. Co-operation with Stiftung Deutsche Kinemathek Berlin and Deutsches Institut für Filmkunde Wiesbaden.
Deutsches Filmmuseum, Schaumainkai 41, 6000 Frankfurt am Main 70. Tel: (069) 212 38830. Fax: 212 37881. Director: Prof. Walter

Schobert. Deputy Director: Jürgen Berger. Film Archive: Rainer Schang. Stock: 3,000 film titles, 14,000 books, 110 current periodicals subscribed to, 300,000 stills, 15,000 posters, thousands of items of cinema equipment, cameras, projectors, ephemera plus musical scores of silent films. The museum incorporates the Kommunales Kino Frankfurt. It has a permanent exhibition on two floors and exhibitions on various themes (up to three per year). It screens 3 different films a day and publishes books and a magazine.

The Museum is organiser of the International Children's Film Festival, now in the 16th year. **Deutsches Institut für Filmkunde,** Schaumainkai 41, 6000 Frankfurt am Main 70. Tel: 617045. Telex: 4–189969. Telefax: 069/62 0060. Director: Dr. Gerd Albrecht. Deputy Director: Eberhard Spiess. Administrative Director: Peter Franz. Stock: 4,200 film titles, 54,000 books, 260 periodicals, 1,000,000 film stills, 30,000 posters, 16,000 dialogue lists, 5,000 scripts. Also programmes, newspaper clippings, advertising material.

Arsenal Kino der Freunde der Deutschen Kinemathek, Welserstrasse 25, D-1000 Berlin 30. Tel: 213–6039. The nearest equivalent of Britain's NFT. Became a model for all "Communal Cinemas" in the Federal Republic of Germany. Programming: Ulrich and Erika Gregor, Alf Bold. The Freunde also run a non-commercial distribution of about 800 films, most of them from the International Forum of Young Cinema, the independent second main programme of the Berlin Film Festival, organised by the Freunde.

Staatliches Filmarchiv der Deutschen Demokratischen Republik, Hausvogteiplatz 3–4, 1080 Berlin. Tel: 2124324. Telex: 112712. Curator: Wolfgang Klaue. Stock: 57,000 film titles, plus documentation material on about 25,000 titles, 1,500,000 stills and 14,000 posters. With its own theatre, the Filmarchiv holds exhibitions and a yearly retrospective on documentaries at the Leipzig festival.

GREECE

Tainiothiki tis Ellados, 1 Canari Street, Athens 106 74. Tel: 3612046. President of D.C.: Aglaya Mitropoulos. Curator: Mona Mitropoulos. Director: Theodore Adamploulos. Stock: 3,800 film titles, 6,000 photos of Greek and international cinema, 500 posters of Greek and 2,500 posters of international cinema, 1,500 film stills. Expanding collection of magic lanterns, praxinoscopes, etc.

HUNGARY

Szinház-és Filmmüvészeti Fóiskola, Vas utca 2/c, Budapest 1088. Tel: (361) 1384 749. Fax: (361) 1294 790. Rector: Ggörgy Iliés. General Secretary; Lajos Tiszeker. Stock: 1,931 feature titles, 8,611 documentaries, 3,693 newsreels, 13,224 books, 3,710 periodicals, 2,708 scripts, 5,381 manuscripts, 143,159 stills, 15,365 posters. The institute, besides housing the archive (Budakeszi ut 51/b, 10 21 Budapest. Head of archive: Mrs Vera Gyürey) also does research into the history of the cinema, particularly the Hungarian cinema, and encourages the development of film culture in Hungary.

Maygar Filmintézet, Budakeszi ut 51b, 1021 Budapest. Tel: 17.67.106. Director: Vera Gyurey. Stock: 7,022 feature titles, 8,713 short films, 3,756 newsreels, 13,224 books, 3,710 periodicals, 2,708 scripts, 5,381 manuscripts, 143,159 stills, 15,365 posters. The institute, besides housing the archive, also does research into the history of the cinema, particularly the Hungarian cinema, and encourages the development of film culture in Hungary.

Szinház-és Filmmüvészeti Föiskola, Vas u. 2/c, 1088 Budapest, Hungary. Rector: György Illes. General Secretary: Lajos Tiszeker.

ICELAND

Kvikmyndasafn Islands (Icelandic Film Archive), Laugavegur 24, 101 Reykjavík. (Postal: P.O. Box 320, 121 Reykjavík.) Tel: 10940. Fax: 627171. Nearly 400 titles in the collection, documentaries being the larger part of it. Numerous sources of information regarding Icelandic films and the national film history.

INDIA

National Film Archive of India, Ministry of Information and Broadcasting, Government of India, Law College Road, Poona 411004. Tel: 51559. Director: P.K. Nair. Stock: 10,798 films, 17,991 books, 214 periodicals, 1,678 disc-records, 108 audio tapes, 1,951 microfilms, 48,685 stills, 4,864 posters, 4,638 song booklets, 19,999 shooting scripts, 5,244 pamphlets and folders and 56,644 press clippings. Daily screenings for Film & TV Institute students at Poona; weekly public screenings at Poona and Bombay, regular special screenings.

National Film Archive of India, Ministry of Information and Broadcasting, Government of India, Law College Road, Poona 411 004, India. tel: 331 559. Director: P.B. Pendharker. Stock: 12,202 films, 532 video cassettes, 19,746 books, 173 periodicals, 20,835 scripts, 7,038 pamphlets/folders, 107,648 press clippings, 85,976 stills, 2, 820 slides, 5,916 wall posters, 5,708 song booklets, 1,822 disc records, 115 audio tapes, 1,957 micro films, 42 microfiches. Daily screenings for Film & Television Institute students at Poona; weekly public screenings at Poona and Bombay, regular special screenings.

INDONESIA

Sinematek Indonesia, Pusat Perfilman "H. Usmar Ismail," Jalan H.R. Rasuana Said, Jakarta Selatan. Tel: 516891. Director: H. Misbach Yusa Biran. Stock: about 257 features plus 114 shorts. Indonesian film titles (50% negatives). Earliest film dates from 1938.

IRAN

National Film Archive of Iran, P.O. Box 5158, Tehran 11365, Iran. Tel: 324 1601. Director: Mohammad Hassan Khoshnevis.

ISRAEL

Tel Aviv Cinémathèque. (The Doran Centre), 2 Sprintzak Street, Tel Aviv. Tel: (03) 217181. Fax: (03) 262817.
Israel Film Archive (Jerusalem Cinémathèque), Hebron Road, P.O Box 8561, Jerusalem 91083. Tel: 724131. Telex: 26358 CANJR IL. Fax: 733076. Director: Lia van Leer. Stock: 14,000 prints in international, Israeli and Jewish collection. Books, periodicals, stills, posters and scripts. Jewish Film Centre, extensive Israeli and Jewish theme collection. Permanent exhibition of early cinema apparatus. 1,200 screenings yearly, extensive morning educational programme for schools. Facilities for film research. Organisers of the Jerusalem International Film Festival (July).

ITALY

Cineteca Italiana, Via Palestro 16, 20121 Milano. Tel: 799224. Sec. General: Gianni Comencini. Stock: 30,000 film titles, 600,000 stills, 8,000 posters.

Museo Nazionale del Cinema, Palazzo Chiablese, Piazza S. Giovanni 2, 10122 Torino. Tel: 4361148/4361387. President: Roberto Morano. Stock: 2,000 film titles, 300,000 stills, 20,000 posters. The Museum is temporarily closed. Films screened every day 4 to 12 pm in three rooms at Cinema Massimo, Via Montebello 8.
Cineteca Nazionale, Via Tuscolana n. 1524, 00173 Rome. Tel: 722941. Fax: 7211619. Interim Curator is presently the General Director of the Centro Sperimentale di Cinematografia: Avv. Angelo Libertini. Preservation Management Consultant: Dr. Guido Cincotti. Head of Archive/Preservation Section: Dr. Mario Musumeci. Head of Access/Screenings Section: Dr.ssa Irene Proietti. Stock: 23,000 film titles, 30,000 books and periodicals, 200,000 stills, 3000 posters. The Cineteca is a department of the Centro Sperimentale di Cinematografia.
Cineteca del Friuli, 26 via Osoppo, 33013 Gemona del Friuli (Udine). Tel: (0432) 980458. Fax: (0432) 970 542. Established in 1982, this excellent Italian archive conceived the idea for the Pordenone Silent Film Festival, and organises regular screenings. Stock: 1,500 film titles, 3,000 newsreels, 5,000 books.

JAPAN

Japan Film Library Council/Kawakita Memorial Film Institute, Ginza-Hata Building, 4–5, 4–chome, Ginza, Chuo-ku, Tokyo. Director: Mrs. Kashiko Kawakita. Secretary: Akira Shimizu. Stock: 500 film titles, 3,000 books, 6,000 periodicals, 50,000 film stills, 100 posters. The Council co-operates with archives throughout the world in supplying Japanese films for screening, makes available stills for publication and publishes documentation of its collections.
National Filmcenter, 7–6, 3 chome, Kyobashi, Chuoku, Tokyo. Curator: Masatoshi Ohba. Stock: 2,100 film titles, 6,000 shorts, animation and newsreels, 4,000 books, 25,000 magazines, 100,000 stills, 1,800 posters, 20,000 scripts. Screenings held twice on Saturday and Sunday.

KOREA (NORTH)

*The National Film Archive of the Democratic People's Republic of Korea, 15 Sochangdong, Central District, Pyongyang. Tel: 34551. Telex: 5345. Director: Pak Sun Tae. Stock: 17,200 film titles, 6,300 stills, 1,100 posters.

KOREA (SOUTH)

Korean Film Archive, 34–5, 3–ka, Namsan-Dong, Chung-ku, Seoul 100. Tel: 755.92915. Telex: 28385. Director: Chung Yun-Koo. Stock: 2,236 film titles, 6,550 stills. Initiated in the mid–1970's and a full board member of FIAF since 1984. Though an independent body, it is funded by the Motion Picture Promotion Corporation.

LUXEMBOURG

Cinémathèque Municipale de Ville de Luxembourg, 19 rue de la Chapelle, L-1325 Luxembourg. Tel: (352) 4796–2644. Fax: (352) 45 93 75. Curator: Fred Junck. Member of FIAF Founded in 1977, the Cinémathèque Municipale specialises in unearthing rare French and American films. Stock: some 8,000 titles (9.5, 16, 35 and 70 mm prints), numerous stills, posters and books. Two screenings per day in a comfortable, Dolby-equipped 180-seat auditorium. Organises "Live Cinema" presentations of silent classics with full orchestra accompaniment, in association with composer-conductor Carl Davis.

MEXICO

Filmoteca de la Universitad Nacional Autonoma de Mexico, San Ildefonso 43, 06020 Mexico, D.F. Tel: 702 6432. Telex: 1777429. General Director: Biol. Ivan Trujillo Bolio. Stock: 7,500 film titles. 120,000 stills.

Cinemateca Mexicana, Museo Nacional de Antropologia, Calzada M. Gandhi, México 6, D.F. Director: Galdino Gomez Gomez. Stock: 1,000 film titles. 500 books, 500 film stills, 300 posters. The Cinemateca Mexicana also has a collection of early apparati dating from 1900.

Cinemateca Luis Buñuel, Calle 5, Oriente 5, Apdo. Postal 255, Puebla, Pue. Curator: Fernando Osorio Alarcon. Established in 1975, this archive has a stock of 100 films, some of them made entirely in Puebla, belonging to the silent period; 300 posters, 500 stills, 200 film books.

Cineteca Nacional, Av. Mexico-Coyoacán 389, 03330 Mexico. Tel: 688 8814. Telex: 1760050 RTCME. Director: Mercedes Certucha. Mexico's main film archive, supported by the Federal government. Stock: 3,700 film titles, 22,000 reels. Documentation department: 21,000 books, 3,000 stills folders, 3,000 posters. Library, bookshop, gallery and four film theatres open Tuesday to Sunday to the public, 14 screenings daily.

NETHERLANDS

Stichting Nederlands Filmmuseum, Vondelpark 3, 1071 AA Amsterdam. Tel: (020) 5891.400. Fax: (020 6833401 Director: Hoos Blotkamp. Deputy Director: Eric de Kuyper. Stock: about 25,000 films, 25,000 film stills, 30,000 posters. The museum has a permanent historic film exhibition and exhibitions with the programme. In two theatres (of 95 seats each) three films a day are shown in thematic programming.

Audiovisual Archive of the Netherlands Information Service, Baden Powellweg 5,2583 KT The Hague; Postbus 20006, 2500 EA The Hague. Head: Mr. R.H.J. Egeter van Kuyk. Permanent collections of films and photographs of the central Government. Mostly documentary material since 1898.

NEW ZEALAND

The New Zealand Film Archive, P.O. Box 9544, 82 Tory Street, Wellington. Tel: 847647. Fax: 829595. Telex: 30386.

NORWAY

Norsk Filminstitutt, Militærhospitalet, Grev Wedels plass, Postboks 482, Sentrum, 0105 Oslo 1. Tel: 472 428740. Fax: 472 332277. Director: Jan Erik Holst. Curator: Arne Pedersen. Head of Cinémathèque: Kjell Billing. Stock: 11,000 film titles, 13,000 books, 130 periodicals and a large collection of stills and posters. Also over five hundred pieces of early cinema apparatus and a fine theatre for screening films. The cinémathèque of the film institute is run by the organisation "The Friends of the NFI."

Henie-Onstad Art Centre, 1311 Hovikodden, Oslo. Director: Per Hovdenakk. Stock: 200 film titles, 100 video works, 500 books and periodicals, 4,000 film stills, 600 posters. A large collection of documentary material on experimental film, and regular screenings.

PANAMA

Cinemateca del GECU, Apartado 6–1775, Estafeta El Dorado, Panama. Telex: 2643 Decla PG. Director: Edgar Soberón Torchia. Stock includes films, books, periodicals, film stills and posters. It has a small theatre in the University of Panama, with three daily screenings.

POLAND

Filmoteka Polska, ul. Pulawska 61, 00–975

Warszawa, skr, poczt. 65. Tel: 455074. Fax: 455074. Telex: 813640.

PORTUGAL
Cinemateca Portuguesa, Rua Barata Salgueiro 39, 1200 Lisboa. Tel: 546279/547732. Telex: 15308 CITECA P. Fax: 3523180. Director: Luís De Pina. Stock: 11,000 film titles, 18,000 film books, 155 current periodicals, 1,000,000 stills. Daily screening sessions, retrospective cycles, publication of film books. New nitrate vaults under construction.

ROMANIA
Archiva Nationala de Filme, Bd. G.H. Gheorghiu dej 68/65 Bucharest. Director: Marin Paraianu. Stock: 7,500 feature titles, 22,500 shorts, 5,350 books, 3,500 stills, 20,000 posters and reference index. Archive also has a collection of clippings, scripts and periodicals.

SOUTH AFRICA
South African National Film, Video and Sound Archives, Private Bag X236, Pretoria 0001. Director: J.H. de Lange. Enormous variety of 35mm and 16mm footage, video and sound material as well as stills, scripts, books, posters and other material. The Archive is a State controlled organisation, dedicated to the classification and preservation of all items relating to the film, video and sound industries.

SPAIN
Filmoteca Española, Carretera Dehesa de la Villa, s/n. 28040 Madrid. Tel: 549 00 11. Fax: 549 73 48. Director: José María Prado. Stock: 11,819 film titles, 4,000 newsreels, 13,500 books, 3,000 posters, 130,000 still files. Thirty screenings a week in Cine Doré. Publishes monographs and useful brochures. Library open to the public.

Filmoteca de la Generalitat de Catalunya, Diputació 281, 08007 Barcelona. Tel: 317 35 85. Excellent Catalan archive that arranges screenings of foreign films also.

SWEDEN
Cinemateket, Svenska Filminstitutet, Filmhuset, Box 27 126, S–102 52 Stockholm. Tel: (46–8) 665 1100. Telex: 13326 FILMINS S. Fax: 08–6611820. Curator: Rolf Lindfors. Head of Documentation: Margareta Nordström. Stock: 13,000 film titles, 36,000 books, 280 periodicals, 1,500,000 film stills, 30,000 posters, and unpublished script material on 6,300 foreign films and 1,700 Swedish films. The collection of

SOUTH AFRICAN NATIONAL FILM, VIDEO AND SOUND ARCHIVE

The aims of this Archive are the acquisition, preservation, storage, adaptation and supply of available films, video and sound material of archival value, with specific reference to South Africa. Further, to provide an information service with regard to film, video, sound material and photographs.

It is a division of the State Archives of the Department of National Education.

Private Bag X236
PRETORIA
0001

South Africa

Isabelle Huppert with Freddy Buache after a tribute screening at La Cinémathèque Suisse

microfilmed clippings holds 50,000 jackets on individual films, 15,000 jackets on film personalities and 6,500 jackets on general subjects classified under 700 headings. Cinemateket has two theatres and four daily screenings in Stockholm. A selection of the yearly programme is also shown in Gothenburg and Malmö. There is also a film club for teenagers, *Filmögat*, with weekly screenings of film classics in four cities.

Asta Nielsen Filmmuseum, Vapenkroken 29, 222 47 Lund. Established in 1946 by G.D. Postén, Head of the Film History section at the Dept. of History, University of Lund. This is one of the biggest, private, non-commercial international collections of published, written materials on motion pictures and the film industry. Included in the collection are stills, programmes, books, magazines, posters, historical materials, etc. with the emphasis on the silent screen. Also the most complete collection of material on Asta Nielsen.

SWITZERLAND

Cinémathèque Suisse, 3 Allée Ernest Anser-

met, 1003 Lausanne. Tel: 237406. Telex: 24430. Curator: Freddy Buache. Stock: 25,000 titles (300,000 reels), 260 apparati, 35,000 posters, 300,000 film references, 15,000 books, and 1,000,000 stills. Three projections each day (except Sunday).

THAILAND

The National Film Archive of Thailand, 4 Chao Fa Road, Bangkok 10200. Tel: 282 0170/ 282 1847. Director: Penpan Jarernport. Stock: 1,680 film titles, 20,000 stills.

TAIWAN

Tien-ying t'u-shu-kuan (Film Library of The Motion Picture Development Foundations R.O.C..), 4th floor, 7 Ch'ingtao East Road, Taipei. Director: Ray Jiing. Opened in January 1979, this archive already has a book collection of some 5,759 titles (in 6,836 copies) and a print deposit of 2,134 films and a video section with five viewing machines and 2,671 tapes, 5,103 stills and 2,708 posters. The library holds regular screenings and special programmes (at 4th floor, 7 Ch'ingtao East Road, Taipei) and organises the annual International Film Exhibition, held in mid December.

TURKEY

Sinema-TV Enstitüsü, 80700 Kislaönü-Besiktas, Istanbul. Tel: 166 983031. Telex: 26439. Director: Sami Šekeroğlu. Stock: over 3,000 film titles, 300,000 stills, original negatives of early Turkish films, 500 books, collections of major world periodicals, 10,000 posters, 12 years' collection of press cuttings, 100 scripts, film music tapes.

U.K.

National Film Archive, 21 Stephen Street, London W1P 1PL. Tel: (71) 255 1444. Telex: 27624 BFILDNG. Fax: (71) 436 7950. Curator: Clyde Jeavons. Deputy Curator: Anne Fleming. Stock: 175,000 film and television titles, 6,500,000 black-and-white stills, 1,000,000 colour transparencies, 12,000 posters, 2,500 set-designs. Viewing service for students and researchers, production library for film-makers.

Imperial War Museum, Lambeth Road, London SE1 6HZ. Tel: (71) 416 5000, Fax: (71) 416 5379. Keeper of the Department of Film: Roger Smither. Deputy: Paul Sargent. Stock: over 40 million feet of actuality film relating to conflict in the Twentieth Century, from Britain and other countries. Viewing facilities for students and researchers *by appointment only*; public film screenings.

The Scottish Film Archive, Scottish Film Council, 74 Victoria Crescent Road, Dowanhill, Glasgow G12 9JN. Tel: (041) 334 4445. Curator: Janet McBain. Established in 1976, the Archive is mainly concerned with the filmed history of Scotland. Stock: 19,000 reels of film, varied collection of non-film material. Viewing facilities for students and researchers *by appointment only*.

URUGUAY

Cinemateca Uruguaya, Lorenzo Carnelli 1311, Casilla de Correo 1170, Montevideo. Tel: 482 460, 494 572, or 495 795. Telex: 22043. Curator: M. Martinez Carril. Stock: 6,500 film titles, 4,115 books, 11,000 periodicals, 13,500 posters.

Archivo Nacional de la Imagen-Sodre, Sarandi 430, Montevideo. Tel: 955758. Telex:

41134. Director: Eugenio Hintz. Stock: 550 film titles, 2,000 stills.

U.S.A.

American Film Institute/National Center for Film and Video Preservation, John F. Kennedy Center for the Performing Arts, Washington, DC 20566. Archivist: Susan Dalton. Stock: 24,000 film titles; no research facilities. All titles in the AFI Collection are housed at the Library of Congress or other American archives where the films are available for study. Screenings are held twice nightly in the AFI Theater at the Kennedy Center.

Harvard Film Archive, Carpenter Center for the Visual Arts, Harvard Univ, 24 Quincy Street, Cambridge, MA 02138. Tel: (617) 495 4700. Curator: Vlada Petrić. Films (16mm and 35mm): 1,000 titles including the Film Study Center collection (Robert Gardner, Producer/Director). Library: 1,100 books, 6,000 clippings files, 700 video tapes. Researchers and scholars may have access by appointment. Public film screenings which are designed in conjunction with Visual Studies courses take place six nights weekly.

The Library of Congress, Motion Picture, Broadcasting and Recorded Sound Division, Washington, DC 20540. Tel: (202) 707 5840. Telex: 64198. Director: Robert Saudek. Stock: 150,000 film and television titles, 4,000 books, 150,000 stills, descriptive material for more than 200,000 films and television programmes registered for U.S. copyright since 1912. Much more extensive book and periodical collection in the Library's general collection. Individual screening facilities are available to serious researchers and scholars by appointment.

Museum of Modern Art, Department of Film, 11 West 53rd Street, New York, NY 10019. Tel: (212) 708 9602. Telex: 62370. Director: Mary Lea Bandy. Curators: Eileen Bowser, Adrienne Mancia, Larry Kardish. Stock: 10,000 film titles, 2,500 books, 250 periodicals, 4,000,000 film stills. The excellent research and screening facilities of the department are available to serious students only by appointment with the supervisor, Charles Silver. 1,000 of its films are available for rental, sale, and lease. Stills Archive open by appointment with Mary Corliss.

George Eastman House/International Museum of Photography, 900 East Avenue, Rochester, N.Y. 14607. Tel: (716) 271 3361. Film Dept. Dr Jan-Christopher Horak, Senior

Curator of Film; Dr. Paolo Cherchi Usai, Assistant Curator. Film collections, including nitrate, rich in American and foreign silents, German, French and American classical studio work, poverty-row and independent documentary. Over 2.5 million stills, posters, scripts and documents related to history of film.

Academy of Motion Picture Arts and Sciences, Centre for Motion Picture Study, Academy Film Archive, 333 South La Cienega Blvd., Beverly Hills, California 90211. Director: Michael Friend. Curator: Daniel Woodruff.

National Museum of Natural History/ Human Studies Film Archives, Rm E307 Smithsonian Institution, Washington DC 20560. Tel: (202) 357–3349. Asst. Dir: Wendy Ann Shay. More than 2,000,000 feet of original film.

The Wisconsin Center for Film and Theatre Research, 816 State Street, Madison, Wisconsin 53706. Tel: (608) 262–585. Head of Archive: Maxine Ducey. Stock: 5,500 feature films, 8,500 short films and television programmes, 2,000,000 stills, 12,000 posters.

Pacific Film Archive, University Art Museum 2625 Durant Avenue, Berkeley, California, 94720. Stock: 6,000 films, 75 periodicals, 3,000 books, 10,000 stills, and 40,000 files of clippings organised by title, person, subject and festival. The PFA's daily international film exhibition programme presents over 750 films per year and covers the history of the cinema, highlighting rediscoveries and rare points, works by independent film-makers, frequent personal appearances by film-makers and scholars, and films for children. The film collection emphasises Japanese features, Soviet silents, international animation, and avant-garde films. Library and research screening facilities are open to the public weekday afternoons by appointment.

American Cinematheque, 1717 N. Highland Ave. (at Hollywood Blvd.), Hollywood 90028. Artistic Director: Gary Essert. A viewer-supported arts complex of state-of-the-art theatres, galleries and gathering places (including a café and bookstore) dedicated *exclusively* to the public exhibition of film and video. Scheduled to open in 1994. Meanwhile, regular film and video programming for the public is underway now at the new Directors Guild theatre complex in Hollywood.

UCLA Film and Television Archive, 1438 Melnitz Hall, University of California, 405 Hilgard Avenue, Los Angeles CA 90024. Tel: (213) 206–8013. Telex: 910 3427597. Director: Robert Rosen. Stock: 55,000 film and television programmes, 5,000,000 stills.

U.S.S.R.

Gosfilmofond, Stantsia Byelye Stolby, Moskovskaia oblast. Tel: 546.05.16, 546.05.13. Telex: 311700 LASTI 007913. Director: Vladimir Malyshev. Stock: 49,000 film titles, 8,160 books, 18,937 periodicals, 359,320 stills, 52,000 posters. Shows films publicly and has viewing facilities for the serious student.

Moscow Film Centre, Museum Dept. of the Film Centre of the Filmmakers' Union of the U.S.S.R., Druzjinnikovskaya 15, Moscow 123376. Curator: Naum Kleiman. Admirable work in restoring Russian and Soviet classics and lost films.

The Central State Archive of Cinema and Photo Documents of the USSR, Krasnogorsk, near Moscow. Director: O.N. Tyagunov.

VENEZUELA

Cinemateca Nacional, Museo de Ciencias Naturales, Edf. Anexo, Plaza Morelos, Los Caobos, Aptdo. Postal 17045, Caracas. Tel: 571

5220. Director: Rodolfo Izaguirre. Stock: 1,012 film titles, 5,000 books, pamphlets and documentation, 12,000 stills, 500-card index.

YUGOSLAVIA

Jugoslovenska kinoteka, Knez Mihailova 19, 11000 Belgrade. Tel: 622 555. Fax: 622 587. Director: Sloboden Šijan. Foreign Relations Consultant: Dinko Tucaković. Stock: 64,610 films, 17,700 books and periodicals, 9,334 scripts, reference index of 200,000 cards, 100,000 newspaper clippings, 185,716 stills, 64,342 negative photos, 10,830 posters, 2,395 programmes.

Stock Footage Libraries

The following is a listing of the major U.S. independent stock footage libraries:

John E. Allen, Inc., North Avenue, Park Ridge, N.J. 07656. Tel: (201) 391–3463.

Archive Films Inc., 530 West 25th Street, New York, NYT 10001. Tel: (212) 620 3955. Fax: (212) 645 2137. Invaluable source of film extracts, newsreels, cartoons etc. Patrick Montgomery's archive contains a vast assortment of material from 1894 through the 1980's.

Producing everything from commercials to full-length documentaries, **Archive Films Inc.** specialises in the use of historical footage. Experts in the utilisation of existing films and tapes, the firm houses a vast collection of archival footage as well as maintaining exclusive arrangements throughout the world with other distributors, archives and libraries. All footage has been transferred to video cassettes for reference purposes and is available on all film and video formats for use.

By definition, historical or "archival" footage is any type of footage, film or videotape, colour or b&w, 16mm or 35mm shot as early as 1898 or as recently as yesterday. Archive Films locates its footage from a number of different origins – acquiring clips from newsreels, silent film comedies and dramas, home movies, Hollywood feature films (primarily those shot outside of the studio system), rare music footage, educational films and cartoons.

Cameo Film Library, 10620 Burbank Boulevard, North Hollywood, Ca. 91601. Tel: (818) 980–9700. Represents stock footage from NBC Productions, Tri-Star, Viacom and others.

Larry Dorn Associates/World Backgrounds, 5550 Wilshire Boulevard, Los Angeles, Ca. 90036. Tel: (213) 935–6266.

Film Bank, 425 Victory Blvd, Burbank, CA 91502. Tel: (818) 841 9176. Fax: (818) 567 4235. President: Paula Lumbard. Stock footage, research, camera service.

The Image Bank Film, 111 Fifth Avenue, New York, NY 10003. Tel: (212) 529 6700. Fax: (212) 529 3469.

Sherman Grinberg Film Libraries, Inc., 630 Ninth Avenue, New York, NY 10036. Tel: (212) 765 5170. Fax: (212) 262 1532. Also, 1040 North McCadden Place, Hollywood, CA 90038. Tel: (213) 464 7491. Fax: (213) 462 5352.

Producers Library Service, 1051 North Cole Avenue, Hollywood, CA 90038. Tel: (213) 465 0572. Houses more than 5 million feet of 35mm colour film from the 1950's to the present, 1 million feet of 16mm colour film from the 1940's and 1950's, and more than 1 million feet of 35mm black-and-white film from the 'teens through the 1940's; it represents stock footage from the productions of ABC Circle, Orion and the Spelling-Goldberg TV series, specialises in Hollywood history and has direct access to stock footage from all Hollywood studios.

The Stock House, 6922 Hollywood Boulevard, Suite 621, Hollywood, Ca. 90028. Tel: (213) 461–61.

BOOK REVIEWS

As befits a year of recession, the publishing trade has been recycling rather than creating new books. And as nearly all the major directors have been consecrated between covers, the output of original monographs has diminished too. We survey below the crop of publications that has reached us during the past twelve months . . .

REFERENCE
Bernard Rapp and Jean-Claude Launy have edited **Dictionnaire des Films** (Larousse, Paris, 1990). This luxurious volume covers some 10,000 films (main credits, a few sentences of comment). Around 200 titles receive more substantial analysis. The dictionary benefits from a genuine cosmopolitan approach at the expense of today's pro-Hollywood vogue. As a reference source, the book surpasses its English-language rivals, without achieving quite the level of scholarship and authority of Passek's monumental *Dictionnaire du Cinéma* in the same format.

Equally heavy, if lacking in pictures, is Tad Bentley Hammer's **International Film Prizes, An Encyclopedia** (Garland Publishing, New York and London, 1991), a labour of love and detail that lists awards in 43 countries. The emphasis is on awards given within a specific country, rather than on festivals that invite a mere handful of titles. Hammer's meticulous research ensures that even Finnish films may be found in their original tongue, while the Title and Biographical indices justifiably, and invaluably, occupy a third of the book.

David Parkinson's **Good Movie Guide** (Bloomsbury, London, 1991) really has few merits, apart from listing the winners at major festivals which Hammer (see above) does not. For the rest, his one-sentence resumés of 5,000 films contain errors and are weighed down with a bizarre system of symbols reminiscent of a bed-and-breakfast guide.

The **Variety Movie Guide** (Octopus, London/Prentice-Hall, New Jersey, 1991) comprises more than 5,000 reviews from the pages of the world's oldest showbusiness newspaper. That means credits as well as savvy analysis from a trade rather than aesthetic standpoint. These no-nonsense notices have stood the test of time rather well, and Derek Elley's competent editorial eye has pruned the more outrageous period solecisms while retaining the much-loved "slanguage" of *Variety*.

HISTORY AND GENRE
Kevin Brownlow brings his study of the silent epoch to a triumphant conclusion with **Behind the Mask of Innocence** (Alfred Knopf, New York/Jonathan Cape, London, 1990). Here he pores over the issues of sex, violence, prejudice and crime in the films of the teens and 1920's. Unlike most film historians, Brownlow really seems to have *seen* every picture he describes, and stuffs each chapter with original quotes from the quick and the dead. His supple, limpid prose rubs alight that vanished era, and his trilogy belongs among the summits of film literature.

Two books on the Australian film. David Stratton's **The Avocado Plantation, Boom and Bust in the Australian Film Industry** (Pan Macmillan, Sydney, 1990) forms a sequel to his previous book, *The Last Wave*, and traces the fortunes of the cinema in Oz from 1980 to 1990. Each film's inception, shoot, and theme is analysed in Stratton's readable and sympathetic fashion; as he was a Film Commissioner in Australia for three of the ten years under review, he knows whereof he speaks. **Le Cinéma Australien** (Centres Georges Pompidou, Paris, 1991), however, surveys the entire landscape. This elegant tome forms a *catalogue raisonnée* to the huge retrospective last summer at Beaubourg, and as always its reference sections and its magnificent photographs make the book indispensable. (Another volume in the same series, **Le Cinéma d'Asie Centrale Soviétique**, breaks even fresher ground and reveals a fertile film-making tradition all too little glimpsed in the West.)

The Pordenone Silent Film Days in Italy continues to publish annual books as an accompaniment to its retrospectives, and **Prima di Caligari/Before Caligari** (Edizioni Biblioteca dell'Immagine, Pordenone, 1990) again offers a bi-lingual (Italian/English) survey of a forgotten period in movie history. Lorenzo Codelli, Barry Salt, and Thomas Elsaesser figure among the contributors and the frame enlargements and pristine stills make the book as intriguing as it is essential.

The Italians, when they try, can produce film books every bit as elegant as their shoes. **Il Cinema dell'Ingegno**, by Ettore Pasculli (Edizioni Mazzotta, Milano, 1990) provides probably the finest appraisal of special effects in the cinema from the silent days to the computerized gadgetry of *Tron*. The array of colour photographs, nearly all of them unfamiliar, enables the English reader to leapfrog the language barrier.

MONOGRAPHS

Naomi Greene's astute study, **Pier Paolo Pasolini, Cinema as Heresy** (Princeton University Press, Princeton, 1990), revives the memory of an all-round intellectual who galvanized Italian artistic rhetoric during the 1960's and 1970's. This is a calm, intelligent book, even when dealing with the most incendiary of topics. In **Cesare Zavattini** (Centre Georges Pompidou, Paris, 1990), Aldo Bernardini and Jean A. Gili go back even earlier, to the 1940's and 1950's when Zavattini seemed to be scripting just about every new masterpiece of Neorealism. A colour section shows Zavattini to have been a painter of some skill, also, and throughout the book the photos summon up vanished faces and occasions. A splendid tribute to a giant among screenwriters.

Antonioni's *Tentato suicidio* was based on an idea by Zavattini and Sam Rohdie's **Antonioni** (BFI Publishing, London, 1990) charts the emergence, chrysalis-like, of this first modernist director from the age of Neorealism, and does so in a mood of graceful scholarship.

Paul Schrader is a ground-breaking screenwriter whose articulate intelligence has not prevented him from trying to be a director too. In **Schrader on Schrader** (Faber and Faber, London and Boston, 1990) Kevin Jackson assembles a host of his writings and interviews. Schrader comes to terms with his puritan background, and freely takes issue with some of the directors who have filmed his scripts.

Philip Kemp pays eloquent, affectionate tribute to Alexander Mackendrick in **Lethal Innocence** (Methuen, London, 1991). This American director, with a Scottish name and an English sense of humour, made some of the most enduring, offbeat masterpieces of postwar comic cinema (*The Ladykillers, The Man in the White Suit, Whisky Galore!*) as well as the cult favourite, *Sweet Smell of Success*, but has never been accorded the recognition he deserves as an auteur, as opposed to the decent professional image he holds in the annals of British cinema.

Foster Hirsch has updated his study of **Woody Allen, Love, Sex, Death and the Meaning of Life** (Limelight Editions, New York, 1990), analysing the deliberateness that has crept into Allen's work in recent years as well as the acerbic Manhattan wit.

SCREENPLAYS

Faber and Faber have continued to put film students and cinephiles in their debt with a stream of screenplay paperbacks. Although some are distinctly arcane (Barry Levinson's **Avalon, Tin Men,** and **Diner**), others break altogether new ground, such as Kieślowski's **The Decalogue,** which contains the scripts for all ten of the TV movies made by the Pole between 1988 and 1989. Kieślowski and his colleague Krzysztof Piesiewicz include minute descriptions of action on screen, which strengthens the value of this volume.

Martin Scorsese and Nicholas Pileggi have written one of the tautest, pithiest screenplays of recent years: **GoodFellas** (Faber and Faber, London, 1990), while Scorsese's old comrade in violence, Paul Schrader, has his script for **Taxi Driver** issued for the first time (Faber and Faber, London, 1990).

Tarkovsky's **Andrei Rublev** (Faber and Faber, London, 1991) is essentially a cine-novel, with stress laid on the description of thoughts and actions rather than dialogue. Philip Strick's introduction helps to unravel the coded passion of this most cerebral of Soviet directors.

Henry Jaglom's **Eating, A Very Serious Comedy about Women and Food** (Rainbow Filmbooks/Samuel French Trade, Hollywood, 1991) is the best kind of screenplay for the armchair buff, because virtually the entire film consists of conversation and repartee. Perhaps the same publishers could do Louis Malle's **My Dinner with André?**

Finally, two paperbacks of Harold Pinter's work: **The Proust Screenplay** and **The French Lieutenant's Woman and Other Screenplays** (both Faber and Faber, London, 1991). The Proust is a travesty, a distillation that contradicts the very virtue for which Proust is most admired: detail. *The Last Tycoon,* in the second volume, however, is well worth re-reading.

VANITY

Julia Phillips's **You'll Never Eat Lunch in This Town Again** (Random House, New York, 1991) is a classic example of showbiz onanism. Written in an appalling, prolix, foul-mouthed stream-of-consciousness, this Hollywood memoir only reinforces one's view of the movie producer as ego-bound and moved exclusively by drugs and the shopping opportunities on Rodeo Drive. Phillips, though, did work on *Close Encounters of the Third Kind, Taxi Driver,* and *The Sting,* so there are anecdotes of passing interest lodged amid the alien corn.

Past Tense (Methuen, London, 1990) is the second volume of the diaries of Jean Cocteau, and covers the year 1953 when Cocteau served as President of the Cannes Film Festival. But alas the diaries are disappointingly bland, if not downright arch.

Film Bookshops, Posters and Records

Australia

Electric Shadows Bookshop, *Upper Level, Boulevard Shopping Centre, Akuna Street, Civic Act 2608. Tel: (062) 488342. Fax: (062) 491640.*
Gaumont Book Company, *123 Little Collins Street, Melbourne 3000. Tel: (03) 63–2623.*
Readings Records and Books, *P.O. Box 482, South Yarra 3141. Tel: (03) 267–1885.*
Soft Focus, *P.O. Box 508, Hawthorn, Victoria 3122.*

Catalogue available listing movie books, magazines, posters, and memorabilia.
That's Hollywood, *Shop 2, 199 Toorak Road, South Yarra, Vic. Tel: (03) 826 3008.*

Canada

Broadway and Hollywood Books, *17 Yorkville Avenue, Toronto, M4W 1L1. Tel: (416) 926–8992.*

Bookstore specialising in stage and screen, and with a comprehensive stock of *biographies*, and out-of-print items. Excellent catalogue available.
Theatrebooks, *25 Bloor Street W, Toronto, M4W 1A3. Tel: (416) 922–7175.*

Founded first as a source of theatre, opera, and dance books, Theatrebooks has since 1982 also developed a first-class film book collection. Worldwide mail order is handled.

Lux, *5220 boul. St-Laurent, Montréal.*
Large stock of European movie posters. Open daily 10 a.m. to 4 p.m.

France

Atmosphère, Librairie du Cinéma, *7–9 rue F. de Pressensé, 75014 Paris. Tel: 45.42.29.26.*
Situated in a leisure complex that includes an art cinema and a café, Atmosphère offers a wide range of film publications, with a special emphasis on science-fiction, fantasy, comics, and pop music as related to the cinema. Also back issues of magazines. Open every day except Tuesday, from 2 p.m. to 8 p.m.
Cinédoc, *45–53 Passage Jouffroy, 75009 Paris.*
Posters, pressbooks, magazines etc.
Ciné-Folie, *14 rue des Frères-Pradignac, 06400 Cannes. Tel: 93.39.22.99.*
Stills, books, posters, postcards.
Cinémagence, *12 rue Saulnier, 75009 Paris. Tel: 42.46.21.21.*
Stills, posters, magazines, books. Mail Order service.
Librairie Contacts, 24 rue de Colisée, 75008 Paris. Tel: 43.59.17.71.
Bookshop established 25 years ago in the film production companies' neighbourhood off the Champs-Elysées. Amply stocked with French and foreign-language books on technique,

Elaine Michaux-Vignes celebrates her 25th anniversary at the helm of Librairie Contacts, the finest film bookshop in France

theory, history, and director monographs. Also magazines. Reliable mail order service. Free "new acquisitions" list. Open year round.

Le Réverbère, *4 rue Neuve, 69002 Lyon.*

Zreik, *68 rue du Cardinal Lemoine, 75005 Paris. Tel: (1) 46.33.65.73.*

Outstanding collection of rare European posters, both films and stars, with more than 300 postcards created from same. Also celebrity pins and other memorabilia items.

Germany

Buchhandlung Dialog, *Gutleutstr. 15, D–6000 Frankfurt 1. Tel: (0611) 23 52 80.*

Filmland Presse, *Aventinstr. 4–6, D–8000 Munich 40.*

Founded in 1977 by H.K. Denicke, this establishment is among the largest film bookshops in Europe, and circulates lists.

Buchhandlung Walther König, *Ehrenstr. 4, D–5 Köln 1.* Also at: *Deutschen Filmmuseum, Schaumainkai 41, D–6000 Frankfurt/Main 70.*

Useful source for anyone in Europe looking for that out-of-print book or magazine. Write for superb catalogue.

Buchhandlung Langenkamp, *Beckergrube 19, D–2400 Lübeck. Tel: (0451) 76479.*

H. Lindemanns Buchhandlung, *Nadlerstr. 4, D–7000 Stuttgart 1.*

Sautter & Lackmann, *Klosterstern 8, D–2000 Hamburg 13.*

Marga Schoeller Bücherstube, *Knesebeckstr. 33, D–1000 Berlin 12.*

One of the fabled literary haunts of western Europe, Marga Schoeller's shop is justly proud of its film book selection.

Verlag für Filmschriften Christian Unucka, *Am Kramerberg 71, D–8061 Hebertshausen. Tel: (08131) 13922.*

Italy

Libreria dello Spettacolo, *via Terraggio 11, 20123 Milano. Tel: (02) 800752.*

"Il Leuto," *via Di Monte Brianzo 86, 00186 Rome. Tel: (06) 656.9269.*

Netherlands

Cine Qua Non, *Staalstraat 14, Amsterdam. Tel: (40) 255588.*

Posters, stills, new and second-hand film books, scripts, and magazine back issues. Specialises in French and Italian cinema.

Spain

Biblioteca del Cinema Delmiro de Caralt, *Escuelas Pias 103, 08017 Barcelona.*

El Espectador, *Consejo de Ciento 475 bis, 08013 Barcelona. Tel: (93) 231 65.16.*

Specialising in cinema and video books, magazines etc.

Filmoteca Nacional, Cine Doré, *Santa Isabel 3, Madrid.*

Well-stocked bookstore dealing with movie topics.

Libreria del Espectaculo, *Almagro 13, 28010 Madrid.*

Specialises in film and theatre books. Wide selection of books from all major countries. Compact and modern.

R. Seriña, *Calle Ariban 114, Barcelona 11.*

A specialist collection of books, photos, magazines, press books, posters and programmes on sale to the public in Spain and abroad.

Switzerland

Filmbuchhandlung Hans Rohr, *Oberdorfstr. 3, CH–8024 Zürich.*

Hans Rohr is one of those rare birds – an advertiser in all 29 years of our book! Over all that time, the shop has remained a paragon of Swiss efficiency and courtesy when it comes to dealing with mail order inquiries for literally any film book or magazine. Libraries and institutions rely on Rohr – even beyond Switzerland.

Librairie du Cinéma, *9 rue de la Terrassière, CH–1207 Genève. Tel: (022) 736.8888.*

Immaculate display of posters, books, stills, film postcards, soundtrack CD's, and videos. A veritable treasure trove for the movie buff. Closed Monday mornings.

U.K.

The Cinema Bookshop, *13–14 Great Russell Street, London WC1. Tel: (071) 637.0206.*

Fred Zentner's film bookshop close to the British Museum has succeeded by virtue of prompt and friendly service, and an eye for rare items.

Cox, A.E., *21 Cecil Rd., Itchen, Southampton SO2 7HX. Tel: 0703.447989.*

This long-established dealer specialises in books, magazines, and ephemera on both theatre and cinema.

Film Magic, *18 Garsmouth Way, Watford, Herts.*

Mail order service for colour and black-and-white stills of film and TV stars, plus books, magazines and posters.

MOMI Shop, *Museum of the Moving Image, South Bank, London SE1. Tel: (071) 928 3535.*

Recently expanded, this shop offers posters, postcards, toys, videos and film books.

Anne FitzSimmons, *The Retreat, The Green, Wetherall, Carlisle, Cumbria CA4 8ET. Tel: 0228.60675.*

A useful source for second-hand and out-of-print books on the cinema, as well as the theatre, puppeteering, etc.

58 Dean Street Records, *58 Dean Street, London W1V 5HH. Tel: (071) 437 4500, 734 8777.*

Specialising in soundtracks, original cast shows (incl. imports), personalities, and nostalgia. Over 7,000 titles both current and deleted items; LP's, cassettes, and CD's. (Mail Order service.)

David Henry, *36 Meon Road, London W3 8AN. Tel: (081) 993.2859.*

Mail-order business.

Ed Mason, *Shop 5, Chelsea Antique Market, 253 King's Road, London SW3. Tel: (071) 352.9695.*

Large and carefully-assembled stock of

memorabilia from the silents to the 1980's. Plus stills, pressbooks, posters. Customers served by post.

Movie Finds, *4 Ravenslea Road, Balham, London SW12 8SB. Tel: (081) 673.6534.*

Teddy Green has built this small firm into a treasure trove of film stills and memorabilia. The range is huge, and the catalogue contains innumerable posters and movie scenes.

Dress Circle, *57–59 Monmouth Street, Upper St. Martin's Lane, London WC2H 9DG. Tel: (071) 240.2227, (071) 836.8279.*

Flashbacks, *6 Silver Place, (Beak St.), London W1R 3LJ. Tel: (071) 437.8562.*

Most impressively stocked establishment, which, in London's West End, caters for those interested in movie ephemera – posters, stills,

Book signings at Samuel French Bookshops. Left to right: Roddy McDowall, and animators Chuck Jones and Leo Salkin

pressbooks – from many countries and every period of cinema history. Also extensive Mail Order service: 4 catalogues per annum.
Zwemmer, A., *80 Charing Cross Rd., London WC2. Tel: (071) 379.7886.*

Zwemmers are of one of the handful of businesses that have survived to advertise in all 29 editions of IFG – a tribute to their solid, professional approach to stocking, and dealing efficiently with mail order inquiries. Location near Leicester Square is also handy.
Movie Boulevard, *Baker House, 9 New York Road, Leeds LS2 9PF. Tel: (0532) 422888.*

Welcome north of England addition to the ranks of shops specialising in soundtracks, videos, and movie memorabilia. Headed by the enthusiastic Robert Wood.

U.S.A.

Applause, *71st Street between Broadway and Ninth Avenue, New York City.*

Now one of the few – and certainly the only uptown – film and showbiz bookstore in Manhattan.
Books of Latin America, *P.O. Box 1103, Redlands, California 92373. Tel: (714) 793–8423.*

Specialist in works on Latin American cinema, and Spanish and Portuguese cinema in general.
Cinema Books, *4753 Roosevelt Way NE, Seattle, Washington 98105. Tel: (206) 547–7667.*

Fine selection of film books and magazines, with space also devoted to TV and theatre. Mail Orders welcome.
Cinema Collectors, *1507 Wilcox Avenue, Hollywood, California 90028. Tel: (213) 461–6516.*

Establishment in Hollywood featuring over 1,700,000 stills (many in colour), 350,000 posters and banners, and marvellous runs of *Photoplay.*
Cinemonde, *1932 Polk Street, San Francisco, California 94109. Tel: (415) 776–9988.*

Installed in a capacious loft-like HQ on Polk Street, Cinemonde may well be the world's leading poster store for cinema buffs. Items are immaculately displayed and stored, and the colourful catalogue is a collectors' item ($8 incl. airmail costs).
Collectors Book Store, *1708 N. Vine Street, California 90028. Tel: (213) 467–3296.*

As well as a commendable range of posters, stills, lobby cards, and magazines, Collectors Book Store stocks movie costumes, set drawings etc.
Samuel French's Theatre & Film Bookshop, *7623 Sunset Boulevard, Hollywood, California 90046. Tel: (213) 876–570.*

The world's oldest and largest play publisher (est. 1830) operates a separate film bookshop. Complete range of new movie books available: directories, reference, writing, acting, biography, screenplays etc.: 3,000 titles and growing! Worldwide mail order service. Note that French's also have a store at 11963 Ventura Blvd, Studio City, California 91604. Tel: (818) 762–535. Gwen Feldman prepares some meticulous catalogues that include more data than most similar efforts.
Gotham Book Mart, *41 West 47th St., New York, NY 10036.*

As its regular "GBM Film Bulletins" will testify, Gotham has achieved a remarkable prominence in the film bookshop field, and has been flourishing since 1920. Philip Lyman, the General Manager, has worked hard to expand the film section.
Larry Edmunds Bookshop, *6658 Hollywood Blvd., Hollywood, California 90028. Tel: (213) 463.3273. Also at 11969 Ventura Blvd, Studio City, California 91604.*

Larry Edmunds is the world's nearest equivalent to a film-book supermart. The stills collection alone is a goldmine for any film buff. Back numbers of movie annuals always available.
Limelight Film and Theatre Bookstore, *1803 Market Street, San Francisco, California 94103. Tel: (415) 864–2265.*

Roy A. Johnson runs this lively store for film and theatre books. Collection includes plays, screenplays, biographies, history and criticism of film etc.

Movie Madness, *1222 Wisconsin Avenue NW, Washington, DC 20007.*

Posters etc. available at this tiny store adjacent to the Key (one of Washington's best repertory cinemas).

Jerry Ohlinger's Movie Material Store Inc., *242 West 14th Street, New York, NY 10011. Tel: (212) 989–869.*

Jerry Ohlinger's emporium stocks a wealth of stills from the 1960's through the 1980's, specialising in colour material. Posters are also plentiful and there are some magazines as well.

Sound Track Album Retailers, *P.O. Box 7, Quarryville, Pennsylvania 17566. Tel: (717) 284–2573.*

Specialists in new and out of print soundtrack albums. Lists issued.

MAGAZINES

The following list amounts to a selection only of the world's hundreds of film publications. Editors wishing to receive a free listing must send sample copies (preferably opening a sample subscription for us). Address: IFG, Variety, 34–35 Newman Street, London W1P 3PD, U.K.

AFTERIMAGE, 1 Birnam Road, London N4 3LJ, U.K. Attractively-produced and intelligent occasional British journal.

AMERICAN CLASSIC SCREEN, P.O. Box 7150, Shawnee Mission, Kansas 66207, U.S.A. Bi-monthly devoted to the preservation of old films; filled with useful addresses.

AMERICAN FILM, 6671 Sunset Blvd., Suite 1514, Hollywood, CA 90028, U.S.A. Glossy monthly featuring articles on video and television, as well as film reviews and interviews.

AMERICAN PREMIERE, 8421 Wilshire Blvd., Penthouse, Beverly Hills, CA 90211, U.S.A. Bi-monthly industry magazine, free to members of the Academy of Motion Picture Arts and Sciences.

ANIMATOR, Oregon Film Institute, Northwest Film and Video Centre, 1219 S.W. Park Avenue, Portland, OR 97205, U.S.A. Entertaining and informative magazine for animators and animation buffs.

AUDIENCE, P.O. Box 7149, Van Nuys, CA 91409–7149, U.S.A. Billed as an "informal commentary on film," this witty, well-informed bi-monthly features articles and reviews, both recent and retrospective.

AVANT PREMIÈRE, Case Postale 418, 1211 Geneva 11, Switzerland. Colourful bi-monthly with lengthy reviews of new releases, as well as updates on Swiss production and distribution.

L'AVANT SCENE CINEMA, 16 rue des Quatre-Vents, 75006 Paris, France. Meticulously researched full screenplays of classic films, ancient or modern. Twenty issues a year.

BIANCO E NERO, 1524 via Tuscolana, 00173 Rome, Italy. Italian quarterly that boasts a reputation for scholarship second to none in its country.

CAHIERS DU CINEMA, Editions de l'Etoile, 9 passage de la Boule Blanche, 75012 Paris, France. Celebrated French journal now enjoying a second lease of life after a long spell in the wilderness.

CAMERA OBSCURA, The Editors, Rush Rhees Library, University of Rochester, Rochester, NY 14627, U.S.A. A journey of feminism and film theory, encourages written responses to issues raised in articles.

CHAPLIN, Box 27 126, S–102 52 Stockholm, Sweden. Sponsored by the Swedish Film Institute and covering world cinema in lively fashion. Recently redesigned for the better.

CIAK SI GIRA, C. so I. Europa 5/7, 20122 Milan, Italy. Glossy Italian monthly, well established, full of lively articles. Similar to France's *Première*.

CINE ACCIÓN NEWS, 3181 A Mission St., San Francisco, CA 94110, U.S.A.

CINEASTE, 200 Park Avenue South, New York, NY 10003, U.S.A. Perhaps the finest anti-establishment movie magazine, never afraid to tackle controversial issues and never prone to Hollywood worship. Interviews are especially good in *Cineaste*.

CINE-BULLES, 4545 avenue Pierre-de-Coubertin, CP 1000, Succursale M, Montréal, Canada H1V 3R2. Remarkable and informative Québécois quarterly that may just be the best in Canada.

CINE-BULLETIN, Swiss Film Centre, Münstergasse 18, CH–8001 Zürich, PC80–1129–6, Switzerland. Serious Swiss monthly in French and German.

CINE CUBANO, Calle 23, no. 1115 Apdo. 55, Havana, Cuba. Vital information on all Latin American cinema, unfortunately only in Spanish.

CINE OJA, Apdo. 50, 446 Sabana Grande, Caracas, Venezuela. Venezuelan monthly.

CINEFANTASIQUE, P.O. Box 270, Oak Park, Ill. 60303, U.S.A. An enthusiastic, well-written, beautifully produced bi-monthly with a special emphasis on fantasy films.

CINEINFORME, Grand Via 64, 28013 Madrid, Spain. Bi-monthly that covers Spanish and international film development.

CINEMA 2002, Adremans 64, Madrid 28, Spain. First-class Spanish monthly packed with pictures, serious articles and interviews, and a great many news items.

CINEMA & CINEMA, 1 via Battibecco, 40123 Bologna, Italy. Respected quarterly.

CINEMA CANADA, Box 398, Station Outremont, Montréal H2V 4NF, Canada. Large-format monthly.

CINEMA IN INDIA, 1 Dalamal Towers, Ground Floor, 211 Nariman Point, Bombay, India. Quarterly published by India's National Film Development Corporation.

CINEMA INDIA INTERNATIONAL, A–15 Anand Nagar, Juhu Tara Road, Bombay 400 400 049, India. Indian quarterly (in English) packed with articles, reviews and interviews.

CINEMA JOURNAL, University of Illinois Press, 54 E. Gregory Drive, Chapaign, IL 61820, U.S.A. A scholarly and respected American magazine, now published twice a year.

CINEMA NOVO, Apartado 78, 4002 Porto Codex, Portugal. Bi-monthly Portuguese magazine dealing with international and Portuguese topics.

CINEMA NUOVO, Box 362, 70100 Bari, Italy. Polemical, academic Italian bi-monthly with excellent articles.

CINEMA PAPERS, 43 Charles Street, Abbotsford 3067, Australia. Excellent large-format Australian bi-monthly is back, packed with information and pictures, useful for anyone monitoring the industry in Oz.

CINEMATECA REVISTA, Lorenzo Carnelli 1311, Casilla de Correo 1170, Montevideo, Uruguay. Bright magazine with international slant published by Cinemateca Uruguaya. Ten times a year.

CINEMATHEQUE, P.O. Box 20370, Tel Aviv 61203, Israel. Fine monthly Israeli magazine (with summary in English) dwelling on seasons at the Tel-Aviv Cinémathèque but also reporting on world festivals etc.

CINEMAYA, B 90 Defence Colony, New Delhi 110 024, India. Informative, elegant new magazine on all aspects of the Asian film industry.

CLASSIC IMAGES, P.O. Box 809, Muscataine, IA52761, U.S.A. Formerly "Classic Film Collector," a good source for film buffs eager to enlarge their library of movies. Bi-monthly.

CULTURE AND CINEMA, P.O. Box 15175–338, Tehran, Iran. Monthly magazine featuring Iranian cinema.

DIRIGIDO POR..., Rbla. de Catalunya, 108 3. 1. Barcelona 8, Spain. This handsomely-produced Spanish monthly throws the spotlight each issue on a particular director of international renown.

DOCUMENTO CINEMATOGRÁFICO LATINOMERICANO, Cra. 19 No. 31–47 of. 205 A.A. 89133–Bogotá, Colombia.

EMPIRE, 42 Great Portland Street, London W1N 5AH, U.K. Glossy magazine with international slant, heavy on reviews and behind-the-scenes. Monthly.

ENFOQUE, Publicaciones y Audiovisuales, Linterna Mágica Ltda., Casilla 15, Correo 34, Santiago, Chile. Occasional quarterly taking an in-depth look at the Chilean/Latin American markets and new-releases.

ENTERTAINMENT HERALD, Corrienres 2817 3–A 1015, Buenos Aires, Argentina.

FARABI, 55 Sie-Tir Ave., Tehran 11358, Iran. Quarterly periodical issued by the Farabi Cinema Foundation.

FATAL VISIONS, P.O. Box 133, Northcote 3070, Victoria, Australia. Lively "junk media" magazine on trash cinema, video and television.

FILM, 21 Stephen Street, London W1 1PL, U.K. Much improved, nicely-printed monthly, issued on behalf of the British Federation of Film Societies.

FILM, Pulawska 61,02595 Warsaw, Poland. Popular Polish weekly with international slant.

FILM (Yeonghwa), Motion Picture Promotion Corporation of Korea, 34–5, 3–ga, Namsan-dong, Junggu,

Seoul. South Korea's only serious film magazine, packed with information. Bi-monthly.

FILMHÄFTET, Storgatan 15, 753 31 Uppsala, Sweden. Egghead monthly with features on international directors, retrospectives, and Scandinavian television. 1991 included a superb issue on banned movies.

FILMKULTÚRA, Népstadion út 97, H–1143 Budapest, Hungary. Essays and reviews on Hungarian and international cinema. Six times a year.

FILMVILÁG, Pozsonyi út 20, H–1137, Hungary. Monthly with reviews and interviews.

FILMS IN REVIEW, P.O. Box 589, New York, NY 10021, U.S.A. Compact bi-monthly journal, reviewing notable new releases with interviews, retrospective articles and television/video reports.

FILM A DOBA, Halkova 1, 120 72 Prague 2, Czecholsovakia. The principal Czech film monthly.

FILM APPRECIATION (Tien-ying hsin-shang), Film Library, 4th floor, 7 Ch'ingatao Road, Taipei, Taiwan. Taiwan's premier serious film journal, published as a bi-monthly. Wide range of material, with the emphasis on the theoretical.

FILM EN TELEVISIE + VIDEO, Haachtesteenweg, 35, 1030 Brussels, Belgium. Extensive reviews of major new film and video releases, profiles and interviews.

FILM BULLETIN, Postfach 137, Hard 4, CH–8408 Winterthur, Switzerland. Informative, straightforward look at international cinema, with useful Swiss material also.

FILM COMMENT, Film Society of Lincoln Center, 140 West 65th Street, New York, NY 10023, U.S.A. Informative, feisty, and usually uncompromising articles as well as interviews on wide-ranging international topics. New video section.

FILM CRITICISM, Allegheny College, Meadville, PA 16335, U.S.A. In-depth articles on international cinema in this quarterly journal.

FILM-DIENST, Am Hof 28, 5000 Cologne, Germany. Fortnightly. Lists all films in West German cinemas and television screenings, with news, credits, reviews, articles.

FILM DOPE, 43 Willfield Way, London, NW11. Not so much a magazine, more a part-work film dictionary, this irregular British quarterly is to be welcomed for its exhaustive research.

FILMIHULLU, c/o Suomen elokuvakerhojenliitto, Annankatu 13 B 11, SF–00120 Helsinki 12. Finnish film and TV magazine with critical approach, appearing eight times a year.

FILM LITERATURE INDEX, Film and Television Documentation Centre, State University of New York, 1400 Washington Avenue, Albany, NY 12222, U.S.A. Manuscripts invited for submission, reviews, interviews or analysis.

FILM MONTHLY, P.O. Box 11365–5875, Tehran, Iran. Reviews and features on the latest releases.

FILM QUARTERLY, University of California Press, Berkeley, California 94720. Now much improved visually, this magazine neatly straddles the barrier between the glossy journals and academic tomes.

FILM REPORT, No. 242, Vali-e Asr Ave., Tehran, Iran. Reports and interviews on international cinema.

FILM THREAT, Box 951, Royal Oak, MI 48068, U.S.A. The world's most outrageous and anarchic movie magazine, lashing out zestfully at all and sundry. Some of it sticks, by the way. The cartoon work is great.

FILM UND FERNSEHEN, Oranienburgerstr. 67–68, 104 Berlin, Germany. Monthly edited by Association of Film- and TV-makers in the G.D.R. Broad surveys, extensive interviews, etc.

FORMATO DIECISEIS, Apartado 6–1775, Estafeta El Dorado, Panama.

FOTOGRAMAS & VIDEO, Consell de Cent 83, 6ª planta, 08015 Barcelona, Spain, Glossy monthly, packed with colourful articles and photographs, also video reviews and television film listings.

FRAMEWORK, 40A Topsfield Parade, London N8 8QA, U.K. Substantial, occasional British magazine, with wide-ranging international essays.

GRAND ANGLE, rue d'Arschot 29, B–6370 Mariembourg, Belgium. Belgian bi-monthly.

GRIFFITHIANA, Cineteca del Friuli, 26 via Osoppo, 33014 Gemona del Friuli (Udine), Italy. Quarterly – living up to its name.

GUIA DE FILMES, Rua Mayrink 28–5 andar, Rio de Janeiro, Guanabara, Brazil. Bi-monthly Brazilian magazine, an equivalent to Britain's *MFB*.

HOLLAND ANIMATION BULLETIN, Stevinstraat 261, 2587 EJ The Hague, Netherlands. Authoritative Dutch bulletin edited by Nico Crama.

HOLLYWOOD, P.O. Box 38010, Los Angeles, CA 90038, U.S.A. A mixture of features, not all cinema-based, for Californians who live in *Hollywood*, not L.A.

IMAGEN, Casilla 1733, La Paz, Bolivia. Magazine of the Bolivian New Cinema Movement.

IMAGENES DE ACTUALIDAD, Rambla de Cataluña 108, 08008 Barcelona, Spain. Glossy, well presented magazine with strong Hollywood bias. Monthly.

IMMAGINE, 1522 via Tuscolana, 00173 Rome, Italy. Much-admired Italian magazine, full of articles and notes on the history of the cinema.

THE INDEPENDENT FILM/VIDEO GUIDE, EFLA, 45 John Street, New York, NY 10038, U.S.A. Quarterly index to the works exhibited by non-commercial film-video show-cases in New York City and New York State.

INTERNATIONAL DOCUMENTARY, 1551 South Robertson Boulevard, Suite 201, Los Angeles, CA 90035, U.S.A. The only publication to focus exclusively on non-fiction film and video. Presents new work and ideas in the documentary field with informative articles, reviews and interviews. Quarterly.

ISKUSSTVO KINO, 9 ulitsa Usievich, 125319 Moscow, U.S.S.R. Chunky, theoretical, officially blessed Soviet monthly.

JUMP CUT, P.O. Box 865, Berkeley, California

94701, U.S.A. Published only once or twice a year, this tabloid contains an extraordinary amount of closely woven text.

KINO, c/o Holloway, Helgoländer Ufer 6, 1000 Berlin 21, Germany. Excellent quarterly devoted to both German and other cinema, with interviews credits and comment.

KINO, Kredytawa 5/7, 00056 Warsaw, Poland. Culturally-inclined Polish magazine with a new, uninhibited editorial board.

KOSMORAMA, The Danish Film Museum, Store Søndervoldstræde, DK–1419 Copenhagen K, Denmark. One of the most beautifully-designed and lovingly-edited of Nordic film magazines. Quarterly.

MACGUFFIN, Paradisgade 7–9, D–8000 Århus C, Denmark. Solid, slim Danish quarterly. Erratic appearance rate.

MAKING BETTER MOVIES, 28 Great James Street, London WC1N 3HL, U.K. Film and video monthly that concentrates on the craft of making your own films.

MEDIUM, Friedrich Strasse 2–6, 6000 Frankfurt am Main 17, Germany. Monthly including articles about mass media politics, TV interviews and portraits of directors, festival reports etc.

MOVIE, 6/F D, Formost Building, 19–21 Jordan Road, Kowloon, Hongkong. Bright new arrival (since summer 1988) on Hongkong's serious movie magazine scene, combining best of the defunct Film Bi-weekly and China & Overseas Movie News.

MOVIELINE, 1141 South Beverly Drive, Los Angeles, CA 90035, U.S.A. Lively, dyed-in-the-wool Hollywood monthly. Poor layout but great interviews.

MOVIES U.S.A., 8010 Roswell Road, Atlanta, GA 30350, U.S.A. Lightweight American monthly, two or three main features and lots of paparazzi.

MOZGO KEPEK, P.O. Box 223, H–1906 Budapest, Hungary. Monthly covering film, TV, and video in tabloid form.

NUOVO CINEMA EUROPEO, Indipendza 13, 50129 Florence, Italy. Chunky bi-monthly report on Italian film industry, in English with Italian summary. Includes industry news, such as box-office, market and foreign sales.

NZ FILM, P.O. Box 11–546, Wellington, New Zealand. News from the New Zealand Film Commission, a monthly round-up of the country's film industry.

ONFILM, P.O. Box 6374, Wellington, New Zealand. A film, television and video magazine for New Zealand with location reports and a production survey.

OFF-HOLLYWOOD REPORT, The Independent Feature Project, 132 West 21st Street, 6th Floor, New York, NY10011, U.S.A. Aimed at independent film makers, this bi-monthly offers interviews, news and sound advice.

PHOTOGRAPH, No. 20, 19th Alley, Gandhi Ave., Tehran, Iran. A monthly magazine by the Young Iranian Cinema Society.

PICTURE HOUSE, 5 Coopers Close, Burgess Hill

.V. Sussex RH15 8AN. Admirable quarterly devoted to the cinema buildings of the past.

POPULAR CINEMA (Dazhong dianying), 22 Beisanhai Donglu, Peking, China. Leading mainland Chinese monthly, also carrying pieces on Hongkong, Taiwan and foreign cinema.

POSITIF, 9 bis, rue Bellot, 75019 Paris, France. In-depth interviews, articles, all immaculately researched and highly intelligent. Still the best film magazine in France.

PREMIERE, 23–25 rue de Berri, 75388 Paris Cedex 08, France. France's glossiest, most down-market monthly, packed with information, reviews and filmographies.

PREMIERE, 2 Park Avenue, New York, NY 10016, U.S.A. Somewhat diluted in size and scope during the past year, but still has its finger on the pulse of Hollywood and retains a huge circulation.

PRÉSENCE DU CINEMA FRANÇAIS, Les Editions de l'Expression, 22 rue Plumet, 75015 Paris, France. On-the-ball, colourfully illustrated bi-monthly that verges on being an industry journal.

PRODUCER, 162–170 Wardour Street, London, W1V 4LA, U.K. Welcome voice for the independent British producer.

PROJEKTIO, Yrjonkatu 11 A5, 00121 Helsinki. 12, Finland. The magazine of the Finnish Federation of Film Societies, appearing quarterly.

QUADERNI DI CINEMA, Via Benedetto Varchi 57, 50132 Florence, Italy. Wide-ranging Italian bi-monthly striving to match cultural politics with an enthusiastic appreciation of film.

RECTANGLE, CAC Voltaire, Rue Général-Dufour 16, 1204 Geneva, Switzerland. Only film magazine in the Suisse romande, and admirably poised between the theoretical and researchist approach to the cinema.

RIVISTA DEL CINEMATOGRAFO, Via Giuseppe Palombini, 6–165 Rome, Italy. Important Italian monthly.

SEGNOCINEMA, Via G. Prati 34, Vicenza. Italian bi-monthly, with particularly useful September issue that lists complete guide to all films released the previous season.

SIGHT AND SOUND, British Film Institute, 21 Stephen Street, London W1 1PL, U.K. Incorporating *Monthly Film Bulletin* which gives full credits for all new films released in Britain. Now monthly, and resolutely opposed to the "foreign film buffery" of its recently-retired editor, Penelope Houston.

SIGHTLINES, 920 Barnsdale Road, Ste. 152, La Grange Park, IL 60525, U.S.A. Excellent quarterly magazine dealing with film education in the United States.

SKOOP, Postbus 11377, Amsterdam, Netherlands. The well-known Dutch movie magazine, with a spectrum of news, reviews, interviews, and a lavish selection of pictures.

SKRIEN, p/a Filmmuseum, Vondelpark 3, 1071 AA Amsterdam, The Netherlands. Excellent Dutch magazine that appears with regularity and enthusiasm.

SORUSH, Motahari Ave., Jam-e Jam Building, Tehran, Iran. Weekly magazine issue by Islamic Republic of Iran Broadcasting.

SOUNDTRACK! 317 Skyline Lake Drive, Box 609, Ringwood, NJ 07456, U.S.A. Excellent quarterly for film music collectors.

SOVYETSKI EKRAN, ul Chasovaya 5–6 Moscow A–319, U.S.S.R. Popular Soviet fortnightly.

SPEKTRI, Box 142, SF–00101 Helsinki, Finland. An independent quarterly aiming at Finnish film buffs. Fresh opinions, no prejudices.

STILL, P.O. Box 432, SF–33101 Tampere, Finland. Lively, very well-informed Finnish quarterly.

STUDIO MAGAZINE, 116 bis, avenue des Champs-Elysées, 75008 Paris, France. Glossy, beautifully designed monthly with reviews, articles and interviews.

TRAVELIN, Valázquez 10, Madrid, Spain. New Spanish fortnightly that sparkles with colour stills and lively articles.

TUSIND ØJNE, Frederiksberg Alle 18, 4 sal,. DK–1820 Frederiksberg C., Denmark. Invaluable for anyone passing through Copenhagen – a tabloid guide to the major films and the issues emerging from them.

24 IMAGES, 3781, rue Laval, Montréal, QC 112W 2118, Canada. Exceptionally attractive French-Canadian quarterly.

VE CINEMA, Hil Yayinlari, Cagaloglu, Istanbul, Turkey. Quarterly published in Turkish.

THE VELVET LIGHT TRAP, University of Texas Press, P.O. Box 7819, Austin, Texas 78713 U.S.A. Bi-annual journal featuring critical essays analysing the history and criticism of the American cinema.

VIDEO MAKER, Oasis Publishing, Media House, Boxwell Road, Berkhamstead, Herts., England. Film and video monthly that concentrates on the craft of making your own films.

VIDEO PROFESSIANAL, Consell de Cent 83, 6°, 08015 Barcelona, Spain. A monthly look at the Spanish video industry, with comprehensive listings of new releases.

VISIO, Ellipsikuja 7, SF–02210 Espoo, Finland. Excellent monthly on technical matters.

WIDE ANGLE, The Johns Hopkins University Press, Baltimore, Maryland 212180, U.S.A. Scholarly thematically arranged journal. Wide range.

Z FILMTIDSSKRIFT, Teatergt. 3, 0180 Oslo 1, Norway. Reliable, polemic, and enthusiastic Norwegian quarterly issued by Norsk Filmklubb-forbund.

ZOOM, Bederstrasse 76, Postfach, 8027 Zürich, Switzerland. Slim Swiss monthly highlighting new releases, with good festival coverage. In German.

National Organs

AFC INFORMATION UPDATE, 8 West Street, North Sydney, NSW 2060, Australia. Monthly.

CHINA SCREEN, China Film Export and Import

Corporation Xinjiekovwai Dajie 25, Beijing, China. Quarterly.

CINEMA, CINEMA, Ministère de la Culture Française, avenue de Cortenbur 158, 1040 Brussels, Belgium.

CZECHOSLOVAK FILM, 28 Václavské námĕsti, Prague 1, Czechoslovakia.

ISRAEL FILM CENTRE INFORMATION BULLETIN, Ministry of Commerce and Industry, 30 Agron Street, Jerusalem, Israel.

KINO, Türkenstrasse 93, 8000 München 40, Germany. Monthly.

NFDC NEWS, Dalamal Towers, 211 Nariman Point, Bombay 400 021, India, Monthly.

Trade and Technical

AMERICAN CINEMATOGRAPHER, ASC Holding Corp., Box 2230, Los Angeles, CA 90078, U.S.A. Monthly.

IMAGE TECHNOLOGY – JOURNAL OF THE BKSTS, 110–112 Victoria House, Vernon Place, London WC1B 4DJ, U.K. Monthly.

BLICK PUNKT-FILM, Kolomanweg 1, D–8019 Glonn, Germany. Strong on box-office returns and marketing, this German weekly also covers Austria.

BRITISH NATIONAL FILM & VIDEO CATALOGUE, 21 Stephen Street, London W1 1PL, U.K. Quarterly that provides essential particulars of all nonfiction films (British and foreign) becoming avail able in Britain.

CINEMA D'OGGI, viale Regina Margherita 286 00198 Rome, Italy. Fortnightly. Interviews with producers.

LE FILM FRANÇAIS, 103 blvd. Saint-Michel 75005 Paris, France. Weekly.

FILM-ECHO/FILMWOCHE, Wilhelmstrasse 42 62 Wiesbaden, Germany. Doyen of the German trade

FILM OG KINO, Stortingsgaten 16, 0161 Oslo 1 Norway. Wide-ranging and well illustrated, covering trade matters but often controversial issues too.

GIORNALE DELLO SPETTACOLO, via di Villa Patrizi 10, 00161 Rome, Italy. Box-office data, legal requirements, technical information etc.

HOLLYWOOD REPORTER, 6715 Sunset Blvd. Hollywood, California 90028, U.S.A. Daily.

MONITEUR DU FILM, 36 rue des Framboisiers, 1180 Brussels, Belgium. Monthly.

MOVIE TV MARKETING, Box 30, Central Post Office, Tokyo, 100–91 Japan. Monthly from Japan – in English.

MOVING PICTURES INTERNATIONAL, 26 Soho Square, London W1V 5FJ, U.K. Launched in 1990, European-orientated weekly trade paper published in London.

THEMATA, Athinon 64, Aharnai, Attikis, Greece. Fortnightly.

VARIETY, 475 Park Avenue South, New York. NY 10016, U.S.A. The world's foremost newspaper of the entertainment business.